MODERN ARABIC DRAMA

INDIANA SERIES IN ARAB AND ISLAMIC STUDIES

Salih J. Altoma, Iliya Harik,
and Mark Tessler, general editors

MODERN ARABIC DRAMA

AN ANTHOLOGY

EDITED BY

Salma Khadra Jayyusi

and Roger Allen

INTRODUCTION BY

M. M. Badawi

A PROTA BOOK

INDIANA UNIVERSITY PRESS

Bloomington and Indianapolis

This anthology was prepared by PROTA,
Project of Translation from Arabic,
founded and directed by Salma Khadra Jayyusi.

The editors and publisher thank Dr. Suad al-Sabah, Kuwait, and
Mr. Jawad Hadeed and the Arab Banking Corporation, Amman,
Jordan, for support of the translations in this volume, and
Mr. ʿAbd al-ʿAziz Saʿud al-Babitain, Kuwait,
for support of its publication.

The paper used in this publication meets the minimum
requirements of American National Standard for
Information Sciences—Permanence of Paper for
Printed Library Materials, ANSI Z39.48-1984.

Manufactured in the United States of America

Library of Congress Cataloging-in-Publication Data

Modern Arabic drama : an anthology / edited by Salma Khadra
Jayyusi and Roger Allen ; introduction by M. M. Badawi.
p. cm. — (Indiana series in Arab and Islamic studies)
ISBN 0-253-32897-7 (alk. paper). — ISBN 0-253-20973-0
(pbk : alk. paper)
1. Arabic drama—20th century—Translations into English.
I. Jayyusi, Salma Khadra. II. Allen, Roger M. A. III. Series.
PJ7694.E5M63 1995
892′.72608—dc20 94-49178

1 2 3 4 5 00 99 98 97 96 95

CONTENTS

PREFACE

In *The Art of the Drama*, Millet and Bentley tell us that "the practical playwright assumes that his work will be submitted to the judgment, will touch the instincts, and will stimulate the emotions, not of a student coolly isolated in his study but of a mass of spectators of varied temperaments gathered in a theater." Like most comments on the drama genre by Western critics, their remarks are based exclusively on models from the European and American tradition. Yet their acknowledgment of dramatic works as pertaining to both text and performance provides a useful link to a relatively youthful tradition of drama in the Arab world and the problems that it has encountered during the course of its development in modern times.

Much has been made of the role of the Arabic language as a spoken medium in the history of the Arabic drama. During the nineteenth century, when Arab intellectuals witnessed performances of drama in Europe and returned to the Arab world to replicate them, certain popular forms of dramatic performance already existed, although their "texts" had rarely been committed to writing. The works themselves certainly do not anticipate anything so formal as a theater building in order to be presented. Such popular presentations were, needless to say, performed in the colloquial language of the region concerned. Against such a background, those writers and producers who attempted to present translations and adaptations of Western drama to such an audience found themselves facing considerable obstacles, the major one being that of the linguistic medium. On one hand, the use of formal written Arabic for dramatic dialogue was markedly inadequate at the turn of the twentieth century, when the Arabic language still carried many pedantic trappings and still retained formal modes of address inherited from older periods. On the other hand, the use of the various regional colloquials faced two major problems. The first was that it introduced a barrier in understanding among the various regions themselves, whose colloquials could differ widely. What is of note here is that the Arab creative talent, when dealing with the main genres of Arabic literature—poetry, fiction, essay, and drama—normally preferred to address itself not just to its local audience but also to the wider Arab audience. Culture and literature in the Arab world have remained a pan-Arab involvement, and the unity of its literary output is instinctively recognized and upheld. The second problem was that the Arab colloquials themselves, during the first decades of the twentieth century, were still unable to express adequately, and with the necessary profundity, the more sophisticated experiences of people. The use of colloquial for dialogue tended, therefore, to de-elevate the dramatic work by considerably simplifying the thematic element to suit a less-evolved colloquial expression. It was through the decades—with the gradual familiarizing of formal Arabic and its wide adaptation to the vast range of subjects addressed by the various branches of the modern media (now widely diffused everywhere) and, at the same time, the steady elevation of the colloquials through the constant infiltration of more formal vocabulary and the absorption of more sophisticated ideas—that an instinctive thrust toward a middle language was felt and has become feasible for the future. It is Arabic drama, and dialogue in the various fictional genres, that are the media to benefit most from this. However, other restraints abounded. The more traditional and orthodox elements objected to the entire principle of public representation, especially where it involved female actresses appearing in public and playing amatory roles. This set of performance characteristics succeeded early in providing the drama genre with a certain notoriety. But perhaps the greatest handicap the drama genre, in its modern sense, complained of at its inception, other than the linguistic factor, was the lack of a theatrical tradition to lean on. Not only was it necessary to learn the craft of writing for a performance art, but it was also necessary to acquire professionalism in the art of directing and acting and to train the public taste to enjoy and interact with theatrical performance. Moreover, it was no easy task to depend on Western examples, and to attempt to render them in Arabic in a way acceptable to the audience, particularly because the basic *Weltanschauungen* of Western and Arab cultures, their interpretation of life and the universe, and the outlook of the two cultures on social and political experience were very different. Within such a context it is not surprising that the task of creating a literary tradition of modern Arabic drama was a long and arduous one, nor that in many countries of the Arab world the popular tradition has continued to flourish. One might suggest perhaps that the most successful examples of modern Arabic drama—as both text and performance—have been those that have discovered a creative common ground between the more literary and the popular modes.

The development of the drama genre has proceeded at different paces in the various parts of the Arab world during the course of this century. Besides the issues of language and audience already noted, at least two other issues have impinged upon the world of the theater. The first is the rapid spread of other modes of communication, particularly cinema and television. In the West, these two media have taken their place alongside a long-established tradition of theater. While the more famous personnel involved in the theater, whether performers or producers and directors, will switch between media, the communities of performers and technicians are essentially discrete. For the much younger and less firmly established tradition of Arabic drama, the advent of such alternative media has tended to have a major impact, not least because of the larger publics and the greater income that television and cinema can offer. Overreaching all these media is the second major issue, that of government control over artistic expression—of which, because of its direct social and political implications, its immediacy and its potentially strong impact on a live audience, the drama was a prime target. As Arab nations gained full independence in the 1940s and 1950s (with Algeria winning the War of Liberation in 1962), both intellectuals and government officials rapidly realized the potential of theater's role as a kind of public platform, a safety valve for the airing of societal problems. As playwrights have proceeded to explore the possibilities of the dramatic medium and to test its limits, governments have set up a variety of means of review and control—in a word, censorship—in order to keep this potentially volatile medium on a tight rein. Only on rare occasions has the relationship been a cordial one, and the result has too often been disillusion on the part of writers and a general sense of ossification.

Faced with these parameters, it has taken a good deal of dedication and courage for writers in the Arab world to persevere in their careers as dramatists. Many talented writers have written a few plays and then turned to other literary genres. Others have given up and either stopped writing altogether or else emigrated. Those who have remained and persevered have faced considerable obstacles in seeing their works published and performed. Since publication has to face government control in most Arab countries, outspoken treatment of controversial topics rarely sees the light of day in printed versions.

That is one reason why some of the more skillful playwrights have resorted to various means of combating this control. One resort was to use symbolism, with its capacity for multiple interpretations, which playwrights hoped would lure the censors away from a clear understanding of the play. A second was to use the historical archetype, an impressively cogent way of employing mythical time to direct criticism at the present. This method reflects great sophistication and has the additional advantage, when resorting to Arab historical archetypes, of orienting Arabic theater to a national experience far removed from the Western one.

English-speaking scholarship on Arabic drama has, with few exceptions, focused heavily on the Egyptian modern tradition and especially on the works of one playwright, Tawfiq al-Hakim. Since translators of Arabic literature mostly belong to the scholarly community, the same holds true for translated anthologies and individual works. In the context of the development of a literary tradition of Arabic drama, such a prioritization was certainly appropriate earlier on. Al-Hakim was the undoubted pioneer in establishing drama as a major genre and placing it securely within the framework of modern Arabic literature. Furthermore, the Egyptian dramatic tradition has, at least until relatively recently, been in the forefront of developments in Arab theater; indeed, the period from 1955 to 1967 is regarded by many as something of a golden age of drama in Egypt. During the course of this century, however, most regions of the Arab world have developed a drama tradition of their own, within their particular local circumstances and subject to the opportunities available, and the last decades have seen significant developments in a number of countries, suggesting that the time has come for a broader perspective on the tradition of Arabic drama as a whole.

It is the aim of *Modern Arabic Drama*, the latest anthology of Arabic literature to be published by the Project of Translation from Arabic, PROTA, to provide such a broad perspective and to try to represent not only as many of the Arab countries as possible but also the more recent developments of the dramatic art in the Arab world. While we have not been able, mainly for reasons of space, to cover the region "from the Atlantic Ocean to the Arabian Gulf" (to quote Jamal ʿAbd al-Nasir's ringing phrase from the 1950s), we have included playwrights from both Tunisia in the Maghreb and Kuwait in the Gulf, as well as a good number from other Arab countries. Several playwrights (and their countries) are represented here in translated works of drama for the first time. In both theme and technique, they present the widest possible variety; the ways in which they make use of various theatrical techniques to address the issues of their own society are as different as the regions from which their writers hail.

It is important to emphasize that despite all the difficulties we have mentioned and the competitive presence of other popular media, such as the cinema and especially television (some serialized programs reflect great banality and a quest for a popularity built on sensationalism, mundaneness, and sentimentalism), a firm place has now been established for Arabic drama, not just in the countries of the Arab heartland, such as Egypt, Syria, Iraq, and Lebanon, but also in many of the other countries, including Palestine and Kuwait, and particularly in the countries of the Maghreb—Morocco, Algeria, and Tunisia—where a thriving and inventive dramatic activity exists. The contemporary cultivated Arab audience has shown great admiration and a deep respect for the dramatic output, now regarding it, with almost ideological fervor, as a pan-Arab literary achievement that will bring modern Arabic drama up to a comparable level with the modern dramatic achievements in the world. This attitude is backed by the incessant experimentation in many aspects of the dramatic art by contemporary Arab playwrights. They reflect an irrepressible, almost compulsive, passion to create, and they confirm an avant-garde theatrical tradition in Arabic which, in its best examples, is certainly equal in originality and effectiveness to the avant-garde examples in the other, highly advanced literary genres in Arabic.

All these considerations underlie and emphasize the necessity of placing this volume before an international audience.

This translated volume now commences the hardest part of its journey, as it attempts to find its way into a Western intellectual community that is presented here with examples of a genre adopted by another culture, returned in a form creatively adjusted to new themes and techniques, and now offered as a contribution to the larger corpus of world drama.

SALMA KHADRA JAYYUSI
AND ROGER ALLEN

ACKNOWLEDGMENTS

The editors of this volume would like to express their warmest thanks to Dr. Suad al-Sabah, a great lover of literature and the arts, for subsidizing both the translation of eleven of the plays included and the preparation of a publisher-ready manuscript. Her spontaneously generous assistance has made it possible for us to surmount many difficulties in this work, which we undertook as a labor of love and a cultural responsibility. Furthermore, it is with profound gratitude that we acknowledge the help of another great benefactor, the Kuwaiti poet ʿAbd al-ʿAziz Saʿud al-Babitain, for generously sponsoring the publication of this large anthology. His passionate patronage of Arabic culture furnishes a prime example of that true sponsorship that seeks its reward from fostering the impetus for greater creative activity in the Arab world. Our sincere thanks also go to Mr. Jawad Hadeed, President of the Arab Banking Corporation, Amman, Jordan, for securing the bank's subsidy for the translation of the experimental Balalin play in this anthology, chosen by us after the initial funds had been exhausted.

Before embarking on the task of selecting the plays, an extensive tour of consultation with several drama critics and directors was undertaken. In this respect, our thanks go to two drama critics, Dr. Ghassan al-Maleh, former Dean of the Syrian Academy of Dramatic Arts in Damascus, and Mr. ʿAli ʿUqla ʿIrsan, head of the Syrian Union of Writers. We also owe deep gratitude to the Tunisian actor and director al-Munsif al- Suweisi, a first-rate specialist in contemporary Arabic drama and a renowned artist, who has dedicated his life to the service of the art of theater and has guided stage production in several parts of the Arab world.

We would also like to express our heartfelt thanks to the playwrights themselves, who have responded with the greatest enthusiasm and warmth to our invitation to include their works in this anthology. The same spirit of enthusiasm and dedication characterizes the way in which the first and second translators, together with the revisers, set about the arduous task of transferring these texts for performance from one language to another, and, one hopes, from one receptive milieu to a second such milieu.

The help received from Dr. Salih J. Altoma, a member of PROTA's Administrative Committee, in the finalizing of publisher-ready copy is acknowledged here with gratitude.

Our profound thanks go to Mr. Christopher Tingley, style editor and good friend of PROTA, for his most fruitful assistance in the final revision of the whole text of the volume after its completion, and for his help in preparing it for the press.

Many thanks also go to Miss Erna Hoffmann and Ms. Kate Kline for their meticulous assistance in secretarial matters.

MODERN ARABIC DRAMA

INTRODUCTION | M. M. Badawi

For much of the first half of the twentieth century, during which the tradition of modern Arabic drama developed, the various aspects of the genre—composition, performance, and criticism—were dominated by the activities of the theater community in Egypt. A combination of historical and cultural forces fostered the development of the dramatic genre in Egypt at a relatively early stage in the cultural movement known as al-Nahda and, in the major figure Tawfiq al-Hakim (1898–1987), achieved considerable literary prestige. Nonetheless, it was in Beirut that the first manifestations of an Arabic drama tradition were born, in 1847, at the hands of Marun al-Naqqash (1817–55), a cultured, widely traveled Lebanese businessman. Al-Naqqash wrote and performed the first modern Arabic play in his own home with the help of members of his family. The play was *al-Bakhil* (The miser), clearly inspired by Molière's *l'Avare*.

It was not long before Arabic drama emigrated to Egypt in search of greater appreciation and official encouragement and patronage. From 1876 onward, Lebanese playwrights (who also served as actors and managers), such as al-Naqqash's nephew Salim (died 1884), and their Syrian imitators, such as Abu Khalil al-Qabbani (1833–1902), took their troupes to Egypt. There they continued the work that had been started quite independently in 1870 by Yaᶜqub Sannuᶜ, an Egyptian Jew who had received part of his education in Italy and who was determined on his return to create a theater in Arabic, comparable to the European theaters, that catered to the increasingly large number of Europeans in Egypt as well as the few Westernized Egyptians. Sannuᶜ's theater flourished for a brief period, from 1870 to 1872, when the Khedive Ismail inexplicably ordered him to close it down.

The Lebanese and Syrian dramatists, together with their Egyptian imitators, succeeded in making the theater a permanent feature of Egyptian urban life, and by 1900 it had even become a political force of some significance in Egypt's nationalist struggle against British occupation. This intense dramatic activity may to some extent account for the fact that it was in Egypt that Arabic drama eventually reached its maturity in the second and third decades of this century. No doubt the fairly continuous history of dramatic and semi-dramatic popular entertainments in that country from the early medieval shadow theater right down to modern primitive farces and Punch-and-Judy-like shows of Qaraqöz, helped in creating a more receptive audience in Egypt.

Both Marun al-Naqqash and Sannuᶜ derived their inspiration from the Western theater arts, particularly the Italian opera, and were heavily influenced by the European comedy of manners and intrigue, specifically the comedies of Molière. Although the pioneers and their immediate followers drew on traditional sources, notably the *Arabian Nights*, for some of their plots, in the main they relied on Western works, which they freely adapted for their popular musical drama. Sannu[c] was the exception in that he dealt (in the Egyptian colloquial language) with certain aspects—albeit on the whole somewhat marginal—of contemporary Egyptian society, such as the blind imitation of Western manners, prearranged marriages, polygamy, and quack medicine. But the search for Egyptian identity continued, strengthened by the rise of Egyptian nationalism and the emergence of a new concept of literature that departed from the still-dominant medieval view, which regarded literature as polite entertainment displaying verbal skill and ingenuity and often inculcating a moral lesson. Instead of being a ruler or a notable, the patron of modern Arabic literature was the newly created, secularly educated middle classes, who were increasingly expecting literature to reflect their contemporary social reality and indeed to attempt to change or reform that reality.

THE DEVELOPMENT OF DRAMA IN EGYPT

The Arabic theater was not able to assert itself in Egypt without a struggle. Quite the contrary. Even when good plays were being written, drama was generally regarded as mere entertainment and not as serious literature, and for a long time the theater continued to be looked upon as a place of immorality with which no self-respecting man (or woman, for sure) should be associated. As late as the early twenties, the illustrious Egyptian playwright Tawfiq al-Hakim had to hide the fact that he was the author of plays; when his secret identity was revealed, his scandalized father decided to send him off to Europe to pursue his higher legal studies in France, in the hope that his absence might help him to break his link with the disreputable theater world at home.

It was not until the early thirties that drama and acting acquired a modicum of respectability. That was due to the increasing number of well-educated and highly born young men who became involved in the theater, either as authors or as actor-managers, together with the rapid growth of theater criticism in newspapers and in several magazines devoted to the theater that began to appear in increasing numbers in the twenties. Of particular relevance was the interest taken in drama, ancient and modern, by the influential literary critic Taha Husayn and his enthusiastic reception of Tawfiq al-Hakim's play *Ahl al-Kahf* (The sleepers in the cave), which Taha Husayn regarded as a landmark in the history of Arabic literature, since in his view it signaled the appearance of a fully fledged Arabic drama.

No less relevant was the fact that the great neoclassical poet Ahmad Shawqi (1868–1932), who was regarded as the supreme poet throughout the Arab world, turned to writing verse drama during the last four years of his life. That, perhaps more than anything else, helped to render drama an acceptable form of literature in the opinion of many people. The Egyptian government began to send scholars on educational missions to Europe to study drama and acting. In 1935 the National Theater Troupe was formed under the direction of the poet Khalil Mutran, with the help of many distinguished men of letters. The first play the troupe performed was al-Hakim's *Ahl al-Kahf.*

By the time al-Hakim appeared on the scene, the main problem that had faced dramatists and indeed Egyptian modernist writers in general—how to produce specifically Egyptian Arabic drama and literature—was gradually being resolved. The process had begun with ʿUthman Jalal's superb adaptation of Molière's *Tartuffe* (*al-Shaykh Matluf*, first published in 1873 but acted much later) and had continued with varying degrees of success in the works of others. It can safely be said, however, that Egyptian Arabic drama came of age with Ibrahim Ramzi's comedy *Dukhul al-Hammam* (Admission to the baths, 1915) and his historical drama *Abtal al-Mansura* (The heroes of Mansura, 1915), Muhammad Taymur's tragedy *al-Hawiya* (The precipice, 1921), and Antun Yazbak's tragedy *al-Dhaba'ih* (The sacrifices, 1925).

Making good use of the dramatic potentialities of either classical or colloquial Arabic, these plays deal in their different ways with genuinely Egyptian problems, be they social, political, cultural, or psychological. *Admission to the Baths* takes up the perennial theme of the opposition between town and country. It describes how the economic difficulties caused by the First World War drive certain poor Cairenes to resort to cheating foolish country folk to eke out a living. It also satirizes malpractice in the courts of law. *The Heroes of Mansura*, inspired by an episode from the history of the Crusades, is an eloquent and subtle expression of Egyptian nationalist feelings and democratic aspirations. *The Precipice* has for its immediate theme the tragic problem of drug addiction, but it is at the same time a plea for responsible relations between marriage partners in modern Egyptian society. *The Sacrifices* deals with relations between husband and wife, among other things, albeit in the context of a mixed marriage (an Egyptian husband and a European wife). It describes the destructive impact of the self-absorbed older generation on the lives of the impressionable and sensitive young, who are often thoughtlessly sacrificed by their elders, caught up as they are in the clashes between them.

TAWFIQ AL-HAKIM

Al-Hakim's remarkably long career as dramatist, during which he wrote more than eighty works, spans more than half a century, from the twenties to the seventies. That is the period which witnessed the full flowering of modern Arabic drama. While still a student, al-Hakim wrote for the popular stage, turning out musical dramas and amusing satires on current political or social issues, such as the British occupation of Egypt and women's emancipation.

After his father sent him off to Paris, he learned, among other things, to regard drama not as cheap, ephemeral entertainment but as a serious form of literature. When he returned to Egypt, he was bitterly disappointed to find that the Egyptian theater, which had been bursting with activity when he left for France only three years earlier, was, for various economic, political, and cultural reasons, virtually dead. It is true that, as noted, when he started publishing his work in the early thirties, drama was slowly becoming a respectable form of literature. Nevertheless, partly because of the world economic crisis, the Egyptian theater was shrinking rapidly, and only the popular commercial stage, with its cheap diet of sensational melodrama and sexually titillating farce, had managed to survive. The rift between drama as literature and drama as stage performance was becoming even wider.

To his credit, al-Hakim resumed writing plays, both in standard written Arabic and Egyptian colloquial, knowing full well that they were not likely to be performed on the stage. These plays show a remarkably wide variety of themes and types, ranging from comedies of manners with an emphasis on the war of the sexes, such as *Sirr al-Muntahira* (The secret of the suicide, written in 1928) and the much underrated *Rasasa fi 'l-Qalb* (A bullet in the heart, 1939), which attacks materialistic attitudes to marriage and upholds the traditional moral values of loyalty and friendship, to dark comedies of social criticism, such as *Hayat Tahattamat* (A wrecked life) and the fascinating one-act *al-Zammar* (The piper, 1930), in both of which the playwright is also clearly interested in probing the psychology of his protagonists. *A Wrecked Life* is a study of failure and moral disintegration, while *The Piper* is a charming and sympathetic delineation of the artistic temperament.

To this period also belong al-Hakim's dramas of ideas, including two of his best-known works, *The Sleepers in the Cave* (written in 1928 but published in 1933) and *Shahrazad* (written in 1927 but published in 1934), in which al-Hakim puts forward his thoughts on time and place, art and life, illusion and reality. These plays demonstrate quite clearly al-Hakim's major contribution to Egyptian Arabic drama: the philosophical dimension he added to it and for which he was partly indebted to the avant-garde European dramatists whose work he came to know in Paris, notably Luigi Pirandello.

The Sleepers in the Cave, an elegant work of considerable originality that displays exquisite sensitivity and humor, is based on the Koranic version of the Christian legend of the Seven Sleepers of Ephesus. It shows how only love and the heart can triumph over time, while reason and intellect fail. Apart from dealing with one of al-Hakim's favorite themes, the play is meant to illustrate his conception of the specifically Egyptian tragedy: unlike Greek tragedy, which he believes represents man's struggle against fate, Egyptian tragedy depicts man's conflict with time.

In *Shahrazad*, which is more of a dramatic poem than drama proper, the action takes place after the passing of the thousand and one nights of the *Arabian Nights*. It depicts the tragic results of human attempts to live on the level of intellect alone to the total disregard of the emotions and the demands of the material world. To this category belongs also a later work, *Pygmalion* (1942), a dramatization of the Greek legend showing one of al-Hakim's main preoccupations: the relative importance of art and life and the need to choose between them. Because of constant indecision, al-Hakim's Pygmalion ends up both smashing his statue and destroying his own life.

In 1950, under the title *Masrah al-Mujtama*ᶜ (Plays on social themes), al-Hakim published a collection of twenty-one plays of varying quality, mostly one-act plays that originally appeared in the newspaper *Akhbar al-Yawm* between 1945 and 1950. Apart from their lively dialogue, these plays have in common a keen observation of the social problems that confronted Egypt immediately after the Second World War. In them al-Hakim satirizes corruption in politics and the machinery of government, favoritism, nepotism, abuse of power, war profiteering, the ugly face of unbridled capitalism, and the prevalence of materialistic attitudes, particularly in marriage. Perhaps the most impressive of these plays is *Ughniyat al-Mawt* (Song of death), arguably the best constructed and the most skillfully written one-act tragic play in Arabic. It is a moving dramatic statement about the clash between the values of traditional peasant society, where revenge, honor, and shame reign supreme, and those of the educated urban class intent on modernization.

In some ways al-Hakim's plays published after the 1952 army coup d'état, which overthrew King Farouk, represent a new stage in his development. Although the difference in political message from his earlier works has been somewhat exaggerated, it is a fact that from then on he came to be regarded as having effected a true marriage between the so-called theater of the mind and the popular theatre, and indeed many of his plays of the fifties and sixties were performed on the stage. Clearly al-Hakim enthusiastically espoused the cause of the revolution in the beginning. In *al-Aydi al-Naᶜima* (Soft hands, 1954), he made a plea for reconciliation between the different classes of society, while in *Sahibat al-Jalala* (Her majesty, 1955), he somewhat crudely attacked the corruption of the ancien régime. *Shams al-Nahar* (1964) is a Brechtian play preaching the values of work and egalitarianism and the need for the military to respect the law. Perhaps the most successful were *al-Safqa* (The deal, 1956) and *al-Sultan al-Haʾir* (The sultan's dilemma, 1960), both of which employ traditional folkloric elements and appeal to the intellectual and the common man alike. It is noteworthy that in *The Deal* al-Hakim made a bold experiment with the language of dialogue, resorting to what is called "the third language," which, while retaining the basic rules of grammar of the classical language, can with the slightest modification be made to sound like the colloquial on stage. He also tried to dispense with stage scenery by setting all three acts in a village public square.

Al-Hakim's experimentation went even further. As a result of a sojourn in France as Egypt's permanent representative at UNESCO, he fell under the spell of theater of the absurd, and in 1962 he wrote *Ya Tali ᶜ al-Shajara* (The tree climber), which reveals some of its influence. Al-Hakim's fascination with the absurdist technique coincided with his disillusionment with the cause of the revolution, clearly revealed in a series of works, full-length plays such as *Masir Sarsar* (The fate of a cockroach, 1966) and *Bank al-Qalaq* (Anxiety bank, 1967) as well as gloomy one-act parables or allegories such as *Rihlat Qitar* (A train journey, 1964) and *Kull Shayʾ fi Mahallih* (Not a thing out of place, 1967). Their mood is best expressed in the message of *The Fate of a Cockroach*, a strange work consisting of two deliberately juxtaposed plays: the grotesque political world of the first play, a fable marked by the savagery of its political satire, provides the context for the absurd human relations of the second play. A society ruled by a cockroach king will end up making the individuals feel like cockroaches.

Before his death, al-Hakim seems to have recovered a little from that mood of unmitigated gloom. His final comment was couched in the wry humor of the title of his last full-length play, *al-Dunya Riwaya Hazliyya* (The world is a farce, 1971), a lightweight pastoral fantasy.

TAYMUR AND BAKATHIR

Al-Hakim's prolific output and constant experimentation tended to overshadow the more traditional work of two other important writers who also wrote plays: Mahmud Taymur (1894–1973), the brother of Muhammad Taymur (author of *The Precipice*), and ʿAli Ahmad Bakathir (1910–1969).

Although Taymur turned to writing drama late in his career, he produced many interesting plays, including what is perhaps the best Arabic farce, *Haflat Shay* (A tea party, 1943), a hilarious though scathing satire on the blind imitation of Western manners; a remarkably subtle comedy of the Chekhovian variety, *Qanabil* (Bombs, 1943); and an excellent historical drama, *Saqr Quraysh* (The hawk of Quraysh, 1955), the hero of which provides a fascinating psychological study. Bakathir managed to create at least two memorable characters, al-Hakim bi-Amrillah (1947) and Lady Julfadan (1962), although his plays, unlike Taymur's, tend to be structurally weak.

EGYPTIAN DRAMATISTS AFTER THE REVOLUTION

Although Taymur and Bakathir continued to write after the 1952 revolution, it was a new generation of dramatists who, together with al-Hakim, tended to dominate the scene. The revolution was in fact a landmark in the history of modern Egyptian and Arabic drama. A remarkable revival of the Egyptian theater occurred during the late fifties and the sixties, following the mood of euphoria and optimism that swept over the country in the wake of the revolution.

The new dramatists were young men more eager to experiment with the form and language of drama than were their older contemporaries, with the obvious exception of al-Hakim. They were less inhibited about the use of the Egyptian colloquial in their "serious" plays, particularly as the new regime adopted socialist and populist slogans. The mood of optimism was expressed in several plays in which playwrights contrasted the hopeful present and future with the corrupt ancien régime. Writers seemed to turn spontaneously to drama instead of other genres as the most suitable form in which to express their preoccupations and impart their message. Because of the banning of political parties and the consequent absence of free exchange of opinion, the theater became an ersatz parliament in which authors expressed their political views, often obliquely—particularly later on with the increasingly active censorship and the growing disillusion with the revolution and anger at the crushing of the individual by a totalitarian regime.

Despite these dramatists' intense nationalism, they were open to foreign influences. Either directly or through translations, they were introduced to the work of playwrights such as Eugène Ionesco, Samuel Beckett, and John Osborne, and they followed with avid interest the news of contemporary experimental productions on Western stages, such as *O, What a Lovely War*. The two European dramatists whose works were most often discussed in the recently established influential monthly periodical devoted to the theater, *al-Masrah* (The stage), were Pirandello and Bertolt Brecht, the latter as much for ideological as for artistic reasons. The interest these Egyptian dramatists took in Western theories about "total" theater, theater in the round, alienation, and the like, coupled with the deepening mood of Egyptian and Arab nationalism, led them to raise fundamental questions about the nature of drama and the role of theater in society, and to search for a specifically Egyptian and Arab form of theater. They tried to establish their plays on the basis of popular traditional village entertainment, such as *al-samir* (a village evening gathering for singing, dancing and storytelling), or to relate their work to medieval Arabic forms, such as the *maqama* (a tale told in rhyming prose with some verse, often about the tricks of an eloquent vagabond who has to live by his wits through impersonating other characters) and shadow theater.

From the start the new regime was aware of the importance of cultural propaganda and therefore pursued a policy that soon led to the flourishing of the theater. The newly created Ministry of Culture and National Guidance set up palaces of culture and the General Foundation for Theater and Music (1960), which established theaters, including an experimental theater; encouraged actors; welcomed distinguished Western directors; and financed the stage production of plays, indigenous and foreign, classical and modern alike. The foundation also financed publication of *al-Masrah*, together with two series of play texts, one consisting of original Arabic plays, the other specializing in translations of masterpieces of world drama. One particularly significant development was the publication on a regular basis of the texts of plays recently produced on the stage. These included many works written in Egyptian colloquial, a fact that helped considerably toward gaining acceptance of the colloquial as a medium for serious drama.

Recent experiments in metrical forms which liberated Arabic verse from the traditional constrictions of monorhyme and monometer made it possible to use the new form for purposes of drama, with the result that there was an interesting large-scale revival of verse drama. A spate of verse plays appeared, beginning with the work of the Egyptians ᶜAbd al-Rahman al-Sharqawi (1920?–88) and Salah ᶜAbd al-Sabur (1931–81). Al-Sabur's *Night Traveler* is included in this collection. Other Arab poets, such as the Egyptian Najib Surur and the Palestinians Muᶜin Bseisu and Samih al-Qasim, joined in, and the vogue spread even to several poets who seemed to know little about the exigencies of drama.

Critics are agreed that the appearance in 1956 of *Il-Nas illi Taht* (The people downstairs), by one of Egypt's foremost dramatists, Nuᶜman ᶜAshur (1918–87), marks the beginning of the new wave. The play is characterized by a new note of harsh realism, of urgency and commitment, together with a bold use of the colloquial. Set in an apartment building in a popular quarter of Cairo, it contrasts the materialism of the self-seeking older generation with the idealism of the young, who reject a secure but soulless life in favor of a more meaningful, altruistic, socialist future. The tragic failure of the Chekhovian character of Ragaᶜi, the only aristocrat in the play, signals the eclipse of the old aristocratic order. The same combination of social and political criticism and popular comedy can be seen in ᶜAshur's other works, which for a while he produced almost at the rate of one play a year.

Social realism is also the hallmark of Lutfi al-Khuli, who provides a vivid portrayal of Egyptian life together with naturalistic colloquial dialogue, but in his plays politics seem to be somewhat arbitrarily superimposed. Saᶜd al-Din Wahba, another playwright who used colloquial Arabic and who began by writing within the social realist school, concentrated on the Egyptian village, at least in his early work. But his sombre comedies gradually acquired an admixture of symbolism, which at times attained considerable subtlety.

The People Downstairs by ᶜAshur was one of the two plays that had a seminal effect upon Egyptian drama, the other being *Al Farafir* (The flipflaps, 1964) by Yusuf Idris (1927–91), who began writing realistic drama as early as 1954. In *The Flipflaps* he claims to have attempted to write specifically Egyptian drama based on the indigenous folkloric theatrical tradition, including the licensed Fool, Juha, the shadow theater, and more particularly the village *samir*. But the play in fact owes as much, if not more, to the Western experiments of Pirandello and Brecht. In an attempt to make drama a genuinely collective, shared experience, Idris deliberately breaks down the barrier between actors and audience, thereby destroying the dramatic illusion.

The play begins with the Author, dressed in a ridiculous costume, explaining to the audience members what they are about to see. He is rudely interrupted by the sudden noisy appearance of the clown, Farfur, a servant in search of a master. One is promptly found for him by the Author. The play proceeds to give an account of the tempestuous relationship between Servant and Master. In the meantime the Author's part grows smaller and smaller until he disappears altogether, leaving the other two to work out their own destiny. The Servant's problem is not solved by exchanging roles with the Master, or even by their death at the end, which only turns Farfur into an electron spinning round the proton of his Master.

Despite its prolixity and digressions, *al-Farafir* is a deeply disturbing play on the social, political, and metaphysical levels. Not only does the play tackle the themes of authority and freedom, the hierarchical structure of society, and the tendency of power to corrupt, but by the gradual shrinking into nothing of the Author, Idris hints at a world that is deserted by God in which men are left to their own devices. The final image of Farfur spinning dizzyingly round his Master like an electron round the proton suggests the all-too-gloomy conclusion that the division of beings into master and slave is a cosmic law. Yet despite its depressing conclusion, *al-Farafir* is full of humor: through his licensed Fool, the author ridicules social injustice, political tyranny, and all forms of hypocrisy and cant.

Idris's rejection of the form of realistic drama, which began with *The Flipflaps*, continued to mark his later plays, in which his vision grows noticeably darker, culminating in *al-Mukhattatin* (The striped ones, 1969), which is an "absurdist" political allegory, lashing out savagely at the totalitarian one-party state; it reminds one of George Orwell's *1984*. It is one of the most outspoken political satires written during the Nasser era, and it is amazing that its publication was not banned by the censor. In it Idris is primarily interested in *homo politicus*; man is reduced merely to his political role, thereby becoming a caricature.

Similar satire on corruption and tyranny in contemporary Egyptian society can be found in the work of Faruq Khurshid (born 1924) and Mikha'il Ruman (1927–73). Khurshid created in *Habazlam Bazaza* a character who is a perfect personification of amoral Machiavellian opportunism. Ruman concentrated on the theme of the freedom of the individual, depicting in more than one eloquent and moving drama, but most notably in his Kafkaesque *al-Wafid* (The newcomer, 1965) and *al-Khitab* (The letter, 1965), the way this freedom is crushed under moral, psychological, and political pressure. Ruman began as a realist in his full-length play *al-Dukhan* (Smoke, 1962), a study of a somewhat existentialist rebel struggling to break free from drug addiction. As his art developed, Ruman relied increasingly on symbolist and absurdist techniques. A curious feature of his work is that he gave the same name, Hamdi, to the protagonists of many of his plays; all of them are highly strung, hypersensitive men, usually of creative artistic talent, driven to the edge of insanity by extreme, often nightmarish experiences. They are all rebels against various forms of oppression.

Alfred Farag (born 1929), on the other hand, avoided the excesses of the theater of the absurd and sought his inspiration in Arab popular and folk literature, such as the *Arabian Nights* and the medieval romances, which he treated in a manner slightly influenced by Brecht, to comment on contemporary social and political reality. He satirized the abuses of the socialist state and attacked dictatorship. Like Ashur, he acknowledged his debt to Tawfiq al-Hakim. He produced one of the best and most thoughtful comedies of the period, *ʿAli Janah al-Tabrizi* (included in this collection), as well as an interesting study of a tragic character in *Sulayman al-Halabi*.

Despite being an entertaining work making full use of the popular dramatic and literary Arabic tradition, *ʿAli Janah* has a deeper social, political, and psychological significance. Both the protagonist and his fictitious caravan lend themselves easily to symbolic interpretation. The author raises several interesting questions, such as the relation between illusion and reality, the thin line separating the prophet or social reformer from the impostor, deception from self-deception.

In marked contrast to the predominantly political drama is the work of Rashad Rushdi, who in a number of plays concentrated on the predicament of the modern Egyptian woman but then turned to more political issues. In his later plays, Rushdi employed rather precious, at times irritating, experimental techniques, making his plays look too contrived, straining after effect.

Of the next generation of dramatists, one of the most outstanding is Mahmud Diyab (1932–83). Diyab, whose work deals mainly with Egyptian village life, began by writing in the realistic mode. His *al-Zawbaʿa* (The storm, 1967) is certainly one of the best plays to be produced by the new wave of dramatists. The dialogue, realistic to the point of faithfully reproducing the local dialect, rises to poetry in moments of deep emotion. In it Diyab, unlike most of his contemporaries, does not preach a facile political or moral lesson. Yet by concentrating on the drama of human relationships and probing deeply into human motives, he manages to raise, in the close and confined world of a tiny far-off Egyptian village, large questions relating to justice and conscience, individual and collective responsibility. With all its earnestness, however, the play is not devoid of humor. In his later plays, Diyab experimented with dramatic form based on the village *samir*; he also shifted his setting to the city, where he succeeded in creating a powerful Pinterlike menacing atmosphere in plays such as *Strangers Don't Drink Coffee* (included here), which operate on political as well as metaphysical levels.

Also outstanding is ʿAli Salem (born 1936), who had firsthand experience of the theater, beginning as an actor. He is probably the most distinguished satirist of his generation, aiming his merciless attacks at three main targets: bureaucracy, corruption, and despotism. His play *The Comedy of Oedipus* is included in this collection. To the same generation belongs Shawqi ʿAbd al-Hakim, who began to write plays in 1960 and who derived his inspiration almost exclusively from the Egyptian folk tale and popular ballad. In this respect he represents one of the most distinguishing features of the new wave of drama: its creative use of popular forms of entertainment and folklore.

THEATER IN OTHER ARAB COUNTRIES

The Egyptian theatrical revival had its impact on many parts of the Arab world, where there soon developed a keen interest in the theater. In Syria the National Theater was established by the government in 1959. In Lebanon the influential Contemporary Theater Troupe was founded by Munir Abu Dibs in the following year. In Iraq the General Foundation for Cinema and Theater was created in 1960, and in Tunisia a drama school was set up in 1959 and was further developed into an important national institute in 1966; festivals for North African drama have been held there since 1961. In Morocco drama institutes were established by the government in 1956, two troupes in 1957, and a center for dramatic art in 1959. The first permanent Sudanese theater was opened in Khartoum in 1961, and in Jordan the Ministry of Information formed the National Theater Troupe in 1965.

Partly under the influence of the Egyptian theater there developed a corresponding search for specifically Arab dramatic forms, based upon either traditional folk modes of entertainment or the medieval Arabic *maqama*. But the emphasis, no doubt inspired by the Western example, tended to be more on staging, acting, and improvisation, on the theater as a "happening" and a living communal experience, than on drama as a written text or a form of literature. Several playwrights and directors of theater companies distinguished themselves, including al-Tayyib al-Siddiqi in Morocco, ʿIzz al-Din al-Madani in Tunisia, Yusuf al-ʿAni in Iraq, and Munir Abu Dibs and others in Lebanon.

SYRIA

In Syria the theater retained its close links with the literary text, and classical Arabic tended to dominate the stage. The most outstanding of the Syrian dramatists is Saʿdallah Wannus (born 1940), who received his theater training in Cairo and Paris. Wannus attained instant fame with his experimental play *Haflat Samar min Ajl Khamsa Huzayran* (An evening party for June the 5th, first published in 1968), a bitter and courageous satire on the politics that led to the Arab defeat in the Arab-Israeli war of June 1967.

Prior to *Haflat Samar*, Wannus had written a number of interesting one-act plays in the tradition of al-Hakim's drama of ideas but employing techniques of the puppet theater. The most notable of them are the sinister *Juththa ʿala 'l-Rasif* (Corpse on the pavement), a somewhat surrealistic portrayal of the callous manner in which the authorities side with the rich against the poor and destitute, and *al-Fil ya Malik al-Zaman* (The Elephant, O King of the World!), a didactic parable demonstrating how people can be totally emasculated and terrorized by a tyrannical and despotic ruler.

Under the influence of Piscator and Brecht, Wannus called for the need to politicize drama, *tasyis al-masrah*, i. e., to use drama as a means of politically educating the theater audience. In several experimental plays he tried, with varying degrees of success, to put his principles into practice, employing various techniques from traditional as well as modern Western sources to ensure the participation and education of his audience. For instance, *Mughamarat Raʾs al-Mamluk Jabir* (The adventure of Mamluk Jabir's head, 1969), *Sahra maʿa Abi Khalil al-Qabbani* (An evening's entertainment with Abu Khalil al-Qabbani, 1972), and *al-Malik huwa 'l-Malik* (The king is the king, 1977) are all set in the world of the *Arabian Nights* and carry overt revolutionary political messages.

In *Haflat Samar*, by strategically placing the actors amid the audience, Wannus extends the stage to the entire auditorium. At an official performance of a play intended to deal with the June war, actors representing eyewitnesses of the war rise from the audience to object to the misrepresentation of the events by the author and director. These eyewitnesses proceed to give a more factual and less flattering account. The lively and open discussion that ensues concerning who was to blame leads the authorities to stop the show and to place the entire audience under arrest. Despite its shortcomings as a play, *Haflat Samar* had a strong impact in its topicality: it was a powerful expression of the mood of disillusion and anger, of self-criticism and soul searching, that enveloped the enter Arab world in the wake of its shocking defeat.

Mughamarat Raʾs al-Mamluk Jabir is described by Wannus in the preface as another experiment in *masrah al-tasyis*, not political theater but politicized theater, theater that engages actors and audience in a lively dialogue. Wannus uses multiple planes of reality. At a café, customers order various drinks and listen to popular songs on the radio while waiting for the Hakawati (Storyteller) to come and entertain them for the evening. The Storyteller arrives, but instead of their favorite medieval romance, which relates the heroic victory of Baybars over the Crusaders, he insists upon telling them the earlier story of the cunning and resourceful *mamluk* Jabir, who during a serious quarrel between a late Abbasid Caliph and his Vizier, manages to get out of Baghdad bearing a secret message from the Vizier for the Persian King, written on the skin of his head after his hair has been first shaved and then allowed to grow again to cover it. When he arrives in the Persian Court, instead of being recompensed for this ingenious device, as he has been promised, with wealth and marriage to the woman he loves, Jabir is instantly put to death by the

Persian King in accordance with the Vizier's instruction, which, unbeknown to Jabir, is part of the message, the other part being an invitation from the Vizier to the Persian King to invade Baghdad and help him depose the Caliph.

The events in the Storyteller's narration are acted out by actors, with the Storyteller performing the function of chorus and the café customers commenting on the action. The audience of the play shares with the audience of café customers the same interest in popular songs but obviously is differentiated, as the latter audience in turn is distinguished from the characters who enact the Storyteller's tale. The dramatist provides many links between these three planes of reality, using various devices, including many topical allusions to the contemporary Arab world. On the whole, this rather complicated structure, in which the same actors are made to play several parts, works reasonably well, despite the author's inability to resist the temptation to bring in a series of very brief scenes depicting the abject misery of the common people, totally neglected by their rulers, who are selfishly engaged in their struggle for power. One also questions the wisdom of making the fate of the mamluk Jabir the central theme in a play dealing with events of such magnitude and import as the struggle for power between the Caliph and Vizier and the treachery of the rulers and their readiness to conspire with foreign governments against the national interest.

Wannus makes another attempt to use history to comment on the present in *Sahra maʿa Abi Khalil al-Qabbani*. Here his immediate objectives are threefold. The first is to recreate the theater of al-Qabbani, the father of Syrian drama (in which Wannus believes there was a kind of direct communion between actors and audience, which he is anxious to recreate in his own work), through a presentation of a slightly modified version of al-Qabbani's play derived from the *Arabian Nights*, *Harun al-Rashid maʿ al-Amir Ghanim ibn Ayyub wa Qut al-Qulub*. The second is a dramatization of the (idealized) career of al-Qabbani as dramatist in Syria, including a semidocumentary episode showing his struggle to establish a theater, the encouragement he received from the Ottoman governor, and the opposition he met with from the conservative men of religion, who eventually managed to close down his theater. Interspersed with this is Wannus's political commentary on the corruption and chaos of the Ottoman rule of Syria. The result is a sprawling work that lacks the necessary dramatic concentration and which even the author suggests in a preface could be abridged for the stage.

By far the most satisfactory of Wannus's experiments is *The King's the King* (included in this collection), which uses as its framework the very tale which Marun al-Naqqash, the father of Arabic drama, had used for *Abu 'l Hasan al-Mughaffal* (1849–50), but with a difference. Here Harun al-Rashid's attempt to amuse himself by having the impoverished and disgruntled merchant Abu ʿIzza drugged and placed on the throne for a day turns sour: once on the throne Abu ʿIzza assumes absolute authority, becomes even more tyrannical than the real king to the extent that the latter's men are forced to acknowledge him as their real monarch, and the tale ends with Abu ʿIzza actually replacing Harun al-Rashid. The play uses a variety of techniques, including farce and puppetry. It opens and closes with the actors in chorus informing the audience what they are about to perform, deliberately destroying the dramatic illusion in the true Brechtian manner. They also comment on the action and at the end point out that the people can, and should, get rid of the very system that makes kings possible, because all kings are the same.

No less political in content are the plays of Mustafa al-Hallaj. For instance, *al-Ghadab* (Anger, 1959) deals with the Algerian struggle for independence and depicts the methods of torture employed by the French colonists. Torture is also the theme of *al-Darawish Yabhathun ᶜan al-Haqiqa* (The dervishes seek the truth, 1970): a totally innocent man is subjected to unspeakable torture and finally condemned to death because he happens to bear the same name as a political activist sought by the secret police, whose primary concern is not to establish a man's guilt or innocence but to prepare a file which they can submit to their superiors on anyone they can force to admit guilt. Though overwritten in parts and with insufficient action, it is a powerful play in which the protagonist becomes a symbol of the heroic struggle of the innocent individual against an all-powerful, unjust system.

Another Syrian playwright, Mamduh ᶜUdwan (born 1941), employs events and characters from early Islamic history to make comments on modern Arab political reality. ᶜUdwan is capable of creating a play with a strikingly cynical twist at the end, such as *Hal al-Dunya* (That's life, 1984; included in this collection), which is written throughout in the interesting form of a monologue, punctuated by the ringing of the doorbell or the telephone.

ᶜAli ᶜUqla ᶜUrsan (born 1940) wrote several plays with political themes, such as *al-Ghuraba'* (The strangers, 1974), a rather naive allegorical treatment of the Zionist immigration to Palestine, and the more subtle *al-Sajin Raqam 95* (Prisoner no. 95, 1974), which ruthlessly attacks political persecution in the Arab world by showing the complete arbitrariness with which sentences, be they death or imprisonment for a limited period or for life, are passed on the innocent and even indiscriminately changed by the authorities. *ᶜAradat al-Khusum* (The opposition demonstration, 1976) is more a political parable or illustrated sermon than a drama, a defense of political idealism and genuine self-sacrifice for the nationalist cause against cynicism and hypocrisy and the use of slogans to promote self-interest. Characters are mere types and undergo conversion instantly, against all probability. It can be argued that the impact of the documentary and Brechtian theater on Arabic drama, as clearly shown in this play, has generally resulted in dramatists' abandoning any serious attempt at portraying character in depth. On the whole the effect has been rather damaging.

Less politically charged and, on the whole, less sombre and more comical in spirit are the plays of Walid Ikhlasi (born 1935), although they are by no means free from satire or social criticism. *Kayfa Tasᶜad Duna an Taqaᶜ* (How to climb without falling, 1973) is a study of the making of an opportunist who, through sheer cunning and resourcefulness, dishonesty and unscrupulousness, manages to rise to the position of cabinet minister. *Hadha 'l-Nahr al-Majnun* (This mad river, 1976), described by the author as "an original tragedy," portrays an elderly woman of a domineering personality belonging to the expropriated class of the ancien régime who is unable to come to terms with the new situation created by the recent land-reform laws, which limited her property and reduced her status. Despite personal tragedies she is determined to struggle on in a world that bears no relation to reality. In *al-Sirat* (The path, 1976; included in this collection), the protagonist is a humble theater cleaner and general factotum who, owing to the illness of an actor, is asked to stand in. He proves such a success as a stage clown that he is encouraged to go on playing the role, but he discovers to his disillusionment that he can only maintain his popularity as a comedian on the stage, and hence his huge financial success, by means of hypocrisy and affirmation of the false values of the establishment. In the end he opts out and is punished by the authorities, being allowed neither to leave his country nor to remain in it, thereby being forced to inhabit an impossible no-man's land. It is through his portrayal of such interesting human types that Ikhlasi presents his criticism of society and reveals its corruption.

The work of Ikhlasi as well as that of other Arabic dramatists often contains poetic elements, but it is in the surrealistic play *al-ᶜUsfur al-Ahdab* (The hunchbacked sparrow, 1967) by poet Muhammad Maghut (born 1932) that we find one of the most powerful and haunting dramatic statements of political oppression and tyranny in the modern Arab world. It is a surrealistic play in four acts with an enormous cast that includes (besides human beings of all ages ranging from grandparents to children) birds, a Birdwoman, and the Voice of the Wind. Characters change from one act to another. In the beginning they all appear as political prisoners in a huge mancage, but the Old Man of Act I is rejuvenated as the tyrannical Prince of Act III, and likewise the sex-obsessed Bachelor is transformed into the Holy Man. The violence of Maghut's imagery and syntax is paralleled in the action of the play, which includes the flogging of prisoners and the shooting of children by a firing squad. However, the absence of a clearly defined plot, a single action with logical progression, would certainly make the staging of *The Hunchbacked Sparrow* an exceedingly difficult task; it is clearly a work more suited for the library than for the theater.

Maghut went on to write a savage satire on Arab regimes in *al-Muharrij* (The jester, 1973), a much more easily actable drama, which makes its point in less surrealistic language. A fantasy in three acts, *The Jester* is a black farce that mercilessly ridicules modern Arab society by means of buffoonery and zany methods, exposing the sham and hollowness in its cherished values as well as the horror of its oppressive, authoritarian governments. It is a powerful, well-constructed play, with plenty of action and humor to sustain the interest of the audience; yet it has the rare advantage, for an Arabic play, of concentrated style and manageable length. It opens noisily with the beating of drums and clinking of a dancer's castanets, announcing the arrival of a troupe of penniless itinerant players, clowns who have turned to acting after having failed in every other trade. They appear on a cart that constitutes the mobile stage and perform in the open space next to a café in an old slum quarter of an unnamed Arab city. The troupe is run by a semiliterate Drummer who acts as Presenter and Commentator, and includes a woman dancer. The inhabitants are attracted by the noise and fascinated by the garish costumes and the gyrations of the female dancer. The Drummer introduces the troupe to the people as young committed actors with a highly developed social conscience, determined to bring the theater to the people's doorsteps. They proceed to entertain them. Their performance is punctuated by angry protests from the owner of the café, patrons' orders called aloud, shouts of annoyance from a solemn elderly schoolmaster because the actors are constantly breaking the rules of classical Arabic grammar, and critical comments from the audience.

They first act a thoroughly distorted scene from *Othello*, leading to the murder of Desdemona. The part of Othello is played by the actor referred to as the Jester, who will subsequently play other parts. He is a comic version of Othello in the exaggerated melodramatic tradition of Yusuf Wahbi, the famous Egyptian stage and film actor, while the female dancer plays Desdemona, appearing in modern costume, swinging her handbag, and chewing gum. In a comment on the action, the Drummer attacks Shakespeare for bringing about the downfall of the Arab national hero Othello, which he sees as a British imperialist plot, in collusion with America, with its nuclear bases. That gives rise to several anti-American and anti-NATO shouts from the audience. The Drummer urges his audience never to give in to such imperialist plots but to derive inspiration and comfort from the innumerable national heroes of their past. At their suggestion the troupe play Harun al-Rashid, the paragon of Arab justice and chivalry. The Jester then appears as Harun al-Rashid comically devouring his food at a feast, dispensing mock justice in an absurdly arbitrary manner to the noisy approval of the audience. This is followed by the Jester's impersonation of the Arab founder of Muslim Spain, the Umayyad ʿAbd al-Rahman, known as the Hawk of Quraysh, who is presented, contrary to historical fact, as a spoiled prince given solely to the pursuit of sensual pleasure. This prompts a comment from someone in the audience that this interpretation would make the Hawk turn in his grave. Immediately the telephone rings, and Act I ends when the proprietor of the café announces that the Hawk is on the phone, wishing to speak to the Jester. Accompanied by thunder and lightning, the Hawk's voice is heard, to the amazement of the stunned audience. From here on, the mood of the play becomes more sombre and macabre.

In Act II the Jester has been transported in a coffin to the court of the Hawk, who is intent on punishing him. The Jester humbly begs for mercy and by a clever trick he manages to distract the Hawk and his courtiers by arousing their interest in the wonders of modern civilization, showing them some of the modern gadgets which, like a traveling salesman, he has brought with him in his coffin. Impressed by the Jester's knowledge and expertise, the Hawk wishes to make use of him by appointing him governor in one of the Arab provinces. He offers him first Spain, then Alexandretta, then Palestine, but he is told that these provinces no longer belong to the Arabs. The Hawk asks the reason for the modern Arabs' failure. The Jester explains how, using the excuse of the Palestinian cause, their despotic rulers have emasculated them, turning them into mere mice and cockroaches, by abusing their freedoms, subjecting them to torture, robbing them of their dignity and destroying their self-respect. He even gives him a practical demonstration of how this is done by inflicting gruesome torture on one of the Hawk's incredulous men, who volunteers for the purpose. The act ends with the disgusted Hawk deciding against the Jester's advice to come back from the dead to restore Arab dignity and manhood and to liberate Palestine. In Act III the Hawk is stopped by immigration officers at the frontiers of an Arab state, on the grounds that he has no passport. When he declares his identity, he is at first taken to be mad, but then his story is believed, and he is surrounded by media men who, uninterested in his mission, ask him all manner of silly questions. But he is soon put under arrest by the Arab authorities and a deal is struck with the emissary of the Spanish government; in return for the significant sum of thirty thousand tons of onions, the Hawk is handed over to the Spanish who are keen to try him for the war crimes he committed when he originally invaded their country in the eighth century. Suspecting the worst, the Jester makes a desperate attempt to persuade the Hawk to escape, but of course he refuses to listen to him.

As can be seen, the play presents a topsy-turvy world in which values are completely reversed. For example, Othello is viewed as an Arab hero destroyed by Shakespeare as a part of a British imperialist plot backed up by the Americans with their nuclear bases and Phantom jet fighters. Harun al-Rashid, the paragon of Arab chivalry and justice, is shown ordering that a plaintiff brought before him for trial be paid a thousand dinars and then have his head struck off for being too talkative. A great Arab national hero from the medieval past is humiliated for not owning a passport and is betrayed by his people and sold to the enemy. Past and present are mixed. The Jester is taken back to the early Middle Ages, and the medieval figure of the Arab founder of Muslim Spain, the Umayyad ʿAbd al-Rahman, known as the Hawk of Quraysh, is brought into the twentieth century. Metaphors are literally translated into the physical reality of their verbal components. An actress described by the Presenter as having been "suckled" on true dramatic art appears on the stage with a dummy (pacifier) in her mouth. Characters are literally "painted" by a house painter with a paint bucket and brush.

LEBANON

Unlike the Syrians, the Lebanese have been concentrating, at least since the 1960s, not on drama as a written literary text but on the revival of the theater as a living experience, both in musical drama and translations and adaptations of Western theatre, benefiting from the technique of the avant-garde and addressing themselves to the local intellectual elite who could appreciate the subtleties of the political satire presented to them. A possible exception to this rule is ʿIsam Mahfuz (born 1939), a poet who became interested in writing for the theater. Among his plays are *al-Zanalakht* (The China tree, written in 1963 but produced and published in 1968), *al-Qatl* (The assassination, 1968), *al-Dictatur* (1970), and *Limadha?* (Why? 1971), the last of which he directed himself.

The China Tree (included in this collection) consists of a prologue and twelve scenes. The setting alternates between the outside of a palace gate and a courtroom by means of dimming parts of the stage. When, near the end of the play, the entire stage is lit, the outside of the palace gate is shown to be a part of the courtroom.

In the prologue Saʿdun, the "hero" of the play, appears on an empty stage caning a chair. He tells the audience he was originally a jeweler and is anxious to tell them his strange story which he himself at times finds incredible, a story in which the main characters are the General, the Clerk, his own Godfather and the Old Lady. Saᶜdun is accused of murdering a young woman and brought to trial in a courtroom full of spectators. Although his guilt is never proved by logical argument, he is sentenced to death. However, before the sentence is carried out, he acts on the advice of a Mysterious Voice claiming to be a Tree, stiffens his body by an act of will, and manages to transform himself into a China Tree. He is carried out of the courtroom horizontally like a tree trunk by two enormous male nurses in white uniforms, to the satisfaction of the people in the courtroom. Immediately afterward a Nun enters ringing a small bell to announce that it is time to eat, at which everyone leaps toward the door, clamoring like school children at the end of classes. They are told by the Nun to wash their hands before eating. Apart from Saᶜdun's sudden change into a tree at the end very little happens in the play. In the courtroom Saᶜdun responds after a fashion to the questions put to him and outside the Palace Gate he is engaged mainly in his desperate attempt to enter the house. He knocks patiently but to no avail. He engages in an "absurdist" conversation with strange Beggars and behaves like one himself. In fact, as in the case of other characters, the exact identity of Saᶜdun is never completely established. Is he a caner, a jeweler, a tramp à la Beckett, or is he Everyman? Equally, the General who tries him is at one and the same time the Judge in the courtroom, the authoritarian father, the military dictator and the ruler of the state. Saᶜdun's desperate attempt to get access to the inside of the palace, his bewildered helplessness as regards a murder charge leveled against him, and a wealth of sinister and haunting imagery make *The China Tree* a cross between a surrealist, nightmarish variation on the Oedipal situation and a strikingly Kafkaesque brand of "absurdist" drama. The play has many remarkable features, such as its sophisticated technical devices, its stychomythia, its impressive Ionescolike style of dialogue, and its rich political, psychological, even metaphysical implications. But it is more the work of an elitist Arab intellectual thoroughly at home in the latest Western vogue than a truly Arab play that can appeal to the average Arab reader or audience.

PALESTINE

With few exceptions, such as the Balalin Company, the collective authors of *al-ᶜAtma* (Darkness, 1972; included here), Palestinians have been primarily interested in drama as literature, and some of them have written verse drama. For obvious reasons, the Arab-Israeli conflict and the need for the struggle to liberate occupied Palestine figure largely in their plays, e. g. *Qaraqash* by Samih al-Qasim (born 1939) and *Thawrat al-Zanj* (al-Zanj's revolution) and *Shamshun wa Dalila* (Samson and Delilah) by Muᶜin Bseisu (1926–1984).

Qaraqash (1970), for which the "time" is described in the stage directions as "always" and the "place" "everywhere," opens with a chorus chanting "Qaraqash is to be found anytime, anywhere." This is followed by a pantomime showing processions first of tired ancient Greeks in chains slowly crossing the stage accompanied by strains of music, herded by a similarly dressed man with a whip, secondly of a procession of ancient Egyptians, and lastly modern Europeans, equally in chains, lashed by a whip, bearing a large photo of Hitler whose voice is heard delivering one of his speeches.

Then ensues a series of four tableaux. In the first, Qaraqash, a one-eyed tyrant, addresses his disgruntled and starving subjects. He urges them to wage war on more fertile, richer land and orders the death of the revolutionary peasant who tries to incite his fellow citizens not to incur any more sacrifices. Tableau I ends with his execution. In tableau II Qaraqash, having achieved victory and enriched his followers with booty, goes on a hunting expedition, is annoyed to find simple folk singing and merrymaking after harvesting for fear that the noise might frighten the wild animals away, and orders them to stop at once. In the meantime the Prince, his son, falls in love with a peasant's daughter, asks the Vizier to persuade Qaraqash to agree to this unequal marriage. In tableau III we see the tyrant Qaraqash sitting in judgment on several citizens with grievances all of whom receive only harsh sentences from him. In tableau IV the gallows are brought on the stage to hang those sentenced to death, including a man whose sole crime is that he could not beget a son to serve in Qaraqash's army. The Vizier tries to sound him out on the matter of a prince marrying a peasant girl, but Qaraqash's prompt reaction is that such a couple ought to be beheaded and he demands to see their heads at once, assuming that what the Vizier mentioned was not a hypothetical case, but something that has actually happened in his kingdom. The severed heads are brought before him and to his horror he discovers that one of them was his own son's. Controlling his grief, however, he proceeds to order his men to go to war. The peasants, however, having had enough of Qaraqash's reign of terror, rise against him and murder him and his Vizier. The play ends with the jubilant peasants being joined by the soldiers in a scene of dancing and singing.

The play is full of contemporary allusions; the one-eyed Qaraqash obviously refers to General Moshe Dayan. Yet it is never really dramatic; the poetry remains lyrical or descriptive and is never transmuted into drama. There is neither real conflict, whether internal or external, nor real characterization, for the author does not dwell long enough on his creations to render them psychologically plausible.

IRAQ

The same preoccupation with politics, social injustice, and corruption and the same call for revolutionary action mark the work of Iraqi dramatists, of whom the most prominent is Yusuf al-ʿAni (born 1927). In his early work, which consisted largely of simple, naturalistic one-act plays, often more like sketches or scenes than properly structured drama, al-ʿAni dealt with such issues as the idleness of civil servants and the corruption of bureaucracy (*Ra's al-Shulayla*, or The gang leader, 1951); exorbitant prescription charges beyond the means of dying patients (*Fulus al-Dawaʾ*, or Prescription charges, 1952); malpractice in private clinics (*Sittat Darahim*, or Six dirhams, 1954); the persecution of political dissidents (*Ana Ummuk ya Shakir*, or I'm your mother, Shakir, 1955); the temptation to embezzle in order to provide medicine for a sick child (*al-Masyada*, or The trap, 1961); and the ill treatment of a mentally retarded young man by his cruel stepmother (*Jamil*, 1962). *Ahlan bi'l-Hayah* (Welcome, life, 1960) treats the abuse of the rights of citizens by a tyrannical regime and the restoration of these rights by the revolution, while *Sura Jadida* (A new image, 1964), a longer play in seven tableaux, shows how a rich merchant who has risen from poverty is saved from the folly of turning out his wife and children and taking on a new wife young enough to be his daughter. Despite its sociological interest, the events in *The New Image* happen too fast and are presented merely externally, without any attempt to portray character in depth. Better known than these are al-ᶜAni's later, longer works: *al-Miftah* (The key, 1967–68; included here) and *al-Kharaba* (The waste land, 1970), in which he makes use of popular traditions and folklore and borrows the technique of the puppet theatre and the documentary.

The Key is a dramatization of a nursery rhyme in a series of tableaux depicting the quest of a young couple for a baby and a life of security, interspersed with political commentary and folk singing, with a narrator filling in the gaps. It is a call for political action and the courage to face reality, dressed as a popular theatrical entertainment. *The Key* is more akin to musical drama with a simple unilinear structure than to drama proper. It constitutes an attempt to make the theater more accessible to the people, serving as a popular and entertaining dramatic spectacle with an obvious social message.

As for *al-Kharaba*, it too is a didactic dramatic entertainment, but it presents a mixture of realism and fantasy, and is deliberately designed to break the dramatic illusion à la Brecht. The auditorium is dressed as an exhibition hall, showing photographs and documents, as well as newspaper clippings illustrating the crimes committed by colonialism and world imperialism. The characters, who remain mostly nameless, are divided into two camps, one representing the wicked evil supporters of imperialism and the other the innocent masses of humanity, the victims of the former who are the villains of the piece. The play offers no detailed characterization, but rather a pageant of characters representing different aspects of injustice suffered or committed by different social groups or classes. It ends with a denunciation of American policy in Vietnam and the Middle East and a recital of quotations from poems by Palestinian poets. After the curtain falls one of the characters urges the audience to have another look at the Exhibition before they leave the auditorium. *The Waste Land* may have been lively theater, but as drama it has several shortcomings, not the least of which is its excessively large number of characters which include figures from Babylonian mythology such as Astarte and Gilgamish; many parts are played by the same actors.

NORTH AFRICA

North African dramatists, deeply influenced by the contemporary French theater, have been less obsessively political than other Arabic dramatists. ᶜIzz al-Din al-Madani (born 1938) of Tunisia and al-Tayyib al-Siddiqi (born 1938) of Morocco are primarily interested in the search for a specifically Arab form of drama. Al-Madani derives his themes from classical Arabic literary figures and works, such as al-Hallaj and al-Maᶜarri, in his plays *Rihlat al-Hallaj* (Al-Hallaj's journey) and *al-Ghufran* (Forgiveness) and from incidents in Arab history such as the Zanj revolt in *Diwan al-Zanj* (The Zanj revolution, 1974; included in this collection). In these plays, al-Madani uses a loose form that mixes dramatic representation with narrative; in the introduction to *Diwan al-Zanj* he claims that it is based upon a traditional structural principle in medieval Arabic writings called *istitrad* (digression). Al-Siddiqi, applying a similar method, dramatized al-Hamadhani's *maqamat* in an attempt to produce a truly popular theater, for which he also wrote works that required audience participation. Younger writers such as the Moroccan ʿAbd al-Karim Ibn Rashid followed their example. Yet despite this hectic formal experimentation, the content of their plays is seldom entirely free of a political component. For instance, in his play *al-Zanj*, al-Madani uses the story of the revolution of the black slaves against the Abbasid Caliph in the ninth century to make a comment on the various revolutions and wars of liberation in today's third world countries, and how they ended in a new form of colonialism: economic servitude.

In fact, with much Arabic drama since the late fifties and sixties, particularly as the mood of anger and frustration deepened in the wake of the traumatic 1967 defeat by Israel, politics has tended to assume enormous proportions. That has given Arabic drama a quality of seriousness and a sense of urgency which it might otherwise have lacked. While it must be admitted that at times politics has dominated Arabic drama to a suffocating degree, this drama, perhaps more than any other literary form, affords incontrovertible evidence that Arab writers have been the political conscience of the Arab nation.

ʿISAM
MAHFUZ

The China Tree

Translated by
Sharif S. Elmusa
and Thomas G. Ezzy

The China Tree (*al-Zanalakht*) was first performed on May 16, 1968, at the Beirut Theater and was very warmly received by an audience eager to see genuine positive change in Lebanese theater. The play not only confirmed current innovations in Lebanese drama, both in form and in methods of production, but also stirred up a controversy concerning artistic compromise, traditionalism, naiveté, and trivia, along with sluggishness and timidity. It was a clear departure from the practice of some playwrights in writing plays couched in a high literary language. In this play, ʿIsam Mahfuz makes effective use of the Lebanese colloquial. In the preface to the first edition, he advocates the use of the vernacular by emphasizing that theater springs from "reality, using the first instrument of this reality: its spoken language, the language of the street and the home." He also expresses his aversion to conservative methods: "[In drama] I am against [pure] intellectual sophistication, rhetoric, oratorical expressions, lyricism, thought [meaning the incorporation of large general ideas], and all that kills actual life in a play. Even though I am a poet myself, I am against the use of poetry in drama." There is small literature, he asserts, and there is big literature. The first treats local problems, but the second begins from the local then widens out to treat the human condition everywhere. He also rejects the idea that Arab theater has to pass through all the stages known in the development of Western theater, claiming that the world has now become small and that cultural and artistic exchange can therefore take place with ease; all barriers are down now, and there is no more Western or Eastern heritage, for both are the heritage of people everywhere. Theater for Mahfuz should take pride of place among literary genres by virtue of its great influence and its capacity to address the audience directly and to embody several other genres at once. It should therefore be exciting and sharp as an arrow. The only condition one may stipulate is that it should maintain its effectiveness vis-à-vis the audience and its constant movement in the very heart of the world. *The China Tree* is an experiment in which the author has been loyal to all these ideas. He chose the theme of madness because he believed a madman was like a child, his behavior a perfect mirror reflecting his world.

S.K.J.

THE CHINA TREE

CHARACTERS

SAʿDUN

GENERAL

CLERK

FIRST BEGGAR

SECOND BEGGAR

THIRD BEGGAR

THE MOTHER

FIRST WITNESS

SECOND WITNESS

THIRD WITNESS

THE LAWYER

THE CHINA TREE

PROLOGUE

SA'DUN *is sitting at stage front, caning a chair. A spotlight shines on him. Surprised, he squints as he looks toward the source of the light. Then he lowers his eyes and stares at the audience.*

SA'DUN Thank you. Thank you very much. I've been waiting a long time to tell you what happened to me. No one believes what happened to me. I don't believe it myself. Every time I look around, I see you, I hear you, I smell your scent.

I want to tell you my story. Maybe you won't believe it, but it's the truth. Imagine, I've lived for forty-five years, working, thinking about myself and other people. I didn't work as a caner at first. I was a jeweler. Caning's a tiresome job. Imagine how many chairs I've caned already. Just think: one chair, two chairs, three chairs; chair after chair after chair. People sitting and people standing, sitting and standing, in a never-ending stream. I've had many thoughts about chairs . . . But what was I going to tell you about? Oh yes, well, here I am. Why am I here? How come I'm here? Let me share the reasons with you. Listen. There was the General, the Girl and the General. There were many people. The Clerk, and my Godfather, and the Old Lady . . . The incident began before I'd seen anybody. Then they started to accuse me. Is it true I killed her? . . . I'd forgotten to tell you, I used to think a great deal. I'd work and think about people. I'd finish my work, sit by my window, and wonder about the passersby. This one, where was he going? Why? And if he cocked his head and looked at me, I'd wonder what he was thinking as he gazed at me. I had many, many thoughts, by the window . . . To this minute, they don't know who she is, or why I killed her. If they'd been with me, they wouldn't have dared open their mouths and blurt out a word. I wish they'd seen the pain I was going through . . . I know them. I know them well, those people from Tyre. Why did they abandon me, then? In their eyes, my worth's measured only in terms of my crime. They believe I committed a crime. But a crime isn't committed: it happens of its own accord. It unfolds like a flower. Only the one who does the killing knows. Do you want to know if I was the one who killed her? Only I know that. Among millions of people, only I know that. If I disclose the secret, what will be left of me? If I tell you, everything will be over. You'll forget me. No one will remember me, no one will ask about me. You'll walk by me as if by a wall, as if I really were a caner, as if I never had such thoughts. You'll shake your heads, as though you knew everything. But *do* you know everything? Is it true? Ask me, "Is it true, Saᶜdun?" (*He stands up.*) No. Some of you might think I killed her for the sake of being interrogated. Maybe . . . But I'm not going to tell you about the murder itself. Instead, I'm going to tell you my own story. I'd love to tell you my story. Ask me. Please ask me, so I can tell you . . . At first, I didn't talk to anyone. All day, I wouldn't talk. They said my being so aloof wasn't a good sign; they took me, and the story began. I'll give it all to you, from A to Z. But you must be patient, please. I have to arrange things the way they happened, as I recall them . . . (*Whispering:*) First, the General, then the Young Girl . . . (*Aloud:*) the Young Girl, the General, the Beggars, the China Tree . . . You must help me, please, so we can understand each other. I'll give you all the details—what they did to me, what I myself did. As I remember. But what point shall I start at? I may make mistakes in the order things happened. As I remember, I was still sitting down, waiting . . . Was I waiting? No, I wasn't . . .

SKETCH 1: BY THE PALACE GATE

The stage is dark. There is the sound of loud knocking, which begins hesitantly, then grows nervous and violent. Lights rise gradually, excluding the left and middle parts of the stage. At the edge of the lit area stands an old-style wall, with a large gate in the middle of it. SAᶜDUN *stands in front of the gate, knocking persistently. At the center of the lit area is a stone bench.* SAᶜDUN *gets tired, gives up, moves slightly backward, looks up at the wall, bends his head down, and turns around. He then trudges off away from the gate, intermittently glancing back at it, and vanishes into the darkness of the left side of the stage. The stage is empty.* SAᶜDUN *returns from the area into which he has disappeared. He looks around dubiously in all directions, moves slowly toward the gate, and knocks, faintly, then quickly and forcefully. He shows signs of being in pain, retreats from the gate, and turns around. His sight falls on the bench. Then he walks up to it, touches it with his hand, and sits down. He lets out a sigh. His eyes are fixed on the gate.*

He utters a short, sharp cry. The reverberations of this cry can be heard. There is a heavy silence, then the sound of a solo violin. SAᶜDUN *begins to feel at a ragged bag dangling from a belt around his waist. His hand plunges into the bag, searching for something inside. Silence. He takes out a pearl necklace, which has a large, gleaming diamond on it.* SAᶜDUN *holds the diamond up and moves it around, admiring it. He drapes the necklace around his neck without fastening it. Then he looks toward the gate and smiles. The necklace falls off his neck. He picks it up, kisses it, glances at the gate and smiles again. He puts the necklace carefully back into the bag. He stands up and goes up to the gate. He raises his hand to knock, then hesitates, turns his eyes upward to the wall, and retreats from the gate without knocking. He sits on the bench, squatting. He searches in the bag, takes out a large apple, and shines it with the end of his sleeve. He munches the apple nonchalantly. His eyes are fixed on the gate. There is light music. His eyelids half-close. The music grows louder. His eyelids close completely. Then the music explodes; he wakes up, frightened; he looks at the gate and all around him. He remembers the apple and puts what's left of it back in the bag. He shifts his position, focuses his gaze back on the gate, and yawns. There is more light music, and his eyelids half-close. Then the music explodes. He trembles, opens his eyes wide and turns them in every direction. He scratches his head. He fixes his eyes, opened as wide as possible, on the gate. There is light music. The stage lights dim gradually. As the stage becomes completely dark, the sound of the music explodes abruptly, then suddenly ceases.*

CURTAIN

SKETCH 2: THE COURTROOM

The stage is wide, with flat and raised areas. The raised areas are uneven. There are two doors, one at the right and one at the left. Small, medium-sized, and large tables and chairs are scattered over the stage and are matching: small tables with small chairs, etc. The small chairs are of children's size, but with men seated in them. At stage front, center, a high wooden chair is placed. On it sits the GENERAL, *an elderly, bearded man, neatly dressed. He is holding a cane, which he leans against. Around the other tables sit men and women of various ages.*

GENERAL (*Continuing his questioning*): Who was there when you entered?

SAʿDUN (*Standing near the door at the left*): Nobody.

GENERAL Nobody? Didn't you say there were three?

SAʿDUN Oh yes, that's right, there were three: the mother, the daughter, and the daughter's husband. We played cards until ten.

GENERAL And then?

SAʿDUN The mother said she was tired, she wanted to go to bed early. She was going to Beirut the next morning to see a lawyer.

GENERAL And then?

SAʿDUN She went to bed.

GENERAL And then?

SAʿDUN I can't remember.

GENERAL When the mother went to bed, what did the rest of you do?

SAʿDUN Nothing . . . I just asked them if they'd like to play another game of cards. The daughter said yes. Her husband said no, that was enough, he preferred that we talk instead.

GENERAL Talk about what?

SAʿDUN What did we talk about? Maybe about the high price of things . . .

GENERAL Alright, alright . . . Clerk, check the second date, the second episode.

CLERK The 14th of July, Your Honor.

Meanwhile, SAʿDUN *has begun knocking gently on the door beside him.*

GENERAL (*Pounding with his cane*): What did you do on the night of the 14th of July?

SAʿDUN Nothing, Your Honor. I didn't do anything.

CLERK (*Writing down*): The defendant did nothing . . .

GENERAL (*To* CLERK): Don't write anything down unless I say so. (*To* SAʿDUN:) Where were you on the night of July 14th?

SAʿDUN Since it was night, I must have been asleep.

GENERAL You were not asleep!

SAʿDUN I was awake . . .

GENERAL You were awake. What were you doing, then?

SAʿDUN Since I was awake, I might have been thinking . . .

GENERAL No, you were not thinking!

SAʿDUN No, I wasn't thinking . . . I was just sitting, sitting down . . . It was probably supper time.

GENERAL Don't say "probably"!

SAʿDUN I won't say "probably." It *was* supper time. My mother was in the kitchen . . . Yes, I was in the kitchen too. We were both sitting down. She gave me a bowl of rice to sift. We were having friends for supper . . . Yes, Aunt Mary, and ʿAbu ʿIzz ad-Din, and his son came later. Aunt Mary's sister sat next to me at the table.

GENERAL Go on!

SAᶜDUN When we were finished, Aunt Mary said to my mother, "Bless your hands, the food was delicious." Of course, she was lying. I'd heard what she said to the person next to her while my mother was out getting the fruit.

GENERAL And then?

SAᶜDUN We talked for a while.

GENERAL Then what?

SAᶜDUN They left.

GENERAL Go on.

SAᶜDUN That was it. (*The others laugh.*)

GENERAL (*Pounding with his cane*): Quiet! Quiet! Clerk, the other episode! The other date!

CLERK (*Mumbling*): The other episode, the other date . . .

CLERK *hums as he leafs through the sheets of paper in front of him. Meanwhile,* SAᶜDUN *moves over to the other gate and knocks forcefully.* GENERAL *pounds with his cane to stop him.* CLERK *then climbs onto* GENERAL'S *high chair and whispers in his ear.* GENERAL *pounds with his cane three times.*

CLERK (*In a loud voice*): The General wishes to speak!

GENERAL Saᶜdun, my son, you know that we love you, don't you?

SAᶜDUN I know, I do . . .

GENERAL Do we love you or not?

SAᶜDUN You love me, you do . . . Let them open the gate for me, then.

GENERAL Do you remember when you fell into the well?

SAᶜDUN I remember, I do . . .

GENERAL It's true that I'm not the one who saved you. But I *was* reciting my prayers out loud, and if I hadn't been doing so, the landlord never would have heard you.

CLERK And if the landlord hadn't heard you?

GENERAL He wouldn't have lowered the rope.

CLERK And if he hadn't lowered the rope?

GENERAL You wouldn't have been able to grab it.

CLERK And if you hadn't grabbed it?

GENERAL You wouldn't be sitting here, safe and sound. And you still say I don't love you?

SAᶜDUN You do love me! You really do!

GENERAL Do you remember when they came to pick you up once? . . .

SAᶜDUN (*Interrupting in a loud voice*): I do remember!

GENERAL Indeed. If I hadn't . . .

SAᶜDUN (*Interrupting*): You love me! You love me a million times over! Let them open the gate for me . . .

VOICE The General is speaking! Listen!

ANOTHER VOICE General, Your Honor . . .

SAᶜDUN *opens the door automatically.* GENERAL *pounds with his cane. Deep silence for a short while.*

GENERAL (*Changing from his gentle tone*): Saᶜdun, why did you do it?

SAᶜDUN Do it? Do what? I've done nothing at all.

CLERK The 14th of September, Your Honor . . .

GENERAL What did you do on the 14th of September?

SAᶜDUN I did nothing, believe me. Nothing.

GENERAL Remember . . . The 14th of September . . . The night of the Feast of the Crucifixion . . .

SAᶜDUN I did nothing.

CLERK (*Writes down*): I did nothing . . .

GENERAL Yes, you did something!

CLERK (*Writes down*): Yes, he did something . . .

GENERAL Don't write down what I'm

saying! (*To* SAᶜDUN): What did you do on the night of the 14th of September?

SAᶜDUN How should I know? I've forgotten. I've lost my diary.

GENERAL It was the night of the Feast of the Crucifixion . . .

CLERK The defendant's diary is available in his file. (*He leafs through the papers.*) The night of the Feast of the Crucifixion . . . I've found it!

GENERAL Read it.

CLERK (*Reads*): "The night of the Crucifixion. I stayed in the shop until 11 P.M. There were some firecrackers I hadn't sold yet. I smoked two cigarettes from the pack Abu Ghazal left on the table. How cheap Abu Ghazal is! In an American cigarette pack he keeps really low-grade stuff. The electricity went off for about fifteen minutes. Maybe the power lines were struck by firecrackers. Umm Fawzi came into the shop and asked for a box of matches. I was out of matches. I caught her eyeing me rather suggestively."

SAᶜDUN (*Shouting*): Lies! Lies!

GENERAL (*To* CLERK): Go on!

CLERK (*Reading*): "I was alone in the shop. Who sent her here? God, keep her away from me . . ."

SAᶜDUN (*Knocks forcefully at the door, shouting at the people behind him*): Open the door! I'm telling you, you sons of bitches, you'd better open up! Have you no fear of God? Have you no fear of the police? Open up! Open the door!

CURTAIN

SKETCH 3: BY THE PALACE GATE

SAᶜDUN *is asleep on the stone bench near the palace gate, as he was at the end of Sketch 1. Silence. Stage lights rise gradually.* FIRST BEGGAR *enters, exhausted. He stops in front of the bench, looks at* SAᶜDUN, *then at the gate, and walks toward it. He knocks. Silence. He knocks again. Silence. He knocks a third time, moves away. He notices the tree, sits on the ground with his back leaning against the trunk.* SECOND BEGGAR *enters, does the same thing.*

FIRST BEGGAR It seems there's no one here.

SECOND BEGGAR Do you *know* there's no one here?

FIRST BEGGAR No.

SECOND BEGGAR Then why did you say so?

FIRST BEGGAR You said there was no one here too.

SECOND BEGGAR I said "it seems . . . " There's a difference. (*Pauses.*) Is this the first gate you've knocked at today?

FIRST BEGGAR No, the seventh.

SECOND BEGGAR (*Pauses*): This looks like a prince's gate.

FIRST BEGGAR No, it isn't. If it was, you'd see a moat.

SECOND BEGGAR It must be the president's gate.

FIRST BEGGAR If it was, you'd see people walking by in fear, praying for protection.

SECOND BEGGAR It must be a minister's gate.

FIRST BEGGAR Then you'd see a few thugs and brokers standing by.

SECOND BEGGAR You speak as though you know something.

FIRST BEGGAR All my teeth have been pulled out.

SECOND BEGGAR It may be the gate of some very important person.

FIRST BEGGAR You'd be seeing maids and servants swarming in and out.

SECOND BEGGAR A liquor warehouse?

FIRST BEGGAR Where are the guards?

SECOND BEGGAR And this guy . . . (*Points to* SAʿDUN:) What's he doing?

FIRST BEGGAR He's dreaming.

SECOND BEGGAR A beggar?

FIRST BEGGAR Of course.

SECOND BEGGAR Why's he sleeping here?

FIRST BEGGAR This must be his gate.

SECOND BEGGAR Every beggar has his own gate?

FIRST BEGGAR I used to have my own gate, a bit smaller than this one. You know what I used to do?

SECOND BEGGAR What?

FIRST BEGGAR I used to sit by it all day long, reading through verses in the Bible. In the morning, I'd wake up to find my breakfast set in front of me. Then lunch was brought by a servant. And in the evening, supper was lowered in a basket.

SECOND BEGGAR Great!

FIRST BEGGAR I sat there for twenty years.

SECOND BEGGAR Great! Wonderful! Which verses did you use to read?

FIRST BEGGAR To be honest, only one: "Behold the birds in the sky, they neither plant nor harvest, and thy Heavenly Father heedeth them. Behold the lilies in the field . . ."

SECOND BEGGAR And why did you leave?

FIRST BEGGAR What can I say? The family petered out . . . They had only one son, who didn't marry. One day they discovered that he'd hanged himself from the tree in front of the house. There were no other legal heirs, although claimants were endless . . . When the Government took over the property, I went back to read my verse, but they chased me away . . .

SECOND BEGGAR (*After a short pause*): Where to now?

FIRST BEGGAR I passed by a gate on my way home. They were cleaning it. They ought to be done by now.

SECOND BEGGAR Are you going?

FIRST BEGGAR In a little while . . . I'm tired. My legs hurt from walking.

(*Silence.* SECOND BEGGAR *begins singing.*)

FIRST BEGGAR Hush . . . Let the man dream. (*Points to* SAʿDUN.)

SECOND BEGGAR (*Pauses*): Let me tell you a story.

FIRST BEGGAR No. (*Pauses.*) Tell me.

SECOND BEGGAR The tale of al-Shatir Hasan?*

FIRST BEGGAR I know it.

SECOND BEGGAR The tale of al-Numrud?

FIRST BEGGAR I know it.

SECOND BEGGAR The tale of al-Zir?

FIRST BEGGAR I know that one too.

SECOND BEGGAR Sayf Ben Dhi Yazan?

FIRST BEGGAR And I know that one too.

SECOND BEGGAR That's amazing! You have a huge brain! . . . Well, how about the tale of Wadha the Gypsy?

FIRST BEGGAR I know it.

SECOND BEGGAR The tale of Bani Hilal?

FIRST BEGGAR I know that one too.

SECOND BEGGAR Al-Zinati Khalifah?

FIRST BEGGAR I know that one too.

SECOND BEGGAR Waddah al-Yemen?

FIRST BEGGAR I know it.

SECOND BEGGAR The tale of the Dove and her Uncle Abu Dirgham?

FIRST BEGGAR I know it well.

SECOND BEGGAR You're very well-in-

*This and subsequent names are of characters from Arabic folk tales.

formed! . . . Okay then, let me tell you the tale of the Olive Jar.

FIRST BEGGAR No.

SECOND BEGGAR Whether you say no or say yes, shall I tell you the tale of the Olive Jar?*

FIRST BEGGAR Tell me.

SECOND BEGGAR Whether you say "tell me" or don't say "tell me," shall I tell you the tale of the Olive Jar?

FIRST BEGGAR *stays silent.*

SECOND BEGGAR Whether you're silent or not silent, shall I tell you the tale of the Olive Jar?

FIRST BEGGAR *stays silent.*

SECOND BEGGAR Laugh! I'm talking to you like this to make you laugh . . .

FIRST BEGGAR *stays silent.*

SECOND BEGGAR Laugh, I beg you . . .

FIRST BEGGAR (*Insincerely*): Ha ha ha.

SECOND BEGGAR Not like that! I want a hearty laugh . . .

FIRST BEGGAR Hee hee hee.

SECOND BEGGAR Not like that either!

FIRST BEGGAR Between you and me . . .

SECOND BEGGAR What?

FIRST BEGGAR Can you keep a secret?

SECOND BEGGAR Like a deep well.

FIRST BEGGAR (*Whispers*): I can't laugh!

SECOND BEGGAR (*Pauses*): Well, cry then.

FIRST BEGGAR No . . .

SECOND BEGGAR Cry, just for my sake.

FIRST BEGGAR Nope.

SECOND BEGGAR Shall I tell you a story that'll make you cry?

FIRST BEGGAR Between you and me?

SECOND BEGGAR Like a well . . .

FIRST BEGGAR (*Whispers*): I can't cry!

SECOND BEGGAR That too?

FIRST BEGGAR Can *you* cry?

SECOND BEGGAR Of course. Listen. Let me try . . . (*He tries to laugh.*) I don't know how to. Strange . . .

FIRST BEGGAR You see?

SECOND BEGGAR You're right . . . When I was young, I used to laugh well . . .

FIRST BEGGAR When you were young?

SECOND BEGGAR (*Looking upward*): Oh God, I ask you, why can't I laugh any more? *You* created us! *You*'re our Father! Do you hear me?

FIRST BEGGAR He stopped listening long ago.

SECOND BEGGAR Maybe you're punishing us! Because we lie? Because we ask for charity?

FIRST BEGGAR Everybody does that.

SECOND BEGGAR But why is it only us that can't . . .

THIRD BEGGAR *enters, goes straight to the gate and knocks agitatedly.*

THIRD BEGGAR (*Speaking rapidly*): You who are sitting upstairs, who are reading the papers and listening to the news of China, Moscow, the Congo, Vietnam, the First War, the Fourth War, Asia, Africa, the Atomic Bomb, the Jews . . . What are you waiting for? These are the signs, there'll be no more putting it off this time! Those of you who've read the Apocalypse in the Bible, *you* must know! There's only one thing missing: the sun isn't rising from the west. But how do you know they won't *make* it rise from the west? Haven't you heard what they've done to the moon? Godlessness, sheer godlessness! . . . Do you want to know what happened to the builders of the Tower of Babel? Who among you would choose this transitory life over a life everlasting? No one! Who

*This is a formula used in a word game played with children, to tease or playfully frustrate them.

among you would prefer the passing pleasures of this life to the bliss of Paradise? No one! . . . What are you waiting for, then? What should you be doing? I'll tell you: good deeds! That's right, good deeds . . .

The lights dim slightly.

FIRST BEGGAR (*Extending his hand*): Alms from God's bounty . . .

SECOND BEGGAR (*Also extending his hand*): Alms for this poor man . . .

THIRD BEGGAR (*Also extending his hand*): Alms for this downtrodden man . . .

FIRST BEGGAR Alms, for the luckless man.

SECOND BEGGAR Alms, for the crippled man.

THIRD BEGGAR Alms, for the blind man.

FIRST BEGGAR Alms, from God's bounty . . .

SECOND BEGGAR For the God-fearing man . . .

THIRD BEGGAR For the poor man, the family man, for the crippled and the blind . . .

CURTAIN

SKETCH 4: COURTROOM

GENERAL (*Pounds with his cane*): The defendant is trying to evade the issue! He's being cagey! The General is quickly losing patience . . .

CLERK Yes, His Honor is quickly losing patience.

GENERAL Hurry up, hurry up, Saᶜdun! Confess that you did it.

SAᶜDUN I've done nothing. Nothing. Ask *them*.

GENERAL We're going to ask them. You! . . . (*He examines the faces in the courtroom, abruptly stops and points to one of them.*) You there. Yes, you . . . Come here.

FIRST WITNESS Me? Of course, me . . . Who else would know *but* me? . . . I've been waiting a long time. I didn't realize it was him until this moment. (*He points to* SAᶜDUN.) Who else could it be but this gentleman? Look, Your Honor, he came to our store a hundred times, and I never once thought of asking him his name. Then one day he signed a check . . . I forget faces. All faces are alike. The only way to tell people apart is by their names. Once a name's written on paper, I take it in. Take Your Honor's name, for instance: your name—pardon me, I don't know your name, but once you write it down on a piece of paper, even if you were to tear it up—please note what I'm saying—and throw it into the sea, if I met you fifteen years later . . .

GENERAL Tell us about the check. About the check, please . . .

FIRST WITNESS Did I say "the check"? Oh yes, of course, the check . . . But how did you know? Ha! Ha! Ha! (*Wags his* ﬁ*nger playfully at* GENERAL.) You're right, we understand each other. You mean to say "the sea." Yes, sir, the sea . . . These are the days of migrations, Your Honor.

VOICE Bird migrations?

SECOND VOICE Maybe Jewish migrations!

GENERAL *pounds with his cane.*

FIRST WITNESS Oh, what were we talking about? May God give me the patience . . . (*Abruptly*:) About the sea. (*Looking at* SAᶜDUN:) Ha! Ha! You thought I'd forgotten . . . So, you thought you'd gotten away with it, Barhum. You thief . . . God is great, Barhum!

GENERAL (*Interrupting*): Saᶜdun. You mean *Saᶜdun*.

FIRST WITNESS That's what I said, Your Honor. They're all like this, I know them all, from grandfather to grandchild. I know them really well. I could recognize him from among a thousand men. I told him "Barhum" . . .

GENERAL Saʿdun. You mean *Saʿdun.*

FIRST WITNESS "Saʿdun, why don't you pay the rent? The boy's dying. I've brought in one doctor after another. You know we're people of modest means, we can't afford illness, but that's God's will . . . What's the matter with you, Barhum? . . ."

GENERAL Saʿdun. You mean *Saʿdun.*

FIRST WITNESS Saʿdun isn't like me. I'm different. He couldn't be like me, how could he? Imagine, Your Honor, if people were all alike . . . How could I say that I'm me and you're you? Just this morning, as I was trimming my beard, I could hardly recognize myself. I've changed, changed a lot . . . I told myself: "Man, God has blessed you, so why bear witness against others?" And then Barhum . . .

GENERAL Saʿdun. You mean *Saʿdun.*

FIRST WITNESS Saʿdun. But Barhum's guilty too, everyone knows that, but it isn't right to gossip about those who aren't here . . .

GENERAL Those who aren't here? Who are they?

FIRST WITNESS Barhum, Your Honor.

GENERAL Saʿdun. You mean *Saʿdun.*

FIRST WITNESS Saʿdun, Your Honor. Saʿdun.

GENERAL But Saʿdun isn't absent. He's here with us, in front of you . . .

FIRST WITNESS I said he was here, he *has* to be here, it would be impossible for him not to be here . . . They're all like that. I know them, from the grandfather to the grandchild. I could recognize him from among a thousand men. Once, we were going to . . .

GENERAL To the seashore?

FIRST WITNESS Which seashore?

GENERAL To the seashore. You haven't told us about the sea.

FIRST WITNESS To the seashore . . . You say you want a story about the sea? It goes like this, sir: once we went fishing, and the women came along. The kids were thirsty . . . Imagine, the sea beside us, and the children went thirsty! Does anyone go to the sea and come back thirsty? But this is the way it happened, Your Honor. I was with Saʿdun . . .

GENERAL You mean *Barhum*!

FIRST WITNESS I was with Barhum. I was with him . . . Then what did we do? . . . May God give me more patience . . . Maybe if we said a few things to each other, Your Honour . . .

GENERAL We *are* saying things to each other.

FIRST WITNESS We were fishing . . . In fact, he was fishing by himself. He was holding the fishhook while his legs were sunk into the sand. He was drenched in sunlight, and I was sitting in the shade, just watching. From morning to evening he held that fishhook, with the wind caressing his hair. A beautiful scene . . . And because I'm a poet I said to myself that this was a poem not to be missed.

GENERAL You didn't hear any screaming?

FIRST WITNESS I'm getting there—did you say screaming? No, I didn't hear any screaming. Perhaps I did, and then thought it was the wind . . .

GENERAL Enough, enough. Thank you.

FIRST WITNESS Excuse me, sir, I'm at your disposal, even though bearing witness against others isn't a good thing to do . . .

GENERAL Back to your seat! Go!

FIRST WITNESS *trudges back to his chair.* GENERAL *looks around in search of another witness. Then suddenly he points to someone in the far corner.*

GENERAL Yes, yes you, why are you being coy? You were with him, correct? (SECOND WITNESS *starts off as though to walk toward the witness stand next to* GENERAL's *chair.*) From your seat . . .

SECOND WITNESS Yes, I was with him, Your Honor, I was . . . In those days there was a wood shortage. There was a war on, people used to steal wooden planks for us so we could make them into coffins. It was wartime. We were hiding in the cellar when he appeared. Look, Your Honor (*turning to* SAᶜDUN), I'm not certain that it was him. But if it wasn't him, it was his father, and if it wasn't his father it was his brother, and if not . . .

CLERK His grandfather!

GENERAL (*Pounding with his cane*): Silence! (*Addressing* CLERK:) You saw him. You confessed you did.

CLERK (*Approaches the witness stand and raises his hand to take the oath*): In fact, Your Honor, I didn't see him. I saw his mother. Everyone knew I wasn't her son, but she was staring at me, and this is as true as my seeing you now, Your Honor . . .

GENERAL Limit yourself to the case. (*Begins to doze off.*)

CLERK He was next to the father and the priest. There was a woman I didn't know. I looked at her carefully and saw her eyes fixed on a door that had been left ajar. I saw . . . I saw a shadow, just like I'm seeing you now. The shadow wasn't clear at first. She was staring obliquely. I just pretended to talk to her. I asked her about her dress. Before she replied, I was facing the door, and she had her back to it, just like I'm seeing you now, Your Honor. I saw nothing. I'd like to say I saw everything, or if not everything then at least more than anyone else in the group. The electric lights were strong, and the shadow clear. I heard the conversation, I looked, but didn't find his mother. She vanished. And I heard him scream, I myself heard him scream . . .

GENERAL (*Opens his eyes*): Scream, Saᶜdun. Let's see . . .

SAᶜDUN (*Screaming*): Waggh!

CLERK Exactly! Except I didn't see him the way I'm seeing Your Horor . . .

SAᶜDUN (*Knocks at the door with all his might*): Open up! Open up, I say! It's unfair! There are people waiting for me! Open up, please, open up! . . .

CURTAIN

SKETCH 5: BY THE PALACE GATE

SAᶜDUN *wakes up. His eyes turn directly toward the gate. He gets up, moves up to the door. He knocks again, forcefully. He looks around.*

VOICE You have to be extremely patient.

SAᶜDUN Who is it?

VOICE *stays silent.*

SAᶜDUN Are you ghost or human?

VOICE Human . . . Although I can't answer you precisely.

SAᶜDUN Alright. Can you please tell me where the owners of this house are? Are they here or not?

VOICE They're here and not here.

SAᶜDUN I don't understand. Good people, like yourself, have told me how to get to this house. The priest, my godfather

. . . and others as well, they've seen her in person. The priest handed me this map . . . (*He searches his pockets for the map, but does not find it.*) They said it was here. This is exactly how they described the house to me: the gate, of course, is here, it ought to be here . . . Everyone I asked, even the children, knew where it was. They overhear things from their parents. True, not everybody who gave me directions had seen it, but they all knew of it. Some had seen it, though . . . But I can't see you. Where are you? Where are you sitting? Your voice sounds so close, as though you were right next to me . . . What are you doing here all alone?

VOICE I'm watching.

SAʿDUN Have you been here long? What is it you're watching?

VOICE *stays silent.*

SAʿDUN Come on, let's bang on the gate together. Your banging may be stronger than mine.

VOICE I can't bang.

SAʿDUN Please tell me, what do you know? Is being patient all you know?

VOICE *stays silent.*

SAʿDUN I'm patient, like you. We're all used to being patient. Still, I'd like to know if there's anyone here. I want a sign.

VOICE A sign?

SAʿDUN Yes, a sign that she'll open up. A sign that she's here. The sound of the maid's clogs, for example.

VOICE Believe me, she doesn't have a maid.

SAʿDUN The sound of the gardener's shears.

VOICE She doesn't have a gardener.

SAʿDUN The sound of the watchman's boots.

VOICE There are no watchmen here.

SAʿDUN Then the dogs?

VOICE She doesn't own any dogs.

SAʿDUN The cat? The cow? The horse?

VOICE She doesn't raise animals.

SAʿDUN That's strange . . . She *could* have a farm.

VOICE No farm.

SAʿDUN Maybe some buildings in the city?

VOICE No buildings either.

SAʿDUN She must rent furnished rooms . . .

VOICE Impossible.

SAʿDUN How does she make a living, then?

VOICE She's rich. She has treasures.

SAʿDUN You know too . . . (*Shyly:*) You think I'm after her wealth . . . Listen: whether you're close to her or not, whether you're acquainted with her or not, I'm not lying to you. I've come only for her sake. I'm not lazy, as my mother keeps saying . . . Hey, see what I've brought with me . . . (*Starts to open the bag, then changes his mind.*) I worked very hard. I used to stay up all night. You may not believe it, but I love her. Come here, let me show you what I've brought with me . . .

VOICE I've already seen it.

SAʿDUN You have?

VOICE Yesterday, while I was asleep.

SAʿDUN While you were asleep?

VOICE I'm always asleep. I'm hardly ever awake. That's why you should seize the opportunity and tell me all you can, before I go back to sleep. If I do, you'll have to wait a long time before you find someone else to amuse you. It will take a year's walking to get to the nearest house.

SAʿDUN I know, I do . . . But now we're just amusing ourselves?

VOICE Of course we are.

SA^c^DUN I'm not amusing *my*self.

VOICE If you're not, then you must be acting as though you were.

SAᶜDUN No, I'm not having fun, or pretending to. You know what I've come for. Why are you frightening me?

VOICE I'm not frightening you. I'm just talking.

SAᶜDUN Talk. I want to keep quiet.

VOICE Keep quiet. I want to go to sleep.

SAᶜDUN Go to sleep, I want to knock at the gate.

A silent pause, then SAᶜDUN *resumes knocking.*

CURTAIN

SKETCH 6: COURTROOM

The stage is dark. The echo of the GENERAL*'s cane being pounded is heard, as is the voice of the* CLERK.

CLERK The court will come to order!

A circle of light is formed at stage front. In the circle, SAᶜDUN *is conversing with an elderly woman.*

SAᶜDUN Is it true that I've done it? Tell them. Tell them, Mother. They don't believe me. Tell them I've done nothing. Tell them he died on his own.

GENERAL (*Lights suddenly flashing on him*): Died on his own? Who died on his own?

The entire courtroom is lit.

SAᶜDUN It's true I didn't love him, but he's still my father. His legs were always hurting. At the end, they were swollen. I heard the doctor say, "If the clotting should reach his heart . . . " Look, I don't know how to lie. I didn't see the swelling, I saw the stolen watch. She was hiding it, during the wake, under her black stockings. She laughed. (*He laughs a short laugh.*) I wasn't laughing at him. She was sitting on the bed across from me, waiting, with her legs wide open. She laughed. (*He laughs, then immediately knits his eyebrows, rushes to his mother, and kneels before her.*) I beg you, Mother, let them know! They don't trust me. No one trusts me. No one loves me. Tell him I wasn't in the house . . . (*He stands up and faces the* GENERAL.) I was playing cards with my friends. Ask them . . . (*He spots a man sitting at a nearby table and pulls at his sleeve.*) Was I playing with you or wasn't I? (*The man looks at him, astonished, denying.*) Maybe it was with someone else . . . I was playing with *you* (*To* GENERAL) . . . I didn't hear him! I swear by God I didn't hear him calling! I didn't, I'm telling you . . . Maybe he needed a drink, how could I tell? How? Why should I want to lie? I always told him everything to his face. And anyway, it's none of your business. I'm a free man, and I want to leave this place! (*He runs to the door on the left and shakes it violently.*) I'm telling you, open up! I must get out of here! (*He looks at* GENERAL) Let them open the door, I want to go, I have an appointment . . .

GENERAL What do you know, Lady?

MOTHER My son—he may be my son—says . . . (*She turns toward* SAᶜDUN:) It's unfair, why are you holding him? In my opinion, he's being held unjustly. Let him leave for his work. He may have a job to go to. Working makes a body healthy. A man doesn't become a real man unless he works. By my children, this man has been unfairly accused! Look, sir, there's nothing in this for me, is there? I don't know him, and he doesn't know me . . . (*She thinks*:) Maybe he *does* know me . . . He kissed my hand . . . Only God knows. Maybe we shared a meal together once . . . (*Forcefully*:) I don't see how this man could be guilty!

GENERAL (*Pounding with cane*): You've eaten, eh?

MOTHER Of course we've eaten! Why not? Everyone eats as much as he can . . . We, for instance, eat meat twice a week.

GENERAL Get away, Lady. Get away from here. God bless you . . .

MOTHER You dare speak of God, you heathen? God is almighty! He can bring you down the same way he raised you up!

CLERK Hey, you, woman! Have you forgotten who you're speaking to?

GENERAL Let her talk about God . . . I haven't heard about him in a long time.

CLERK This woman is hallucinating, Your Honor.

MOTHER Look, sir, release this man. I don't see how he can be guilty.

CLERK (*Shuts his eyes*): I'm tired . . .

CURTAIN

SKETCH 7: STAGE FRONT

The intensity of the lighting increases gradually over the circle at stage front. The MOTHER *is standing.* SAᶜDUN *is sitting on the floor, a few steps away from her. Silence.*

MOTHER Excuse me, do you know my children? Asaᶜd, Saᶜdun, Fuad, Bahiyyeh, Lulu, Linda . . . Too many, eh? God keep them! Listen, I sent them to the best schools. All the Ottoman gold coins I've given to college presidents! Just like that!

SAᶜDUN I'm asking you, Mother, why are you shutting the door on me?

MOTHER Arthritis, son, it's killing me . . . You seem to be an intelligent man. Do you know of a good remedy? And don't say bay leaves or camomile . . . We used to have a Moroccan doctor who'd visit us, you may know him. You don't seem to be a stranger . . .

SAᶜDUN I know, I do . . . When Sabibah was lost, we were all down and it was damned hot . . .

In the ensuing dialogue, SAᶜDUN *and his* MOTHER *speak in over-lapping snatches. When one pauses, the other will continue, but* SAᶜDUN*'s snatches will always be shorter than the* MOTHER*'s.*

SAᶜDUN (*Continuing*): I didn't think about her any more. I just stood there. People were pushing me from all sides. I spent every penny I had. I used to take money from the till at the shop. I thought no one would notice. It wasn't stealing, I don't steal. Abu Ghazal's a liar, they're all liars. I did nothing . . . You see, Your Honor, I know that nobody loves me . . . They should have told me! They should have told me everything! I'd closed the windows, I didn't know that people were watching. I'd closed the windows and the lights were off. Yes, they were off, they were . . . I honestly can't remember anything any more, maybe they weren't off. It's such an old story, I've forgotten . . . I was alone, there was no one with me. I closed the windows, I wanted to have some fun. I didn't know people were watching. I always shut the window. Do you know that I don't see anyone? I enjoy myself, Your Honor, and no one can see me. The window's small and there's no door. All the windows are small, even the cat can't get through them. There were no carpenters, they were at work, they needed to make a living. I heard a whistle, the children's whistle. I went out, but saw no one, and it was hot . . . (*He turns to the* MOTHER:) Are you listening? I'm glad you're listening. I meant to tell you long ago, but there was no time . . . (*He lowers his voice to a bare whisper, while the* MOTHER *continues to talk.*)

MOTHER How should I know? May God keep them all . . . Every one of those Ottoman gold coins was so big! What a waste! . . . So many houses, but no one in them . . . She's a loose woman. Wealth's being squandered. My mother's house at the edge of the Druze neighborhood is a castle. The rabbits may have died. I can't hear them breathing any more. Maybe they're dead . . . God forgive him, if only I'd gone with him to Huran.* How unfortunate you are, Saᶜida! He was at the peak of his youth, and the Shaikh of the church . . . Do you think I'm old, son? It's from worrying, too much worrying. I live by myself. It's true, I don't remember. Everyone forgets . . . (*To* SAᶜDUN:) Excuse me, do you know my children—Nabih, Asaᶜd, Saᶜdun, Lulu, and Nabihah? So many of them, may God grant them long lives . . . I sent them to the best schools, the Americans' schools. Many's the large gold coin I'd send to the college president, *and* the jugs of *qawarma*,† God bless them! . . . Let them eat. Health's the most important thing. This damned arthritis, it *loves* me! It must find me pretty . . . (*To* SAᶜDUN:) Be honest, am I pretty? . . . Hey, do you know my children? They're young, like you are, or perhaps a little older. Have you seen them in Beirut? Saᶜid, Jamil, Saᶜidih, Emile, Lulu, Amalaine . . . I sent them to the best schools. I don't know when . . . Milia, I want to go to Milia, but I don't know where she got married. Her husband used to come to visit me. (*Looks at* SAᶜDUN:) Excuse me, do you know her husband? He's tall and dark, like yourself. He doesn't come by any more. God protect them . . . What's this? No one thinks they have a mother who needs being visited? . . . (*She cries and looks at* SAᶜDUN:) Hey, if you see the children, tell them I'm not having anything to do with them any more. If I die I don't want anybody weeping for me or visiting my grave . . . (*She pauses.*) So many homes, but everything's drifting, what's the use? The vineyards and the olive trees . . . The climate isn't what it used to be. This is God's wrath. They may have dried up . . . (*Pauses.*) But why not? The sons of Adam are used to being alone . . . God protect them, I don't want anything from them, they may have gotten married. Please tell me, do you know Emile, Fuad, Nabih and Saᶜida? They're my children. Look, I sent them to the best schools . . .

MOTHER *continues her chatter, while lights gradually dim.*

SKETCH 8: STAGE FRONT

SAᶜDUN *is alone in a small circle of light at stage front. He is kneeling back on his haunches, but bent forward from the waist so that his head is tucked between his hands, which are clasped over his knees. Only the top part of his body is visible. Silence. The* CLERK *comes out of the dark area. He approaches* SAᶜDUN, *stands behind him, and places both his hands on* SAᶜDUN'*s shoulders.*

*A mountainous part of western Syria.

† The meat of very young lambs, cooked in their own fat and preserved for winter.

CLERK I've caught you!

SAʿDUN *looks up at him silently, then returns to his original posture.* CLERK *takes his hands off* SAʿDUN*'s shoulders and sits next to him.*

CLERK What are you doing?

SAʿDUN *remains silent.*

CLERK Are you dreaming?

SAʿDUN *remains silent.*

CLERK Thinking?

SAʿDUN *remains silent.*

CLERK Are you thinking about her?

SAʿDUN (*Straightens up abruptly*): Who is she?

CLERK *Her*. . . . Is there anyone else?

SAʿDUN *returns to his original posture without replying.* CLERK *looks behind him, scratches his hand, and shouts.*

CLERK She's coming! She's . . .

SAʿDUN *leaps to his feet, looks around, and doesn't see anyone.*

SAʿDUN Liar! I know you're a liar . . . Listen, you're a good man. Can you tell me why you're so dead set against me?

CLERK:: I'm not against you.

SAʿDUN I thought you'd forgotten. I didn't know you could hate.

CLERK I don't hate. Emotions are one thing, and deeds are another . . . And besides, everything belongs to Him . . . He's the one with the power to decide. He alone can raise a man, or bring him down. He can grant life, or will death . . .

SAʿDUN Who are you talking about? God?

CLERK No, the General. Nothing can be hidden from his sight; he knows even what's been concealed. Do you hear what I'm saying? No one can deceive him. Justice must take its course. Why are you defending yourself, tormenting yourself?

SAʿDUN I'd like to know why I'm stuck here.

CLERK So that the case can be closed.

SAʿDUN When will that happen?

CLERK It'll end; it will . . . Everything has a beginning and an end. Your case with my sister: did it end or didn't it? It did.

SAʿDUN So that's why you're against me. You're holding a grudge.

CLERK I'm not holding any grudges against anyone. Not even after all you did.

SAʿDUN It's your fault. You should have disciplined her better.

CLERK No one can discipline anyone these days. Besides, what she did to you was your fate.

SAʿDUN (*Agitated*): My fate? My fate? You all say that! If it weren't for her, I wouldn't be here. To hell with her! Let her take the boy, what do I need kids for?

CLERK What do you need kids for . . . Kids aren't for us, kids are for those who can bring them up well.

SAʿDUN *I'm* the one who knew how to bring him up! Whenever I hit him, he never said a word. I had a good idea of how I wanted him to be. Sometimes I pushed him, and other times I let go. That's how to bring kids up. How else? Do you want to know how I fed him? "Look, boy, soft-boiled eggs are better than the hard-boiled, and the hard-boiled better than the scrambled, and best of all are the baked eggs. Eat plenty of bread, it's full of vitamins, and also lentils. When the French army came here, it bought up all the lentils in the country. Lentils are chock full of iron, which fortifies the blood . . . And tomato juice, keep the napkin around your neck so as not to spill it all over your clothes. Don't tear the newspapers, papers are for the toilet. Good boys also kiss their fathers' hands when they wake up. Like this. Very good . . ."

CLERK (*Interrupts*): Very good? Me?

SA^cDUN Not you, the boy. You should've seen when I set out to teach him to read: "Capital S, small t, small u, d, y . . . Study! "The Fox and the Rooster": It's said that once a clever fox saw a rooster on the roof of a house, and said to him, "Good morning, Rooster, why don't you come down so we can play together?" The rooster answered, "Since when does a fox play with chickens?" And the fox said, "Have you heard what happened in town today?" . . .

CLERK I heard he had a breakdown before she took him away.

SAᶜDUN No, not at all. When she took him he was in great shape, nothing in him was broken. She's a liar, and a big liar at that. Once when I beat him with a stick, his earlobe came off, but I glued it back on. And the same thing happened when his right toe was broken, I glued it back to normal with my own hands. If you saw him, you'd never be able to tell anything in him had ever been broken. I told you she was a liar.

CLERK My sister doesn't lie.

SAᶜDUN Of course she does.

CLERK I told you she doesn't!

SAᶜDUN She does.

CLERK She doesn't!

SAᶜDUN Okay, she doesn't . . .

CLERK *laughs hysterically and places his hands over his head in the shape of two horns. At the same time, the stage is lit. He runs among the tables, to the shock of those present. They watch him in disbelief as he yells:*

CLERK He confessed, he confessed, he did!

GENERAL Who confessed?

CLERK Saᶜdun, Your Honor! Saᶜdun's just admitted that she doesn't lie!

GENERAL My dear Clerk, how many times must I tell you to keep your own case separate from the others?

Silence.

GENERAL (*Presenting* FIRST WITNESS): Saᶜdun, do you recognize this man facing you?

SAᶜDUN Yes, Your Honor.

GENERAL (*Presenting* SECOND WITNESS): Saᶜdun, do you recognize this man facing you?

SAᶜDUN Yes, Your Honor.

GENERAL (*Presenting* THIRD WITNESS): Saᶜdun, do you recognize this man facing you?

SAᶜDUN Yes, Your Honor.

GENERAL (*To the three witnesses*): You may begin. Let's see . . . (*Starts to doze off.*)

FIRST WITNESS Saᶜdun, do you recall the wife of Abu Ghazal, your relative?

SAᶜDUN Saᶜdun maintains: "Thou shalt not covet thy relative's wife."

SECOND WITNESS Saᶜdun, Abu Ghazal's wife was found dead in the bathroom, with her jewels stolen.

SAᶜDUN Saᶜdun maintains: "Thou shalt not fornicate; thou shalt not kill; thou shalt not steal; thou shalt not covet thy relative's wife."

THIRD WITNESS Her father died of sorrow.

SAᶜDUN Saᶜdun maintains: "Be kind to thy father and thy mother."

SECOND WITNESS It was her husband who died, not her father.

FIRST WITNESS You're wrong, her husband remained alive. It's the mother who was murdered in the bathroom.

SAᶜDUN Saᶜdun maintains: "Thou shalt not fornicate; thou shalt not kill."

THIRD WITNESS One of you must be

mistaken, because I saw both father and mother walking in her funeral.

SECOND WITNESS They may have been walking in a funeral, but it was their neighbor's funeral, not their daughter's.

FIRST WITNESS Not one of their neighbors has died in six years. That was the funeral of her husband, Abu Ghazal.

SAʿDUN Saʿdun maintains: "Thou shalt not fornicate; thou shalt not kill; thou shalt not marry."

SECOND WITNESS You're mistaken. Her husband didn't die—everyone knows it's *she* who died. Abu Ghazal's still alive, healthy as a horse.

SECOND WITNESS Strange . . . How could they have been walking in the funeral when it was so emotional? . . .

FIRST WITNESS And the one that died was a dog.

THIRD WITNESS I used to own a greyhound. I sold it for six thousand liras. I hired a Moroccan trainer for it.

SECOND WITNESS There are poodles that hunt better than hounds.

FIRST WITNESS Impossible. There can't be hunting and nonhunting dogs. There are dogs that hunt birds, others that hunt people, and still others that don't hunt at all.

SECOND WITNESS The dogs that aren't hunting now either hunted before or they'll go hunting in the future.

THIRD WITNESS Dogs are honest.

FIRST WITNESS There are dogs and there are dogs. The Great Dane's honest, excellent, but it doesn't bark.

SECOND WITNESS The boxer barks, but it isn't honest.

THIRD WITNESS The German shepherd's honest, *and* it barks.

FIRST WITNESS There are dogs that don't bark. Basset hounds love women.

SECOND WITNESS Huskies love women, too.

THIRD WITNESS Women don't like huskies; they love spaniels, which are prettier.

SECOND WITNESS Women don't love either poodles or huskies; women love men. Yesterday I saw a woman following her husband.

FIRST WITNESS Maybe it wasn't her husband, maybe it was her son.

THIRD WITNESS Maybe her daughter.

FIRST WITNESS Like mother, like daughter . . . After a mother marries, she gets her own daughter married.

SECOND WITNESS She marries her off to a rich old man, who buys her clothes and jewelry.

THIRD WITNESS And then they steal the jewelry.

SECOND WITNESS And after they steal the jewelry, they kill the woman.

FIRST WITNESS Saʿdun, why did you kill Abu Ghazal's wife?

SAʿDUN (*Suddenly snaps out of his distractedness to pay attention to the question*): I didn't kill.

SECOND WITNESS How can that be? People saw you walking in her funeral.

SAʿDUN I didn't walk in her funeral.

THIRD WITNESS How can it be that you didn't walk in her funeral when you're the one that killed her?

SAʿDUN I didn't walk in her funeral, because I don't know her.

FIRST WITNESS Of course you do.

SAʿDUN No, I don't know her.

SECOND WITNESS Yes, you do.

SAʿDUN No, I don't know her.

THIRD WITNESS You do.

SAʿDUN No, I don't!

FIRST WITNESS You do!

SAʿDUN Not at all!

FIRST and THIRD WITNESS Yes, you do!

SAʿDUN No, I don't!

SECOND and THIRD WITNESS Yes, you do!

SAʿDUN No, I don't!

FIRST, SECOND, and THIRD WITNESS Yes, you do!

SAʿDUN Okay. I know her . . .

THE THREE No, you don't know her.

SAʿDUN Yes, I know her!

THE THREE No, you don't!

SAʿDUN I know her!

THE THREE You don't!

SAʿDUN I don't know her . . .

THE THREE Yes, you do.

SAʿDUN I don't!

THE THREE You do!

SAʿDUN I don't know her! I don't! I don't!

SAʿDUN *starts knocking on the door.*

CURTAIN

SKETCH 9: BY THE PALACE GATE

Scene as at beginning of Sketch 3. FIRST BEGGAR *enters, sits on the floor next to* SAʿDUN. *A silent pause.*

SAʿDUN Who are you?

FIRST BEGGAR A beggar. Do you have something to offer?

SAʿDUN No.

FIRST BEGGAR And who are you?

SAʿDUN A beggar, eh? . . . You know, you look like my godfather.

FIRST BEGGAR Could be . . .

SAʿDUN How old are you?

FIRST BEGGAR Fifty, thirty, forty . . . Something like that.

SAʿDUN My godfather's age.

FIRST BEGGAR Could be . . .

SAʿDUN What's your name?

FIRST BEGGAR Which one do you want?

SAʿDUN Why, how many do you have?

FIRST BEGGAR Many. My first name was Nineveh. I found it heavy, stuffed with history. During the time of the Turks, I called myself Hikmet. Then I fell in love with a beautiful girl who found the name ugly, so I changed it to Zuzu. More recently, I called myself Michael, like my father's cousin, an old, rich man. He was about to die, then changed his mind. And now, because I've become poor, and to shock people, I call myself Ford.

SAʿDUN Strange, Mr. Ford . . . Your name's like my godfather's. Which town are you from?

FIRST BEGGAR From Dahr Safra.

SAʿDUN That's weird, too . . . My godfather's from the same place. You must have known him.

FIRST BEGGAR Did you say his name was Ford?

SAʿDUN Yeah!

FIRST BEGGAR Fat?

SAʿDUN Yeah.

FIRST BEGGAR Works as a lawyer?

SAʿDUN Yeah.

FIRST BEGGAR I don't know him.

SAʿDUN Too bad. I wanted to . . .

FIRST BEGGAR What are you doing here all by yourself?

SAʿDUN I'm waiting.

FIRST BEGGAR Waiting for who?

The lights dim. The stage is filled with the clamor of the courtroom, the sound of the pounding of the GENERAL's *cane. The lights come back on.* SAʿDUN *is still on the stone bench.* BEGGAR *moves from his right side to his left side, takes* SAʿDUN's *hand and begins to read his palm.*

FIRST BEGGAR (*Continuing*): You were working when she came in . . . No, maybe her father came in first. (*Mimicking her father's voice*:) Have you got an elegant jewel, Saʿdun?

SAʿDUN Of course, sir.

FIRST BEGGAR (*Continues mimicking*): I'm not a sir! I'm your Master! Your King!

SAʿDUN And I'm your slave . . .

FIRST BEGGAR The jewel and the necklace, I want them for my own daughter. Have you met my daughter?

SAʿDUN No, I haven't.

FIRST BEGGAR No, *Master*!

SAʿDUN No, Master . . .

FIRST BEGGAR How come you don't know my daughter?

SAʿDUN I haven't had the honor, sir.

FIRST BEGGAR How dare you say you haven't been honored?

SAʿDUN Because, as I told . . .

FIRST BEGGAR And she—she, who loves you . . . She who's sacrificed her youth for your sake . . . She's been waiting for you all her life; she's still waiting for you.

SAʿDUN Waiting for me, Sir?

FIRST BEGGAR Of course. Who else would she be waiting for? Aren't you Saʿdun, son of Umm Saʿdun?

SAʿDUN Yes, sir.

FIRST BEGGAR How dare you make these denials to my face! What's this? Isn't that her picture? There, hidden on your chest? You coward!

SAʿDUN No, this isn't her picture. It's my mother's.

FIRST BEGGAR Let me take a look.

SAʿDUN (*Aloud*): No, I won't . . . (*Aside*:) As a matter of fact, it *was* her picture, but I was afraid of him. He began yelling at me again.

FIRST BEGGAR If you're brave enough, show it to me!

SAʿDUN (*Aloud*): To tell the truth, although I'm not as brave as a lion, still I could tell him: "Here it is. Have a look . . ."

FIRST BEGGAR See? Poor woman, you're her only hope. You betrayed her . . . She's rejected many suitors: the sons of princes, of my colleagues and friends, the sons of kings, the King of Iron, the King of Wood, the King of Razor Blades, the King of Brooms, the Oil King, the King of Swimming, the King of Restaurants . . .

SAʿDUN I'm sorry, Master. I had no idea . . .

FIRST BEGGAR That's alright. We'll manage. Mistakes can be mended.

SAʿDUN I'm at your disposal.

FIRST BEGGAR And my daughter's at your disposal.

SAʿDUN Really?

FIRST BEGGAR Really.

SAʿDUN Will you let her marry me?

FIRST BEGGAR Yes, I will.

SAʿDUN I'm poor, penniless . . .

FIRST BEGGAR It doesn't matter.

SAʿDUN And I'm ugly.

FIRST BEGGAR I don't care.

SAʿDUN I dream a lot, and I'm afraid of death.

FIRST BEGGAR My daughter won't love anyone *but* a man who's afraid of death.

SAʿDUN I've been unlucky since birth.

FIRST BEGGAR That's a prime requisite.

SAʿDUN I get tired quickly.

FIRST BEGGAR Everyone's like that.

SAʿDUN I also get discouraged easily.

FIRST BEGGAR That's as it should be.

SAʿDUN (*Whispering*): There's one important problem . . .

FIRST BEGGAR What could it be?

SAʿDUN I don't wash my feet before I go to bed.

FIRST BEGGAR I don't give a damn.

SAʿDUN Will you still let her marry me?

FIRST BEGGAR (*Pausing at* ﬁ*rst*): She's all yours.

SAʿDUN As if you were here . . .

The lights dim again. The clamor of the courtroom returns. Then the lights are turned on all at once. SAʿDUN *is lying on the ground, while* FIRST BEGGAR *is pacing back and forth in front of him.*

FIRST BEGGAR Are you sure it's her?

SA^cDUN Who? You mean the landlady, of course . . . Do you know her?

FIRST BEGGAR Every other day, she hands me out a loaf of bread and two onions.

SAᶜDUN What's she like?

FIRST BEGGAR You tell me.

SAᶜDUN Fair?

FIRST BEGGAR No, dark.

SAᶜDUN A slender brunette?

FIRST BEGGAR Her thighs are hefty.

SAᶜDUN Her thighs . . . Ah, her thighs, they're full, they quench the appetite . . . Her lips are tender?

FIRST BEGGAR Her upper lip's thick.

SAᶜDUN Exactly.

FIRST BEGGAR And so's the other one.

SAᶜDUN And so's the other one.

FIRST BEGGAR Her hair reaches down to her legs?

SAᶜDUN Yeah, she has long hair.

FIRST BEGGAR No, she has short hair, actually.

SAᶜDUN Exactly.

FIRST BEGGAR The landlady . . . I know her well. She gives out alms to me three days a week. Are you sure it's her? . . .

SAᶜDUN *walks toward the gate and begins knocking once more.*

CURTAIN

SKETCH 10: STAGE FRONT

LAWYER *and* SAᶜDUN *are alone at stage front, with* LAWYER *pacing back and forth. He stops a few steps away from* SAᶜDUN, *who is sitting on the ground staring at him.*

LAWYER Are you tired, Saᶜdun?

SAᶜDUN (*Lifts his head*): You're my godfather, and you're a lawyer. Maybe, a long while back, you loved me. Tell me the truth: will my case take long?

LAWYER That depends on the facts of the case.

SAᶜDUN The facts?

LAWYER Of course. The facts . . . And they must be supported by evidence, and evidence in turn must be supported by facts. When facts are found, evidence is also found, and vice versa. But the most significant thing in every case is the existence of facts; if they're not there, they must be created. The court, however, doesn't accept fabricated facts. And that's why fabricated facts must be made real, being, as we've just said, not real to begin with, because they were fabricated. So how can facts be real and at the same time unreal, and vice versa?

SAᶜDUN Yes, how can that happen?

LAWYER That's the one thing I can't answer. Neither can the General, or his predecessors.

SAᶜDUN Truly, this is a strange story . . .

LAWYER Which story?

SAᶜDUN Which story's true?

LAWYER (*Irritably*): The story of facts! . . . Take this, for example. (*Resumes pacing.*) You're riding in a speeding car, which will travel the distance between Village A and Village B, via Village C. Which of these is fact? Your riding in the car? Your passing through Village C and arriving in Village B? They all are. On your trip, you see people quarreling, and other people watching them. Where's the fact? Both the people quarreling and the people watching are facts. But these are only apparent facts. Apparent facts aren't real facts. Facts have more than one aspect to them. The fact of the people quarreling and the fact of the people watching could actually mean that the people who are watching are the ones who *were* fighting, and are just standing and watching the people who came to reconcile them.

SAʿDUN I didn't get that.

LAWYER What matters is that you mention all the facts.

SAʿDUN All the facts . . .

LAWYER All the facts. Because there are facts which you might believe will work against you, when in actual fact they could serve your interest. So you'd be mistaken not to mention them.

SAʿDUN Mistaken?

LAWYER Of course. By judicial standards, a fact is a fact regardless of its merits. Sometimes an unfavourable fact will work in your favor, while a favorable one will hurt your case.

SAʿDUN I understand now. I do.

LAWYER You haven't understood a thing, because the facts that are mentioned are not as significant as those that aren't mentioned, and unmentioned facts aren't very important either, because they'll be brought out later on. I, for one, have many unmentioned facts.

SAʿDUN Relating to my case?

LAWYER No, relating to mine.

SAʿDUN Why? Have you got a case, too?

LAWYER No, I don't, but one must always be ready for future eventualities, especially since I don't like prisons.

SAʿDUN Why? Does a case always have to end up in jail?

LAWYER Whether it begins or ends up in jail isn't the point; what matters is the existence of imprisonment: life imprisonment, imprisonment with hard labor . . . many, many types. You may have heard of them.

SAʿDUN No, yes, of course I have. I'd like to say that I haven't experienced jail, I have no ideas about it, I've been busy all the time thinking of other things. But I understand that prisons have improved these days.

LAWYER Not all have. It depends. Cells for solitary are still the way they were in the days of King Solomon.

SAʿDUN I've heard about those.

LAWYER Then there are special jails and detention centers.

SAʿDUN Those I'm not aware of.

LAWYER There are many things you're not aware of, because you're busy, you have other things to think about. But that's my job. I can tell the difference between what's authentic and what's fake with my eyes closed . . . (*In a low voice*:) Between ourselves, imports are multiplying. (*In a loud voice*:) We don't know what to do with them. There are many jails that are empty, while jails for the common people are so crowded that inmates have to sleep standing up, like chickens . . . (*In a low voice*:) Between ourselves, the administrative apparatus is corrupt. Chaotic. (*Looking around cautiously*:) It's the same in all countries . . . Also there's another type, where they offer traditional vocational training in such things as tailoring, business, handicrafts, etc. And still others that offer a more modern kind. That's good, a man comes out of prison old, but at least with a skill. Do you know, however? The means of entertainment there are scarce: dominoes, backgammon, checkers, sometimes chess . . . That's the opposite of political and ethical prisons, which offer everything a person might desire, I'd even say that they have a certain degree of luxury: refrigerators, telephones, hot water . . . Except for the elevators, which break down often. At any rate, the government's ordered new elevators from overseas, that's something new . . . Then there are radios, TVs, comfortable mattresses, built-in closets, metal drapes, porcelain kitchens, pressure cookers, washers and dryers, calculators, cinemas, cafés, restaurants, nightclubs, stereos, cars, pajamas, shirts, underwear, cups . . . (*He hears the reverberations of the* GENERAL's *cane being pounded. He looks around, frightened, doesn't see anybody, regains his self-confidence.*) Be that as it may, not all of them are like that; there are filthy jails. And I'm afraid. Time turns like a wheel; one day it smiles at you and another it frowns. I'm a smart man, I know how to smooth things with the General . . .

SAᶜDUN How?

LAWYER At the expense of the defendant, of course. When I feel that the General wants the client's neck and has sharpened his teeth to pounce, I deliver. You may want to ask *how* I deliver. It's simple. You're aware, I'm the only lawyer in town. When I don't defend a client, I give the General the opportunity to do as he pleases. I let him arrange the facts to suit himself. I know they're wrong, but I close my eyes. And then—and this is for your ears only . . . (*Leans over to* SAᶜDUN *and whispers.*)

SAᶜDUN You're related to the General?

LAWYER Naturally. And I'm honored to be . . . (*Begins to hum a tune*:) Ta-rum, ta-rum, ta-ra-ra-rum, tum . . . (*Resumes pacing back and forth.*)

SAᶜDUN My dear Godfather, you weren't like this then. You used to be committed, a lover of justice. At least that's what you used to claim. Remember when you used to write poems on the subject?

LAWYER Bygones are bygones. I was naive. In those days, I didn't know how to stroke egos. Life's a game; only the intelligent understand it. Look at my forehead.

SAᶜDUN (*Sadly*): I see, I do . . .

LAWYER Don't worry, Godchild. You're different. I'm going to take you under my wing, and defend you in a way that will save you without offending the General. But be careful. Remember, as I told you, the facts! The facts, the facts . . . (*He begins to laugh.*)

CURTAIN

SKETCH 11: COURTROOM

CLERK What do you think, Your Honor?

ALL (*Repeating*): What do you think, Your Honor?

CLERK (*Eyes them disapprovingly*): The reason . . .

ALL The reason . . .

CLERK . . . that Saᶜdun . . .

ALL . . . that Saᶜdun . . .

CLERK . . . doesn't want to confess . . .

ALL . . . doesn't want to confess!

CLERK . . . is probably that he hasn't done anything. If he really isn't guilty, we've been a bit hard on him.

GENERAL Not just a bit: a great deal . . .

CLERK Why?

ALL Why? Why?

GENERAL (*Pounding with his cane*): Because it's not possible that he isn't guilty! I know, I'm certain! If he weren't guilty, he wouldn't be here. If he weren't here, I wouldn't be here either. And if I weren't here, the Clerk and the witnesses wouldn't be here either. And if we weren't here, none of you would be needed here. And if that were the case, none of this would exist . . . But it's impossible that nothing at all has happened. Something must have, and that something requires the existence of a crime, and a crime implies the existence of a guilty party, and a guilty party requires that there be a verdict, and a verdict requires the presence of a judge. And a judge, these days, must be a General.

That's the reason why I'm here, and you're here, and so is Saᶜdun. (*Calling out*:) Saᶜdun!

VOICE His blood is on us and on our children!

GENERAL (*Pounding with cane*): His blood is on him alone. I'm an easygoing man. You know I am. But not to the point where I'll permit you to speak nonsense ...

VOICE Nothing's nonsense!

SECOND VOICE We want to know what he's guilty of!

ALL We want to know what he's guilty of!

ALL He's guilty of being the first on the list submitted to me by the Clerk. A list on which all your names are placed ...

CLERK Yes, all of your names ...

VOICE It can't be!

ALL It can't be! It can't!

GENERAL (*Pounding*): Yes it can! (*Menacing*:) Yes it *is*!

ALL (*Subdued*): You're right, you're right ...

GENERAL Does anyone disagree?

ALL No, not at all.

GENERAL Saᶜdun!

CLERK Hey, Saᶜdun!

SAᶜDUN *who is standing next to the* GENERAL *but does not answer him, points intently to the* CLERK. CLERK, *in turn, points to another man, who has the appearance of a hangman. Both men drag* SAᶜDUN *so that he is facing the* GENERAL.

GENERAL Don't you intend to confess, Saᶜdun?

CLERK Your file's grown thick, and your case even thicker. It's been stretched to the limit. You must find a solution.

GENERAL There are many aspects to your indictment now. If you wanted to confess, where would you begin? We're going to resort to a method we abandoned a long time ago.

CLERK What do you mean, we abandoned?

GENERAL Hush!

HANGMAN *moves close to* SAᶜDUN *and starts to whip him with a lash he was concealing.* SAᶜDUN *endures the beating stoically.*

GENERAL Are you going to confess?

CLERK Saᶜdun wants to confess, but he isn't able to because he can't remember.

GENERAL (*To* HANGMAN): Enough. We'll make him remember. We will.

SAᶜDUN (*Remembering*): Ah, what wonderful days those were! A little devil with tiny horns used to visit me here. He didn't cost anything, he didn't even drink tea ... (*He* ¤*xes his eyes somewhere in the space of the courtroom.*) Why don't you want something to drink, go ahead, have something. Ha! Ha! (*Laughs, looks at* GENERAL:) He had a nice dimple when he laughed. The Doctor was a good man, he knew how to make him laugh. He loved simple folk. (*Reciting*:) "Blessed are the meek, for they shall inherit Heaven . . ." He kissed me and said he wanted to wash my feet. He was laughing, and his hands were resting on my shoulders. I said, "Doctor, I'm a sinful man." He began to laugh, his eyes got smaller and smaller, to the point where I couldn't see them. I grabbed his neck and squeezed . . . (*He squeezes an imaginary neck.*) I kept squeezing ... (*He begins to pant.*)

GENERAL You know that I know you're lying, Saᶜdun.

SAᶜDUN *abruptly lets go of the imaginary neck. He looks rather stupidly at those present. Silence.* SAᶜDUN *starts walking around in the courtroom.*

SAᶜDUN When the Priest asked me to confess, I did ... I told him everything. He asked me to recite ten Our Fathers and twenty Hail Marys.

GENERAL Did you?

SAᶜDUN I was praying, and while I was still on the second set I heard a voice. I looked, and found him sitting in a rear pew. He was dressed in the Doctor's uniform. But I recognized his horns. He was laughing. I spoke to him; he didn't answer. I asked him why he was wearing the Doctor's uniform. He didn't say a word. His horns began to grow. I was afraid. I made the sign of the cross, but he didn't go away. I called on Jesus to help me, but he didn't go. I covered my eyes (*He covers his eyes with his hands*) and pretended to ignore him, so that he might go away. He didn't. I glanced at him from the corner of my eye. How did I know that I did it? A liar . . . he's a liar. His horns kept growing. I began to wonder, how was this possible in the middle of a church? My eyes must have been tired, and I couldn't see well. I ran to the altar. (*He runs.*) I burned some incense in the thurible . . . (*He waves an imaginary thurible.*)

GENERAL You're hallucinating, Saᶜdun. You know these are fantasies. You're making the case more complicated. This has nothing to do with it.

SAᶜDUN (*Continues his monologue without paying attention to the* GENERAL): The incense clouded my eyes. I couldn't see the creature any longer. I thought he was gone; then, when the smoke had cleared, I found him still in his place. His horns had already become enormous, and he was laughing. (*Addressing the devil in a loud voice:*) What's the matter, why are you laughing? If you need something, just let me know . . . Don't laugh, I beg you! I haven't done anything! *She*'s the one who asked me to! Believe me! She did! She deceived me . . . I was young and didn't know the difference between Mortal Sin and Original Sin, believe me . . . I was still young, stupid, a jackass . . . Don't laugh! Where are you going? (SAᶜDUN *shrinks back, frightened.*) Why are you crowding me? Stay away! Stay away, I say! You're wrong! I'm telling you, it was her, stay away, I say! I thought we were friends! Do you smell the scent? That's the incense . . . (SAᶜDUN *still retreating.*) Don't come any closer! Don't, I say, don't! Stop there! . . . (*His back hits the wall. He turns around and begins to knock at the door.*) Open up for me! Open up!

Lights begin to dim.

GENERAL Witness Ahmad Sulayman al-Abd!

CLERK Witness Ahmad Sulayman al-Abd . . .

WITNESS Present.

SAᶜDUN *begins to knock at the door, cautiously at first, then more forcefully. Meanwhile,* GENERAL *keeps calling witnesses.*

GENERAL Witness Ibrahim Yusuf Mneimneh!

CLERK (*With fading voice*): Witness Ibrahim Yusuf Mneimneh . . .

WITNESS Present.

GENERAL Witness Muhammad Ahmad al-Kishi al-Sarayfi!

CLERK Witness Muhammad Ahmad al-Kishi al-Sarayfi. . . .

WITNESS Present.

CURTAIN

SKETCH 12: BY THE PALACE GATE

SAᶜDUN *wakes up, gets off the bench. Comes up to the door, knocks. Silence. Knocks. Silence. Knocks for a third time.*

VOICE I hear you.

SAᶜDUN I thought someone must be listening . . . Otherwise, why would I be knocking? (*Silence.*) I didn't hear a thing, not a sound, the whole night . . .

VOICE The whole one thousand and one nights I've spent here . . .

SAʿDUN How long shall I keep knocking on the door?

VOICE When you were knocking on the door in the middle of the night, I thought you were just sleepwalking.

SAʿDUN I used to do that often. My mother tells me that when I was little I'd walk in my sleep. I'd go to the garden, climb the plum tree, pick one of the fruit, and put it to bed beside me. (*He laughs.*) I never ate it, my mother tells me.

VOICE May God keep her.

SAʿDUN You're a good man.

VOICE Don't mention it.

SAʿDUN (*In a faint voice*): Do you love me?

VOICE *remains silent.*

SAʿDUN I'm asking you, do you love me? I love you . . .

VOICE I don't know, I haven't loved before. But I think I know how to . . . Do you love her?

SAʿDUN Of course I do, why else would I have traveled all this distance, forty years?

VOICE Forty years?

SAʿDUN Yeah, working for her . . .

VOICE Does she love you?

SAʿDUN Of course she does.

VOICE Do you know her?

SAʿDUN Naturally.

VOICE How does she look? Is she tall?

SAʿDUN Yeah, tall . . .

VOICE Blonde?

SAʿDUN Exactly: blonde.

VOICE Does she have green eyes?

SAʿDUN Oh yes, her eyes are green.

VOICE Is she slender? Does she wear a white headcloth?

SAʿDUN Right, that's right. But how do you know all this? You must have seen her. Tell me the truth, where did you meet her? You must have seen her. What did she say about me? She said she was waiting for me, didn't she? I know. They wouldn't believe me when I said so. They began to laugh. (*He laughs.*) I told them to come along and I'd make them rich, right down to their grandsons. They started to laugh. Maybe because my clothes were filthy. I was working and I hadn't had time to change, you know how work is . . . Why don't you come with me yourself? I'll make you rich, you believe me, don't you? (*Silence.*) Hey, why don't you answer? Where are you, where have you gone? I'm talking to you. Do you hear me? Why don't you answer any more? You, what's your name? You, who don't know how to love, do you hear me?

VOICE I hear you. But I'm losing my voice. Soon I won't be able to speak at all. I'll become a tree.

SAʿDUN Become a tree?

VOICE I forgot to mention that you've been talking to a tree. I thought you wouldn't believe me. Do you want me to tell you the story from the start?

SAʿDUN Go ahead.

VOICE I said to myself, "Man, wouldn't it be better if you became a tree?" I stood up, and turned into a tree.

SAʿDUN Why? Why did you become a tree?

VOICE It's a long story, and I don't have time for the details. Why don't you join me, and turn into a tree yourself?

SAʿDUN I can't, really. You know I've been waiting for her . . . Besides, I don't know how to be a tree.

VOICE It's the simplest thing in the

world. Just think that you want to become a tree. You'll feel a shudder as the cold penetrates your bones. Then it's all over.

SAᶜDUN How come it's not all over for you?

VOICE I've been thinking about what kind of tree I'd like to be. I tried the apple first. It didn't suit me.

SAᶜDUN Why not?

VOICE Then I tried the oak tree. Same thing.

SAᶜDUN Why didn't it suit you?

VOICE Then I tried the palm tree, the fig, the banana, the lemon, the loquat, and the pear . . . None was agreeable.

SAᶜDUN Why not? Why not?

VOICE Then, after I'd tried them all, I finally realized what it was I'd been looking for. Only today have I known what to become.

SAᶜDUN What?

VOICE A China tree.

SAᶜDUN A China tree? Why? (*Silence.*) Answer me, I'm asking you, answer me! . . .

VOICE Who'll answer you? The tree? The tree can't.

SAᶜDUN You must speak! You must say something before you change into a tree! What's the last thing you wish to say?

VOICE Why don't you become like me, a China tree? We'll keep each other company, and live carefree.

SAᶜDUN What'll we do?

VOICE Nothing. Just watch people. We'll grow tall, become old comfortably, and die without knowing we're dying. We'll die standing up.

SAᶜDUN Are you sure we'll die standing up?

VOICE Effortlessly.

SAᶜDUN Effortlessly?

VOICE We'll suffer no pain for the rest of our lives.

SAᶜDUN No pain?

VOICE We'll live happily.

SAᶜDUN Happily? (*Then he remembers the first answer.*) How can we suffer no pain? Some kid might come by and carve his name on our trunk.

VOICE Even if he does, we won't feel pain. I'm speaking from experience.

SAᶜDUN But why a China tree?

VOICE When locusts invaded our country, they devoured everything except the China tree. The China tree stood erect, like the Roman columns at Baalbek.

SAᶜDUN The China tree has thin leaves. It doesn't give any shade.

VOICE That's very good.

SAᶜDUN And it only grows among houses.

VOICE That's good, too. That way it can watch people's misery, and can laugh to itself.

SAᶜDUN But the China tree doesn't know how to love.

VOICE That's even better.

SAᶜDUN Who says so?

VOICE I say so. Come on, try to become a China tree. You'll see . . .

SAᶜDUN I told you, I can't.

VOICE I'm just asking you to try. You've got nothing to lose.

SAᶜDUN Okay . . . What shall I do?

VOICE Think China tree.

SAᶜDUN I'm thinking.

VOICE Concentrate on the coldness.

SAᶜDUN I'm thinking.

VOICE Make yourself very stiff.

SAᶜDUN I have.

VOICE (*Pauses*): Are you feeling the coldness?

SAᶜDUN No.

VOICE Concentrate harder on thinking about the coldness.

SAᶜDUN I am.

VOICE And now?

SAᶜDUN I'm still not cold.

VOICE Of course you won't get cold!

SAᶜDUN Why?

VOICE Because you're thinking of other things at the same time.

SAᶜDUN Like what?

VOICE Maybe about her . . .

SAᶜDUN You're right, I *am* thinking about her, terribly . . .

At this moment the sound of approaching footsteps can be heard. SAᶜDUN *jumps, looks at the door, turns around.*

SAᶜDUN Hey, listen! Are you listening? She's come! She has! I told you she'd be back! I knew! No one believed me, no one! Not even *they* (*Pointing at the audience*) would believe me! . . . Now we'll go inside together; you must be hungry, we're all hungry . . . We'll go inside and drink some wine, you'll warm up . . . (*He hears the squeaking of the hinges of a gate as it opens: an imaginary gate.*) Here she is, I told you! She's opening the door now . . . Answer me! Answer me, I love you! Don't say it's too late; it's never too late. Here I am; I've been waiting a long time, but here she comes. If you keep knocking at the door, the door will open. Ask for a fish and you won't get a snake. Come on, I'll make you a cabinet minister in my government. And if you don't want to do any work, fine: I'll pay you a salary while you hang around. I know why you're upset. Maybe you haven't been getting paid very much . . . Look, here she is! I'll have her invite you in . . .

He looks at the door and finds it still shut. He listens to the sound of the footsteps, but discovers they're already receding. In the midst of a heavy silence, SAᶜDUN *stands up, his eyes bulging and his mouth open, rigid as a statue. Meanwhile, an ugly doll in bridal costume is lowered from the ceiling, until it faces him. He is startled. He stares at it for a second. Holds it. Then he begins to tear it apart. He throws it on the floor and steps on it violently.*

A silent pause. Then an unpleasant guffaw issues from the same part of the stage the VOICE *has spoken from.* SAᶜDUN *does not look toward the source of the guffaw. He attacks the door, banging it with all the strength in his two fists. He bangs without saying a word, then collapses by the door. The lights dim for a short while. Then the entire stage is lit. The entire stage must be shown clearly. This place, which has seemed to be separate from the Courtroom, is actually a part of it, and the door where* SAᶜDUN *has fallen is one of the two doors of the Courtroom. The* GENERAL *pounds three times with his cane.* SAᶜDUN *becomes attentive. He turns over and stares at the* GENERAL.

GENERAL Saᶜdun!

SAᶜDUN (*Gets up*): Your Honor . . . I didn't know he'd deceive me. I didn't. I should have, though. I was stupid, a jackass, to believe him. Who could have told that this is how it would end? For forty years I've been carrying this diamond; forty years, Your Honor. He deceived me.

GENERAL Who was it, Saᶜdun? Who?

SAᶜDUN Maybe that's the reason you're mad at me. I didn't know it'd turn out like this. I spent my life engraving it. Look (*He searches his pockets for the diamond*), how beautiful it is. A perfect gem . . . (*He searches again, to no avail.*) For forty years I carved on it, forty words each year, and in each word were forty letters, and on each letter were forty vowel marks.* I even did it in Farsi script. That's what her

*In classical Arabic script, marks are placed above and below consonants to indicate short vowel sounds. Today they are used mainly as decorative elements in calligraphy.

father wanted, Farsi, Your Honor . . . (*He despairs of finding the diamond.*) The necklace is lost! The necklace, too, Your Honor! This is just what I needed! It's as though I've done nothing, all's been wasted . . . Even the souvenir's lost! I thought I'd be left with a souvenir, at least . . . (*He begins to cry.*) I thought he was a real king, but he turned out to be a liar! I thought kings didn't lie . . .

CLERK Are you talking about the King of the Djinn?*

SAʿDUN No, no, about a king I thought had stature. I didn't know he was lying. He had no daughter, Your Honor, he hadn't any. He was a dirty tramp, a son of a bitch. No one knew. Ask them (*Points at the audience*), they've all been deceived . . . Ha! He told me he'd give me his daughter and half his kingdom. I set to work (*He goes back to searching for the necklace*) on the necklace. It isn't lost, it can't be! Impossible! Now who'll marry an old jeweler who's not worth a penny? I should have known from the start, this is unfair, I should have . . . No one could have believed he was such a liar; no one wants to believe . . . (*He collapses slowly onto the floor, repeating the last sentence.*)

GENERAL (*Pounds with his cane*): The Defense! The attorney for the Defense!

LAWYER It's greed, Mr. President, greed is the reason. If only the world could go back to the way it was during the days of Noah, peace be upon him! . . . Look, Mr. President, I've scrutinized all my books for a legal article on which I can base my defense, but to no avail . . . And if we were to give him a sentence that was commensurate with all his crimes, we'd have to hang him thirty times over, and jail him for 360 years with hard labor, in solitary confinement. His crimes are heinous. But in truth he doesn't deserve all this punishment. It's unfair. (*He slaps* SAʿDUN *absentmindedly.*) I've known him since he was in his mother's womb. I held him in my own hands. He used to slither like a fish. And, like all kids, he used to play and fight and insult people. And like other kids he had a family and a home, and his mother sent him to school until he acquired a skill and began to make money. Like everybody else, he was supposed to get married and have children, to have his own house, to visit people and be visited on holidays. He was supposed to do all of any number of things, and to rear his children, grow old, wet his bed like all old men, and have his kids care for him. I know him well, Your Honor. I don't know what hit him. Maybe he started to think more than he ought to. No one should think any more than necessary . . .

SAʿDUN (*Abruptly wakes from his daze, as if he's remembered something*): I remember, Your Honor, now I remember! There was one condition I had to fulfil. I'd forgotten it, and that's the truth. I wasn't thinking about the condition, I'd stopped worrying about it and become absorbed in her. If I hadn't forgotten, things wouldn't have taken the turn they did. He knew how to set me up. First, he made me fall for her; then he added the condition. I remember now, I do, Your Honor . . . Uh . . . I forget. I've lost it. Lost it . . .

LAWYER I'm not only his godfather, Mr. President, my grandmother is his mother's aunt's cousin, and my grandfather is her brother-in-law's cousin; he married her stepdaughter; her daughter's also my father's first cousin's daughter. My father married, by mistake, his sister, who in

*Spirits, demons.

turn was born to neither his father nor mother. And after the mother died, my father married her stepdaughter. His second wife is his first cousin on his father's side. In other words, Saᶜdun is . . .

GENERAL And so? Go on . . .

LAWYER And so I want to tell you, Mr. President, that this defendant, standing before you, is my own brother. And that's the only reason why Your Honor may want to pardon him.

GENERAL You're wrong to think that. Duty comes before feeling; duty takes precedence over everything else.

Silence. GENERAL *and* LAWYER *exchange some whispered words.* CLERK *returns to his place.*

GENERAL Saᶜdun, would you like to make any statement before the judgment is pronounced?

SAᶜDUN (*Shivering*): I'm cold, Your Honor . . . A wave of coldness has penetrated the marrow of my bones . . . I'm not sure, I may be turning into . . . (*Shivering*:) unh . . . unh . . . unh . . .

GENERAL *pounds three times with his cane.* SAᶜDUN *is still shivering.* CLERK *walks up to* GENERAL *and hands him a large sheet of paper.* GENERAL *examines it. Silence.*

CLERK The General will now read the sentence!

GENERAL (*Pounds with his cane to call the court to order; he clears his throat, then starts to read the sentence in a mechanical, monotonous tone, without any pauses*): On the basis of the Prosecution's decision for distinguishing the absurdity of life by honoring the terminology appeal profoundly and justice behavior by Fate the High Court in considering in place and consideration of the liberty to inquire about testimony of any fees liberated to socialism we the conferees in case and because of the people's solidarity people and masses coming close to the holy battle on the pathways freedom justice the crisis situation cited above based legally on justice and considering that behavioral probation and local consumption in the various circles and real estate in kindness to our brothers and since the speculations ending the lawsuits in Geneva and the arms at the stock market, the Lebanese broadcasting, according to sources in the West the right path in research about wakes, ending and finishing the projects of Saihun and Jaihun and the Kalb River and colonialism toward national banks a nationwide presidency appealing first from the state, making use of superior references in the state the duty of being honored by bringing forth decisions, the written texts, adopting the grandiose republican picture on the passports of the blessed country, for love and dignity, and the formalities of appeal and maintaining security, the Government of the Separate Peace and because of colonization, the confiscations, the secretariat, the general common market at the service, the country a government consortium for advancement and construction . . .

CLERK *goes up to* GENERAL *and whispers a few words in his ear.*

GENERAL (*Continuing*): In accordance with all of this, and to save time, we declare the judgment of the people against Saᶜdun ibn Bishara ibn Saᶜdun ibn Bishara ibn Ismail ibn Bishara ibn Simaan ibn Bishara ibn Ismail ibn Yahya ibn Saᶜdun ibn Yahya ibn Bishara ibn Qarih . . .

CLERK Etcetera, etcetera . . .

GENERAL . . . to be death by gunfire.

CLERK Or on the guillotine.

GENERAL Or by hanging.

CLERK Or stoning.
GENERAL Or in the gas chamber.
CLERK Or by poison.
GENERAL Or by being beheaded with a sword.
CLERK Or by the pen.
GENERAL Or by being buried alive.
CLERK Resurrection by burial.
GENERAL Death by lashing.
CLERK Or by being run over by a car.
GENERAL Or a train.
CLERK Or by acid.
GENERAL Or by starvation.
CLERK Or by gluttony.
GENERAL Or thirst.
CLERK Or cold.
GENERAL Or terror.
CLERK Or drowning in the river.
GENERAL In the sea.
CLERK Or in a drop of water.
GENERAL Or by being pierced with an arrow.
CLERK Or a needle.
GENERAL By handgun.
CLERK By mortar.
GENERAL By hunting rifle.
CLERK Or the atomic bomb.
GENERAL Or the hydrogen bomb.
CLERK By falling from a building under construction.
GENERAL Or from a threshold.
CLERK By being dragged behind a truck.
GENERAL Or being brought to the stake.
CLERK By being fed to rats.
GENERAL Or to industrialists.
CLERK By heart attack.
GENERAL Or by cirrhosis.
CLERK Or intestinal fever.
GENERAL Pneumonia.
CLERK Cholera.
GENERAL The plague.
CLERK Typhoid. Paratyphoid.
GENERAL By having his teeth pulled.
CLERK By working.
GENERAL Or not working.
CLERK By sleeping.
GENERAL By insomnia.
CLERK By coincidence.
GENERAL By order.
CLERK Or life imprisonment.
GENERAL Or permanent death.
CLERK Or permanent life.
GENERAL Or, as our audience sees fit . . .

During this exchange, SAᶜDUN *stops shivering. His body stiffens until it resembles wood. Voices are heard in the courtroom: "Hang him!" "Scaffold!" "Bullets!" "Life imprisonment!" The din grows louder, becomes deafening. Suddenly there is the squeaking of a gate being slowly opened. The din subsides, and fear grips the place. The* GENERAL *gets down from his chair, frightened, losing his solemnity. He hides behind the chair and peers intermittently at the gate. Two enormous male nurses, in white uniforms, enter through the gate. They move cautiously toward the center of the courtroom, where* SAᶜDUN *stands stiffened. One of them listens to his heartbeat, then signals to his companion to carry* SAᶜDUN *out. They carry him horizontally, like a tree trunk. They exit. They shut the door behind them. The people in the courtroom express satisfaction. The other gate opens. A* NUN *enters, ringing a small bell she holds in her hands.*

NUN Time to eat! To the refectory!

Everyone leaps toward the door where she entered, clamoring like pupils when the bell has rung announcing the end of classes.

NUN Don't forget to wash your hands before you eat!
ALL (*In mechanical unison*): Yes, Sister; yes, Sister . . .

CURTAIN

MAMDUH

ʿUDWAN

That's Life

A MONODRAMA

Translated by Robin Ostle

That's Life (*Hal al-Dunya*) is the first attempt in Syria at writing a monodrama. Mamduh ʿUdwan wrote and published it in 1984, and it was performed that year, first in Jordan, then by the same theatrical group in Kuwait and Tunisia. In 1985, the play had its first performance in Damascus. Acclaimed at once by critics in many parts of the Arab world, it was considered by the Cairene journal *al-Musawwir* to have revived the art of the monodrama in Arabic. Its success prompted the author to write three more monodramas: *Doomsday, The Garbage Collector,* and *Man Eaters.* All four appeared in a single volume in Damascus in 1993. In a letter to the editors detailing his purpose in writing a drama with a single actor, ʿUdwan said, "I wanted to expose a man's life, so I let him talk at will. Being the male, the man, the husband, the father, and the breadwinner, he represents social authority par excellence, an authority parallel in kind to both political and economic authority." ʿUdwan describes him as a man unused to discussing matters with anyone, one who, because he is a kind of autocrat, can renounce logic and truth, contradicting himself unashamedly. His only weapons are the values of existing culture, for it is such traditions, wisdom, religion, and customs which cement his authority. "The fact that no one can interrupt him," ʿUdwan says, "means that he can choose what he likes to represent reality, can leap over all hindrances and opposition. As he enjoys the opportunity to speak, uninterrupted, he exposes his hypocrisy and inhumanity." Although the woman is absent from the stage, her presence is felt there, with all her feminist issues. ʿUdwan regards this play as "an adventure in drama" in which he chose to defend woman through the pronouncements of a male chauvinist who despises and exploits her, affirming his religious, social, and sexual supremacy over her. In casting such light on the logic of dictatorship in the family, the author feels he is also helping to cast light on the logic of dictatorship in all other spheres of Arab life.

S.K.J.

THAT'S LIFE

A sitting room in an ordinary house, with a telephone, a desk and some chairs. On the wall, a photograph of a woman looking at the audience and a photograph of a man—Abu ʿAdil, star of the stage—but the photographs date from their youth. There is another photograph of a group of children of various ages. Near the door there is a mirror. The house has a vaguely chaotic air. The chairs look as though they have been pulled from their places, suggesting that people were there and that the house has not yet been put in order after their departure. The lighting is dim, appropriate to just before sunset. There is some fruit on a tray in a corner of the room.

Abu ʿAdil is aged fifty but still retains a fine healthy appearance. He enters by a side door [from the kitchen] holding a coffeepot and turns on the light. He sits on one of the chairs, pours himself some coffee, and lights a cigarette. He smokes calmly and drinks the coffee with evident enjoyment. He relaxes. Silence. Someone knocks at the door of the house. Abu ʿAdil doesn't move, as if he hadn't heard. He carries on smoking and drinking coffee. The knocking on the door stops. He pours himself another cup and drinks.

Suddenly he gets up with an unexpected burst of energy as if he had remembered something important, and takes hold of the telephone wire to put the plug back in. He looks at the woman's photograph.

"Blessed is He who never forgets." There I go again forgetting to plug the telephone back in its place. It's been unplugged since yesterday. How do I know now whether the children called? Perhaps they heard the news and called to make sure.

He smiles at the photograph and sits down.

You know how much the children thought of you. Dreadful news like this always makes people afraid to have it confirmed. Wasn't it Mutanabbi who said: "The news raced round the Peninsula until it reached me, and I hoped against hope that it lied." If Mutanabbi had been alive today he'd have used the telephone to make sure, or perhaps he'd have sent a telegram.*

The telephone rings. He gets up, lifts the receiver, and speaks gently.

Hello? Yes. On my own? Of course I'm on my own. I'd forgotten to plug in the telephone. No, no. Not at all. Why should I be angry? There's no need for that sort of talk now, ʿAdil. (*In a voice close to tears:*) No problem. No problem. (*He sighs.*) Of course the house is desolate. No. I can't come. I don't want to see anyone. I don't want to be consoled. You're young, you can get over it and forget, but broken bones don't heal so easily when you're old. I'm shattered, ʿAdil. The loss of your mother has crippled me. (*The tearful note*

*Abu al-Tayyib al-Mutanabbi (d. 965) is the most renowned of the classical Arabic poets.

in his voice increases.) I don't want to forget her. I shall stay here to be with her. (*He looks at the photograph.*) Leave me alone. Look after your guests and don't bother about me. No. No. When the condolences are over you must stay with your wife. She's young and she needs you. I can look after myself. Fine. Fine. Give me Faʾiz. Hello son. I'm glad you arrived safely. I'm so sorry, but what can we do? That's life. You're right, your brother's house is near the bus station. What's the difference between my house and your brother's? Your sister Faʾiza? Perhaps she'll arrive today. She must have heard. You're all a long way off, son. What was the point of waiting? The Lord God bade us make haste to bury the dead. That's the way of the world. The important thing is for you to be a man and help your brother ᶜAdil, especially when your brothers and sister come. That's honoring your mother, Faʾiz. God be with you. I'll see you tomorrow.

He puts down the receiver, walks to and fro, slowly and silently. He sits down, drinks his coffee, then gets up and walks to and fro.

Whatever things were like, it's not easy to forget thirty years of living together. I can't sit still. This silence is stifling. The house seems bigger or wider. God, is this what the disappearance of a single person can do? They leave us, then the house becomes a void, and the world becomes a void, a wasteland. Is this why they say, "Better a bachelor for a lifetime than a widower for a month"? I didn't think her passing would be as painful and hurtful as this. Her shadow's everywhere. She was the one who organized this house as painstakingly as an ant. Thirty years she worked in this house. Only when absolutely necessary did she ever go out for a few hours. Then back to work here. I always used to wonder: what is this strange creature called woman that can find constant occupation day in day out for thirty years in one place? She was the house and the house was her. Now the house without her really is a great void, as though it's become a forest or a desert. It's become deserted like damp, mouldering ruins.

He sits down, stretching his legs over the chair, speaking in a distracted manner as he drinks the coffee.

This was the time I used to wake up from my siesta and she'd bring me a cup of coffee. (*He looks at the photograph.*) I couldn't sleep this afternoon because of you! (*He turns away from the photograph.*) When I was asleep her only care in the world was for me to rest and not be disturbed. No ringing the doorbell and no callers. She'd turn off the electricity in the house and disconnect the telephone. ᶜAdil would say to her, "Mother, you shouldn't disconnect the telephone. There could be an emergency call." And she, God bless her soul, would say, "What emergency can't wait until your father wakes up?" Often we'd forget to put the plug back in when I did wake up. (*To the photograph:*) We're a family that unplugs the telephone. Every family has its peculiarities, and you got us used to this one. You began it for our sakes. (*Addressing himself:*) All her life she took more care of me than she did of ᶜAdil. After coffee she'd sit alone, waiting until my temper improved or until I'd finished reading and went into the kitchen. I'd get home from work and find her in the kitchen, because she knew what time I'd be back. I'd ask her, "Umm ᶜAdil, how do you know that when you can't tell the time?" And she'd reply with that laugh of hers that meant the whole world to me:

"My heart can tell the time." If I didn't speak to her, then she kept quiet. She knew I was tired or tense because of work or the traffic. No sooner did I ask for food than it was put before me in an instant. Fresh, hot, delicious food, into which she'd put her heart and soul. Yes, cooking's a gift, so they say. The food was never the same in my family's house, in my friends' houses, and even in my son ᶜAdil's house; ᶜAdil, who all my life I'd hoped would have a house of his own. It's true that ᶜAdil's wife's young and beautiful, but how could she ever be as skillful as Umm ᶜAdil? That's what I was telling Abu Yasin as we came back from the cemetery. Abu Yasin honors and respects you, and he was grieving for you just as much as he was for me. Abu Yasin, now there's a fine man. No wonder he's worked for twenty years as a judge. He's a well-balanced fellow with a fine sense of judgment. Since he retired and came to live in our quarter, he's become an unofficial judge for all of its inhabitants. Everybody consults him and has recourse to him. He considers things judiciously; he reasons, and then gives judgment. Only he could understand my plight, especially since he was stricken like me with the death of his wife, Umm Yasin. He was broken-hearted until God requited him with an upright woman who bore him a son to gladden his declining years. I told him how we'd known about the illness for six months, and how you insisted from the very beginning on going on looking after me, in spite of your illness. It's true that it was your duty to look after me, but was it necessary to overburden yourself and land us in this mess and cause us to waste all this money? Poor Umm ᶜAdil! You wanted so much to take care of me that you sacrificed yourself and me as well! The only thing you had which tied me to you was this endless care you took of me. But why so stubborn? You got old, Umm ᶜAdil. You became an old woman, and this looking after me was no use to you any more. Now the illness forced you to recognize you were weak and couldn't hang on to me any more. You needed rest. And this was a heart disease, no laughing matter. Was it necessary for you to carry on regardless, until you collapsed twice in the kitchen? During the third attack I had to carry you to bed. If you hadn't had a strong and still youthful husband who was able to carry you, you'd have stayed stretched out on the floor until someone dropped by. But I carried you, drooping and limp like a tattered old dress. Only then did you admit that standing exhausted you and that you were dizzy. Six months in bed. By God, Abu Yasin, those six months were enough to wear down mountains. If I'd been just a bit older, it would have been a problem. (*He smiles with a certain bitterness.*) I would have needed someone to look after her and to look after me. But thank God I'm still strong. Thank God as well that the neighbors love and respect us. My son ᶜAdil, his wife, the neighbors, and all our relatives, all came to look after her and to look after the house in her place. None of them would accept a word of thanks from her. "You've done so much for us, Umm ᶜAdil," they'd say. Even your new wife, Umm Samir—may God keep him and preserve him to grow up under your care—was constantly with us, and no doubt she told you how much she did for hers. She must have told you, otherwise you wouldn't have been so keen to discuss the subject as we were coming back from the cemetery. Our house was full of people. She was certainly a much-loved woman. No woman had a funeral procession like that before. Even the men haven't had such funeral processions. Our area hadn't seen a procession like it since the death of the late Hussein Bey, who was the leader of the district. Even I was amazed. I know that she had a good standing in the neighborhood, and that my son ᶜAdil has a certain status too, and has his friends. And me! I too have my own status. But I didn't imagine that a woman's cortège could be as big as that. My goodness, Umm ᶜAdil, you should have seen them, then you'd have known what people thought of us. Everyone was there! All the women wept, and even the young men. I wept myself. I couldn't control myself. When the condolences beside the tomb were finished, and I made to leave, it seemed that what was happening was a joke or a farce. You couldn't have died! ᶜAdil was standing by me, receiving condolences. His stubble had grown, he hadn't shaved for five days. How much we suffered in those last five days! I'd tell him to shave every day, but he wouldn't. But he's a young man and a little stubble won't matter! But I couldn't do it. White hair looks dreadful; it makes a man look older than he really is! When the condolences were over, I looked at him and was on the point of saying, "Call your mother. Let's go home!" The words nearly came out of my mouth. From his sad, tired, grief-stricken face and his unshaven beard, I realized that you were dead. I nearly collapsed. I lost my balance a little and leaned on ᶜAdil's shoulder. I was afraid I'd go mad, and I burst out crying. My weeping was sincere and moving; it made everyone cry too. (*His eye falls on the mirror.*) Acting? Does acting make people cry? I defy any actor in the world to cry like I did! Why should I act? A man pretends in order to convince others of something. Instead of pretending to cry, I could have pretended to control myself as men are supposed to do. I wept the way women do. I wept and made everybody there weep. ᶜAdil didn't weep. I wept for a lifelong companionship, the companionship of thirty years. He's young, he can control himself. I was in great pain. Yes, the loss of a wife is like a blow to the elbow; it's extremely painful at first. That's why I collapsed onto ᶜAdil's shoulder. When I fired the gunshots to alert the neighbors of your death, my weeping set off a lamentation which was like the wailing of a bunch of gypsies. They all reacted to the calamity and gave vent to their feelings. They didn't use their minds and well-chosen words as they did later. They used their eyes and their tears. And after that there were some who said, "God have mercy on her. She's at rest. She died with dignity, honored by her husband, her children, and her family. She died without burdening anyone." They didn't know what they were saying! Who says you weren't a burden to anyone! Weren't you a burden to me all through your illness? What could I do about those constant doubts about yourself? What was I to do about your feelings of inadequacy?

You had doubts about whether I loved you, because you doubted your own value, and thought you didn't deserve to be loved by a cultured and educated man like me. So you used to think my feelings for you were merely courtesy, and my show of love mere acting! Acting? How could you know acting from the truth? Acting, silly woman, belongs to the cinema, the stage, and television. In your whole life you never went to the theater or the cinema. You never even watched television, except for a few songs. When a series or a play began, I'd look at you and see you'd fallen asleep, and always the same excuse: tired from the day's work. You're right. You really were tired, and that's why you fell asleep as you followed the series. But how could you know what acting is? Acting's knowledge and art. Understand? Acting's an art about which more books have been written than there are hairs on your head. That's why you can't say your heart tells you and teaches you about it. Your heart can only tell you about the truth of my feelings, and it can tell you the time I get home. Isn't that right? You went on trusting your heart and relying just on that, until you see where that heart of yours got you! In fact you wore your heart out by insisting on relying on it. You'd even say about my behavior toward other people: this is acting or this isn't acting. What's it matter to you whether I'm acting or not? My fault was that I'd open my heart to you when we were alone. If a man can't speak as he wishes in his own house with his wife, then who can he speak to? With you I'd say everything that was on my mind, even though I was certain you didn't understand all I said. But I had to tell somebody what I thought about Hussein Bey and Taysir Bey and ʿAmmar Bey . . . and express my opinion without coming to any harm. They're all big shots and they're all vile and despicable. But when they're in my house, when I invite them, I have to treat them with respect and do my duty. My reputation and the family's honor are at stake. And why shouldn't I invite them? It's in my interest, because they can make or break me. They can promote me, help me to get on, and even protect me. If I ask for help against some injustice, they might help me. That's why I treat them nicely and pretend to respect them. What have I to lose? The proverb says, "Kiss the hand that you can't bite, and pray for it to break." That's what I used to do. I'd kiss the hand, and then when I was alone with you, I'd pray for it to break. I wanted you to know what a strain I was under in this life, mentally and physically, how clever I am at dealing with these big shots who are as cunning as wolves. That's the value of education, the value of the books you used to grumble about because they took all my time. They want to sit with me to enjoy my conversation and benefit from my education. I know that. I know these big Beys are empty vessels who don't understand a thing and who have books in their houses just for show and one-upmanship. Even sitting with me is for show and one-upmanship! They want to have cultivated people all around them in their entourage. I know all that and I'm telling you so that you know my real worth. But instead of being proud of your husband's worth, you became like a scorpion. How was I to know that you've got a mind like a prosecuting counsel, that you'd turn my frankness with you into evidence against me! You want to prove anything against me. I know you. You're afraid of me, so you keep quiet! But I can read your thoughts in your eyes! I can see that you're full of accusation and indictment, and that you're silently shouting "hypocrite!" What on earth will satisfy you? Tell me! Didn't I look after you? Didn't I exhaust myself for your sake? Weren't you a burden to Samira as well? Yes, even Samira, who doesn't want to take responsibility for anyone and who didn't get married because she didn't want to be bothered. She came and looked after you throughout your illness. She didn't leave you for a single day. Even your daughter Faʾiza didn't look after you like she did. Your daughter is with her husband. She'd come to visit you for one or two days, then she'd go back to her husband. And don't forget how before she left she'd thank Samira, and leave you in her charge, saying, "God help us to repay your kindness!" But Samira doesn't expect any reward. Like me, she worked expecting nothing in return, and no doubt like me, she's now suffering, sad, and exhausted. I'm tired too, tired after six months of your illness, and the last five days of crisis. Then the final night. I didn't sleep a wink last night. Up till now I haven't slept. I could see in everybody's eyes the looks of pity being cast in my direction; they all know I'm old and tired, and that I've suffered alone; they know how much I need amusement and rest. That's why I told ᶜAdil to give me a rest and to have the mourning ritual in his house. I want to rest a little, I want to take a breather. People know I'm like a man whose crops and barns have been destroyed by fire, and who wants to count his losses when the fire's been put out. And to count them he has to be alone. So here I am, alone, alone, and not knowing how to count my losses. My material losses are the simplest. Everybody knows I was ready to sell the roof over my head and the floor under my feet for your treatment and your nourishment. (*He goes to the fruit bowl, takes an apple and a knife, and begins to peel it and eat it.*) There was always fruit in the house, but all to no avail. The money spent, the care, the effort, were all in vain. God's will! And on top of it all, I shall be sharing the costs of the mourning ritual and the burial. I'll give ᶜAdil what I can, if his brothers don't chip in. So what if they spend a little money because of their mother's death? They're civil servants as well, and have their salaries. Does the whole loss have to fall on my shoulders? Isn't all I've spent on the illness enough? (*He goes to a batch of medicine boxes.*) I sweated blood to pay for all this. (*He throws the medicines into the wastepaper basket.*) And what about my other losses which nobody else feels? My biggest loss is in losing you. You know how much marriage costs these days. The price of gold's gone up, and clothes as well. However undemanding a woman is, she can't get married without a wedding ring and some dresses and a new bedroom. Those are expenses to burn a hole in the pocket. If you hadn't died, I wouldn't have been forced to get married again! What does it matter to you? You're dead and at rest. Perhaps you wanted to die. Perhaps you wanted to be free of the torture of the illness and its pains. For a month you talked of nothing but death. It's as though you wanted to put death into our minds so that we'd accept it when it came for you. Even I began to think of your death. I mean, I began to wonder, "What shall I do when she's dead?" You wanted it. After every attack, after every call to the doctor, and after the treatment you'd burst out crying, and turning to God you'd shout, "Oh God. Be gentle, oh God. Have mercy on me, oh Lord!" I understood. I understood that God's mercy you asked for was death, to deliver you from the torture of illness. During every attack you hovered between life and death. The doctor, ᶜAdil, and I, in the grip of our anxiety, tried to revive you and bring you back to life. (*To himself*:) What else could we do? What would people say? "They abandoned her during her last days. They begrudged her the price of the medicine and the doctor's fee." A fine thing if they talked about us like that after all our expenses. All your life with me you lacked nothing.

He goes quickly into a neighboring room and comes back with a large bag, which he throws on the floor.

All these were clothes belonging to you. (*He opens the bag and takes out a few clothes.*) Doesn't all this cost money? (*He looks at the clothes in front of him.*) So what if they're secondhand? Everybody buys secondhand clothes. And you never used to go anywhere. You didn't need clothes except to cover yourself, and here at home anything would do. Even now they're still good. Two days ago I began collecting them in this bag. Samira said to me, "We can give them to the poor"; now that you're not using them. (*To the mirror*:) Now she's gone, what use are any of the other things? What use are the clothes, the medicines, and everything else connected with her? Even this picture, does it have to stay here? Perhaps the children would like to have a picture of their mother. I really should have taken the picture to ᶜAdil's house. A picture of the deceased should hang where the mourning is. (*He shouts*:) Sure, I began collecting her clothes two days ago! It was obvious she was going to die. If not today, then tomorrow. A man must be prepared for things like this so that they don't take him by surprise. (*To the photograph*:) Don' t look at me like that. I don't tell lies. You know I didn't begrudge you anything, that I did everything that had to be done. Yes, the thought had crossed my mind. (*To the mirror*:) There isn't a man in the world who hasn't thought of the death of his wife. Sometimes one thinks of the death of one's sons. Man's like that. He imagines the loss of those he loves. That's what books on psychology say. Man wants to try a life without strings. He needs ties with others at a certain stage so that he doesn't feel alone and abandoned, but after a while he feels those ties have become fetters which limit his liberty. So he dreams of being free of them. But that doesn't mean that every time a thought crosses our mind, we're ready for it to become real. Otherwise humanity would be exterminated, or men would have reverted to their original bestial state; a father would kill his sons, the people would kill those they love. In other words, people would become wild animals. I'm like other people, I have thoughts like those, but I can't carry them out. I'm not a killer. If I'd wanted to kill her, I wouldn't have bothered when she had the attack at midnight, and we were alone. Samira wasn't in the house. After all, she's free. She's a friend who helps us, but she doesn't have to explain herself to us, nor do I have any right to ask her. She said she wouldn't be able to sleep here. She told you that as well, when ᶜAdil was here listening. Even ᶜAdil said you were comfortable, so I told him to go and sleep at home. Five days and nights he'd been by your side. I told him to go. Poor fellow, he has a young wife and he shouldn't leave her for longer than that. I was alone with you when the attack came. Was it my fault that the mere mention of the subject put you into such a state? Don't you know that I may marry again after your death? I can get married again while you're still alive, without even consulting you! I can do that by law. Yes, I can marry up to four wives, so what's all the fuss? And since when do you dare to accuse me of lack of good taste? Such recklessness is positively suicidal, it's the recklessness of one who has given up on life. (*He imitates her*:) "If you had any taste you wouldn't bring that up now!" You know that for saying much less than that, I could have made you see stars, but I was patient and kept a grip on myself because you were ill. If you had had any taste you would have understood the limits of this patience of mine. If you had had any taste, you would have broached the subject yourself! If you'd had any taste you'd have said, "Mahmud, you've put up with me so much, why don't you look for a nice wife to look after you?" You might have wanted me to spend the remainder of my life in happiness. No such thing would occur to you! Even when you were fussing and talking to me like that, without laying a finger on you, what did I do? I shouted at you. Of course I shouted at you and cursed you. It was the least I could do. All my life I've shouted at you and cursed you, and beaten you, and you put up with it. So what, if you remember all that when you have a heart disease? The doctor told you that you had to avoid distress and tension, but you went on recalling that I used to beat you, and counted out the times that I beat you. So what if I used to beat you? I'm your husband and your master. I could beat you till you were black and blue, you still remained just as you were when you left the village, a dumb peasant without a clue how to respond to my desires. That's why I was forced to beat you now and again. My nerves would be on edge and you didn't understand. Perhaps you didn't feel my tiredness; you didn't know how hard life is for the breadwinner in his job, with the bosses, and out in the street with all the people. That's why I used to close my door and immerse myself in reading. I'd withdraw from the world and follow it in books and magazines. I'm a stranger in this town and any insult could humiliate me. They all want to try it out on us! They're all-powerful, and don't distinguish between big or little. I'd walk along alone, avoiding everyone, shunning contact with anyone. Keeping away and avoiding people, even trying to make myself small and insignificant in the street so that no one would see me until I arrived home with my dignity intact. Only at home, after closing my door, did I feel that I could be comfortable and relax. Even the place where I worked didn't give me that feeling any more. I don't know how often I had to stick to the law to suit so and so, or how often I had to break the law because so and so was one of the big shots, and I had to do it because of him. All my life my only security was at home. But you don't take any account of all that. I'd get home, sigh with contentment that the day was well over, then you'd ask me to go back to the market to buy provisions or get bread. You didn't know how to do the shopping. (*Shouting*:) Is it your privilege not to know things? To remain ignorant of everything so that you forced me to leave the house and go into that jungle? The children were too little or they were at school, and they couldn't jostle for position in the queue at the bakery door. As if *I* could fight in the queue! Was I supposed to stand up to people if they took no notice of the queue? I'm an educated man, not a wrestler or a boxer. I don't want to become a laughingstock, even to the grocers. The greengrocer won't let me choose the fruit and vegetables, he just puts in what he wants. If you'd been able to go out to do the shopping, perhaps they'd have treated you differently. Perhaps they'd have felt more restrained with women. But then again there's another problem. If one of them's rude to me, I can pretend not to hear, especially if there's nobody around. I can swallow the insult and go away. But what can I do if one of them insulted you, and you came complaining to me? You're just the same as you were when you left your village. You still think that it's impossible to keep quiet in the face of an insult. You'll come and complain to me that one of them's insulted you. You won't understand that I can't go back and face up to him. No, you'll think that my silence and acceptance mean that I'm not man enough to protect my wife and children. Yes, even the children were a source of misery for me. I couldn't stop them from going out to play in the neighborhood or from playing at school, and children get into fights. How could I make the children understand that they had to put up with the hurt caused by their friends, so as not to drag me into trouble? They all think their father's the strongest man in the world. You know what happened to Saʿid al-Hardan's son because of a fight with another boy. Three armed men in an official car came round and beat up the boy in school. Then they took him home and beat up Saʿid al-Hardan himself in front of his wife and children. Just imagine if I were humiliated in front of you and the children! . . . Not a day goes by in the market without my seeing them beat up someone or other, for no apparent reason . . . but still, as soon as I get home you ask me to go back to the market. Then I get back from the market, and your complaints begin. The vegetables are no good. The zucchini are no good for stuffing. The beans are big and hard. The tomatoes are too ripe or too green. I don't understand these things. Manage your own business. Cook anything. That's all I could bring. But still you go on: "They've been laughing at you. We'll have to throw out half of what you've brought because it's no good." To hell with it! Chuck out everything in the house and stop this croaking of yours! I'm not a child. I know I've been cheated. I know, but I keep quiet. Keeping quiet doesn't mean we don't know. It just means we can't do anything about it. But you don't let up until I fly into a rage and beat you. Then I sit down to relax, and you begin the list of complaints. "This child needs an exercise book." "Fine." "That one needs a new school bag." "OK. I'll take care of it." "This one's been beaten up by one of the neighbors' sons." "I'm not the kids' *qadi*! Listen, Umm ʿAdil, children fall out, then they always make it up again. We mustn't interfere." But still you go on. "The neighbor's son who beat him up's a big boy, and he hit little Samir." "What am I supposed to do? Go and fight with him? Lower myself and become a laughingstock? Your son's a rascal. You must teach him how to behave with those who are older than he is. If he weren't such a rascal, then the neighbor's son wouldn't have hit him." But still you're not satisfied, and still you go on. I say to you, "A big strong boy won't hit a child." You say, "Your son saw him peeping into the house through the keyhole, so he cursed him." "Shut up and don't talk to me about things like that! Shut up, or I'll force you to be quiet! I'll beat you!" "Look at the paraffin seller, the bastard. He didn't fill the tin properly. The paraffin's half water." "What have these things got to do with you? I work to earn the money, and I keep quiet about it. How much does the paraffin seller steal? One or two liters from the tin? I forgive him. That's better than shame and disgrace." But you keep prattling on, and I know you're not satisfied. Why are you so stubborn? Why can't you be content? I'll have to soften that thick head of yours, or break it. Whatever I say, you have to take it as given. Don't argue with me! I can't bear anyone to argue with me. If you can't accept what I say without arguing, I'll beat you. Even the Holy Qurʿan has advised us to beat our wives: it says, "and those women whose recalcitrance ye fear." And what is the meaning of *recalcitrance* if it isn't being contrary to your husband or being a nuisance to him? Aren't men responsible for women? "And as for those women whose recalcitrance ye fear, admonish them." I admonish you, but you don't accept it! "And keep ye apart from them in their beds." I used to do that occasionally. "And beat them." Do you hear that? "Beat them!" I beat you as is my right. I beat you to give vent to my anger. And where should a man give vent to his anger if not in his own home? So I give vent to my anger, I curse you, and I beat you. You must put up with me and be quiet. All your life you put up with me. Why, on this occasion, did my cursing and shouting bring on a heart attack? If I'd wanted to bring on the attack, I wouldn't have rushed to call the doctor. I left the house immediately. Yes, I could have called him by telephone, but we'd unplugged it when you went to sleep in the evening, so its ringing wouldn't wake you. It was for your own comfort. When you had the attack I rushed to the telephone, but it was dead. The telephones are often out of order. Any change in the weather puts the telephones out of order. Bad lines. I thought the telephone wasn't working. I was blinded by confusion and haste. I forgot that we'd unplugged it. ʿAdil did it. That's why I went out to get the doctor. His house is close by and you know him. I rushed there to wake him and bring him. Of course I rushed. I rushed as fast as a man of my age could. Don't forget that I'm fifty-five years old! And I'm a respected man with a position to consider. That's why I slowed up a bit when I got to his house. It's a matter of good taste. Didn't you accuse me just a little while before of a lack of taste? I thought of how much it would disturb him to be woken up at this hour! His little sons might wake up terrified. I'm not selfish. The man looks after us extremely well. But we must always show good taste. Yet in spite of that, I knocked on his door. It was just as I expected: not only did he wake up to open the door, but everyone in his house was wakened by the knocking. His children with eyes half asleep; his wife in her delicate diaphanous nightdress, trying to cover her beautiful body from my eyes. I had no time for that; I had no interest in her or her body, but still it was embarrassing. The sight of her and the children made me beg the doctor's pardon. But he understood, and left me standing with his wife while he went to get his bag. But how long did I stand hesitating at his door? Just a few minutes. A few minutes, then I brought him back here. My reward was that insult which his wife hurled at me. I heard her whispering to her husband before he came out behind me: "This wretch has eyes like the Devil himself." Of course if she hadn't been upset by my waking them up, she wouldn't have spoken like that. My eyes! What's wrong with them? Nothing's wrong! It's not because I was looking at her body. I just looked normally, a passing glance. No man can stop himself looking at a virtually naked body through a transparent nightdress. She meant that my eyes were swollen because of my staying awake with you.

The telephone rings. He goes toward it eagerly, but controls himself and looks at the photograph.

You're always the same. This suspicion won't ever let me relax, even after your death. So what if Samira calls to ask about me? Do I have to be forgotten by everyone? (*He picks up the receiver.*) Hello? (*He appears disappointed.*) Who? Abu Yasin? Hello! How nice to hear you! Thank God. Yes? No, nothing's happened. ʿAdil can't stop me from doing what I want when I want. I know, I know what your sons did when you wanted to get married again. Children! They think the world belongs just to them. No, of course you didn't make a mistake. On the contrary, I'm grateful. You're the only one who feels for me, and understands me. My dear fellow, neither ʿAdil nor anyone else. They can bang their heads against any brick wall they choose. I'm doing nothing against the law and custom. That's life, Abu Yasin. If necessary I'll surprise you. God preserve you. God willing, I'll see you tomorrow. Goodbye. (*He hangs up the receiver.*)

Everything is preordained and prescribed. "Say, nothing shall befall us save what God hath prescribed for us." (*To the photograph:*) Man only dies when his time has come. You would have died, even if I'd arrived with the doctor a few minutes earlier. These lives of ours are given by God Almighty to us his servants. They're things held in trust which He then reclaims. We can't end these lives unless He wills. It's God's will that has been done. God Almighty has reclaimed His trust. Don't put the blame on me, blame your weak heart, which couldn't hold out for those few minutes. I did slow down a little but not intentionally. When I slowed down I wasn't just thinking of not disturbing the doctor and his family, I was thinking of you! Yes. Just at that moment I thought of you and your desire for death. You wanted to die. You wanted to be at peace, and you were suffering with the illness. You wanted me to help you. You didn't dare ask me clearly and directly; as usual you were being shy and using your cunning. But I knew what you wanted. This is something which happens all over the world. The newspapers are always writing about it. Everywhere they're discussing the rights of the family and the doctors to help someone who's hopelessly ill, to deliver them from pain by making death easier for them, or by hurrying it along. Exactly as they help a dying horse by shooting it in the head. It's a point of view which is discussed in the most civilized countries of the world. I didn't invent it. (*He takes a book from the desk, looks through it till he finds a certain page, and reads:*) "The doctors must take care of those citizens who are sound in body and mind. As for the rest . . . "(*He addresses the photograph:*) That's Plato, listen. "As for the rest, we shall let those with sick bodies die. The citizens themselves will decide the fate of those whose minds have become warped and whose natures have become abnormal." (He closes the book and puts it back in its place.) Yes, Plato. Go on, tell me you're not impressed by Plato either! For you to start casting doubts on Plato is all we need! Does Plato say all that just because he doesn't like you? Or does he love another woman and wants you to die? I was thinking of your death just to bring you relief. It's a civilized point of view in which I happen to believe, but I can't put it into practice. There are other similar civilized ideas just like that one I read about, but they wouldn't suit our society, or they wouldn't be accepted by it. So I only did what duty demanded.

I got the doctor in his nightshirt. He knew how serious your condition was. I told him to go on ahead of me, so that I could get ʿAdil. All that couldn't go on without your son being there. He had to come in any case. So let him witness everything; I would have needed him anyway. I'm getting old and I can't rush about the streets looking for a chemist if you needed medicine. And perhaps if I hadn't fetched him he would have blamed me. For all I know he might have accused me of not caring. I woke him up and he left his young wife's bed too, and came in his nightshirt. Even his wife got up in her delicate nightdress. It's true she's not embarrassed with me, she's just like a daughter to me. But still, she's not a blood relation. It's not right that I should have seen her in a transparent nightdress which reveals the parts of her body. Do you see now how I've disturbed people because of you? I rushed after ᶜAdil until we reached the house. We found the doctor standing at the door. Why didn't he go in? He was ringing the bell and nobody opened the door. (*To the mirror:*) I swear it was the confusion. I forgot that Samira wasn't in the house. "Blessed is He who does not forget!" I'd got used to having her around with us and relying on her. Umm ᶜAdil was on her own and couldn't get up to open the door. Perhaps she didn't hear the bell. Perhaps she was dead before we arrived. How do I know? I wished the earth would swallow me up when I realized I had gone out in my nightclothes without the key. The worry! (*To the picture:*) Worrying about you made me forget it. We began to push the door, but it was useless. I almost killed myself pushing the door with my shoulder. Then ᶜAdil jumped through the bathroom window and opened it for us. The doctor examined you, gently raised his head, and said he was sorry. I was the one who cried then, especially when the doctor said, "Perhaps we could have done something if only you'd telephoned." I said to him through my tears, "What bad luck. Look, Doctor, the telephone's out of order." Then ᶜAdil remembered that we'd unplugged it; he did it himself. I'd said to him, "Unplug it so that the telephone ringing won't disturb your mother; we aren't expecting any important calls." The doctor shook his head in confusion. No doubt he thought that any further talk on the subject would be embarrassing, especially at a time of grief. And after all, he's not an investigator and he isn't concerned with matters like that. We're free to reply to his questions or not, and I'd just burst out crying and there wasn't any more room for that sort of talk. I wept and got out the pistol and fired it in the air to tell the whole world about your death. Once, twice, five shots altogether. That's all there was in the magazine but it was enough. It's a small town and there's no better way than firing a gun to tell people something quickly. We're used to that. (*The telephone rings; he lifts the receiver.*) Hello? How're you! God preserve you and keep you always. What can we do? You're right. It comes to us all. That's life. We're in God's hands. No, the mourning's at ᶜAdil's house. I came here to rest a little. I'll try. Goodbye. (*He puts down the receiver.*) The neighbors came and then each began to tell the other that Umm ᶜAdil had died. By morning, the whole house was swarming with people, and the whole neighborhood as well. I wept like a child in front of them all, not just for myself but for you. The tears had to flow because of you. I wept for you until I made all the people weep with me, and I wept when I saw Samira. I don't know who told her. Perhaps she heard the gunfire. Noise travels a long way at night, so it must have reached her house. When I saw her I thought that everyone would think I was embarrassed because you'd died on the one night when she left you alone, as though I'd let you down. As though she'd entrusted me with something and I hadn't been able to keep that trust, as though I'd failed.

I know how you two were friends, and

the neighbors know it as well. The neighbors respect her just as much as you. It's true that she's over forty and she's never married, but there's nothing wrong with her. She's got a good reputation. It was just her fate. That woman's a real mother. You remember how she looked after you when you were ill, how necessary her presence was. She'd wash you and look after you. I didn't know how to look after you. Your own son didn't look after you like she did. Me? Never! I was grateful to her, but I was a bit abrupt with her. I'm not used to dealing with women. Her constant presence in the house confused me. I'd sit down in silence with her, reading a magazine or a book, or getting out the cards. Do you blame me for that? Should I have gone to my room and left her with you? That would have been bad taste, and indifference on my part. I began to sit with her and try to maintain some conversation, and sometimes we'd spend the time near you playing cards. In the end she began to ask me to go to my room to rest. She began to feel for me, because she knew how much I was doing for you. She began to look after me and you. She became a part of the house. She was the one who cleaned, cooked, washed, and saw what was needed for the house and got me to provide it every morning. What else could she do? After she'd finished all the work, she'd sit and read a magazine or newspaper, waiting for a sign from you to get you some medicine or anything else you needed. In the end she began to nod off in the chair. I told her she could sleep here, indeed you were the one who begged her to sleep in your room. Nobody forced her to do it, nobody forced her to sleep in the house of a stranger. And you know that people who are asleep can't control themselves. The blankets may fall off, and their bodies may appear naked, or virtually naked. I could have walked into the room at any time and seen Samira naked. Nobody forced her to reveal herself to a stranger. Of course I'm not related to her, and I forgot sometimes that she was there. I'd open the door and go into the room in the middle of the night to see that you were all right, and so I'd see her with the blankets off. Of course I didn't try to cover her up. She might wake up. You might wake up and then where would I be! So I'd go quietly back to my room. Even when I opened the bathroom door while she was taking a bath, how did I know she was there? I heard the sound of the water and thought you were taking a bath, so I opened the door. That often happened with us; but she was the one who was bathing. Of course she was embarrassed. Is it easy for a woman to be surprised naked in the bath? I quickly closed the door and apologized, but it means that she'd exposed herself to embarrassment which was quite unnecessary. All that was because of you! Through looking after you she showed me the sort of body I'd been dreaming of all my life. Her body hadn't yet run to fat like yours. Nobody could have imagined that beautiful body was hers. It's as though she was twenty. A body white as milk. Bright shining thighs. When I saw them in the bath, her bosoms were just like pangs of hunger. Yes, two breasts like pangs of hunger. I'm not a poet, but I can only describe them like that. (*The telephone rings. He lifts the receiver.*) Hello? Yes. Yes. Abu ʿAdil here. God preserve you and have mercy on the souls of your dear departed, my friend. Of course. Of course. She's an irreplaceable loss. But what can we do? We're in God's hands. That's life. If she's such a loss to you, what can I say? (*His voice trembles.*) Pardon me! I couldn't control myself. I must have patience. Of course. No, please! I want to sleep awhile. You went to ʿAdil's house and didn't see me? As I told you, I'm tired and I've come to rest. Goodbye. (*He hangs up.*) Poof! What a lack of taste. For heaven's sake, is it such a favor that you went to ʿAdil's house to offer condolences? Who are these people? One wants to let me know he went, the other tells me he wants to go.

The doorbell rings. He goes and looks through the peephole in the door, then comes back without opening, talking as though addressing the person at the door.

I won't open it! You can see the door's closed. That means the mourning ceremony's at ʿAdil's house. (*The doorbell rings again.*) You can stand there till morning if you like. If you've come to offer condolences, then do the honors at ʿAdil's house. Otherwise, why have you come? Do you think you can just sit here and amuse yourself? (*He goes quietly and looks again through the peephole. He sighs with relief.*) Thank goodness! He's gone. He can say what he wants. (*The telephone rings and he rushes eagerly toward it.*) Hello? Yes. Hello! I'm sorry, I don't remember you . . . In any case, how nice to hear you. God preserve you. No, at ʿAdil's house. Near the bakery. Yes. Yes. You'll know when you see the lights. Ask any grocer there. Goodbye. (*He hangs up.*) His friend, he said! His friend, and he doesn't even know his house. What sort of friendships are those? The world's become a jungle. Nobody bothers about anyone else. People have lost their real ties with each other and nobody cares what happens. That's happened to me, and now I'm alone. (*He addresses himself in the mirror:*) You're on your own, Mahmud. Alone, and nobody cares about you. No. These people are merely offering condolences, they're not really concerned. They don't come because of me. They come because of her. Or to keep up their social image. They want to prove to themselves and to others that they're doing their duty unstintingly. Nobody bothers about me. I might spend the rest of my life alone in this house. I could die and the stench rise from my body before anyone realized I was dead. I can't rely on anyone, not even my son. I can't blame him. He has his own family and responsibilities. And he has his beautiful young wife. He must stay with her, especially as she says she's afraid to stay alone in the house. So let her cuddle her husband if she wants, and let him cuddle her as well. I know she's not scared. She's lying. So's he. Otherwise how did she spend the last five days on her own without being afraid? They want to be together. They're free, so let them be alone together. And now let them have the bother of the mourners. Let them wish everyone would go away so that they can be alone in their embraces. Everyone's free to do what he wants, and so am I. You live your life, my son. I won't stand in your way; I've no right to stand in your way. But just leave me to live out the rest of my life. You mustn't stand in my way either; you've no right to stand in my way. In fact, you can't stand in my way, because I'm not bothered about you or your opinion. I'm your father and you're my son. You do as I tell you and not vice versa. (*The telephone rings. He lifts the receiver.*) Yes? ʿAdil! Haven't we done enough telephoning? I told you I wanted to rest. Faʾiza's arrived? Let me talk to her. Faʾiza, my darling. How are you, my girl? Don't cry on the telephone. I want to hear your voice clearly. Please. Faʾiza, my girl, that's life. Now you'll take your mother's place.

You've shown this tenderness all your life. Your tender nature will make you understand your father and look after him. Crying again? Give me ʿAdil. ʿAdil? No problem. No problem. Of course she'll cry. Let her cry a little. She must. You know how women are. But listen. I don't want to hear this crying on the telephone any more. Good. No. No. I can't come. I'm exhausted and I want to rest. ʿAdil, my son, I'm old. I can't endure all this any more. You're young. You're the one to shoulder the burden. You're the eldest. Let them sleep at your house. It's no problem. The mourners? What about them? So what if they're my friends and of my generation? You do your duty. ʿAdil, they haven't come to play cards or backgammon. They've come to offer condolences. It's not a question of my friends or your friends. I know it's out of respect for the deceased, that's why you must show them great respect. She's your mother, not mine. With all due respect, I'm tired. I'm at the end of my tether. I'm a wreck. No. No. I don't want anyone. I don't want any dinner. I'll look after myself. I'll unplug the telephone so nobody disturbs me. Don't get in touch again. Tomorrow's another day. Goodbye. (*He hangs up.*) Her worth! With all due respect to her worth! You and your mother have done us such an honor! But what are we supposed to do? Kill ourselves? She's the one who died. Do we have to die as well? The living are worth more than the dead. You should think of me. Your mother's dead and at peace. I'm the one you have to bother about now. Her value! And me? Don't I have any value? Will you all neglect and abandon me? I appreciate your circumstances, so why won't you appreciate mine? Why was I avoided like the plague when Abu Yasin mentioned the subject? Do you think I run after women like you do, you rascal? Then what did it have to do with me? He was the one who brought it up. He's got my interests at heart, while you don't care. Quite simply, he understood matters. I'm alone, and my children have grown up. They're not even in the same town. Some are studying, some have their jobs, and you're the only one left in town. Do you have any time for me? You, with your beautiful young wife? I need someone to look after me. Must I spend the rest of my life like this? I don't know how to fry an egg or make a cup of coffee. I'm not used to it. I'm a man. I always had someone to look after me, so I never learned anything of all this. I never learned how to rely on myself in these matters. So who'll prepare my food or wash my clothes? You? Your wife? Of course you don't have the time. You won't be able to spend the night by my side as I used to spend the night by your mother's side. You'll find a thousand excuses to go home and be alone with your wife's young body. What will you care about me when you embrace her and stretch out beside her in bed? Let your father go to hell! You're right. She's a warm-blooded young woman and you're a young man. But what am I to do? What shall I do if I'm still a vigorous man? Should I go running after the whores in the street the way you do? I can't do that. I'm not cut out for that. I don't dare go after forbidden fruits like you. I'm not after illicit sex which has been forbidden by Almighty God. As Abu Yasin said, I shall get married according to the law of God and His Prophet. Anything wrong with that? It's the law of creation. That's life. The man has our interests at heart. And the words weren't out of his mouth before your voice rose like a gypsy's . . . The first move should have come from you and not from him. You're the educated one who understands everything. Instead of using your knowledge against me you should have used it for your father's interests! If you'd been a real human being, you'd have thought about your father and taken great care of him. Precisely because your mother died, so as not to lose your father as well, or at least so that I wouldn't be angry with you? Didn't God Almighty warn you against the wrath of your parents? You want to appear wise and educated in people's eyes, but your wisdom only shows itself when I'm involved. (*He imitates his son:*) "If it had been my father who'd died, would you have been thinking about marrying off my mother?" Idiot! Good for nothing! To hell with you and your education! "If it had been my father who'd died!" You'd like to see me dead, isn't that it? You were only thinking about my death so that you could marry off your mother. My God, you were shouting at me with other people present, while your father was devastated and a nervous wreck. I'm the one who can put a price on thirty years of marriage, not you. I'm the one who lived through them. And what's that got to do with loyalty? Of course she wouldn't have got married if I'd died. That's life. Instead of trying to reform me, reform the world. A man remarries after the death of his wife but a woman doesn't remarry after the death of her husband. Life's like that. If a mother remarries, that's a sign of her weakness, her disloyalty, her bad faith, her inhumanity, her disregard of the sacred bond of motherhood. That leads to tragedy. Don't you remember *Hamlet*, which I asked you to read? The book's still here. (*He takes the book off the shelf.*) Here it is. A young man whose father dies and whose mother then remarries. The speed with which she remarried led the young man to suspect wrongdoing. Of course he was suspicious! Are we supposed to believe in ghosts as well? He began to see the ghost of his dead father urging him to avenge him, but naturally, it was the speed of the operation that aroused his doubts. If things had taken their natural course, there would have been no need for such haste. How the young man suffered! Just imagine. If it had been his mother who'd died and his father married another women, would that have led to tragedy? Of course not! Hamlet's an understanding sort of fellow. His father's strong and healthy, still full of virility. That's more important than being a king! So what would have happened? Hamlet would have been a little sad, just as any man can be sad over someone he loses, but in the end he'd have thought about the present. He'd have thought about his father. I'm convinced that this fellow Hamlet would have thought about the remarriage of his father, because he understands! Because he's not a bastard like you. But who knows? Perhaps Hamlet was a bastard. Maybe he was only thinking about the inheritance problem. Maybe that's what you're thinking about. You don't want me to remarry so that you won't have any more brothers to share your inheritance. What is this great inheritance which makes you want to tie down my life? Is it our land in the village? All your life you never bothered about it; it's only now that the price of land's risen that you've started thinking about it again. Now you understand why a woman doesn't remarry after her husband's death. Her children won't allow it! Hamlet couldn't stop his mother? He's a liar! He wasn't grief-stricken because of his father. The mere fact of his mother's remarriage meant the loss of the throne for him. His mother was a weak woman who'd fall under the control of the man who married her. She'd do as he said, according to how he saw his power, and not hers. As for a man, he remarries because they can't stop him. A man's strong and doesn't fall under a woman's control. He possesses everything: the house, the wife, and the children. And I am a man. I'm the master of the house, the breadwinner of the family, and the father of the children. Obedience to me is part of obedience to God. Who can stop me from doing what I want? Nobody can lord it over me. I'm the one who can lord it over all the rest. I fed them, brought them up, and spent my money on them. So then I'm free to do what I like. I shall remarry if I wish. (*He opens the book and reads:*) "O God! a beast that wants discourse of reason, would have mourn'd longer."

He throws the book angrily away, then pulls himself together and controls himself.

That's because she's a woman. I'm a man who wants to lead a decent life in his old age, as Abu Yasin would say. If it hadn't been for the need to do that, I wouldn't have thought about the issue at all. (*Addressing the photograph:*) Your son believes I think about women for other reasons. But you know that I endured six months of your illness without touching you, though I had every right to do it. Even when another woman was around. Yes, Samira was always around. She'd come into my bedroom to wake me or to bring me coffee as I was reading. She'd wash my clothes. Even my underclothes. That's why I said to myself that Samira was a woman well suited to my home. She knows it so well already. Besides, she's an outstanding housewife. It's much better than to bring a strange woman into the house. Then what woman would agree to marry a fifty-year-old widower? Only one who herself was a widow or a divorcée. And why should I take a woman that some other man's known? How do I know whether she won't go on remembering him? She might go on thinking about him, even when she's with me in bed! Then she might already have children. No man's touched Samira before. We know she's never married. I asked her. I'd never have believed it if I myself hadn't tried it on with her. I mean, I tried to flirt with her, just to test her, but she refused. She threatened to leave the house. She told me literally: "No man will touch me except by the Law of God and His Prophet." Then, she's educated. She can read and write. Because she didn't marry she's had the time to mix with people and benefit from their knowledge and experience. (*He shouts:*) It's my right! You were virtuous and utterly dedicated, but times have changed and the world's changed. Even I've changed. I'm no longer the country boy who married his village girl when he was twenty years old. I'm no longer the naive, simple chap I was in the village. We've lived in the city for thirty years. All that time I've been growing and changing, learning and developing, while you stayed at home, just the same as the day you left the village. For thirty years I'd look at the townswomen, then come back home to see you with your clothes stinking of cooking. Cooking isn't a mark of distinction for a woman any more. There's plenty of food in tins and restaurants. You can send the washing out. A man wants something else. If I'd stayed in the village I wouldn't have known what more a man wants than that, but I didn't stay in the village. I came to the city and I changed. I changed in this city. How would it have been if I'd gone to a bigger town or to the capital? And I've got older. I'm nearly sixty and I've only got a little time left. I've a right to enjoy the little that remains to me. Yes, enjoy! In every sense of the word! Enjoy, even my relaxation, walks, and conversation, with a civilized, educated woman.

Of course you don't understand at all. If only you'd understood, then you wouldn't have put up with being a prisoner in the kitchen, and you wouldn't have exhausted yourself with your bad heart, with the result that you were prostrate in bed for six months, dependent on me. After all I've put up with in my life, do I have to end up by serving you? Did I marry you to serve you, or for you to serve me? And how long do I have to look after you just because you're ill? What do you think? Should I go on being cooped up in this house because of you? Surely it's enough that I imprisoned myself with you for thirty years? You're not ambitious. All you want is to look after your children and the house. You think the whole of life revolves around food, bed, and childbirth. Even animals can manage those things, and I'm not an animal. I'm a man of ambition. I didn't stop at you and the house. My family only got me to primary school, but I worked hard, got a job, and brought you here from the village. Here I studied with my own resources until I got through secondary school. If I hadn't been so old I'd have gone to university, but I sacrificed myself and was content with private study. I was happy to shut myself up in the house and read. I read everything. I read more than the students at the university. I borrow books and read, and buy them when I have enough money . . . I sacrificed myself for you and the children. I supported them for their education. Now it's my turn. I want to live, I have the right. Even the blessed Prophet said, "You have a duty toward your soul and you have a duty toward your body." So I have to fulfill my duty toward my body, just as toward my soul. I need somebody to love me. You don't love me. You never loved me. We got married, that's all. We got married because we were related, because as we grew up, there was nothing else for us peasants to do. Then we just went on with our life together, and were too weak to think about our life. I'd come back home because it was my duty, and you did all the work for me in the house because that was your duty. Even when you came to bed, you came because it was your duty. I never once felt in thirty years that you came out of desire. Do you know that in other countries married couples split up for a lot less than that? We didn't split up because we didn't understand, and because we didn't dare. We didn't know we wanted to split up . . . Well, I knew, but you were illiterate and ignorant, you didn't know. Nevertheless, I shut up, put up with it and sacrificed myself, sacrificed myself because of the children, and because of what people would say. I resigned myself to a life of thirty years without love. Now I can dare to say it. No, I didn't love you either! For thirty years I was a coward and didn't dare to think about it. But I hated coming home. I began to hate everything in this house. I hated the furniture, the kids, the kitchen, the food, the bed. Everything in it took on a hateful flavor. So I'd fly into a rage on the slightest pretext. I'd fly into a rage, bellow and curse, beating you and the children. Everybody said that Abu ᶜAdil was a harsh fellow, but they didn't know why I was so harsh. Living in a house that I hated, with a woman that I hated, unable to leave the house because I hated the world around it and was afraid of it. A world that tortured me with everything it had. Even with its beautiful women. I didn't dare look at any other woman. A married man with grown-up children. Shameful, sinful! Just imagine! Sinful! Is it sinful or stupidity? The stupid fool's the one who puts up with life with a woman like you he can't stand. He sleeps with her when he doesn't love her, and knows that she doesn't love him. That's sin! That's adultery! That's sinking to the level of an animal! "A sinner," they say! Just imagine, then, that you're my lawful wife and Brigitte Bardot's the forbidden fruit. Or let's leave Brigitte Bardot out of it. Just imagine that you're lawful to me and the beautiful girls who fill the town are out of bounds to me. Or let's forget about the town girls. Imagine you're lawful to me and to have Samira would be a sin. The sin lies in the crime I've committed against myself, being buried with you in this house for thirty years. Thirty years without loving you. Thirty years I've been forced to be content with you in the eyes of God and other people. Long years I've been deprived of warmth. Yes, warmth! The feeling that someone you love has gone to bed before you and warmed it up for you. The feeling of a warm body that you'd be happy to embrace, and then you'd doze off without wanting anything else. ᶜAdil doesn't understand that, but that's his business. Let him think what he wants. I'm not forced to give explanations to him. I'm not responsible to him, and I'm no longer responsible for him. I no more have any duty toward him. I've done my duty fully, to the children, and to you. Even to Samira. Samira, who won't have me except by the law of God and His Prophet, and who wouldn't become my second wife along with you. So what does that mean? What does it mean that she'll only marry me on that condition? It means she wouldn't marry me until after your death. She didn't exactly say that, but an intelligent person can take a hint. Even your friend Samira wanted you to die. Your presence got in the way of all of us and stopped us living. That's why you had to die. You dragged out your illness for no good reason. If I'd let you have your way, you'd have been ill for another two years, maybe more. The situation needed some decorum. Yes, some taste! Whoever can't live should die. And if they can't do it, then others should do it for them. Did the whole of life have to stop because you were ill? Did God create only you in this world? We want to live as well. It's enough what you've deprived us of. You had to die. Your existence had no point any more. You couldn't even be of service any more. And so what if you're dead? Must life come to an end? On the contrary. It's a relief for you and for others. I've the right to feel relieved, and nothing in the world's going to come between me and my happiness.

The telephone rings. He picks up the receiver.

Hello? Samira? Hello! Of course I've been waiting for you. If you had a telephone I'd have called you. Where are you speaking from? (*He bursts out laughing.*) From your mouth? I thought you might be using some other orifice. (*Guffaws.*) No. No. On my own. The mourning's at ᶜAdil's house. I told them all I was tired and wanted to rest. I said I'd unplug the telephone, so nobody will disturb us. Yes. Why? I'll take you back at night. Don't complicate things, why tomorrow? Time's slipping away from us, Samira, and every day that passes takes away a part of our lives. Alright. Listen, I'll come to you. It's dark and nobody will see me. Why should we wait? I can't wait any more.

Either you come or I come to you. Do you want to start disagreeing and arguing with me now? I know. I know, you're not Umm ᶜAdil, but I can't bear anyone arguing with me. Everything's fixed. All her clothes are in the bag. Tomorrow I'll give them to Sheikh Ahmad, so that he can give them to the poor (*He laughs*) in memory of the dear departed. There's nothing else here except her photograph, and the children are sure to take that tomorrow. I understand you. I won't leave any trace of her in the house, but you mustn't be jealous of a dead woman. I swear the two rings have been in my pocket for two days. I didn't tell you because I was waiting for the right time. Of course, I'm smart. I'm coming now. What? Tired? Who told you I was tired? So you thought I was an old man? Old, at forty-five? All right, forty-six, just for you! You'll see now whether I'm old or not. Just the time it takes to get to you. Don't worry. We'll meet today and tomorrow. I'll face all of them. I've prepared myself for everything. Bye bye!

He kisses the telephone and puts down the receiver. He goes to the mirror, adjusts his clothes, and sprays some perfume on his face. He picks up the bag of clothes and throws it into the kitchen. With a vigorous step he goes to the door, puts out the light, and leaves.

The light remains as if drawn into the house from the street lamp. It falls onto the wife's photograph. Total darkness, except for the woman's face looking at the audience.

SAʿDALLAH
WANNUS

The King Is the King

Translated by
Ghassan Maleh
and Thomas G. Ezzy

The King Is the King (*Al-Malik huwa 'l-Malik*) is the most recent in a series of plays in which Saᶜdallah Wannus, one of the Arab world's most prominent dramatists, has experimented with a variety of multilayered presentations on the stage, often involving a complex relationship between the actors and the audience. The basic story, that of Abu al-Hasan, the henpecked husband in the *Thousand and One Nights*, is set in a frame like the original tale, involving two characters, Zahid and ᶜUbayd, who orchestrate the actions and explain their implications. The central tale tells how Abu al-Hasan (whom Wannus calls Abu ᶜIzza in the play) is tricked by the King: brought to the palace in a drunken stupor, Abu ᶜIzza is put on the throne and made to believe he is King. The actual King's plans immediately start to go badly awry, as Abu ᶜIzza assumes the royal mantle with great ease, reducing the redoutable Police Chief to a whimpering underling. The Queen seems entirely unworried by the change. At the end of the play, Abu ᶜIzza is still King, and it is left for Zahid and ᶜUbayd to draw conclusions about the nature and abuse of authority. In this play as in others, Wannus makes skillful use of framing and distancing techniques. As usual, he also has very specific instructions regarding performance: the actors are to use a very histrionic approach, and the costumes are to be elaborate, all with the purpose of exaggerating social differences and pointing to the play's primary message.

R.A.

THE KING IS THE KING

The mottoes on the POSTERS *(or slides) should be read aloud by either* ᶜUBAYD *or* ZAHID *or both in unison. These preliminary remarks may be made while the actors make their entrances. This is to emphasize the role of* ᶜUBAYD *and* ZAHID *as leaders of the game.*

PROLOGUE

Characters in costume: KING, VIZIER, EXECUTIONER, POLICE CHIEF, MAYMUN *the courtier*; ABU ᶜIZZA *the fool*, UMM ᶜIZZA *his wife*, ᶜIZZA *their daughter*, ᶜURQUB *their servant*; HEAD MERCHANT *and* SHAYKH TAHA; ᶜUBAYD *and* ZAHID.

The actors enter like a group of circus players, with agile, acrobatic movements. They will assume stylized formations that correspond to various parts of the Prologue.

HEAD MERCHANT *and* SHAYKH TAHA *stand in a corner pulling on puppet strings.* ᶜUBAYD *and* ZAHID *separate from the group. They are running the game.*

ᶜUBAYD (*Shouting to be heard*): This is a game!

ABU ᶜIZZA This is a game.

KING We're the players . . .

The word "game" is now repeated by everyone, in varying tones and in disorder. ᶜUBAYD *beats on the floor with a stick he carries. Silence.*

ᶜUBAYD Ready?

ALL (*Individually*): Yes, ready.

ᶜUBAYD Let's start, then.

EXECUTIONER Let me ask first: am I a headsman or a woodsman?

ZAHID What's the difference?

EXECUTIONER Here I am carrying an ax, not a sword.

ᶜUBAYD Never mind, you'll be a headsman with an ax. Now let's go!

The actors now form into two groups: ZAHID *heading* ᶜURQUB, ABU ᶜIZZA, UMM ᶜIZZA *and* ᶜIZZA; ᶜUBAYD *heading* KING, VIZIER, EXECUTIONER, POLICE CHIEF, *and* MAYMUN. *The two groups stand opposite each other.*

SHAYKH and HEAD MERCHANT What about us?

ᶜUBAYD Get to your corner and play with the puppets.

MERCHANT *and* SHAYKH *act accordingly.* ᶜUBAYD *and* ZAHID *stand in the corner directly opposite them.* ᶜUBAYD *strikes on the floor with his stick, announcing the start of the game.*

ᶜURQUB (*Standing at the head of the* ﬁ*rst group*): Allowed!

EXECUTIONER (*Standing at the head of the second group*): Forbidden!

ᶜURQUB Allowed!

EXECUTIONER Forbidden!

ᶜURQUB The war between the Allowed and the Forbidden is as old as Adam. We the rabble, the mob, the plebes—we have hundreds of these names—we never tire of asking for the Allowed.

EXECUTIONER And we the great—the kings, the princes and the lords—we have a hundred such names—we never tire of asking for the Forbidden.

ʿURQUB We pull . . .

EXECUTIONER And *we* pull.

ʿURQUB For centuries they've been pulling and we . . . (*He pauses, lets fall his arms to indicate no more pulling.*) Well, to make a long story short, our sovereign state has settled down into a wise old fate: you may, and you may not, in equal measure.

EXECUTIONER Exactly! In equal measure: safety in equality; security in equilibrium.

ʿURQUB To dream . . .

EXECUTIONER Allowed.

ʿURQUB To fancy . . .

EXECUTIONER Allowed.

ʿURQUB To dream . . .

EXECUTIONER Allowed . . . but carefully!

ʿURQUB To let dream become reality . . .

EXECUTIONER Not allowed.

ʿURQUB Or fancy become riot . . .

EXECUTIONER Not allowed.

ʿURQUB Or collective dreams become action . . .

EXECUTIONER Not allowed.

ʿURQUB That's the good old fate our great sovereign state has settled down to: you may and you may not in equal measure.

MAYMUN We're in an imaginary state.

ʿIZZA And ours is a tale of fancy.

KING Indeed! A fanciful, fanciful tale . . .

ʿURQUB And we dream . . . Let everyone have his dream—a companion as faithful as his shadow . . . (*Cries out:*) Dream, all of you! Go ahead and dream! You may dream; it's allowed!

EXECUTIONER Yes, but carefully.

ʿURQUB Yes, of course . . . But these are only individual dreams, which can never unite and act. (*He cries out again:*) Dream! Dream! All of you, dream! You may! It's allowed!

The two groups now mingle, with each person trying to speak of his dream.

ABU ʿIZZA (*Spinning like someone in a swoon*): I become Sultan of the realm. . . . I tighten my fist on my subjects, even if it's only for a day or two. (*Singing:*) There goes my seal, / Done is my will . . . Ah, Taha! That treacherous, devious Shaykh . . . He shall ride backwards on a donkey in the midst of everyone, and then shall be hanged in the unfurled cloth of his turban! And that great merchant, Shahbandar, along with the silk dealers who control the markets and regulate goods and trade, they shall be flogged to my heart's content and then they shall hang, but not before I've taken over all they possess, money and land. And as for those old friends who snubbed me when I was broke, they'll rot in cells, as examples for all ungrateful swine . . . (*Singing:*) We shall then do what we may, / And turn the night into full day . . .

UMM ʿIZZA (*Pushing him*): You'd better empty your head of these fancies first.

ABU ʿIZZA And then I'll change this hag of a wife for a thousand favorites, fair and full of life . . .

UMM ʿIZZA (*In a matter-of-fact tone*): Who can I turn to? What can I do with such a man—poor in spirit and small in skull? Bastards, who far outnumber legitimate sons these days, have made a scavenger of him. His money and his business are gone. Everything's been sold except the house that now shelters us. My husband drowns himself in drink and illusions, and while we're in this condition my only daughter stands no chance of a good marriage . . . But who can I go to? I wish I could get an audience with the King. No one else can give us justice and snatch us out of the pit we've been thrown into . . .

ABU ʿIZZA Now that I am Sultan of the realm, / The envious shall feel my hand at the helm.

ʿURQUB Dream! Dream! Dream, all of you, dream!

VIZIER I am Barbir, the famous Vizier. My only wish is to stand by the King: to help and accommodate, direct policy and offer advice.

KING I am the dream, the dream itself. What do I want? (*Languidly*:) Absolutely nothing. My Vizier, I'm bored. (KING *withdraws, followed by* VIZIER.)

VIZIER I am your shadow, which extends behind you and follows you.

MAYMUN I am Maymun, the King's private chamberlain. My ultimate dream is that I should cross my Lord's mind when he's bored.

ʿIZZA (*Shyly, with dreamy eyes.* ʿURQUB *watches her lovingly*): He'll come from far, far away and enter the city like the wind or a storm. His face will be sun and marble, and his glances will glint like daggers. Frightened by them, men will run to their houses. The streets will be empty. Triviality will go into hiding . . . And he shall cut through the city, purging its pestilent air and purifying its cruelty and its insult-infested atmosphere. Like the wind or a storm he shall cut his way to me. His face then will be a green meadow, and his glances wet grass. We'll exchange no words: just passion meeting passion, two locks of hair in a braid . . . Then we'll go away—where to I don't know, but far, far away, to some place where the air is clean, where there's joy and light, where people are equal and don't die by the score like dogs, of hunger and insults . . . Where to I don't know, but far, far away, to a place where the air is clean and there's joy and light. For him I wait, and will not tire of waiting . . .

ABU ʿIZZA (*Singing*): We shall do what we may, / And turn the night into full day . . .

ʿURQUB (*Crying out*): Dreams! You're all dreaming!

EXECUTIONER Feeble hearts think that chopping off heads isn't much of a profession. Simple hearts even imagine that the life of a headsman like me is an endless, sleepless night. But *I* say—and I know very well what I'm saying—that this profession of mine leaves me simply drunk with pleasure and joy. Oh the ecstasy of it all, when I let fall that ax of mine, when the head goes tumbling off, when the blood spurts out in gushing fountains! It's more than ecstasy . . . The sensual pleasure is absolutely indescribable . . . The King himself had a taste of this pleasure once. I don't know what gave him the idea of playing executioner, but the smoothness of his movement showed that he was enjoying that ecstatic moment no end. I could see his face lit up with jealousy . . . If I lose this job I'm finished . . . What else can I be? . . . Nothing: shadow, or mere dust.

ʿURQUB Now what about ʿUrqub? What does he dream of?

ABU ʿIZZA (*Singing*): Off goes my seal. / Done is my will.

ʿURQUB (*Pointing to* ABU ʿIZZA): This man is my master. I entered his service when he was a man of means. Although his fortunes have been at a constant ebb, I haven't left him. He hasn't paid me for ages, and he's even swallowed up all my savings. It's all been recorded, of course. Staying with him has been a problem: it's just ridiculous that he should be the master and I the servant. Some people say that I'm even more stupid than he is, and some think that it's noble of me to stay. But I know that I'm neither stupid nor noble. The thing is, I'm in love. I'm burning with desire for my master's daughter. If I leave now, I'll lose what he owes me; if I stay, he'll incur more debts, which, added up, will amount to a suitable dowry. With the debts all recorded in the books, they'll be forced to summon a Shaykh for a quiet marriage. It will be their only way out—their salvation, as well as my own, by God . . . But when, when exactly, will the day come when I can embrace ᶜIZZA in reality, and not in dreams?

ABU ᶜIZZA Come along, ᶜUrqub . . . Off goes my seal, / Done is my will.

ᶜURQUB The day will come when you come around . . . (*Cries out before he exits:*) Dream! Dream! All of you, dream! It's allowed! It's allowed!

SHAYKH TAHA and MERCHANT (*Together*): We, from pulpit and *souk*, / Hold the string and hook.

SHAYKH TAHA One string for the rabble . . .

MERCHANT Another for trade and crops . . .

SHAYKH TAHA and MERCHANT And a third for palace, King, and politics. We, from pulpit and *souk*, / Hold the string and hook.

They exit, playing with puppet strings. ᶜUBAYD, *helped by* ZAHID, *places a cushion up the back of his shirt to look like a hunchbacked beggar.* ZAHID *slings a porter's rope around his shoulder.*

ᶜUBAYD As for us, we'd better sew our lips together and not part with a single thought that crosses our minds.

ZAHID In this tale we'll keep to a corner, as we do in life.

ᶜUBAYD We'll appear here and there, but only in brief interludes, and certainly outside the movement of the game.

ZAHID Our lips will be closed tightly on our dreams, which we'll never reveal. At least, not now . . . (*Police whistles are heard.*)

ᶜUBAYD Let's go.

They run out. Enter POLICE CHIEF, *as though chasing someone. Walks about, exits.*

SCENE ONE

POSTER: WHEN THE KING IS BORED HE REMEMBERS THAT HIS SUBJECTS ARE AN AMUSING LOT, IN POSSESSION OF TREMENDOUS ENTERTAINMENT POTENTIAL

The Throne Room in the Royal Palace. Velvet-covered steps lead up to a dais, on which stands the throne, which is made of ebony and ivory inlaid with coral. There are dragon heads at the ends of the arms. Otherwise the room is cold and empty, exuding an atmosphere of barren magnificence, unreal and inhuman. Upstage and back, winding steps lead to the Royal Chamber. The KING, *on the throne, should look like a bundle of brightly colored and heavily embroidered cloth. These clothes should look like a mold encasing him. On the outside is a gold and silver-woven cape. His crown comes halfway down his forehead; in the middle of the crown, just above the forehead, is a glittering jewel. The* KING *is sunk into his throne, his hand holding lightly on to the sceptre. Beside him stands the* VIZIER, *starched and coarse-looking. His robes as well are like a mold encasing him, but more tight-fitting than those of the* KING. *Out of this mold juts the turbaned head of the man. At the far end, by the door, stands* MAYMUN, *head bent down in a state of attentiveness. Near him stands the* ROYAL BAND.

The movement in this scene should be mechanical, to match and accentuate the coldness and emptiness of Court.

THE BAND Lord over all of us,
Master of the realm,
Son of Kings bounteous,
Stay healthy at the helm
In celestial bliss.

Joy is on his forehead borne,
Good by his gentle hands is wrought;
This peerless monarch is with dignity fraught:
God keep him, for us and all who will be born,
In celestial bliss . . .

KING *looks bored. He motions with his hand for the* BAND *to stop. They stop immediately.*

VIZIER (*To* BAND): Go.

They leave in silence. MAYMUN *returns to his position, head bent. Embarrassed silence.*

VIZIER Would His Majesty care to see to some urgent affairs of state?

KING Nothing is urgent when I happen to be in a bad mood.

VIZIER Heaven forbid that My Lord should be in a bad mood . . . (*Hesitating.*) There are a few issues that we should perhaps consider . . .

KING (*After a short pause*): Maymun, rub my fingers for me, will you?

MAYMUN (*Approaching* KING *religiously, eyes fixed on the floor*): What an honor My Lord graces me with! (*Kneels before the throne, takes* KING's *hand the way one picks up a precious jewel. Starts massaging. Pause.*)

VIZIER The Notables met yesterday to choose gifts for Coronation Day. They also drafted a few suggestions regarding the next stage . . .

KING Don't they ever get tired of drafting suggestions?

VIZIER They're concerned over the laxity they see in things. They're afraid that it might grow and pose grave danger to His Majesty and themselves.

KING His Majesty has long left grave dangers behind. He will not allow a few bubbles here and there to disturb him.

VIZIER (*Hesitant*): Still, there are some affairs to see to and some measures to take . . . Coronation Day isn't far off . . .

KING (*Distractedly*): I've been on this throne for years and years . . .

VIZIER Yes, My Lord; years as happy as the blessed stalks . . . The country will look like a beautiful bride. It will witness unprecedented festivities. The bazaar leaders have chosen their presents for this historic occasion. The goldsmiths will present you with a full-sized statue made of gold and gems. The silk merchants are draping the entire procession with . . .

KING (*Interrupting sharply*): Are you trying to impress me? Are you implying that the King might not deserve such trivial gifts?

VIZIER Heaven forbid that . . .

KING How often has this land had a King like me?

VIZIER Never. Even the founders of this realm seem like mere shadows in comparison to Your Majesty. They are all dwarfed by your glaring light . . . What King could ever have kept his throne for as long as you have? What monarch has revitalized the land the way you have? What King has ever brought this realm such stability and prosperity? What other monarch has been a monarch like you?

KING Sometimes I feel this country doesn't deserve me . . . (*Pauses.*) Maymun, the Queen herself should be envious of the softness of your hands . . .

MAYMUN The precious gem they are touching makes them soft . . .

KING (*Trying to pull his hand away*): My fingers aren't numb any more . . . (MAYMUN *continues to rub them dotingly.* KING *pulls his hand away.*) That's enough!

MAYMUN (*Startled, steps back in fear*): I'm sorry! Forgive me, my Lord . . .

KING (*Rising, stepping off the dais*): Oh, how bored and ill-tempered I am today!

VIZIER Heaven forbid that you should ever be . . . Why don't you go in to your concubines? There are hundreds of them, all beautifully shaped . . .

KING Oh, my concubines . . . it's like sinking in foam! Sometimes I feel I'm masturbating . . .

VIZIER What about Rihana, the new one?

KING Yes, she's the only one left, but not now . . . My boredom lies heavier on me than a mountain . . .

VIZIER Emir Wirdshah is giving a party tonight. Everybody will be there: the Emirs, the administrators . . . My Lord may wish to embellish this party with his presence. It will be a chance to talk in an atmosphere of fun and joyousness.

KING I know these parties: I'll just end up discussing politics and affairs of state . . .

VIZIER Shall I call in the chess master?

KING No . . . I know I'll beat him.

VIZIER Shall I send for your jesters?

KING I'm sick and tired of their jokes . . . The more I reflect on how this country doesn't deserve me, the worse my boredom gets . . . I want to play a game—a cruel and vicious one. (*Pauses.*) Yes, that's what I want: to have some violent and savage fun!

VIZIER The Vizier shall always join in his Lord's games with respect and gratitude . . .

KING You? No, that's not what I need . . . I want something more violent, more vicious! I want to have some fun with the country! With the people! (*Walks up and down, thinking. Suddenly stops, turns to* MAYMUN, *who is standing at the door:*) Maymun, you may disappear.

MAYMUN (*Withdrawing*): Yes, my Lord.

KING Listen, what about going into the City?

VIZIER That's exactly what I was afraid you were going to suggest, my Lord. Could you please think of something else?

KING I'm not interested in anything else just now. Why is it that every time I talk of going into the City, you panic?

VIZIER I don't know . . . Forgive me, my Lord, but these incognito expeditions always leave me restless and tense—even till long after we return . . .

KING Could it be that you worry about the throne going—and with it your position as Vizier?

VIZIER What traitor would dare! . . . No such thoughts ever cross my mind! But the people are like frogs . . . they never cease croaking or grumbling . . . Your Majesty must have noticed that on our past expeditions everyone we met had a grievance to tell of or a complaint to make. Ingrates have such long tongues . . . I'm afraid their poisonous spray might anger my Lord, or put him in a bad mood. Security reports bring the City naked to you in this very hall . . . Why should you expose your august personage to contact with stench and filth?

KING Because there are times when that amuses me. When I listen to the people's little problems, when I watch their comings and goings in search of a penny or a mouthful of food, I'm overwhelmed by a sense of cunning pleasure. Their stinking lives are more interesting than anything a court jester could imagine or invent. And today there's something else: I have my own invention, a game to play, with my country and my people. Since the idea crossed my mind, every part of my body has been throbbing with life. Bring us the disguise.

VIZIER Is this really His Majesty's desire?

KING It is His Majesty's *order*, which is not open to debate or argument.

VIZIER (*Somewhat unhappily*): I'll bring them at once.

VIZIER *exits in the direction of the Chamber. Meanwhile* KING *paces up and down, thinking.*

KING (*Smiling, his eyes lighting up*): This will be a *vicious* new game! I'm going to laugh until the emptiness my boredom's created in me is filled up! (*His excitement rises; he knocks on the floor with his sceptre.*) Maybe I'll even mention it in my Coronation Day speech . . .

MAYMUN (*Hurrying in answer to the knocking*): At your service, Awesome One . . .

KING Maymun, my hand's numb again.

MAYMUN (*Holding dotingly the hand extended to him*): I would give my very life for this irradiant hand to relax . . .

KING I think I'll be turning in early tonight.

MAYMUN May you sleep well, and dream even better . . .

KING Should the Queen inquire about me, tell her I'm tired and don't wish to be disturbed.

MAYMUN Done, my Lord.

KING Wake me up with the first rays of the sun. Do it by rubbing my toes. But carefully: I don't want to be awakened suddenly or harshly.

MAYMUN I shall turn into a gentle breeze, my Lord. (VIZIER *enters.*)

KING Now you may go.

MAYMUN (*Withdrawing*): Yes, my Lord.

VIZIER I wish my Lord would change his mind.

KING Is your houseboat ready?

VIZIER Always ready to receive my Lord.

KING See that everything's prepared, and then we'll leave. Do you know where we're going?

VIZIER Anywhere you say . . . All houses are ready to receive Your Majesty.

KING Do you remember that man we promised to call on, for an evening of singing and fun?

VIZIER That fool who dreams of power and revenge on his many enemies?

KING That's the one! What is his name?

VIZIER Abu . . . Abu ʿIzza, I think.

KING We'll visit him tonight. You'll see what fun the King has in store for you . . . This time, I want our disguises to be complete. Maymun thinks I've gone to bed. We won't tell a soul. We'll leave by that secret passage that ends up way beyond the walls.

VIZIER Won't we have a guard or two following us?

KING Not a soul, I said.

VIZIER In the past we've had guards trailing us at a distance . . . One can't be too careful, my Lord.

KING Not a soul! Help me take this off . . . (VIZIER *helps* KING *out of his heavily embroidered cloak.*)

VIZIER How does my Lord feel when this awe-inspiring cloak slips off his shoulders?

KING A little lighter.

VIZIER Is that all?

KING What a question! Yes, that's all.

VIZIER (*Taking his cloak off*): I—I must

admit that when I take my cloak off I feel . . . well, like my body's softer. You may laugh at me, but the fact is that my legs give way—or rather, the ground becomes less solid beneath me.

KING I think if you lost your job as Vizier, you wouldn't live to see another day . . . Where are my breeches?

VIZIER With the gold stripe? Here they are . . .

Lights fade to blackness as they go on changing.

FIRST INTERLUDE

POSTER: SUBJECTS ARE NOW DESTINED TO GO INCOGNITO.

A darkish secluded corner somewhere in the City. ᶜUBAYD, *bent forward with a hunched back, leans on a stick. He seems to be waiting for somebody. He looks around surreptitiously.* ZAHID, *dressed as a porter, soon arrives.*

ZAHID If I'd run into you on a street, I wouldn't have known you.

ᶜUBAYD Let's hope the Police Chief's spies and informers don't recognize me.

ZAHID (*Staring at him*): What a bruise!

ᶜUBAYD It's real . . . Does it look bad?

ZAHID Blue and swollen.

ᶜUBAYD An added touch . . . Quite useful.

ZAHID You weren't involved in a brawl, were you?

ᶜUBAYD No, it was more like a farce. It happened in the fruit market . . . The greengrocer had arranged his apples in such a way that I just couldn't control my hands: they looked so red and delicious, and I thought the man wasn't looking . . . But as soon as the two apples were in my bag the man attacked, with the ferocity of a hyena that's just smelled a corpse. I thought that if I ran I'd give myself away and if I stayed the police would come. So I just let him go on hitting and kicking until people began to have pity on me and made him stop. (*Smiling.*) Still, I managed to keep one of the apples . . .

ZAHID What a risk to take for an apple! Suppose they'd taken you for questioning and found out you're the man the Police Chief's been hunting for?

ᶜUBAYD Well, you know how fond I am of that girl . . . It was her I was thinking of when my hand reached for the apples. If it weren't for her, I'd have no place to go. The houses of friends won't do, and the Mosque isn't a safe place any more, now that it's full of disguised police agents.

ZAHID Still, in your situation, one more false step could lead to total disaster.

ᶜUBAYD I don't know . . . You see, I was thinking of her, and I wanted so much to take her an apple . . . It was she who talked her mother into putting me up. She treats me kindly and takes an interest in what I say. I feel so safe there . . . Except for that servant, who makes no secret of how much he hates me. He's angry they're letting me live there. I avoid him as much as I can, but I'm afraid he might be setting a trap for me . . .

ZAHID Haven't you been able to win him over? I thought people like him would naturally be on our side.

ᶜUBAYD I'm fairly certain we won't be able to count on any servants. They're a special, complicated case. It would be the logical thing for them to be on our side, but in actual fact they're not. Their masters' lives fascinate them and leave them in a state of imbalance, swinging between humble obedience and secret longing to become copies of their masters . . . But we're not here to discuss that. What have you got for me?

ZAHID We've found a place where we can all meet from time to time.

ʿUBAYD Good news. It's time we made our meetings regular. Have you managed to contact almost everyone? (*A* MAN *appears at a distant corner.* ʿUBAYD, *on seeing him, nudges* ZAHID *and changes position.*) Alms . . . Alms . . . May God protect you . . . May the Lord preserve your children for you . . .

ZAHID (*Noticing the* MAN *and taking up his cue*): And may the Lord provide for you . . . (ZAHID *moves away to a corner, while the* MAN *comes close to* ʿUBAYD.)

ʿUBAYD (*Reciting*): One act of charity is like a seed that will grow into seven stalks . . . (*Grabs onto* MAN's *jacket.*)

MAN Hey! Let go, will you!

ʿUBAYD Please . . . May the Lord bless you and your children . . .

MAN (*Pushing him away*): I said let go! (*Moves away.*) Some day you'll be begging with knives and daggers! . . . (*Once he is gone,* ZAHID *comes back.*)

ZAHID What a day!

ʿUBAYD That man's just said that some day we'll be begging with knives and daggers . . .

ZAHID That'll be the end of begging.

ʿUBAYD And the end of a long history of painful masquerade. We'd better hurry. It's prayer time, and there'll be many more people around. Tell me what's happened.

ZAHID Everyone's agreed on the letter. Abdullah's taken it to make the necessary copies. It'll be ready for the night of Coronation Day.

ʿUBAYD What about distribution?

ZAHID It's all taken care of. But some of our friends are having doubts about our plan . . .

ʿUBAYD But why?

ZAHID They think Coronation Day's an opportunity for something bigger.

ʿUBAYD For what? To shout out "Down with the King!" and then all go to prison together?

ZAHID They think there's a widespread feeling of hardship and disillusionment. Any organized effort would accentuate the explosive feeling. First of all, it would shake up the regime; second, it would create an atmosphere more conducive to our work.

ʿUBAYD That's true. There *is* a feeling of hardship and disillusionment. The people are becoming more and more resentful; their fear and misery are growing worse. But the contradictions aren't yet *ripe* enough! I'm telling you—and please pass this on to our doubting friends—that the King has only one course to follow: more terror and repression.

ZAHID Isn't there anything else he could do? A little reform here and there might calm things down for a while . . .

ʿUBAYD That won't do any more. The regime, even if there were a new King, has no choice now but to resort to more terror and repression. Are we to provide it with the excuse it needs and offer ourselves as victims?

ZAHID Then what do we do about spontaneous outbreaks?

ʿUBAYD We turn them to our advantage, but without risking any of our units. At this stage we must plan our course carefully. The more they repress, the more we perfect our camouflage. That way, our movement will gain strength while the contradictions grow. We must strike at exactly the right moment—not a second too early or too late. (*The call for prayer is heard. Two men appear in the distance.*) And there's something else: we've got to work harder! It isn't safe to stand here any more . . . The East Cemetery, the day after tomorrow. Alms . . . Alms, for the love of

God, alms . . . (ZAHID *extends his hand to him as if to give him a coin.*)

ZAHID At sunset. (*Moves away. The two men approach.*)

ᶜUBAYD Charity for the deformed . . . For the love of God, alms for the poor . . .

FADE OUT

SCENE TWO

POSTER: REALITY AND ILLUSION CLASH IN THE HOUSE OF A SUBJECT CALLED ABU ᶜIZZA.

Typical Arab house. Spacious courtyard with two doors upstage that lead to rooms inside the house. Downstage right, a wide door that leads to the street. ᶜIZZA *enters, lights the two oil lanterns on the wall, then moves upstage left to spread a worn mattress on the floor.* ᶜURQUB *enters, moves up toward her.*

ABU ᶜIZZA (*From inside*): A Sultan I shall be, / The envious shall know me . . .

ᶜURQUB Has Her Radiant and Perfect Ladyship called for me?

ᶜIZZA (*Surprised, coolly*): I called for no one.

ᶜURQUB I thought I heard a voice, more melodious than the strings of a lute, call out, "ᶜUrqub!"

ᶜIZZA You're imagining things.

ᶜURQUB Isn't there some service I can do for the Beautiful One?

ᶜIZZA There's nothing I need.

ᶜURQUB My heart breaks when I see your hands stained with the dirt of that hunchback . . .

ᶜIZZA Don't worry about my hands. And don't say anything bad about that man . . .

ᶜURQUB It's odd, but I just can't stand him.

ᶜIZZA Why?

ᶜURQUB Ever since that man moved in, the Peerless Beauty of this world has been constantly either distracted or absent-minded. The care you lavish on him! You'd think he'd worked some kind of spell on you. Who knows . . . I wouldn't be surprised if he turned out to be some wily magician.

ᶜIZZA Why can't you have pity on the man's deformity?

ᶜURQUB And what about *my* deformity? Who'll have pity on that?

ᶜIZZA What's wrong with you?

ᶜURQUB Listen to that! "She wrings your heart out, and then she asks what's wrong!" Don't you know what's wrong with me? My hump's bigger than his, except that it's growing out here, in my chest, and pressing in on my heart . . .

ᶜIZZA (*In an even cooler tone*): Not again!

ᶜURQUB I don't want to hear this! I've told you, time and again . . . (*He draws closer to her, tries to touch her somewhat indecently.*) Have mercy on me! There's a fire burning inside me! *You* are my illness, and my cure . . .

ᶜIZZA (*Pushing him away angrily*): Have you gone mad?

ᶜURQUB Your beauty would drive anyone mad!

ᶜIZZA Get out of my sight, or I'll call my father!

ᶜURQUB Will this torture never end?

ᶜIZZA I just can't stand the very sight of you! Get out!

ᶜURQUB One day you *will* be mine! You'll see . . .

ᶜIZZA I'd rather die! If I call out, my father will throw you out, but not before he breaks his stick on your back!

ᶜURQUB (*Nonchalant but defiant*): Your

father! Throwing *me* out? Ha! Ha! That's a joke! He'll have to recover his sanity and settle his debts first. You're going to have to wait a long time before that happens!

ʿIZZA (*Somewhat crushed*): How can you be so insolent and mean?

ʿURQUB It comes from rejection and depression.

ABU ʿIZZA (*From inside*): ʿUrqub, where are you?

ʿURQUB The Master's calling . . . (*Heads in the direction of the voice.*)

ʿIZZA (*Pulling at her hair*): Oh God! How can anyone live in this hell? (*Withdraws as* ABU ʿIZZA *enters.*)

ʿURQUB Yes, Master?

ABU ʿIZZA Come here. (*Looking around*:) I heard voices. Is that woman back?

ʿURQUB Who? My mistress, Umm ʿIzza? No, she isn't back yet.

ABU ʿIZZA Where were you?

ʿURQUB The call of nature, sir.

ABU ʿIZZA The call of nature couldn't have come at a less opportune moment. You missed seeing your master ascend the throne.

ʿURQUB Your face is all sweaty. You must be worn out.

ABU ʿIZZA From what?

ʿURQUB From your ascent. It must have been quite a climb. That's just how I've always pictured the ascent to a throne would be: stairs and stairs, going straight up and spiraling round and round, as in a minaret.

ABU ʿIZZA How stupid you can be!

ʿURQUB Your wisdom, sir, is enough to make up for my own and anyone else's stupidity.

ABU ʿIZZA Still, I don't really blame you . . . What else can you expect from plebes and commoners? Their little brains can imagine the ascent to a throne only in terms of climbing to the top of a building . . . If only you'd seen it! Guards on both sides, standing like two rows of aspen trees . . . And there I was, walking between them as though I were flying—or rather, as though I were walking on some carpet of quicksilver. The band walked before me, and all the men of state behind. As I ascended the throne, heads bowed and silence prevailed. It was truly a solemn moment . . . It felt like looking at the world from the top of a hill . . .

ʿURQUB And in that solemn moment, my master forgot all about me . . . This is what I get for all my service and companionship. Why didn't you tell me? You could have postponed the ceremony.

ABU ʿIZZA You fool . . . Royal ceremonies can neither be delayed nor postponed.

ʿURQUB And the Ministry? Don't tell me *that* went while I was answering the call of nature.

ABU ʿIZZA Relax, relax. I haven't named my vizier yet.

ʿURQUB (*Hanging by his neck to kiss him*): I can breathe again! What are you waiting for? Name him at once! You'll never find a better man than ʿUrqub.

ABU ʿIZZA I'm still undecided.

ʿURQUB But why?

ABU ʿIZZA Well, of course, I do need a vizier to advise and look after me. To drink my health / and walk before me to death.

ʿURQUB Heaven forbid! No servant may walk ahead of his master! Are you sending me to death for the sake of a rhyme?

ABU ʿIZZA A *royal* rhyme! . . . You see why I'm still undecided. You certainly do have ability, but I'm afraid you're not made for the job . . . It's your birth that stands in the way. A vizier must be descended from nobility, and be well-off. You—and you should take this bravely—are only one of the people. A commoner, if you will . . .

ʿURQUB One of the people? A commoner? What about you? . . . Are you hanging from a tree whose roots stretch back to the House of Muhammad? Are you sitting on a mound of gold? (*Walks away.*)

ABU ʿIZZA Me? Are you talking about me? Where are you going?

ʿURQUB To look for your birth . . . And mine!

ABU ʿIZZA Come here.

ʿURQUB Leave me alone!

ABU ʿIZZA Your master is ordering you to come here!

ʿURQUB What do you want?

ABU ʿIZZA Come here. You want to talk about my birth? Look at me, then . . . Examine my features, my eyes . . . Tell me what you see. (ʿURQUB *holds* ABU ʿIZZA *by the ears and turns his face harshly to the right and left.*) Take a good look, ʿUrqub . . .

ʿURQUB Ah yes . . . What do I see? . . . Two distraught eyes, inhabited by two giants and a retinue of *djinn*. I see dusty skin, with pores that exude the Yellow Disease. I see a beard that . . .

ABU ʿIZZA Forget my beard. Tell me about my features.

ʿURQUB The only features I can see are those of disease and old age.

ABU ʿIZZA (*Pulling his face back and pushing him away*): This man's blind! These are royal features! Can't you see them? Look at them! . . . The cheeks are shining like stars . . . Light radiates from the eyes . . . When I saw them in the mirror I nearly went blind!

ʿURQUB Plebes can't perceive such features.

ABU ʿIZZA Now I understand! You've been blinded by anger! I never thought the truth could hurt so much . . . You know how I feel about commoners and crowds. Their very smell in the marketplace makes me sick. Touching them gives me a rash all over my body. Nevertheless, for old time's sake, His Royal Majesty has decreed that you be the Vizier.

ʿURQUB Master! Please hold me! I'm about to faint with joy!

ABU ʿIZZA Man, pull yourself together.

ʿURQUB Well, it isn't every day that a person becomes a Vizier . . . (*Looking at his master's face*:) These features . . .

ABU ʿIZZA What about them?

ʿURQUB They're radiating such a light and fire . . . I don't mind being burned by them.

ABU ʿIZZA You mean you see them?

ʿURQUB Yes, ever since I became Vizier.

ABU ʿIZZA I don't think I'm going to regret my decision . . . Provided you continue this way.

ʿURQUB You can depend on me. And now, where do we start? Vengeance on that treacherous Shaykh? Torture for that damned Merchant?

ABU ʿIZZA All enemies shall know the weight of our hand . . . But let's intensify our pleasure by the taking of some wine. (*Starts humming*:) Awake, awake, and fill the cup / Before life, soul, and body are up . . . (*Pauses, turns to* ʿURQUB.) Aren't you going to deposit some money into the Treasury?

ʿURQUB Now we come to the heart of the matter . . . I haven't got anything left to deposit.

ABU ʿIZZA You mean you're beginning your career penniless?

ʿURQUB No, let's forget about the Vizier and his career . . . Let's get to this question of money . . .

ABU ʿIZZA Don't you trust your Master?

ʿURQUB Heaven forbid! Of course I do! But my Master isn't in a position to return what he takes . . .

ABU ʿIZZA You'll be sorry for saying this! What are your deposits to date?

ʿURQUB Well . . . It takes time to calculate, but they're all in the books.

ABU ʿIZZA Alright then. Add a new item—"diverse expenses"—and enter the sum in the books.

ʿURQUB (*Jumping up, listens*): Shh! I hear footsteps! It must be my Mistress . . .

ABU ʿIZZA (*Pulling him down*): Impossible! I can smell her coming before you can hear her footsteps! Don't you try weasling out of this . . .

ʿURQUB But she's warned me not to give you anything . . . You're my Master and she's my Mistress and I never know which to obey . . .

ABU ʿIZZA What? Which to obey? Who's the Master here? Tell me!

ʿURQUB Well . . . I hope you won't mind my saying this, but sometimes I think it's you, and sometimes I think it's her . . . Still, it's none of my business. You're my Master and she's my Mistress. I can divide my obedience equally between you.

ABU ʿIZZA Stay still, my anger! Are you insulting your Master, who gave you a job and brought you up? I am the Master here! Your loyalty goes to no one else! Understand?

ʿURQUB I'm glad to hear it. Have you decided to take over the reins with an iron hand?

ABU ʿIZZA With a steel hand. I'll tell you a secret . . . The moment I took my place on the Throne, I felt that all around me was confusion and chaos. All I had to do was to be firm . . .

ʿURQUB Let's forget about the Throne for a moment. Can I say that, from now on, yours is the final word in this house?

ABU ʿIZZA But of course.

ʿURQUB And that you will be obeyed by everyone here?

ABU ʿIZZA If I'm not, I'll tear the whole house down!

ʿURQUB That's my Master! You make things easier for me. We both understand each other, and it's time I spoke. . . .

ABU ʿIZZA Is it a serious matter?

ʿURQUB Serious enough to determine whether I'll be spending my life in happiness or in grief . . . And it's of interest to all of us, as well . . . But first I want my Master to give his word that he will agree to my request.

ABU ʿIZZA You meet *my* request before you put yours. That way we shall listen better and act quicker.

ʿURQUB Wouldn't it be better if we finished with the matter at hand? Let's do it while there's still peace here. I can't control my passion any longer. It's an affair of the heart . . . And a word from you, sir, will send me flying up to the Seventh Heaven.

ABU ʿIZZA An affair of the heart? How can one discuss affairs of the heart without the necessary stimulation of the palate? Add a new item—"diverse expenses"—and record the sum in the books. And let's have it before you go flying up to the Seventh Heaven!

ʿURQUB (*Reaches into his pocket for a small notebook and pulls at a small pencil tied to a string around his neck*): Well, now that we've gotten this far, we might as well go ahead . . . I'll put down, "price of half a bottle" . . .

ABU ʿIZZA I've never been a man for happy mediums.

ʿURQUB Half a bottle and no more. Sign here.

ABU ᶜIZZA It would be easier to use my seal . . .

ᶜURQUB I'd rather you signed.

ABU ᶜIZZA Alright . . . (*Signs.*) There. We pay for goods before delivery.

ᶜURQUB (*Snatching notebook and moving away to fetch the drink*): And *he* talks of payment! That man's swallowed up all my savings . . . If I don't get what I long for, my fury will be greater than Samson's . . . ᶜIzza, you're caught in my net!

ABU ᶜIZZA Don't be long . . . (ᶜURQUB *turns, shakes his head and leaves.*) Ah! . . . Now that I am Sultan of this realm, / The envious shall feel my hand at the helm . . . Off goes my seal, / Done is my will . . . (*Pauses.*) What's this I see? The Head Merchant himself? On his knees, crying and pleading? . . . (*Places his foot on the imagined shoulder of the kneeling man.*) Didn't you swear, before the biggest merchants in the *souk*, that you'd see to it my business was ruined and I was driven out of the market entirely? So you've come to beg my pardon, have you? To declare you're sorry in front of everyone? You thought you'd seen the last of me, that day you declared me bankrupt and had my creditors strip the very clothes off my back! . . . You never expected we'd meet again, did you, with the scales tipped in *my* favor? . . . With you on the floor, kneeling and begging forgiveness, and me taking revenge in my own time and loving it . . . Ha! Shaykh Taha! Don't try to hide behind the nine hundred and ninety-nine beads of your rosary! I can see you there, behind all those faithless friends who sold me out the minute I was down! You accused me of madness . . . And now there you all are, the lot of you! Your fates all hang on a word from me! . . . It was the Shaykh who started it. Then the Head Merchant went along with him, and then so did all my faithless friends . . . Every one of you plotted to bring me down, to cast me into abject poverty and humiliation; I had a place among you, but you forced me out and divided the spoils . . . But now we meet again! Things are different now, and my revenge shall know no bounds! No, no, it's too late for sorrow and regret! Too late for tears! Now, *I* am your Lord and Master . . .

Enter ᶜIZZA; *walks toward her father. She has obviously been crying.*

ᶜIZZA Are you alone, Father?

ABU ᶜIZZA No. I'm with my enemies, my love.

ᶜIZZA Father . . .

ABU ᶜIZZA Don't ask me to have pity on them! I'll strip their skins off and pluck out every hair of their beards . . .

ᶜIZZA Will you please listen to me?

ABU ᶜIZZA If it weren't for them, you'd be a jewel by now, decorating the palace of some prince . . .

ᶜIZZA (*Exploding*): I don't want a palace! I don't want a prince, or servants! I don't want anything!

ABU ᶜIZZA (*Pauses; wakes up as from a trance*): ᶜIzza . . . What is it, my love?

ᶜIZZA (*Staring aimlessly at him*): Mother's late. It's already dark and she isn't back yet.

ABU ᶜIZZA I wouldn't worry. You know your mother . . . When she gets started talking and complaining, there's no stopping her—at least, not until she's given everyone around her a bad headache.

ᶜIZZA She's out working for *us*, Father . . .

ABU ᶜIZZA You too, ᶜIzza? . . . Your mother's broken my back with her insinuations about what she's done and what she's doing for us . . . (*Somewhat sadly and distractedly*:) People call me a fool, and say I live shamelessly on my wife's earnings . . .

ʿIZZA Believe me, I didn't mean *that* . . .

ʿURQUB (*Walks in humming*): Awake, awake, and fill the cup . . .

ABU ʿIZZA (*Recovering his liveliness*): Before life, body, and soul are up . . . (*To his daughter, in a serious tone*:) You needn't worry, my love. She should be back any minute now.

ʿURQUB (*Moving toward* ʿIZZA): I wish my mistress would command me to do some service for her . . . (ʿIZZA *steps back in obvious disgust*; ʿURQUB *steps forward, is pulled back by* ABU ʿIZZA.)

ABU ʿIZZA Alright, let's have it, ʿUrqub . . .

ʿURQUB Here it is. Vintage stuff. And now you've got what you wanted, it's my turn to get what I want. You will pay attention, won't you? And if Mistress ʿIzza has already hinted at something, that will make it easier for us to get right into the subject; to have a man-to-man talk . . . I'm sure we'll have no problem coming to an understanding.

ABU ʿIZZA No, let's talk master-to-servant. (*Opens bottle.*) No . . . No need for glasses . . . I prefer it straight from the bottle. (*Humming.*) Fill the cup that clears / Today of past regrets and fears . . . (*Lifts bottle to his mouth; freezes motionless.*) She's back! She's here already! She's at the door! My God, get rid of those glasses! (*Closes his eyes, gulps down the wine, as* ʿURQUB *looks around, frightened and agitated.*)

ʿURQUB (*Angrily*): Another chance missed! I wonder who the real fool is here . . .

UMM ʿIZZA (*Entering*): Well, well, well . . . All we need now is some singing and dancing to go with it. And why not? This house is so rich and prosperous . . .

ABU ʿIZZA Why don't you try to catch your breath first?

UMM ʿIZZA You never give me a chance to. I'm off working in other people's houses while you sit here drinking to your heart's content. How in hell did you get the stuff, anyway?

ʿIZZA *reenters.*

ABU ʿIZZA It was dropped on the roof by courier pigeons.

ʿURQUB (*Keeping very close to* ABU ʿIZZA, *trying to mask his confusion*): That's a good one!

UMM ʿIZZA (*Sternly*): ʿUrqub!

ʿURQUB From the market, Mistress, from the market . . .

UMM ʿIZZA And the money? Where did the money come from? Is there going to be another man knocking on our door for what we owe him?

ʿURQUB (*Nudges* ABU ʿIZZA *angrily, whispering*): My Master's going to have the last word in this house, eh? Like hell!

UMM ʿIZZA (*Grabbing* ʿURQUB *by the neck, shaking him*): What are you mumbling about? *Is* there going to be someone else knocking on our door for what we owe him?

ʿURQUB No. It'll be the same old person.

UMM ʿIZZA What do you mean?

ʿURQUB Me, Mistress. Me . . .

UMM ʿIZZA (*Almost strangling him*): Didn't I warn you not to give him any money? Who'll pay you? How can we pay you? How can we pay anybody?

ʿURQUB (*Trying to loosen her grip on him*): Master! Help, Master!

ABU ʿIZZA (*Drinking from bottle*): Leave my Vizier alone, woman!

UMM ʿIZZA (*Lets go of* ʿURQUB, *turns to her husband and takes hold of him*): And you! You're driving me crazy! You've ruined our lives, broken up our household, and now you want to drive us all mad!

ᶜIZZA (*Holding her mother back*): Mother, what's come over you?

ABU ᶜIZZA The cane, ᶜUrqub! The cane!

UMM ᶜIZZA Yes, ᶜUrqub, bring the cane! I'm either going to bring you back to your senses or die trying! This time you've got to wake up and listen to what I have to say! Otherwise we're going to lose the only thing we've got left—our house!

ᶜIZZA *tries to calm her mother, while* ᶜURQUB *attempts to hold* ABU ᶜIZZA *back.*

ABU ᶜIZZA The cane, ᶜUrqub!

ᶜIZZA If this doesn't stop, I'll kill myself!

ᶜURQUB Take it easy, Master . . . Think of God, who is loving and merciful.

ᶜIZZA (*Putting her arms around her mother*): Mother, has anything happened?

UMM ᶜIZZA (*Collapsing with her daughter*): My heart feels as swollen as a boil! I'm worn out from fighting our misery all by myself! (*There is a knock at the door*; ᶜURQUB *goes to answer it.*) We're as low as we can get, and there's not one person who'll help us . . . I spent the whole day at your uncle's. My brother! My flesh and blood! I wore my tongue out, begging him; solid stone would have yielded. But not my brother! He never even blinked an eye!

ᶜURQUB (*Returning, whispering to* ABU ᶜIZZA): Master, it's Haj Mahmoud and Haj Mustapha. They've finally come.

ABU ᶜIZZA (*Somewhat disturbed*): This isn't the right time. The mood's wrong . . .

KING *and* VIZIER, *in disguise, walk in and stand by the door.*

UMM ᶜIZZA Imagine, ᶜIzza, my brother tried to bargain with me over our house . . . My very own brother wanted to rob us of our home and turn us out! Blood has turned to water . . . There's no one left to turn to . . . (*Turns to her husband, sharply*:) Do you hear me? You've got to open your ears properly this time! Do you hear? We're as low as we can get, and there's nothing around us but daggers!

ᶜURQUB (*Trying to draw his master's attention to the entrance of the two guests*): Master . . .

ABU ᶜIZZA Those daggers shall become banners when *I* am Sultan of this land! I'll know how to treat all those villains then . . .

ᶜURQUB They're in here . . .

UMM ᶜIZZA (*Attacking her husband*): I can't take it any more! Will you put that bottle down?

ABU ᶜIZZA (*Evading*): The cane! The cane! Where's the cane?

UMM ᶜIZZA Will you put that bottle down and wake up?

ABU ᶜIZZA (*Stops before* HAJ MUSTAPHA *and* HAJ MAHMOUD; *tries to compose himself*): This is indeed an honor! You are most welcome, Haj Mahmoud and Haj Mustapha. Do come in . . . Although you may find there's too much dust in the air.

MUSTAPHA Your honor, my friend, is enough to clear the air of any dust—or boredom.

UMM ᶜIZZA (*Stops, eyes the two men curiously*): And who are these people?

ᶜURQUB This is Haj Mahmoud and Haj Mustapha. They've been here once before (*Lowers his voice*) and were not ungenerous, with advice and things . . .

UMM ᶜIZZA Come and meet them, ᶜIzza.

ᶜURQUB Yes, ᶜIzza. You should . . .

ᶜIZZA *gives him a dirty look and withdraws.* ABU ᶜIZZA *leads his guests in.*

MAHMOUD We've been here once before, and we got to like the people here so much that we promised ourselves we'd come again. If it weren't for our work, we would have called long ago . . . But it seems as though we've chosen a bad day for our second visit. Something must have happened here to disturb your peace and happiness. If our presence is burdensome or undesirable, please let us know. We know the way out. Friends needn't stand on ceremony.

ABU ʿIZZA It's noble and generous of you to say so. But your visit has been long awaited, and you are most welcome . . .

MUSTAPHA (*Mischievously*): I hope there are no serious causes for your distress . . .

UMM ʿIZZA Since you ask, there's no point in hiding things from you . . . Causes of distress are abundant here.

ABU ʿIZZA I wouldn't listen to her if I were you. She's a wet blanket.

UMM ʿIZZA A wet blanket! And don't I have reason to be? Oh, if only these guests weren't here . . .

MUSTAPHA (*Drawing close to her*): Don't let that worry you, my dear sister . . . We feel quite at home.

UMM ʿIZZA What can I say? I've had enough! This man's driving me insane . . .

MUSTAPHA If there's anything a friend might do to help you make up, we'll do it.

ABU ʿIZZA (*Moving to join* MAHMOUD): I shall make peace with her only if she acknowledges me as her master and pledges loyalty to me as her lord and sovereign.

From now on there are two camps: MUSTAPHA *and* UMM ʿIZZA *on one side,* MAHMOUD *and* ABU ʿIZZA *on the other, and* ʿURQUB *in the middle.*

UMM ʿIZZA Listen to that! Is this the way a sane man talks?

ABU ʿIZZA Are you accusing your lord and sovereign of being mad?

MAHMOUD Don't be so quick to get angry . . . Calm yourself.

UMM ʿIZZA But who can I turn to? Who can I complain to?

MUSTAPHA You have to accept him the way he is.

ABU ʿIZZA Poor hag of a woman . . . No doubt she's the victim of some magic spell that's sailed off with her senses.

UMM ʿIZZA There was one disaster, now there are two. First those swine came to ruin us; then he went crazy and started fantasizing. It's too heavy a burden for anyone. I wish I knew who to turn to . . . If only I could meet the King!

MUSTAPHA What would you say to him?

UMM ʿIZZA What would I say to him? Lots of things! I'd say: "Our Mighty Lord, this land is being run by thieves, who plunder the wealth of all your subjects. Justice lies dormant, and there's no one to investigate or call them to account. They cheat everyone; not even your own security and dignity are safe from them." No, no, you needn't worry. If I met the King, I'd know what to say.

MUSTAPHA You must be exaggerating.

UMM ʿIZZA Let him come and see for himself! If I were exaggerating, would we be in the condition you see us in? This house is ruined, and its master's brain has scattered with the winds . . .

ABU ʿIZZA Why, just why do I have to live with this wet blanket when I have a thousand beautiful women . . . ʿUrqub, where are the sofas, the carpets, and the cushions?

ʿURQUB Sofas, carpets, and cushions! Oh Mistress, help!

UMM ʿIZZA You are obviously gentlemen . . . You won't mind if what we have to offer doesn't befit your station.

ABU ʿIZZA ʿUrqub, get the silver cups. Then you may set the table.

MAHMOUD No, please don't, there's no need for ceremony. We've come to take you with *us*. We enjoy your delightful company and your clever conversation. This time, you will be our guest.

ʿURQUB And what about my Master's servant?

MAHMOUD You may come too.

ABU ʿIZZA If you weren't so set on my going with you, I wouldn't be settling for anything less than a royal banquet here for you.

UMM ʿIZZA Now I ask you, what am I to do?

MUSTAPHA I have a way. Maybe we can help . . .

ABU ʿIZZA Fill the cup that clears / Today of past regrets and future fears . . .

MUSTAPHA (*Taking* MAHMOUD *aside*): Give me a signed and sealed audience card.

MAHMOUD What are you up to?

MUSTAPHA We're going to let this woman meet the King.

MAHMOUD Haven't we had enough of her lashing tongue?

MUSTAPHA (*Reaching for the card*): By mere chance, this game is working out perfectly . . .

ABU ʿIZZA (*To* MAHMOUD *in a whisper*): Don't mind me saying this, but your friend is a bore, and a pain in the neck . . .

MAHMOUD Give him a chance . . . Wait until we've had a drink or two. You'll find him wittier and more entertaining then.

MUSTAPHA My dear sister, I hope you know how to keep a secret. I have access to the King, and will arrange for you to appear before him.

UMM ʿIZZA (*Startled*): Appear before the King? But what about all those things I've just said about him?

MUSTAPHA Never mind. Just promise me that you won't let anyone know.

UMM ʿIZZA (*Still awestruck*): I feel as though I'm in a deep, deep well . . .

ABU ʿIZZA ʿUrqub, the sceptre!

ʿURQUB Yes, Master.

MUSTAPHA Take this piece of paper. Give it to the palace guards tomorrow, and they'll take you straight to the Throne Room.

UMM ʿIZZA God bless you and all those like you, my son. Already, I'm at a loss for words. May I take my daughter with me? She may help me, and give me strength.

MUSTAPHA Alright.

MAHMOUD Haj Mustapha, shall we go?

MUSTAPHA With God's speed, let's go. You have a good sleep, and we'll take your husband along with us and enjoy his company.

UMM ʿIZZA God bless you!

MUSTAPHA (*As he walks with* MAHMOUD *toward the door*): What a wonderful family this is! (*They exit.* ABU ʿIZZA *and* ʿURQUB *follow.*)

ʿURQUB Shouldn't we lock the door? We don't want that hunchback coming in while the women are all alone in the house.

ABU ʿIZZA Never mind, ʿUrqub. The girl thinks that God will reward her for her kindness to him.

UMM ʿIZZA (*Crying out happily*): ʿIzza! ʿIzza! (*Her daughter enters.*) God is great, ʿIzza! Prepare yourself! . . . Do you know where we're going tomorrow? You'll never guess, no matter how hard you try . . . We're going to the Palace, to see the King!

ʿIZZA The King?

UMM ʿIZZA Himself! We're going to tell him everything, and beg for justice . . . Come here. Let's have something to eat and think about what we're going to do tomorrow.

ʿIZZA But Mother . . .

UMM ʿIZZA Don't worry. I haven't taken leave of my senses. Come here, and I'll tell you how it all happened . . .

FADE OUT

SECOND INTERLUDE

POSTER: A STORY OF THE HISTORY OF THE MASQUERADE, AND THE SECRET OF THE HAPPY FAMILY

Nighttime in ABU ʿIZZA'S *house. Only the corner with the mat on the floor is lit, supposedly by moonlight.* ʿUBAYD *is sitting on the mat and leaning with his back comfortably against the wall. He is busy writing something.* ʿIZZA *enters. He is startled and confused. He hides the piece of paper and bends forward, away from the wall, as if in pain.* ʿIZZA *stares at his back.*

ʿUBAYD (*Confused, yet happy*): Hasn't the young lady gone off to sleep yet?

ʿIZZA (*Somewhat depressed*): I can't . . .

ʿUBAYD The look of sadness on your lovely face is so very unlike the beauty of this night . . . What is it?

ʿIZZA (*With difficulty*): This has been a hard and terrible day . . . I'm afraid . . .

ʿUBAYD Of what? Come on, get it off your chest . . . What is it? Speaking of our troubles to others can help us feel better . . .

ʿIZZA I don't know . . . (*Exploding*:) I can't bear it any more! It's sheer hell! This house is inhabited by misery and madness! All the time I feel I'm living with crazy ghosts in a dark, dreary, airless cave!

ʿUBAYD Still, it just so happens that the cave is our house, and the ghosts our family . . . It really is a hell. But it can't last.

ʿIZZA I can't take any more of it!

ʿUBAYD It's only at times of utter misery that man feels he can't take it any longer. But, as a matter of fact, there are no limits to what he can take. He can stand any hell because he knows, by instinct, that it can't last.

ʿIZZA Yes, but this misery, *our* misery—when will it end?

ʿUBAYD When I was your age, and on nights like this, I used to feel my heart beat happily, softly promising something vague and joyful . . .

ʿIZZA I'm sick and tired of waiting! Sometimes this uncertainty makes me feel so empty that I'm afraid and desolate . . . Are you sure there is something that will come one day?

ʿUBAYD Of course.

ʿIZZA Don't you know where it is now?

ʿUBAYD It might be in this city . . . It might be more than one—perhaps a huge gathering . . .

ʿIZZA In this city? What's he waiting for, then? Why doesn't he show himself, and cleanse the air, and drive out misery, and then . . . come . . . (*Pauses shyly.*)

ʿUBAYD (*Searching in his bag*): No doubt they have a carefully worked-out plan, and they'll appear at the right time . . . (*Takes out an apple.*) Look what I've brought you. When I saw these apples, I thought of you . . . I wanted to bring you a few more, but with apples being so expensive, what could I do?

ʿIZZA I don't want you going to any trouble for my sake . . .

ʿUBAYD Take it. It will make me feel very happy to see you relax into the beauty of this night . . . To see you bite peacefully into the apple and wander away into lovely visions of the days to come . . .

ʿIZZA You're very kind . . . When I listen to you, I feel your words are washing away all the dirt and ugliness of the world . . . (*Hesitates.*) But you puzzle me. There's something mysterious about you. A couple of days ago—please don't be angry, I promise I won't tell, even if they cut my tongue out—a couple of days ago, I saw you adjust that cushion you wear as a hump on your back . . .

ʿUBAYD (*Distractedly*): So you've found me out . . .

ʿIZZA I don't know why you do it; I'm confused. Why?

ʿUBAYD To complete my disguise.

ʿIZZA Why a disguise?

ʿUBAYD Because we need one.

ʿIZZA (*Shyly but eagerly*): Are you the something I'm waiting for?

ʿUBAYD Are you tired? Sleepy?

ʿIZZA No.

ʿUBAYD Then I'll tell you the story of the masquerade: how it began and how it developed.

ʿIZZA You haven't answered my question.

ʿUBAYD Don't you want to hear the story?

ʿIZZA Yes, but I want very much to know . . .

ʿUBAYD The answer can wait. Let's begin the story . . . (*His eyes stare into the night, and his voice assumes a different tone.*) Once upon a time—and that was a long, long time ago—there was a community of people who led a life that was as simple as a lovely song. They were all equal, and all free. They worked together on land they held in common; they worked as one hand, and as one family they all partook of the common wealth. They had all they needed to eat and wear. In those days, men's faces were lucid, and their eyes transparent. What was inside was outside: no one was devious, or malicious, or envious. Life, simple as it was, flowed like a clear stream, or a harmonious melody . . . But one day—and that day is already history—the song went off-key. One man—a stronger man, or, say, a craftier man—broke up the community's land and kept the larger share for himself. He set himself off from the others and stood apart. He was different; he got himself a fine, colorful gown; he changed the way he looked and adopted a new demeanor; he took a disguise; he turned into a landowner. That was the beginning. Then he put on even finer garments and surrounded himself with pomp and magnificence. The landlord now turned into an overlord, a king: a logical extreme of the masquerade. From this developed an endless series of disguises. The simple, translucent life fell to pieces. The united community now became a host of masks divided: men disguised as princes and officers; others disguised as servants or slaves, as beggars or destitute vassals. Countless groups wore different masks and costumes and played a variety of roles. Some took on disguises in order to rule; some were forced into theirs so that they might serve and be ruled. And at the top stood the king—the noble descendant of that ingenious first inventor of the masquerade—who is the most attentive of all to his disguise. All this, my dear ʿIzza, happened a long time ago but has continued ever since. But it can't last forever.

ʿIZZA (*Contemplatively*): But how can this masquerade end? Will people's eyes and faces ever be clear again?

ʿUBAYD We're told in history books of one group that did get fed up with misery, hunger, and injustice . . . They went into a furious rage, slaughtered their king, and ate him.

ʿIZZA (*Shocked*): Ate the king?

ʿUBAYD That's what the history books tell us.

ʿIZZA Didn't they get poisoned?

ʿUBAYD At first some had upset stomachs and got sick; but after a while they recovered and settled down to enjoy life without masks or disguises.

UMM ʿIZZA (*From inside*): Aren't you asleep yet? We have to be up before sunrise!

ʿIZZA I couldn't sleep. I'm coming.

UMM ʿIZZA We're going to need clear minds and lots of strength tomorrow. Come!

ʿIZZA (*Whispering*): I promised her not to tell, but never mind, I'll tell you . . . Tomorrow we're going to meet the King.

ʿUBAYD The King!

ʿIZZA I'll tell you all about it tomorrow . . . (*Hesitates.*) Now that I know that you're what I've been waiting for, you'll never lose me. (*Goes inside.*)

ʿUBAYD If she only knew how painful a note she's struck . . . I've always longed for this moment, and yet I've always feared it, too . . . Tomorrow, if I can, I must find a new place to live and a new disguise . . .

FADE OUT

SCENE THREE

POSTER: KING GIVES HIS BED AND CLOAK TO HIS SUBJECT ABU ʿIZZA

Corner close to Royal Bedchamber. HAJ MUSTAPHA, HAJ MAHMOUD, *and* ʿURQUB, *standing. Dim lighting. The sound of heavy snoring comes from inside the chamber.*

MAHMOUD Good God! Is that snoring or braying? He'll wake up the whole palace . . .

ʿURQUB Shame on you, Master . . . If you knew where you were sleeping, you'd be holding your breath.

MUSTAPHA That drug we gave him with his wine was pretty strong.

MAHMOUD (*In a whisper*): If any of the men of the palace woke up now, there'd be quite an uproar.

ʿURQUB (*Taking a dirty, worn handkerchief from his pocket*): I'll put this in his mouth.

MUSTAPHA Why should you? His Majesty might find this most interesting. After all, it isn't every day that he gets to listen to his subjects snoring.

ʿURQUB (*Taken aback*): His Majesty? Did I hear you say His Majesty?

MUSTAPHA That's right . . . It's time we brought you in on this. You'll be useful.

MAHMOUD Go easy, Haj Mustapha . . .

MUSTAPHA (*Sharply*): Mahmoud, don't interrupt! We, ʿUrqub, are two of the King's courtiers. We've planned this on his orders, and for his entertainment. We told him about Abu ʿIzza and his fantasies, and then he gave us permission to set up this game. Your master is now lying in His Majesty's chamber.

ʿURQUB (*Jumping up and down*): His Majesty's chamber! Good God! I must stop this snoring at once!

MUSTAPHA Never mind that. Listen to me carefully: we'll need all your skill and wit. This morning your master will be wearing the Royal Crown. He'll be King all day, and you'll wear the Vizier's clothes.

MAHMOUD *My* clothes! (*Correcting himself:*) The Vizier's gown?

ʿURQUB The Vizier's!

MAHMOUD Perhaps the Vizier wouldn't like anyone wearing his clothes . . .

MUSTAPHA (*Sharply*): When the King wills, the Vizier has no choice but to will the same thing.

ʿURQUB (*Stunned, feeling his body*): Me? . . . In the Vizier's gown? . . .

MUSTAPHA Yes. You'll wear the Vizier's gown and act with your master in the same way a Vizier acts with his lord and king. But you must be careful: one slip of the tongue may spoil the whole thing and bring Abu ʿIzza back to reality prematurely.

ʿURQUB You needn't worry, Haj Mustapha. In this kind of game I have skill and experience.

MUSTAPHA Following this game in the course of the day will give the King great pleasure.

ʿURQUB And may I see the real King afterwards?

MUSTAPHA Of course you will. *And* you'll taste his bounty . . . But first, the trick must work.

ʿURQUB You needn't worry.

MUSTAPHA Let's get some rest before the night's over. You go to bed, ʿUrqub, but make sure you're up before sunrise.

ʿURQUB I'll be up at dawn . . . Your Eminences, I'll take my leave now . . . I hope you sleep well. (*While withdrawing, pauses by the Royal Chamber.*) Snore, Master, snore . . . For tomorrow you cross into a world of madness. (*Exits.*)

MAHMOUD My Lord, there's still a chance to change your mind. It's my duty to remind you that this whim of yours is leading us down a slippery path.

MUSTAPHA You worry too much; it's affecting your sense of humor. I've told you: I want *fun*; it's an irresistible desire with me. I feel like a child who's set his trap with such care that all he has to do is wait for something to come along and get caught in it. My dear fellow, we have before us a whole day of fun and laughter.

MAHMOUD Your trap's made up of *my* cloak . . . (*Remembering*:) Mine *and* yours . . .

MUSTAPHA There you go again, harping on *cloaks* . . . Don't be ridiculous!

MAHMOUD Forgive me, sire. But even when I have my cloak on, I feel insubstantial . . . How will I feel when I see that man wearing it?

MUSTAPHA It's not fitting that my Vizier should seem to be a dilapidated rag . . . Pull yourself together! Why all this worry?

MAHMOUD Because it's a dangerous game.

MUSTAPHA And all the more interesting for being so . . . I know it's dangerous. I know that by the end of the day that fool may have lost what's left of his wits . . . But I just can't repress this fierce desire I have for fun! I can imagine everyone's confusion . . . That effete young Maymun will be the first to be bedeviled; then they'll all be acting as though the palace were haunted by *djins*. And then there'll be an endless series of impossible situations. And come evening I'll laugh in everybody's face; and I'll have taught them a lesson about how important it is that the sovereign should fit his sovereignty, and that his sovereignty should fit the sovereign . . .

MAHMOUD Well, suppose the impossible situations become impossible to resolve . . .

MUSTAPHA We can interfere any time we wish.

MAHMOUD My Lord, just to make sure we can maintain control over this game and enjoy ourselves without worry, let me remain as Vizier. I'll stay close to him, advise and guide him so as to avoid any mistakes or foolishness . . .

MUSTAPHA No, that would spoil the

fun. You'll be where I am. For God's sake, can't you give up your position as minister for one single day? And to such a person? You're being ridiculous! Now let's go get some rest and get ready for tomorrow.

MAHMOUD Once upon a time a fisherman pulled his net out of the water, to find in it a sealed bottle. As he held it he heard a voice moaning and crying inside . . .

MUSTAPHA Tonight I can go to bed without anyone telling me a story.

MAHMOUD As you wish, My Lord . . .

KING *exits.* MAHMOUD *looks at him angrily and contemptuously as he goes.*

MAHMOUD The beginning of the end . . . No King can afford to forget his ribbons, or to treat his robe and crown lightly . . . Still, I mustn't allow the strings to slip from my fingers. What I must do is keep my robe; he can go to hell. I must think of some contingency plan . . .

FADE OUT

THIRD INTERLUDE

POSTER: REMEMBER, THIS IS A GAME. PLACE YOUR BETS.

As in Prologue, ʿURQUB *and* EXECUTIONER *are engaged in acrobatic movements.* ʿUBAYD *and* ZAHID *stand in a distant corner.*

EXECUTIONER You can't be too careful. A good memory always comes in handy.

ʿURQUB We must keep our memories so that we don't forget. So that our thoughts don't wander from that . . .

EXECUTIONER This is an imaginary kingdom . . .

ʿURQUB An untrue story. We're dreaming . . .

EXECUTIONER And dreams are private.

ʿURQUB (*Jumps*): Fantasies, illusions, dreams . . .

ʿUBAYD No king gives up his throne willingly.

ZAHID No king lends his crown for fun.

ʿURQUB We're playing . . .

EXECUTIONER A game that, so far, is progressing innocently.

ʿURQUB Today, my Master ascends to the Throne. He'll rule and govern. He's one of us, a commoner. Let's see what he has in store for us . . .

EXECUTIONER He's not a commoner; he's one of *our* select elite. Let's see what he'll grant us.

ʿURQUB No! He's one of us, a commoner.

EXECUTIONER And I say he's one of our elite! (*They are on the verge of coming to blows.*)

ʿURQUB He'll be generous to *us*!

EXECUTIONER To *us*!

ʿURQUB He's one of *us*!

EXECUTIONER One of *us*! (*They come to blows.*)

ʿUBAYD (*Separating them*): Let's watch, shall we? We'd better keep track of the story . . .

SCENE FOUR, PART ONE

POSTER: SUBJECT ABU ʿIZZA WAKES UP A KING.

The Royal Chamber. MAYMUN *is busy rubbing the King's feet dotingly. Every now and then he bends down and kisses the King's feet.* ABU ʿIZZA *raises his head, sees* MAYMUN, *closes his eyes and buries his face in the pillow.* MAYMUN *notices that* ABU ʿIZZA *is awake.*

MAYMUN (*Bending over* ABU ʿIZZA*'s feet*): A very good morning to my Lord and Master!

ABU ᶜIZZA I'm dreaming! How wonderful . . .

MAYMUN May the Lord make all my Master's days perpetual bliss, whether he's dreaming or awake . . .

ABU ᶜIZZA (*Tickled*): My feet! Take it easy . . .

MAYMUN I beg your pardon. Have my hands been guilty of a rude touch?

ABU ᶜIZZA No, they couldn't be softer . . . They're tickling me to ecstasy! I hope I don't wake up from this dream . . .

MAYMUN Your Majesty asked to be awakened at sunrise.

ABU ᶜIZZA Then ask the sun to wait a little before rising.

MAYMUN Glory to God! Could it be that sleep is more powerful than the Royal Strength?

ABU ᶜIZZA *sits up in bed with a jerk and looks around in great astonishment.* MAYMUN *is still on his knees, his head bent down.*

ABU ᶜIZZA (*To himself*): Dreams! How completely they gain control over you! Am I awake or not? (*Feels his chest, then the bed, and reaches for a silver objet d'art on a bedside table.*) My hand tells me that what I'm touching is hard and real. But what my eyes seem to be seeing can't be true . . . This bed, the furniture, the gold and the silver, the silk and the velvet . . . It just can't be true!

MAYMUN I hope that my Lord slept well, and that he isn't feeling in any way indisposed . . .

ABU ᶜIZZA (*Staring at* MAYMUN; *hesitantly*): Who are you, young man? Where are we?

MAYMUN Does His Majesty wish to punish me by acting as though he didn't know me? You're in your bedchamber, my Lord, and I'm Maymun, your loyal servant and guard.

ABU ᶜIZZA Come closer, young man.

MAYMUN (*Approaching, eyes cast downward*): At your service, my Lord. (ABU ᶜIZZA *feels* MAYMUN'S *face with trembling hands. Then he fondles the young man's cheeks and hair.*)

MAYMUN Kind is the hand that touches, my Lord.

ABU ᶜIZZA Dreams, please stay with me!

ᶜURQUB *enters in* VIZIER'S *costume. He is walking and acting somberly.*

ᶜURQUB A very good morning to my Lord and King.

ABU ᶜIZZA (*Covering his eyes with both hands*): Here comes the owl! The destroyer of my dreams and the ruiner of my pleasures!

ᶜURQUB Will my Lord rise? The sun is up, and affairs of state await your wise command and supervision.

ABU ᶜIZZA Go away! What's the sun got to do with me? *I* never asked him to rise, and I won't leave this blissfulness just because he does!

MAYMUN (*In a whisper*): Your Eminence, I'm afraid His Majesty is slightly indisposed this morning.

ᶜURQUB Step aside, and I'll see what's going on.

ABU ᶜIZZA (*Staring at* ᶜURQUB): ᶜUrqub! What's that you're wearing?

ᶜURQUB ᶜUrqub? His Majesty's sense of humor is always with him, even in the early morning. No doubt, my Lord is calling me by this vulgar name to tease me.

ABU ᶜIZZA (*Angrily*): Your master never jokes on an empty stomach! Who are you? And who am I?

ᶜURQUB You are the mighty King Fakhreddin, and I am your loyal servant Barbir, whom you've been bounteous enough to call your vizier.

ABU ᶜIZZA *gets up violently, still somewhat confused.*

MAYMUN There rises Perfection . . .

ᶜURQUB Justice and Magnificence . . .

ABU ᶜIZZA What did I do last night?

MAYMUN Last night my Lord was feeling tired and went to bed early.

ABU ᶜIZZA Dream, reality . . . (*Walks about, touching and feeling everything.*) Dream, reality . . .

ᶜURQUB It's time His Majesty put on his ceremonial costume, and took up his crown and sceptre . . . Maymun, send for the courtiers.

ABU ᶜIZZA ᶜUrqub . . .

ᶜURQUB (*Interrupting*): Please, Your Majesty, do not call me by this vulgar name in front of the courtiers. It will affect my prestige.

ABU ᶜIZZA Come here. I want to investigate the line that separates dream from reality. Slap me.

ᶜURQUB My Lord?

ABU ᶜIZZA Slap me. (ᶜURQUB *slaps him with such force that* ABU ᶜIZZA *sways and puts his hand to his cheek.*) Oh, God! I wish I had a thicker beard! (*Reaches angrily for* ᶜURQUB.)

ᶜURQUB Forgive me, my Lord, and slap me a hundred times! Had my Lord not insisted, I would not have dared lift a finger!

ABU ᶜIZZA (*Somewhat distractedly*): This isn't a dream, then . . . (*Pauses.*) Now tell me—I haven't been thinking straight this morning. How long is it that you and I have been King and Vizier?

ᶜURQUB In a few days, the country will be celebrating the coronation anniversary of His Majesty, Fakhreddin the Mighty. And I've been by your side all along, as your loyal and obedient Vizier.

SCENE FOUR, PART TWO

POSTER: SUBJECT ABU ᶜIZZA EVAPORATES BIT BY BIT.

Commotion. MAYMUN *enters, followed by two* VALETS, *who are followed by the* ROYAL BAND.

BAND Lord over all of us,
Master of the realm,
Son of Kings bounteous,

Stay healthy at the helm
In celestial bliss
In celestial bliss

ᶜURQUB Dress him—Fakhreddin the Great—with vestments of glory, might, and stateliness!

The two VALETS *bow respectfully.* MAYMUN *massages* ABU ᶜIZZA's *shoulders and strokes every article of clothing lovingly. The dressing of* ABU ᶜIZZA *should be performed slowly, like a ritual or holy ceremony. Touches of makeup may be added.*

ABU ᶜIZZA (*As* VALETS *help him to first article*): Can this be true? Or has something happened to my mind? . . .

BAND Dress him, the magnificent one,
In vestments of glory and deep
meaning . . .

ABU ᶜIZZA The line between sleep and wakefulness seems like glass, made up of light and mirage . . . Is this magic? A dream? Or has something happened to my mind? . . .

BAND Awesome and bounteous . . .

MAYMUN (*Feeling* ABU ᶜIZZA's *rigid body, whispering*): I wish my Lord would let his body relax.

ABU ᶜIZZA I feel as though I were walking on wet ground . . . My feet aren't sinking; and they aren't getting wet . . . They're just sliding along a shimmering glaze, while the wind carries everything far, far away, behind me . . . Is this magic? A dream? Or has something happened to my mind? . . .

BAND Radiant and glorious . . .

ᶜURQUB Be careful with the crown. Handle it with care.

ABU ᶜIZZA The wind's gone. My memory's dead. On I go, with nothing behind me but a dark, dark wall. Can this be true?

MAYMUN (*Reaching for* ABU ᶜIZZA'*s hand*): Let me cover this with emeralds and rubies . . .

ABU ᶜIZZA The light! The faces! I'm beginning to see . . . (*Places the crown on his head.*)

BAND Perfect and peerless . . .

ABU ᶜIZZA It seems as though I've just arrived here . . . As though I've just been born . . . I'm entering a huge hall, empty and spacious, flooded with a light that's as fierce as daggers . . . I'm alone!

ᶜURQUB And here's the mighty King's sceptre.

ABU ᶜIZZA *holds the sceptre; his features assume a somber look; his body becomes erect and his demeanor firm.*

BAND Prince of the realm,
Noble, mighty, awesome and firm;
Radiant of visage,
Bounteous of lineage,
Great and just,
Rule he must.

KING (*Beats on floor with sceptre*; BAND *stops*): Now We shall proceed to the Throne Room, where We shall see to the affairs of state.

VIZIER You are dismissed.

FADE OUT

SCENE FIVE, PART ONE

POSTER: THE KING HAS TWO MORE COURTIERS.

HAJ MUSTAPHA *and* HAJ MAHMOUD *stand whispering in the corner where the Bedchamber and the Throne Room meet.*

MUSTAPHA (*Gaily*): Did you notice how off-tune they were? I can just imagine their eyes popping out of their sockets! Their tongues turning stiff with fear and astonishment!

MAHMOUD (*Irritably*): I did not notice that they were off-tune. Nor did I notice any swelling of their tongues.

MUSTAPHA You're not quite yourself this morning.

MAHMOUD Why should I be? Aren't we on a holiday today?

MUSTAPHA We are. And we're having fun, too. Do you still feel that lightness?

MAHMOUD Yes, and in my head as well. I feel that . . . (*Enter* MAYMUN, *who walks to his position by the Throne Room door.*)

MUSTAPHA (*Interrupting*): Here comes Maymun! Let's see how bewildered he gets!

MAHMOUD He doesn't look bewildered in the least.

MUSTAPHA Maymun, Maymun . . . (MAYMUN *looks at them with surprise.*) Come here.

MAYMUN Who are you? What is it you want?

MUSTAPHA Who are we!

MAYMUN Have I seen you before? I'm surprised you know my name. How did you get in here?

MUSTAPHA (*In a rage*): Maymun!

MAYMUN Sir: knowing my name doesn't give you the right to shout at me.

MUSTAPHA (*Changing his tone, trying very hard to control himself*): Never mind, young man. It's just that we're surprised you didn't recognize us, since we're two of His Majesty's intimate courtiers. We've been here quite frequently and know almost everybody by name. Unfortunately, however, not everybody here seems to know us . . .

MAYMUN I didn't mean to insult you, sir. I would give my very life for my Lord and Master; to his courtiers, I certainly owe courtesy and respect.

MAHMOUD Well said. Is His Majesty comfortably up already?

MAYMUN At first I thought, Heaven forbid, that he was slightly indisposed. I was quite frightened, sir. But soon he was shining like a full moon . . . (*Feels his face dreamily.*) And I will never forget that he, the King himself, with his Royal hands, touched these cheeks and this hair of mine . . .

MAHMOUD A great occasion. You should have it tattooed on your face.

MUSTAPHA Tell me, Maymun, did you look hard into your Master's face?

MAYMUN The questions you ask, sir! Who would dare stare into the sun while it's shining?

MUSTAPHA Well, my face then. Look at it carefully. Look . . .

MAYMUN (*Impatiently*): I have, sir, and for much longer than my time permits.

MUSTAPHA And you don't recognize me?

MAYMUN I'm sorry, but I don't remember seeing you before.

MUSTAPHA And these fingers? (*Showing him his hand.*) Don't you remember ever having touched them?

MAYMUN (*To* MAHMOUD): What is it with your friend? Has he gone (*Pointing to his head*) round the bend? Next he'll be telling me that he's the King . . . Now may I leave? My Lord and Master will be here any minute. (*Moves away, shaking his head.*)

MUSTAPHA I always knew Maymun was no more than a stupid fool!

MAHMOUD I hope he's not the only one.

MUSTAPHA What do you mean?

MAHMOUD Nothing.

MUSTAPHA Tonight I'll cut off those fingers of his and feed them to the dogs!

KING *enters, followed by* ᶜURQUB. *He walks solemnly and firmly. His face has acquired a look of seriousness and noble sadness.*

MAHMOUD I think the King . . .

MUSTAPHA (*Startled*): The King? You mean our stupid friend . . .

MAHMOUD See how confidently he's walking! How well he's playing the part! And look at ᶜUrqub, stuffing my robes with vulgarity! (*Makes for them.*) I'd rather have my eyes put out than stand by and watch this!

MUSTAPHA (*Pulling him back*): The game's just started! Don't spoil it!

MAHMOUD He's wearing my skin . . . I've lost my very skin . . . I feel so weak . . . (*He stops* ᶜURQUB *and whispers:*) Be careful with the cloak!

The KING *stops.* ᶜURQUB *is somewhat discomfited, as* MAHMOUD *fondles* ᶜURQUB*'s cloak.* MUSTAPHA *tries to pull him back.*

KING Who is it that's interrupted Our procession? Where are the guards?

ᶜURQUB (*Resorting to humor to hide his discom*□*ture*): No need for the guards, my Lord. I don't know how I could have, but I must have forgotten to inform His Majesty: these are two dervishes we once met on our tour of the province of . . . of . . .

MUSTAPHA (*Sarcastically*): East Anbar.

ᶜURQUB Yes, my Lord, it was the province of East Anbar.

KING I don't remember them. Nor do I

remember that there is a province of East Anbar in my Kingdom.

ᶜURQUB That's a good one! Trust a man with a sense of humor not to miss a chance!

KING (*Curtly*): Briefly, ᶜUrqub, who are they?

ᶜURQUB Briefly, sire, these dervishes have been in the Palace since yesterday. They've come from far, far away in the hope that the King will add them to his retinue and let them serve him as entertaining jesters.

KING I have enough of *them* around me. They're all so boring.

ᶜURQUB But, my Lord, Mustapha and Mahmoud are different . . .

KING What can they do?

ᶜURQUB They can imitate kings and viziers, tell amusing stories, and bark.

MUSTAPHA (*Shouting*): Bark?

MAHMOUD (*Hitting* MUSTAPHA *on the back*): Is this what it's come to, Haj Mustapha? Barking?

ᶜURQUB I meant—I meant, what jesters call *singing*! And besides, my Lord, these two are good at magic and sleight-of-hand, and they are not altogether ignorant about erotic love.

KING Add these two to my jester roster. I'll test them tonight. But let me tell you something neither of you knows: I don't like seeing jesters in the morning.

Turns his back to them and proceeds, slowly but steadily. ᶜURQUB *gives them a meaningful look, shakes his head, and follows.*

MAHMOUD Happy, Haj Mustapha? We've got the job.

MUSTAPHA I beg your pardon. Did I hear you call me Haj Mustapha? Have you forgotten yourself?

MAHMOUD (*Pulling him into the corner*): Let's hide here, so he can't see us if he turns around.

SCENE FIVE, PART TWO

POSTER: LE ROI C'EST LE ROI: SUBJECT ABU ᶜIZZA FORGETS HIS ENEMIES.

The Throne Room. KING *solemnly climbs up the steps leading to the throne, sits on it with habitual self-assurance.* ᶜURQUB *is still playing a game: he is restless; he feels the throne, sniffs at it.*

ᶜURQUB Now that I am Sultan of the realm / The envious shall feel my hand at the helm . . .

KING (*Eyeing him with astonishment*): What is this nonsense?

ᶜURQUB Your enemies, my Lord. The time has come for revenge. Whom shall I summon first?

KING Which enemies? And can't you stand still? What do you think you are, a vizier or a jester?

ᶜURQUB (*Bows his head, assumes a serious look*): My Lord, forgive me. I just couldn't control myself: it must be the happiness of knowing that now we can take our revenge . . .

KING What enemies? What revenge?

ᶜURQUB (*Imitating* ABU ᶜIZZA's *voice*): "That devious and treacherous Shaykh Taha . . ."

KING Devious and treacherous? Why?

ᶜURQUB Because he robs—left, right, and center—even orphans, and . . .

KING On Fridays, doesn't he pray to God to preserve the King?

ᶜURQUB (*Confused*): He does . . .

KING Has he urged the people to rebel or mutiny?

ᶜURQUB No, he hasn't . . . He wouldn't dare. All I meant was that he isn't very honest, even when it comes to orphans' money.

KING The trouble with this country is that God seems to have put serpents, instead of tongues, in people's mouths.

ᶜURQUB Alright: what about Shahbandar, the Head Merchant?

KING What about our friend Shahbandar?

ᶜURQUB Friend? Your Majesty calls him a friend? The man who ruined our business?

KING What's come over you this morning? Are you trying to tell me that the very pillars of this realm are my archenemies? Do you want my state to collapse?

ᶜURQUB Heaven forbid, my Lord. But somehow I thought I once heard you speaking of revenge on certain enemies ...

KING When?

ᶜURQUB Yesterday, perhaps.

KING *tries to remember. Knocks on the floor with his sceptre.* MAYMUN *hurries to him.*

MAYMUN My Lord?

KING Young man, what were you doing this time yesterday?

MAYMUN (*Frightened*): This time yesterday? I was spraying perfume around Your Majesty's throne.

KING And why are you delaying today?

MAYMUN I was just about to, my Lord, when Your Majesty knocked on the floor with his sceptre . . . (MAYMUN *sprays perfume on and around the throne.*)

KING (*To* ᶜURQUB, *after a brief pensive pause*): I too see strange things in my sleep, or when I'm alone . . . But I avoid talking about them, and tend to forget them as soon as I wake up.

ᶜURQUB You are right. It must be a dream I had, or a mere figment of my imagination. Let's forget about enemies and revenge, and . . . well . . . Let's do what we may / And turn the night into full day.

KING (*Interrupting angrily*): Vizier! (ᶜURQUB *stops;* KING *stares suspiciously into his face.*) Come here! Turn around ... (ᶜURQUB *approaches, turns around like a model in a fashion show.* KING *examines him closely, then startles him with*:) Are you really Barbir, my Vizier?

ᶜURQUB My Lord, are you having doubts about your own Vizier?

KING Let's not talk about this now . . . Who is to see me first?

ᶜURQUB Well, the usual, my Lord. The same as usual ...

KING (*Stares into* ᶜURQUB*'s face again, beats on the floor with his sceptre.* MAYMUN *enters.*): Let my first visitor appear before me!

MAHMOUD *and* MUSTAPHA *emerge surreptitiously from their corner.*

MAHMOUD See, he's beginning to have suspicions about ᶜUrqub.

MUSTAPHA Who would have thought that he'd be such a good actor?

MAHMOUD Who said he was acting?

MUSTAPHA What is he doing, then? Can a man change completely overnight?

MAHMOUD Sometimes you don't need that long. Remember what happened some years ago?

MUSTAPHA What happened?

MAHMOUD More or less what's happening now ...

MAYMUN (*Calling out*): Let the Chief of Police appear before His Majesty!

MAHMOUD (*Spitefully*): Are you still waiting for him to trip or slip up? I haven't seen you laughing yet, Haj Mustapha ...

MUSTAPHA This time you go too far!

MAHMOUD At this point, neither of us can go any farther than being Haj Mustapha and Haj Mahmoud, employed to entertain our Lord and Master the King.

MUSTAPHA Barbir!

MAHMOUD Who's he, I wonder . . . *Where* is he? Let's see how the Chief of Police will react. This man knows when every man in the Kingdom sleeps with his wife.

MUSTAPHA Yes, *he'll* see what's happening, I'm sure of it . . .

SCENE FIVE, PART THREE

POSTER: LE ROI C'EST LE ROI. FORMER CITIZEN ABU ᶜIZZA FOLLOWS HIS NATURAL COURSE.

Enter CHIEF OF POLICE, *carrying a whip. He is walking like one who knows that he is both important and indispensable; he is nonchalant to the point of arrogant defiance.* ᶜURQUB, *catching sight of* CHIEF OF POLICE, *hides behind the throne.* KING'*s face stiffens. Obviously, he senses that he is being defied and pushed into a fight.*

MUSTAPHA Look, the Chief of Police seems to have found him out! Notice how insolent and indifferent he is . . .

MAHMOUD I've noticed that frequently —*and* pointed it out.

KING (*Gradually managing to control his discomfiture*): How did my Kingdom spend the night?

CHIEF OF POLICE As it spends every night: in peace and tranquility.

KING You mean nothing serious happened?

CHIEF OF POLICE Nothing. Just the usual minor incidents.

KING And beneath the surface? Are there no plots being hatched in the dark?

CHIEF OF POLICE Sire, my men can see in the dark.

KING You are overconfident. Overconfidence can make a man less vigilant, and careless.

CHIEF OF POLICE (*Sharply*): This is a tone I'm not used to!

KING Every now and then kings must change their tone, if they don't want to see their thrones evaporate into the dark.

CHIEF OF POLICE (*Somewhat confused*): Is my Lord alluding to anything in particular?

KING Your Lord should not have to resort to alluding. This kingdom is not free of darkness . . .

CHIEF OF POLICE His Majesty seems to be suspecting something . . .

KING A king without suspicions is like a king without a throne.

MAHMOUD (*Admiringly*): Bravo! That's what I've always thought myself!

CHIEF OF POLICE I say it's a dirty trick! Who was it that informed on me?

KING (*In control of the battle*): You are here to report to me, not to question me. (*Raises his voice*:) Do you call subterfuge loyalty to your King?

CHIEF OF POLICE (*Crumbling*): My Lord, I . . . I didn't mean to. I was confused, and I . . . I just felt there was no need for me to be bothering Your Majesty with an incident as simple as that. I've already had those responsible for his escape burned to death, and right now we're hunting him down everywhere. I assure you, neither he nor his band will manage to elude us.

KING *rises from the throne, walks up to* CHIEF OF POLICE. *Circles him, looking him up and down contemptuously.*

MUSTAPHA (*Obviously worried for the first time*): What is this about?

MAHMOUD Yesterday, Haj Mustapha, when you were King, there was a serious matter I wanted to bring up with you, but you were so terribly bored . . . I also meant to tell you that today the leading citizens of the realm were supposed to come to see you.

MUSTAPHA Did I hear you say when I . . . *was* King?

MAHMOUD That is, I believe, the tense used to indicate what is past.

MUSTAPHA Barbir!

MAHMOUD Who is it you're talking to?

KING (*Standing before* CHIEF OF POLICE, *angrily pounding on the floor with his sceptre*): A man escapes from prison! There are bands, contacts, secret plots that shake the Throne! And the Chief of Police appears before his King as though he were walking into one of his slave women's chambers, and what does he say? "Sire, my men can see in the dark!"

MAHMOUD Good show! That's the spirit! Go on, go on, Your Majesty!

CHIEF OF POLICE (*On his knees*): Forgive me, my Lord, it was a mistake, and I promise it'll never happen again. It isn't as serious as all that, Sire.

MUSTAPHA The Chief of Police, the State's secret eye, can't identify his own king. Is this what it's come to? Am I dreaming?

MAHMOUD No, this time you aren't.

KING (*Goes back to throne and sits with assurance*): What do you mean, it isn't all that serious? Your King does not like to sit on a throne that isn't secure.

CHIEF OF POLICE He's nothing but a scoundrel, my Lord, who has only a few rogues around him.

KING And these few rogues, what do they want?

CHIEF OF POLICE To cause trouble, sire. But I shall have all of them roasted before they can lift a finger.

KING And how will you do that? You have to find them before you start roasting them.

CHIEF OF POLICE (*Startled*): We're doing everything to find them, my Lord.

KING You mean you haven't arrested one single person other than the man who broke out?

CHIEF OF POLICE But we have, sire. We caught another of them, but he died in the torture chamber without having confessed a thing.

KING So . . . This throne is being threatened by a force that's both secret and tenacious? A force that may strike anywhere and at any time without our knowing a thing about it?

CHIEF OF POLICE You needn't worry, sire. I pledge that I'll hunt them down in no time.

KING Listen, you: I dislike vague promises. If you don't get them before Coronation Day, you might as well hang yourself.

CHIEF OF POLICE My Lord!

KING (*Hitting on the floor with his sceptre*): Not another word! Your very interesting report is enough for today . . .

CHIEF OF POLICE (*Withdrawing humbly*): Yes, my Lord.

ʿURQUB (*Jumping up and down happily*): You got him, my Lord! You got him beautifully! He came in a peacock and went out a mouse! He'll repay us generously for this, I'll bet . . . What a service we've rendered him!

KING Him? Who?

ʿURQUB Oh, nothing, nobody . . . I was just talking to myself.

KING Talk to yourself quietly, and don't interrupt my thoughts.

MUSTAPHA Can it be true? My own Chief of Police is double-crossing me! What's happening in my kingdom?

MAHMOUD There are things happening that should make a king hang on tight to his sceptre and stay close to his vestments.

MUSTAPHA You mean you've known all along?

MAHMOUD Well, when I was Vizier and you were King, I often felt like slapping your face.

MUSTAPHA (*Failing to control himself any longer, grabbing him by the collar*): Slap *me*! You, Barbir?

MAHMOUD Calm down, Haj Mustapha, or you'll give us away. The ones who set you up don't like a King who gets bored or a Vizier who doesn't know what's going on in the state. For some time they've been meaning to talk to the King and ask him to do exactly what he's doing now.

MUSTAPHA What he's doing now? This fool?

MAHMOUD This man you call a fool has managed to find out what's happening in this country.

MUSTAPHA (*Collapsing*): I'm going mad! What's the meaning of all this?

MAHMOUD It's very simple: Our Lord and King is clinging to his gown the way a baby clings to his mother's womb; you'd think his sceptre was his umbilical cord. He would have done the exact same thing yesterday that he's doing today.

MUSTAPHA I can't believe it! It can't be! This must be a nightmare! I must put a stop to it right away! (*He rushes forward, but is pulled back by* MAHMOUD.)

KING (*Coming out of his meditations; bangs on the floor with his sceptre*): Let the Executioner appear before me.

ʿURQUB The Executioner! God have mercy on my soul, what for?

MUSTAPHA When that Executioner comes in, I'll put an end to this farce! His ax will have mercy on no one!

MAHMOUD This farce was begun by a king; only a king can put an end to it. Haj Mustapha is nothing more than Haj Mustapha.

MUSTAPHA I can't believe it . . .

EXECUTIONER (*Standing before* KING, *bowing from the waist*): Executioner at your service, Your Majesty.

MUSTAPHA Can it be? I can't believe it! Is it possible that the Executioner hasn't noticed that the King's face and features are different?

MAHMOUD A King has no face and no features.

KING *eyes* EXECUTIONER'*s ax blade voluptuously.*

ʿURQUB My God, what a fearful blade! We've been given a whole day with . . . this. (*Points to ax.*) The lovely creatures await your loving caresses.

KING (*Giving* ʿURQUB *a dirty look*): Executioner, you stand here beside me. Let your ax be within reach. (EXECUTIONER *stands on the* KING'*s right, at attention, holding his ax parallel to the armrest of the throne.*)

ʿURQUB (*Shrinking back, obviously disturbed*): Good God! What's come over him?

KING (*Feeling the blade sensuously*): That's better. That's the way I want it—within my reach . . . I love the solid feel of its blade . . . I want that steel to break through these fingers and into my veins, to go up through my arms and into my heart . . . I want to unite with it, become one with it . . . Stay where you are, Executioner. Let that ax support my hand, penetrate my body . . . Let the King and his blade be one.

EXECUTIONER Yes, my Lord.

ʿURQUB My God, I can hardly recognize him! Who is he? And what about the game, and all the fun our Lord's waiting for? . . . ʿUrqub doesn't understand any more.

MAHMOUD My heart's racing. I want my gown so badly that I can hardly breathe. This is the moment when a minister wants to be close to his lord and king. I can feel his radiance from here . . .

MUSTAPHA This can't be true! Have I gone mad? (*Tries to hold himself together.*) Minister, anesthetize him!

MAHMOUD Anesthetize the King, Haj Mustapha? Etherize steel?

MUSTAPHA I order you to end this game at once!

MAHMOUD Then the fisherman discovered that the crying was coming from the bottle he'd caught in his net. Inside it was a little *djinni*, locked up. "Please, please, set me free," said the *djinni*. The fisherman's heart softened, and he opened the bottle. At that moment a mighty giant emerged and stood roaring with laughter. His voice shook the high hills and the deep, deep valleys. This giant now moved to destroy the man who had set him free.

MUSTAPHA (*Obviously unbalanced now*): It can't be true! Or else I *am* mad!

MAHMOUD If this is where things end, I'll feel sorry for you. But I must look to myself now, and see what I can do.

All is still, except for KING*'s fingers fondling* EXECUTIONER*'s ax.*

FOURTH INTERLUDE

POSTER: GIVE ME GOWN AND CROWN, AND A KING YOU WILL HAVE.

Same scene, but all is still. MUSTAPHA *leaves his corner and begins to walk about the stage. He is distraught and on the verge of total collapse.* ʿUBAYD *and* ZAHID *enter from opposite corners and meet downstage center. They speak their words lightheartedly, but not without solemnity.*

MUSTAPHA (*Turning around*): Not one person has looked at his features or his face! Can it be true, or have I gone mad?

ʿUBAYD He put on the gown, and then he was King. That's quite a normal, natural transformation.

ZAHID In any regime of masquerade, / This is the rule you should postulate: / Give me gown and crown, / And a King you will have.

MUSTAPHA What's happening? What's true and what's false? What's dream and what's reality?

ZAHID It isn't a matter of dream and reality. The whole story is that the gown has changed its stuffing. Details may differ, but not the essence.

ʿUBAYD The man who rests his rump on that throne seems firmer. The man whose rump seeks to rest on that throne *was* firm, and sooner or later would have become firmer. Conditions demand that a shaky throne be protected, so a king *has* to become firmer.

ZAHID and ʿUBAYD (*Together*): The Royal Rule is: details may differ, but not the essence. This is the rule, wherever kings rule.

MUSTAPHA (*Still turning, stopping to stare into everyone's face, his eyes protruding*): Mirrors, nothing but mirrors . . . I feel as though I were locked alone inside a room made up of mirrors—on the floor, the ceiling, the walls, the windows, everywhere . . . I clap my hands, only to see hordes clapping. I cheer, and there go the cheers of thousands and thousands of men . . . I bow, and millions bow before me. I walk, and huge crowds walk with me, shaking the very earth on which they step . . . Hordes and crowds, repeating my words, emulating my movements, all ready to respond to the slightest signal . . . Mirrors . . . Myriads of mirrors . . .

ᶜUBAYD Pride and arrogance alone make kings forget that basic rule . . .

When old Korosh made the rounds of his royal place,
And thought that he alone was in full grace,
He forgot that those who built the town
Were obeying simply his sceptre and his crown.

ZAHID And when Khofo looked at the tall pyramid
And thought he was mightier than all kings,
He forgot that those who'd built with sweat and tears galore
Had been obeying his sceptre and crown, and nothing more.

ZAHID and ᶜUBAYD (*Together*):
Under regimes of masquerade,
It is safe to postulate
The Golden Rule remains:
Give me gown and crown,
And a King you will have.

ZAHID *and* ᶜUBAYD *withdraw.*

MUSTAPHA (*Continues to move distraughtly among the frozen personages until he reaches his former place with* MAHMOUD): No one's recognized him . . . Mirrors, all mirrors, followed by still more mirrors . . . Can it be true, or have I gone mad?

SCENE FIVE, PART FOUR

POSTER: LE ROI C'EST LE ROI. FORMER CITIZEN ABU ᶜIZZA NO LONGER RECOGNIZES HIMSELF OR HIS FAMILY.

The frozen scene comes to life again. MAYMUN *approaches the throne and bows.*

MAYMUN Your Majesty, two of your subjects, women, carrying audience permits duly signed and sealed, wish to appear before you.

ᶜURQUB (*Rubbing his hands together*): Women! Good! We're in for better weather . . .

KING Let my subjects in.

MAHMOUD How I love this incisive, decisive tone!

MUSTAPHA The two women! That's right, I'd forgotten about them . . . The truth will soon be out!

Enter UMM ᶜIZZA *and her daughter. They falter as they walk. Their faces reflect fear and anxiety.*

ᶜURQUB Good heavens! What brings *them* here? The game's gone full circle. Now the real fun begins . . .

KING (*To* ᶜURQUB, *who has hidden his face behind* KING's *shoulder*): I don't like ministers who talk to themselves like idiots.

ᶜURQUB (*Confused, stuttering*): But Master, I mean Your Majesty, look! They're . . .

KING When the morning's business is over, I'll look. I'll look into *your situation*! Now what is it that these two women want from their sovereign?

UMM ᶜIZZA (*Drops suddenly to her knees, speaks in a studied manner*): Our Lord and Master, to whom we owe obedience and loyalty, we've come to beg for restitution. We've been made to drink poison and suffer injustice.

KING And we are here to give justice . . . But your Lord and Master doesn't like crying and the shedding of tears. Rise, women. Rise and tell us your story.

ʿURQUB (*Now stands erect, overcoming his initial confusion*): This is only a game, so why should I come out of it empty-handed?

UMM ʿIZZA (*Helped by her daughter to stand up*): Sovereign Lord of All Times: the likes of us are unable to do anything but mourn our fate and complain of our condition. We've come to you for justice and restitution. It was my lot, Your Grace, to marry a witless and helpless man . . .

ʿURQUB (*Assuming a grave tone*): You haven't come here, woman, to tell His Majesty of your marriage problems and the ineptitude of your husband.

ʿIZZA (*Her eyes grow wide as she sees* ʿURQUB): Mother, look! He looks like ʿUrqub!

UMM ʿIZZA (*Whispering angrily*): Don't be stupid! How could you confuse ʿUrqub with the awesome Vizier?

KING Leave the woman alone. I love to see my subjects display their dirty linen, and talk about their petty woes.

MUSTAPHA That sounds like me! That's an extension of myself speaking! Who is he? Who am I?

UMM ʿIZZA (*With* ʿIZZA *clinging to her in fear and glancing stealthily at* ʿURQUB *and* KING *in turn*): When a man falls, all there is to show is dirty linen. My husband, my Lord, is both witless and helpless, and the times, Your Majesty, are not for the likes of him: they're for the schemers and plotters. His father had left him with a piece of land and some money, and had appointed Shaykh Taha as guardian over his son's affairs. This Shaykh Taha, my Lord, is quite a man; he would sell his own beard, along with his religion, for a handful of coins. He wanted to swindle my husband out of the whole inheritance, but we managed to salvage half of it. We went to the judge, but this got us nowhere. Shaykh Taha left no possible stone unturned and kept swallowing up one portion after another, until he left us with hardly anything and sent us off with abundant reprimands. Then we put together the little we had left, and with it my husband opened a cloth shop in the great *souk*. It was alright at first; business was brisk. But bastards, my Lord, far outnumber the legitimate. Other merchants, the great Shahbandar prominent among them, grew envious and began to set traps for my husband. And he, witless and helpless as he is, simply walked into them. Overnight he went bankrupt. How they did it, we don't know. All we know is that it was the work of Shahbandar and his friends. Oh, the way they acted! The way they stabbed that fallen beast, who soon went completely insane and took to drinking and despair! And here we are, with nothing we can call our own except for this daughter of mine; I can hardly arrange a decent marriage for her . . .

ʿIZZA Mother!

UMM ʿIZZA You needn't feel ashamed of it. He's our Lord and Master, and should know about all our problems. Mighty King and Lord: you alone can bring us justice and restore what's been forcibly taken from us! . . .

KING, *distracted, is stroking the ax.*

MUSTAPHA This woman is his wife; the girl, his daughter. Yet no one recognizes anyone. Am I bewitched, or have I just gone mad?

MAHMOUD Both.

ʿIZZA (*Frightened, drawing closer to her mother*): Mother, look! The King! I'm afraid . . .

UMM ʿIZZA (*In a whisper*): Afraid! I brought you with me to give me strength, not to be afraid!

ᶜIZZA (*Whispering in a faltering voice*): But . . . He looks like my father!

UMM ᶜIZZA What's come over you, child? You must have a fever. Or maybe it's the palace's somber atmosphere that's affected your mind . . .

KING (*Suddenly, to* ᶜURQUB): Vizier, do you know these two women?

ᶜURQUB (*Startled, confused*): My Lord? Perhaps we, ah, met them on one of our little jaunts . . .

KING Do you know them or not?

ᶜURQUB But . . . Does His Majesty remember seeing them before?

KING No. It's His Majesty who's asking. You're supposed to just answer.

ᶜURQUB I know them and I don't. I might have run into them once . . .

KING To the point, ᶜUrqub! I don't like beating around the bush . . . How do you know them?

ᶜURQUB (*Hesitates, but soon becomes decisive*): I'll come to the point, and I hope my Lord won't mind . . . Your Vizier is in love. I saw this young lady once, and I've been moaning and sighing ever since.

KING When it comes to love, my Vizier talks like a servant.

ᶜURQUB Mine are honorable intentions, my Lord. I want her for my wife. And if you grant me this favor, I shall grow wings and fly up to the Seventh Heaven . . .

KING I can do without a flying Vizier.

MAYMUN Your Glorious Majesty: The Queen, my Mistress, says that she is waiting for you to join her for breakfast and relaxation.

KING We shall go to her as soon as this audience is over.

MAYMUN (*Withdrawing*): Yes, my Lord.

UMM ᶜIZZA The King's consulting with the Vizier about our case. That's a good sign.

ᶜIZZA I wish it were over . . . I'm getting more and more frightened all the time! I'm too afraid to look at either of them . . .

UMM ᶜIZZA You'll feel much better once justice has been done. Just wait . . .

KING Your complaint, woman, is a serious matter. It reflects both on the state and on those in charge. Your story is truly a sad one, so much so that long before this audience, my Vizier has been wanting to obtain justice for you.

UMM ᶜIZZA Long live our King and his Vizier!

KING I have been saddened, woman, by your adverse fortunes. Nothing ever grieves me so much as when fate turns against my subjects, for this is what causes envy, dissension, and hatred. I am only one of the people, and I know very well how hard it can be for those whom fortune has betrayed. They become bitter souls, always dissatisfied and finding fault with everything. I've been holding my temper with you, woman, because I know that bitterness can blind. But let me just ask: have you come here to tell me that this throne is worthless? That I am a worthless King and that the whole state is a handful of dust? The moment your husband opened that shop of his without reaching an understanding with Shahbandar, he made himself a rival and an enemy. No one ever robbed him or cheated him. He simply entered into a duel that he had little chance of winning. No wonder he lost: after all, the other had the right to win as well. It's your husband that you should have been complaining to, for he's the cause of all your trouble: a man who, weak in will and poor in skill, found it easier to blame others for his own shortcomings; then, on top of that, he resorted to drink, and despair . . . I become distressed when fortune turns against my people. This session has lasted too long. Here are my decisions, to be recorded by the Vizier . . . (KING *assumes a very serious tone.* ʿURQUB *starts up, still somewhat dazzled, to try to record the judgment.*) This woman's husband shall be put to public shame, paraded through the whole Bazaar from the Small Gate to the Central Square. This woman shall receive an annual allowance of five hundred dirhams, to be paid by the Vizier. In return for this, the woman shall entrust him with her daughter, whom he may make use of, as his wife or as a slavewoman, in his palace.

ʿIZZA (*Leans against her mother for support; cries out*): My Lord! . . .

ʿURQUB Five hundred dirhams! My mind's numb!

MUSTAPHA What's going on? Can it be true? The man's just sold off his family, passed sentence on himself, and no one's recognized anyone!

MAHMOUD A king doesn't have to know all his subjects, my dear Haj Mustapha.

MUSTAPHA His subjects? Who was talking, anyway—him or me? No one's recognizing anyone . . .

UMM ʿIZZA (*Musing*): Except for the bit about public shame, everything the King has just said we've already heard from the Imam, the Judge and the Head Merchant . . . You'd think they were all one man, one tongue, one family . . . Who knows? Maybe you'll become the Vizier's wife . . . Who knows, indeed . . . God is great!

ʿIZZA Mother, no! I don't want to go and live in his palace! I'm engaged!

UMM ʿIZZA Engaged? Who to?

ʿIZZA To someone who'll come to put an end to all misery, and all forms of the masquerade . . .

UMM ʿIZZA You too? Haven't I got enough with your father? Won't there be *one* of us left with a grain of sense?

EXECUTIONER (*Pushing the two women out*): Come on now, off you go. Someone will call for your daughter tomorrow.

UMM ʿIZZA Alright, ʿIzza, let's go. (*They exit, followed by* EXECUTIONER.)

MUSTAPHA No one recognizes anyone . . . But wait! The Queen! She's often green with jealousy on account of Rihana . . . *She*'ll bring everything out into the open! . . . I can just see it. (*As though hallucinating deliriously*:) She'll let out a scream, and the game will be disclosed. Then I'm going to break all those mirrors and slaughter everyone—every single one—the actors in this game as well as the spectators! . . . Every single one! . . . Go ahead, my darling Queen! Scream! Lay everything open! I'm coming . . . (*He rushes across the hall.* MAHMOUD *follows.*)

MAHMOUD Where are you going, Haj Mustapha?

MUSTAPHA I shall appear in their midst like a war cry! I shall break all those mirrors and slaughter every one of them! This is the right moment!

MAHMOUD *gives him a pitying, sarcastic look.* MAYMUN *tries to stop* MUSTAPHA, *but the latter pushes him aside roughly.*

MAHMOUD This is indeed the right moment . . . His Majesty has been nagged by suspicions all morning . . . It shouldn't be too difficult to get rid of a Vizier who isn't totally convinced he is Vizier . . . And as to His Majesty, my Lord and Master, he shall remain my Lord and Master . . . (*He takes a letter out of his pocket and turns towards* MAYMUN:) Maymun . . .

MAYMUN What's come over that friend

of yours? He's been acting strange and aggressive . . . He just pushed by me and ran off toward the Queen's chamber.

MAHMOUD It was only this morning that the King admitted us to his court. My friend's jests tend to be a bit extreme. But you needn't worry . . . Kind sir, can I rely on you for a favor?

MAYMUN I'll oblige if I can.

MAHMOUD This message is urgent. Will you please hand it to His Majesty immediately?

MAYMUN It will be done, sir.

MAHMOUD (*Handing him the message*): God bless you. (MAYMUN *exits.*) We know that you are not the King. We also know that the man who stands before you in the vestments of the Vizier is not the Vizier. *He* knows it, and has told us so . . . This is the final test, Your Majesty: either you will continue to wear the crown, or he who has gone raving mad will recover it. In either case, the grip of the State will be firmer, and the Vizier shall be more powerful still . . . But first I must recover my cloak.

Enter EXECUTIONER, *squats by the throne and starts to fondle his ax lovingly.* MAHMOUD *approaches.*

MAHMOUD You'd think it was a bride on her wedding night. Do you love that ax of yours that much?

EXECUTIONER Much more than you can imagine . . . But I feel it slipping away from me.

MAHMOUD Why?

EXECUTIONER (*With a lump in his throat*): My Lord and Master is now as much in love with it as I am.

MAHMOUD You're right. I saw him feeling its blade as though he wanted to melt into it.

EXECUTIONER He's been stealing it away from me bit by bit . . . Its solidity, which had been deeply embedded inside me, has been abandoning me and going over to him. I feel so weak . . . You'd think my legs were made of dried-up reeds . . .

MAHMOUD I know what you mean very well. That's how I feel now.

EXECUTIONER Really? But who are you?

MAHMOUD One of my Lord's courtiers—admitted to his service only this morning.

ʿURQUB *enters, running.*

ʿURQUB Haj Mahmoud, where are you? Help!

MAHMOUD What is it?

ʿURQUB He's gone completely mad! Tell His Majesty—I mean *His Majesty*!—to intervene and do something . . .

MAHMOUD What happened?

ʿURQUB It was unbelievable! Maymun walked in with a letter. The King read it and blew up like a volcano. He stamped on the floor with his foot and shouted: "My Vizier? False? But what about the King? Do they think the King is a joke? A King is a King! I'll show them! . . ." Then he roared: "Where's my Executioner? Send for him! Close the Palace gates!"

EXECUTIONER (*Jumping up*): Is my Lord summoning me? I'd better run! (EXECUTIONER *exits.*)

MAHMOUD And the Queen?

ʿURQUB The Queen? The Queen herself, in the flesh, was fondling him and feeding him with her own hands. And when he stood up shouting, she threw herself down on the floor before him, clutched his feet, and kissed them, saying, "Do what you wish, my Lord and Master! Torture me, if you want to! You alone are my Lord and Master . . ."

MAHMOUD (*Sensuously ecstatic*): What

a moment to watch! . . . And what about Haj Mustapha?

ᶜURQUB Mustapha! He's some courtier! . . . In he walked, in a fury, to declare that he was the King! We all burst out laughing. Then the Queen took her sash and put it around his neck. Now he's spitting insults and walking on all fours at the end of a leash . . . But where's my Lord?

MAHMOUD You've just left him.

ᶜURQUB Haj Mustapha! Are we all going mad in this game? Where's the real King?

MAHMOUD I've just told you. And you'd better take off this cloak before the jailer gets hold of you.

ᶜURQUB Take it off? No, don't try to confuse me . . . He's my Master, and I know him.

MAHMOUD Our Master, ᶜUrqub. Take it off . . .

ᶜURQUB Have I gone mad enough to leave this party empty-handed?

MAHMOUD Are you trying to sell me my post?

ᶜURQUB *Your* post? *My* Master is the King—why shouldn't I be the Vizier?

MAHMOUD Because he's found you out. He knows you're not real. The jailer's after you now, so let's exchange clothes before he gets here.

ᶜURQUB How much will you pay?

MAHMOUD You shouldn't hope for much.

ᶜURQUB (*Striking his own forehead*): But the girl! . . . She's not part of any deal. I'll sell you the post of Vizier, but not the girl.

MAHMOUD The King gave the girl to the Vizier. So take some money, and don't let your hopes run too high . . . I hear His Majesty coming. Let's go.

ᶜURQUB (*Withdrawing*): There's madness everywhere—in the King's palace as well as in the house of Abu ᶜIzza.

SCENE FIVE, PART FIVE

POSTER: LE ROI C'EST LE ROI. THE ONLY COURSE OPEN TO HIM IS OPPRESSION, AND STILL MORE OPPRESSION.

KING *enters, raging with fury, followed by* EXECUTIONER *and* MAYMUN.

KING Steel! . . . Only steel can protect this throne! This ax shall be my hand, my arm, my heart! My gown and my bed! (*To* EXECUTIONER:) From now on you'll be able to rest!

EXECUTIONER But an Executioner's pleasure is to execute his Master's will . . .

KING From now on the King will execute his own will!

EXECUTIONER Heaven forbid that I should let my Lord and Master get his hands dirty . . .

KING For Kings, nothing cleanses like blood! I shall bathe in it! It shall be my incense and perfume!

EXECUTIONER (*In a faltering voice*): And what will the Executioner do, my Lord?

KING He shall stand at his Lord's side, and prepare the rituals . . . But *when* are they going to attack? The Commander of the City Garrison wants to storm the Palace; the Chief of Police allows plotters to slip between his soft hands . . . No, now is the time to tighten our grip!

MAHMOUD (*Rushing to the side of the* KING): Yes indeed, my Lord! Now is the time! I was lured away from your side this morning by a treacherous trick, but thank God, we've crushed the mutiny! It wasn't the Garrison Commander at all—it was a handful of agitators . . . The town crier will announce to everyone that the plot has been uncovered, and we shall arrest all the suspects—along with anyone else who looks suspicious.

KING There's another measure I want you to take: set up a security organization to watch over the Chief of Police's security organization.

VIZIER A very wise decision, my Lord. It shall be done immediately.

KING And that rascal who was pretending to be Vizier?

VIZIER We'll get him, my Lord.

MAYMUN My Lord, a delegation of prominent citizens wish to have the honor of appearing before Your Majesty.

KING The honor is mine . . . Let them in.

IMAM and SHAHBANDAR May peace be upon our Lord and Master.

KING May peace be upon the Imam and the Head Merchant.

SHAHBANDAR Has the great Vizier told Your Majesty of . . .

VIZIER I'll break the good news. There's no need to tell His Majesty about anything. Since this morning, he has been holding his sceptre with a hand of fire and steel.

KING It was a passing disturbance. But chaos shall be consigned to the dungeons, and the ax shall snuff out every breath that's found to be out of tune.

VIZIER The town crier will tell of the discovery of a plot. People will flock to the Palace to renew pledges of loyalty and support. Other measures, prompt and decisive, will follow.

SHAHBANDAR That's good news!

IMAM Good news, indeed!

KING We must work on the people . . . We must develop their adherence to both exalted principles *and* exalted officials. We are depending on the Imam to draw up new subject matter for the schools, and new material for the preachers and town criers.

IMAM I'd call this telepathy! Exactly what I was about to propose . . . *And* urge!

VIZIER Didn't I tell you? There'll be no more need for demands or delegations. The sceptre is being wielded by a hand of steel! Now to more interesting matters: the gifts, and the celebrations . . .

SHAHBANDAR The gifts are ready. So is everything needed for the celebrations.

VIZIER And on our part, measures shall be taken without delay.

KING *pounds with his sceptre.*

SHAHBANDAR (*On his way with* IMAM *to the door*): Do you find the King's changed?

IMAM Yes. He's become more of a king.

They run out, laughing. Scene freezes.

EPILOGUE

Life returns to scene. Actors appear as in Prologue.

MUSTAPHA (*Walking around, the* QUEEN'*s sash dangling from his neck like a leash*): It's a game, it must be a game . . . I am he, or he is . . . Mirrors, nothing but mirrors, shattered, like my face, into a thousand thousand pieces. Who'll put them together? Where's the Vizier? Where are the Guards? The Slave Women? . . . I am the King! It was a game, I am the King! I am the King! . . . Off goes my seal! Done is my will! . . .

ᶜURQUB No, no . . . ᶜUrqub won't be there to give his help . . .

MUSTAPHA With my face in a thousand thousand pieces . . .

ᶜURQUB Even the money I got for the

Vizier's robes has turned out to be counterfeit . . . I've lost the woman I always dreamed of having for a wife . . . Was this a game, in which I was both spectator and victim, simultaneously? . . . But have I learned a lesson? I'm afraid it might be too late already. I didn't know how to stick to my own kind, and I didn't know how to climb any higher. I'm afraid it might be too late already . . .

MUSTAPHA We played and we played . . . A game . . . Who am I?

UMM ʿIZZA I went for justice, only to have my daughter turned into a slave woman and my husband scandalized and put to public shame. If only I knew where he is . . . This is a game, and I've got my share. But have I learned anything? Yes . . . Perhaps I've learned that they're all a part of one and the same family . . . But so what?

EXECUTIONER (*Shaken and weak*): In this game I was both participant and victim. The King's taken my ax, and I've become dust, a mere shadow . . . What can dust or a shadow learn?

ʿIZZA This was a game that I was dragged into unawares. Now I'm a slave woman in a hideous house. When I lie down, on top of me lie spider webs and a worm, a great, big worm . . . Who is my father? Who is the Vizier? Who is ʿUrqub? Who is the King? . . . I turn around and around, and I don't know anything, except that I'm being crushed between a bed and a worm . . . That's all I know . . . But the moon! Where's the moon? Why has it been extinguished? . . .

MUSTAPHA Let's say it was a game: the King is the King, and I am he . . . I am the King . . .

KING, VIZIER, CHIEF OF POLICE, MAYMUN, *and* EXECUTIONER *now form a group standing downstage left. Behind them stand* SHAHBANDAR, *the* HEAD MERCHANT, *and* SHAYKH TAHA, *the* IMAM, *pulling at puppet strings as they did in the Prologue. Opposite this group stand* ZAHID *and* ʿUBAYD.)

KING A game? It *may* have been a game . . . (*Assumes commanding tone*:) You may not play!

GROUP You may not play . . .

KING You may not fancy!

GROUP You may not fancy . . .

KING You may not imagine!

GROUP You may not imagine . . .

KING You may not dream!

GROUP You may not dream . . .

SHAHBANDAR *and* SHAYKH TAHA *applaud.*

ZAHID Even when a King is exchanged, the only way open to him is more terror and repression.

ʿUBAYD We must wait for the right moment: not a second too early or too late.

ZAHID This *right moment*—is it any nearer now than before?

ʿUBAYD Anyway, it can't be *too* far off . . .

All take off character costumes and begin to take turns in speaking the following lines. Voices rise, and ultimately unite.

History tells
Of a group that got fed up
With misery, hunger, and injustice.
They went into a furious rage.
They slaughtered their King
And ate him.
At first
Some had stomach aches
And others got sick.
But after a while they recovered
And sat down to enjoy life
Without masks or disguises,
Without masks or disguises.

History tells of a group that got
Fed up with misery, hunger,
And injustice. They
Went into a furious rage, they
Slaughtered their King, and ate him.

At first some had stomach
Aches, others got sick,
But after a while they
Recovered, and sat down to
Enjoy life without masks or disguises.

WALID IKHLASI

The Path

Translated by
Olive Kenny
and Thomas G. Ezzy

A story of the unsatisfactory answer to a question concerning migration of ʿAbd Rabbo, who is known as an actor by the name of Abido, and who is still contemplating a means to escape from the path.

The Path (*al-Sirat*) was written in 1975 and published in Damascus in 1976. The first performance took place in Aleppo in December 1977, after which the play was performed by several theatrical groups, both in Syria and in other Arab countries. It is an attempt by the author to throw light on a social reality dominated by hypocrisy and oppression, a reality that compels the main character, Abido, like others in the Arab world, to attempt to walk a narrow path between good and evil, besieged by danger on both sides. Not an action play—there is no single event that produces conflict and thereby change—it examines the way ideas and a mode of expressing them slowly affect the mind of the protagonist and impose a major change on his attitudes and behavior. Because of a constant fluctuation between cunning and stupidity, spontaneity and design, resistance and capitulation, Abido remains unpredictable for the major part of the play. In the last act he surrenders to the forces of the establishment and the secret police and is shown in compete harmony with them. One of the most famous plays in modern Arabic, *The Path* is a successful representation of the crisis of the contemporary Arab writer and artist, who have had to function under totalitarian regimes that have deprived Arabs of political stability.

S.K.J.

THE PATH

THE PLACE:

The events of this semidocumentary play take place between the wings of the theater and its stage, or in other places impossible to designate at present.

THE TIME:

Night and day, and the time in between.

THE CAST:

ʿABD RABBO, who plays the role of the famous actor Abido. A skinny young man devoid of all physical beauty, or love of beauty.

The DIRECTOR of the theatrical company.

The JOURNALIST, a young lady called Salma.

Actors and actresses in various successive roles: masked men—journalists—police—judges—powerful security police—lovers—television advertising and theater actors—critics—prisoners.

COMMENTS:

In the second act of the play the producer has the right to add to or cut out some of the advertising scenes. He may also use colloquial language in these scenes.

THE PATH

ACT ONE

SCENE ONE

One side of the theater stage is quite bare. Suddenly the place is alive with the clamor of boisterous music, like circus music. Two masked men in the form of modern-day devils begin working at something. They are seen to be drawing, rapidly sketching what turns out to be a straight line. One of them sets up a sign which reads: This is the Straight Path. The first man attempts to walk along the line like a tightrope walker, but quickly loses his balance and falls to the right of the line. This action is repeated by the second man, who falls on the left side. They both straighten up and stand aside to watch ᶜABD RABBO, *who enters slowly, in a costume that hides his features. He reads the sign, then stands lost in thought.*

ᶜABD RABBO Here we are facing the Straight Path again. Wherever I turn I'm confronted by this path. Keep your balance and you'll do it. Being balanced within yourself is the best way. Danger, pain, whatever the ordeal, it can be overcome by the measure of equilibrium. (*He walks the line to the end without faltering.*) There! We're to be congratulated on crossing safely. (*He retraces his steps with perfect balance.*) This is the true story (*Hesitating*), or rather the more or less true story of the mendicant of the Most High, ᶜAbd Rabbo son of ᶜAbd Rabbo. I am he, ᶜAbd Rabbo. Whoever requires proof of my claim may ask (*To himself*:) ask whom! (*Forcefully*:) Ask his Lord. (*He crosses the line nimbly.*) I am ᶜAbd Rabbo, known as the simple-minded, or at least that's what my friends in the alley call me. (*Hesitating.*) Did I have friends? Let's say my companions then. Did I have buddies? Hear me, did I have relatives? (*Shouting*:) Those of you who are without friends, acquaintances, or family, remember my name today, tomorrow, and until the judgment day. (*To himself*:) Amen. (*Pulling a bottle of wine from his pouch, he takes a long swig.*) Now then, when we were advised to be silent, we loved, and when we were advised to love, we were silent; if we were silent, we were ordered to kneel. We were silent, we spoke, we loved, we knelt, and we walked. (*A moment of silent thought.*) We walked the Path. (*He walks along the line, correcting his balance as he drinks from the bottle, halting at every step and contemplating.*) Whoever wishes to walk the Path, let him follow me, and whoever doesn't wish to follow it (*Meditating*), let him follow me too. (*He raises the bottle as if drinking a toast to someone.*) There's a cure for people in here. I drink; I'm happy and (*After a moment's hesitation*:) I'm ᶜAbd Rabbo. (*He laughs, then frowns.*) I drink and I'm ᶜAbd Rabbo; I get drunk, therefore I exist. (*Stepping off the line, he takes a swig. Then, as if making a speech*:)

That's how it is. We had nothing to do with the affair, so they deliberately involved us in it and then made us walk the Straight Path. The Straight Path, oh you ... (*As he is advancing and talking, he meets two men hurrying to enter the theater. One is the* DIRECTOR *of the company.*)

DIRECTOR (*Sadly*): Have you heard the terrible news?

ʿABD RABBO Who's died?

DIRECTOR I wish I could die instead of living to see a disaster like this one that's hit us.

ʿABD RABBO So someone has died. (*Shaking hands.*) May you live out your days.

DIRECTOR (*Holding him back*): Where are you going, idiot? I tell you it's a disaster, but no one's died yet. (*Ruthlessly*:) Now you've made me forget what I was going to say.

THE OTHER (*Trying to whisper in* ʿABD RABBO*'s ear*): Here's your chance, you fool.

ʿABD RABBO Take your time, tell me about the disaster, sir. I've finished cleaning the theater.

DIRECTOR But I don't have the time. Time's against us, stupid. Don't you realize that in a short while the hall will be filled? The tickets have been sold and the disaster's almost on us.

ʿABD RABBO Congratulations, sir.

DIRECTOR What do you mean congratulations, you son of a ... (*Suddenly backing off, he humors him*:) You shall definitely help us, Mr. ʿAbd Rabbo ... you gallant fellow.

ʿABD RABBO (*Dumbfounded*): Mr? (*Laughing.*) Mr. ʿAbd Rabbo!

DIRECTOR Are you surprised to hear me address you like that, an artist like you?

ʿABD RABBO (*In amazement*): An artist like me!

DIRECTOR I'll never forget the marvelous monologues you give to the members of the cast backstage.

ʿABD RABBO But they're just for local consumption ... So I ...

DIRECTOR (*Interrupting*): So we're agreed. Let's get down to business.

ʿABD RABBO We're agreed! Right. I told you I'd finished the cleaning. Go and see for yourself.

DIRECTOR (*Laughing*): What cleaning, sir? (*With emphasis*:) You're the one who's going to play the role of the Shaikh in *Horseman of the Desert.*

ʿABD RABBO (*Objecting*): What am I going to act in? *Horseman of the Desert?*

DIRECTOR You're the revered Shaikh, dispenser of justice to all the tribes.

ʿABD RABBO Are you crazy? You expect me to act the part of the main character?

DIRECTOR (*Impetuously*): You're the one who's mad; you don't understand.

THE OTHER Get it into your thick head, ʿAbd Rabbo! Get a grip!

DIRECTOR Don't waste our time, stupid.

THE OTHER The hero fell ill suddenly; his appendix burst.

DIRECTOR And you're going to take his place.

ʿABD RABBO (*Objecting*): You expect me to take the place of the principal star? Who's drunk, you or me?

DIRECTOR There's nothing to it, ʿAbd Rabbo; you'll see.

ʿABD RABBO But I'm not prepared; I don't know my lines. You know only too well that the monologues I entertain you with are impromptu performances. I write them on my sleeve and chant them.

DIRECTOR Don't talk so much. It'll work out.

THE OTHER I'll be hidden behind the big chair in the scene, and all you'll have to do is repeat what I tell you.

DIRECTOR Surely you're smart enough to repeat what's said to you.

ᶜABD RABBO Like a parrot.

DIRECTOR Exactly like a parrot.

ᶜABD RABBO But I'm not a parrot, I'm ᶜAbd Rabbo.

DIRECTOR Mr. ᶜAbd Rabbo.

ᶜABD RABBO Main cleaner of the theater.

DIRECTOR Don't argue with me. I don't have much time and I might kill you, you son of a . . .

ᶜABD RABBO Kill me and there won't be any play.

DIRECTOR (*Jubilantly*): I knew you'd agree.

ᶜABD RABBO Who said so? Did I say I would?

DIRECTOR (*Grabbing him*): You son of a . . .

ᶜABD RABBO There won't be a play, because the police will arrest the murderer.

DIRECTOR What murderer?

ᶜABD RABBO Didn't you say you'd kill me? You're the murderer.

DIRECTOR (*Impetuously*): You scamp, I really will end up murdering you!

ᶜABD RABBO Now we're agreed. You've just given me my proper name. (*Seriously*:) I'll try to save your failing company. (*The* DIRECTOR *kisses him on the head.*) I'll accept on one condition.

DIRECTOR (*Eagerly*): I agree to all your conditions. But hurry up and put on your makeup.

ᶜABD RABBO I want to charge the battery.

DIRECTOR What battery? Is this the time for charging batteries, you . . . (*Smiling*:) sir.

ᶜABD RABBO (*Drinking*): With the aid of this marvel drink we face the world.

DIRECTOR (*Leaving the place*): I won't forget the way you helped us out like this.

THE OTHER (*Leaving*): I'm with you to the end.

ᶜABD RABBO (*Alone and intoxicated*): I'm Mr. ᶜAbd Rabbo, performing in the one and only *Horseman of the Desert*. Applaud my eloquence. My fluency will leave them stunned, and make the foolish crowd cry. (*Drinks from the bottle.*)

DARKNESS

SCENE TWO

Part of a stage scene for the play Horseman of the Desert. *Open curtains separate this area from an invisible hall. Central to the scene is a huge chair on which ᶜAbd Rabbo sits crosslegged, dressed like a venerable shaikh. The prompter is concealed behind the chair. A guard and influential people are to one side of the scene. Singers and musicians are visible or concealed. A singer opens out into a song that so delights the shaikh that he begins to sway to it, disregarding his station in life. Meanwhile the prompter cautions him to calm down and conform to his position in the play. A young horseman enters. The singing stops, much to ᶜAbd Rabbo's consternation. He sits up and finds that the approaching young man has reached the center of the stage.*

HORSEMAN Peace be upon the exalted shaikh.

PROMPTER And the peace and mercy of God be upon the horseman.

ᶜABD RABBO (*Angrily*): If you hadn't greeted me before you started speaking . . .

PROMPTER (*Quickly*): And the peace and mercy of God be upon the horseman.

HORSEMAN (*Suddenly realizing his fellow actor's situation, repeats*): Peace be upon the exalted shaikh.

ᶜABD RABBO (*Impetuously*): We understand, brother, you said greetings and peace and we say greetings and peace to you. Let's listen to the music, man.

The hall bursts into uproarious laughter. ʿABD RABBO *turns to the singer and asks him to resume.*

ʿABD RABBO Go on with your singing, my dear.

The hall roars with laughter again. The DIRECTOR *appears from the wing, points, and the curtain is drawn. He makes for* ʿABD RABBO *and grabs him by the neck.*

DIRECTOR So much for you, you idiot. Now look what you've done. Didn't I tell you only to repeat what you heard from the prompter?

ʿABD RABBO The idiot spoiled that lovely singing for me. I'll kill him if he does it again!

DIRECTOR You lunatic, I'll kill you if you leave the part again! Do you want to ruin the company? If that's what you're trying to do, I'll see you dead, I swear it!

ʿABD RABBO (*Grasping the truth of the threat*): I promise you I won't listen to the singing.

While the DIRECTOR *returns inside to give instructions for the show to begin again,* ʿABD RABBO *prepares himself by taking a swig. The curtain lifts to reveal the original setting.* ʿABD RABBO, *forgetting himself, sways to the rhythm of the song. The* HORSEMAN *enters and the singing stops.*

HORSEMAN Peace be upon the exalted shaikh.

PROMPTER And the peace and mercy of God be upon the horseman.

ʿABD RABBO (*Stammering*): And on the peace be the horseman.

Laughter in the hall.

PROMPTER The peace and mercy of God be upon the horseman, dummy!

ʿABD RABBO (*Quickly*): The peace and mercy of God be upon the horseman, dummy!

Laughter in the hall.

PROMPTER Don't you know how to answer a greeting, you imbecile?

ʿABD RABBO Don't you know how to answer a greeting, you imbecile?

Laughter in the hall.

HORSEMAN (*Confused, he tries to begin again*): Peace be upon the exalted shaikh.

ʿABD RABBO And peace be upon you, worthy son, come in, by the Great God, come in.

The hall roars with laughter.

PROMPTER God damn you, you scamp!

ʿABD RABBO (*Sticking to his orders*): God damn you, you scamp!

The hall roars with laughter.

PROMPTER (*Tearing his hair in exasperation*): I'm telling you, and peace be upon the horseman!

ʿABD RABBO I'm telling you, and peace be upon the horseman!

The hall surges with laughter. The DIRECTOR *attempts to lower the curtain, but voices and clapping prevent him from doing so; whereupon* ʿABD RABBO *takes off his headdress and the rest of his makeup and costume and throws them to the floor.*

HORSEMAN Peace be upon the exalted shaikh.

ʿABD RABBO This is the last time I'll play a shaikh in the desert (*Clapping*) or in the city (*Clapping*). (*To himself:*) Who would have thought a tramp like me would be elevated to the role of a venerable shaikh? (*Clapping.*) I wouldn't be any good even as one of the shaikh's guards. (*Clapping.*) (*Looking up,* ʿABD RABBO *notices that he has attracted the attention of the admiring audience and tries to escape, but the audience's protests prevent him. He comes to a halt and addresses the audience*:) Ladies and gentlemen. (*Stammering.*) Good evening. (*Clapping.*) I'm called ʿAbd Rabbo. You won't know me, as I'm only a cleaner here, a theater stagehand. (*Clapping.*) I'll tell you frankly, I've been forced to assume the role of an exalted shaikh, and act out the part, and not only that, but to play the part in the desert. I swear I know nothing of the desert. (*Calling*:) Oh, horseman! (*To the audience*:) Ask the horseman. (*The* HORSEMAN *appears from backstage, disturbed.*)

HORSEMAN (*Reverting to his role*): Peace be upon the exalted shaikh.

ʿABD RABBO (*Impetuously*): Peace be upon the shaikh; peace be upon the shaikh! What do you want? I'm tired of your greetings. Come on, let me know what you want. Let's get these preliminaries over with. *The* PROMPTER *creeps back to his place to take up his role.*

PROMPTER And the peace and mercy of God be upon the horseman.

ʿABD RABBO *grabs the* PROMPTER *and pulls him out of his place.*

ʿABD RABBO Aren't you going to stop this crazy whispering of yours? Leave us alone. I want to reach an understanding with this man. Get out and let me say what I want. (*Clapping.*) Go or I'll kill you, you spy. (*The* PROMPTER *exits.*) Ladies and gentlemen, we've got rid of the main cause of the disturbance. (*Turning around, he sees the* HORSEMAN *still standing in the same place.*) Welcome; so what is it you want, brother?

HORSEMAN (*Getting into his role again*): The savage gypsy tribes are gathering on our borders, oh exalted shaikh.

ʿABD RABBO And what have I to do with the gypsies?

HORSEMAN (*Hesitatingly*): The savage gypsy tribes are gathering on our borders, oh exalted shaikh.

ʿABD RABBO Let the gypsies gather.

HORSEMAN (*Confused; however, an indication from the* DIRECTOR *instructs him to carry on*): But they may attack us, oh exalted one, if we remain indifferent, and then we'll lose our grazing lands.

ʿABD RABBO By God, I don't have a horse, or land either.

HORSEMAN (*Repeating*): But they may attack us, oh exalted one, if we remain indifferent, and then we'll lose our grazing lands.

ʿABD RABBO (*Looks to the* DIRECTOR, *who waves to him threateningly to carry on*): Aren't you a horseman who can cut off a hair with the edge of his sword?

HORSEMAN (*Bowing*): I am one of your generals.

ʿABD RABBO God forbid, brother. (*Laughter in the hall.*)

HORSEMAN (*Repeating the previous script*): They may attack us, oh exalted one, if we remain indifferent, and then we'll lose our grazing lands.

ʿABD RABBO So you go and destroy them.

HORSEMAN I'm waiting for a sign from you.

ʿABD RABBO Give us the sign.

HORSEMAN What about the council, your excellency? Won't they confer with you in the war tent?

ʿABD RABBO (*Impatiently*): You're making a mountain out of a molehill. If you want to fight, go ahead.

HORSEMAN And what about the desert traditions?

ʿABD RABBO (*Interrupting*): You and the desert traditions can go to the nearest (*Thinking*:) to the nearest stinking stream (*Emphatically*:) and drink from it. (*Laughter in the hall.*)

HORSEMAN (*He tries to leave, but the* DIRECTOR *signals to him to stay*): I'll give my opinion in the war council, then.

ʿABD RABBO (*Walking around the* HORSEMAN, *thinking and scrutinizing him*): I've often seen you in this city. Tell me, horseman.

HORSEMAN (*Bewildered*): What shall I tell you?

ʿABD RABBO Aren't you the one who owns a big house on the eastern borders?

HORSEMAN Perhaps.

ʿABD RABBO And aren't you the one who owns a green strip of date palms and fruit trees?

HORSEMAN A gift from God. My father left it to me and I've looked after it.

ʿABD RABBO There . . . now we know the truth. If you're afraid for your property, horseman, go and defend it by yourself.

HORSEMAN The danger doesn't simply threaten my house and grazing lands; it threatens all our lives.

ʿABD RABBO What have our lives to do with a personal problem of yours?

HORSEMAN But it concerns everyone, your excellency, sir.

ʿABD RABBO What kind of lie do you want to make me believe! Do you intend me to sacrifice my poor men to protect your interests?

HORSEMAN But if the gypsies cross our frontiers they'll kill and steal.

ʿABD RABBO And why not? They're hungry, brother.

HORSEMAN They're always hungry.

ʿABD RABBO That's the reason they raid and attack horsemen.

HORSEMAN So shall we wait for them to attack first, so that we can attack them afterward?

ʿABD RABBO Feed them.

HORSEMAN (*Disapproving*): Feed them!

ʿABD RABBO Fill their stomachs; stuff their mouths with food. You'll soon find they'll keep the peace.

HORSEMAN How can we feed them?

ʿABD RABBO With God's bounty. His earth is vast.

HORSEMAN And where is God's bounty?

ʿABD RABBO You'll find it all around your big house.

HORSEMAN Are you suggesting I share my wealth with them?

ʿABD RABBO Yes, do it, before they make you share hellfire.

HORSEMAN I'm afraid I don't understand.

ʿABD RABBO I'll make you understand. (*Taking off his sandal, he rushes at the actor, who takes flight.*) You son of a . . . (*To the crowd*:) He wants to start a war, the son of a . . . I'll sack him and turn his sword into a broomstick. He'll be a straw horseman, I'll make him even forget his name. (*He drinks from the bottle.*) Here's health to the poor! (*Loud clapping.* ʿABD RABBO *is cheered while the* DIRECTOR *of the company struggles to close the curtain.*)

DARKNESS

SCENE THREE

Backstage, two JOURNALISTS *are embracing* ʿABD RABBO, *who appears drunk rather than intoxicated with the effects of his theatrical success. A young lady* JOURNALIST *looks on and takes photographs. On the other side, the* DIRECTOR *surveys the scene with astonishment.*

JOURNALIST 1 It was clear from the first moment that you were going to be the star of the season.

ᶜABD RABBO The olive season.

JOURNALIST 2 (*Visualizing*): Birth of a Great Comedy Star. That's the headline I'll use.

ᶜABD RABBO What about the address of your new house?

JOURNALIST 1 I've never seen an audience so pleased with an actor as I did tonight. You've amazing talent.

ᶜABD RABBO It's true, I have amazing talent in emptying bottles.

Passing the bottle around and getting no response to his invitation, he drinks.

JOURNALIST 2 We'd like to interview you at length, sir.

ᶜABD RABBO Or in breadth.

JOURNALIST 1 (*Takes a photograph*): These will be the pictures of the season.

ᶜABD RABBO I'd rather you took a picture of my backside. It's more eloquent.

JOURNALIST 2 Have you any previous experience in acting?

ᶜABD RABBO Once at most.

JOURNALIST 2 I knew it.

ᶜABD RABBO I played the part of the thwarted lover.

JOURNALIST 1 Where? With what company?

ᶜABD RABBO No, under the balcony.

JOURNALIST 1 Romeo and Juliet!

ᶜABD RABBO The role of ᶜAbd Rabbo, a poor man on earth, with a beautiful lady who to this day doesn't know who ᶜAbd Rabbo is.

JOURNALIST 2 Could we have full details about your life?

ᶜABD RABBO By all means, provided you agree to one condition.

JOURNALIST 2 What's that?

ᶜABD RABBO Not to write about any of it!

They laugh. One of them takes another picture of him.

JOURNALIST 2 My heavens, there are no limits to your wit.

ᶜABD RABBO Everything has its limits. The country has its boundaries.

JOURNALIST 1 Where and when were you born?

ᶜABD RABBO I was born on the day the last happy man died, and the moon hid his face.

JOURNALIST 2 (*Exchanging looks with his companion as though he had stumbled on a piece of treasure*): You grew up in artistic surroundings, of course.

ᶜABD RABBO Of course. My late father was a connoisseur of the arts.

JOURNALIST 1 What's the relationship between your personal life and art?

ᶜABD RABBO The same relation as a cat has with a mouse.

JOURNALIST 1 I don't quite understand.

ᶜABD RABBO Do you really want to understand?

JOURNALIST 1 That's my job.

ᶜABD RABBO Then have a drink; charge the battery. (*He offers him the bottle.*)

JOURNALIST 1 Thanks, but I don't drink on the job.

ᶜABD RABBO Send in your resignation and then have a drink.

JOURNALIST 2 We've noticed, Mr. Abido . . .

ᶜABD RABBO (*Objecting*): Abido!

JOURNALIST 1 Your professional name.

ʿABD RABBO You want to change my name?

JOURNALIST 2 ʿAbd Rabbo's a compound name which doesn't suit a great comedian like you.

ʿABD RABBO I'm as happy with my name, brother, as I'm satisfied with you having only one stomach.

JOURNALIST 2 Mr. Abido. (*Drawing back as* ʿABD RABBO *looks at him angrily.*) Mr. ʿAbd Rabbo, what are your future plans?

ʿABD RABBO To get better results from my work.

JOURNALIST 1 You mean in relation to the theater, or in other projects you're turning over in your mind?

ʿABD RABBO I'm more concerned with what I'm turning over in my hand.

JOURNALIST 1 I don't understand?

ʿABD RABBO The project of cleaning, of course.

JOURNALIST 2 Cleaning the arts!

ʿABD RABBO No, cleaning the theater.

JOURNALIST 1 Is the theater (*Hesitating*) not clean? I mean is it dirty?

ʿABD RABBO It's obvious that after every show dirt will have gathered.

JOURNALIST 2 And where does the dirt usually gather?

ʿABD RABBO Look around you.

JOURNALIST 1 (*Laughing as he catches on*): We noticed you were hard on the horseman because he owns a big house and gardens.

ʿABD RABBO (*Seriously*): Do you really want my opinion?

JOURNALIST 1 Very much so.

ʿABD RABBO And will you really take it seriously?

JOURNALIST 1 We're all ears.

ʿABD RABBO No one ever came by wealth honestly.

The two JOURNALISTS *sit stunned. The* DIRECTOR *of the company hurries to intervene.*

DIRECTOR Would you care to hear some news of great importance?

JOURNALISTS Certainly.

DIRECTOR My friend, Mr. Abido. (*Hugs* ʿABD RABBO.) I should like to announce to our distinguished audience news that they will be the first to hear.

ʿABD RABBO I suppose he's going to announce I'm sacked.

DIRECTOR It'll be the event of the season.

ʿABD RABBO (*Finishing*): Write, "Dirty Theater's Main Cleaner Sacked."

DIRECTOR (*Proudly*): Mr. Abido will be the star of the forthcoming production.

ʿABD RABBO One of the stars at noon is what I'll see. May God protect you from seeing them.

JOURNALIST 1 (*To* ʿABD RABBO): You're a deep one, Mr. Abido. You didn't tell us that.

ʿABD RABBO (*To the* DIRECTOR): And who's going to clean the theater for you?

DIRECTOR God forgive you, man. A talented artist like you will cleanse the human heart of grief.

ʿABD RABBO That's wonderful! Hurray!

DIRECTOR Go ahead and announce it . . . The star of the season, beyond all shadow of doubt, is Abido.

ʿABD RABBO (*To himself*): They're still determined to make me forget my name. Let's call him Abido . . . Fareedu, Huwaydu.

An actor enters reading a slip of paper he is holding.

ACTOR (*Derisively*): My God, the director of television requests a personal interview. (*Dramatically:*) May God protect him, with ʿAbd Rabbo!

ʿABD RABBO My friends are over the moon with joy. Soon I'll be face to face with the director of television, the lord of color, the terror of the world!

The director of television enters holding out his hand by way of a greeting to ʿABD RABBO, *who draws back cautiously.*

DARKNESS

SCENE FOUR

The set represents part of a television studio. There is no talking, but constant movement. By way of preparation, cameras are being placed in position, and the PRODUCER *is giving instructions to the actors.* ʿABD RABBO *in the disguise of a donkey receives instructions from the* PRODUCER. *The other actors—the* JUDGE, *the* MERCHANT, *the* POOR MAN, *and the* POLICEMAN *are preparing for action. The lady* ANNOUNCER *appears.*

PRODUCER Stand by. Lights. Signature tune.

ANNOUNCER In a moment, children, you'll be seeing a new episode in the series "The Accused Donkey." Starring in the series is your favorite actor, Abido. (ʿABD RABBO *brays like a donkey, this being a standard introduction for each episode.*)

Music, then the POLICEMAN *appears driving* ʿABD RABBO, *who is kicking at the air in protest.*

POLICEMAN A stubborn donkey. (*Beating him.*) By God, we'll make you sorry for what you've done. (*The donkey stops, so he scolds him.*) Approach his honor the judge. (*To the* JUDGE, *who is sitting cross-legged in an attitude of profound wisdom:*) Here he is, your honor.

JUDGE The charge?

POLICEMAN He'll tell you himself, your honor. (*He jerks* ʿABD RABBO.) Confess, you criminal.

JUDGE Come on, confess, Mr. Donkey. I have many important cases on hand.

ʿABD RABBO Ask the policeman; he knows the truth.

POLICEMAN What this donkey has done, your honor . . .

JUDGE (*Interrupting*): I would ask you to keep within the bounds of the law, officer. The accused is innocent until he's pronounced guilty. (*To* ʿABD RABBO:) State your case, my son; we're here to establish justice, not to enforce injustice.

POLICEMAN (*Reproaching* ʿABD RABBO): Hurry up, confess.

ʿABD RABBO I'm only a poor miserable donkey, your honor. I've never been in a court of law before, and I've never in my life stood in front of a venerable man like yourself, so please excuse my confusion and shortcomings, your honor.

POLICEMAN And who is it who brings an animal like yourself into the presence of a distinguished man like his honor the judge?

ʿABD RABBO The one who accused me falsely.

POLICEMAN And am I going to accuse you falsely, you . . . (*Controlling himself.*) Your honor, there are witnesses on behalf of the prosecution.

JUDGE First witness.

The MERCHANT *advances arrogantly.*

MERCHANT Your worship, this donkey can only be regarded as a murderer. He was on the point of killing me with premeditated intent and purpose. His baser self would have induced him to kill a noble, peace-loving citizen and distinguished merchant who wouldn't think of harming an ant, and pays his charity and alms tax at their proper times, and performs the ritual prayers at the times prescribed, and . . .

JUDGE (*Interrupting the* MERCHANT *with a sign and directing the proceedings to* ʿABD RABBO): What have you to say, Mr. Donkey, about this accusation?

ʿABD RABBO Do you believe, your honor, that a poor donkey is capable of murder? Have you ever before come across a donkey who kills?

MERCHANT You're more than capable of murder, you . . .

JUDGE (*Interrupting, speaks to the* MERCHANT): What's your evidence?

MERCHANT Your honor, I hired this donkey with my honestly earned money to convey me to my business. My firm, your worship, has a good reputation. Ask the people in the market about it. Little profit, but an honest living. No sooner had I mounted this donkey than he rose up on his two hind feet in the manner of a thoroughbred horse. On my second attempt to mount, he threw me off his back. He was about to trample me underfoot with the intention of premeditated murder. (*Moaning.*) Oh my poor bones, worn out in the earning of an honest living!

JUDGE What does the accused have to say by way of defense?

ʿABD RABBO I admit I refused to allow this respected gentleman to mount me.

MERCHANT Didn't I pay the price set by law?

JUDGE So you confess that you threw this respected gentleman to the ground.

ʿABD RABBO No, I just refused to have a man like him on my back.

JUDGE (*Astonished*): Why then (*Sternly*:) the charge of murder is justified!

ʿABD RABBO Your honor, I never for a moment contemplated disobeying the law.

JUDGE So why did you throw this respected gentleman to the ground?

ʿABD RABBO Because he isn't worthy of respect, your honor.

JUDGE What grounds do you have for making such a suggestion about this man?

ʿABD RABBO Shall I speak the truth, your honor?

JUDGE And nothing but the truth.

ʿABD RABBO This merchant isn't honest. He robs people by cornering their food and other necessities, hoarding his unlawful gains without fear of conscience or . . .

JUDGE (*Interrupting*): And who set you up as a judge over people, donkey?

ʿABD RABBO I'm not a judge, your honor, but I'm free to decide who shall ride me. Take this man, for example. (*Pointing to the* POOR MAN, *who steps in front of the camera.*) He is of humble origins, but good. Have I ever demanded payment from you, brother?

POOR MAN I swear, your honor, that this good donkey has never once asked me for payment.

JUDGE (*Rebuking him*): No one summoned you as a witness. Stay where you are.

ʿABD RABBO But surely children, the poor, and the well-intentioned deserve assistance?

JUDGE (*Becoming angry and losing his dignity*): Do you want to change the world order according to the humor of your back or your ears, you wretched donkey?

MERCHANT (*Tearfully but defiantly*): I want my rights, your honor.

POLICEMAN This creature is a menace to our society, your honor.

POOR MAN On the contrary, he's a benefit to society, your honor.

JUDGE The charge is quite plain. Moreover, it's a more than proven charge, as to which our law is clear.

ʿABD RABBO I don't plead for pardon, your honor, since I've committed no crime. But I ask you in the name of justice to avail yourself of this ready opportunity to impose a penalty on this avaricious merchant in view of the countless charges that can be brought against him.

JUDGE (*So angry he rises*): And you aggravate the case against you by attempting to influence the impartiality of the judiciary. You will go to prison; I sentence you to a year's imprisonment without fodder.

ʿABD RABBO I may die.

POLICEMAN Long live justice!

MERCHANT Long live justice at your judicial hands!

ANNOUNCER (*Advancing from the crowd*): And in the next episode we'll continue this story of "The Accused Donkey."

DARKNESS

SCENE FIVE

The events in this scene take place in ʿABD RABBO*'s dressing room. The* JOURNALIST *Salma takes a picture of him while he prepares for the stage.*

JOURNALIST The children love Abido.

ʿABD RABBO They love the donkey first and the accused second.

JOURNALIST But I can't tell you how much they love you.

ʿABD RABBO What about the adults?

JOURNALIST They like serious actors.

ʿABD RABBO But I don't know how to be serious.

JOURNALIST Who said so?

ʿABD RABBO You all say so. Your press talks about the comedian Abido.

JOURNALIST The gravity of laughter outweighs that of tears.

ʿABD RABBO You're satisfied with me then?

JOURNALIST As long as you remain serious like this, we're with you all the way.

ʿABD RABBO And if I change!

JOURNALIST You'll still have our support.

ʿABD RABBO And if I'm neither one nor the other?

JOURNALIST We'll be against you.

ʿABD RABBO You too!

JOURNALIST I'm just a member of my profession.

ʿABD RABBO Even you, Salma?

JOURNALIST Even me . . . (*Briefly searching her memory*) ʿAbd Rabbo.

ʿABD RABBO Thank you, you're a great comfort to me.

JOURNALIST Take care of yourself . . . We'll stay behind you.

After applying his makeup, ʿABD RABBO *gets up and approaches the* JOURNALIST. *He looks earnestly into her eyes.*

ʿABD RABBO I'll promise one thing . . . I'll take care of myself as long as you're with me.

JOURNALIST (*Emotionally*): Thank you. (*Alertly*:) It's time . . . Come on. (*They leave.*)

DARKNESS

SCENE SIX

The setting represents a stage scene from which the curtain has been drawn. We see an open square in a small, quiet city. The DIRECTOR *appears from the wings and makes an announcement over the microphone.*

DIRECTOR Ladies and gentlemen, in a few minutes your favorite actor, Abido, will come on stage (*Clapping*) in a new play, "The Lovers Struggle for Life." (*Clapping.*) It also gives us great pleasure to announce that the famous actor Abido will continue his theatrical performances for another month, ignoring innumerable commitments, in order to show his devotion to you, his loving audience. (*Clapping.*)

Overture music to the play. ʿABD RABBO *enters to the applause of the audience. His appearance arouses pity as he is seen to be carrying his lute. He contemplates the hall intently, searching for someone.*

ʿABD RABBO Coo, coo . . . hou, hou . . . Hey, people of this city. (*Waits for an answer to his call.*) Even the cats are on holiday. (*Looks up at the sky.*) Where are the birds? (*Sits on the curb.*) Where have the people gone? (*He sniffs the air to detect a scent.*) There's no smell of food. A stingy city. Perhaps the place is abandoned or else the people eat canned food. (*Calling out:*) Hey, you people in there behind the walls! Come out, peace and safety be upon you! (*Questioning:*) What are these people afraid of? It's as if a plague had struck the city.

After some minutes he begins to fiddle with the strings to amuse himself. Meanwhile a pretty young GIRL *appears and stands at a distance contemplating him. He doesn't see her picking up on the rhythm. When he does see her he stops playing, dazzled by her beauty.*

GIRL Why have you stopped, uncle?

ʿABD RABBO (*Astonished*): Are you a human being?

GIRL What do you think I am? A jinn?

ʿABD RABBO How could anyone believe that a girl of your beauty could have human parents?

GIRL (*Approaching a little nearer*): Who are you? You're not from this city.

ʿABD RABBO I belong to this land. In fact that land (*Pointing into the distance*).

GIRL We all belong to this land.

ʿABD RABBO You have your roots. I have none.

GIRL (*Approaching him good-humoredly*): Then you're a jinn, a demonic being.

ʿABD RABBO When I saw how splendid you are, my roots began to grow, and I wished I lived in this city.

GIRL (*Downcast*): Don't expect any good from this city.

ʿABD RABBO (*Standing up*): Your presence alone is sufficient to show what good is. (*Approaches her.*) I was hoping for some food and drink, but seeing you has quite fulfilled my needs.

GIRL What a truly charming man you are.

ʿABD RABBO How unlucky I am not to have known you before.

GIRL Go on with your playing.

ʿABD RABBO Did you like it?

GIRL Play for me and I'll dance for you.

ʿABD RABBO (*Intoxicated with joy*): I'll play for you! I won't stop till it kills me. (*He begins playing while she sways coquettishly. The playing continues for a short while, then gradually diminishes.*)

ʿABD RABBO And if I sing for you?

GIRL I'll listen to you.

ʿABD RABBO (*Starts to sing*):

> I'll ransom him if he keeps his love
> or loses it.
> King of my heart, what else should I
> do?

GIRL I can't think of anyone like you in this city.

ʿABD RABBO I can't think of another like you in this world.

GIRL (*Overcome with sadness*): The city's cold.

ʿABD RABBO You make it warm.

GIRL And yet it knows nothing but hate and the hoarding of money.

ʿABD RABBO It's a cold world. Half of it's plunged in darkness, but you're the shining half.

GIRL (*Pleading*): I wish you'd stay in the city. Perhaps you'd manage to change its harshness!

ʿABD RABBO I wish you'd stay there in front of me and warm the bones of a man who's been a wanderer without end.

GIRL (*Hopefully*): Stay with us.

ʿABD RABBO Stay with you! I promise you I won't leave this city, this very place, as long as you're here.

GIRL Who knows, you may manage to earn a living by keeping these miserable people happy.

ʿABD RABBO I only want to win your affection; that will make up for everything else.

A YOUTH *appears from a corner of the place. The* GIRL *approaches him with evident delight. They meet like lovers, around whom* ʿABD RABBO *hovers with misgivings.*

GIRL (*To ʿAbd Rabbo*): This is my sweetheart. You'll like him.

ʿABD RABBO (*Regretfully*): Your sweetheart. (*Restraining himself.*) Why shouldn't I like him? I'll like him.

GIRL Play some of your tunes for us. It's so long since there's been any tenderness in this city.

YOUTH (*Contemplating* ʿABD RABBO): A wandering singer?

ʿABD RABBO A wandering wretch.

GIRL (*To the* YOUTH): I'd like to introduce you to the man who's brought joy to this miserable place.

YOUTH (*Holding out his hand to greet* ʿABD RABBO, *who occupies himself with the pretense of putting his lute in its case*): Welcome.

GIRL Where are you going?

ʿABD RABBO God's world is wide.

GIRL Are you leaving us? (ʿABD RABBO *is on the point of going.*) You can't just slink away like that!

YOUTH Why don't you stay with us?

ʿABD RABBO A wanderer doesn't know how to stay rooted in one place . . . The time and the place are both against me.

GIRL Someone like you is loved by the time, the place, and the people.

ʿABD RABBO This was a dream from which I've awakened. Everything's over now. I have to go back.

GIRL Where are you going back to?

ʿABD RABBO To the place all the homeless come from, those without a roof or loved ones.

GIRL There's a roof here . . . and loved ones.

ʿABD RABBO I never said I didn't care for you.

GIRL Stay with us then.

ʿABD RABBO (*Hesitating, then drawing his lute out of its case*): There's no harm in stopping at a place where there's a flower (*Looking at the* YOUTH) or two.

GIRL (*Joyfully*): You're the one who made the flowers open. Your coming may be of help to two unfortunate lovers. Look at us.

ʿABD RABBO And what possible use could a poor middle-aged man be to two lively young people?

GIRL Don't be misled by youth.

YOUTH The elders of the city lay traps for us.

GIRL No one blesses our love!

ʿABD RABBO Who's the idiot who doesn't bless this love?

YOUTH Her father . . . her relatives, the mean-spirited people of this city.

GIRL The age-old problem: she's rich and he's poor.

ʿABD RABBO The disease of this globe.

YOUTH What globe?

ʿABD RABBO The one you're standing on. Earth's solid, but its people are frail.

YOUTH What's the answer then?

ʿABD RABBO The problems of love can only be treated by a further growth of love.

GIRL (*Kisses* ʿABD RABBO*'s forehead in her joy*): Play for me. I want to dance and fly. I love the air of this city now.

ʿABD RABBO *plays for the* GIRL, *while the* YOUTH *fixes his eyes on the* GIRL *as she dances.* ʿABD RABBO *appears to watch her rather sadly, but soon the radiance of his smile reveals his warmth toward the couple, and his melody grows more lively. Suddenly the* GIRL *stops dancing and stares in alarm at a stout, sullen man—her* FATHER.

FATHER (*Yelling at the* YOUTH): Have you come back again? Didn't I forbid you to come near my daughter? (*He lunges at the* YOUTH, *whom* ʿABD RABBO *protects.*) I'll kill you, you coward, if ever you dare to approach her again or talk to her.

ʿABD RABBO Take it easy, brother. It's not the end of the world.

FATHER (*To his daughter*): Who's this foreign busybody?

GIRL (*Hesitatingly*): He's . . .

ʿABD RABBO (*With persistent boldness*): I am the liberating king in a land of fettered feet.

FATHER What's this madman talking about?

ʿABD RABBO I'm saying what only the wise can understand.

FATHER I don't understand a word. (*He looks at* ʿABD RABBO*'s squalid appearance.*) Who is this person who presumes to be familiar with his superiors?

GIRL Father, he's our guest and also a stranger.

ʿABD RABBO I became a stranger when I saw your malice toward two lovers.

FATHER This scoundrel had better get out of these parts, before I call my men.

ʿABD RABBO Men! So I've been privileged to visit a land of men. I can't wait to see their manly fists engage the gentle face of love.

FATHER (*Lunges angrily at* ʿABD RABBO): I'll teach you manners, you impudent lout.

ʿABD RABBO (*Flourishing the lute*): Teach manners to this wretched lute. Cut its strings if you like. That's more in your style.

FATHER (*Furious*): I'll kill this creature if he doesn't get out of my sight.

ʿABD RABBO (*Coldly*): I'll get out of your sight when you show a little compassion and give your blessing to these two lovers.

FATHER (*Lunges at* ʿABD RABBO, *but the* GIRL *intervenes to protect him*): You'd protect him, would you, you little hussy?

ʿABD RABBO She's protecting you from the anger that I haven't unleashed yet.

GIRL This isn't right, father. The man's a guest.

FATHER More like a snake in the grass.

ʿABD RABBO Have I squirted venom in your face, man? (*To the young people:*) Stand together, stay close, I can see men over there coming toward us, men who've never learned how to smile. (*The* YOUTH *stands close to the* GIRL.)

FATHER (*Angrily turning on his heel*):

I'll come back with my supporters and that'll be the end of you, you . . . (*To the* YOUTH:) The end of you, too. (*To the* GIRL:) And I'll teach you some manners.

ʿABD RABBO And we'll teach you how to love, you mean-spirited wretch. (*Clapping.*) (*The curtain falls.*)

DARKNESS

SCENE SEVEN

The scene takes place in the wings. ʿABD RABBO, *seated crosslegged on a chair, is relaxed and paying no attention to the advertising* AGENT *who has come to negotiate with him. A* BOY *stands on call to assist* ʿABD RABBO, *massage his neck, or bring him a glass of lemonade.*

AGENT Mr. Abido, I can't understand the reason for your refusal.

ʿABD RABBO What does it matter to me whether you understand or you only pretend to . . .

AGENT I beg you, sir.

ʿABD RABBO Do you want me to accept?

AGENT (*Eagerly*): That's what I'm here for, sir. Heavens, of course that's what I want.

ʿABD RABBO Then don't bring up the subject again.

AGENT You're shaking the company's confidence in me.

ʿABD RABBO (*Interrupting*): May God never shake you up.

AGENT (*Repeating his sentence*): You're shaking the company's confidence in me. I've been commissioned to have you sign the contract this evening.

ʿABD RABBO Are you sure you want me to sign the contract?

AGENT (*Full of hope, reveals the contract*): That's what I'd like you to do, sir.

ʿABD RABBO Then tear it up.

AGENT (*In desperation*): Doesn't the payment come up to your expectations? I'm authorized to raise the price.

ʿABD RABBO Rewards are in God's hands, brother.

AGENT We'll double it.

ʿABD RABBO (*Hastily*): Do you want us to resolve this business?

AGENT That's what I'm here for, sir.

ʿABD RABBO Well, I refuse. Let's talk about your affairs instead. Are you married?

AGENT I'm not just married; I have a wife, six children, and a mother to support.

ʿABD RABBO If I had a mother, I'd send her to you.

AGENT Thank you, sir. But to return to the contract, be so good, darling of the people, as to agree.

ʿABD RABBO (*Continuing*): And do you believe in this job of yours?

AGENT It gives me a living, and a reason for existing, too.

ʿABD RABBO You told me you direct a visual advertising company for television and other associated interests.

AGENT I'm just a junior employee in the company.

ʿABD RABBO And do you believe in the benefits of advertising?

AGENT (*With the repetitious manner of a student who has memorized his lesson*): We offer a twofold service, to the good consumer and the go-ahead manufacturer. We find a market for our national products and one for our merchants' imports, too. (*Sighing*:) The advertisement will only take a few moments of your time. I beg you.

ʿABD RABBO And what did you tell me about the advertisement you requested?

AGENT (*Delighted*): Manufactured goods, sir, products. And the rest will follow. One for underwear, the other for carbonated drinks. Your appearance in the advertisement will ensure sales, seeing that you're the people's idol.

ʿABD RABBO You too!

AGENT Of course I like you.

ʿABD RABBO Look, Mr. Advertising Man. Because people idolize me, I don't want to swindle them.

AGENT Swindle them. God forbid! Who said anything about that? You have my word of honor.

ʿABD RABBO (*Interrupting*): Wait, I'll accept.

AGENT You're a great fellow.

ʿABD RABBO But on one condition.

AGENT You have a free rein, idol of the people!

ʿABD RABBO It's the only condition.

AGENT Go ahead.

ʿABD RABBO I want to give my frank opinion of the products I'll advertise.

AGENT Say what you wish. (*Thinking.*) And what is your frank opinion?

ʿABD RABBO I want to say your underwear's bad, uncomfortable, and made from synthetic fabrics. Your company doesn't care about anything but profit.

AGENT (*Interrupting*): Sir!

ʿABD RABBO (*Interrupting*): As for your pop, the chemical mixtures make the people who drink it sick. I found a fly in one of your bottles myself; in fact I found two.

AGENT Aren't you exaggerating a little, sir?

ʿABD RABBO To hell with you, your advertisements, and your companies.

AGENT We'll triple the fee.

ʿABD RABBO And I refuse any offer.

AGENT (*Gathering up his stuff*): This is insufferable! What does he have to do with underwear or mineral water? (*Muttering as he leaves.*)

BOY Did you hear what that man said?

ʿABD RABBO He said I was an imbecile.

BOY He was scoffing at you? Aren't you going to do anything?

ʿABD RABBO He's only telling the truth you . . . idiot.

DARKNESS

SCENE EIGHT

The set represents part of a television studio. The scene takes place in a prison, where ʿABD RABBO, *still playing the role of the accused donkey, is with three other prisoners. The lady* ANNOUNCER *appears.*

ANNOUNCER Today, children, we bring you a new episode in the series "The Accused Donkey," with your favorite actor, Abido.

ʿABD RABBO *brays, as at the beginning of each episode. Music follows, and the actors take up their positions.* ʿABD RABBO, *with his face to the wall, kicks up his hind feet and brays.*

PRISONER 1 I don't understand what's up with this donkey.

PRISONER 2 Shut up, he might hear you.

PRISONER 3 (*Calling*): Hey, brother, Mr. Donkey.

PRISONER 1 He won't answer you. He's been like this all day.

PRISONER 2 He'll get tired in the end and join in. Prison's so boring.

PRISONER 3 Hey, Mr. Donkey, aren't you going to tell us why they put you in prison? (ʿABD RABBO *doesn't respond.*) Do you want me to tell you why I'm here? (ʿABD RABBO *still doesn't respond.*)

PRISONER 2 Go ahead, go on, tell us.

PRISONER 3 My story is that I hit a policeman on the nose and his blood got mixed up with his snot. (*Everyone laughs except* ʿABD RABBO.) So they beat me until I couldn't think any more. I was sentenced to three months, and I've one more to serve. Nothing's worth getting upset over.

PRISONER 2 I'm new here, like our friend, the donkey. Ten days of my year have gone by, and they've seemed an eternity. We robbed a fat man on the bus. A dozen policemen moved heaven and earth investigating it, and then came the venerable judge. And the worst of it was, the man had hardly anything in his wallet, the cheat! Not even enough to feed the children for two days.

PRISONER 1 I'll be here for two years, and that's a blessing as far as I'm concerned. It means I'm free of having to look after a huge family. A mother, paternal aunt, wife, ten children, and three cats. My charge is ludicrous. I borrowed my colleagues' money at work, with every intention of repaying them. But when they called me a thief, I went along with it. They sentenced me, and I went along with that, too.

PRISONER 3 Those are our stories; so what's yours, new boy?

ʿABD RABBO (*Shouting weakly*): I'm hungry.

PRISONER 3 Were you jailed because you were hungry?

ʿABD RABBO No, I'm hungry because I'm in prison.

PRISONER 2 I don't understand.

ʿABD RABBO And you'll never understand anything.

PRISONER 1 Don't treat us like idiots.

ʿABD RABBO May God protect your reason; but I could never make you understand my problem.

PRISONER 2 Tell us and we'll understand.

ʿABD RABBO I said my piece before, and the judge didn't understand.

PRISONER 3 We'll shut up, then.

PRISONER 1 So you can talk.

ʿABD RABBO I'd rather talk about your problems than dwell on my own.

PRISONER 1 We're OK, thank God.

ʿABD RABBO You're happy, then.

PRISONER 1 Yes, thank God.

ʿABD RABBO That's the problem. You like being in prison.

PRISONER 3 No one's happy in prison.

ʿABD RABBO So the prospect of getting out pleases you.

PRISONER 3 There's the truth of it.

PRISONER 1 And our only hope.

ʿABD RABBO No one's thought of anything else. (*He becomes perplexed.*) Would you allow a donkey like me to tell you what's wrong with you?

PRISONER 2 (*Angrily*): What's this donkey saying?

PRISONER 3 Let's listen to him. Go on, tell us the rest, Mr. Donkey.

ʿABD RABBO Hasn't any one of you given a moment's thought as to why you're in prison?

PRISONER 1 Fate.

PRISONER 2 Luck.

PRISONER 3 Whatever happens to us, it's our destiny.

ʿABD RABBO (*Angrily*): By God, if I were the judge here, I'd double the length of your sentence.

PRISONER 3 Are you out of your mind?

ʿABD RABBO No. But I'm amazed you've given no thought to why you're in prison.

PRISONER 2 I know. I'm a thief.

ʿABD RABBO Why did you steal?

PRISONER 2 (*Hesitating*): Because it was a habit. (*After a moment*:) And because the children were hungry.

ʿABD RABBO And why are the children hungry?

PRISONER 1 Because they've no food.

PRISONER 2 It's their lot in life.

ʿABD RABBO What do you mean by lot! Why haven't the children the necessary food? Surely that's the question. Do you realize why I was put in prison? You don't? I'll tell you. Because I refused to carry, on my back, one of those merchants whose avarice leaves children hungry.

PRISONER 3 (*Whispering*): Heavens, this donkey really does have a brain.

PRISONER 2 What can we do?

ʿABD RABBO Do you want to know what to do?

PRISONERS Go on, tell us.

ʿABD RABBO No . . . I'm not going to tell you.

PRISONERS Come on . . . please.

ʿABD RABBO (*Preparing to go to sleep*): I'll talk to you . . . but not now because I want to get a little sleep. Good night.

ANNOUNCER For those of you watching, this ends another episode of "The Accused Donkey." We say goodnight and hope you'll join us again next week.

DARKNESS

SCENE NINE

The events take place backstage in ʿABD RABBO*'s dressing room. He is sitting on a cushion, crosslegged like a magician or prince.* JOURNALISTS *and* CRITICS *are scattered about the place. The* JOURNALIST *Salma has taken up a position a good way off. The* DIRECTOR *stands beside* ʿABD RABBO*, addressing those present.*

DIRECTOR We have the pleasure of welcoming distinguished critics and members of the press to this artistic and intellectual conference. The star of our theater and the arts, Mr. Abido, is ready to answer any questions. Please keep them brief, as Mr. Abido has a busy schedule.

CRITIC 1 In recent months you've been working extremely hard in the theater and on television. Are there any signs that you're now beginning to go downhill?

ʿABD RABBO This is the age of going downhill. We all decline, but I'm declining less than any of you.

CRITIC 1 Does that mean things aren't going as well as you anticipated artistically?

ʿABD RABBO The financial aspect's remunerative, but the artistic side's impoverished.

JOURNALIST You're making a criticism of art in our country, then?

ʿABD RABBO No, I'm criticizing the artistic side.

JOURNALIST 1 But isn't the artist Abido part of the artistic life of this country?

ʿABD RABBO I'm the bad part of it, sir.

JOURNALIST 1 Isn't that just being modest?

ʿABD RABBO Modesty isn't a usual characteristic of the artist.

JOURNALIST 1 Then why are you the bad part?

ʿABD RABBO Because I still haven't said all that should be said.

JOURNALIST 1 But you say things no one else has dared to say, and in addition the people approve of you and love you.

ʿABD RABBO What I've done is only a beginning.

JOURNALIST 2 You've unsheathed your weapons, and they're sharp and exacting.

ʿABD RABBO Only a glancing edge has

been shown so far. That's all I've been allowed to do, gentlemen.

JOURNALIST 2 What more do you expect to do? You've exposed human wrong, attacked errors, and said this is futile and that's unlawful.

ʿABD RABBO But I haven't as yet provided a solution. The things I've pointed to as futile haven't changed. Whatever I attempt is like pissing in the wind.

CRITIC 1 I take it from what you're saying that you'd like to be a guide to society.

ʿABD RABBO Believe me, my friend, I can't even guide myself.

JOURNALIST 1 You want to be a politician.

ʿABD RABBO I want to be ethical.

CRITIC 2 (*Cunningly*): Then there's a distinction between politics and ethics.

ʿABD RABBO You can't compare things at opposite poles.

DIRECTOR (*Intervening*): May I ask you, on behalf of my dear friend and illustrious actor Abido, to switch your questions to more important subjects? Why not ask him about his plans for the future?

JOURNALIST 1 What are your plans for the future?

ʿABD RABBO Not to act.

JOURNALIST 2 (*Astonished*): Don't you wish to remain an artist?

ʿABD RABBO Who said I didn't? I want to be an artist.

CRITIC 1 And not act!

ʿABD RABBO I want to be myself.

JOURNALIST 1 And who are you now?

ʿABD RABBO I'm a man called ʿAbd Rabbo. (*Sarcastically*:) Send my greetings to all the imposters and clowns on the stage, and in the audience as well, and wish them constant good health. We're all well here and we send you this song.*

CRITIC 1 (*Interrupting*): Is this part of a new play?

ʿABD RABBO (*Turns toward the* CRITIC *seriously*): Let me tell you something, Mr. Critic. You and I are part of a conspiracy against the theater, art, people, history, geography, national information, and chemistry. You write what you please (*Pointing to his head*) about what you please (*Pointing to his palm*). I don't blame you. Inflation's rampant, salaries lose their appeal, the public are gullible, the actors criticize, and the critics act.

DIRECTOR (*Intervening*): Gentlemen, no one's inquired about Abido's personal life.

JOURNALIST 1 Every artist has his emotional side, but we don't know anything of your life.

ʿABD RABBO (*Returning to his seat*): Write this down: I love innocence, so I adore children, and I love childhood because it's still uncorrupted. I like women who generate compassion and human warmth. I hate women who exchange their sex for bank accounts. For that reason I haven't married. (*He takes a ®eeting look at the woman* JOURNALIST.) Does that meet with your approval? I'll tell you the truth: women have no desire to look at me. Who could imagine an intelligent woman looking at a handsome man like me? (Laughter.) Besides that, I make a habit of bathing in buffalo milk to keep my skin clear in imitation of famous actresses. But as I haven't found the pure milk, I more often have to resort to water. That's cleanliness, gentlemen: merchants clean out pockets and agents clean out minds. (*Shouting calmly*:) I'd like to play the role of a merchant who's honest, but I can't find a model to copy. (*Imitating a folk story teller*:) Al-Jurjany, gentlemen—

*This is an imitation of radio announcements sent by expatriates to their friends and families.

he was, I believe, an Arab writer who died (of frustration, I think) probably a thousand years ago—says the following:

> "There is nothing but ignorance these days.
> A climber ascends only to reach depravity.
> Here am I sitting on a platform
> And they rise to the top of the ladder."

What do you think about our friend al-Jurjany's saying?

The scene becomes frozen, until brought to life by a CRITIC.

CRITIC 1 There's one more question.

JOURNALIST 1 Two more questions.

ʿABD RABBO In fact there are many more questions, and I'm the one who wishes to pose them. Why do we lie? Why do we play act? Why do we deceive and let ourselves be deceived? What's the use of all this clowning?

WOMAN JOURNALIST But we haven't seen you clowning.

ʿABD RABBO What's the use of one voice in a forest of loud noises that drown out everything? (*Seriously*:) Gentlemen, the interview is over. (*He gets down off the cushion and, in leaving, is overtaken by the director of the company.*)

DARKNESS

SCENE TEN

Events of this scene take place in an official office, indicating that it is the premises of the authority in charge of investigation. The place is simple and austere: a table, a floodlight, wooden chairs. Two men acting as ASSISTANTS *in the office receive* ʿABD RABBO, *who enters apprehensively.*

ASSISTANT 1 Come in . . . come in, Mr. Abido.

The other ASSISTANT *invites him to sit down on a chair. No sooner has he done so than he pulls it out from under him, making him fall on the floor. The two* ASSISTANTS *burst out laughing.*

ASSISTANT 2 Did the trick amuse you? (ʿABD RABBO *says nothing.*) It's not so very different from one of your stage plays.

ʿABD RABBO The first act's over. When shall we start the second?

ASSISTANT 1 (*Offers a cigarette to* ʿABD RABBO, *who takes it and thanks him.*) You smoke, don't you?

ʿABD RABBO We smoke, and drink to intoxication.

ʿABD RABBO *lights the cigarette, which explodes in his face, causing the* ASSISTANTS *to burst out laughing.*

ASSISTANT 2 A great trick.

ʿABD RABBO Has the second act finished?

ASSISTANT 1 Plays have three acts, don't they?

ʿABD RABBO That's a bad theatrical habit. Most stretch to five.

ASSISTANT 2 We hope it will be five and not three.

ʿABD RABBO And I wish to limit it to two acts.

ASSISTANT 1 Aren't you happy here?

ʿABD RABBO (*Sarcastically*): Does that make sense? Such a great reception and such smiling faces?

ASSISTANT 2 What will you have to drink?

ʿABD RABBO We have no objection to wine.

ASSISTANT 1 Don't you see it's an official office, sir?

ʿABD RABBO So just a little wine without alcohol.

ASSISTANT 2 We'll bring you what you want. But first tell us, what's the latest joke?

ʿABD RABBO A man's standing on the stage (*The two listen to him attentively*) when two men arrive. One's dim-witted and the other's an idiot. (*The two* ASSISTANTS *show visible signs of annoyance.*) They say to him, "Come with us for a stroll." So he accompanies them. (*He stops.*)

ASSISTANTS So what happens next?

ʿABD RABBO Nothing. They give him a cigarette that explodes noisily. (*He laughs loudly, but no one joins him.*)

ASSISTANT 1 Is that a joke?

ʿABD RABBO And is this the way to entertain a guest?

ASSISTANT 2 You're here to answer our questions, not ask them.

ʿABD RABBO Good. Now the last act's begun. I'm ready.

ASSISTANT 1 Your full name.

ʿABD RABBO With no titles. ʿAbd Rabbo junior, son of ʿAbd Rabbo senior.

ASSISTANT 2 Profession.

ʿABD RABBO An actor by chance.

ASSISTANT 2 Can't you talk seriously just for once?

ʿABD RABBO I swear to you by this holy place that I'm telling the truth.

ASSISTANT 1 (*Grabbing* ʿABD RABBO *by the collar*): You're making fun of us, you clown.

ʿABD RABBO (*Offering no resistance*): I swear by your gentle fingertips that I'm not laughing at you.

ASSISTANT 1 (*Squeezing cruelly*): I'll show you how we treat perjurers.

ʿABD RABBO I've learned enough already. Would you be so good as to release my neck?

ASSISTANT 1 This clown's going to drive me mad.

ASSISTANT 2 Let him go. He'll regret what he's done.

ʿABD RABBO Yes, I'm really sorry for what I did, gentlemen.

ASSISTANT 1 You were really making fun of us.

ʿABD RABBO I'm regretting the fact that I'm here with you.

ASSISTANT 2 Do you consider you're here at your own choice?

ʿABD RABBO If I've no choice, then I'm forced to be here.

ASSISTANT 2 You've hit the nail on the head, smart guy.

ʿABD RABBO Shall I say that I'm detained?

The CHIEF *enters suddenly.*

CHIEF What's all this nonsense? You're our guest, Mr. Abido.

ʿABD RABBO (*To himself*): A new peacock.

CHIEF I apologize for being late. Have these two fools been annoying you? (*He motions to the two* ASSISTANTS, *who leave.*)

ʿABD RABBO Thanks, you came just at the right time.

CHIEF Anyhow, welcome. What will you have to drink?

ʿABD RABBO I'm fine, thanks. Your men have already offered me their hospitality.

CHIEF So let's talk. You don't have any objections to speaking to me?

ʿABD RABBO I don't mind talking to you.

CHIEF What's your opinion of democracy?

ʿABD RABBO I'm not very well up on technical terms.

CHIEF (*Somewhat angrily*): Do you believe in it?

ᶜABD RABBO Who doesn't believe in it?

CHIEF And what is democracy according to you?

ᶜABD RABBO I'm practically illiterate, sir. But I've heard it said that it's government by the people for the people. Sometimes they say it's the climate in which freedom grows. And they also say . . .

CHIEF (*Interrupting*): But what do you say?

ᶜABD RABBO Do you care a fig about my opinion . . . sir?

CHIEF Your opinion affects a large number of people in the theater, and on the television screen and the radio.

ᶜABD RABBO You're exaggerating my importance, sir.

CHIEF (*Importunately serious*): What is your honest opinion of democracy and freedom? Can't we speak directly?

ᶜABD RABBO You direct me.

CHIEF What is your view of someone who exploits democratic government and the freedom of speech that entails?

ᶜABD RABBO He should be punished like a student who hasn't prepared his lesson.

CHIEF And will that kind of punishment be enough for someone who misuses the most sacred concepts of the ages?

ᶜABD RABBO Beat him on the nape of the neck until he learns his lesson, or the contrary, sir.

CHIEF We have better means at our disposal to deal with those who violate the law.

ᶜABD RABBO What's my role now? Have I become a disciplinary consultant?

CHIEF (*Like a former teacher*): Don't you see that the individual members of society, and those on its fringes, are like a compact building? Whoever's instrumental in pulling down part of it threatens the collapse of the whole.

ᶜABD RABBO I agree with you.

CHIEF And that a certain class of society, like merchants, for example, at least the more honest ones, form a part of this integral structure.

ᶜABD RABBO A part, sir.

CHIEF And that the police are the protective part incorporated into that society.

ᶜABD RABBO A part, sir.

CHIEF So why your continual attacks and recriminations against certain classes and ideas that are continually at work for the betterment of all members of society?

ᶜABD RABBO It's a part of the action, a part.

CHIEF (*Stirred to anger*): You've used art as a tool for your own evil ends. (*Taking* ᶜABD RABBO *unawares*:) Tell me, who are you?

ᶜABD RABBO (*Standing up*): ᶜAbd Rabbo junior, son of ᶜAbd Rabbo senior.

CHIEF What I want to know is your real identity; what party do you represent, when do you meet, and where?

ᶜABD RABBO (*With droll politeness*): I am citizen ᶜAbd Rabbo. (*In the manner of a radio announcer*:) I represent myself; I have no party, and I ask you to end this investigation as quickly as possible so that I may return to my work. The curtain is about to be raised on tonight's performance.

CHIEF Take it easy. I must, unfortunately, advise you to forget about the stage from now on.

ᶜABD RABBO (*Sitting down in surrender*): If I must contemplate a different future, have you more suitable work, sir?

CHIEF (*Calmly*): As I see it, you have a choice, Mr. Abido; you either return to your work or you don't.

ᶜABD RABBO Do you want the truth? I want to return . . .

CHIEF (*Quickly*): Then confess. Who are you, and what party do you represent?

ʿABD RABBO (*Resuming his former position*): I am citizen ʿAbd Rabbo; I represent myself and not a party; I send my greeting to . . .

CHIEF (*Interrupting angrily*): Can't you be serious for a minute?

ʿABD RABBO Two or even three minutes, sir.

CHIEF (*Maliciously*): Do you know how we punish those who attempt to subvert the state?

ʿABD RABBO It can only be with hell and a bad end.

CHIEF Something far worse than hell and damnation.

ʿABD RABBO Vitriol?

CHIEF First comes loss of the means of livelihood.

ʿABD RABBO It's better to be sentenced to death than lose your job.

CHIEF Are we coming to an understanding?

ʿABD RABBO No more work on the radio or television. Closing the theater. If that's not cutting off my livelihood!

CHIEF That's the first stage.

ʿABD RABBO And what's the second?

CHIEF Documents to establish cooperation with enemies of the state.

ʿABD RABBO That's grounds for a death sentence.

CHIEF The final part entails life imprisonment in one of the cells.

ʿABD RABBO We've heard of those, sir. The place is air conditioned with love and kindness. Hotels that cherish their guests.

CHIEF Since you're informed of the penalty, why this obstinacy?

ʿABD RABBO I'm a social animal; I don't know how to be stubborn. What do you wish me to do, sir?

CHIEF You're a great actor, so join our ranks.

ʿABD RABBO My every breath is with you, sir.

CHIEF If you're with us, the sky's the limit for you.

ʿABD RABBO And if not?

CHIEF You'll be so winded you'll forget your own name.

ʿABD RABBO In fact I have forgotten it, sir.

CHIEF (*Holding out his hand to confirm their pact*): We're agreed, then.

ʿABD RABBO What are we agreeing to?

CHIEF That in future you'll be more positive with regard to people's interests, regulations, and traditions. You understand the rest.

ʿABD RABBO We do, sir.

CHIEF When you've established your good intentions, you can return to your public.

ʿABD RABBO Really?

CHIEF (*Making fun*): No one ever came by wealth honestly, eh?

ʿABD RABBO But they do, they do!

CHIEF (*In farewell*): I shall recommend a special rate for you for television work.

ʿABD RABBO Who said we'd raised our price! The Ministry of Food may get angry.

CHIEF (*Shaking hands*): That's settled, then.

ʿABD RABBO The agreement's irrevocable. God is my witness to what I say. May the flag of unity flutter above our heads until God's decrees are fulfilled. Amen.

CHIEF (*Leaning toward him confidentially*): I trust you'll treat our pact with confidence, and that not a word will escape your lips.

ʿABD RABBO It will be more secret than anything you've ever done, sir. (*He bows in salutation like a corporal.*)

DARKNESS

SCENE ELEVEN

The set is bare. ʿABD RABBO *is alone, soliloquizing.*

ʿABD RABBO Who said everything's wrong with this world? They're kind people who let you choose between prison and money. Surely only a fool would choose prison. (*Silence.*) What did I do to end up going through this kind of ordeal? Things were better when we used to sweep the theater and draw the stage curtains. What shall I say to my fans now? Shall I tell them merchants are honest men and deceit leads to a better world? (*To himself*:) Deceit really does lead to a better world. Frauds, agents, and pimps are the big shots. Who'd deny that? (*After a moment's silence*:) Shall I become a martyr? But why, and for whose sake? If I go to prison, there's nothing there but brutality. Why should I be beaten?

If you're smart, ʿAbd Rabbo, you'll think about the inspector's words. What can the artist do?

What can I do?

People crave amusement, and I can entertain them so that even the most stony-faced will lose their inhibitions; the respectable woman will take off her wig; the old man's dentures will fall out; the police officer will lose his dignified bearing; the merchant will devote part of his income to charitable organizations; the hypocrites will say they can't compare with me; and the liars will feel embarrassed by their own honesty. Let me die with the Philistines!

The peace and mercy of God be upon you.

He falls upon his knees, weeping.

DARKNESS

ACT TWO

SCENE ONE

The events of this scene take place in a photographer's studio, where proofs for small business advertising films are being taken. Movable stage decorations form the various sets. Present are the DIRECTOR *of the company, who has become a shareholder in the film corporation, the lady* ASSISTANT *to the producer, and the actors who are going to alternate in playing the secondary roles in the films.*

DIRECTOR I believe we're ready for action. (*To his* ASSISTANT:) Is that right, my dear?

ASSISTANT The sets are all arranged.

PHOTOGRAPHER The films are loaded.

ASSISTANT We may be able to shoot all the inside scenes today.

DIRECTOR Yes, we really must shoot all the inside scenes today. (*Joyfully*:) I can hardly believe our luck.

ASSISTANT Thanks to Abido, things are going marvelously.

DIRECTOR Abido's a dear friend of mine. If only he'd started in this business earlier, we'd have been rich in no time.

ASSISTANT Why did he refuse to make advertising films before?

DIRECTOR Bullheaded. But he's loosened up now. We've had contracts for making films showered on our company, hundreds of them. This man's a real magician. The people are crazy about him. He tells them, "I like the biscuits," and the markets are sold out of them. He says, "Milk is black," and they believe it. (*Anxiously*:) He's late, isn't he?

ASSISTANT He's putting the last touches to his makeup. He'll be here in a moment.

DIRECTOR (*Anxiously*): Our time's worth gold.

*ᶜ*ABD RABBO *enters, accompanied by the* JOURNALIST *Salma.*

ᶜABD RABBO (*Commenting*): And our speech is worth silver. (*To the* ASSISTANT:) How many shots have we today? (*To the* JOURNALIST:) They'll say a dozen.

ASSISTANT About that many.

DIRECTOR Scores of them, sir. Scores!

JOURNALIST (*Surprised*): Do you shoot more than one film a day?

ᶜABD RABBO We shoot, we act, we eat and sleep, all at the same time. This is the age of technology. (*To all of them*:) To work, you champions of the fine arts! (*He plunges headlong into work.*)

FIRST FILM

The backdrop represents the enlarged cover of a magazine depicting a seminaked woman. Seated in front of the cover, a YOUNG MAN, *who manifests signs of stupidity, is thumbing through the magazine.* ᶜABD RABBO, *who is playing the role of the father, approaches him, dressed in robes that resemble a priest's. He watches things out of the corner of his eye and makes for his son as though in the act of catching him redhanded.*

ᶜABD RABBO I've caught you in the act, you wicked boy. I'll straighten you out, reading a magazine when you should be studying!

STUPID YOUNG MAN (*Con□dently*): I love it because it teaches me life's secrets.

ᶜABD RABBO (*As the camera comes into closeup, he examines the magazine with manifest pleasure*): *Naked Virtue* magazine! Beautiful! (*To the audience*:) Buy it, it's the greatest! (*Taking a step forward.*) They enjoy this magazine from the Atlantic Ocean to the Persian Gulf. A magazine of art, love, and youth. (*He turns the pages of the magazine without looking at them.*) *Naked Virtue* teaches us the art of living. Don't forget to get your copy when it comes out every week. (*Whispering*:) And beware of the black market because everyone, without exception, is looking for *Naked Virtue* magazine. (*Smiling.*) With greetings from the editor-in-chief, Dr. A. L. Fadil.

The shooting ends. ᶜABD RABBO *throws the magazine down and approaches the journalist, while preparations begin for the second film.*

ᶜABD RABBO (*Sarcastically*): *Naked Virtue* teaches us the art of living. Do you read it, my dear? Don't forget to look at the horoscope. It'll promise you wealth and love.

JOURNALIST I've never had any wish to read it. It's colors are so glaring.

ᶜABD RABBO To hell with them and their nude magazine!

He vanishes backstage to be met by the ASSISTANT, *who will act in the next film.*

DARKNESS

SECOND FILM

A huge backdrop representing a nature scene upon which is written in conspicuous lettering: "No to dirt. Yes to Freedom Detergent." An actress sits on a chair in an exaggeratedly emotional pose, while the spotlight plays over her amorous face. The camera moves in on ᶜABD RABBO, *who appears in a swimming costume, showing off his muscles to his sweetheart.*

ᶜABD RABBO Your love makes me strong. (*He addresses an imaginary moon*:) Heaven be my witness that I love you deeply. (*He kneels at her feet.*) I place my heart and future in your hands. (*The* GIRL *acts coyly.*) I love you, I really do.

GIRL I don't believe it.

ᶜABD RABBO What shall I swear by?

(*Stands up.*) I promise you I'm offering you the greatest love that's ever been!

GIRL I don't believe it.

ʿABD RABBO What proof do you want, apple of my heart and eye?

GIRL (*Coquettishly*): Will you really give me what I ask?

ʿABD RABBO You can ask for the moon or the stars, and I'll give them to you.

GIRL (*Standing beside him*): I don't want the moon or the stars. I want Freedom Detergent.

ʿABD RABBO *kneels submissively. Then they both become fixed.*

VOICE Yes, Freedom Detergent. Don't just use it to clean your clothes. It cleans everything. Use it once, you'll love it forever. You'll find it everywhere, because it's like freedom.

The shooting ends. Getting up in disgust, ʿABD RABBO *approaches the* JOURNALIST. *Meanwhile preparations are being made for the third film.*

JOURNALIST (*Clapping*): What a long advertisement.

ʿABD RABBO It's because they pay more. (*Sarcastically*:) Just one lira and you clean up dirt. It's as if our lives depended on their filthy soap!

JOURNALIST It seems it does.

ʿABD RABBO I don't understand these clever advertising executives. They persuade everyone to buy imported powders and upset everyone around them with all their noise and tricks.

JOURNALIST (*Joking*): But you were totally sincere. People will love this Freedom Soap.

ʿABD RABBO (*Preparing to go in*): Even you, Salma. (*He disappears.*)

DARKNESS

THIRD FILM

A background representing a voluminous book and various other educational aids. ʿABD RABBO *is one of* THE THREE *men dressed like young schoolboys.*

THE THREE Don't be sad. Don't despair. Put fear to one side and start your studies again.

ʿABD RABBO Thanks to the Private Righteous Schools, I've begun my life anew.

THE THREE Take up a course with Private Righteous Schools, and you too can find new confidence.

ʿABD RABBO Is mathematics your weak subject?

THE THREE Go to the Private Righteous Schools.

ʿABD RABBO Are you poor in languages and science?

THE THREE Go to the Private Righteous Schools.

ʿABD RABBO Knowledge just grows and the fees are modest.

THE THREE The Private Righteous Schools will see your children get ahead. They're the best in education.

The shooting ends. ʿABD RABBO *approaches the* JOURNALIST. *Meanwhile preparations are made for the fourth film.* ʿABD RABBO *is still dressed as a pupil.*

ʿABD RABBO An intelligent boy like me, under the tutelage of the Private Righteous Schools, can't possibly get tired.

JOURNALIST They seem to be exceptional schools.

ʿABD RABBO They've gathered into their fold the cream of the rising generation, the builders of a super civilization built on pills.

JOURNALIST They seem to be exceptional schools.

ʿABD RABBO And I proposed a badge of honor for them.

JOURNALIST No, you put the seal of approval on them.

DIRECTOR (*Entering the argument*): That isn't our business, Miss. We're paid to dress up facts.

ʿABD RABBO Cosmetic surgeons. Now for the next set. (*Disappears.*)

DARKNESS

FOURTH FILM

A backdrop on which a huge shoe has been drawn. A POLICEMAN *is directing traffic.* ʿABD RABBO *crosses the street carrying a pair of shoes around his neck.*

VOICE Our shoes, with their strength and elegance, have knocked at the door of history.

ʿABD RABBO (*Comes to a standstill, an expression of delight on his face*): Life has no meaning for me without plastic King Shoes.

POLICEMAN The height of civilized taste.

ʿABD RABBO (*To the crowd*): Only plastic King Shoes can withstand time.

The shooting ends.

ʿABD RABBO ʿAbd Rabbo, popularly known as Abido, is going to make advertising films for the plastic shoes of the people of the republic. We're in the service of shoes. We're here to pay tribute to shoes of all sizes. (*The* JOURNALIST *claps and* ʿABD RABBO *bows to her in deference.*) Abido's scientific advertising films salute the gleaming shoes of the press. (*To the* DIRECTOR:) Is there anything else?

DIRECTOR We'll take a break.

DARKNESS

SCENE TWO

The events of this scene take place in ʿABD RABBO*'s room. The* DIRECTOR *of the company and the* CHIEF *investigator are waiting in the middle of the place. As the* DIRECTOR *looks at his watch, he hears the applause of the crowd in the hall, indicating that the performance is finished.* ʿABD RABBO, *entering a few minutes later in his stage clothes, is taken aback by the two seated there.*

DIRECTOR Surprise, eh?

ʿABD RABBO (*Staring at the* DIRECTOR): I thought for a moment I'd come back to a place I won't easily forget.

CHIEF I should like to have attended the play, but my time, as you know . . .

ʿABD RABBO Is limited, sir. I realize that. But do us the honor of sitting down for a while.

CHIEF (*Handing over an envelope to* ʿABD RABBO): Here's something that will make you happy.

ʿABD RABBO Notice of exemption from taxes.

CHIEF Something more important. Aren't you going to open it? Go ahead.

DIRECTOR Read it, my friend, go on. This man comes bringing nothing but blessings.

CHIEF The Chamber of Commerce has paid for four complete performances and the Building Contractors Association for seven.

DIRECTOR A dozen performances.

ʿABD RABBO A sudden new awareness in the arts. I'm optimistic for the future of artistic appreciation. How did you discover that, sir?

CHIEF We didn't need to discover anything, my dear fellow. We have our own ways and means of supporting people like yourself.

ʿABD RABBO May you continue with your patronage. Through you, art will be revived.

CHIEF I knew you'd be delighted, my dear Abido.

ʿABD RABBO It's your presence that affords us such joy.

CHIEF (*Makes to leave*): You'll find the checks for the prepaid performances inside the envelope. I'll leave it to you to schedule the dates. So, until we meet again.

DIRECTOR (*Accompanies the* CHIEF *as far as the door*): God keep you a benefactor of the arts, sir. Your kindness will not be forgotten. (*He returns from escorting the* CHIEF.) That's action for you, ʿAbd Rabbo.

ʿABD RABBO (*Clapping*): May God keep you a supporter of the arts, sir.

ʿABD RABBO *takes out a bottle to pour himself a drink.*

DIRECTOR A really fine man.

ʿABD RABBO Fine and elegant.

The JOURNALIST *Salma enters.* ʿABD RABBO *raises his glass in a toast.*

ʿABD RABBO Health to the mobile press.

JOURNALIST (*Copying him*): Health to the stationary stage. (*To the* DIRECTOR:) How are things?

DIRECTOR Great. To tell you the truth, they've never been better.

ʿABD RABBO We're the beneficiaries of an angel's kindness.

DIRECTOR Art's on the rise again. The old dark days are over, and a new sun has risen. (*To the* JOURNALIST:) Listen, Miss, any new play we present now will be worth a dozen of our past performances. And why? Demand, performances, rewards. It's no secret that the responsible authorities have nominated Abido for a glittering artistic prize. (*To* ʿABD RABBO:) Isn't that wonderful news?

JOURNALIST Congratulations.

ʿABD RABBO (*Without emotion*): May God grant a long life to those responsible for the decision. And God damn the irresponsible ones. (*Takes a sip.*) I drink to those responsible people, and to those who wonder, and those who'll ask questions from now until judgment day.

DIRECTOR (*Happily*): Your success in the arts has been rapid. One day people will say, "Lucky like Abido."

ʿABD RABBO Cheers to the lucky people, spread over the map of the world like exclamation marks.

JOURNALIST Or question marks.

ʿABD RABBO Or the commas between clauses.

JOURNALIST Or the clauses between the commas.

ʿABD RABBO Or the commas between the periods.

JOURNALIST Or the periods between . . .

DIRECTOR (*Interrupting*): Hey, this kind of talk's driving me crazy. I'm not going to stay here a minute longer, or I might change into an exclamation between two periods!

When he starts leaving, ʿABD RABBO *yells at him in earnest.*

ʿABD RABBO Who gave you permission to leave?

DIRECTOR (*Perplexed*): Goodnight. (*Questioning*:) Are you serious?

ʿABD RABBO I've never been as serious in my life as I am at this moment.

DIRECTOR (*Trying to regain his composure*): Have you forgotten who I am? I'm the one who directs the company . . . I direct your work.

ʿABD RABBO And that means that you must bow in deference to me.

DIRECTOR Have you lost your mind? (*Pretending to be hearty*:) You're joking as always.

ʿABD RABBO (*Yelling*): I'm telling you to bow in deference to the chief source of your prosperity.

DIRECTOR The chief source of my prosperity! Have you forgotten, ʿAbd Rabbo?

ʿABD RABBO The artist Abido. I won't allow anyone to address me except by my real name.

DIRECTOR ʿAbd Rabbo's your real name.

ʿABD RABBO You reactionary, you're talking about a past that's dead. (*Shouting*:) Bow to me or . . .

DIRECTOR And if I don't?

ʿABD RABBO Everything will collapse over your head and mine.

DIRECTOR (*Struggling with his perplexity, he looks at the* JOURNALIST): Is this alright for you?

ʿABD RABBO (*Suddenly*): It will satisfy us. Now go.

DIRECTOR (*To himself*): A mad world. He's contemplating ruining everything. (*He goes out, mumbling unintelligibly.*)

ʿABD RABBO (*Bursts out laughing*): Did you see, my dear . . . (*After a moment*:) how terrified he was?

JOURNALIST You were cruel. What's happened to you?

ʿABD RABBO I'm the despised citizen ʿAbd Rabbo, who was treated with a cruelty he's learned to direct at others.

JOURNALIST An unjustified rebellion.

ʿABD RABBO How do you explain this undermining of the mind and soul? They're depraving my soul, trying to set my ideas in a mold.

JOURNALIST You chose the way you went.

ʿABD RABBO (*Laughing bitterly*): Do you really believe that, my dear?

JOURNALIST (*Approaching him*): What's happened to you then? You've changed overnight from the enemy of greed to the advocate of greed and avarice.

ʿABD RABBO Would you like to know the truth?

JOURNALIST What good will that do, when you're making commercials by the dozen?

ʿABD RABBO Even you, Salma!

JOURNALIST I'm with you.

ʿABD RABBO What do you think about things in general?

JOURNALIST Does what I think matter to you?

ʿABD RABBO (*Crumbling emotionally*): Your opinion's fundamental. Don't you understand?

JOURNALIST I don't see anything.

ʿABD RABBO (*Approaching her*): I understand. I'm too presumptuous at times. A girl as clever and pretty as you couldn't possibly feel attracted to a man of my looks. (*Smiling bitterly*:) Thanks for even putting up with the sight of me.

JOURNALIST (*Although disconcerted she tries to evade the issue*): What's this? Is this a new part for tonight's performance?

ʿABD RABBO In fact, tonight will be decisive, and it will bring down the theater.

JOURNALIST As far as I can see, it's already fallen.

ʿABD RABBO It's gone under, my dear, and my career's over. (*He drinks.*) A toast to falling into the sea of business. (*Sarcastically*:) And a toast to falling into the sea of committed art.

JOURNALIST You still haven't answered my question.

ʿABD RABBO What question?

JOURNALIST What's happened to you? Overnight the avenger of greed has become its champion.

ʿABD RABBO (*In a hollow voice*): No one ever came by wealth honestly.

JOURNALIST But why this sudden change?

ʿABD RABBO Because money's always dirty.

JOURNALIST (*Sarcastically*): It's earned by the sweat of a man's brow.

ʿABD RABBO There's no honest wealth.

JOURNALIST So the constant heat of the lights has worn you out.

ʿABD RABBO No one ever . . .

JOURNALIST So you've collapsed under the strain of inner pressure.

ʿABD RABBO No one ever came . . . No one ever . . . but I collected money, and in turn it collected me. (*He collapses on the floor.*)

An ominous silence like that preceding a storm.

JOURNALIST (*Helping him to his feet*): It's time for a new beginning.

ʿABD RABBO (*Staying on his feet*): What kind of revival is it that comes after a fall? I rise up like one submerged in mud. I'm finished, Salma. Forgive me everything.

JOURNALIST Why do you ask my forgiveness?

ʿABD RABBO Forgive me for . . . (*Hesitating*) for loving you.

JOURNALIST I knew that. Why should I forgive you for that?

ʿABD RABBO I loved you the moment you told me—and your eyes were shining when you said it—to keep on living by my motto: "No one ever came by wealth honestly."

JOURNALIST And you never told me!

ʿABD RABBO I was ashamed of myself.

JOURNALIST And you want me to forgive you.

ʿABD RABBO I hope you will.

JOURNALIST I may not forgive you, because you're very late . . .

ʿABD RABBO (*Sighing*): Am I really late?

JOURNALIST You're late in confessing that you've come to ignore your motto.

ʿABD RABBO (*Sadly*): I'm not late, my dear, nor shall I ever forget my motto.

JOURNALIST And you still haven't told me why everything's changed with you.

ʿABD RABBO I'm not able to, Salma. I can't do it.

JOURNALIST Since when couldn't you do it?

ʿABD RABBO Ever since it was prescribed for me what I should say and what I shouldn't.

JOURNALIST Who prescribed it for you? Who dared!

ʿABD RABBO (*Bitterly*): Look at me, young lady. Look at me well; we may never meet after this. Let's say words we won't forget, words we'll remember always.

JOURNALIST I can't believe you're serious.

ʿABD RABBO There was never any boundary between seriousness and humor with Abido. But ʿAbd Rabbo is careful to make the distinction.

JOURNALIST Which one's speaking to me now?

ʿABD RABBO Which do you think?

JOURNALIST Most probably . . . ʿAbd Rabbo.

ʿABD RABBO Thank you. (*Very sadly*:) Goodbye.

JOURNALIST Don't go until we've spoken.

ʿABD RABBO The beginning was delightfully candid, so let the end be the same.

JOURNALIST You seem to be talking about things that are really going to happen.

ʿABD RABBO Matters are quite clear to

me now. (*He lives through some moments when his two personalities are intermeshed.*) The Path . . . the Straight Path. A man walks along the path. He encounters hellfire, paradise, falsehood, truth, greed, abstinence, compassion, and Salma's there, too. Here or there?

A gust of wind blows you here, a teardrop of doubt deflects you there. Which place do you choose?

And who decides for you? Who thrusts you aside from the path . . . and why anyhow did you choose to travel the Straight Path?

JOURNALIST Why did you choose the Path?

ʿABD RABBO I wanted to find safety.

JOURNALIST And what did you want for your soul?

ʿABD RABBO What soul and what safety? (*Calmly*:) Shall I tell you something? (*Shouting*:) I don't deserve anything . . . I don't deserve love. (*In despair*:) The only one of my actions worth remembering is that I failed in everything.

DARKNESS

SCENE THREE

The events of this scene take place on the small stage. The DIRECTOR *watches the action apprehensively from backstage.* ʿABD RABBO *bows to the audience's excessive applause. The setting represents part of a city square.* ʿABD RABBO *is playing the part of an imbecilic beggar. The other actors are stationed around the square. One represents an important* MERCHANT. *The* DIRECTOR *and the* JOURNALIST *Salma are engaged in conversation.*

DIRECTOR I don't understand what's come over him. He doesn't seem to be himself today.

JOURNALIST Are you afraid he'll forget his lines?

DIRECTOR I'm more afraid he'll change his lines. It wouldn't be the first time.

JOURNALIST But the other time was what made him into an actor.

DIRECTOR And I'm afraid this one will make me into a beggar.

(*The scene in the stage play begins.*)

ʿABD RABBO (*To a* POLICEMAN): Did you see them eating camel liver?

POLICEMAN (*Making signals as if directing the traffic while at the same time driving off the beggar*): Clear off, don't obstruct the traffic.

ʿABD RABBO (*Going toward a man reading a newspaper*): Did you see them eating camel liver?

READER (*After a pause*): You're interfering with my grasp of world affairs. Leave me alone.

ʿABD RABBO (*Going toward an important-looking* MERCHANT *seated on a raised chair*): Did you see them eating camel liver?

MERCHANT (*Throws the beggar a bag of coins*): I saw them eating it and they left you nothing.

ʿABD RABBO Is this my portion, oh Prince of Merchants, oh Prince?

MERCHANT We don't forget the poor and the good.

ʿABD RABBO God grant you a long life, oh Prince, you are noble-minded.

MERCHANT (*Assuming the role of a preacher*): It is written that we are noble-minded, my son.

ʿABD RABBO The generous hand is better than the mean hand. We poor live on your leftovers and they keep us alive.

MERCHANT (*Throwing him another bag*): Take this, and pray for us, man.

ʿABD RABBO (*Stands calling out*): Long

live the poor in the shadow of the rich. (*He suddenly looks at the crowd*:) What's the matter with you? I'm saying to you, "Long live the poor in the shadow of the rich."

(*Laughter in the hall, but the* DIRECTOR *is evidently disturbed.*)

DIRECTOR What's happened to you, ʿAbd Rabbo, why are you changing the lines?

JOURNALIST But he's urging the audience to believe in the idea of the play. (ʿABD RABBO *addresses the audience, and it appears he has indeed changed the lines.*)

ʿABD RABBO Whoever believes in the poor, let him leave this hall ashamed to face me. And whoever believes in the merchants, let him clap for a clown like me. To hell with art sponsored by merchants and agents. (*Clapping and commotion.*)

ʿABD RABBO *leaves the stage angrily. The* DIRECTOR *grabs him in a rage.*

DIRECTOR Quickly, draw the curtain. (*To* ʿABD RABBO:) What on earth have you done, you lunatic?

ʿABD RABBO I've come to my senses.

The DIRECTOR *rushes outside.*

JOURNALIST Is this ending like the beginning?

ʿABD RABBO Didn't I tell you?

JOURNALIST What did you tell me?

ʿABD RABBO Goodbye, Salma.

JOURNALIST Where are you going?

ʿABD RABBO Somewhere I can think clearly and review everything.

JOURNALIST And what will you do after that?

ʿABD RABBO We may meet again, and I may have the chance to tell you that I love you without being ashamed of myself.

JOURNALIST But where are you going?

ʿABD RABBO I don't know, but I'm no longer wanted here.

He takes her by the hand, and after a time he kisses it. Their eyes meet. He lets go of her abruptly and rushes outside.

DARKNESS

SCENE FOUR

The events of this scene take place in an uninhabited area on the border. Office of the border patrol, a guard. ʿABD RABBO *is seen carrying a bundle and traveling equipment; he walks behind the security* OFFICER. *The sound of a car starting up is heard.* ʿABD RABBO *looks anxiously toward the origin of the sound.*

ʿABD RABBO The car's leaving. (*Calling*:) Hey . . . wait a moment . . . it's leaving, officer . . .

OFFICER Don't worry, sir. We'll examine your papers, and God will take care of the rest.

ʿABD RABBO (*Entering the office behind the security* OFFICER): And where am I going to find a car on this deserted border?

OFFICER God will look after it. (*Coldly*:) You told me your name was ʿAbd Rabbo.

ʿABD RABBO ʿAbd Rabbo, sir, ʿAbd Rabbo.

OFFICER (*He makes an entry in the record open before him on the table*): Widely known as Abido.

ʿABD RABBO That was my former name. Now, please, let me catch up with the car.

OFFICER (*Thumbing through the index file in front of him*): I'm very sorry to have to inform you that you can't travel, Mr. ʿAbd Rabbo.

ʿABD RABBO I must travel. I'm ill. As you see, I'm sick, and I need to be examined by doctors. I've got to have treatment. Rest.

OFFICER Isn't there treatment and rest in our country?

ᶜABD RABBO There is, sir, there is. I've really tried everything. I need a change of scene.

OFFICER (*Still turning over the papers*): You're not happy with the system here.

ᶜABD RABBO Of course I'm happy.

OFFICER People are never happy. (*Mumbling unintelligibly.*)

ᶜABD RABBO I'm satisfied; I swear it.

OFFICER I'm sorry, Mr. ᶜAbd Rabbo, but you can't travel.

ᶜABD RABBO Why?

OFFICER The instructions are quite clear; it's an order.

ᶜABD RABBO I don't understand, sir. A citizen wants to travel. His papers are legal, so where's the hindrance?

OFFICER Your name tops the list of those who are forbidden to leave the country.

ᶜABD RABBO I don't believe it. Show me.

OFFICER (*He screens the papers from* ᶜABD RABBO): These are official documents; they aren't a perfumer's bill, Mr. ᶜAbd Rabbo.

ᶜABD RABBO What's the solution, sir? I must leave.

OFFICER Doesn't your homeland please you?

ᶜABD RABBO What has my homeland to do with this?

OFFICER (*Sharply*): One's country is everything.

ᶜABD RABBO I love it as I've never loved anything before.

OFFICER Theatrical talk.

ᶜABD RABBO It may be theatrical or television talk, but that's my business.

OFFICER Whether it's your business or not, it's no business of mine.

ᶜABD RABBO Then let me travel.

OFFICER Are you giving me orders, you . . .

ᶜABD RABBO Am I in a position to do that? I'm entreating you.

OFFICER The regulations are clear. (*He stands up.*) The interview is over.

ᶜABD RABBO This means I'll have to go back and get new permission and new papers.

OFFICER That's your affair.

ᶜABD RABBO (*Picking up his stuff*): We may meet again.

OFFICER Who knows?

No sooner does ᶜABD RABBO *leave than the* OFFICER *summons him again and he returns.*

OFFICER Mr. ᶜAbd Rabbo, I forgot something.

ᶜABD RABBO (*Joyfully*): I hope you've had news my name's been dropped from the blacklist.

OFFICER (*Thumbing through other papers*): This is the list for those entering the country, so I hope it won't be . . . (*All of a sudden*:) Your name's at the bottom of the list, Mr. ᶜAbd Rabbo.

ᶜABD RABBO (*He sits on a chair in resignation*): So the story's come full circle. Why am I forbidden to enter my country, sir?

OFFICER The list's very clear.

ᶜABD RABBO (*To himself*): I can't leave; I can't enter. Am I supposed to stay here until God works it out?

OFFICER Do you think my office is a waiting room, Mr. ᶜAbd Rabbo? A coffee house? An amusement center?

ᶜABD RABBO What am I expected to do now?

OFFICER That's none of my business. Peace go with you.

ᶜABD RABBO (*Laughing*): Peace go with me. And where will peace accompany me?

OFFICER God's world is wide.

ᶜABD RABBO No doubt God's world is wide. Goodbye. (*The* OFFICER *becomes absorbed in studying the papers in front of him.*)

ᶜABD RABBO Goodbye to official documents.

ᶜABD RABBO *goes out into the open country. He puts his luggage on the ground, and walks back and forth perplexed.*

ᶜABD RABBO I can't leave the country. I can't enter the country. I just don't understand. Where shall I go? Where will you go, ᶜAbd Rabbo? I was here and I wanted to be there. I can't be here and I can't be there. God's world is wide. What consolation's that? I can't find a foot of ground to settle in. There are plenty of people, but I can't find anyone. (*Calling*:) Hey, hey . . . isn't there anyone to tell me where to go? (*As if he has hit on a new idea*:) I've found it. I've found my place. Do you remember, ᶜAbd Rabbo, those imaginary lines that separate one state from another? I've discovered those imaginary boundaries and they're mine. I can walk along them without observation, interdiction, or obstruction. I'm free, I'm free. (*He starts walking on an imaginary line like a tightrope walker in a circus.*) You've found it, ᶜAbd Rabbo. Now you'll adopt the rules of the Straight Path. You'll walk in accordance with your character. You'll balance in compliance to the path. You'll play the real balancing game. (*Calling*:) Salma, are you watching? I'll soon get this perfect. It's my territory. I'll walk along it without anyone's permission.

He comes and goes several times and darkness falls gradually until everything is pitch black.

ʿIZZ AL-DIN
AL-MADANI

The Zanj Revolution

Translated by
Nazeer El-Azmeh
and Richard Davies

The subject of *The Zanj Revolution* (*Diwan al-Zanj*) is taken from the Zanj (or Black) rebellion, which occurred in southern Iraq in A.D. 879–883 on account of social, racial, and economic differences between the black "slaves" and other communities in the Abbasid Empire. The Blacks seized power for fourteen years, shaking the central government of the Abbasid Caliphate in Baghdad, before they were finally defeated. The Tunisian playwright, ʿIzz al-Din al-Madani, has used the historian al-Tabari's account of this revolution, not only from a dramatic point of view but also from a humanistic one, telescoping events to explore matters of universal concern: those of social justice and freedom. The local Abbasid setting was deliberately chosen from the past to express a crucial human issue still persisting in the present. This use of mythical time, employing episodes or personalities taken from Arab history, has been one of the major oblique approaches used by modern Arabic literature in all its genres to voice a contemporary protest of major significance. In the production of this play, Al-Madani used teamwork, cooperating with al-Munsif al-Suweisi, one of Tunisia's most prominent drama directors and producers, to revolutionize theatrical traditions. This landmark play was produced in 1974. Three theatrical stages are employed. The first is the usual dramatic stage where the original text of the play is performed. On the second stage the playwright himself appears to address the audience, saying that he has written the play under the influence of the various revolutions, uprisings, and coups d'état which have taken place in the second half of the twentieth century in a number of third world countries. The author poses many suggestive questions about what content contemporary Arab plays should have and why they should be written, questions which he leaves unanswered. Then a number of other poetic personalities appear on this second stage and, through their poems, represent contrasting views of the Zanj Revolution. On the third stage, the historian al-Tabari appears to address the audience, first justifying his account of the revolution as seen through the eyes of the central Abbasid power, then moving on to monologues and dialogues with the author, who defends his text vis-à-vis al-Tabari's account. Al-Tabari, however, subsequently reverses his method, presenting many poems of complaint by people suffering poverty and the high cost of commodities, advising or threatening the Caliph, and recounting his administration's defeat in battle by the Blacks. The play ends with al-Tabari declaring that the Zanj Revolution was not a simple insurrection, nor its leader a mere outsider. People, he asserts, should review their history and heritage. This method of teamwork, and the use of the flashback, reflects an originality of presentation unprecedented at this level in Arab theater. The digressions support the dramatic work and engage the audience. The play proved stimulating and won pan-Arab fame. What is exciting is its fidelity to a well-entrenched method in Arabic writings, one in which digressions are the norm. In other plays, al-Madani employs various other Arabic methods of storytelling faithful to his firm belief that the Arab theater must achieve an Arab dramatic form. He believes that a minute study of the old social history will lead to the discovery of the roots of an Arab theatrical method "still buried in the sands of history, and awaiting someone to unearth it from oblivion."

R.A. and S.K.J.

THE ZANJ REVOLUTION

CHARACTERS

The Revolutionary Council of the Zanj, or Black, Revolution

ᶜALI IBN MUHAMMAD
The leader of the Black Revolution. He is forty years old. A Negro, his face shines like the sunrise. He has black hair that flows down around his shoulders and a black beard. His features are large and powerful. His movements are controlled and well-balanced. He is imaginative, resourceful, and cunning.

KHALIL IBN ABAN
The leader's right hand. Dark-complexioned, tall, and thin. He carries the weight of his years with fortitude, but his age is a mystery to everyone. His expression is one of openness, yet he moves nervously. His face becomes blank in the presence of his leader, before whom he bows his head. He has considerable patience.

YAHYA IBN MUHAMMAD
The leader's left hand. He is middle-aged, more than fifty years old, and of medium height. He has a paunch and a large chest, strong shoulders and strong arms. His large head is bald. He walks heavily, speaks slowly, and his silences command respect.

RAYHANA
A brunette, as fresh as the coolness of evening. Her eyes are two shooting stars. Her body is honey-colored, like amber. Her beautiful figure is perfectly proportioned. Her hair flows down her back, and is long enough for her to be able to sit on it easily. Her gestures are graceful and free, and she has the loveliest of voices. She is the Flower of the Black Revolution.

MUHAMMAD IBN SALIM
A prominent member of the Zanj Revolutionary Council. Of mature age, though signs of youth are still visible in his features. He is short, skinny, and small-boned. He has a chronic illness. He loves to talk; words flow out of him in a passionate torrent. It is said that he began his career as a clerk in one of the departments of state during the reign

of the Caliph, al-Wathiq Billah. He has a biting, bitter sense of humor and a contemptuous laugh.

SULAIMAN IBN JAMIᶜ

Was the last to join the Revolutionary Council. Has been named general of the army by ᶜAli Ibn Muhammad. He is a Negro, as black as olives, with thick features and a heroic appearance. His manners are impeccably smooth. On the field of battle he is an expert strategist who draws up battle plans, a man who carries out his orders quickly and fruitfully.

RAFIQ

A young man in the Revolutionary Council, brought up by Ibn Salim, who adopted him. He is argumentative, reads a lot, and criticizes a great deal. The hair on his head, his beard, and his mustache are unkempt. When he is alone, he has the air of a poet. Essentially shy, he did not participate in the struggle for liberation but was born because of it, and so he has inherited its consciousness.

Official Abbasid Delegation to the Zanj Council

SALIH IBN WASIF

Ambassador of the Caliph, al-Muᶜatimid ᶜAla Allah ("The One Who Depends On God"), to the Zanj Revolutionary Council and head of the delegation. He is also assistant to Musa Ibn Buga the Great, chief of staff of the Abbasid army. He is a venerable old man, blond and handsome. His beard and mustache are dyed with henna. He is blue-eyed and well-proportioned in build; he wears elegant, fancy clothes, and his sword is studded with fine jewels. He has the accent and tone of a Turk.

ABU JAᶜFAR IBN JARIM AT-TABARI

A little old man with a neatly-trimmed beard. An enlightened, upright Muslim, he is the author of The History of Prophets and Kings.

ABUL-MAHAMID YAᶜQUB AS-SAYMARI

The head of the Merchants' Guild. He is a tall, skinny man. His back is stooped, his complexion is pale, and he has a beaked nose. He is agile, and proud and graceful in all his movements.

YAHYA IBN KHALID

The court poet of the Caliph. He is elegant in everything, wearing exotic silken gowns, and makes no bones about it. He is jumpy, and has his own prejudices, opinions, pretensions, and hypocrisies. He has a vile temper.

ABU JAᶜFAR AL-ASQALANI

A cunning judge in Baghdad and head of the Department of Justice, who does not do his job. He is short and skinny, and highly observant. Although he says almost nothing, he does not miss a thing.

THE ZANJ REVOLUTION

ACT I
PREPARING TO BUILD THE CITY OF AL-MUKHTARA ("THE CHOSEN")

Seven actors enter, carrying wooden planks and construction tools. They are wearing overalls.

ᶜALI Bring the planks! . . .

KHALIL At last, the day of joy is here!

ᶜALI Bring the bags over here! . . .

YAHYA At last, the time to build is here!

ᶜALI Put the picks and hammers over there! . . .

SULAIMAN Before, we were wasting our lives . . .

ᶜALI Bring up the wagons! . . .

MUHAMMAD Today, we're showing that we exist!

ᶜALI Let the craftsmen and laborers come forward! . . .

RAFIQ In the days to come, we want our city to be the Virtuous One.

ᶜALI And on this spot . . .

RAYHANA Every garden will provide a swaying, fully blooming flower for the city . . .

ᶜALI Khalil, where are the iron bars?

KHALIL Since when have we started building our houses with iron bars? Our iron's the strength of our arms!

ᶜALI Yahya, where are the panes of glass?

YAHYA We'll make them out of our pure desert!

ᶜALI Sulaiman . . .

SULAIMAN At your service.

ᶜALI Where are the cement arches?

SULAIMAN We'll cut them out of the mines.

ᶜALI Muhammad, where are the compass, the square, the level, the plumbline?

MUHAMMAD We'll make them all from our thoughts and our heritage. Truly we are profoundly original people . . .

RAFIQ Sing with me, then: Tomorrow is the Best!

RAYHANA And ᶜAli is our Savior!

YAHYA And our life is the happiest life!

KHALIL And our destination is the greatest destination!

SULAIMAN And our thought is the purest thought!

Silence.

ᶜALI Well, members of the Revolutionary Council, what do we do now? After this anthem and these hopes, now that we've liberated the people from slavery and exploitation and won our first battle against the Abbasids, what do we do now? You know that just singing about freedom isn't enough to make it real. We must put it into practice. But how? Tell me, how?

SULAIMAN We'll carry on with our struggle. There'll be no truce between us and them. The battles must go on. Our first aim is to conquer Basra, the headquarters of the merchants, brokers, and landlords.

ᶜALI It is our intention, our decision,

and our will to carry on the struggle. But we're trying to find an oasis of peace in the desert of these battles, so that we can build there the Great House of the Revolution.

RAYHANA The Oracle of Yaʿmara used to be able to see anything that walked, crept, crawled, or flew within a distance of twenty miles. Behold, now *I* can see the merchants of Basra, who seared our bodies with the lashes of their brokers, who tortured us in the marshlands and poured barley mush down our throats: surprised by our swords, they've taken refuge in flight!

ʿALI But where are our weapons? We're fighting with cleavers and scimitars, and a few swords. We still have no armories.

SULAIMAN We'll loot our weapons from our enemies.

ʿALI Muhammad, do you remember how we started our struggle?

MUHAMMAD We started it in secret, and we started it openly.

RAYHANA With call after call . . .

YAHYA Smuggling messages into the mosques . . .

MUHAMMAD From one jail to another; from those in exile to those who stayed behind.

KHALIL Like bandits, for ten years we attacked the caravans of the merchants.

ʿALI With three dull swords, plenty of clubs, and a few arrows . . .

RAFIQ So! . . . You remember the history of our struggle as if it was a tale from *A Thousand and One Nights* . . .

ʿALI By God, they were the fiercest battles we'd ever had to face. But we endured them, with all our strength and firmness of heart, with all our righteous thinking and all our cunning . . . Those battles were fought between a strong force and a weak one; but our hearts were, and still are, full of faith.

SULAIMAN We endured them by standing together, with our pure consciences and our clean intentions and our devotion to Truth. Our motives were good.

RAFIQ But you're always living on memories that I've no way of recalling!

KHALIL (*Addressing* RAFIQ): Look: among us there are Sudanese, Abyssinians, Gypsies from the marshes, Kurds from Iraq, Bedouins from the deserts, mountain people, Berbers from Africa, and Majis from India and Sind . . .

SULAIMAN What brought them all together? What united the wills of this mixture of men, this riffraff, these dregs of society? What induced them to live free, noble, and strong; to eat when they were hungry, drink when they were thirsty, and put on clothes when they were naked?

YAHYA The credit belongs to the man who united their spirit and wakened their hearts. His summons was like a fresh breeze that came to refresh their starved souls.

RAFIQ (*Interrupting*): One catapult's better than a thousand of those men!

SULAIMAN But who can handle the catapult? Our friends have no experience . . .

MUHAMMAD Then let them learn the secret of the technique from their enemies.

RAFIQ Why don't we fight as one front?

SULAIMAN Battles today no longer involve the tactics of attack and retreat. We no longer operate just in deserts or plains or valleys; we're in the hills, in the marshes, and on the rivers.

ʿALI Let's fight them on every front, battle after battle!

RAFIQ Let's fight them in small groups!

RAYHANA And in guerrilla bands scattered through the jungles and the forests, like crocodiles that sit on banks in the marshes and pretend to be asleep! . . . Like old vultures that keep watch from the lofty peaks! . . .

SULAIMAN We want this to be a war that will wear them down!

KHALIL Exhaust them!

MUHAMMAD Devour them!

YAHYA Cut them to pieces!

RAFIQ A war that will consume, waste, and destroy!

ʿALI (*Interrupting*): No more rhetoric! It's more dangerous than opium . . .

RAFIQ ʿAli, didn't you say that the war wasn't our real problem?

ʿALI Yes. Peace is the problem; the problem is peace. As for the war, we'll carry on with that immediately, now! (*Addressing* SULAIMAN:) Sulaiman, begin!

SULAIMAN Your wish is my command.

ʿALI Take twenty thousand fighters with you, march on Basra, and conquer it. Let Rafiq help you.

RAFIQ But I'm only the clerk of the Revolutionary Council . . .

ʿALI We want you to drench your hands in blood, so that you can understand the meaning of our struggle.

RAYHANA I know the language of the Sudanese and the dialect of the Abyssinians; I know the tongue of the Berbers and I can translate the language of the Kurds . . .

ʿALI I want you to go out and help Sulaiman because you burden the men of the Council with your questions.

YAHYA Oh, ʿAli, leave him alone. He's more suited to the Council.

MUHAMMAD Let him be. If the younger generation were as sure of themselves as we are, and nothing shook them up, then God help them. I brought him up to ask questions, to discuss, to think, to search . . . The embarrassment is when the people asked are afraid of the questions.

ʿALI Start out, Sulaiman, and take this flag with you. (*He hands him a red flag, on which is an image of the Anqa.*)* What are you going to say to the oppressed people in Basra? What good news are you going to take them?

SULAIMAN I'll take them what God has said in his noble Book: "God has bought from the believers their souls and their fortunes, and given them Paradise. They struggled along the Path of God; they killed and were killed. . . . " Truly, this has been promised in the Bible, the Gospel, and the Qurʾan. And who has ever fulfilled his promise better than God? "Be happy with the bargain you have made, it is the ultimate triumph. . . ."

ʿALI Go ahead, Sulaiman . . . Don't leave Basra until you've wiped out the merchants, crucified the brokers and burned the slave traders with fire; until you've liberated the slaves and restored the money and possessions of the Muslims to the Treasury.

SULAIMAN Oh, ʿAli, leader of the Revolutionary Council, your wish is my command. Riding a horse and carrying the red flag is my proper role. The merchants, brokers and slave traders will be destroyed, I promise you that. (*Exits.*)

A sound of blowing horns and beating drums announces the beginning of the battle. There is a moment of silence. Then only one sound is heard: all of them saying, "Allahu Akbar."

ʿALI (*After a moment of silence*): As I was saying, war isn't the problem. We shall be victorious. We shall seize Basra, and then Kufa, and after that we'll threaten Baghdad and Samarra . . . (*Suddenly*:) Only, we want to build the Great House of the Revolution. What do we do then?

MUHAMMAD I believe it's much too

*A mythological bird similar to the Phoenix.

soon to be speaking about building. We haven't finished the battle yet.

ᶜALI Sulaiman Ibn Jamiᶜ will dominate the battle.

YAHYA I believe we should slow down a little, and start building once we've seized Basra.

ᶜALI Sulaiman Ibn Jamiᶜ will be in charge of Basra.

KHALIL I believe the fortunes of the merchants in Basra will help us to buy the tools for building—the cement, the iron, and the glass . . .

ᶜALI Sulaiman will lay hold of the fortunes of the merchants. They won't disappear, or run out, or melt away.

MUHAMMAD It's a fact that you can't overcome the world in one battle. Revolution doesn't mean a magical solution to every problem.

ᶜALI I've become confused, I can't see events clearly. You're not making any distinction between mirage and reality . . . Open the door of this meeting room! Listen! (*Shouts, cries and groans are heard*: "*We're hungry*!" "*We're thirsty*!" ALI *resumes*:) An entire people is suffering from hunger. Securing their daily bread, that's building, if you like. And so is establishing a daily supply of water, and providing clothes to wear . . .

MUHAMMAD But the more important thing comes first, and the less important thing comes second! Battle's the more important; peace and construction come second to that.

ᶜALI I want us to strengthen ourselves. There's no harm in waging a struggle and building at the same time . . . We capture towns, we destroy the cities of the Abbasids, *and* we build our own. One hand fights and the other builds.

MUHAMMAD That would be a waste of our efforts. This situation calls for concentration. There's a time for war and a time for peace. War is a contagious disease that spreads like darkness, like death, and destroys all that's been built.

KHALIL We have half a million fighters, ready and waiting . . .

MUHAMMAD What you mean is, we have half a million men, women, and children—including the chronically ill, the weak, and the exhausted. The thousands of children weigh on us all . . .

RAFIQ They're all suffering because the food's so bad and so scarce.

MUHAMMAD So how will you build a city with an army of beggars and hungry men?

ᶜALI What do we do then?

RAYHANA Let's confiscate every woman's jewelry!

MUHAMMAD Have you seen anyone wearing as much as a thread of silver? You're dreaming of gold and jewelry and pearls, Rayhana . . .

KHALIL Let's have an alliance with the Carmathians of Bahrain. Their revolution's rich. They have jewelry and pearls. Their treasuries are full. Diving in the Gulf for the finest pearls is their industry. And you certainly know that the Caliph's afraid of their attacks and their bribes and their leaders . . . They're advancing strongly on Syria in the north, Persia in the east, Egypt in the west, and Oman in the south. What will you say to their messenger, who's been standing for days at the door of our Council?

ᶜALI The Carmathians (*Chuckling*) . . . What have they got to do with Bahrain?

RAFIQ They're rebels, like us . . .

ᶜALI Their beliefs are strange and farfetched, foreign to us. They believe in sharing everything equally—even women!

RAYHANA They imported that from Azerbaijan, or the other side of the mountains, where a man doesn't know whether his wife might be his sister, his daughter, or his mother. We too practice equality, and we believe in it regardless of race or color. We don't believe there should be separate cultures or regions or nations. We believe in freedom and the elimination of all class distinctions. Among us, there's no leader or led, and no shepherd or king. The equality of the Carmathians is a forgery, a decadent fabrication, a patchwork quilt of lies.

RAFIQ I disagree! I really must protest! Don't be misled by what people may say about fabrications and lies . . . "Imported principles!" Damn those words! (*Addressing* MUHAMMAD:) Have you ever read any of their books?

MUHAMMAD They're people of principle, of Divine Law and judgment. All they possess, they share . . .

ʿALI Away with these myths!

RAYHANA Admit it, Muhammad, they're illusions!

MUHAMMAD I'll vouch for what I've read . . .

ʿALI (*Interrupting*): You've misread! You've misinterpreted, and missed the point!

MUHAMMAD I worked in the Department of Postal Services in the Abbasid civil service. With the scholars of Kufa, I studied the *Books of the Animals*; with the scholars of Basra, the *Book of Horses and Idols*; with the scholars of Baghdad, the verses of Sulaik. I've never mispronounced one word, or read it wrongly. That gives me the authority to say what I say.

ʿALI I told you, your beliefs aren't original, they're imports, alien and strange. (*Addressing* RAFIQ:) Enough! Your arguments are rejected! Stay in your place!

RAFIQ Since when have you had a monopoly on opinions? What do you mean by "imported beliefs"? What do you mean by "unoriginal principles"? I don't understand a word of what you've said! Are you one of the Esoteric School, or a Sophist? Are you able to solve all the problems of peace and war yourself, by the principle of equality alone?

ʿALI Equality is our great governing principle.

RAFIQ Can you feed the hungry with equality? Can you build the City of Al-Mukhtara with equality? If you can, you have the magic key that can solve everything!

MUHAMMAD The Prophet—may peace be upon him—has said that the goal of the believer is wisdom.

ʿALI (*Interrupting vehemently*): "Imported" means, what doesn't apply to our circumstances and what doesn't answer to our needs.

RAFIQ Hamdan Qirmut and his supporters are learned men. Knowledge doesn't stumble and go astray, or go wrong. Knowledge doesn't allow any loopholes for whimsicality . . . We want our revolution to be a secular and scientific revolution.

MUHAMMAD That's what the books of the Carmathians say.

YAHYA But in reality our books are far apart . . .

KHALIL Then what do you say to the messenger?

ʿALI What about the quarrels that have broken out among them and destroyed their unity? One group's made Bahrain its stronghold, another's wandering in Hijaz, and the third's roaming the deserts of Syria. Each of them posits its own Master as being the Supreme Rebel, and describes his adversaries as schismatic infidels and atheists.

YAHYA Which shall we believe, Ibn Salim? And which should we make an alliance with?

ʿALI (*Frowning and prophesying*): The revolution of Hamdan Qirmut won't leave a trace, any more than the revolutions of Abi Dhar, Babik, Ghailan the Damascene, and the Man of the Donkey . . . They're gone with the wind.

RAFIQ Listen, Ibn Salim! Listen, as though he were the mouthpiece of Fate!

MUHAMMAD But Fate's defined its terms for us. (*Laughing.*) Isn't that so, ʿAli?

YAHYA Let's put an end to this dispute! Khalil, give the messenger of the Carmathians a general statement, saying that we support them and bless their endeavors. But don't let on that some of us oppose them. (KHALIL *exits and returns after a short while.*)

ʿALI Why are you so silent, Rayhana? You used to back me up . . . (*The two are alone in a corner of the stage.*)

RAYHANA My dear ʿAli . . . If I had spoken it would have added oil to the flames. I'm afraid the Revolutionary Council may split up. For the cause of togetherness and unity, I sacrifice my freedom of speech.

ʿALI Black Flower . . . That's how you always are, and that's how I was in my youth . . . I hid my opinions, I concealed my beliefs . . . I roamed over all the countries of the Bahrain, I roamed Ahsaʾ and Yamamah, stayed in Muscat and traveled to Oman. And on the coast of the Arabian Gulf I ran into you, collecting clusters of pearls . . .

RAYHANA Then we went as pilgrims to Mecca.

ʿALI For a month, day and night we walked, toward the Place of Pilgrimage. The message of our doctrine spread among the pilgrims, and the eyes of the spies followed us to Mecca. During the holy months we settled there, before the screens of the Kaʿba, praying together . . . That the world be brought down on the heads of its oppressors.

RAYHANA That all mankind should be honored . . .

ʿALI But in those countries I found brother betraying brother. The son failed his father, and the citizen was false to his neighbor. My revolution in the countries of Bahrain was suffocated in the cradle.

RAYHANA The time for living underground has gone forever! The time for openness has arrived! . . . Our pilgrimage has been justified! Faith has dawned, and our cause is victorious! . . .

INTERLUDE

THE SEVENTH (*Indicating the beginning of the Council*): Salamasai!*

THE FIRST (*The lantern bearer*): Salamasai! Agum Mizdadagh!

THE SECOND (*The book bearer*): Salamasai! Sinbanar the Council of the Blacks!

THE THIRD (*The rosary carrier*): Salamasai! The Guide of the Council of the Blacks!

THE SEVENTH Kalman Telhab Desh Raquz—the Secrets of the Council of the Blacks!

THE SECOND (*Nods his head, then reads from the book as though it contained the list of names of all the Council members*): Namajair!

THE SEVENTH Ahourta!

THE SECOND Bazai . . .

THE FIRST Ahourta!

THE SECOND Shazaar . . .

*This word and those following are nonsense words, meant for theatrical effect.

THE THIRD Ahourta!

THE SECOND Delhook . . .

THE FIFTH Ahourta.

THE SECOND Rayhana . . .

THE SIXTH (*In a female voice*): Ahourta! Salamasai the Black Revolutionary Council!

THE SEVENTH Lucah arbei, let us hear the words of our good and virtuous brothers.

THE FIRST The time of light and openness has come.

THE SECOND The cause is victorious and the veil is removed.

THE THIRD Hooray for the men of the Revolution!

THE FOURTH Now, the cause is victorious . . .

THE FIFTH . . . and joy is over all!

THE SIXTH Take off your masks!

THE SEVENTH Come out from the marshes, the jungles, and the forests!

Each removes his mask. The Interlude is finished, and the main scene is resumed.

ACT I (RESUMED)

RAYHANA The time for living underground has gone forever! The time for openness has arrived! . . . Our pilgrimage has been justified! Faith has dawned, and our cause is successful! . . .

KHALIL Why don't we seek protection with the Fatimid Caliph? Between him and us . . .

OTHER MEMBERS (*In surprise and denial*): The Fatimid Caliph?

KHALIL Why not? His enemies are ours, aren't they?

The rest of the members express strong disapproval.

KHALIL Okay, I withdraw my suggestion . . . I'm sorry you don't like it. We should seek help from Yaᶜqub Ibn Laith as-Safaar!

RAYHANA Do you want to send us back to slavery and exploitation?

KHALIL I was thinking . . .

MUHAMMAD My Lord and Master, Khalil, is thinking! And what is he thinking? About cooperation, with Yaᶜqub Ibn Laith as-Safaar! (*He laughs bitterly.*)

RAFIQ There can be no cooperation except with our equals, with those whose hearts God has purified of all oppression and whose plans God has cleansed of all corruption.

YAHYA What's the matter with you? Throwing ourselves on kings! . . . We have our dignity, our pride and manhood! . . .

MUHAMMAD But people—praise be to God!—how do hunger and dignity go together?

YAHYA (*Interrupting* MUHAMMAD): A young girl who's free will go hungry; she won't eat by selling her breasts!

MUHAMMAD Hunger is a merciless infidel. To be hungry is to lose all dignity.

YAHYA (*Addressing* KHALIL): Now you want to be loyal to the Fatimid Caliphs, and then you want to form a coalition with Yaᶜqub Ibn Laith as-Safaar! Another time, it will be someone else . . .

RAFIQ (*Interrupting*): We don't want East or West! We're the Zanj, the Black Ones! We're nonaligned!

YAHYA (*Resuming*):Would you like us to ally ourselves with the Umayyads of Andalusia?

RAYHANA Is it true that the Fatimid Caliph has a thousand concubines, a thousand young men, and a thousand eunuchs?

RAFIQ The truth is, he has all Africa as a colony, and he drains away all its wealth from its rightful owners.

MUHAMMAD There are pairs of things which are never in contradiction: conquering countries and possessing their women; enslaving men and exploiting their resources; the tyranny of a king in his kingdom and the oppression of a father in his household; and so forth and so on . . . Like engenders like.

ʿALI We know you've read Plato's *Republic*! Enough of these philosophical hallucinations! Tell me, how are we going to solve the problem that's facing us?

RAFIQ You mean war or peace?

ʿALI I mean how to build the Great House of the Revolution, and how to build this city . . .

YAHYA We haven't yet discussed the matter of reclaiming the salt mines, and selling the salt . . .

KHALIL Mountains of salt are piling up in the mines. How do we sell it? The Abbasids have placed an embargo on the trade routes over land and sea, and they've blockaded the ports of Basra. If we'd allied ourselves with the Carmathians, we would have been able to sell our salt to *them*.

ʿALI (*Angrily*): Here we go again! The Carmathians! . . .

KHALIL (*Apologetically*): They're rich, and they have hard currency.

RAYHANA (*Interrupting*): Their money's false! Their pennies are false! Their dinars are false! No one will accept them . . . and on top of all that they do business with the capitalists and the merchants, with sea captains and Chinese pirates!

KHALIL Does that mean they're committed to the Fatimid State?

RAFIQ You don't understand anything! You have the body of an elephant, and the head of a cuckoo!

MUHAMMAD *laughs harshly.*

YAHYA We must find a way to market the salt, because it's our last chance . . .

RAYHANA (*Interrupting*): Enough of this!

ʿALI Leave the salt alone. Oh yes, it won't run out or go moldy . . . Let's talk about feeding and housing the people.

MUHAMMAD Who are you going to get to construct the walls of al-Mukhtara?

RAFIQ Have you got architects?

KHALIL Who'll build its bridges? Who'll pave its roads? Do you have experts? Arches? Technicians?

MUHAMMAD How will we build the city? In Abbasid style or Andalusian style? In Fatimid style or Byzantine style? Chinese or Pharaonic?

RAFIQ Or are you going to take a little of each and bring them together in a patchwork? Or take them apart, modify them, and forge them together? What we'll have is the Crazy City!

KHALIL And once we've laid its foundations, who's going to teach the Qurʾan to our children?

YAHYA And who'll teach our young people science and wisdom?

MUHAMMAD And who's going to care for our sick?

YAHYA And who's going to manage our markets?

RAFIQ And who'll be in charge of the ships?

MUHAMMAD And who'll be the judge?

KHALIL Who'll be the chief of police?

MUHAMMAD Who'll manage its public departments?

RAFIQ Who'll supervise the coinage?

ALL (*Except* ʿALI *and* RAYHANA): Who? Who?

YAHYA Those whose cause we're fighting for are ignorant, all of them ignorant! Absolutely ignorant!

KHALIL They only know how to lift heavy loads.

MUHAMMAD They only know how to dig ditches and fill them up again.

RAFIQ They only know about driving camels.

RAYHANA They only know how to have babies.

ʿALI They're ignorant people. You see how much easier war is for us than building a city?

ACT II
THE PROBLEM OF MARKETING SALT FROM THE MINES OF BASRA

SCENE 1

The Revolutionary Council is still in session, discussing, arguing, and talking, while the news comes from SULAIMAN *that the army of the Zanj has occupied Basra, liberated the slaves, and burned the houses of the merchants.*

ʿALI We've seized Basra. And soon we shall overwhelm Ahwaz, and triumph there as well.

KHALIL We should take pride in this great victory! Our congratulations are due to you, Leader of the Zanj . . . But for you, we'd never have been liberated. But for you, we'd never have sprung to life.

RAFIQ You, the Inarticulate One, you've suddenly become a poet!

RAYHANA Under your victorious leadership, ʿAli, we shall expand along the banks of the Tigris and Euphrates. We shall march on Baghdad, and to the mountains of the Kurds. We've succeeded because we're Faith, Love, and Hope.

MUHAMMAD (*Responding to the words of* KHALIL): But for this elite, but for this chosen group, but for this firm unity, we'd never have accomplished anything . . . O, God, guide our steps! Unite us, and unite our word! Banish our differences!

KHALIL (*Addressing* ʿALI): Why don't we conquer Wasit before Ahwaz?

ʿALI The inhabitants of the Kufa are Shiʿites—you, of all people, ought to know that. Even if the scholars of Kufa did kick you out of their city, it's still a stronghold of opposition to the Abbasids. It's still a thorn in their flesh.

KHALIL So when will be the time to strike at Wasit?

ʿALI Wasit's no more than a dusty settlement, tossed about between whirlwinds. There are no merchants or landlords there, and no farmers or slaves. There's nothing in it but the ruins of an old postal station and a miserable tavern for bandits, and the rebels and outcasts banished by the Abbasids.

RAYHANA And when will we attack Ahwaz?

ʿALI Within a week . . . It stands at the borders of Persia and the Gorge, on the trade routes to Hawazan and Abadan, and it's defended by a regiment led by Musa, chief of staff of the Abbasid army.

YAHYA If *that* regiment's defending it, what's the use of moving in?

ʿALI We're only going to engage them in skirmishes, as though we intended to take it. We'll camouflage our purpose. The Caliph won't guess that our plan's to conquer Kufa, which is the next logical step after conquering Basra. We'll move on Ahwaz, and then attack Baghdad from the rear.

YAHYA You really are a sly fox!

RAFIQ (*Suddenly, in a high-pitched voice*): Members of the Revolutionary Council, hear me! . . .

The members of the Council listen, and keep listening: the echo of pipes approaching can be heard. Slowly, the sounds become more distinct.

RAYHANA Who is that? Is it Sulaiman, returning like Hercules?

YAHYA But we gave him orders to remain in Basra . . .

ᶜALI Where are the guards?

A black FIGHTER, *wearing a leopard skin, runs into the Council chamber. He is carrying a bundle in his hands and wearing a large colorful mask on his face.*

FIGHTER A troop of the Abbasid army, carrying a white flag, wish to parley! They'll be here soon.

ᶜALI (*As though dreaming*): Abbasid troops?

RAYHANA How could they find us?

YAHYA They wish to parley?

RAFIQ But we're at war with them!

MUHAMMAD And who's leading the troop?

FIGHTER I don't know him. He's a fair-complexioned, bowlegged man with blue eyes, and he wears his clothes like a prince.

ᶜALI That's the Caliph's brother.

FIGHTER On his turban there's an exotic plume that shines like a peacock's feather . . .

YAHYA Silence, everybody! Let's be calm, and prepare ourselves to receive them.

FIGHTER He has another flag, a black one . . .

ᶜALI Put on your masks!

They put them on, and listen.

INTERLUDE
INTRODUCING THE OFFICIAL DELEGATION TO THE AUDIENCE

AUTHOR Salih Ibn Wasif! . . .

SALIH Who's calling? Who's called me by my name, without my titles?

AUTHOR I have. I'm the author of this play. How many villages do you own?

SALIH One thousand! . . . My Lord, the Caliph, bestowed them on me.

AUTHOR And you, Abu Jaᶜfar, have you ever thought that Truth has many faces, which might contradict each other?

AT-TABARI Truth is one and unique: it is one, Islamic, Orthodox, and Abbasid! Official!

AUTHOR What about you, Abul Mahamid?

ABUL MAHAMID I have my own interests in the Basra. They're all laid waste, and useless. I had tons and tons of wheat and cotton, tons and tons of furniture and feathers. They've all been consumed by fire in the holocaust of the Basra. I'm a poor man now! . . .

AUTHOR And you, Yahya Ibn Khalid?

YAHYA IBN KHALID Please don't disgrace me!

AUTHOR You little Court rhymer! . . . You drummer! You piper! . . . Didn't you say: "May God bless you, descendant of proud rulers, / Men of iron will and unshakable honor, / You have wiped out the rebel band / And left your enemies bitter / Only waiting to be destroyed . . . "? The people have found you out for what you are. They've broken the drums, and broken the pipes!

YAHYA IBN KHALID *remains silent.*

AUTHOR Jaᶜfar of Asqalan, you are the chief judge in the Justice Department. You make judgments, but you don't govern; you investigate, but you never settle one case.

AL-ASQALANI I'm a consultant to the Caliph al-Muʿtamid. I only give him my opinions on the cases . . .

AUTHOR Your work might seem to be innocent, but in reality it's a fraud! . . .

Interlude ends here. Scene 1 is resumed.

SCENE I (RESUMED)

SALIH (*Contemplating the* MEMBERS OF THE REVOLUTIONARY COUNCIL, *one by one*): Peace be with you, members of the Council . . .

COUNCIL MEMBERS *remain silent.*

SALIH My Lord and Master, the Caliph of the Messenger of God, al-Muʿtamid, the One Who Depends on God, has sent me as his delegate to you.

COUNCIL MEMBERS *remain silent.*

SALIH And these famous scholars are with me . . .

AT-TABARI Abu Jaʿfar Ibn Jarim at-Tabari, at your service!

ABUL-MAHAMID Abul-Mahamid Yaʿqub as-Saymari, at your command!

AL-ASQALANI Abu Jaʿfar al-Asqalani, at your disposal and under your protection!

COUNCIL MEMBERS *remain silent.*

YAHYA IBN KHALID Yahya Ibn Khalid, devoting himself to the praise of your merits, your virtues, and your beauties!

COUNCIL MEMBERS *remain silent.*

SALIH We have carried the white flag from the City of Peace. At the public gate of Baghdad, our Lord and Master, the Caliph of the Messenger of God, bade us farewell . . .

COUNCIL MEMBERS *remain silent.*

AT-TABARI The Caliph, our Master, has sent us with an oral message.

ABUL-MAHAMID He says: "In the name of God the Merciful and Compassionate, this letter comes from the Caliph of the Messenger of God to the inhabitants of the marshes and mines and their leader, Ali Ibn Muhammad. We have sent a delegation, led by Salih Ibn Wasif and other men from our side, to negotiate our differences, to eliminate everything that separates us and to unify our word under the protection of the flag of Islam."

COUNCIL MEMBERS *remain silent.*

AL-ASQALANI What do you say? What is your answer? We are loyal messengers.

YAHYA IBN KHALID (*Looking around from side to side*): The Prince of the Faithful truly desires that we live together in peace, love, security, and harmony. Whoever has judged you by the sword has treated you badly. Woe to anyone who accuses you of ingratitude . . . For you are part and parcel of us, and we of you, lock, stock, and barrel.

COUNCIL MEMBERS *remain silent.*

SALIH Your silence isn't going to solve our complicated problems at all.

AT-TABARI ʿAli Ibn Muhammad is your commander-in-chief. Where is he?

COUNCIL MEMBERS (*In one voice*): Each one of us is ʿAli!

SALIH Praise be to God who moves your tongues to speak!

YAHYA IBN KHALID You are articulate and expressive . . . You speak the Arabic language, the language of the Qurʾan, the language which distinguishes good from evil . . . May grace be bestowed upon him who speaks it . . .

AT-TABARI If what we've heard is true, ᶜAli, you really are ᶜAli son of Ahmad, son of ᶜAli, son of Isa, son of Zayd, son of ᶜAli, son of al-Husayn, son of ᶜAli, son of Talib, may God honor his face.

ONE COUNCIL MEMBER I don't care which dynasty I'm related to!

SECOND MEMBER (*In female voice*): I'm an ordinary man, one of the masses, a member of the lower orders, an outcast, a man from the depths of degradation . . .

THIRD MEMBER My grandfather was a Persian. He was a builder, a silversmith, and a porter . . .

FOURTH MEMBER My father was an Arab, a rough nomad, a laborer, a peasant. He planted seeds of barley and wheat, but all he reaped was revenge, and rage at his landlord.

FIFTH MEMBER My mother was a Sindi concubine. She worked as a singer and dancer in the taverns. My father freed her, and she taught me that the world stands on two horns—the horn of Good and the horn of Evil, the horn of the strong and the horn of the weak—and that the conflict between them goes on forever.

SIXTH MEMBER My uncle was a noble black from among the elite of the Baluba tribe. He was captured by nets in the deep jungles of the region of Ghana. He was sold in the slave markets of Basra, and then he was given a broom to sweep up the salt. The mosquitoes, the hunger, the thirst, and the terrible sexual frustration finished him off.

SALIH AND THE OTHER DELEGATES (*In one voice*): We swear that we are innocent of all this. We swear that we are not responsible for it, and that we know nothing about any of it.

COUNCIL MEMBERS That was the only existence we ever knew. And so we gathered the Zanj together, declared war, and marched into battle.

SALIH War's become old-fashioned. It *used to be* the rule between nations, peoples, and tribes . . .

AT-TABARI Why should we fight one another?

ABUL-MAHAMID Why don't we work together for the good of man, whether he be Abyssinian, Arab, Persian, or Berber?

YAHYA IBN KHALID War destroys nations and brings death. It reaps lives and sows shame. A good life is one of peace: this needs to be thought on carefully, and not casually dismissed.

A COUNCIL MEMBER And Truth is something that demands conditions . . .

SECOND MEMBER That all our rights be restored.

THIRD MEMBER Our rights to a steadfast liberty . . .

FOURTH MEMBER . . . Our right to equality. And despite the fact that our Lord and Master the Caliph possesses an army of one thousand horsemen and a million foot soldiers, and a thousand camps, strongholds, and regiments, he must be completely dedicated to peace.

SALIH We accept all your terms. And bear in mind the fact that—may God keep you healthy and well—Yaᶜqub Ibn Laith as-Safaar has been given command of Persia, as have Hamdan Qirmut of Bahrain and Ibn Tulun of Egypt.

ONE COUNCIL MEMBER How did this happen? (*Addressing another* COUNCIL MEMBER:) How did this happen? Yaᶜqub Ibn as-Safaar? And Nageer Dagh Ahen?

SECOND COUNCIL MEMBER Nash? Hamdan Qirmut? Ahourta?

THIRD COUNCIL MEMBER But our spies, who are spread out all over this land, haven't informed us of these great events!

SALIH We haven't come to you in fear!

AT-TABARI We're up-to-date. We've left the idea of war to the old men, may God have mercy on them . . .

FOURTH COUNCIL MEMBER What are the terms of the cooperation between us?

SALIH This is the Caliph's rosary. Take it. It is the token of the covenant of security and peace between us. (*He gives the rosary to one of the* COUNCIL MEMBERS.)

FOURTH COUNCIL MEMBER I accept the rosary. I accept the pardon and general amnesty. I accept the peace. Salamasai Jibran, shabnaar maglis Zanj Sarbut litham!

COUNCIL MEMBERS *all unmask themselves at once.*

YAHYA IBN KHALID Bravo! Bravo! Look at those shining lights! How beautiful those faces are!

RAFIQ What are your conditions for peace?

SALIH First, ᶜAli Ibn Muhammad shall be the Governor of the Marshes of Basra. He will be responsible for all of you, in all matters, large and small, before our Lord and Master, the Caliph.

MUHAMMAD But that won't be enough . . .

AT-TABARI Take it easy, may God be good to you! . . .

SALIH Second: That the marshes of Basra shall remain in your possession until the land, and those who are on the land, have passed back into the hands of God.

KHALIL IBN ABAAN That means we're completely liberated from bondage and exploitation!

RAYHANA And it means they've freed the concubines and the slaves!

AL-ASQALANI Take it easy, Khalil! From the abundance of His generosity and His good deeds, God has bestowed on you His grace . . .

SALIH Third: That you manage together the affairs of your people, and choose any system you like—tribal, monarchical, democratic, or regional. Our Lord and Master will not interfere in any particular.

YAHYA IBN MUHAMMAD We've already chosen the form of our rule. I swear, this term is truly a miracle of our time!

YAHYA IBN KHALID Yahya, my brother, I am inspired! A beautiful poem in your praise has just occurred to me. I will recite it immediately . . .

RAYHANA Watch out! They don't like poetry . . .

SALIH Fourth: That we should settle our dispute concerning the marshes of Basra. Our Lord and Master, the Caliph al-Muᶜtamid, is offering to buy from you the salt of the mines of Basra.

ᶜALI All of it?

ABUL-MAHAMID Yes. And he will pay one dinar for every qantar of salt.

AT-TABARI Look, this is an Abbasid dinar. (*He gives it to* KHALIL.)

KHALIL (*Pretends to bite it*): I swear, it's pure gold! (COUNCIL MEMBERS *pass the coin among them, except for* ᶜALI *and* RAYHANA.)

RAFIQ (*Addressing* ᶜALI *alone*): I'm skeptical about every one of these terms.

ᶜALI (*Whispering*): They've given us general amnesty!

RAFIQ (*Whispering*): Are we going to trust the Abbasids? Don't you remember what they did to the descendants of ᶜAli?

ᶜALI (*Whispering*): We're almost making things right . . . Don't spoil it!

RAYHANA How beautiful this dinar is! I'll make bracelets, necklaces, and rings from the gold . . . (*The dinar goes back to* AT-TABARI.)

SALIH Fifth: That you should sell no salt to Caesar of Byzantium or the Emperor of China . . .

ʿALI We accept this term.

SALIH Sixth: That you should perform the Five Prayers in the name of our Lord and Master, the Caliph. Also, his name is to be proclaimed from the tops of the minarets. Also, a land tax is to be collected in his name.

ʿALI We accept these terms as well.

SALIH Seventh: What are your demands?

ʿALI We want engineers to construct our city, which, by God's blessing, we have named al-Mukhtara. We also need craftsmen and laborers, plasterers and archmakers, architects and artists, painters and sculptors.

SALIH Record this, Abul-Mahamid. Write down what the Governor has requested. Are there any other demands?

YAHYA IBN MUHAMMAD Yes, I would like to ask for instructors and teachers, professors and masters, to teach our children science, literature, philosophy, and the Arabic language.

SALIH Hurry and write down his demands, Jaʿfar. And with them, send along a library of the Caliph's rare books, which include books on grammar, books of prose, books of proverbs, books on philosophy, books on mathematics, and books on athletics.

KHALIL We would prefer the books of Sufiyan the Revolutionary, the biographies of Abu Thar al-Ghaffari and Waraqa Ibn Nawfal, and *The Two Cups of Eternity* by al-Hallaj.*

SALIH All that is instantly granted.

RAYHANA: And we would like you to send a delegation of cooks and goldsmiths, fashion experts and tailors, seamstresses and embroiderers.

SALIH Yahya Ibn Khalid, write down what this lady has requested and carry it out at once.

YAHYA IBN KHALID Your wish is my command.

MUHAMMAD We need doctors, pharmacists, and male and female nurses.

SALIH We have doctors, surgeons, pharmacists, and all the instruments of medicine. And we will send you that famous wise man and doctor, Bukhtishuh himself, the physician of our Lord the Caliph.

AT-TABARI And, as a present, I will give you my book, *The History of Prophets and Kings*.

ʿALI We accept it with love and honor . . . and we will include it in our course of studies.

SALIH And I, as a present, will give you my clothing!

YAHYA IBN KHALID And I will give you my turban and sash . . .

AT-TABARI Here are my gown and slippers . . . Take them!

AL-ASQALANI Here is my burnoose . . .

ABUL-MAHAMID Here are my sash, my stockings, my trousers . . .

SALIH Dress yourselves up, members of the Council! Wear the silk and the muslin! Be as colorful as you can! All of these are gifts to you! Enjoy yourselves! . . .

Together, the COUNCIL MEMBERS *put on the clothes of the Abbasid delegation—all except* RAFIQ, *who has been sitting in a corner ever since the end of his conversation with*

*Sufiyan: a religious thinker and theologian of the eighth century. Al-Ghaffari: one of the Prophet's companions. Waraqa Ibn Nawfal: a pre-Islamic thinker. Al-Hallaj: a mystic crucified in Baghdad for heresy (A.D. 922).

ʿALI. *One member puts a sash on his head, another wraps a burnoose around his body, and a third finds another idiosyncratic way of wearing the Abbasid clothes. A fourth powders his face and puts on perfume, wearing a gown as though it were a pair of pants. A fifth mimics exaggeratedly the poise, walk, and speech of the Abbasid nouveau riche, and has fun making sophisticated jokes.*

SALIH And this is our last present! . . . *He throws down a steel ball, which is covered with brightly colored electric eyes of a thousand shades. It stands on two legs. If someone touches it, it immediately springs into action and rolls along the ground, making loud noises and blinking its eyes on and off. When it stands still, it sparkles fire.*

ABUL-MAHAMID This instrument will help you to sweep up all the salt in the marshes. It is yours. We will equip your laborers with one hundred balls exactly like this one. Keep it!

The members of the delegation exit, saying, "See you next year." Meanwhile, the COUNCIL MEMBERS *stay behind to work with the instrument. They are very much frightened of it.*

SCENE 2

A year later. SULAIMAN IBN JAMIʿ *has not returned from Basra, and all the* COUNCIL MEMBERS *look as though there were a nightmare of sorrow and regret looming over their heads.* ABUL-MAHAMID *is presiding over this session. He wears shining black clothes that emphasize his swarthy complexion. His face is brown, his features are faded, and his eyeballs are constantly swiveling from side to side, and staring. His shoulders are wide, like two large wings. In front of him he has placed a large pair of scales. In one of the pans there are bundles, and in the other, raw salt.*

ABUL-MAHAMID We've carried out our promises. We've sent you the doctors, the engineers, the teachers, and a hundred sweeping machines to help you sweep up the salt in your mines . . . And still you haven't built the city!

ʿALI We've been faced with many obstacles . . . During this time, our chief engineer passed away . . .

ABUL-MAHAMID You haven't set up all those institutions. You haven't built the secondary schools, and the primary schools.

KHALIL The Arabic language is difficult to master . . . It requires years of memorization, and exercises, and . . .

ABUL-MAHAMID (*Interrupting*): And you haven't organized any medical centers, clinics, or hospitals. Disease has increased and spread.

MUHAMMAD There are so few physicians, and so many sick . . . Our workers are still not used to Abbasid methods of treatment.

ABUL-MAHAMID And every one of the hundred machines you've broken. They're completely destroyed!

YAHYA IBN MUHAMMAD Our workers aren't used to machines yet.

RAYHANA They're afraid of them. The machines make them tremble and shrink back.

ABUL-MAHAMID Has production increased? Of course not! It's declined, drastically . . .

RAFIQ (*Angrily*): Did you expect production to double in one year? Since when has that been a law of labor? Production's not a gown that changes color every second!

ABUL-MAHAMID (*Waving a piece of paper in front of the Council*): Here's the agreement made between us. It includes a doubling of production in the first year. You yourselves signed this agreement . . .

MUHAMMAD But you didn't allow for the psychological factors, and all the other circumstances . . .

ABUL-MAHAMID We loaned you a million golden dinars, didn't we?

COUNCIL MEMBERS *remain silent.*

ABUL-MAHAMID When they were in charge of the mines, the Abbasid managers achieved results. Under them, your workers were producing 1,500 qantars a year. But today the mines are under your supervision, and the workers are yours, and the government's in your hands. And production's declined and deteriorated. The estimate for last year was 1,000 qantars. What's happened to the other 500? Where are they?

RAYHANA We told you, we had many obstacles to overcome. We replaced the old mine managers with new, young ones.

ABUL-MAHAMID Why don't you say you've been hindered by other kinds of obstacles, like the worker demanding higher wages and holding demonstrations, as well as combining against you in innumerable strikes? That's what's brought down your production!

RAFIQ If you please, Abul-Mahamid, don't interfere in our affairs. You yourselves accepted these terms completely, which include the condition that the Caliph and his clerks won't interfere in any of our affairs.

ABUL-MAHAMID (*Shouting, protesting*): Then what's happened to the gold we loaned you? Where did you spend it? Answer me! I don't want to interfere in your affairs. But first, answer me, where did you squander the loan? It was *our* money, which we dedicated to raising *your* standard of production! Tell me!

ᶜALI (*Coldly*): To train foremen for the mines, of course. Training requires a lot of money.

ABUL-MAHAMID That's fiction! I swear by God, it's a fabrication! Foremen should be trained on the job!

KHALIL IBN ABAAN In organizing the labor in the mines . . . in cleaning, supervising, writing, calculating, weighing and measuring, and in transportation . . .

ABUL-MAHAMID The loan's gone into administration? Vanished into the pockets of the clerks? Another fabrication! How is it possible that a million golden dinars could disappear into the bellies of clerks, into their houses and their toilets? Look at your own bodies! Your bellies have got round!

RAYHANA Don't forget, we also had to pay salaries to the physicians, engineers, and instructors that you yourselves sent to help us.

ABUL-MAHAMID Don't forget that a substantial portion of the loan's been spent on cosmetics, bracelets, rings, dresses, and feathers! Look at your face in the mirror! Look how ugly it is now! And the rest of the money's gone to pay for ᶜAli's son's trips to Byzantium. Did my lord and master, the son of ᶜAli Ibn Muhammad, travel to Byzantium on nothing? Or on just his own money?

MUHAMMAD We need to become open-minded, to know the world . . .

ABUL-MAHAMID We know all about that myth! We know all about the open-mindedness that's professed by the filthy rich of Baghdad! So, open-mindedness is obtained by having the son of ᶜAli Ibn Muhammad go on a pleasure trip to Byzantium . . . Why don't you say you've built a villa for yourself? Where's the money for that come from? From the loan, of course!

MUHAMMAD The villa I had built was made of ordinary red clay . . .

ABUL-MAHAMID But it includes a recreation room, and a bar . . . And you plan to invite Ziryab, the singer. Who's going to pay for that?

YAHYA IBN MUHAMMAD His villa's a model for Zanj housing projects. It's like those houses they're building of red clay in the Sudan nowadays. In this way we'll fulfill our destiny, revive our heritage, and give new life to the personality of our people.

ABUL-MAHAMID Words! Words! Words! . . . Calamities! . . . You're hanging on to them so you can camouflage your failures in production! You make me laugh . . . You speak of your originality, and forget that you're no more than a mere ragbag of nationalities and tribes, every one of you clamoring to make your mark. And why? Simply to challenge Abbasid civilization. But Abbasid civilization's universal, whether you like it or not. All these differences will be absorbed in it, because we believe in knowledge.

RAFIQ You're going too far, man! You're smearing us! You're cunning and sly, like a fox! You're full of tricks and ruses! You're a reactionary! (*He tries to hit* ABUL-MAHAMID, *but a* COUNCIL MEMBER *holds him back.*)

ABUL-MAHAMID (*Enduring all this with contempt*): I'm malicious, am I? A conspirator and plotter? A reactionary? . . . Cursing will get us nowhere, my son. I suppose you're a progressive revolutionary?

RAFIQ You thrive on the exploitation of labor!

ABUL-MAHAMID This man calls himself a progressive revolutionary, while at the same time he refuses men freedom of speech, freedom of production, and the freedom to strike! . . . May God bring you good health for being so progressive! . . . Look at Baghdad! It contains all opinions and factions: the Zaidites, the Malakites, the atheists, the Caysanites, the Ultra-Shiʿites, the Kharajites,* the scoundrels, the sophists, and the theologians.

RAFIQ Oh yes, Baghdad! Baghdad's a very large zoo!

ABUL-MAHAMID Can someone call himself a revolutionary when he doesn't respond to the demands of mine workers for better wages? And all this time we've been giving you land and villages, opening gardens for the people, and financing you with a vast loan.

RAFIQ There's trickery in your loan! And there's evil in your machines!

ABUL-MAHAMID What is there in your "model homes" but sly cunning and wasted money? Members of the Council, let's be brief. Here's the text of the new agreement. I'll read it to you, and we'll meet again next year.

RAFIQ No, we won't! We don't want a new agreement! We'll sell salt to Byzantium, to China, and the Fatimids of Egypt!

ABUL-MAHAMID But they all buy their salt *re¤ned*, from our markets.

RAFIQ ʿAli, don't sign this agreement!

ABUL-MAHAMID Well, your salt's as hard as rock . . . We need to refine it before people can use it in their food. Where will you get the refineries? . . . We're taking back our doctors.

ʿALI and YAHYA You mustn't do that!

ABUL-MAHAMID And taking back our engineers . . .

*All of these are religious, philosophical, or political sects.

ᶜALI and KHALIL Please don't do that! He's immature! He doesn't know what he's talking about!

ABUL-MAHAMID And taking back our teachers . . .

ᶜALI and RAYHANA We beg you, don't do that! We'll sign the agreement, here and now!

RAFIQ Let me break his neck! I'm going to kill him, wipe him out! (*They restrain him.*)

ABUL-MAHAMID You, lad, you shout too much, and you don't do anything.

RAFIQ (*Addressing the* COUNCIL MEMBERS): You're traitors, traitors! Cowards! You're the shadows of the Abbasids, their slaves! Are you really going to sign this agreement and cast us into slavery?

RAFIQ *is taken away and isolated.*

ABUL-MAHAMID Is this how our sincerity's rewarded? With malice and ingratitude?

ᶜALI We'll remove him. We'll expel him from our party.

ABUL-MAHAMID There is no strength or power except in God . . . (*Pretends to weep.*)

YAHYA IBN MUHAMMAD Wipe away your tears, Abul-Mahamid. We'll put him in jail. Don't let yourself be bothered.

RAFIQ Traitors! Puppies! Dogs of the markets!

ABUL-MAHAMID (*Still pretending to weep*): Allah will be our sustenance! Praise be to Him, the One we depend on! . . .

KHALIL We'll cut his roots, we promise you! We'll throw him in jail!

ABUL-MAHAMID (*Suddenly wiping away his tears*): Here is the text of the new agreement. "In the name of God the Merciful and Compassionate. First: With regard to the reduction in the mining of salt, in view of certain difficulties which have stood in the way of the doubling of production, and because the first financial loan has been spent on behalf of things beneficial to the Country of the Zanj, the Caliph al-Muᶜtamid will buy all their raw salt, production of which is estimated to stand at 2,000 qantars for the coming year. He will pay a silver dirham for every qantar that is delivered to the public gate of Baghdad, the City of Peace . . ."

RAFIQ Brum brum! Shrum brum! Shrum brum shrum!

COUNCIL MEMBERS Agreed.

ABUL-MAHAMID "(A) If the Council of the Zanj does not fulfil this condition, then the Caliph, al-Muᶜtamid, reserves the absolute right to alter this agreement . . ."

RAFIQ Brum shrum brum shrum brum shrum!

COUNCIL MEMBERS Agreed.

ABUL MAHAMID "(B) If the Council of the Zanj does not make 2,000 qantars of raw salt available by the end of the month of Hijja in the coming year, then the Caliph, al-Muᶜtamid, reserves the absolute right to reprice the salt as he sees fit, with regard to every qantar delivered to the public gate of Baghdad . . ."

RAFIQ Shrum brum shrum! Brum brum!

COUNCIL MEMBERS Agreed.

ABUL MAHAMID "(C) If the amount of raw salt stated above has not been delivered on the said date, then the Council of the Zanj will be obligated to make a financial compensation, the amount of which will be 5,000 dinars, cash . . ."

RAFIQ Shrum brum shrum! Brum shrum brum!

COUNCIL MEMBERS Agreed.

ABUL MAHAMID "(D) If, after investigation, it has been proven beyond any shadow of a doubt that the Council of the

Zanj has sold raw salt to Byzantium, or China, or any other nation than the Abbasid Caliphate, then the remaining amount of the production of the mines is to be confiscated and brought to the public gate at Baghdad . . ."

RAFIQ Brum shrum brum shrum!

COUNCIL MEMBERS Agreed.

ABUL MAHAMID "Secondly: In the interests of underdeveloped humanity, and with the objective of raising the standard of production, and in support of your political and social system and the maintenance of economic and financial relations between the Abbasid Caliphate and the Council of the Zanj, our Lord and Master, the Caliph al-Muʿtamid, decrees the following: he will continue to send you physicians, engineers, theologians, mechanics, technologists, grammarians, bankers, scientists, poets, cooks, tailors, gravediggers, housekeepers, and dramatists . . ."

COUNCIL MEMBERS May God support the Caliph, our Lord and Master!

RAFIQ Traitors! Sheep dogs!

ABUL-MAHAMID "Thirdly: In regard to the various difficulties which have stood in the way of achieving increased production during the past year, and in consideration of the needs of the Council in the field of technological training, it has been decided to grant you a loan of twenty thousand gold dinars, which the Council will pay back over a period of ten years, beginning with the current year, at an interest rate of fifteen percent . . ."

COUNCIL MEMBERS (*Speaking among themselves, and trembling*): Let's sign . . . (*They sign.*)

ʿALI (*Shaking hands with* ABUL-MAHAMID): This is how genuine cooperation ought to be! And if it isn't like this, then there's no point to it!

ABUL-MAHAMID We're not asking for any reward, or thanks . . . All we're doing is serving the public welfare of this nation.

ʿALI In the name of the Council . . .

RAFIQ Not in *my* name, you traitor!

ʿALI In the name of the Council, I ask you, Abul-Mahamid, to present our many thanks to our Lord the Caliph, al-Muʿtamid.

ABUL-MAHAMID (*Preparing to leave*): In the name of all love and dignity, there is still one matter I want to inform you about, members of the Council. The Caliph, al Muʿtamid, has seen fit to retain the twenty thousand dinars in his treasury, as well as the money that is to pay for the salt. This has been arranged in case of robberies, or holdups, or bandit raids—may God not allow these? Who knows? Therefore your money is safe from all these calamities. It is secure and protected in the treasury at Baghdad, and you can withdraw it any time you wish.

ʿALI We're not going to argue about that. Trust is everything.

YAHYA It's a mere formality . . .

KHALIL The treasury of the Muslims belongs to us . . .

RAFIQ Abul-Mahamid, listen to me! You're a thief, and the Caliph's a bandit!

ABUL-MAHAMID (*Contemplates* RAFIQ *closely, then begins praying in supplication to God*): O God, bestow your mercy upon us! Preserve our minds from madness! You are the Almighty Being, who rules over all . . .

RAFIQ Abul-Mahamid, you crook! You drinker of the sweat of the hungry! This evil trick's worked on these cowards, but I can see what you've done!

ABUL-MAHAMID There's just one more thing that I wish to say. The Caliph appeals to you to release the prisoners in your jails. He sees no justification for imprisoning those whose opinions differ from your own. That is his recommendation.

ʿALI We will carry this out, and you will please convey to our Lord our loyalty to him, and our thanks for his favors. Convey to him our gratitude.

ALI, KHALIL, *and* RAYHANA *bid farewell to* ABUL-MAHAMID, *while* MUHAMMAD *and* YAHYA *stand restraining* RAFIQ *from attacking* ABUL-MAHAMID.

The COUNCIL MEMBERS *reconvene.*

ʿALI Are you crazy?

RAFIQ Are you so naive?

RAYHANA Lower your voice before our leader!

RAFIQ As of today, he's no longer my leader. How can he be a leader? A leader over whom? The leader of the new slavery?

ʿALI Didn't you see how we obtained a new loan?

RAFIQ And how will we pay it back? With what money? Where is it? We're besieged on all sides—by land, sea, and river—and you offer your neck to the one who'll slit your throat from ear to ear! . . .

KHALIL How can you curse us when we're being faithful?

RAFIQ Faithful? What do you mean? Faithfulness isn't enough to build the city of al-Mukhtara!

RAYHANA It is! We are the true believers . . .

RAFIQ Truthfulness isn't enough to build the city of al-Mukhtara!

ʿALI Are you denying that we're faithful?

RAFIQ Faithfulness is always prejudiced. Truthfulness is always biased. Forget my accusations . . . look carefully around you . . . You're so naive! How can you be truthful with people whose intentions are evil, whose thoughts are evil, whose plans are evil? How? Tell me! Do the wolf and the lamb meet together and live under one roof and unite in the same cause?

ʿALI But they've pardoned us. They've sent us their instructors . . .

RAFIQ To warp your minds!

KHALIL They've sent their engineers . . .

RAFIQ To make you prisoners of your own lives and habits!

RAYHANA Well, what about the physicians?

RAFIQ To camouflage the situation; to make the camouflage look like the real thing; to cover up their falseness and dazzle your eyes and your minds . . .

ʿALI If I'd been firm with you and sent you with Sulayman, you wouldn't have done these ugly things to us.

RAFIQ Muhammad! Yahya! Khalil! Say something! Am I to blame, or is he? Judge fairly . . . You traitor! I'm washing my hands of you and your agreements with the Abbasids and your loyalty to them! And you, Khalil, how can you support this naive simpleton, who said farewell to that thief and schemer Abul-Mahamid, saying, "Tell the Caliph how very loyal we are"? And you, Rayhana . . . Have you forgotten the Battle of the Naharwan, when we wrung the necks of the Abbasid spies in the mines and on the boats? Today you're hunting for cosmetics, bracelets, and dresses! Who's for the workers, and who's for you, and who's for me? Who? Who?

KHALIL The marshes are our country. We love it and we'll defend it, and we won't let the Abbasids harm us.

RAFIQ Yes, we're free patriots—who doubts that? But social issues are more important than political ones. Have any of the problems you've had in erecting the Great House of the Revolution since the Liberation had anything to do with the staging of a revolution, Khalil? I'm a product of the Liberation, and I can't understand a thing you're talking about. Where is the revolutionary program?

ʿALI Haven't we proclaimed equality for all?

RAFIQ That was equality among the workers in the mines—there's still no equality between you and them.

ʿALI Haven't we abolished servitude, and the exploitation of the slaves?

RAFIQ That was merely a phase. It's over. It's past history. Why are we cheering about it?

ʿALI What about our unity?

RAFIQ What about the demonstrations and the strikes? What about the gangs? What about all the opponents you've thrown in jail?

ʿALI You're talking about the revolutionary program! (*He laughs.*)

RAFIQ Yes, the revolutionary program . . . It maps out the path of our future. It plans our economy and sets the agenda for our efforts. It's our freedom, our dignity, our bread . . .

ʿALI But you know the people are ignorant. We've got to educate them, to teach them how to build the city.

RAFIQ The workers have rebelled because they carry the truth of revolution in their hearts. They know which is the free man and which is the slave. Whoever knows that is *not* ignorant!

MUHAMMAD I think the lad's right . . .

ʿALI So . . . You too?

MUHAMMAD But I say, if we'd kept on with the war and not signed the peace treaty with the Abbasids, we wouldn't be all caught up in loans and schemes of interest. We could have been more self-reliant.

ʿALI But where would we have gotten money from?

YAHYA As an example, I wish we'd allied ourselves with the Carmathians . . .

KHALIL You too, Yahya? But we've been treated fairly, and justly . . .

ʿALI Your solutions will get us nowhere! War has only one end: destruction.

RAFIQ The world stands on two horns, the Horn of Good and the Horn of Evil, and violence moves them. The strong eat the weak. He who has no power starves to death, and his neck's broken.

KHALIL You young pup! These are theories, slogans, and fantasies!

RAFIQ Oh Master, it's the truth! Look at your position now! Instead of fighting you with weapons, with swords and spears, Abul-Mahamid can suck your strength away with his money, until your brains are empty and he can throw you in the garbage. Long live the Revolution!

ʿALI Take it easy!

RAFIQ Abul-Mahamid's created two classes among you: you, the members of the Council, have taken the place of the Abbasids and become lords; and the workers of the marshes, who can't hear what I'm saying, have become slaves once more—slaves of the members of the Council!

ʿALI The issue's more complicated than you claim!

MUHAMMAD Yes, that wicked thief *has* deceived us!

YAHYA How can we straighten things out?

RAFIQ We should cancel our agreement with the Abbasids and declare war on them. We should write our future with our own hands!

KHALIL That's infantile! How can you throw away thousands of dinars?

RAFIQ Our maximum production is 1,000 qantars?

KHALIL That's right.

RAFIQ And our interest payments come to 1,000 dinars?

KHALIL True.

RAFIQ Then how will we pay back the loan?

KHALIL (*Silence, reflection, then suddenly*): You're right! The loan's a burden on our shoulders! It's useless!

ʿALI So, you too?

RAFIQ Let's go to war! Long live the Revolution!

RAYHANA Come to your senses!

RAFIQ Long live the Revolution! Let's go to war, so that the Abbasids will never enslave us again!

ʿALI War's no solution! *Peace* is the question!

RAFIQ War's for destroying agents, traitors, and the disloyal!

ʿALI Our only course of action will be to attack Baghdad! . . .

RAFIQ Because you've sat on the throne of the Abbasids, and you've built up the houses of the Abbasids, you've become warped!

RAYHANA You're crazy!

RAFIQ The people who demonstrated are ready for war! They're the majority, and you're the minority! Let's go to war! Long live the Revolution!

MUHAMMAD I agree with you, and I'll support you to the last days of my life! You've awakened me, my son! I feel sorry and sad for what's happened . . . I ask myself how the situation could have changed, reversed itself to the point that the workers we liberated from bondage are demonstrating against us . . .

KHALIL And how we could have thrown them in jail . . .

YAHYA And robbed them of the freedom of speech . . .

KHALIL And fed them the worst food . . .

YAHYA Workers of the marshes, listen to my words! This is my flesh! To win justice for yourselves, you can do whatever you want with it!

MUHAMMAD I don't understand anything any more . . .

KHALIL That's because we were blinded, and our consciences dulled.

RAFIQ We've been shown the truth . . . Let's declare war! Long live the Revolution!

ʿALI Take it easy! . . . If you declare war, you won't build the city. It's either one thing or the other!

RAFIQ Out of my way! Long live the Revolution! (*He snatches up the red flag.*)

RAYHANA I'm going back to the Land of the Sind. It will be my refuge and my sanctuary.

ʿALI That's not the solution . . . You'll be back, because the problem still has to be solved . . .

Darkness

WRITTEN AND PRODUCED BY
THE BALALIN COMPANY OF JERUSALEM

Translated by
Aida Bamia
and Thomas G. Ezzy

The Palestinian Balalin Company was formed in 1971 in Jerusalem, giving as its first performance in the same year a play called *A Piece of Life*. In 1972, the group embarked on an ambitious avant-garde experiment with the play *Darkness* (*al-ᶜAtma*), which the company wrote, prepared, and performed collectively. The producer was François Abu Salim, and among the actors was the musician and lute player Mustafa al-Kurd. The collective and pioneering nature of this experiment and its successful performance attracted great publicity, and the group enjoyed immediate fame and popularity. In 1973, the company embarked on an ambitious program by arranging a theater festival in Ramallah at which it offered three plays: *The Treasure, The Emperor's Robe*, and *Weather Report*. After this climactic success, the company began to have differences of opinion and disbanded in 1974. Abu Salim, al-Kurd, and some others continued their theatrical careers and, in 1977, Abu Salim founded the Hakawati Group in Jerusalem containing Palestinian members from both the territories occupied after 1967 and Israel proper. The activity of this new theatrical group culminated in the building of its own theater in 1984. But, being faithful to a political commitment that aimed at exposing the evils of Israeli occupation, the theatrical program of this group, as of other Palestinian theatrical groups, was constantly jeopardized by the Israeli authorities.

S.K.J.

DARKNESS

The play opens while the audience is entering the hall. MILAD *is sitting at one end of the stage; he is holding a few balloons, as well as a bottle and a cigarette pack containing one or two cigarettes.* MILAD*'s mood indicates that he is sad, yet despite his sadness he seems self-confident and takes an occasional drink from the bottle. He toys with the balloons and the cigarette pack. In an effort to amuse himself, he may get up to pick something up off the floor. He may speak to a person in the audience and ask for a light or a cigarette. The audience may make comments, continually, on* MILAD*'s condition. He will not pay any attention to their words unless he likes what they say and finds it funny—especially if their comments relate to his psychological condition and to his role on the stage. Only then will he respond and answer the person who speaks to him.*

Light music is heard as the people enter. Lights are projected onto the stage curtain, which is closed.

When the performance begins, the sound of the music gradually subsides. Meanwhile, MILAD *lies down slowly on his back, until he is totally flat on the stage. The curtain opens, announcing the beginning of the play.* MILAD *stays on his back. The audience waits for twenty or thirty seconds for something to happen, then the curtain is closed. Voices can be heard behind the curtain, asking for* MILAD. *The curtain is partly open—a technical problem. We see* FRANÇOIS *running from stage left to stage right, where* MILAD *is lying.*

FRANÇOIS (*Calling aloud*): Milad! Milad! Hey guys, where's Milad? Where did he go? ʿAli! Husam! Have you seen Milad? Damn him, why is he behaving like this at the last minute? Don't you see how serious it is? The hall's full, and people are waiting! Listen to them shouting . . . Go look for him in the back room . . . He was here a minute ago, then he left . . . Where did he go? He went to the hall, he took a bottle with him . . . Oh-oh, what does that mean? Is this a time for drinking? I'll show him, now! Milad! Milad! (FRANÇOIS *goes from one end of the stage to the other, calling; also, he looks out into the hall. Then he spots* MILAD *lying on his back.*)

FRANÇOIS Hey, Milad, what do you think you're doing? Are you crazy?

MILAD Ha! Ha! I can see the stage through your legs.

FRANÇOIS Milad, do you know that the curtain's been raised?

MILAD Yes, I know, I saw it go up—but upside down. And I saw it lowered, but also upside down.

FRANÇOIS Milad, this is no time for joking. Get up and go back to your place on the lighting switchboard, may God grant you long life. The hall's full, and we have to begin.

MILAD Forget the play for now, man . . . We still have a few minutes. Why don't you lie down beside me and observe the world? Have you ever seen it overturned?

FRANÇOIS That's enough! Don't make me swear!

MILAD (*Continuing*): No, I have a better idea. Let's have all the audience lie down on the floor and then watch the performance. Let them see a play presented upside down! (*He laughs, pleased with his idea.*) I'm a genius, aren't I?

FRANÇOIS (*Nervous and angry*): Why are you being such an ass? I was talking to you like I would to a human being. When I say get up, I mean get up! The play's about to begin! All the actors are very tense, and the hall's filled with people that are waiting for "Your Highness"! Everything's ready! All we're waiting for is for you to get up and go to your post to operate the lights! We want to begin!

MILAD Please, François, don't shout. I've had it up to here today!

FRANÇOIS But, my friend, people are waiting. (*He repeats this sentence several times.*)

MILAD (*Edgily*): Let them wait a little while longer! What would it matter to them if they stayed in the hall two hours and ten minutes instead of two hours?

FRANÇOIS Ten minutes? Are you out of your mind?

MILAD Even half an hour. What would it matter? They'd be a little late for a TV program featuring the singing of Samira Tawfiq, or for an evening with the neighbors, which they'd spend eating food and sweets, stuffing themselves and gossiping about other neighbours. What are those important responsibilities that are waiting for them? What have they got to do? What?

FRANÇOIS (*Calmly*): That's none of our business. We have a responsibility that we must assume.

MILAD I know *my* responsibility very well, but you don't. All you think of is yourselves. You're all selfish. You think a human being's like a machine, you only have to press a button to make him work.

FRANÇOIS No, my dear Milad, man is certainly not a machine, and I never said he was. A human being is a responsible person; if he has faith, he's capable of behaving responsibly. But if he becomes slack and says God will provide, he proves that he has no faith and can't be entrusted with a job to do. In short, he can't be considered a human being.

MILAD (*As though interrupting* FRANÇOIS): A human being's more than that. He's flesh and blood, he's emotions and nerves, and problems, too. You're worrying about the time, you're worrying because it's seven o'clock already, and the curtain's been raised, and the hall's full of people. Yet neither you nor the audience know that today, in order to get the performance started at seven sharp, I was fired from my job. It's even possible that the doctor who fired me, along with his wife, is sitting in the hall and looking forward to an enjoyable evening.

FRANÇOIS I know, I know you have problems at work. I also know that every one of the actors has more problems than he can handle. I have problems too. But we can't all lie on our backs and give in to our problems. We can't allow our personal problems to interfere with the activities of the Company, either. This is certainly no way to act, Milad. (*In a recriminatory and imposing tone*:) For seven months we've been working on this play. We've worked hard, we've sweated, we've stayed up late. Each of us has had a responsibility and has tried very hard. We all have personal problems, but we put them aside because we believe that in order to produce something worthwhile we must endure our problems. We have no right to block others. Look at yourself: because of one small problem, you and this bottle are destroying what we've built.

MILAD Ha! Do you hear what he's saying, madam? Do you like it? (*He turns toward* FRANÇOIS) I want to introduce you to Mrs. Khadra—Mrs. Green Bottle. She's the product of the labors of priests—you probably know that priests take good care of women. Khadra at least stays with me whenever I have a problem. She entertains me. She comforts me. She doesn't philosophize, she doesn't dramatize, and she doesn't shout at me like Mrs. Umm Elias does.

FRANÇOIS Oh no! This isn't the right time to be discussing Umm Elias too!

MILAD No, no, listen, I'd like to tell you something about this Umm Elias, the wife of the doctor who employs me. I mean who used to employ me. As God is my witness, when I was done at the clinic she used to send me to work in the garden, then she'd call me to help in the kitchen. Then she'd send me to clean the garage and wash the car. She'd send me up to the roof, then down to the garden again, and later to the market and the post office. Then I had to check whether the doctor needed anything at the clinic. By the time the day was over, François, I was totally finished! I can't find anyone better, kinder, and quieter than Mrs. Green Bottle. We enjoy each other's company.

FRANÇOIS (*To the bottle*): Pleased to meet you. (*He grabs* MILAD *by the shoulder*) Take your bottle and come with me; let's begin the play. Every actor is at his position, waiting. You too must be at your post. It's already ten minutes after seven.

ʿADIL (*Intervening from the audience; his voice is loud and can be heard by everybody*): It doesn't matter, brother! We sympathize with you. But tonight, do try and make an effort. Let's see this play.

SAMIR (*Speaking loud enough to be heard by all*): Take it easy, man! We'll soon find you a better job. Tonight it's only a matter of two and a half hours. The play will soon be over. Do it for our sake.

ʿALI (*Loud enough to be heard by all*): Once the play's over, I promise you a bottle of the priests' product. But now, let's see the play.

MILAD (*To* ʿALI): For your sake only . . . for the sake of your eyes! True friendship's the best there is. (MILAD *goes with* FRANÇOIS *to the right side of the stage, in the direction of the lighting board. He stops and turns toward* ʿALI:) Don't forget . . . after the play's over, you give me a bottle of the priests' product! (MILAD *continues walking until both disappear backstage. The curtain falls.*)

The lights go off; the curtain rises. The lights are very weak. We see a suicide scene.

FRANÇOIS Let them learn.
Death ends everybody's troubles,
The fastest way to die is suicide.
I'll explain to you, I'll explain to you.
All you need is an open window, a fourth floor;
A clean suicide and the next day
Your name is in the papers. Why go on living
A life where you're constantly being
Punched in the nose? At home they're unfair to you,
In the street they're unfair to you, and at school.
I want to explain to you so I can teach others.
I am not weak, I can do something big, I can

Commit suicide, I can shake up the whole town.
The road to fame is an open window
On the fourth floor.

The scene lasts thirty seconds, long enough to get the spectators' attention. Suddenly the lights go out. Total darkness. For twenty seconds, not one voice is heard.

FRANÇOIS (*In a hoarse whisper*): Milad, what happened?

MILAD (*His voice is normal*): How would I know?

FRANÇOIS (*Hoarse whisper*): Lower your voice, Milad! Have you gone out of your mind?

MILAD I want you to hear me.

FRANÇOIS (*Raises his voice slightly*): What happened to the lighting? Why did the lights go out?

MILAD I don't know. It happened suddenly.

FRANÇOIS I said lower your voice!

MILAD But I want you to hear me . . . As for the lights, come and see for yourself. I don't know what happened.

FRANÇOIS (*Nervously, in a hoarse whisper*): How come you don't know?

MILAD Try it yourself.

FRANÇOIS (*In a normal voice*): Did they go off just like that? You must have been playing around with them, or not using them right. Otherwise they couldn't have just gone off by themselves!

MILAD Don't shout! By God, they went off by themselves! I was even taking a drink from the green bottle when it happened. If you don't believe me, ask Mrs. Green Bottle!

FRANÇOIS Damn you, and damn the bottle! This is no time for green bottles! Tell me what happened, I want to understand. Let me see what I can do.

MILAD Goodness, I told you I don't know! Ask the lights why they went out!

FRANÇOIS So this is what I get from you. Where's your hurricane lamp? What will we tell the people? What will we say?

MILAD Explain to them in a few words, precise and to the point.

FRANÇOIS You'd better stop talking and hand me the lamp.

FRANÇOIS *goes out on the stage and addresses the audience. While he is talking,* MILAD *enters carrying a gas lamp. He places it on the stage or on a piece of furniture. Then he returns backstage so that he can, inconceivably, drag out the whole lighting system.* FRANÇOIS *requests help from the audience in repairing the lighting system.*

FRANÇOIS We're sorry, folks. The lights went out unexpectedly, and we don't know why they failed. Will everyone please remain in his seat and keep quiet? The lights will be repaired any minute now.

Some comments from the audience are heard.

ʿALI Do we lose our tickets if the system isn't repaired?

FRANÇOIS No, you won't. Everybody will get his money back.

ʿALI How annoying! If we'd used the twenty piasters* to go to a café, we would have enjoyed ourselves. We would have played backgammon, drunk a soda, and listened to Umm Kulthum sing.† Such an inexpensive treat!

*Approximately fifty cents.

† Famous Arab woman from Egypt who dominated the art of singing in the Middle East for half a century.

FRANÇOIS So, according to you the theater's a twenty-piaster ticket, and two hours to kill and have fun in. But the theater isn't an easy task; it's rather difficult. Lights going off is nothing compared to the nervous tension of the actors backstage. Any one of us might have panicked, or fainted, and been unable to perform. In the past, that's happened very often.

MAJID Praise the lord, nervous tensions and breakdowns are signs of the corruption of souls, and their degeneration. This darkness is a reflection of the opacity which fills people's hearts and consciences . . . Like the man in charge of the lights: his life consists of a cigarette to smoke and a glass to drink . . . Do you think that God isn't aware of all these sins? He is, and this darkness is our punishment for deviating from the right path.

HUSAM Oh boy! Maybe the Power Company's decided to cut the electricity—or the Municipality even!

MAJID (*Angry*): Shut up, man, or I'll break your teeth!

EMILE (*Intervenes to calm the uproar*): Allow me to say a word on behalf of the audience, and let's see if you're capable of answering. The people who are here aren't responsible for what's happened. Some of them have been working all day, and they're tired. They've come to have fun, and not to listen to stories about the exploits of the theater.

SAMIR Suppose that you've been wounded in the street and you're bleeding. The cars pass you by without stopping. Since they work, and they're tired, all the drivers can say that it's not their fault. Meanwhile, you're bleeding . . . Isn't that selfish? Wouldn't it be better to stop and and ask about their problem and see if you can help?

ʿADIL *leaves the rows of the audience in a dreamy state, feeling very romantic.*

ʿADIL You can't imagine, brother, how happy I am to help the theater! For a long time, I've been wishing for such an opportunity! What can I do to help?

FRANÇOIS What do you know? Do you have any expertise in electricity?

ʿADIL I like the theater, art, nature, and birds . . . For me, the theater's a breath of fresh air in a monotonous and stifling life!

FRANÇOIS Thank you, I appreciate your feelings. But the theater's more than mere emotions. How can you help us?

ʿADIL Frankly, I'm waiting for you to tell me what to do.

FRANÇOIS Do you know anything about electricity?

ʿADIL I have an idea about it. Let me see what I can do . . .

FRANÇOIS *leads* ʿADIL *to the lighting system in order to show it to him.*

FRANÇOIS Have you ever seen equipment like this?

ʿADIL What a lovely piece of equipment! There's not another like it on the whole West Bank!

FRANÇOIS This isn't the time for that kind of talk. What I meant was, have you ever worked on equipment like this? Have you ever repaired any?

ʿADIL Anyhow, we must do our best to repair the lighting system.

FRANÇOIS I agree, but how?

ʿADIL Art must prevail! The electricity must be brought back! We must see the play, even if it's by candlelight!

EMILE *comes out, interrupting.*

EMILE You're wasting your time, brother. This boy won't be any use to you. He's talking about art, nature, and birds, while the situation needs someone who understands electricity, who knows how light functions . . . If we asked him about Ohm's law and the relationship between voltage and amperes, we'd soon find out how little he knows.

ʿADIL Does a person need to know all the theories of the world in order to repair an electrical malfunction?

EMILE Of course, of course . . . The whole world's basically linked by a system very similar to the system of electricity. The stars and the constellations, for example, have their own orbits, exactly like the electrons in electricity. A simple example, that *you* can understand, is that of the stars, which shine at night like electric bulbs. There you can see how complex electricity is, and how important theories are in repairing equipment like this.

FRANÇOIS Well, then, seeing that you know all this information by heart, you must be able to repair the system.

EMILE Before I start repairing this system, I must tell you that it was developed in 1911 by a German scientist. This was, naturally, before World War I. At that time all companies were busy producing military goods. In 1928, the Siemens Company bought the patent from that scientist, and the system you see now is the result of the genius of Hans Zimmermann.

FRANÇOIS This is useful, accurate, and interesting information. But let's apply these theories to the equipment.

ʿADIL Yes . . . We don't want to hear theories; we want to see work done.

EMILE Work isn't really possible without theories and laws. Speaking of work, what's your job?

ʿADIL I'm a carpenter.

THE SCENE OF THE CANDLES

ʿADIL I have an idea that might work. Why don't we get candles? Since no one's able to repair the equipment, let's go buy candles. Then you could perform your play by candlelight.

FRANÇOIS Why not? Let's try it . . . But where can we get candles at this hour?

ʿADIL From the shops, from the churches, from the mosques, from the houses . . . From the people! All the people!

FRANÇOIS Alright. Take some money and see what you can get with it.

ʿADIL No, no, I have money. Come on, pal.

MILAD Where to?

ʿADIL Get up! Don't you want to help me? We're going to buy candles! (ʿADIL *says this last from the rows of the audience, because he is in a hurry.*)

MILAD (*Catching up with* ʿADIL): By god, this is how youth moves! I'm old and done for! (ʿADIL *exits, followed by* MILAD.)

ʿADIL *and* MILAD *will be absent for about two minutes. During their absence,* EMILE *remains on stage, talking in an oratorical manner, using his hands to clarify the meaning of his words. He talks about a variety of subjects, addressing the audience,* FRANÇOIS, *and himself.*

EMILE Ladies and gentlemen, until the lighting system is repaired, we'll talk to you about the history of the theater. Every educated person who is worthy of the designation knows that the theater has had a long history. It has known many problems and has been divided, over the years, into many schools, such as the Realistic School, the Romantic, the Classical, the Experimental, and the Experiential; into Popular

Theater, Theater of the Poor, and Elizabethan Theater, with its giant, Shakespeare. There has also been Revolutionary Theater, Proletarian Theater, Abstract Theater, Comedy, Tragedy, Live Theater, Theater of the "Happening,"* and Psychodrama.

In order to save time, I will not make this list of names any longer. Now, let us enter into the subject of the history of the theater. As any intellectual worthy of that name knows, theater is a complex art, and fine literature. You can ask me about the art of drama, because I've written a few plays. And let me tell you frankly, I haven't found, up to now, a group of actors worthy of performing one of the seven plays I've written. My plays require people who understand them, and must be acted by lots of intellectuals. Also, it's important that an intellectual should produce them ... At any rate, the history of the theater is very long, and we can say that after the age of the Greek and Roman theater ...

EMILE *pursues his talk on the theater, but it gradually deteriorates into incomprehensible words and meaningless sounds. As this happens, the movements of his body, head, and hands change to synchronize with the sounds. His action evokes a surrealistic scene and lasts forty seconds.*

The audience is bored and irritated. ʿADIL *and* MILAD *enter from the outside, bringing candles.*

ʿADIL and MILAD Candles, candles, candles! We've brought the candles! Now we can continue the play ...

FRANÇOIS Great! How did you do it?

MILAD We pulled him out of bed.

FRANÇOIS Who did you pull out of bed?

MILAD The shop owner who sold us the candles.

FRANÇOIS Let's begin passing them out to the audience.

EMILE Wait! Don't pass them out until we've organized the distribution operation. (ʿADIL *and* MILAD *look at each other in a way that shows they believe him.*)

EMILE (*Pursuing*): We must take into consideration the fact that there are young children and older people in the audience. We run the risk of exposing everyone to a possible fire. We need to know the time it would take a fire brigade to reach the building. This is our first responsibility ... Then there is the question of the electric bulbs: since there are some that have a power of 75 watts and others 100 or 200, we must know the number of candles we will need in order to replace the original lighting ... And as for fire, you mustn't forget that we are living in the Industrial Age, and clothes today are made of easily flammable substances. Also, there are in the hall many women whose hair is quite long; it must be remembered that either their hair or their dresses could easily catch fire ... By the way, we must also know how many extinguishers there are in the hall. Count them for me please. You, and you, too ... (EMILE *points at* ʿADIL *and* MILAD, *and they act like people who have been convinced by him, and are reluctant to distribute the candles.*)

In the midst of the audience, SAMIR *stands up, with obvious energy, and shouts.*

SAMIR Enough is enough! Damn you, and damn all intellectuals like you! You've killed us! Have some consideration! Have

*This English word is used in the Arabic text.

mercy on the nerves of the people who are sitting here! . . . But how could you, since you're made of stone! . . . What can I tell you? You're thoughtless. You're a living symbol of despair, as well as fear and weakness. You're made of stone, you're dead, without feelings . . . Every sentence you pronounced was a dead sentence, lifeless, because life springs from the heart and you're heartless.

Your theories are all superficial; they're nothing but glittering words that you memorize and repeat without understanding their true meaning, because their true meaning's known by the one who discovered them and wrote them down.

Walk in the streets, man! Eat cookies! Play with your son in the park! Stroll the boulevards, sing, look at the world, and you'll see it's colorful, red and green, with a blue sky and a beautiful sun! Don't look at the world through printed words.

You're a man of darkness! The obscurity we see around us comes from you and people like you, from those who live in the world only to show us despair and teach us fear . . . Your heart's full of fear! All you know is: don't dirty the curtains; watch out, the wood of the stage can catch fire; don't pass out the candles.

All the time you were talking, you didn't say one thing from the heart, one sentence of your own. That's the reason I said you're a dead person. (SAMIR *looks at* ʿADIL, MILAD, *and* FRANÇOIS *accusingly*:) Are you still here? Were you really convinced by him?

FRANÇOIS, *as though awakening from a sleep, intervenes. He gives orders to* ʿADIL *and* MILAD.

SAMIR Can I do something to help?

FRANÇOIS Come on, Milad, go with him and pass the candles out to the people.

MILAD *and* ʿADIL *carry handfuls of candles and distribute them to the audience, saying a few words to them as they do.* EMILE *accompanies them. He tries to discourage people from taking the candles, and recommends that they take his advice. He keeps doing this until he reaches his place and sits down. He will remain seated until the presentation of the scene on the theater by* HANI *and* FRANÇOIS.

MILAD Now, everyone will hold a candle, a little flame . . . We're all responsible. If the candles remain lit, it means that the hall and the stage will be lit, and we'll be able to watch the play; otherwise, we'll return to a state of darkness. We'll see who'll hold on well until the light's restored. Every person's holding a candle; whoever doesn't have one must ask for one. If *we* don't hold the candles, no one will come from outside to hold them for us, and we could remain in the dark forever . . . Take care of the candle. It's your responsibility; accept it gracefully, and think of more important ones.

MILAD *takes his place in one of the corners of the theater.* ʿADIL *goes back to* FRANÇOIS.

ʿALI Let's get it over with! We've been waiting half an hour in the dark, we've held a candle, but when do we see a play? You must either give us our money back or show us a play.

ʿADIL Do you think you'll be able to go on with the play now?

FRANÇOIS I don't think so. The lighting isn't enough.

ʿADIL What should we do?

FRANÇOIS I think the only solution would be to have a qualified electrician repair the equipment.

While ʿADIL *and* FRANÇOIS *are talking, another dialogue begins between* NADIA *and* HANI. *Their voices are low, but can be heard by the people sitting around them. Gradually their voices rise to a degree that allows them to be heard by the entire hall. This change in volume takes place after* FRANÇOIS *has addressed the audience and asked for a qualified electrician.*

NADIA Hani. Hani . . .

HANI What do you want?

NADIA Listen . . . Look at me for a minute.

HANI What else do you want?

NADIA Why are you talking to me with your head turned? Why don't you face me?

HANI Well here, I'm looking at you! What's wrong?

NADIA What do you think of the things that are happening here?

HANI It's a farce! I think they're taking advantage of us.

NADIA I don't mean that . . . Did you hear what the producer said?

HANI Oh. He admitted that he's an ass, and that he's incapable of repairing the equipment, and *huf*! (*He blows out his candle.*)

NADIA Why did you blow out your candle?

HANI One candle less won't make any difference; and anyhow, it's useless.

MILAD *holds the audience witness to* HANI'S *attitude. He directs the light onto* HANI *and* NADIA.

MILAD Do you see? Do you hear? We gave the gentleman a small candle and told him that it was *his* responsibility, so that we could all sit in light. He failed to assume it . . . What difference can one candle make, he says! If everyone thought like him, we'd be sitting in darkness again.

NADIA They asked for an electrician; I think I can help them. I'm going onto the stage.

HANI That's all we need! Do you want to provoke a scandal? What do you mean, going onto the stage?

NADIA What's wrong with that? I understand electricity and I want to go help them repair the equipment.

HANI Will you please keep quiet and stay where you are? Don't cause a public scandal . . . You belong to a respectable family, and you can't mix with their kind.

NADIA What does respectability have to do with it? Why did I go to school, and then to college? Why did I major in electrical engineering? Why the sleepless nights, the fatigue, the exams? Day in and day out I used to sit with piles of books, closed in by four walls, seeing neither sun nor blue sky . . . Why did I do all that? Why?

HANI Because a girl of your social position has to have a university degree . . .

NADIA (*Interrupting* HANI): In order to frame it and hang it on the wall for guests to look at! While I, the one who took the degree, don't count! The diploma's become more important than the knowledge that earned me the degree . . . It's not the education you want, but a degree, a social position! That's what you want!

HANI Don't start in with your fancy logical and scientific discussions. I'm a man who dislikes stubborn people. Obey me the way you've been doing until now. No more discussions. The subject's closed.

NADIA What do you mean, "the subject's closed"? Do you think that because you're my fiancé you have the right to talk to me that way? Slavery's over! The sultan's harem is history! . . . I'm determined to go onto the stage to help; you must respect my wish. There must be equality . . . I will go onto the stage to help the group and put the theories I've learned into practice. I must work, because a diploma's knowledge, not a mere object to hang on a wall for visitors to admire.

HANI So, that's it?

NADIA Yes, that's it!

NADIA *stands up, but* HANI *pulls her by the arm and she sits.*

HANI Sit down and listen to me! Have a little self-respect . . .

NADIA I don't want to listen!

ʿADIL *intervenes from the stage.*

ʿADIL She has an impressive degree in engineering while we're sitting in the dark, and you don't want her to come onto the stage to make the necessary repairs? A while ago you were blaming Milad, saying that the electricity was his responsibility. Your responsibility, however, is greater: to give her her freedom and the chance to help.

MILAD *is sitting in one of the corners, reading a newspaper aloud.*

MILAD "Society News: One of our rising generation, the engineer Di'a Kahrabawi,* has returned home after having obtained a bachelor's in electrical engineering, with honors. Well-wishers will be welcomed at the engineer's father's house, 75 Misbah† Street . . . " (*Sarcastically*:) Anyone reading about "our rising generation" in the newspapers would think the world imports progress from us . . .

HANI If you get up on that stage, I'll leave, and you won't see me again. What do you say?

NADIA I respect you as my fiancé, but I won't accept conditions and orders of this kind. The fact that you're my fiancé doesn't give you the right to exploit me. You must also understand that you can't control my freedom like this.

HANI I'm not restricting your freedom. I'm only telling you how a girl of your status ought to behave . . .

NADIA I'm a girl, a girl called Nadia! Not so-and-so's daughter and from such-and-such a class . . . I'm a girl and a human being; a human being who knows electricity. That's why I want to help, and you have no right to stop me! And no one in this hall, or even in the whole world, has the right to stop me . . .

MAJID (*Interrupts* NADIA, *infuriated by her words*): No! It's not true! In my opinion, everyone has a duty to stand and speak out! It's the duty of every person in this hall, and of anyone who deserves to be called a human being and has at least a minimum of respect and consideration for our traditions and customs. Here, I protest, even if the whole audience doesn't. I'm sure they'll all agree with every word I say. A girl who rejects her fiancé's orders and goes against his will is unheard of! Such a girl deserves to be burnt!

NADIA Why? Aren't I a human being? Don't I have the right to express my opinions, and act according to my opinions and my will?

MAJID (*Addressing* HANI): Sir, how can you allow your fiancée to talk like this? Aren't you a man? Shut her up, don't let her talk! The woman's a devil!

HANI Nadia, if you say one more word, I'll have to leave the hall and take you with me by force.

NADIA I won't stop talking and I won't go with you!

NADIA *stands up to get into the aisle, but* HANI *pulls her back.*

*Literally, "electric light."

† Literally, "lamp."

HANI Nadia, come and sit down! I'm beginning to believe the man who said you were a devil is right.

MAJID Go ahead, sir! Beat her if necessary! Beat her, I give you the permission to do so!

NADIA (*Shouting*): I don't want to listen to anything anymore! I want to do whatever I want! (*She breaks away from* HANI*'s grasp.*) I'm fed up!

HANI (*Runs toward the stage after* NADIA *and grabs her hand*): If you want to get on the stage, do. But, as I told you before, you won't see me again!

NADIA I'll do what I want! If I want to help out on the stage, I'll go up there! You can do whatever you like. And if I feel like seeing you again, I'll see you.

NADIA *runs away;* HANI *runs after her and catches her.*

ʿALI This is getting really hot!

HANI (*Catching* NADIA *for the last time*): No! You won't do as you like!

NADIA (*Shouting*): I certainly will! (*She runs away and appears seconds later on the stage.*)

ʿALI Things are looking bright! Really bright! By God, don't you think things have brightened up?

MAJID God's curse upon her! Why did you let her get on the stage? May Almighty God forgive us!

HANI (*Looking dazed*): This is my problem . . . It's my business . . .

MAJID May God forgive me! He has every right to be angry with us and spread this darkness on us!

HANI (*Talking to himself and to* NADIA): I wanted to provide you with the life of a princess . . . to buy you the best clothes, the most beautiful dresses, the latest fashions . . .

ʿALI: Don't answer him, beauty! And don't worry . . .

Talking to himself, repeating the previous sentences, HANI *gradually nears the stage, then gets up on it. He approaches* FRANÇOIS, *while* ʿADIL *and* NADIA *are working on the equipment.*

HANI Hello. Are you the producer? Excuse us, my fiancée's nervous. But she can help you—without a doubt, certainly. She's studied, and she's bright. She has a degree, a degree in electrical engineering.

FRANÇOIS By God, this is great! Then she'll be sure to repair the equipment quickly, and we'll be able to see the play!

HANI Of course! I told you, she studied and studied, for four years. Also, her degree's from a reputable university in Germany, and then she went to America to specialize. She's mad about the theater, and art in general. To tell you the truth, I like the theater and art too, but the theater in our country's still poor, very poor. I'm telling you this because I've seen a large variety of theaters; the quality in our country isn't so good.

FRANÇOIS You say that you like the theater and that the quality isn't so good . . . tell me, what have you done to improve it?

HANI Frankly, if you don't mind my saying so, I like the theater from a distance. That is, I don't like to participate in artistic activity because the life of artists is never settled. They don't know what will happen to them from one day to the other.

FRANÇOIS You don't have to act and participate directly in the process of acting. Theater work's also encouragement and help. It consists of seeing a play, telling one's friends about it, and bringing them along. Everyone can help, according to his means and potential. Tonight the theater needs an electrician; tomorrow it may need a printing machine, or a seamstress, a carpenter, a bricklayer, a doctor, and so many other things. Everyone can help the theater according to his own capacities.

HANI I've seen many theaters and met many producers, but not in this country.

FRANÇOIS Where?

HANI In Europe, all over Europe . . . You know, I once saw a play, a very nice play, and there was a delay, but not because of electricity. One of the actors got sick. They brought in a replacement immediately. He knew the role, he really did, and they didn't have to sit and wait.

FRANÇOIS Frankly, we're in a difficult situation. The electricity here . . .

HANI (*Interrupting*): I appreciate you, and I appreciate your work and efforts. Tell me, have you been doing this for a long time?

FRANÇOIS Almost a year—just over a year.

HANI If you need any help, I personally am ready to oblige. I might be able to do something for you. My fiancée would offer her services, too. I encourage her, because I'm not a reactionary. I hate reactionaries, and I love emancipation. I believe that women must work, like men . . .

FRANÇOIS We're in real need of people to help and encourage us, especially girls . . .

HANI Look! Look at her, notice how adroit she is . . . She's knowledgeable; after all, it's her job. See how she holds the screwdriver and the wire! She's so skillful—better than the carpenter sitting beside her!

FRANÇOIS In fact, she does seem to be quite skilled . . .

HANI She doesn't only *seem* to be skilled! . . . I tell you, she has a degree in electrical engineering. You must visit us one day and see her diploma, prominently displayed in the room. Her father ordered the frame from Spain. In that country there's a person who specializes in exotic frames. He worked three weeks to finish it. It's an antique piece, a thing of value. Very nice indeed! It's made of wood, with birds and flowers carved on it. It's breathtaking! That's what you call art! And you should see the color of the silk curtains in the sitting room, which exactly match the color of the wood of the frame. You ought to see my fiancée wearing an evening dress and sitting on the sofa, under the frame . . . She looks like a rare piece of art painted by the most famous of painters.

NADIA Enough, Hani! I'm neither a painting nor a doll that you dress up and display on a sofa. I'm a human being with a mind that thinks and eyes that see. I also have a heart that beats, and will power. Five years went by while I was studying, and after all that effort you see nothing in me but a doll wearing an evening dress, clean and wearing makeup, a beautiful and reasonable person, a housewife in a plastic bag . . . a woman that sees the world, but has no contact with it, as though tucked away in a bag, imprisoned and unable to reach people. I want to work! I want to help! I want to move, and think, and use my knowledge; I want to be in the center of life, not on the fringes.

The light projected onto the equipment is turned off and directed toward the front part of the stage, where a shift to another time takes place. Accompanied by HANI, NADIA *goes behind a white curtain. Then, with* HANI, *she emerges wearing a sack and hops toward the lit area.*

HANI (*Describing* NADIA *in telegraphic style*): My fiancée . . . height, 163 centimeters; weight, 120 pounds; dark-skinned, black hair, dark eyes; feet, size 36; bust, 90; waist, 60; pelvis, 90. And, as you can see . . . (*Asks* NADIA:) Is there something you'd like to tell the audience?

NADIA *nods her head affirmatively.*

HANI What do you want to say?

A loud, unintelligible sound is heard from inside the sack.

HANI My fiancée tells you that she's happy, and says hello.

NADIA *shakes her hands in a way that indicates disagreement.*

HANI What did you say, then?

More unintelligible sounds are heard.

HANI Oh! . . . She's telling you that she's happy because we're getting married soon, and because I intend to provide her with a life worthy of a princess. I shall buy her the best dresses, and have her wear the most expensive clothes, and give her her pick of the latest fashions . . .

NADIA *moves again inside the sack, indicating disagreement and uttering unintelligible sounds.*

HANI My fiancée says that all the women envy her. Our house will be beautifully furnished; it will be a model house. The kitchen will be the best there is, with silver cutlery; everything will shine and glitter. The whole house will glitter. Nadia's happy because she'll be working at home, with the electricity of the house, as she pleases. She advises all girls to do like her . . .

While he is talking, NADIA *is moving violently inside the sack as a sign of her disapproval.* HANI *takes hold of the sack and moves off toward the white curtain, repeating sentences on dresses, kitchen furniture, silver cutlery, etc. He and* NADIA *disappear behind the curtain. The light is taken off the front of the stage and turned back onto the equipment, where we see* ʿADIL, FRANÇOIS, *and* NADIA *and* HANI, *who have returned from behind the stage.*

NADIA (*Continuing her conversation as though she has not left the place*): Do you understand that I don't want to be a doll in a sack? And now I don't want us to remain in darkness . . . Enough talking. Let's get to work.

HANI Alright, alright . . . I'm very happy you're helping the group. I haven't objected. (*He turns to* FRANÇOIS, *continuing his previous conversation with him:*) What were we saying about the theater? Oh yes, I wanted to tell you about my experiences abroad . . . There, the theater's a part of people's lives. They appreciate the theater and art; they're ready to sacrifice a great deal for the development of the theater. I've met important and famous actors and directors. Let me tell you that the best thing you can do as an enthusiastic group, desirous of achieving something, is to leave this country. You'll get nowhere here, because it's impossible to teach these people to appreciate art and become as aware of the value of the theater as they are in Europe. It's impossible . . .

FRANÇOIS I'm convinced that what you're saying isn't at all true, because we produced a play before this one and got great encouragement, considering the situation in this country. What's even better is that the encouragement wasn't phoney or affected or commercial. Moreover, people didn't come to the theater out of trendiness, or habit. On the contrary: we felt that they were participating with their hearts; they were very decent. And as for going abroad, if everyone who planned to do something positive left the country, who'd remain in it? It would become like a desert, without seed . . .

FRANÇOIS *continues, but* HANI *interrupts him, not willing to give him a chance to outweigh him in the discussion.*

HANI You won't convince me. Over there, journalism, artistic revivals, and theatrical activities are beyond description, and discussion! If only you'd been at the theater festival at Avignon during the summer of '68!

EMILE Did you say Avignon? In France? The summer of '68? Unbelievable! Impossible! I never thought that there were people interested in the theater to that extent! I must congratulate you, not in my own name, but in the name of all theater lovers! Can you imagine? Can you believe it, folks? After four years, two persons meet again—on a stage! This is a sign of their love for the theater, and of their support of it.

I too was at Avignon. Where were you lodging? But let me first introduce myself, my name's Emile, I'm a teacher and one of those who like the theater and support it because I consider it educational.

HANI Pleased to meet you. My name's Hani; I'm a journalist.

EMILE A journalist . . . how interesting!*

HANI Actually, first I studied journalism, then I concentrated on art and theater criticism as a journalist.

EMILE I too am organizing theatrical activities at our school, and I support the local groups.

HANI Great. But don't you feel isolated? I mean, does anyone help you?

EMILE Frankly, not very much . . . But you know that every beginning is difficult. It's our responsibility, and because no one cares, the whole burden falls on my shoulders. It's a huge responsibility . . .

A flashback shows EMILE *with one of the producers of a young, local group who is asking for his help in selling tickets for his production. At first,* EMILE *offers to help. He makes promises. But the days go by—Monday, Tuesday, Wednesday . . . Saturday and Sunday—and on the day of the show he tells him, "I'm sorry." The lights are faint. The characters seem like ghosts. The events of the flashback are related by* MILAD.

We return to EMILE, HANI, *and* FRANÇOIS.

EMILE And up to now, I believe I've been doing my duty as any concerned person should.

HANI Great! My fiancée too has this sense of responsibility, and I share her opinion.

FRANÇOIS Responsibility doesn't consist in the simple act of following your fiançée, who likes to repair things and feels responsible. You must share her work, and give her the opportunity and the facility to practice her responsibility.

HANI Of course! I do give her the opportunity. (*He looks at* FRANÇOIS *in a very special way.*)

HANI'*s contradictions, and looks, disturb* FRANÇOIS; *he abandons the discussion and goes to the equipment.*

EMILE You haven't told me yet who was with you in Avignon.

*This expression occurs in English in the original text.

HANI The fact is that in '68 I was alone. You know the sense of freedom one can have, and the possibility of meeting new people.

EMILE I agree. I too am alone on most of my trips. There's nothing like freedom.

HANI What a coincidence . . . You seem to like being on your own the way I do.

FRANÇOIS (*Nervously, having despaired of seeing the equipment repaired; also, fed up with discussions and talking*): What luck! If we keep on this way, we'll be in the dark until dawn! With my luck, the sun might not even rise! . . . We happen to have equipment that's not working, and we want to see a play! We've asked for help, for people who work, not chattering away like pigeons! . . . .

MILAD Have you noticed, guys? By God, we're really unlucky . . .

ᶜALI (*Leaving his place*): Forget all that, Mr. Producer. I'm coming! You just relax somewhere and watch me deal with the situation. (ᶜALI *goes up on stage.*)

FRANÇOIS What do you plan to do?

ᶜALI My dear man, we want to have fun and amuse the audience. Haven't you understood by now that the electricity won't be restored? The fact is, I saw the moon appear on the stage, and I wondered, why not sing for it? And here I am. Excuse me . . .

ᶜALI *leaves* FRANÇOIS, *while* HANI *and* EMILE *are having a side conversation in low voices, not at all concerned by what is going on around the equipment.* ᶜALI *approaches* NADIA *and* ᶜADIL.

ᶜALI Hello! We've come to help. My name's ᶜAli.

ᶜADIL Hello! My name's ᶜAdil. Are you an electrician?

ᶜALI Forget about electricity and all that rubbish . . .

ᶜADIL *and* NADIA *stop working for a moment and look at* ᶜALI *in disbelief and suspicion.*

ᶜALI (*Going back on his former position*): Well well well, you certainly believe what you're told! I was joking! . . . Can't you take a joke? Of course I know about electricity! As a matter of fact, I understand everything! There's nothing I can't do! . . . But, madam, we haven't been introduced . . .

NADIA *makes no reply.*

ᶜALI Don't you have a name?

NADIA This is no time for introductions! ᶜAdil, give me the long screwdriver.

ᶜALI Yes, do, please give her the most beautiful long screwdriver . . . (*In a low, sweet voice*:) And as for your name? Have you made up your mind? Don't you want to tell me your name? How can we work together without knowing each other's name? . . . Well, I shall call you "Moon," because you look like the moon.*

NADIA Young man, if you're here to help and contribute something useful, you're very welcome. But if you're here to make speeches about the moon, and about names, you should know that I don't like speeches. If you push it too far, I'll ask you to get off the stage.

ᶜALI No, young lady, don't be angry! I don't want to upset you, or cause problems, or make you shout. A beautiful woman mustn't get upset . . . I'm a well-meaning man; I don't want to cause problems.

A period of silence. ᶜALI *leaves his place and*

*This sentence is in English in the original text.

moves around the equipment, trying to get NADIA *away from it.*

ʿALI This wire seems to be cut! Come and see . . .

NADIA *leaves the equipment and goes to the spot where* ʿALI *is standing.* ʿALI *gets close to her in order to smell her hair.*

NADIA (*Angrily*): Oh!

ʿALI (*Lovingly*): Don't you want to tell me your name?

NADIA (*Upset*): Will you stop that!

ʿALI When I saw you wearing a Charleston dress and getting up on the stage, I thought you were emancipated. But you seem to be very bad-tempered.

NADIA Keep your distance! Show me more respect than you do your own kind!

ʿALI Don't be upset, lady, it's alright . . . What can I do for you? For your sake, and to make your task easier, I'm prepared to learn about electricity. I don't want you to dirty your soft hands . . . What lovely hands! (ʿALI *tries to reach out and touch* NADIA*'s hands.*)

NADIA (*Loudly*): Enough's enough! Stop talking, and let's work seriously. If you can't keep quiet, leave the stage.

FRANÇOIS What's happening here?

ʿALI Listen, brother producer, I've come to help. You should at least thank me, not shout at me. I'm a nervous man . . . I can't stand anyone shouting at me; I won't be responsible for the consequences.

FRANÇOIS We don't want any favors. If you want to help, you're welcome; if you don't, it's fine with us. No one's forcing anyone else to help, and we have no time to lose.

ʿALI Alright, I'll shut up, but on one condition—that you tell me the name of the beautiful young lady working on the equipment.

FRANÇOIS So *that*'s your reason for coming on the stage . . .

ʿALI Of course, brother! What did you think? I'm looking for a bride . . . I said to myself, in the theater there must be beautiful girls—among the actresses, I mean.

FRANÇOIS But this girl has no name.

ʿALI Hey, are you making fun of me? I told you, I'm a nervous man . . . (ʿALI *grabs* FRANÇOIS *by the collar.*) Don't use your flighty ways with me . . . Don't think that because I'm on the stage you can boss me around!

They are on the verge of fighting, and attract the attention of EMILE *and* HANI, *who have been discussing their trips. Both of them approach* FRANÇOIS *and* ʿALI.

EMILE (*Sarcastic*): I don't think that *this* is the way to repair the equipment! . . . Now you're shouting, and soon you'll be fighting. The situation requires organization; this can't go on . . . (*He addresses* HANI, *who nods his head approvingly*:) We have to hold a meeting.

EMILE *calls* ʿADIL, NADIA, MILAD, ʿALI *and* FRANÇOIS. MILAD *refuses to participate. The meeting is held.* ʿADIL *withdraws, then* NADIA; *the meeting continues with* HANI, EMILE, ʿALI *and* FRANÇOIS. ʿADIL *and* NADIA *are near the equipment; they succeed in bringing the lighting back for a short period; it is unsteady, and its unsteadiness affects the meeting. For ten seconds, the set expresses hope and expectancy. We hear some comments.*

EMILE Please, everyone, stop working! (*To* ʿADIL:) Didn't you hear? Stop working! (*To* NADIA:) You too, sister. Stop your work! Come on, all of you! You too, producer. (*To* ʿALI:) And you, too. Don't make me repeat my request ten thousand times!

HANI At last, some order . . .

EMILE (*To* MILAD): You're responsible

for the electricity, and here you are, sitting apart and drinking! Come here, this is your responsibility!

MILAD Not only are you doing nothing, you want people to stop working as well. Is that your duty?

EMILE Do you hear what he's saying?

MILAD I don't understand how they can be obeying you . . . Leave me alone and don't nag me. I've had enough!

EMILE We're all working on some broken equipment. We're trying to repair it. But things have gotten out of hand, because, essentially, before undertaking any work we must know *why* we're working, *why* we're repairing; in other words, the purpose of our effort. Yes, the purpose; are we working for the same purpose?

MILAD (*Sarcastic*): Are we working for the same purpose!

EMILE Even if the purpose is the same, the question is: is everyone following the same path to reach this purpose?

ʿADIL Will you stop that? Let me tell you: your aim is the aim of the aim of the aim! . . . Have pity on us, man! We have equipment to repair, *that*'s our purpose! And once it's repaired, we'll watch a play: this would be our secondary purpose . . . It's simple. It doesn't need a meeting or organization.

EMILE (*Interrupting*): Haven't you seen how disorganization spreads?

ʿADIL Of course . . . Any work involves disorganization. Wait and see how your meeting becomes disorganized. (ʿADIL *withdraws to go to the equipment.*)

EMILE There won't be any disorganization, because one of the purposes of this meeting is to know each other, and to study each other's personalities. We'll see if there's anyone who's not serious, so we can refuse his help.

HANI By God, you're right! Imagine, I'm talking and working with people whose family names I don't know . . . It's very good of you to remind us of this, Mr. Emile.

EMILE It's my duty to remind you of all these things—and of others, too . . .

NADIA That's enough, sir! You're wrong in everything you say! (NADIA *leaves them and returns to the equipment.*)

FRANÇOIS I agree with her, because from our experience I've discovered that people who come from different social backgrounds are capable of working together and producing. It's on the job, and in assuming responsibilities, that they get acquainted. That can't be achieved in a meeting. There, no one would say, "I'm not serious." Everyone seems serious. But in the heat of the work, it's possible to find out who's serious and who isn't.

EMILE You can't convince me. The equipment we're repairing is scientific equipment, and every step in repairing it must be scientific. Even our getting to know each other must be scientific. And I repeat, we *must* know each other's purposes. If our opinions are different, we shouldn't work, even in a matter that seems trivial and insignificant. The fact is that these little things are very important, no matter what we say . . .

It's strange that one should discover one's mistakes after one makes them. I wish we could discover them before we make them; there wouldn't be so many catastrophes in the world. Can you imagine how many catastrophes happen in the world because of a lack of awareness and organization? . . .

While EMILE *is talking,* FRANÇOIS, ʿADIL, ʿALI, *and* NADIA *try to interrupt him.* HANI *invents sentences to agree with* EMILE. *People talk together in pairs, and the meeting deteriorates into chaos. At that moment* ᶜADIL *succeeds in moving the light. The light goes off.* EMILE, HANI, *and* ᶜALI *turn on* ᶜADIL, *blaming him and insulting him in loud and angry voices, until* NADIA *interrupts them.*

NADIA In fact, it's no one's fault, and the young man's doing his best. This equipment can't be repaired with a screwdriver and simple pliers. It needs an electrician's tools: a volt meter, and . . . (NADIA *lists a number of tools she needs.*) Isn't there anyone who knows an electrician?

ᶜALI I know the best electrician in town, and he has the best tools, too.

NADIA Alright, can you go call him? He might come and help us.

ᶜALI Just ask, my beauty! I'll be back in five minutes! I'm flying . . . (ᶜALI *sings the song "I'm Flying," and disappears.*)

The light focused on the equipment becomes very weak. People seem like ghosts. A stronger light is projected onto the front stage. Here a second time sequence takes place, and we see a scene in a coffeehouse. ᶜALI *enters the coffeehouse.*

ᶜALI Munir,*
My brother, we need you for a while . . .
There's a power failure in the theater . . .
People are waiting in the dark . . .
Come help us, and bring your tools . . .
Munir,
We need the tools . . .
People are in darkness . . .
We have to repair . . .
Let's help . . .
We've waited too long . . .
Munir,
The theater . . .
Darkness . . .
People . . .
Tools . . .
Time . . .
Our responsibility . . .

During the coffeehouse scene we can hear exchanges between NADIA, FRANÇOIS, *and* ᶜADIL.

NADIA Why's he taking so long? Is the coffeehouse far?

ᶜADIL It's only a matter of two minutes, both ways.

FRANÇOIS That means he won't come back.

NADIA He must come back!

The coffeehouse scene is over. The light is taken off of it and projected back onto the equipment, where we see FRANÇOIS, ᶜADIL, NADIA, HANI, *and* EMILE.

FRANÇOIS I don't think we should wait any longer.

NADIA But how can I work without tools?

ᶜADIL Don't you have your own tools, sister?

FRANÇOIS Yes, that's right . . .

NADIA Certainly. But my house is too far, and I don't know if my fiancé will agree to drive me there.

ᶜADIL He must agree! I'll persuade him . . .

NADIA *I'll* talk to him. (*From where she is standing,* NADIA *turns to* HANI.) Hani . . . Hani, can you drive me home to get my tools?

HANI (*Surprised and disdainful*): Me?

*The name is symbolic and means "one who provides light."

(*He continues his conversation with* EMILE.)

NADIA Yes, you . . . Are you afraid of getting tired?

HANI *makes no answer and continues his conversation with* EMILE.

NADIA Hani, please . . . It won't take us more than ten minutes.

HANI What is it? I said I won't go—that means I won't go!

From the side where EMILE *and* HANI *are standing, we hear voices in the background.*

EMILE I hear your fiancée's house is a long way away . . .

HANI Yes, but I have an Alpha-Romeo, the latest model. I bought it in Italy. There's not one like it in the country.

EMILE I'm like you, I love Italian cars. Mine's a Fiat 124, a coupe.

NADIA (*Angry*): Answer me, at least!

HANI (*To* EMILE): I tell you, that day we drank five bottles of Arak in two hours . . .

NADIA So . . . That's it. I won't forget this!

HANI I wish you'd been at my birthday party that day . . . It was more than words can describe . . .

The light goes off. Everyone except NADIA *and* FRANÇOIS *goes behind the white curtain.*

THE PARTY SCENE

This scene is divided into three sequences. The first involves games, and the voices of all the actors. In the foreground we see SAMEH, SAMIR, MAJID, *and* EMILE; *the others are in the background.*

The second phase is the distribution of gifts. It begins with SAMIR'S, *which is a bottle of whiskey. All move as though they are opening the bottle; then they participate in pouring and drinking it.*

The second gift is from ʿALI, *a song entitled "The Threshold Is Glass." It is accompanied by appropriate movements of dancing and singing.*

The third gift is from MAJID: *a Big Ben clock. The accompanying movement is that of oscillation.*

The fourth gift is from MILAD, *a yacht. The accompanying movement is raising the knee to form a ninety-degree angle, and moving the hands. They all form a circle around* HANI, *which is constantly growing larger and smaller.*

The fifth gift is from ʿADIL: *it is a car. The accompanying action: they all lie on their backs and move their legs in the air, imitating the noise of a beeping horn.*

The sixth gift is from HUSAM. *It is a shaving brush, king-sized. Appropriate accompanying action.*

The seventh gift is from EMILE: *it is an island. The accompanying action consists of everyone swimming in front of each other.*

The eighth gift is from SAMEH: *a hair from Brigitte Bardot's armpit. The accompanying movement consists of everyone moving toward* HANI *and touching him.*

In the third phase, HANI *is carried while they sing "Happy Birthday" for him. They force him to put on a silk tie and gold cufflinks. They chant: "Make him drink! Throw him away, throw him away, throw him away . . . " He is then placed on a cart, and* EMILE *pulls him away, out through the audience. Slowly they disappear through the rear of the hall.*

MILAD Our theatre has no money to buy an electrical system . . . But we mustn't be surprised: that's how money's spent.

MAJID God won't forgive us! We'll remain in darkness until that girl comes down off the stage . . . Do something, people! We have a responsibility to our customs and traditions, our history and civilization! The appearance of this girl on the stage means that we've opened the door to Sin! It means the dissolution of our society, the disintegration of our civilization! If we care about seeing our civilization continue on a strong foundation, we shouldn't lose control over our girls! . . .

MILAD What you're saying, honorable man,
Means that we should assassinate the cycle of time,
Means that we should lose our place in life,
Means that we should live like ancient tribes.

MAJID (*Very angry*): You're not an Arab! You've no pride; you don't recognize your Arab feelings!

MILAD (*Very calm*): If you want to call me an Arab, do; if not, don't. But I *feel* like an Arab, and I feel that this girl's more of an Arab than those we saw in the coffeehouse, or at the party, because she's sincerely trying to repair the equipment. Anyhow, where is this Arabism of yours? Show it to us! . . .

MAJID (*To the audience, very agitated*): Do you see, people? We're losing our children to the stage, boys and girls alike! We're losing our control over them!

HUSAM Father, I'm bored with all this.

MAJID Shut up, and don't interrupt me!

HUSAM Father, you can see that everyone's bored and fed up . . . Instead of shouting at them, let's get up and get acquainted, enjoy ourselves. We might make some friends . . .

MAJID Since when have you become so pretentious as to dare answer back to your father? You're still as small as a frog!

HUSAM A frog! I'm a man! I'm twenty one years old! How can you say I'm a frog?

MAJID Shut your mouth before I break your bones!

HUSAM Why? (*The situation is very tense.* MAJID *beats* HUSAM; HUSAM *runs toward the stage and gets up on it.*)

MAJID (*Standing among the audience*): My son! . . . You've even corrupted my son! God will never forgive you! (MAJID *goes to the rear of the audience, repeating the previous sentence.*)

HUSAM (*Addressing* FRANÇOIS, NADIA, *and* ʿADIL): Don't worry about him. That's the way my father is. He's nervous, and always shouting. Just go on working and don't be bothered by his ideas. He'll never change. If we're going to get anywhere, it'll be through your work. (*Addressing the audience*:) What do you think? I won't take such treatment! You may have been taken in by his talk, but I wish you'd been with me the other day, you would have seen what he did . . .

The light is taken off of HUSAM *and the equipment and turned onto the front of the stage.* MAJID *enters, carried on a cart. From behind the white curtain enter a woman and her husband. For four minutes, we see a childbirth scene.* MAJID *keeps repeating, "The rent!" while the husband begs him to postpone the matter until after his wife has delivered.*

When the scene is over, MAJID *goes back, on the cart, to the rear of the audience. Then he returns to the hall and tries to deny what has happened. He is angry at his son and at* NADIA.

MAJID (*Hysterical*): You've corrupted my son! This is the result of mixed company! It's this girl! *She*'s to blame, *she* is! Take her away! Make her come down off the stage! We're losing control of our children, all of them, boys *and* girls, we're losing them . . . All this is incredible! It's not right!

HUSAM It is right! I can prove what I'm saying . . .

NADIA (*She has reached a very critical psychological condition*): I can't go on working this way! It's impossible, it's really impossible! If you want us to go on working, do something! Get him out of here! I can't anymore, I can't! . . . Get him out! Get him out!

MAJID No, people, if you want to protect the foundations of our civilization, you must get her down off the stage.

MILAD One of two things: either we let the girl work and help us, or we take her down off the stage and stay in darkness for a hundred thousand years.

MAJID (*Angrily, and in an aggressive tone*): Get her down, people! Get her down!

NADIA (*Querulous and tired*): Get him out! I can't take any more . . . I'm going to have a nervous breakdown . . .

The scene between "Get her down" and "Get him out" lasts for some time. The light goes off. NADIA *moves toward the front of the stage; so does* MAJID. *The light is projected onto the front of the stage.*

MAJID (*Holding a plastic bag; he is experiencing mixed emotions: he is angry, upset, and gratified at what he is about to do*): What brings you onto the stage, you? What takes you out of the sack? Your place is inside the sack! You must return to your place! You mustn't be free! You must remain a woman . . . Do you understand what it means to be a woman? Get back to your sack! Woman was born to live in a sack . . . You mustn't breathe . . . If you're free, if you're emancipated, what will happen to us men? Who will I control then? Who will I shout at? Only man has the right to enjoy his freedom . . . Man must impose his authority on you! Man must beat you and insult you as he would a slave! And that will only be possible as long as you're stifled inside the sack . . . We're the masters! Only men are the masters! . . .

MAJID *has finished putting* NADIA *inside the sack. As he leaves the hall, he addresses the audience.*

MAJID Women mustn't be free; otherwise, we won't be masters . . . There won't be master and slave, and there must be master and slave. Man's the master, and woman's the slave. She mustn't be free. Only man enjoys his freedom. We men give the orders and prohibit, we do and undo, beat and humiliate, allow and forbid . . . We men are the masters! We *are* the masters!

MAJID *disappears through the back door. Focus of action returns to the equipment.*

HUSAM I want to help . . .

FRANÇOIS (*Bored*): You see, I'm nervous. And do you know why I'm nervous? Everyone wants to help and no one knows how to. There's a difference between wanting and knowing.

HUSAM Does that mean you don't want me to help?

FRANÇOIS No, my dear man, that's not what I mean—not at all. Help if you know how to help; if you don't, learn! Because a man who works without knowing how to does more harm than good.

HUSAM You mean to say I'm ignorant?

FRANÇOIS (*Losing his temper, as does* ʿADIL): Ahh! Oh no, you're not ignorant! . . . (*He walks away from* HUSAM.)

SAMIR *gets up from the audience.*

SAMIR Listen to me . . . I don't know how to help, but I do know how to play music. I notice you're all bored and fed up, and the people are bored too. Let me entertain you and calm your nerves . . . (*He goes up onto the stage.*) Don't you have a musical instrument?

FRANÇOIS Look backstage. There's no theater without a musical instrument . . .

SAMIR *goes backstage, and we hear him speaking to the actors he meets there.*

SAMIR Are you still waiting? There are people here . . . If you've got no play, prepare a show for us, something interesting . . . Amuse us. I'm willing to play music for you . . . (SAMIR *comes out carrying a guitar; he speaks to the audience*:) Well, there are people backstage . . . The actors are still there, waiting for the electricity to be restored . . . (*Addresses the people backstage*:) Go ahead, get ready! . . . (*Addresses the audience*:) Well, what shall we sing? . . . Sitting in darkness . . . I suppose people who are doing that usually sing about—what? The appearance of the sun . . .

SAMIR *begins to sing a well-known old Arabic song: "It Appeared, How Beautiful Is Its Light."* ʿALI *enters, wearing a mask and carrying a drum. He sings with* SAMIR. *Then the backstage actors, wearing masks, join in with the movements of a show. The scene lasts until* MILAD *wakes up from his dream.*

MILAD Enough, enough! Stop! Do you think this is a marketplace? You've turned this place into a circus! The theatre's really progressed—rest in peace, Shakespeare! A circus! . . . Shakespeare, rest in peace . . . What a sleep! What a dream! . . . (MILAD *speaks to* FRANÇOIS, ʿADIL, SAMIR, *and the audience*:) I've had such a wonderful dream! . . .

EVERYONE What did you dream?

MILAD Shsh! Quiet! . . . A silent dream's better than words.

The light goes off; everyone comes out from the back part of the stage for the Dream Scene. During the Dream Scene, all lights are lit, in the hall and on stage, until the end of the dance. Then the lights go out suddenly.

MILAD Folks, this has been a dream . . . We're still in the dark. But frankly, wasn't it a wonderful dream? Imagine: people dealing with each other without fighting and without shouting and in an orderly way . . . There's understanding and harmony between them; they join hands . . .

While MILAD *is talking, the actors take their places for the Scene of the Flies.*

FRANÇOIS (*Interrupting him in a painfully realistic way*): Stop dreaming! . . . Look, look at them, see how ugly they are, piled on top of each other like corpses . . .

We see the Scene of the Flies.

SAMIR (*Repeats, during the scene*): Put your trust in God, He'll solve it. Who's responsible? I'm not responsible, He's responsible . . . Let's help; you begin; God will provide a solution. Go on, you first, not me. Put your trust in God . . . (*Everyone repeats these sentences, in a disorderly fashion.*)

FRANÇOIS Shoo! Shoo, damn you! . . . Like flies, shoo! Shoo! . . .

Everyone exits; only FRANÇOIS *and* ʿADIL *remain, exhausted. A period of silence of thirty to forty seconds, until someone comes to speak.*

SOMEONE If we can't repair the equipment, it means we're worthless. We're sick . . . And what's the remedy? Responsibility!

FRANÇOIS The remedy's that you should shut up, brother. The remedy isn't a responsibility in words. Talking has proved its total failure. It's an old song we've heard often—let's change the record. I have a remedy, here! . . . (*He points to* ᶜADIL, *who is sitting near the equipment.*) This young man works, and doesn't talk. The remedy's work. The cure is that I too stop talking. (FRANÇOIS *stops talking and goes beside* ᶜADIL *in front of the equipment.*)

Suddenly, one light is lit. The actors start moving from among the audience, proud that the light is back "due to their efforts." The first one is ᶜALI, *the second is* HUSAM, *the third is* MILAD, *then* SAMIR *and* NADIA, *then* EMILE *and* HANI.

The second light is lit. HUSAM *and* ᶜALI *dance and joke.* MILAD *and* SAMIR *hug each other.* NADIA *interacts with the various groups.* EMILE *and* HANI *engage in a show-off conversation.* FRANÇOIS *moves among them all.* SAMIR *inquires about the blond young man, looks at him, touches his shoulder.* ᶜADIL *drops dead.*)

Everyone is silent except for HANI *and* EMILE, *who pronounce the final sentence.*

HANI and EMILE You see?—the result of our work and efforts . . .

They all go up to ᶜADIL *and lift him onto their shoulders. They go from the stage to the hall and leave through the rear door.*

ʿABD AL-ʿAZIZ AL-SURAYYIʿ

The Bird Has Flown

Translated by
Salwa Jabsheh
and Thomas G. Ezzy

^{c}Abd al-^{c}Aziz al-Surayyi^c wrote *The Bird Has Flown* (*Tara 'l-Dik*) in 1971, and it was performed in 1972 under the direction of the Kuwaiti playwright and director Saqr al-Rushud. It was presented in broad Kuwaiti dialect, but when al-Surayyi^c prepared it for publication, he worked on the language, making it more comprehensible to readers in other countries of the Arab world, without however putting it in high Arabic and, by this, making it lose its approximation to real life and its dramatic immediacy. The play revolves around the great difference between European (here British) and traditional Arabic culture. The playwright here resorts to a convincing ploy when he has one of the sons of the rich old man represent British culture, thus giving legitimate reason for his intimate entry into the conservative family. This son is the fruit of an early second marriage of the father with an Indian woman when he was in his youth. This was during the pre-oil days when the most pertinent occupation of men was commerce and pearl diving and they spent many months at sea, their ships traveling to India and farther. On one of these trips eastward, he fell in love with an Anglo-Indian woman and married her, but divorced her at her own request after their son, Yusuf, was born. Both disappeared from his life for many years, his ex-wife having gone back to England with her British mother. Now Yusuf, a young man, is coming, with his Western outlook and values, to meet his Kuwaiti family for the first time. The meeting brings out the many deep differences between conservative Eastern and modern Western values. The major point the play tries to bring out is the inner contradictions of the new generation of post-oil Kuwaitis and the way they deal with the shock that a liberal Western culture can produce. The question here is this: can the new Kuwaitis, aspiring to Western civilization, accept that which they seek? Can what seems to them as enlightenment be translated into harmonious action with which they can live?

S. K. J.

THE BIRD HAS FLOWN

CAST

YA^c^QUB AL-^c^ALI
The father, approximately sixty-five years old; a sailor in the pre-oil days of Kuwait, he now makes his living from property he rents out.

SHARIFA
The mother, YA^c^QUB AL-^c^ALI*'s Kuwaiti wife; she is over fifty.*

SALEM
Their eldest son, approximately thirty years old; a government employee.

FATIMA
Salem's sister, several years younger than he is.

^c^ALI
Salem and Fatima's younger brother, a student.

YUSUF
YA^c^QUB AL-^c^ALI*'s son by his second (Indian) wife; he is over thirty and speaks broken Arabic.*

UNCLE ABU-^c^ABDALLAH
YA^c^QUB*'s eldest brother; he is a little over seventy and very wealthy.*

SARAH
UNCLE ABU-^c^ABDALLAH*'s daughter, a young lady of around eighteen.*

ABU-FALAH
An elderly Bedouin man, a neighbor of YA^c^QUB AL-^c^ALI*'s.*

MUTLEQ
The son of Abu-Falah; a student.

ABLA
The maid.

THE BIRD HAS FLOWN

ACT ONE

SCENE ONE

The Diwaniyah—an Oriental room with seats that are no higher than fifty centimeters above the floor. Between the seats, every meter or so, are cushions to lean on. Facing this area is a wall telephone. Behind that falls a brightly-colored curtain. To the right is an opening on to a hallway that leads to the outside door. To the left is another entrance, which leads to the inside of the house. Close to the entrance, on the left, is a television, while a medium-sized transistor radio has been placed on one of the seats. An iron coal-burning stove is set to one side, with coffee and tea pots placed on it; behind it stands a trolley carrying whatever else might be needed.*

The scene seems very quiet, although FATIMA *and her mother have been talking. As soon as the curtain is raised,* FATIMA *gets up and turns on an extra light. Her movements are naturally graceful; she looks back at her mother and speaks dreamily.*

FATIMA What does this brother look like? I can't imagine how he looks . . .

SHARIFA He looks English, of course. What else? Just like the ones we see on television . . .

FATIMA Mother, why are you so set against him?

SHARIFA (*Stands up*): The one who's making my life a misery is your father. Who would have thought that he might be so quietly deceitful?

FATIMA Father has committed no sin.

SHARIFA Of course you're taking your father's side . . . I hope my reward will be in heaven, for no one seems to be taking my side. You're all supporting *him*.

FATIMA Mother, this is something that happened a long time ago. Now, he's got no one but you.

SHARIFA How could he have taken a second wife? He didn't even tell me!

FATIMA Mother, what's the matter with you?

SHARIFA He goes and gets married, gets himself a son, names him Yusuf, and then he gets divorced! The whole world turns upside down, and I never know a thing about it!

FATIMA Only yesterday you told me that you'd felt something was going on.

SHARIFA I did feel something was going on. I felt it, and I'd heard several rumors. But I didn't want to believe them, and he swore by his youth that he was innocent. He kept on saying sweet words until I believed him and disbelieved myself.

FATIMA Mother, don't upset yourself with that kind of talk now. He married and divorced her before I was born. What good is all this talk now?

*A room where Kuwaiti men usually receive guests.

SHARIFA Why did he lie to me? Why?

FATIMA If he hadn't lied to you, and had told you the truth, what would you have done?

SHARIFA I would have asked him for a divorce! I would have left him!

FATIMA So you see the reason why he had to lie to you! If he had divorced you, neither ᶜAli nor I would have come into existence, and my brother Salem would have been like an orphan between the two of you, not knowing where he belonged . . . And besides, what would you have gained from a divorce?

SHARIFA Oh . . . And what have I got now? Look at him! He's old, and nearly blind, and I'm still in the prime of my youth.

FATIMA (*Makes a sound of protest*): Your calling my father blind is a ridiculous exaggeration, may God protect him!

SHARIFA What is he then? Don't say he's young.

FATIMA Don't be sarcastic, Mother. He may be old and nearsighted, but he's kind and loving. He loves you, and never says no to anything you ask for.

SHARIFA (*Infuriated*): Oh! I feel I'm suffocating in this anguish! Where did that devil of a son come from?

FATIMA He's my brother . . . He's *my* brother . . .

SHARIFA Have you seen him? (*The following dialogue goes on rapidly.*)

FATIMA No.

SHARIFA Do you know him?

FATIMA No.

SHARIFA Had you heard of him before this dreadful week?

FATIMA No . . . And this is not a dreadful week.

SHARIFA All girls are kind and supportive to their mothers, only you're against me! (*Exits angrily.*)

FATIMA (*Shakes her head in astonishment*): God help us!

MAID (*Entering from the other side, in a hurry*): Where's the mistress?

FATIMA What do you want?

MAID I want her.

FATIMA What food have you prepared?

MAID Meat *makbous* and *dakkous*.*

FATIMA Why meat *makbous*?

MAID And why not?

FATIMA How could he be familiar with meat *makbous*? If he's spent all his life in London, he might not even know Arabic.

MAID Don't exaggerate. They say he's learned Arabic in London.

FATIMA Well, that's right . . . But he doesn't know *makbous*.

MAID You mean he wants English food. (*Leaves hurriedly.*)

FATHER (*Enters, just misses bumping into* MAID): What's wrong with you? You act as though someone's chasing you.

MAID (*Conceals a smile and exits*): Sorry.

FATHER Just like an airplane . . . (*He appears clearly now. He is wearing eyeglasses, but has his hand placed like a shade over them. He looks fixedly at* FATIMA. *He hears the horn of a nearby car.*) Fatoum . . . Run and open the door for them, Daughter.

FATIMA Yubah,† how many times have I told you? If you love me, don't call me Fatoum. My name's Fatima.

FATHER You're teaching me your name when I was the one to name you. What's wrong with "Fatoum"? It's better than "Fatim."

*Kuwaiti dishes.
† "Father," a form of address in the Kuwaiti dialect.

FATIMA I'm neither Fatim nor Fatoum. I'm Fatima.

FATHER It doesn't matter now . . . Go and open the door for them.

FATIMA First of all, the door *is* open . . . And besides, who are the "they" I should be opening the door for?

FATHER Your brothers—who do you think we're waiting for? Can't you hear the horn?

FATIMA Yubah, may God have mercy on you, that's not our car. They're not coming right now—it's still too early. It's only 7:30, so if the plane was on schedule it will have just landed. Not to mention the time they need to get home, and the customs search . . . Have you forgotten?

FATHER What search? They're not robbers.

FATIMA Why robbers? The customs search applies to everybody.

FATHER My children are never searched. They're well-known.

FATIMA Father, you don't even know Yusuf yourself . . . How can the customs officers know him?

FATHER What do you mean, I don't know him? Isn't he my son?

FATIMA He might be your son, but have you ever seen him? Do you know him? Are you sure he's your son?

FATHER No . . . No . . . (*Suddenly*:) Where's your mother?

FATIMA My mother's angry.

FATHER (*Angrily*): That mother of yours!

SHARIFA (*Enters and hears his last words; becomes furious*): What's wrong with her mother? Is she mad?

FATHER (*Startled*): God help us!

SHARIFA What? Have I suddenly turned into a demon?

FATHER Woman, what's happening? Why don't you relax and think straight? What's turned you upside down? What's happening? . . . Do you think I went out looking for him, or even asked about him?

SHARIFA How would I know? How do you expect me to believe you, after what I've seen from you? We were just newlyweds, and young, and you went and took another wife, and tormented me . . . Why?

FATHER (*Smiles sarcastically*): Again! Haven't we exhausted this subject over the past week? What's happening to you? Anyone who heard you now would think that I'd just been to India and married that beautiful Indian woman, Theresa (*Dreamily*) and was living with her . . . Oh, the long-lost days of youth and strength! . . . God is strongest, for "if Death leaves you alone, Old Age won't."

SHARIFA (*At his last word, starts stamping the floor with her feet, like an angry child; her tears fall despite herself*): Did you hear? Can you see? To this moment, he still loves her! (*She exits.*)

FATIMA Yubah, why do you have to make her miserable?

FATHER By God, she's crazy! I'm still in her hands, even now . . . She's always played me around as she pleased.

FATIMA Yubah, how come you married the Indian woman?

FATHER (*Looking at her woefully*): That's another story . . . But I married her legally.

FATIMA I know. But how come you married her when your marriage to my mother was still recent?

FATHER (*As though trying to relieve himself of a burden he has been carrying for years*): Ah . . . After I married your mother, I had to be away for long stretches of time. During the diving season I was a diver, and during the traveling season I went on voyages. I used to leave the house and come back four or five months later—sometimes even eight. I went on like this for five years, and we had no children. In the first years of the Great War, I had to go to India. Do you know how old I was then?

FATIMA How old?

FATHER Thirty. Ah, youth! . . . I used to hang from the mast of the ship like a monkey . . . And if anything happened, your father could do the work of five men—neither the captain nor the first mate were a match for me. I didn't stay put one year. I was a real man then—not like now . . .

FATIMA (*Interrupting him*): Yubah, I asked you how you married Yusuf's mother, the Indian woman . . .

FATHER (*As if waking up from a dream*): Ah—I married her when we were stranded in India. The sea was rough, and the world was rough, and the war left no one in peace. Even we, who had nothing to do with it, were harmed.

FATIMA How come? How? Why?

FATHER Haven't you any patience? Wait a minute, let me catch my breath.

FATIMA Yubah, you're making a short story long.

FATHER How do you know it's short?

FATIMA I know . . . It's a habit of yours.

FATHER (*Sarcastically*): Make your complaints to God—you've no patience with your father. Your father's grown old, Fatoum—I mean Fatima—Fatima, don't be angry.

FATIMA (*Feels ashamed*): Forgive me, Yubah.

FATHER No, Child, it's not your fault. You're all like that, always in a hurry.

FATIMA So, how did it end, Yubah? Tell me.

FATHER I'll tell you, I will . . . (*Laughs.*) I'll tell you quickly!

FATIMA That's better.

FATHER I saw her and she saw me. I loved her and she loved me. And we got married.

FATIMA Is she a Muslim?

FATHER She wasn't, but when I married her she became a Muslim.

FATIMA What's her name?

FATHER Theresa.

FATIMA (*Laughs*): Theresa? That's a funny name!

FATHER Their names are different.

FATIMA Why did you divorce her?

FATHER I was afraid of your mother . . . I don't know how she became aware that something was wrong . . . I don't know whether I may have talked in my sleep once, or one of my friends told her.

FATIMA Didn't you warn them not to tell?

FATHER Of course I did. I specifically asked them to be careful.

FATIMA Did they refuse to keep your secret when they found out she wasn't a Muslim?

FATHER Yes, they did, and they were cross with me. But the Mulla,* God rest his soul, helped me to convince them.

FATIMA But he's a man of religion. How could he do that?

FATHER He told me that I'd be rewarded by God, he said a lot of wise words, because I'd converted her to Islam. So when my friends heard that, they shut up . . . She got pregnant. I left India, and when I came back on my next voyage I found that she'd given birth to a child, whom she'd named Yusuf. I stayed for twenty days, divorced her, and went back to Kuwait.

FATIMA Why did you divorce her?

FATHER She was the reason . . . She told me God had given me one of three choices:

*A Muslim religious official, sometimes called simply the *shaikh*.

either remain in India with her, take her with me to Kuwait, or divorce her.

FATIMA And you divorced her?

FATHER I divorced her in spite of myself. I tried to convince her, I wanted to change her mind, but she insisted on her conditions. What was I supposed to do? Stay with her? I couldn't . . . Take her to Kuwait with me? I couldn't . . . I had no choice but to divorce her.

FATIMA Couldn't you have convinced her? She might have been more patient.

FATHER I couldn't . . . She took me to court and I had no time to deal with that . . . The *boum** was about to leave, and I was morally obliged to return to your mother . . . I divorced her . . .

FATIMA Did you love her?

FATHER That's a shameful question to ask.

FATIMA There's no shame in that.

FATHER There's no point in talking like that now.

FATIMA How about Yusuf?

FATHER The mother was dearer to me than Yusuf . . . He was never more precious than she was.

FATIMA And you abandoned a young infant?

FATHER I did . . . What a world!

FATIMA You never made inquiries about him?

FATHER I did . . . I made myself dizzy with asking. On my third trip to India I went looking for them, but I couldn't find them . . . I got no news of them . . . I went back to Kuwait sick and miserable.

FATIMA But why? Wasn't it you who divorced her?

FATHER It was just one divorce† . . . I still had hope.

FATIMA Of remarrying her?

FATHER Yes, but I couldn't find her. On every trip I asked about her, until I found out that she'd left for London with her mother. It was then that I cried, for I knew I'd lost her forever.

FATIMA Why did she go to London?

FATHER Her mother was English and her father Indian. She left with her mother after her father died.

FATIMA And your son?

FATHER I never gave up hope of finding my son. I always felt that when he grew up and became a man he'd inquire about me, and find me . . .

FATIMA You were right . . . He's searched for you until he found you.

FATHER But first, I've got to test him . . . I'll question him. He might be faking his identity.

FATIMA I don't think so . . . (MAID *enters.*) Yes?

MAID Mistress is sick . . . (*She exits.*)

FATHER Oh!

The sound of a nearby car horn is heard. FATHER *prepares himself.* ʿALI *enters first, in a hurry, laughing, followed by* SALEM, *who is carrying suitcases. Behind them appears* YUSUF, *wearing a strange outfit: ordinary pants, a shirt, and an old-fashioned waistcoat; on his head is an embroidered kufiyya, and over it is an old, thick igal.*‡ *He looks agile, and is smiling in a strange way. He is carrying a medium-sized suitcase in his hand.*

ʿALI (*Laughing*): Yubah! . . . Yusuf's arrived.

FATIMA *remains silent and motionless, watching anxiously. When she sees* YUSUF

*An old Kuwaiti sailing ship.

† A Muslim divorce is easily rectified: remarriage is possible after up to three divorces.

‡ *Kuﬁyya* and *igal*: items of Kuwaiti head-dress for men.

she doesn't realize that he is her brother, because of his strange dress.

ʿALI (*Walks toward* YUSUF *and takes his hand*): Fatima—this is my brother, Yusuf.

FATIMA *is completely bewildered and doesn't know what to say.* YUSUF *smiles and nods his head to greet* FATIMA. *He speaks to* ʿALI, *repeating* ʿALI*'s words in broken Arabic.* ʿALI *laughs and corrects his pronunciation.*

YUSUF My sister—well, hello, my sister.

FATIMA (*Pulls herself out of her silence*): Hello, my brother. Welcome . . . Say hello to your father.

YUSUF (*Kisses her; she panics*): Fatima—beautiful Fatima . . .

ʿALI (*Laughs*): What's wrong, Father? Why are you glued to the spot?

FATHER (*Clears his throat*): Is this Yusuf? . . . Why is he dressed up like this—as though he were a teacher of the last generation?

YUSUF (*Looks astonished*): Daddy! . . . Daddy is old—very old . . . Hello, Dad!

FATHER (*Comes closer*): Who would believe . . . I *can't* believe it! Take that outfit off him, and let me see him properly!

ʿALI (*Laughing*): Shall we undress him completely?

FATHER No, just take off that *igal* and—

YUSUF (*Doesn't understand what is being said*): Daddy . . . Daddy . . .

FATHER (*Annoyed*): Salem, why don't you come in here? Where have you gone?

SALEM (*Returns, bringing in the suitcase he was carrying*): Yes?

FATHER Why is your brother dressed up like this?

SALEM What was I supposed to do? He came from London dressed that way.

FATHER God have mercy! Let him sit down—let him sit down.

YUSUF (*In English*): What? What? What?

FATHER What's he trying to say?

YUSUF (*Relaxed and happy*): How are you, Dad?

FATHER (*Touched*): Poor lad . . . (*To* FATIMA:) Do you know why he's calling me "Daddy," and not "Yubah"?

FATIMA (*Amid her astonishment*): Why?!

FATHER Because he never said it when he was young.

YUSUF How are you, Father?

FATHER May God protect you, what do you want?

YUSUF (*In English*): What?

FATHER What's wrong with him? . . . No, no, that's not my son! Never!

SALEM Yubah, what's wrong?

FATHER No, he can't be my son!

ʿALI What's he supposed to do? He can't understand what you're saying . . .

FATHER You shut up! . . . As if *you* could understand! . . . He's tall, and broad-shouldered . . . But still, all he's been able to say so far is "What? . . . What?"

FATIMA Yubah, he's just learned Arabic—the written Arabic, that *you* don't understand . . . When he says "What?" he's trying to ask you to repeat what you said!

FATHER So if he doesn't understand my language, how can he be my son?

FATIMA How come you loved and married his mother when she couldn't understand your language?

FATHER Shut up! Shame on you . . .

SALEM Nothing shameful's been said . . . Really now, how did you come to marry a woman who couldn't understand your language—and whose language you couldn't understand?

FATHER I knew some Hindi, and she knew some Arabic . . . We could understand each other . . . And besides, she was my wife—not my daughter. But here's a man, tall and strong, who's unable to understand his own father—the eldest of my children! . . . Oh, what misery!

FATIMA Did you say you were going to test him?

FATHER Well . . . He *looks* as if he's mine . . . I hope it turns out otherwise.

FATIMA Yubah, how could you? You want to deny your own son!

FATHER You—come here. Come on.

YUSUF *looks very odd; he will have an expression of bewilderment on his face throughout the following conversation.*

SALEM Yusuf . . . Yusuf . . . Joe!*

YUSUF (*In English*): Yes?

SALEM It's no use, Yubah. He's grown up speaking a different language for thirty years. You can't expect him to switch and speak a language he's had only a few lessons in over the past two years.

YUSUF (*Angry*): What's that? What's that? . . . I can't understand a single word you're saying! Please speak in Arabic—leave off that other language, now, for my sake! . . . I learned Arabic specially so that I'd be able to speak to you!

SALEM Calm down, Yusuf, calm down . . . We're speaking in the Kuwaiti dialect, which is Arabic as well.

YUSUF But I can't understand anything!

FATHER Why's he so angry? He's talking like some actor on the radio.

SALEM Why don't you ask him, Yubah?

FATHER Come closer.

YUSUF (*Does not understand, hesitates; then, like a person finally surrendering, comes closer*): Yes? What does my father want?

SALEM He wants to ask you a few questions.

YUSUF Yes . . . Yes, what are those questions?

FATHER Listen, what's your mother's name?

YUSUF Yes?

FATHER What's this "Yes"? Get out of here!

SALEM (*Holds him*): Patience, Father . . . What's wrong with you?

YUSUF Father . . . (*Apologetically*:) What . . . What can I do?

SALEM (*In English*) He asked you what is your Mother's name?

YUSUF Oh, sorry Father, Dad, I'm very sorry. (*He kisses him.*)

FATHER (*Furious*): What's going on, Salem?

SALEM Calm down, Father . . . I only translated your question for him.

YUSUF My mother . . . My mother . . .

FATHER Yes, your mother! What's her name?

YUSUF Thérèse. Thérèse.

FATHER (*More cheerful*): Yes, by God, Thérèse! . . . Theresa, that's her name! . . . Damn him, he's reminded me of her . . . She used to pronounce her name the way he did just now! . . . (YUSUF *is about to speak.*) Wait, wait, a second question—what special peculiarity did she have?

YUSUF What?

FATHER Explain to him, Salem . . . Ask him if his mother had any special distinguishing marks.

YUSUF (*Understands*): Yes, she had. She had a spot here . . . (*He points to the top of his thigh.* FATHER *sees this and gets up.*)

FATHER OK, OK, that's enough. (YUSUF *keeps pointing.*) That's enough, I said. I understand . . . What's my name?

YUSUF Yes?

FATHER God save us! (FATIMA *and* ʿALI

*"Yusuf" is "Joseph" in English.

laugh; YUSUF *joins in without understanding.)*

SALEM (*Pointing to his father*): What's his name?

YUSUF (*With sly astonishment*): Doesn't he know his own name? (*Laughs.*) Jacob al-ᶜAli.*

FATHER (*Excited*): That's enough! He's my son! He's my son! By God, he's my son! . . . God save you, my son! Come and greet me properly!

YUSUF *does not understand.* SALEM *pushes him into* FATHER*'s open arms, and they embrace. Silence.*

FATHER (*Touched*): May God protect you!

YUSUF (*After embrace is finished*): How are you, my father?

FATHER I'm fine, thank God. How are you?

YUSUF (*In Arabic*): I'm well . . . My father sends her greetings.

FATHER What did you say? (*Everyone laughs.*)

SALEM He means his mother sends her regards.

FATHER Thank you . . . (*Excitedly:*) How is she? . . . (*Anxiously:*) How's she getting along?

YUSUF Very well . . . She's fine.

ᶜALI (*Laughing*): His teacher must have been Lebanese, or Syrian.

FATHER Come on, Salem, go and buy your brother a *dashdasha.*† Take him to the tailor . . . Then, take him to the *souk* and buy him a proper *ghutra* and *igal* . . . What's that thing he's wearing?

SALEM (*Laughing*): It must be our friends who are studying in London that dressed him up this way. It must be, there's no other explanation.

YUSUF *is trying to follow by moving his head in all directions.*

SALEM What are those clothes?

YUSUF (*Holding the waistcoat in his hand*): They're Daddy's—my father's.

SALEM (*Looking surprised*): Yubah, is that your waistcoat?

FATHER That's strange . . . How come?

YUSUF My mother . . . My mother.

SALEM His mother gave it to him to wear. You must have left it there with her.

FATHER (*Surprised, pleased*): Poor Theresa . . . She kept my waistcoat . . . What a world!—you never know what your fate in this life will be.

YUSUF *points to the igal.*

SALEM And the *igal* as well . . .

FATHER Oh! That's my wedding *igal*—the night I married his mother. They dressed me in the captain's *igal* . . . So, she's looked after it . . . Where's Theresa now? Where's your mother?

MAID (*Entering in a hurry*): Mistress is very ill! How can you leave her all alone? . . . Go and see her.

FATHER Yes, by God . . . We've forgotten all about your mother, children.

SALEM (*Leaving*): What's wrong with my mother?

FATIMA *and* ᶜALI *follow* SALEM. FATHER *calls to* ᶜALI, *and goes after him inside.* YUSUF *stays alone.* MAID *eyes him suspiciously.* YUSUF stands staring at his surroundings. He smiles at MAID. *She is startled.*

MAID (*To herself*): What is this?

YUSUF (*Sharply*): Yes?

* "Jacob" is the English form of "Yaᶜqub."

† Kuwaiti national dress for men, worn both summer and winter.

MAID (*Frightened*): What is this? What do you want? What brings you here?

YUSUF Who are you? Mummy?

MAID (*Surprised*): What are you saying? Mummy?—Me, your Mummy?

YUSUF Don't you speak Arabic?

MAID What are you blabbering about? What do you think I'm speaking—Hindi? What do you want? What brings you here? Don't just stand there like a log—speak! (YUSUF *smiles, embarrassed.*) So, you're smiling! Are you making fun of me? (*To herself*:) I'm sure he's either deaf or mad. (*Silence.*) You! . . . (*She tries to make him understand by her gestures.*) What are you doing here? Or, in plainer words, who let you into this house? (YUSUF *keeps smiling.*) No—I'm positive now that you're insane . . . Who do you think I'm talking to now? (YUSUF, *understanding the situation, tries to tease her. He moves in a way that frightens her.* MAID, *annoyed, steps backward*:) Hey, watch out! I'll scream! (YUSUF *stands smiling.*) That's right, behave like a sane person—for your own good! (*Exaggerating his movements,* YUSUF *puts his hands out and suddenly moves closer to her.* MAID *shouts in terror.*)

SALEM (*Rushes in*): Hey, what's going on?

YUSUF *bursts out laughing.*

MAID Salem, sir, please look at that!

SALEM (*Realizes what has been going on and smiles*): Don't you know who he is?

MAID No.

SALEM That's my brother Yusuf.

MAID (*Stiffening*): He—he frightened me.

YUSUF Who's she?

SALEM Go on inside . . . (MAID *leaves dejectedly.*) That's our maid, Abla.

YUSUF A—B—L—A . . .

SALEM Come on, come and see your room.

YUSUF My room . . . Thank you.

They exit. The stage remains empty for a moment. Then in rushes SHARIFA, *followed by* FATIMA *and then the* FATHER.

SHARIFA (*Ferociously*): Where is he? Where is this man who's made my life so miserable, who's made me sick with grief?

FATIMA Yumma,* Yumma, calm down. (*Tries to restrain her mother, while her mother struggles to get free.*)

FATHER (*Stands in front of her angrily*): Are you going to behave rationally or not?

SHARIFA (*Defiantly*): What is this? What do you plan to do?

FATHER (*Slaps her hard*): *That's* what I'm going to do!

SHARIFA, *shocked, collapses into her daughter's arms.*

FATHER (*Furious*): Take her inside!

FATIMA Yubah, she's fainted! My mother's fainted!

FATHER (*Exasperated*): Then run and get her some water! (*He takes hold of the mother.*)

CURTAIN

SCENE TWO

Same setting. FATIMA *is facing the audience, watching* YUSUF*'s movements, and smiles every now and then.* YUSUF *is wearing a new dashdasha, kufiyya, and igal, and muttering to himself as he walks back and forth.* YUSUF *is repeating to himself some of the Kuwaiti words he has learned, pronouncing them wrong. Bursting into laughter,* FATIMA *corrects him and asks him to repeat.*

*Kuwaiti form of address for "Mother."

FATIMA Well done! . . . By God, brother, you're bright!

YUSUF (*In a broken accent*): It's very tiring . . . I've been practicing for six hours—once with Salem, once with ᶜAli, and now you.

FATIMA How about Father? Haven't you learned anything from him?

YUSUF Very little . . . His language is much too difficult for me.

FATIMA *is trying to teach* YUSUF *the numbers when the* FATHER *walks in, wearing his indoor clothes.*

FATHER Good evening.

YUSUF Good evening.

FATIMA Good evening, Yubah.

FATHER Hello, Yusuf.

YUSUF What?

FATIMA (*Laughs*): No—when you can't understand something you should say, "Excuse me." You shouldn't use that kind of language to your father, or to any other person you respect.

YUSUF I respect everyone.

FATHER What's your aunt's name?

YUSUF Sharifa.

FATHER (*Smiling*): Good, you know her name now. How are things between you and her?

YUSUF They're OK.

FATHER Fine. Why don't you eat our food? Don't you like it?

YUSUF I do eat.

FATHER Yes, but not enough for a man your size.

YUSUF (*Uneasily*): Give it time . . . I'm trying to get used to it.

FATIMA (*Interceding*): Yubah, our food's different from what he's used to.

YUSUF Yes, that's true.

FATHER If there's anything special you feel like eating, do tell us. What would you like to eat from now on?

YUSUF Your food's fine . . . But I've noticed there's one thing you never cook.

FATHER What's that? Just ask for it.

YUSUF Just a minute, I don't know the word for it in Arabic. (*He searches in his pocket, takes out a small notebook and starts looking.*)

FATHER That's strange . . . You write your food down in a notebook?

FATIMA Say it, Yusuf . . . I'll help you.

FATHER Say it . . . What is it?

YUSUF One moment . . . This one, Dad—this is a good dish. I haven't eaten it for ages.

FATHER Say it, what is it?

YUSUF Pork.

FATHER (*Dumbfounded*): What?

FATIMA No, Yubah, he means lamb.

YUSUF (*Surprised*): No—pork.

FATHER Pork yourself, you scoundrel! Have you no fear of God?

MAID (*Walks in suddenly*): Uncle Abu-ᶜAbdallah is at the door.

FATHER Get up, Fatima, go inside. My God! Pork?

FATIMA Let me say hello to my uncle.

FATHER No, you won't. Go inside.

FATIMA (*Exits*): Alright.

FATHER (*Calls out*): Come in, Brother! Greetings!

ABU-ᶜABDALLAH (*Walks in, an elderly man wearing eyeglasses; has a white beard; his appearance indicates wealth and power*): Greetings!

FATHER and YUSUF (*Together*): Greetings.

ABU-ᶜABDALLAH How are you?

FATHER Fine . . . What's been happening?

ABU-ᶜABDALLAH Nothing but good news . . . We went to the gentleman and spoke to him. Let's hope for the best.

FATHER (*Distraught*): No, you pig!

ABU-ᶜABDALLAH What!—Why?

FATHER No, Brother, it has nothing to do with you . . . Someone has asked if he could eat pork!

ABU-ᶜABDALLAH Is that what's bothering you? Has the world turned upside down? . . . So. Why should you care?

YUSUF (*Smiling*): I don't know.

FATHER You be quiet.

ABU-ᶜABDALLAH (*Laughing*): I hope it's not Yusuf?

FATHER It is.

ABU-ᶜABDALLAH Well, you can't blame him. He's been living abroad. He's gotten used to their food, and to doing what they do, without knowing the difference. You should blame the ones who live here all their lives, go away for only six months, and come back talking with twisted tongues, with their hair all strange and different, and with pork and similar things among their recent accomplishments.

YUSUF Pork's good—everyone eats it.

FATHER You mustn't say that, my son.

YUSUF Why not?

ABU-ᶜABDALLAH Because God has asked us not to eat it, my son.

YUSUF I didn't know . . . I've never heard that.

FATHER No, this is unacceptable! He needs religious instruction! . . . Do you know how to pray?

YUSUF Of course . . . I've always gone to church with Mummy.

ABU-ᶜABDALLAH Well, what can you expect?

FATHER Go and call your brother Salem.

YUSUF *exits.*

FATHER What have you got done, Brother?

ABU-ᶜABDALLAH It was difficult . . . But may God make things easier.

FATHER Why difficult? I'm a Kuwaiti national, and he's my son.

ABU-ᶜABDALLAH Yes, but your son's English.

FATHER My own son, English! . . . Abu-ᶜAbdallah, let anyone else say that, but please, not you!

ABU-ᶜABDALLAH Well, everyone else *has* said it. He's a man who knows nothing about Kuwait.

FATHER So what do they want from him? They're not appointing him chief . . .

ABU-ᶜABDALLAH Don't you want citizenship for him?

FATHER Yes, but . . .

ABU-ᶜABDALLAH Well then, let things take their course. We'll keep on trying and we'll put our trust in God.

FATHER What did Abu-Khalaf say?

ABU-ᶜABDALLAH He didn't hesitate. He tapped his chest* and said, "Leave it to me!"

FATHER Does he know me well enough?

ABU-ᶜABDALLAH Yes, and he knows that you don't lie . . . Moreover, he knows the story of your marriage?

FATHER And we found a witness . . . (SALEM *enters and stands, with* YUSUF, *waiting for his father to finish.*) What stupidity!—I, testifying that my son is my son! . . . Whoever heard of such a thing?

ABU-ᶜABDALLAH Do you think that things happen just like that? That as soon as you say "I've got a son" they'll give him citizenship? Where's his birth certificate?

FATHER What birth? What certificate? News of that birth has turned everything upside down!

SALEM He's talking sense, Yubah. Do

*In Arabic culture, tapping one's chest means "Rely on me."

you expect them to change the law for your sake?

FATHER What law? There's no *law*! There's only God's Law! Does the Law say that Yusuf isn't my son? How would it ever know, one way or the other?

SALEM They're only asking for proof . . . Prove it to them.

FATHER Don't you believe me, Swailem?*

SALEM (*Sarcastically apologetic*): What does it matter what I believe? I can't do anything anyway.

ABU-ᶜABDALLAH It isn't done! You can't just say, "That's my son!" without proofs and identification! Do you think life's the chaos it used to be in the past?

FATHER Oh, the good old days! Chaos or no chaos . . .

ABU-ᶜABDALLAH What do you miss? All it was was hard work, and fatigue, and indignation.

FATHER What joyful fatigue it was! I wish things would go back to what they used to be!

YUSUF I don't need citizenship. I've got a British passport.

SALEM That's better for him. He'll be hired right away as a consultant.

FATHER What? Are you trying to say that if he gets naturalized, then he'll be jobless?

SALEM No, he won't . . . But he'll be a Kuwaiti, and not a consultant.

FATHER So what's the solution? Leave him as he is, so he'll stay British while I'm Kuwaiti?

ABU-ᶜABDALLAH If you'd registered him in your family's file, his citizenship would have been automatic.

FATHER How was I to know he'd be turning up after all these years?

SALEM Then how are *they* to be expected to know?

YUSUF *exits.*

FATHER So, what am I to do? Disown my own son?

ABU-ᶜABDALLAH God forbid . . . But Abu-Khalaf has offered his help, and all you have to do now is write a letter declaring . . . (*Angrily*:) You've got nothing! Not even your marriage certificate, or divorce papers! What can we do? Your case is complicated!

FATHER Now don't get angry . . . We've written the letter and witnessed it. What else should we do?

ABU-ᶜABDALLAH Take it to the notary public.

FATHER The notary public!? Why? I'm going crazy!

SALEM Take it easy. He'll be naturalized. Just do as I say.

FATHER You see? That's what this modern world's all about: instead of you doing as I say, I have to do what you say!

ABU-ᶜABDALLAH Don't worry, Yubah.† Write all the necessary papers, and we'll ask the *mukhtar*‡ to sign them. Don't worry.

FATHER (*Angrily*): No!—I'll have nothing to do with the *mukhtar*. He's only my son's age, and you expect me to . . .

ABU-ᶜABDALLAH Yubah, it's just routine

*"Swailem" is the nickname for "Salem."

† Used by a peer, "Yubah" does not mean "Father," but something like "Old Boy," a friendly form of address.

‡ A *mukhtar* is an official chief of a district or a quarter who supervises community legal matters.

. . . What's wrong with you? Relax, and leave it to God's will.

FATHER There's no God but God.

ABU-ᶜABDALLAH Yubah, the boy himself told you he's got a British passport, and he's not a child. So why are you worrying yourself?

FATHER (*Hurt*): You've tried your best, Brother, but why didn't you say you were unable to deal with this, and the whole matter's impossible to handle?

ABU-ᶜABDALLAH What am I supposed to do with you? You don't want to listen to me, or to the boy, and what you do want is impossible!

FATHER Ai! My complaints are only for God! I'm only a helpless old man—my words and requests don't count.

SALEM You're not helpless, Yubah! Thank God for what you've got.

FATHER I do thank God! I haven't said a word . . . But I'm frustrated: your uncle Abu-ᶜAbdallah's words carry weight; *his* suggestions are valuable, but mine are nonsense! My complaints are only for God!

ABU-ᶜABDALLAH Listen, Yubah, you're exaggerating things. The whole matter's straightforward. We've spoken to Abu-Khalaf—Abu-Khalaf said it was easy enough. He'll testify with you, and so will I. We'll take the papers to the *mukhtar*, and then we'll take them to the committee, and we'll write a word on your behalf.

FATHER A letter on my behalf!?

ABU-ᶜABDALLAH What's wrong with you? Why are you about to eat me up? You're treating me as though I were the youngest of your children, and forgetting that I'm your eldest brother. Don't you think that Yusuf matters to me as well? He's like one of my own—I don't consider him any different from Salem. Even if he asked for the hand of one of my daughters, I'd gladly accept.

FATHER *If* he asked . . .

ABU-ᶜABDALLAH And why wouldn't he? That would be his lucky day!

FATHER That's enough—don't get heated up—of course it would be his lucky day . . . After all, she is his cousin.

SALEM Yubah, right now the issue is his citizenship: can you get it for him or not?

ABU-ᶜABDALLAH That's right. Let's get the citizenship out of the way first, then everything else will be easy. I'll leave you in peace now.

SALEM Wait, Uncle, you haven't had anything to drink.

FATHER So now you remember!

ABU-ᶜABDALLAH Allow me to refuse now. Some other time.

FATHER What's the hurry? Just a glass of tea . . .

ABU-ᶜABDALLAH (*Heading out*): Next time . . . After all, this is my home, and where I belong.

FATHER God be with you. Forgive us.

ABU-ᶜABDALLAH (*Leaves, laughing*): Don't you worry. (SALEM *follows him.*)

FATHER (*Alone*): So, now I'm an idiot! I'm the one who doesn't think straight, who doesn't know what's what! My complaints are only for you, God! How did I end up in all this trouble? What a mess!

SALEM (*Returning after seeing his uncle out*): What's the matter, Yubah? Calm down.

FATHER Come over here, you! Why don't you behave properly?

SALEM I do.

FATHER So, instead of standing up for me you stand by your uncle!

SALEM May God protect you, Yubah!

FATHER Go and call that brother of yours! Go on!

SHARIFA *enters, angry.*

SHARIFA You'd better watch out! I've run out of patience! It's either me or that son of yours in this house!

FATHER Now what's wrong with you?

SHARIFA I've told you, and it's final! It's either me or your son!

FATHER So! You want me to kick out my own son, who's a total stranger here. (*Angry*:) Do you want me to be a laughing-stock for everyone? Will that satisfy you?

SHARIFA It's no concern of mine.

SALEM Yumma, what's going on? Have some tolerance . . . Has he said anything to annoy you?

FATHER She just hates him—as though he were cutting in on her profits.

SALEM No, something must have happened. Go ahead, say it. Is there anything wrong?

SHARIFA No, there's nothing in particular. But I don't want him in my house!

SALEM Yumma, shame on you! That's so childish.

SHARIFA It's none of your business, don't interfere! I'm talking to your father . . . If you don't want me, I'll leave!

FATHER (*Laughs painfully*): God help us, where will you go? Go on, tell me—where?

SHARIFA So, you do want me to leave! . . . I will, don't worry about me. May God keep my brothers safe, *they*'ll take me in!

YUSUF, *wearing a suit, walks in, followed by* FATIMA.

YUSUF (*Haltingly*): Will—you—go with me?

SALEM No, I've got something to do.

SHARIFA You've got no business talking to my son!

SALEM Yumma!

FATHER What's the matter with her, eh? What's the matter with her? (*To* YUSUF:) Have you told her anything to upset her?

SALEM Yusuf—your father's talking to you.

YUSUF What?—me?

FATHER Yes, you. What have you been saying to your aunt?

YUSUF Me? I haven't said anything to her.

FATIMA Yubah, I know the whole story. Salem, you leave, and you too, Yusuf. Go on, don't worry.

FATHER Well said! Go on, Yusuf.

YUSUF First I've got to understand what's wrong.

FATHER Just go!

YUSUF That's not right . . .

SALEM Come on, come on, I'll go with you.

YUSUF But you just said you had something to do.

SALEM That's enough! Come on.

SHARIFA Let him be! Stop pampering him!

FATHER Why don't you listen to me, go with your brother!

SALEM As you say, Yubah . . . Come on, Yusuf.

FATIMA Please, Brother, for my sake . . . Leave now, and everything will be OK.

YUSUF (*Angrily*): Alright, alright, I'll go . . .

SHARIFA May you leave and never come back!

FATIMA No! Enough, Yumma!

SHARIFA All of you! It's as though you weren't mine! That son of an Indian's bewitched all of you! (YUSUF *stands looking at her, his anger apparent.*) Why don't you hit me? Go on, get him something to hit me with!

SALEM (*Takes* YUSUF'*s hand and tries*

to pull him out of the room): Come on, Brother . . . (YUSUF *turns violently and leaves, followed by* SALEM.)

FATHER Now, you . . . Tell me what's the matter with you! I'm sure he couldn't understand half of what you said. If I'd been in his place, I would have hit you with the heaviest thing I could lay my hands on.

SHARIFA The one who'll lay his hands on me hasn't been born yet! I'm Umm-Swailem!

FATHER This is strange . . . Now you've turned into my enemy. What is it you want? Do you want me to kick out my own son? What has he done to you?

FATIMA Yubah, I'll explain the whole thing to you.

SHARIFA You keep quiet! It's none of your business!

FATIMA You can do whatever you want to, but I'm telling my father! This is intolerable, Mother! You've no right to do this to us! All our lives we've lived respectably, as respected citizens . . . What will people say now?

FATHER Well said, Daughter! You've turned out to be saner than your mother.

SHARIFA What! Are you trying to say I'm crazy?

FATIMA (*Interrupting*): Yubah, he told me that he'd written asking his mother to come here. I let it slip, and told my mother.

FATHER (*Surprised*): What?

SHARIFA Yes, he's bringing your Indian bunny rabbit! . . . Rejoice and be happy! *Samosas* and *chapattis*!*

FATHER I was wondering what had happened to you. What's wrong? I haven't remarried the woman, it's just that my son's come to me. Nothing's happened.

SHARIFA He's bringing his mother *here*!

FATIMA So what? Let him bring his mother . . . What's that got to do with you?

SHARIFA So what, you say? There's a limit to my patience! . . . You're allowing him to flaunt my rival before my very eyes, and you expect me to keep quiet! That's absolutely intolerable!

FATHER You're asking me to forbid him to see his mother . . .

SHARIFA No, don't forbid him! Divorce me, and throw me out!

FATIMA Yumma, God forbid! What kind of talk's that?

FATHER (*Angrily*): Your thoughts and actions haven't been well-balanced lately. I've been very patient with you, not for your own sake but for your children's. Now, are you going to start thinking straight, and leave those idiotic thoughts behind, or what?

SHARIFA (*Impatiently*): Divorce me. I don't want you!

FATHER Will you shut your mouth, or else!

SHARIFA (*Crying out*): That's just my luck!

FATHER So, what's been wrong with your luck? Who's ever hurt you, but yourself? A man wants to see his mother—what is it to you? She's a woman I divorced in the prime of my youth—thirty years ago—not just now. Are you insane? Are you trying to finish us off with your tongue? You're blathering and talking nonsense, and it's pointless!

FATIMA (*Tenderly*): Yumma, in God's name, why are you working yourself into a fury for nothing? My father loves you, and cares for you, and has no one but you.

*Typical Indian food.

FATHER Tell her more.

SHARIFA (*Calming down*): What's the use? . . . Did you hear what he said just now?

FATIMA Don't mind what he said when he was upset . . . He's not minding what you said.

FATHER If I'd taken seriously everything she says, I wouldn't have lived with her all these years.

SHARIFA Did you hear? What's so bad about me?

FATHER (*Laughs*): Before God, it's the truth! That's your nature: you exaggerate things, throw out words you don't mean, and then later everything goes back to normal. That's your nature—what can I do about it?

SHARIFA You mean I'm not all there . . .

FATHER Oh! We're right back where we started!

FATIMA Come on, Yumma, go wash your face.

SHARIFA You haven't told me what you're going to do if he brings that Indian woman here, to lord it over me, and *sit* on me!

FATIMA (*Laughs*): No, Yumma, there's no need for that! We have enough chairs.

FATHER Don't worry, he's not bringing her now. First, he's got to get his citizenship, and work. Later he'll get his own place, and then he can bring his grandmother as well as his mother.

SHARIFA (*Laughs*): Ai! Why didn't you tell me that before and cheer me up?

FATHER So now I've cheered you up. You see, Fatima, your mother's just a child.

SHARIFA (*Laughs*): Why? . . . Because I'm soft-hearted and say what I feel, you call me a child. If I were mean, you'd be thinking I was good!

The door bell is heard.

FATIMA (*Gets up*): Well!

FATHER Where's Abla gone?

FATIMA I'll get it. (*Goes to open door.*)

SHARIFA She's cleaning. (*Meaning* ABLA.)

In walks SARAH*—merry, joyful as a peacock, very beautiful and elegant. She talks coyly; she's young, and she calls herself Sou Sou. She's artificial to the point of being funny. She tries to act dumb, while in reality she is very intelligent and cunning. She sashays about; everything about her is exaggerated.*

SARAH Hello . . . (*Embraces* FATIMA.)

FATIMA (*Embraces her warmly and kisses her*): Welcome back . . . When did you arrive? Yumma, Sarah's here.

SARAH I got back only last night . . . How are you, Uncle? (*She kisses his head.*)

FATHER Welcome back, Sarah. Hello.

SHARIFA *gets up to greet and kiss her.*

SARAH Fou Fou . . .

FATIMA (*Smiles*): My name's Fatima . . . (FATHER *laughs.*)

SARAH Why? . . .

FATIMA That's my name, Sarah.

SARAH And my name's Sou Sou—if you don't mind! . . .

FATHER (*Goes on laughing*): How strange! I thought those were cats' names.

SARAH (*Coyly*): Uncle, you're just like my father—an old fuddy duddy!

FATHER Your father's my brother; we have the same father and the same ancestors . . . But I don't know who *you* take after!

SHARIFA How's your mother?

SARAH Mummy's OK. She sends her love.

FATHER (*Laughs again*): So, what's Fatima's name again?

SARAH (*Slyly*): Fatima . . .

FATIMA Yubah, you gave me my name, and you don't know it!

FATHER (*Laughs again*): Why don't you want me to call you " Ftaim" or "Fattoum"?

SARAH Oh! (*Disgustedly*:) Such old-fashioned names!

FATHER (*Gets up*): What's your mother's name then, Sarah? (*Continues laughing as he leaves the room.*)

SARAH (*Acting stupid*): Ha—Ha—

SHARIFA Sabika, of course. Have you forgotten her name?

FATHER (*Pauses before disappearing from stage*): I meant, what's her name now?

FATIMA (*Laughing*): It must be Sou Sou!

FATHER *exits, laughing loudly.*

SARAH (*After he disappears, smiles*): My uncle's cute! Cute!

FATIMA Sit down, Sou Sou.

SHARIFA I'll go and call the maid. (*Exits.*)

SARAH (*Innocently*): Where's Yusuf?

FATIMA You mean Salem?

SARAH Is Salem here?

FATIMA He left with Yusuf.

SARAH Where have they gone?

FATIMA They'll be back soon.

MAID (*Entering*): Yes?

FATIMA Make us some tea.

SARAH No, it's OK. I've got to go . . .

MAID One minute, I'll make some tea . . .

SARAH No, sorry, I couldn't have any . . . When will Salem be back?

FATIMA In a little while . . . Wait for them.

SARAH No . . . No, Fou Fou . . .

FATIMA I told you—Fatima.

SARAH OK, as you wish: Fatima.

FATIMA Why don't you wait a little?

SARAH No, I've got my car roof open, and someone might fool around with the car . . . The weather is nice, isn't it?

FATIMA Yes, very nice.

MAID What shall I do?

FATIMA Nothing. Just go. (MAID *leaves.*) How was your trip?

SARAH Very nice . . . Is it true that Yusuf's English?

FATIMA You mean like *the English*?

SARAH They say he's typically English—blue eyes . . .

FATIMA No . . . His eyes are just like yours and mine. Yusuf's my brother, and your cousin.

SARAH I'd like to see him.

FATIMA You can if you stay.

SARAH I'll come back . . . When will he be here?

FATIMA Have you seen Salem?

SARAH No, not yet. Maybe he hasn't heard I'm back.

FATIMA I don't think he has . . . Or else he'd have come straight home to see you.

SARAH Well, then . . . I've got to go. Good-bye . . .

FATIMA God be with you . . . (*As she is leaving with* SARAH, YUSUF *walks in.*) This is Yusuf.

SARAH (*Enchanted*): Yusuf . . .

YUSUF We've had an accident.

FATIMA An accident?

YUSUF Yes.

FATIMA Where's Salem? I hope he's all right . . .

YUSUF He wasn't hurt . . . He's talking to a policeman.

(SARAH *is standing erect, staring at* YUSUF.)

FATIMA My brother! . . . I hope nothing's happened to him . . .

YUSUF No, nothing; but the car was crushed a little.

FATIMA I should go and call my father.

YUSUF There's no need. Salem will be back any minute and see him.

SARAH (*Enchanted*): Hello, Yusuf . . .

FATIMA Yusuf, I haven't introduced you to Sarah, my cousin.

YUSUF Uncle Abu-ʿAbdallah's daughter?

FATIMA Yes . . . I'll go and tell my father. (*Exits.*)

YUSUF Hello . . . You're very beautiful.

SARAH (*Happily*): Is it true? Am I really beautiful?

YUSUF (*Surprised*): Yes, very. Very . . . (*They look at each other in apparent confusion.*)

SALEM (*Entering*): Greetings . . .

SARAH (*Notices him, and so does* YUSUF): Hello, Salem.

SALEM Oh! Sarah! . . . When did you get back?

SARAH (*Still enchanted, looking at* YUSUF): Last night . . .

SALEM (*Takes her hand with love and longing*): Welcome back—welcome back . . . Why didn't you tell me? I would have come to the airport . . . By the way, this is my brother, Yusuf.

YUSUF (*Nods his head*): Hello.

SALEM This is my cousin, Sou Sou . . . (*Stops, looks at one, and then the other.*)

CURTAIN

ACT II

SCENE ONE

A ground floor porch, one afternoon a few days later. In the background, stage right, is a garden with typical trees in it—one of which is growing in such a way as to cover part of the porch. Along two sides, chairs are set up parallel to each other. At the center of the porch are two small extra seats. To the left are the main entrance gate and a small door beside the porch that leads into the house.

The curtain rises. The FATHER *walks in, followed by* SHARIFA, *who has been telling him something that has made him burst out laughing.*

SHARIFA Just sit down and rest . . .

FATHER (*Walks to one of the chairs and sits down*): And then? . . .

SHARIFA (*Flirtatiously*): And then what, Abu-Salem? . . . We're too old for that! . . .

FATHER (*Interrupts her*): Don't call me Abu-Salem.

SHARIFA And why not?—Salem's your son.

FATHER I've been called Abu-Yusuf by everyone, including you, all my life—long before Yusuf came or we set eyes on him.

SHARIFA So? . . . Nothing's happened.

FATHER Yes, something *has* happened . . . At first, people called me Abu-Yusuf because my name's Yaʿqub.* Now, it's become more appropriate: Yusuf's come back, and he's the eldest . . .

SHARIFA So?

FATHER So, call me Abu-Yusuf.

SHARIFA As you wish.

FATHER Say, "Abu-Yusuf."

SHARIFA Yusuf, may God show him the right way, is a bit odd . . .

FATHER Not again! . . .

SHARIFA You think I hate him . . . I swear, I don't. He's your son, and the brother of our children. But . . .

FATHER But what?

SHARIFA He's different from us.

FATHER Of course he's different! Did you expect him to be like us?

SHARIFA Well, naturally! As long as he's living with us he should be like us. You're his father, and you should give him some advice.

FATHER What's he done?

*Through association with the Biblical-Quranic story, any person named Yaʿqub is called Abu-Yusuf, i.e., father of Yusuf, even before he has any children.

SHARIFA I don't know . . . I'm afraid that if I say anything, you'll tell me I hate him and I'm spreading gossip about him.

FATHER So you won't tell?

SHARIFA We've got our children, and Fatima is a girl . . . I don't want them to be aware of the things Yusuf's doing. May God show him the right way . . .

FATHER What's he done?

SHARIFA He brings strange girls into our house.

FATHER (*Gets up*): What!?

SHARIFA Calm down . . .

FATHER What girls?

SHARIFA The day before yesterday, he came into the house with a girl. I don't know where he'd met her.

FATHER Speak clearly!

SHARIFA Don't eat *me* up! . . . What have I done?

FATHER A girl, you say—what girl? Whose daughter?

SHARIFA An English girl . . . Like him . . . When I asked him about her he said she worked with him in Ahmadi.*

FATHER That's incredible!

SHARIFA I really didn't want to tell you, but you've forced me to.

FATHER No! . . . That shameless . . .

SHARIFA Blonde hair, blue eyes . . . A short, transparent dress that showed everything.

FATHER That's enough! That's enough, may God forgive us!

SHARIFA I'm just describing her . . .

FATHER Stop describing her! God curse the both of them! The scoundrel! . . .

SHARIFA I honestly didn't want to tell you, but I was worried that one of our neighbors or relatives might see him, and then we'd have become a laughingstock . . . So I thought I'd tell you, and you could advise him, and explain to him. He might not be aware of how things are . . . Set him straight . . .

FATHER That's enough, keep quiet. Where's he gone now? Isn't he back from work?

SHARIFA Not yet . . . (SALEM *walks in, worried.*)

SALEM Good evening . . .

FATHER Good evening. Come here . . . (*To his wife*:) You, go inside.

SHARIFA Very well. (*Pleased, she smiles secretly and leaves.*)

FATHER What are we going to see next from that brother of yours?

SALEM Why? What's happened?

FATHER The unacceptable's happened! —and how come it's happened in my own house without my knowledge?

SALEM I don't understand what you're talking about.

FATHER Aren't you concerned? Have you lost all sense of honor?

SALEM Why? What's wrong, Yubah?

FATHER So—now Yusuf has turned my house into a brothel?

SALEM How?

FATHER Don't act dumb. I'm positive that you're in with him on this, and that you're aware of everything he's been up to . . . You listen to me, carefully: all my life, I've had a good reputation. I've taken pains to care for you and bring you up to maturity, and I'll not tolerate anyone, no matter who he is, coming along and ruining everything I've accomplished! . . . No, never!

SALEM I really don't know what you're talking about, Yubah.

FATHER So try to understand now: he's

*An area about half an hour's drive from the city of Kuwait. The Kuwait Oil Company is located there, and many English people used to live there.

brought girls into my house—girls into my house! Do you understand now, or not? *Girls*— and in *my* house!

SALEM Girls? It's not possible . . .

FATHER I can't believe you didn't know.

SALEM By God, I didn't know! Do you think I would have kept quiet about it if I had?

FATHER So, what's to be done now?

SALEM I'll have a word with him, Yubah. He doesn't realize the implications . . .

FATHER What are you trying to say?

SALEM He doesn't understand our traditions . . . He's acting the way he's been brought up to act. No matter what, Yusuf is intelligent, and he'll understand the situation. I'll talk to him.

FATHER Explain to him clearly that this mustn't happen again. Otherwise, he'll have to go back where he came from . . . What a scoundrel! In my own house!

SALEM Don't worry, Yubah, it's a simple matter. I'll deal with it.

FATHER What time is it? I hope we haven't missed prayers because of that heathen . . . (FATIMA *walks in.*)

SALEM No, we haven't missed them.

FATHER (*Exits*): What a son!

FATIMA Hello. Why's Father angry?

SALEM He isn't angry.

FATIMA Who was he talking about?

SALEM The problem's Sou Sou.

FATIMA Sou Sou?

SALEM She's not back home yet.

FATIMA Who told you that?

SALEM They called, asking for her. She left the house this morning and hasn't come back yet. I've looked everywhere I could think of. Do you have any idea where she might be?

FATIMA No . . . Have you asked about her at her friend Amal's house?

SALEM I've asked everywhere.

FATIMA Where's she gone? . . . (YUSUF *enters, wearing his office clothes.*)

SALEM I don't know whether to go to the police or call the hospitals. She might have had an accident . . .

FATIMA Don't rush. Wait a little.

YUSUF Hello . . .

SALEM Wait a minute, Yusuf, there's something I want to talk to you about.

YUSUF Yes? What is it?

SALEM I'll tell you later . . . But be careful, Father's mad at you. Don't let him lay eyes on you.

YUSUF Why? What's happened?

SALEM I'll just go make a phone call, and I'll be right back. (*Exits hurriedly.*)

YUSUF What's wrong with Salem?

FATIMA Sou Sou's late getting back home, and he's worried about her.

YUSUF Sou Sou?

FATIMA Yes . . . Sarah . . .

YUSUF She's just gone home.

FATIMA That's strange . . . How do you know?

YUSUF She was at Ahmadi, and she said I should come back with her.

FATIMA What are you saying?

YUSUF (*Smiles*): Yes.

FATIMA What about your car?

YUSUF I left it at Ahmadi . . . She said I'd better ride with her in her car.

FATIMA You mean she drove you here?

YUSUF Yes.

FATIMA Why?

YUSUF I don't know . . . I'm hungry. Tomorrow . . . (*He attempts to leave.*)

FATIMA Wait, Yusuf. Just a moment . . .

YUSUF Yes?

FATIMA Last night, did you take Sou Sou to Ahmadi?

YUSUF Yes.

FATIMA Did you invite her?

YUSUF No . . . She'd said several times

she'd like to go there with me, so last night I took her.

FATIMA And why didn't you take me?

YUSUF (*Smiles*): It's not your kind of place.

FATIMA Why?

YUSUF You're too proper . . . And besides, you never said you wanted to go there with me.

FATIMA Your lunch is ready.

YUSUF *exits, smiling.* FATIMA *moves around nervously, but when she sees* SALEM *approaching, she restrains herself.*

FATIMA And? . . .

SALEM She's back safely, thank God.

FATIMA Did you speak to her?

SALEM Yes.

FATIMA What did she tell you? Where had she been?

SALEM She said she'd been visiting a friend of hers at the hospital . . . Thank God she's safe!

FATIMA (*After a period of silence*): Were you worried about her?

SALEM A lot. You know how much I love her.

FATIMA Then why don't you marry her, and have some peace of mind?

SALEM What?

FATIMA Marry her . . . What are you waiting for?

SALEM Your question startles me . . .

FATIMA As long as you love her . . .

SALEM She loves me, as well.

FATIMA All right—then trust in God and marry her.

SALEM I never thought it should be so soon . . . The matter was agreed on some time ago . . .

FATIMA Personally, I feel the sooner you get married, the better.

SALEM Why?

FATIMA Because you aren't young any longer, and then she . . . How long do you want to go on waiting?

SALEM (*Smiles*): Now you've made me wonder . . . Although the whole thing's really simple—we can marry whenever I wish . . . I'm wondering whether she isn't the one who's pushed you to bring up the subject . . .

FATIMA (*Cutting in*): No—not at all . . .

SALEM In any case, I'll give it some thought . . . By the way, call her. She wants to talk to you.

FATIMA If God wills it . . .

SALEM I say . . .

FATIMA Yes?

SALEM Where's Yusuf gone?

FATIMA He's gone to have lunch . . . (FATHER *can be heard, clearing his throat.*) I'll go and call Sou Sou . . .

SALEM And I'll go too, before Father catches me . . . (*He hurries off.*)

BLACKOUT

SCENE TWO

The lighting comes back on. FATIMA *and* ʿALI *are sitting down.*

ʿALI It won't take you more than five minutes—you'll give me my half a dinar, and come back.

FATIMA I can't just now . . . In a little while . . .

ʿALI Please, Fatima . . .

FATIMA No, I'm not moving from here. I'm waiting for Sou Sou.

ʿALI It doesn't matter—you'll get it before she comes.

FATIMA ʿAli, darling, don't be so insistent.

ʿALI Please, Fatima . . .

FATIMA God Almighty! Can't you wait just fifteen minutes?

ʿALI Give me the key, and I'll get it.

FATIMA Why are you in such a hurry?

ʿALI I told you, I'm going to the cinema.

FATIMA There's plenty of time for that . . .

ʿALI No, there isn't. I've already missed the commercials.

FATIMA Please, be patient.

ʿALI That's the last time I leave my money with you . . .

FATIMA O.K., I'll go . . . It seems there's no other way . . . (*Begins to leave with him.*)

SOU SOU (*Enters, wearing dark glasses*): Good evening.

FATIMA Hello, Sou Sou . . . (*Kisses her warmly.*) One moment: I'll just give ʿAli his money and come back.

SOU SOU Wait a minute . . .

ʿALI Please Sou Sou, let her just give me my money and she'll be right back. I'm in a hurry to go to the cinema.

FATIMA Have you got half a dinar?

SOU SOU (*Opens her purse*): Yes, one second . . . (*She takes out one dinar*:) Take this . . .

FATIMA No, I've got a dinar—see? (*She shows it to her.*) But I'm worried he might spend it all—have you got a half?

ʿALI That's O.K.! . . . (*Snatches the dinar and hurries off, smiling.*)

FATIMA (*Smiles*): Naughty boy! Give me back the money, or else! . . . (*Failing to catch him, she returns. To Sou Sou*:) Take the dinar, please.

SOU SOU No, I won't . . . Whatever is the matter? He's my cousin, and just like my own brother.

FATIMA As you wish . . . (*Silence.*) Why are you wearing those glasses?

SOU SOU What?

FATIMA (*Smiles*): The glasses—whatever for?

SOU SOU Fatima—I have to tell you something I can't tell anyone else . . .

FATIMA (*Worried*): What?

SOU SOU Yusuf . . .

FATIMA What's wrong with him?

SOU SOU I don't know.

FATIMA (*After a pause*): Do you love him?

SOU SOU *nods her head affirmatively.*

FATIMA What about Salem?

SOU SOU *remains silent.*

FATIMA There's nothing wrong with that . . . I—

SOU SOU No—Yusuf and I—(*She stammers and stops.*) I mean—

FATIMA (*Clearly worried, she stands up*): Don't tell me? . . .

SOU SOU Yes . . . But it was my fault. I loved him, and gave myself to him.

FATIMA Oh! . . . Oh no, Sou Sou! . . . No! . . .

SOU SOU That's what's happened . . . I don't know what the consequences will be.

FATIMA (*After a period of silence*): Don't worry . . . Everything will be all right . . . (FATHER *enters.*)

FATHER Where's Yusuf? . . . Who's that? Sarah?

SOU SOU Good evening, Uncle.

FATHER Good evening . . . How's your father?

SOU SOU Very well.

FATHER Fatima, go and call Yusuf.

FATIMA (*Moving closer to* SOU SOU): Go in to my room . . . (*Then to* FATHER:) OK, Yubah.

FATHER Sou Sou . . . (*Laughs.*) Sou Sou! . . .

SOU SOU *exits.* MAID *enters, carrying a pot of coffee in her left hand and a coffee cup in the other.* FATHER *sits down.* MAID *hands him a cup of coffee.*

FATHER (*Taking it*): How many times have I told you not to let it spill! . . .

MAID It hasn't spilled.

FATHER Don't put so much in . . . The pleasure of coffee is a sip or two . . .

MAID Yusuf likes it full.

FATHER Damn you *and* Yusuf! . . . So, now he dictates how we're to drink our coffee! . . . Get out of here! To hell with him and you! . . . (MAID *leaves.*) Where's he gone to?. . . .

YUSUF *walks in, whistling. He sits in one of the chairs close to* FATHER *and stretches his legs comfortably, nonchalantly.*

YUSUF Hello! . . .

FATHER No hello! No nothing, God damn you!

YUSUF (*Stunned*): What?

FATHER You shameless creature! You walk in here, whistling! . . . You will prevent God's angels from entering this house! . . . You, the enemy of God and of His Prophet!

YUSUF Why, Dad?

FATHER Stop asking your stupid "why"! . . . And besides, how dare you put your legs up in my face! Haven't you got any manners?

YUSUF Why?

FATHER God help us, this is a real tragedy! . . . Where were you brought up, anyway? With animals?

YUSUF Why, Dad? You're the one who's always screaming and shouting . . . That's not right . . .

FATHER You bring girls into my house and you expect me to keep quiet?

YUSUF What girls?

FATHER Who was the girl you brought into our house? . . . May God forgive us!

YUSUF Which one?

FATHER You stud! Have you brought more than one?

YUSUF Why are you so angry, Dad?

FATHER I'm asking you, who was that English girl you brought home? Who was she?

YUSUF Someone from Ahmadi.

FATHER I know she's from Ahmadi! What were you doing with her?

YUSUF She's just a girl friend.

FATHER I don't understand.

YUSUF A girl friend . . .

FATHER Speak precisely . . . What does "girl friend" mean?

YUSUF It means she's my girl friend: a friend . . .

FATHER God forgive us! How am I expected to get anywhere with this person?

YUSUF Why are you so angry?

FATHER Yusuf, Yubah, this is not done . . . This is our house, where our women live. Your sister's a woman; she's old enough to be married. This is an embarrassment before all God's creation.

YUSUF Why, Dad? It's all the same to me, but . . .

FATHER (*Interrupts him*): Incredible! . . . All the same? . . . No, Yusuf, it's not all the same! . . . We're a well-known family. We've got neighbors, we're not living on a desert island . . . You might be taking after your mother's brothers, but their habits aren't acceptable here.

YUSUF Why not?

FATHER (*Shakes his head with great sorrow*): I'm trying to tell you. Don't keep on asking why—See! . . . If you can't live the way we do, leave us.

YUSUF (*Perplexed*): What?

FATHER Don't you work at Ahmadi?

YUSUF Yes, I do.

FATHER All right, then go and live in Ahmadi, and take your problems away from us . . . I'm worried that your brothers might see you, and act the way you act . . . No, Yusuf, you leave, and may God keep you always.

YUSUF You mean I should go and live at Ahmadi?

FATHER Yes . . . Find yourself a house and live there. Then you can't do whatever you want. You can visit us once a week, if you wish . . .

YUSUF Why?

FATHER (*Angry*): Don't you know any word except why? Every time I say something, you ask, "Why?"

YUSUF (*Smiles cunningly*): Why?

FATHER (*Gets very angry*): You're defying me! You stupid fool! Get out of my sight, God damn you!

YUSUF Never mind, Dad, never mind . . . I'll go and live at Ahmadi.

FATHER Yes, go then! Do whatever you want, away from my eyes and my mind! . . .

YUSUF Never mind, I'll leave . . . (*Exits.*)

FATHER (*Alone*): Only what God wishes will prevail . . . Whoever has brought worry onto himself—

SHARIFA (*Entering, followed by* FATIMA): What's wrong.

FATHER Come in. We're free now . . . He's going to live in Ahmadi.

FATIMA Who is?

FATHER Yusuf.

SHARIFA Well done! If he wants, he can visit us once or twice a month, and he'll be quite welcome . . .

FATIMA Whose idea is this?

SHARIFA Ha! So now you know better than your father?

FATIMA I'm not more knowledgeable than he is . . . But this isn't right.

FATHER Why not? He's not under age . . . Nor is he a girl.

FATIMA But what reason have you got for kicking him out?

FATHER Whoever said I've kicked him out?

FATIMA You mean he's asked to leave?

SHARIFA Why are you interfering in something that's none of your business?

FATIMA Why, Mother, isn't he my brother?

SHARIFA He is, but he's *his* son . . . He hasn't thrown him out on the street.

FATHER Doesn't he work in Ahmadi? . . . Well, he'll be better off living there. He'll do whatever he likes. He'll live among his own kind, who understand his ways and can get along with him.

FATIMA This isn't fair, Yubah . . . You'll make him feel abandoned.

FATHER He's not fit to live with us. His habits are too different from ours; they can't blend in with our customs. They're completely different—*different*, don't you understand?

FATIMA He hasn't done anything . . .

FATHER You don't know anything of what's been going on.

FATIMA I know . . .

FATHER (*Alarmed*): What?—what do you know?

SHARIFA No—no, she doesn't know . . . Just ignore her.

FATHER Fatima, if you want to please me, and be dearer to me than you already are, drop this subject.

FATIMA Yubah—

FATHER (*Interrupts her angrily*): I said drop it! (SALEM *enters.*)

SALEM Hello! (*He smiles cheerfully at* FATIMA.)

FATHER Hello.

SALEM Where's Sou Sou?

FATIMA In my room . . . Oh, God! I'd forgotten all about her! . . .

SALEM Don't neglect Sou Sou . . . Go to her . . . Yubah, when can you spare me a moment? (FATIMA *gets up.*)

FATHER What is it?

SALEM (*As* FATIMA *pauses, worried*): It won't take long.

FATHER (*To* SHARIFA): Go inside now.

SHARIFA Why?

FATHER (*Angry*): Don't ask why!

SHARIFA (*Warily*): Ho! . . . You're not sane today . . .

FATHER I said go inside! (FATIMA *exits.*)

SHARIFA I'm not leaving . . .

FATHER Why are you being so obstinate?

SHARIFA I'm his mother . . . What concerns you concerns me.

FATHER Maybe it's something private . . .

SHARIFA I'm not leaving!

SALEM It's all right—my mother should know as well.

FATHER All right, say it.

SALEM Yubah, I . . .

FATHER Yes?

SALEM Be patient . . .

SHARIFA Come on, speak!

SALEM Have patience! . . .

FATHER You're carrying a burden . . . Relieve yourself of it . . .

SALEM Yubah, I'm old enough now . . . and my situation, thank God, is excellent . . .

FATHER Yes . . . What are you leading up to?

SALEM Patience, Yubah . . .

SHARIFA Come on, say it!

SALEM OK, then! . . . Father—I want to get married. How's that?

SHARIFA Most joyful news, Son! (*Breaks into ululations.*)*

FATHER This is a most blessed moment! . . . Why not? It's our dearest wish! . . . So, whatever you want from me, ask, and you'll get it.

SALEM I ask for nothing but your well-being . . . The truth is, I wasn't thinking much about this matter until it was brought to my attention by Fatima . . .

FATHER Your cousin's been waiting for you: we spoke for her a long time ago . . .

SHARIFA Ever since you were children we've said that you were hers and she was yours—unless you have someone else in mind . . .

FATHER I don't think so.

SALEM You're right, Yubah . . . It's Sou Sou, and no one else.

FATHER Sarah . . . Yes . . . If the patches on a dress come from the same material, Son, they add to its beauty . . . Your cousin's worthy of you.

SALEM So . . .

FATHER So?

SALEM Will you go speak to my uncle?

FATHER It seems you're in a hurry . . .

SALEM No, Yubah—whenever you can . . . But, as the proverb says—

FATHER "The sooner, the better" . . . It's done! I'll go and speak to your uncle, and the matter will be finalized.

SHARIFA (*Joyful ululations*): Thank God I'm alive to rejoice in your happiness, Salem! . . . May we rejoice for ʿAli and Fatima . . . (FATIMA *rushes back in.*)

FATHER (*As he is leaving, very excited*): Congratulate your brother, Fatima!

FATIMA Yubah? . . . (FATHER *stops.*)

*Ululations are shrill songs of joy, made by vibrating the vocal cords ending with a rapid oscillation of the tongue, made by women in celebration of happy occasions, such as weddings and births.

SHARIFA (*Ululates again*): May I rejoice soon for you, daughter—and for your brother ʿAli as well. . . .

FATIMA Congratulations, Yubah. May God keep you for us . . . (*She kisses her mother.*) Congratulations, Yumma . . .

FATHER *and* SHARIFA *exit.*

SALEM How about that? I've done what you asked me to.

FATIMA God be with you, Brother. You've moved quickly . . .

SALEM Wasn't that what you wanted?

FATIMA (*After a short pause*): I didn't expect it so soon . . .

SALEM As Father says, the sooner the better . . . Sarah and I have been very patient. We must enjoy each other before we get too old, and discover that our bloom of youth's gone . . .

SOU SOU *enters reluctantly.*

SALEM (*Rushing up to her and taking her hand happily*): The long wait's over, Sarah . . . Now you're mine and I'm yours, thank God.

SOU SOU Thank God in any case . . .

SALEM We'll talk to Uncle and discuss the details of the marriage dowry . . . Then we'll go and buy our furniture and organize things—What's wrong with you? (SOU SOU *is staring away, absent-mindedly.*) What's wrong, Darling? Aren't you happy? . . .

FATIMA (*Breaking in*): You surprise her like this, and then you expect her to be ecstatic? . . . Wait a minute—let her catch her breath . . .

SALEM She isn't happy . . . Sou Sou, what's wrong?

FATIMA Salem, why don't you postpone the marriage for a while?

SALEM You're weird! Why? . . . You have a different suggestion every minute!

FATIMA Well, that would enable Sou Sou to finish her education . . . She's only got this year left of high school—let her finish it.

SALEM I never said she couldn't . . . The wedding won't be today—we'll get ready, and prepare ourselves, and buy whatever we need. Then we'll go through the legal ceremony, and we can have the wedding whenever she pleases.*

FATIMA But her future? . . .

SALEM (*Interrupting her*): Her future's with me. We'll get married . . . Then she can go on studying until she's an old woman. Even if she decides not to have children, I won't mind.

FATIMA Sou Sou . . .

SOU SOU Yes?

FATIMA Go now.

SOU SOU Where?

FATIMA Home . . . Her mother called for her . . . Don't be late. Go . . .

SALEM Wait, I'll take her.

FATIMA No, why should you? She has her own car.

SALEM Fatima? . . .

FATIMA Go now, Sou Sou.

SOU SOU (*Rigid as a statue*): Goodbye.

SALEM Wait!

FATIMA *You* wait . . . (*She holds him back, and keeps restraining him after* SOU SOU *has disappeared.*) Wait . . .

SALEM I don't understand anything!

*An Islamic marriage consists of two stages: first the legal signing of documents, then the actual wedding ceremony after which the marriage is consummated. The two ceremonies may take place on the same day or may be years apart. If so, the couple are regarded only as fiancés, although they are legally married.

FATIMA Salem . . .

SALEM Fatima, what's happening? I'm sure you must have a good, convincing explanation for all this . . .

FATIMA You're rushing about like a child . . . Wait. Sit down . . .

SALEM I'm not going to sit down!

FATIMA Sit down. I have something important to tell you.

SALEM Go ahead, say it. (*Sits down.*)

FATIMA Salem . . .

SALEM Yes?

FATIMA Salem, Sou Sou isn't right for you.

SALEM I'm controlling myself again now, and asking—why?

FATIMA Sou Sou and Yusuf—the thing is—

SALEM (*Gets up*): What?!

Suitably dramatic music.

CURTAIN

ACT III

SCENE ONE

The same place, a few minutes later: SALEM *and* FATIMA.

SALEM (*His extreme anger apparent through his irregular and furious gesticulations*): I must know how this happened! How? . . . You knew something was going on—how come you kept quiet? How dare that coward eat his own brother's flesh. How could he? . . . I'll die! . . . I'll die if I don't—but *she's* to blame! She's despicable! Contemptible! . . . I would have taken anything from her, but not this depravity! . . . Is this my brother? My own brother? . . .

FATIMA Keep your voice down . . . before someone hears us . . .

SALEM If anyone hasn't heard yet, let him hear!

FATIMA Calm down, Salem . . . Calm down and think . . . What's done is done . . .

SALEM Are you crazy? He's no brother of mine! . . . I wouldn't have done this to a stranger even if it had meant my life! But he did it to me! . . . Oh! How miserable I am! . . .

FATIMA Salem, Brother, wait . . . What will happen to us if you go on like this?

SALEM Be quiet, Fatima! . . . I'm going to kill her! It isn't *his* fault—*she's* the cause of this, that murderess! She's stabbed me in the back! . . . It's so pitiful! So pitiful! . . . All that love I had for her . . . How could I have loved a girl like her? . . . I won't be patient! I'll get even with her! I'll kill her, and be free!

FATIMA (*Holds him tightly*): No, Salem! No! . . . Don't be hasty! . . . What's happened to you? You've always been so reasonable . . . What's happened to you?

SALEM I've got no brains left in me . . .

FATIMA Salem, think for a minute . . . What if you do kill her? What happens next? . . . You'll spend the best days of your life in prison, *and* ruin us! . . . You'll turn our lives into misery and sorrow! No, Salem, you're wiser than that. Just think . . .

SALEM But the scandal! The scandal, Fatima! . . . What if people find out? How can I face them? . . . What a disaster!

FATIMA Our reputation and honor are in your hands . . . You must behave in the correct way.

SALEM What *is* the correct way? What? What?

FATIMA Think calmly and find a solution . . . *You've* always been the one who guided and directed us. Anger shouldn't stop you from thinking straight.

SALEM I've got no more brains, or wisdom . . . Oh, Fatima! What if Father knows? I hope he doesn't!

FATIMA (*Frightened*): Oh no! I hope not! . . . No . . .

SALEM It's best neither Father nor Uncle should know. That low, despicable bitch—because of her, a whole family would disintegrate! (*Silence.*)

FATIMA The best way is to meet Yusuf, and talk to him.

SALEM Meet Yusuf? No . . . It's better that I don't lay eyes on him. Otherwise, I'll kill him with my bare hands . . . Oh!

FATIMA Don't go back to that! If you break down, you'll ruin our lives. Pull yourself together.

SALEM What has Yusuf brought us, but problems?

YUSUF enters. The tension intensifies. He greets them with a smile. This infuriates SALEM even more, but he controls himself and looks harshly at him. YUSUF stops, and FATIMA walks up to him. She takes hold of him and tries to move him away from SALEM. Slowly, SALEM begins to exit, and as he comes closer to YUSUF, he turns abruptly away and leaves.

YUSUF What's wrong with Salem? What's the matter?

FATIMA Come here, Yusuf . . . Yusuf, you've killed us.

YUSUF What?

FATIMA This business of yours with my cousin Sou Sou . . . What have you done to us?

YUSUF Sou Sou?

SALEM (*Returns, having calmed down*): Fatima . . .

FATIMA (*Startled, runs to him in alarm*): Yes?

SALEM Leave me with Yusuf.

FATIMA Salem . . .

SALEM Don't worry. I'm just going to talk to him.

FATIMA Salem, please don't cause a scandal . . . Let me stay here with you . . .

SALEM Go, and don't worry. I told you, I'm just going to talk to him.

FATIMA Why can't I stay here?

SALEM Fatima, you're not supposed to be listening to such talk! You're too innocent and pure for all this . . . Oh! . . .

FATIMA Salem, stop it! OK, I'll leave . . . But please, by our mother and father's lives . . . (*She gives him a quick kiss on the head.*) You—

SALEM I said go . . . (*FATIMA leaves reluctantly. YUSUF comes nearer to SALEM.*) Come here.

YUSUF Yes?

SALEM Just relax . . .

YUSUF What's wrong with you?

SALEM You're still asking what's wrong with me? Just relax! . . .

YUSUF OK . . . (*He sits down.*)

SALEM Yusuf . . . You must marry Sou Sou.

YUSUF (*Stands up*): Why?

SALEM What do you mean, "Why?"

YUSUF Why should I marry Sou Sou?

SALEM Because you've done wrong by her, and you ought to rectify your mistake.

YUSUF I don't know what you're talking about. She never said I should marry her—there was no agreement as such. I'm not ready to marry now . . . And besides, I wouldn't want Sou Sou for a wife.

SALEM This is incredible! . . . It isn't up to you!

YUSUF What isn't up to me?

SALEM Are you crazy? Don't you understand?

YUSUF Why are you shouting?

SALEM (*Controls his temper*): Listen, Yusuf, Sou Sou is my cousin. My uncle—her father—is older than my father, which means he's the oldest male in the family. He's the family's name and reputation. Uncle has no sons—we are like his sons. He only has girls . . .

YUSUF So?

SALEM So, if he becomes aware of what you've done, he'll die.

YUSUF Why?

SALEM You're still asking why? I'm trying to explain things to you calmly . . . (*Masters his anger.*) Yusuf, do you realize that if she did have brothers they'd slaughter you, kill you?

YUSUF (*Frightened*): Why? What have I done?

SALEM What more could you have done? You've raped her, dishonored her.

YUSUF I didn't rape her . . . She—

SALEM Don't say any more than what you've said! You don't realize the extent of your mistake—and that's a calamity in itself . . . If I'd thought you were aware of the seriousness of the situation, I wouldn't have spoken to you—I would have killed you with my own hands.

YUSUF You're saying a lot of things I can't understand . . .

SALEM And that's the tragedy; there's no common language. Sou Sou is my fiancée, and I've loved her for years. She loved me, as well.

YUSUF (*Astonished*): I didn't know! I didn't know . . . I swear, I didn't know! . . . Why didn't you tell me? Why didn't she tell me? I swear, I didn't know! . . . This is weird! . . . This is weird! . . .

SALEM I'm not the issue now. The important thing is that the parents don't find out; otherwise, a tragedy will happen. We've got to settle things. You marry her, and everything will end peacefully.

YUSUF Me marry her? No . . . Me marry her while you love her? . . . No—*you* should marry.

SALEM, *infuriated, gets up, and is about to take hold of him when* FATHER, *clearing his throat, can be heard approaching.* SALEM *controls himself, but his eyes burn with hatred.*

YUSUF Salem, you must be feeling sick . . .

SALEM We'll finish this conversation later.

FATHER Greetings . . . (*They don't answer.*) Can't you hear?

SALEM Hello! . . . Yusuf, I'll see you at Ahmadi.

YUSUF (*Starting off to leave*): OK.

SALEM Don't forget what I told you . . . Think about it . . .

YUSUF OK. (*Exits.*)

FATHER What's the matter? (SHARIFA *enters.*)

SALEM Nothing's the matter.

FATHER What do you mean, "Nothing's the matter?" What's all this about going to see him?

SALEM Nothing, really . . . He's just selling his car, and I've found someone who's interested.

FATHER Why does he want to sell it?

SALEM He's tired of it.

SHARIFA Ha! He's had it for barely four months!

SALEM He doesn't like it, he doesn't want it . . .

FATHER If he didn't like it, why did he buy it?

SHARIFA Too much money! . . . Whoever told you to buy it for him?

FATHER I didn't know he was a fool . . .

SALEM No—he might not sell it after all.

FATHER Yes, you advise him, and bring him to his senses. After all, you're the smarter . . .

SALEM I'll try, Yubah . . .

SHARIFA This has nothing to do with Salem! Why should you put the responsibility on him?

ʿALI (*Rushing in hurriedly*): Yubah!—My uncle . . .

FATHER My brother?

ʿALI Yes! . . .

SALEM Go inside, Mother, go inside.

SHARIFA Wait a minute . . . At least let me say hello to him.

SALEM Yubah, he's in a hurry . . .

FATHER Umm Salem, go inside!

SHARIFA All right, don't kick me out—I'm leaving . . . (*She exits.*)

FATHER Where is he? Come on in! . . . (ʿALI *rushes out.*) Now we'll talk to him about Sou Sou . . .

SALEM Yubah, please don't talk to him just now.

FATHER Why not? The sooner the better . . .

SALEM No, Yubah . . . Please put it off for now.

FATHER OK, you're right . . . To talk to him now wouldn't be appropriate. The proper thing is to go to his house and do it. OK.

ABU-ʿABDALLAH Where are you, Brother?

FATHER Greetings, Brother! Come in . . .

ABU-ʿABDALLAH I've got something private to talk about—just between you and me.

FATHER All right.

SALEM Good evening, Uncle.

ABU-ʿABDALLAH Go inside.

SALEM I hope there's nothing wrong . . .

ABU-ʿABDALLAH Go on inside, I said! Don't you understand?

SALEM All right, all right.

FATHER I hope nothing's wrong, Brother.

ABU-ʿABDALLAH Everything's wrong!

FATHER God save us!

ABU-ʿABDALLAH Oh, Brother, it's a disaster! . . . Death would have been more merciful!

FATHER Nothing's wrong with the "Mother of the Children," I hope.

ABU-ʿABDALLAH It's worse! Something much worse! . . . If death had taken us, it would have been kinder!

FATHER Tell me, Brother, tell me! . . . You're killing me!

ABU-ʿABDALLAH It's news you wouldn't wish on your worst enemy! It's dishonor, Brother! . . . We've been ruined, and it's happened right under our noses!

FATHER What's happened?

ABU-ʿABDALLAH Your son, Brother! . . . Your son, Yusuf . . .

FATHER (*Gets up*): No—don't worry—I've kicked him out of my house, the criminal!

ABU-ʿABDALLAH So you know . . .

FATHER Yes . . . (*Laughs*) I found out, and I was shocked! . . . But I kicked him out of the house. I'm your own brother and I wouldn't allow him to make us a laughingstock in front of our own people.

ABU-ʿABDALLAH Did you know about his carrying on with Sarah?

FATHER What? Don't tell me . . .

ABU-ʿABDALLAH It's happened, it has . . . God help us! God protect us! . . . God, if I've committed sins in my lifetime, forgive me! I'll never do it again! . . . God, I've got gray hair! Don't shame me like this! The grave would be kinder!

FATHER Oh God! . . . Oh God! . . . And who was it?—My son? My own son? . . . Kill me! Destroy me! It's all my fault! . . .

ʿALI (*Rushes in*): Yubah . . . (FATHER *and* ABU-ʿABDALLAH *fall silent.*)

FATHER Yes?

ʿALI Abu-Falah's at the door.

FATHER Tell him I'm out. Tell him I've gone away . . .

ʿALI But I've already told him you're here.

FATHER What does he want me for this time?

ABU-ʿABDALLAH Let him come in . . .

FATHER I wish death had taken us before this happened, Brother . . . How could we have known?

ABU-ᶜABDALLAH It's her mother! . . . God damn her and her mother!

ABU-FALAH (*Entering; his voice can be heard before he is seen*): Abu-Salem? . . . Abu-Salem? . . . Where are you?

FATHER Come in . . . Welcome. How are you?

ABU-FALAH *approaches. He is an old man, obviously nearsighted, who is holding a cane that he leans on when he walks. His son,* MUTLEQ, *a young man, is wearing his school uniform and is helping his father hold the cane.*

ABU-FALAH May you have a long life, Abu-Salem . . . How are you?

FATHER Very well . . . Please sit down.

ABU-FALAH Thank you . . . (*To his son*:) Sit down there.

FATHER This is my brother, Abu-ᶜAbdallah.

ABU-FALAH Good evening.

ABU-ᶜABDALLAH (*Wearily*): Good evening.

ABU-FALAH And this is your obedient servant, Mutleq, my son . . . Greet your uncles, Owl-Face!

MUTLEQ (*Stupidly*): Uncles?

ABU-FALAH Yes . . . Greet them properly—don't behave like an idiot!

MUTLEQ (*Frightened*): Of course, Father . . . Greetings.

FATHER To you, too.

ABU-FALAH And the other one . . .

MUTLEQ (*Quickly*): Greetings!

FATHER Yes.

ABU-FALAH He's giving me so much trouble, this boy . . . He's had to repeat his grade three times.

MUTLEQ Twice.

ABU-FALAH And this is the third year, God damn you!

FATHER Take it easy, Abu-Falah . . .

ABU-FALAH Ai!

FATHER Welcome . . .

ABU-FALAH Hello . . . (*Silence.*)

FATHER Welcome, welcome . . .

ABU-FALAH Thank you, may God protect you. (*Silence.*)

FATHER Yes?

ABU-FALAH May God bestow on you.

ABU-ᶜABDALLAH (*Impatiently*): I hope everything's all right . . .

ABU-FALAH I hope everything's all right. (*Silence.*)

FATHER Greetings . . .

ABU-FALAH Greetings to you.

FATHER Yes?

ABU-FALAH May God bestow on you . . . (*He laughs quietly.*) It looks as though you're pressed for time . . .

FATHER Yes, I mustn't lie to you . . . There's an urgent matter that I must discuss with my brother.

ABU-FALAH Don't worry, I'm in no hurry . . . You finish whatever you have to discuss first.

FATHER No—you go first.

ABU-FALAH No; it's all the same . . .

ABU-ᶜABDALLAH Come on, out with it!

ABU-FALAH As God wishes, as God wishes . . . (*Silence.*)

FATHER Go on . . .

ABU FALAH Thank you. (*Silence.*)

FATHER (*Angrily*): Go on, Abu-Falah! . . . (*Calms down.*) You see, it happens that I'm busy . . .

ABU-FALAH (*Laughs*): Where's the wall-gecko?

ABU-ᶜABDALLAH What do you mean?

FATHER What wall-gecko, Abu-Falah? . . . May God grant us further patience!

ABU-FALAH The fair Englishman.

FATHER Yusuf?

ABU-FALAH (*Laughs loudly, then stops*): Is his name Yusuf?

FATHER Yes.

ABU-FALAH I thought his name was

Shar Shar . . . Mutaileq, you never said his name was Yusuf—what's written in your book?

MUTLEQ (*In a studentlike way*): Tom.

ABU-FALAH Yes, Tom—Tom . . . You've reminded us of the days of the war . . .

FATHER Abu-Falah, we don't understand yet. Please explain to us . . .

ABU-FALAH Yes, where is he?

ABU-ᶜABDALLAH (*Agitated*): Who?

ABU-FALAH Shar Shar.

ABU-ᶜABDALLAH We told you, his name is Yusuf, may God take him away!

FATHER (*Stands and calls out*): Salem! . . . ᶜAli! . . .

ABU-FALAH Don't get angry—take it easy . . . Yusuf? OK, let it be Yusuf, whether I like it or not!

ᶜALI (*Entering*): Yes, Yubah?

FATHER Go and call Salem . . . (SALEM *enters unexpectedly*.)

ᶜALI Here's Salem.

FATHER Salem, come sit with Abu-Falah, and try to understand what he wants . . . Come on, Brother, let's go inside.

ABU-FALAH Have I annoyed you?

FATHER No, but I've got some urgent business to attend to.

ABU-FALAH Is this the way to treat your neighbor?

FATHER Here's Salem . . . He'll take care of you.

ABU-FALAH We've come for *your* help! . . . but it's to God that we complain!

ABU-ᶜABDALLAH Come on, forget about him! . . . (*Goes inside*.)

FATHER Salem's reliable; take care of him, Son.

SALEM Don't worry, Yubah.

ABU-FALAH Abu-Salem, what's happening? The world isn't disappearing, is it? . . . (FATHER *goes inside after* ABU-ᶜABDALLAH; ABU-FALAH *sits down again*.)

SALEM Yes? . . . How can I help you?

ABU-FALAH God bless you . . . I want to go to London, to have my eyes examined.

SALEM (*Going closer*): There's nothing wrong with your eyes.

ABU-FALAH Nothing but sickness and misery!

SALEM They're just irritated because they're dirty . . . Any doctor here can treat them.

ABU-FALAH How do you know? . . . Are you crazy? Medicine and eyedrops haven't done me any good.

SALEM All right . . . So what can we do for you?

ABU-FALAH Seeing that your brother Yusuf's family is in London, let him ask his relations there to look after me—take me to a good doctor . . . I want to ask him a few questions . . . (ᶜALI *walks in*.)

ᶜALI Brother?

SALEM Yes—come here and stay with them . . . I have to go inside for a moment.

ABU-FALAH Where are you going?

SALEM I've got some work to do.

ABU-FALAH This is unheard of! Curse your house, you're kicking me out! . . . Well, I'm not leaving!

SALEM (*Turning to exit*): Give me a minute . . . I'll be back.

ABU-FALAH And even if you don't come back—I'm staying right here! (SALEM *exits. Laughing,* ᶜALI *moves closer to* MUTLEQ *and touches him*.)

MUTLEQ Don't touch me . . .

ᶜALI (*Puts his finger to his head as though thinking*): What do you want? . . . I'm Yusuf.

ABU-FALAH What? Is it you?

ᶜALI (*In English*): *Yes*.

ABU-FALAH Mutaileq—Mutaileq—come on! Hurry up, talk to him!

ᶜALI *Yes*.

MUTLEQ *Yes* . . . I know that word. *Yes*.

ᶜALI *No.*

MUTLEQ *No . . .*

ᶜALI *He is.*

MUTLEQ *He is . . .*

ᶜALI *She is.*

MUTLEQ *She is . . .*

ᶜALI *Back window.*

MUTLEQ *Back window . . .* (*Laughs.*)

ABU-FALAH God damn them! . . . All this proficiency, and they failed you in English! . . . How could they?

ᶜALI *Naughty people . . .*

ABU-FALAH Have you explained to him about my eyes?

MUTLEQ No.

ABU-FALAH Then what have you two been talking about?

MUTLEQ I told him a lot of things.

ABU-FALAH Yes? Like what?

MUTLEQ Yes and no, he is and she is, book, window. . . .

ABU-FALAH Book and window? You ass.

ᶜALI Why don't you tell me what you want?

ABU-FALAH Hey! He knows our language.

ᶜALI Yes, I do. What do you want?

ABU-FALAH I want to have my eyes cured.

ᶜALI Right . . . I know just what you need.

ABU-FALAH May God grant you the best of everything! . . . What?

ᶜALI Have you got money?

ABU-FALAH Yes, thank God.

ᶜALI Right.

MUTLEQ Yubah . . . I say! (*He laughs.*)

ABU-FALAH You shut up!

MUTLEQ Yubah, I say . . .

ᶜALI Don't say anything, you fool!

ABU-FALAH What is it?

MUTLEQ This is their son! . . . His name's ᶜAli . . . He's the one who opened the door for us . . .

ABU-FALAH This is the last straw! . . . You mule! . . . (*He raises his cane to hit* ᶜALI, *then directs it at his son.*) Where were you? Why did you keep quiet, and chatter away with him? . . . You scoundrel! . . . (*He gets up to leave.*) You'll see! . . . I'll get my revenge on you all . . .

ABU-FALAH *curses* ᶜALI *and exits. Laughing,* ᶜALI *heads for the door to inside, while his* FATHER *comes out through it, hesitantly.*

FATHER Ha! . . . So he's gone?

ᶜALI Yes, Yubah. (*Exits.*)

ABU-ᶜABDALLAH (*Entering*): Come on, Brother, God be with you . . . (*To* ᶜ*Ali*:) Go on; call Yusuf . . . (ABU-ᶜABDALLAH *looks exhausted, the situation having drained him.*)

FATHER Have faith in God . . .

ABU-ᶜABDALLAH I do have faith in God . . . (*Makes toward exit.*)

FATHER (*Following him*): Rely on God . . . God willing, nothing but good will happen.

ABU-ᶜABDALLAH Oh, God! . . . Your protection, God! Your protection! . . . (*Exits.*)

FATHER (*Returns, defeated*): God help us!

SHARIFA (*Enters*): So . . . Has Abu-ᶜAbdallah left?

FATHER Yes.

SHARIFA What did he want?

FATHER Nothing.

SHARIFA Hmm . . . All this time, and he wanted nothing? . . . (*Silence.*) Have you talked to him about Salem?

FATHER Salem?

SHARIFA Yes . . . Salem and Sarah . . .

FATHER (*Angry*): Be quiet, woman!

SHARIFA What's wrong with you?

FATHER Nothing—just leave me alone.

SHARIFA I hope nothing's wrong . . .

FATHER Nothing's wrong. Just go, and leave me alone.

SHARIFA Why? What have I done to you?

FATHER Nothing! . . . Just leave me alone—can't you understand?

YUSUF (*Walks in*): Good evening . . .

FATHER (*To his wife*): Get inside!

SHARIFA What's going on?

FATHER Will you leave now or not?

SHARIFA I will, I will . . . You're embarrassing me in front of your son . . .

YUSUF Yes?

FATHER (*To* SHARIFA, *who is standing at a distance*): I said go! . . . (*She exits.* YUSUF *sits down.*)

FATHER Yusuf . . .

YUSUF Yes?

FATHER (*Hesitates—doesn't know how to begin*): You're now . . .

YUSUF Yes?

FATHER (*Angrily*): Wait! . . . (*Silence.*) I can't say anything . . . It's pointless to talk now—what's happened has happened . . . How could you? How? . . . Your own blood, and honor . . . What's the use?—it's happened, over and done with . . . Now listen—what's today?

YUSUF Monday.

FATHER On Thursday we'll have the wedding and marry you to your cousin, and let bygones be bygones . . . She's a heathen, but thank God my son isn't a stranger . . .

YUSUF What is it, Dad?

FATHER Don't call me Dad! . . . I'm not your father!

YUSUF Why?

FATHER Still asking why? . . . (*He controls himself.*) Listen, Yusuf, didn't you understand what I said just now?

YUSUF I didn't understand.

FATHER I'll explain it to you: on Thursday, you're getting married.

YUSUF To Sarah?

FATHER Yes, to Sarah!

YUSUF No, Dad . . . No!

FATHER What's this no? . . . You will, whether you like it or not! . . . You can't abandon her—who'd marry her then? . . . It would be a scandal for us . . . You'll marry her whether you want to or not, or I'll kill you with my own hands and bury you in this house! You filthy—

YUSUF Why?

SHARIFA *appears; she has obviously been eavesdropping. She looks shocked, but takes care that they don't see her.*

FATHER Don't ask why! . . . God damn you and your whys! . . . On Thursday you're marrying her, whether you say yes or no! . . . This is staggering!—my God, do you want me to go mad?

YUSUF Father, listen . . .

FATHER I don't want to hear anything!

YUSUF (*Shouts*): No, Dad, you must listen!

FATHER (*Warningly*): Don't raise your voice! . . . What am I supposed to listen to?

YUSUF Dad, I didn't know that Salem loved Sarah . . . Salem must marry Sarah! He must!

FATHER You fool! Do you want my son to grow horns? . . . Don't even think of it! . . . This kind of thing may go on where you come from, but never here!

YUSUF Yubah . . .

FATHER The wedding's on Thursday. Prepare yourself and get everything organized. No one should know . . . And once we're finished with that we'll see what happens . . . Do you hear me? Otherwise, you'll see—something you never imagined could happen to you will happen! . . . We'll call Mullah Hammoud and get you married, and afterward you can both go to hell! . . . You bastard! She's your cousin! . . . Haven't you seen the grief that's been eating away at your uncle? (*Silence.*) Thursday—do you hear?

YUSUF Thursday—why? I didn't say I wanted to get married. There's been no agreement as such . . .

FATHER (*Furious*): What agreement?

YUSUF Sarah never talked about marriage . . . She said I was just a boy friend.

FATHER (*Places his hands on his head*): God is great! God is strong!

YUSUF Dad! . . . You've got to listen to me . . . I can't marry every girl friend I know! If that were the case, I'd have a hundred wives! . . . Do I have to marry every girl I see?

FATHER (*Stands, agitated, not knowing what to do; gesticulates furiously, but the words don't come to his rescue*): God! . . . Is this *my* son, of my own flesh and blood? And I'm supposed to be his father? God forgive me!

YUSUF Look, Dad, I can't get married . . .

FATHER You'll marry her whether you want to or not! . . . You're crazy! . . . I'll kill you!—by our gracious God I'll slaughter you with my own hands! (*Walks toward him and takes hold of him.*)

SHARIFA *comes clearly into view. She gives an agonized scream and faints.*

CURTAIN

SCENE TWO

Same setting. MAID *is putting the final touches on the cleaning, moving cheerfully.* FATIMA, *carrying an incense holder, is scenting the room.* SOU SOU, *dressed up very elegantly, enters and pauses.*

MAID I haven't been to a wedding in ages . . . I was expecting you'd be getting married first . . .

FATIMA Be quiet, Abla.

MAID But, thank God, Sou Sou's wedding will be before yours . . . (*To* SOU SOU:) Rejoice, be happy! . . . Enjoy your London husband! . . . He's special! There's no one like him—fair hair, tall, broad-shouldered. . . .

SOU SOU *goes back inside without saying a word.*

FATIMA Abla, why don't you keep quiet? . . . You interfere in everything.

MAID What have I done?

FATIMA Go and throw out that trash you're carrying . . . My father and uncle will be back from prayers at the mosque any minute, and if they find us still prancing around—don't look at me like that! (MAID *exits, angrily.*)

SHARIFA (*Walks in, sad and unhappy*): Don't put yourself to any trouble . . .

FATIMA Why, Yumma?

SHARIFA This won't be an easy night, Fatima . . . My son's losing the wife he was promised.

FATIMA It's all the same, Yumma . . . After all, Yusuf is his brother.

SHARIFA I feel so angry at him! . . . Even if I cut him up into pieces, I wouldn't be able to get rid of it all!

FATIMA Come on, Mother . . . Marriage is destiny. Whoever Salem marries will be lucky. Kuwait's full of girls—all he's got to do is choose.

SHARIFA Couldn't he have found someone other than his brother's fiancée? How will my son get through this night? May he who caused him such unhappiness suffer the worst ever! . . .

FATIMA That's enough, Yumma . . . Have some pity . . . (SALEM *enters.*)

SALEM Hasn't Yusuf come?

FATIMA No—not yet.

SHARIFA Oh, Salem! . . . May he taste your agony some day!

SALEM Yumma, stop that talk . . .

Come on, Fatima, go and get yourself ready.

SHARIFA (*As she is leaving*): May God take him away! . . . May God take him away!

FATIMA (*Leads her mother offstage*): Come on, Yumma . . .

SALEM *stands waiting for his* FATHER, *who appears first, followed by the* IMAM *and then by* ABU-ʿABDALLAH, *who is walking with difficulty and looks tired and unwell.*

FATHER Come in—welcome . . .

IMAM God bless him . . . (*Looks at* SALEM:) Is this the bridegroom?

FATHER No, this is my son Salem, his eldest brother . . . The bridegroom is Yusuf.

IMAM God bless them . . . The happiest moments of my life are when I join two people together in matrimony . . .

ABU-ʿABDALLAH God bless you . . .

IMAM Because marriage, as we were taught by God, is that great glory by which Muslims increase . . . And we must not forget that the Prophet—God bless him—made marriage the equivalent of half of religion . . .

FATHER The Prophet spoke the truth . . .

ABU-ʿABDALLAH God bless you . . .

IMAM And the best marriage is an early marriage, because it prevents sin and disobedience . . . And when will you be getting married, Salem? (*Laughs.*)

FATHER When God wills.

IMAM Yes, that's a good answer . . . Where's the bridegroom? We're late.

FATHER Where is he? . . . Go and see.

SALEM He hasn't arrived yet.

ABU-ʿABDALLAH Didn't you make sure he knew the exact time?

SALEM Yes . . . He'll be here any minute.

FATHER Go and look . . . He might have just got here.

SALEM I'll go phone him. (*Exits.*)

IMAM It seems he's going to be late . . . Aren't you hungry? I'm worried you might be getting hungry.

ABU-ʿABDALLAH It's still early.

IMAM The Prophet said, "We are people who don't eat until we're hungry, and when we eat we're never full" . . . There's no shame in eating. I'm hungry—I've eaten nothing since breakfast.

FATHER All right, come on, Shaikh . . . Come and eat. The food's ready—I asked them to have it ready.

IMAM We'll eat, then we'll perform the marriage ceremony. (SALEM *enters.*)

SALEM Yubah . . .

FATHER Yes? . . . (*He stands up.*) Is the food ready?

SALEM Yes, but I need to have a few words with you, please.

FATHER What's the matter? (*Takes* SALEM *to one side.*)

SALEM Yubah, Yusuf's left the country.

FATHER (*Freezes*): What?

SALEM He's tricked us . . . He's gone.

FATHER I thought you—

SALEM Yes, I made arrangements with him . . . And he said not to worry.

FATHER Who told you he's left?

SALEM I called and found he'd left a message with a friend.

FATHER What does he say in it?

SALEM Just a few words—"Sorry I have to leave, because I don't want to get married."

FATHER So, what do we do now?

SALEM I don't know.

ABU-ʿABDALLAH (*Approaches, worried*): What's going on?

FATHER Nothing.

IMAM Hasn't the bridegroom arrived?

FATHER Be patient, Brother . . . Come

on, Shaikh, have some lunch . . . Salem, stay with the Shaikh.

SALEM (*Leading* IMAM *toward the interior*): Come on, this way.

IMAM How about the others?

FATHER Right behind you, right behind you. (IMAM *and* SALEM *exit.*)

ABU-ʿABDALLAH What's happened?

FATHER Come and relax . . .

ABU-ʿABDALLAH I won't relax! . . . Tell me, has he refused?

FATHER No . . .

ABU-ʿABDALLAH Thank God!

FATHER He's left, Brother . . . He's run away, the coward!

ABU-ʿABDALLAH Oh! (*Overcome by consternation, collapses into a chair.*)

FATHER He's gone, the coward! . . . He went away.

ABU-ʿABDALLAH Gone?

FATHER Gone.

ABU-ʿABDALLAH For good?

FATHER Gone.

ABU-ʿABDALLAH Gone? . . . Left the country? (*Falls silent.*)

FATHER *is sunk into a worried silence.*

ABU-ʿABDALLAH What, then?

FATHER *remains silent.*

ABU-ʿABDALLAH What do we do now?

FATHER *remains silent.*

ABU-ʿABDALLAH What about the girl?

FATHER *gesticulates and mutters incomprehensible words.*

ABU-ʿABDALLAH What about me?

FATHER I don't know.

ABU-ʿABDALLAH How about Salem?

FATHER No! . . . No, Brother . . .

ABU-ʿABDALLAH Then what?—what? (*Silence.*)

FATHER I don't know . . .

The stage lights dim. ABU-ʿABDALLAH *walks twice around the stage, then faces his brother, who stands up. They hold each other's hands, then drop their hands and turn their backs on each other. Overcome by sadness, they exit in different directions.*

CURTAIN

YUSUF
AL-ᶜANI

The Key

Translated by
Salwa Jabsheh
and Alan Brownjohn

Yusuf al-ᶜAni wrote *The Key* (*al-Miftah*) in 1967-68. In this play he resorted to the use of folklore, one of the oblique methods employed by modern Arab writers to bring resonance and poignancy to the treatment of contemporary issues. An unprecedented experiment in Iraqi theater, *The Key* succeeded marvelously. "The story is ancient," says Alan Brownjohn, one of the translators, "and the themes eternal. Yusuf al-ᶜAni employs vividly modern images . . . in this haunting fable about human hope and fulfilment. Haira desires a baby, but her bewildered husband refuses to father one in a conflict-ridden world that 'boils and seethes.' Nouar, his younger brother, joins the two on an entertaining and touching quest for a solution. It takes them first to Haira's ancestors, the seven grandfathers, then off to some exhausting travels in search of a symbolic key which will eventually provide security and a child." The essential theme of the play is the contradiction, in the contemporary Arab world, between those like the couple in question who still dwell in a world of myths and traditions and those, represented by Nuwar, who believe in striving toward the achievement of something worthwhile, on the basis of knowledge and a scientific approach. The play ends by asserting the folly of running after an empty goal. The final triumph of the couple, reflected in the imminent birth of a child, is gained only after long search. As such, the child symbolizes the coming generation, which needs to have solid goals. This play is regarded by ᶜAli al-Raᶜi, a prominent drama critic, as one of "universal appeal, which can be performed easily not only in the Arab world, but on the world stage." Brownjohn, an English poet, suggested substituting *Erbil* for *Acca* as is in the Arabic version. He wanted to write the songs in meter and rhyme, and *Acca* was intractible. Since *Acca* was originally used just for the rhyme and not for any specific geographical reason, I thought that the substitution made sense, and it reads very well indeed. I changed the translation of *raᶜi* to "herdsman" instead of "shepherd," as the original translation had it, because the character has only cattle and not sheep.

S.K.J.

THE KEY

CHARACTERS

NARRATOR

NOUAR
The brother

HAIRAN
The husband

HAIRA
The wife

FIRST GRANDFATHER

SECOND GRANDFATHER

THIRD GRANDFATHER

FOURTH GRANDFATHER

FIFTH GRANDFATHER

SIXTH GRANDFATHER

SEVENTH GRANDFATHER

BLACKSMITH

BRIDESMAID

HERDSMAN

BRIDE'S PROCESSION

VOICE OF THE WELL

CHORUS

GARDEN'S ECHO

THE KEY

INTRODUCTION

The NARRATOR *sits behind a small table of the kind used in schools; in front of him is an open book.* HAIRAN, HAIRA, *and* NOUAR *face the audience, under spotlights.*

NARRATOR We have this story which we'd like to tell
—Though *story*'s the wrong word for what's no more
Than a small fable which —we all feel sure—
No one recalls particularly well.
Besides, it's an odd tale: it has no tail
And no head either; and no size, or weight.

NOUAR But if you listen, you can hardly fail

HAIRA —to find some things to like—

HAIRAN (*Exeunt all three.*)—and some to hate!

NARRATOR Once upon a time, long, long ago these events happened—happened like a delusion, or like a dream once the darkness has vanished, or like the truth once the morning sun has risen. The tale of "The Key" is based on an old folk legend everyone's familiar with, an ancient fable that everyone knows by heart. It starts with several rapid repetitions of the same idea, and it ends with questions and sincere appeals and prayers.

Darkness covers the stage; and when the lights come on again we see a crowd of children carrying colored balloons, and swinging happily on wooden swings. One or more of the swings is moving at any given moment, and it is this particular swing to which the children are referring in the poetry of their song. A small empty crib is seen in the middle of the stage.

THE SONG

Swing me, swing me to and fro,
Take me where I long to go,
Where my grandfathers live still,
On the outskirts of Erbil.
They'll give me a robe and cake,
Both of which I'll proudly take
And store the cake in—store the cake—

But where *can* I store the cake?—I know, I'll store the cake inside my trunk!

But!—the trunk will need a key
Which the blacksmith makes for me,
And the blacksmith must be paid,
And the young bride, I'm afraid,
Has the money he will want,
And she's in the bath and can't
Find the money, in the dark,
Without a lamp to throw a spark
Of light, the lamp which fell,
Through some mishap, down the well,
And the rope has gone! The rope
Is tied up tightly round (I hope!)
The horns of the bull, and alas,
The bull must have some grass,

And the garden where it grows
Is parched and dry, and no one
  knows
How to bring the rain but God,
But God himself and only God,
No God but the one God.

The voices gradually die down.

FIRST SECTION: THE JOURNEY

FIRST SCENE

In the land where HAIRAN, HAIRA, *and* NOUAR *live there is a long oval street that begins at the middle of the stage and ends back in the middle, as if it goes nowhere.* HAIRA *and* HAIRAN *sit close to the small, empty crib, and* NOUAR *stands alongside watching them.*

HAIRAN (*Moves forward, addressing the audience*): My name is Hairan.

HAIRA (*Moves forward as well*): And mine is Haira ...

HAIRAN Haira is my wife.

HAIRA And Hairan is, of course, my husband.

HAIRAN Haira wants a child and I say ... No ... No ... No ...

HAIRA But I say: I want a child, I want a child!

HAIRAN No ... No ... No ...

HAIRA (*Moves forward toward the audience*): My friends! Have you heard of any husband in this world who doesn't want a child?

HAIRAN Not one.

HAIRA (*Faces Hairan, and they start arguing*): Then why don't you want a child like every other husband in the world?

HAIRAN What world are you talking about? This world that we don't even know? This world that boils and seethes? This world where people can't tell the difference between black and white? I'm so scared. I'm so bewildered.

HAIRA What shall we do then? (*A silence. Then Haira looks at him as if a brilliant idea has occurred to her.*) Hairan ... let's go to a *different* world. Is there any other world we can reach? Come on, let's go there.

HAIRAN I want security for my son. I want him to have a pleasant, peaceful life from the minute he opens his eyes right up to the time he becomes an old man leaning on a stick.

HAIRA And where do we find this security?

HAIRAN I don't know. I told you I was scared: I told you I was bewildered. (*He walks up and down with a worried expression.*)

HAIRA (*Sits down and watches him; after a pause, she speaks*): You'll soon be forty-one years old and you're still without a child.

HAIRAN Thirty-eight.

HAIRA Forty-one.

HAIRAN Say forty.

HAIRA No, forty-one. (*They fall silent.*)

HAIRAN You'll soon be thirty-one, yet you still want a child.

HAIRA Twenty-seven.

HAIRAN Thirty-one.

HAIRA Twenty-seven.

HAIRAN Say thirty.

HAIRA Twenty-seven.

HAIRAN Thirty.

NOUAR *enters carrying a paper and a pen—he had disappeared at the beginning of the scene while they were introducing themselves.*

NOUAR Thirty-one. Thirty-one African countries joined the United Nations in ten years, meaning that thirty-one countries became independent and proved their existence. And in that time nine other countries from different parts of the world also joined. A total of forty countries in ten years. Do you know how many countries the United Nations was founded with?

Hairan and Haira look at him with astonishment—not understanding what he is talking about.

NOUAR The United Nations was established in 1945 with just fifty members. Now it has 124 members. That means that the difference between what there was and what there is, is seventy-four new members. This shows that the rights of the nations will win out in the end.

HAIRAN What rights are you talking about?

NOUAR The rights of the nations—people's rights.

HAIRA How about me? Aren't I one of the people?

NOUAR Of course you're one of the people.

HAIRA Where are my rights then? Isn't it my right to have a child?

NOUAR Of course it is.

HAIRA Then why does your brother refuse to have one unless he can give him security?

NOUAR He's right.

HAIRA If he's right, then tell us how we can find that security?

NOUAR *thinks briefly.*

HAIRAN Why don't you answer her?

NOUAR You don't believe what I say, and sometimes you tell me I'm only philosophizing.

HAIRA No, this time we'll believe you.

NOUAR Security will come when the world becomes a world of love and goodness.

HAIRAN And when will the world be like that?

NOUAR I can't tell exactly.

HAIRAN There, you see! He doesn't know either. I'm not the only one.

NOUAR But one day it *will* happen.

HAIRAN I want to know *when* it will happen.

NOUAR I told you—I can't tell exactly.

HAIRA *bursts into tears and draws away from them.*

HAIRAN Don't cry. (*Exit.*)

NOUAR Haira, don't you realize that crying and wailing is a kind of defeatism? It's true that crying can be a relief for people, but mostly it's a sign of weakness.

HAIRA Please, do be quiet. You're philosophizing again.

NOUAR (*To the audience*): What did I tell you? They don't believe anything I say. (*Exit.*)

HAIRA, *left alone, looks at the small crib, then approaches it and rocks it, repeating a song to herself, softly at the beginning, then with increasing volume.*

HAIRA Swing me, swing me to and fro,
Take me where I long to go.

(*She repeats these lines several times, then the echo of the verse is heard in the theater, and the other lines follow.*)

Swing me, swing me to and fro,
Take me where I long to go,
Where my grandfathers live still,
On the outskirts of Erbil.

(*Haira looks around to the source of the echo, and listens. When the echo dies out, she repeats to herself:*)

Where my grandfathers live still,
On the outskirts of Erbil.

(*Then suddenly screams:*) Hairan! . . . Hairan!

HAIRAN (*Rushes in*): What?
HAIRA I've found a way out.
HAIRAN A way out?

Enter NOUAR.

HAIRA A way to find security, we'll go to Erbil.
HAIRAN Haira, what's happened to you, are you all right?
HAIRA The story . . . the story says that . . . (*She comes closer to the crib.*) Listen! (*She repeats the first lines.*)

Swing me, swing me to and fro,
Swing me, swing me to and fro,
Swing me, swing me to and fro.

(*The song is heard all over the theater, and when the song ends she looks at* HAIRAN:) Did you hear it?
HAIRAN Hear what?
HAIRA The story . . . the song that tells the story.
HAIRAN I know the story. (*He repeats it quickly.*)

Swing me, swing me to and fro,
Take me where I long to go,
Where my grandfathers live still,
On the outskirts of Erbil.

HAIRA Go on, what comes next?
HAIRAN That's what I've learnt from the story.
HAIRA Come on, let's start.
HAIRAN Start for what?
HAIRA For our grandfathers' village—we'll ask for their help. What do you think? Come on, Hairan, don't hold back.
HAIRAN (*After a little while*): All right, as you wish. We'll go.
HAIRA Nouar, you come with us too.
NOUAR I don't believe the story, and I see no purpose in going, so why should I go with you?
HAIRAN Come with us for my sake. You can help us on the journey.
NOUAR Only on one condition: that I won't be expected to change my mind.
HAIRA As you wish.
HAIRAN But—how do we get there?
HAIRA The story will take us there . . . (*She repeats the story.*)

Swing me, swing me to and fro,
Take me where I long to go,
Where my grandfathers live still,
On the outskirts of Erbil.

Their singing merges with the echo of the song heard in the background as they walk. Then the sound dies out and the light dies down.

SECOND SCENE

HAIRAN *and* HAIRA *arrive in the place where their grandfathers live.* NOUAR *carries a sign with "Erbil" written on it, and sets it down on the stage.*

NOUAR So—we've reached Erbil.
HAIRAN How do you know?
NOUAR It says so on the sign: Erbil.
HAIRAN So it does.
HAIRA Hairan.
HAIRAN Yes.
HAIRA Do you know your grandfathers?
HAIRAN Which one of my grandfathers?
HAIRA Your father's father, your father's father's father, your father's . . .
HAIRAN (*Interrupts her*): I only know my grandfather, my father's father, and I only know him from the picture on the wall in our house, because he died when I was very young. As to the others, I never met them or saw their pictures, and as to my other grandfather, my mother's father, I didn't know him at all and he didn't know me.
HAIRA How about Nouar? Doesn't he know him?
NOUAR (*Laughs*): How can I know him

if my older brother never knew him, or saw him?

HAIRA I suppose you're right.

The seven GRANDFATHERS *appear on a hill humming the same tune and beating the floor with canes in time with it. They are all dressed in white. The last one of them carries a poster bearing the words "The seventh generation," meaning he is the seventh grandfather. Suddenly they speak, all in high voices and in unison.*

THE GRANDFATHERS Hello! Hello! Welcome! Welcome!

HAIRAN *and* HAIRA *draw back, frightened.* NOUAR *contemplates the grandfathers.*

HAIRAN and HAIRA (*In a choked voice*): Hello!

HAIRA (*To* HAIRAN): Is that them?

HAIRAN What do you mean by "them"?

HAIRA Your grandfathers.

HAIRAN (*Looks at them intently*): The one in the front is my grandfather in the picture, but . . .

HAIRA But what?

HAIRAN He hasn't got his *nargila* with him.

HAIRA What *nargila*?

HAIRAN They were inseparable, he and his *nargila*. He had it in the picture with him.

THE GRANDFATHERS We said hello! We said welcome! No one answered us.

HAIRAN Excuse us, we did answer you. Perhaps you're a little deaf.

THE 7th GRANDFATHER Us? *deaf*?

HAIRAN I mean—perhaps we didn't speak clearly enough.

HAIRA *nudges him;* NOUAR *laughs.*

THE 1st GRANDFATHER Hairan, what's wrong with you, are you scared?

HAIRAN No, grandfather, but I'm shivering with cold.

THE 1st GRANDFATHER Go and stand in the sun; you'll feel warm there.

HAIRAN *stands in the sun.*

THE 1st GRANDFATHER How you've changed, Hairan! You were only four when I left you.

HAIRAN *starts to cry.*

THE 1st GRANDFATHER Hairan, why are you crying?

HAIRAN I've remembered the day God took away your soul and we buried you.

THE GRANDFATHERS *laugh.*

THE 2nd GRANDFATHER How can you remember that if you were only four?

HAIRAN My father, God rest his soul, used to tell us how it was a cold and rainy day, and they didn't have any wood to light the fire.

THE 1st GRANDFATHER (*Interrupts him*): What about your father? Why didn't he come with you?

HAIRAN My father passed away fifteen years ago.

THE GRANDFATHERS May God rest his soul.

HAIRAN May He rest your fathers' souls also.

THE 1st GRANDFATHER I haven't seen you for a very long time. It must be thirty-six years.

HAIRA (*In a low voice*): Thirty-six years ago he died—add on four—that means you're forty now. How do you make out you're thirty-eight?

HAIRAN This isn't the time to talk about that.

THE 1st GRANDFATHER What are you saying, Hairan?

HAIRAN I said I feel warmer now and I'll come back to my place. (*He returns to where he stood before.*)

HAIRA Grandfather! We came to consult you on a most important matter.

THE 6th GRANDFATHER What kind of a voice do I hear? Is it a woman's voice?

HAIRAN Yes, grandfather. That's my wife, Haira.

THE 5th GRANDFATHER Your *wife*?

HAIRAN Yes, my wife.

THE 4th GRANDFATHER Meaning your woman.

HAIRAN (*Hesitates*): Yes, my woman.

THE 3rd GRANDFATHER What's her name?

HAIRAN Haira. I married her fourteen years ago, and now we've come to you . . .

THE 7th GRANDFATHER (*Interrupts him*): How dare she speak in your presence!

HAIRAN Why shouldn't she dare?

THE 6th GRANDFATHER The wife doesn't dare ask or answer if her husband is present.

THE GRANDFATHERS *all nod their agreement.*

HAIRAN Grandfather! In our day the woman speaks in front of the man—and behind the man! She walks in front of him. She's started going to school and getting educated, she's become a teacher and a doctor. She can even drive a car.

NOUAR (*Joins in enthusiastically*): She's also become a member of parliament, and a prime minister, and an astronaut.

THE 2nd GRANDFATHER Who's this talking?

HAIRAN This is my brother Nouar. None of you saw him.

THE 1st GRANDFATHER Nouar?

NOUAR Yes, Nouar. I came with them only as a companion on their journey. I'm not convinced of their point of view.

HAIRAN *signals to him to be quiet.*

THE GRANDFATHERS That's strange . . . how the world's changed . . . it's changed so much.

HAIRAN Of course it's changed. Cars are more numerous than camels! Anyone who doesn't read or write is called an illiterate. The airplanes fly without propellers.

NOUAR People will go to the moon, and the world's become a very small place. We have breakfast in Baghdad and supper in Japan.

HAIRAN And neon lighting's now used instead of lanterns. But life's become so very, very expensive!

NOUAR Working hours are shorter, and weekends are now two days a week, and art has become as essential a nourishment as bread.

HAIRAN But in some places children fade away from malnutrition, and thousands and thousands of Arab refugees are dying from the heat or the cold. They were driven out of their land on a black, dark night . . .

NOUAR A new Nazism has planted itself in our land, a modern Nazism; the United Nations is asleep drinking the health of the napalm bomb and of all twentieth-century barbarism.

HAIRAN A new Hulagu is trying to crush humanity and destroy the world.

NOUAR The blacks have revolted against him and threatened his power. Guevara has shaken the regimes of two entire continents. He's become a symbol like the sun. Debray was imprisoned when he was twenty-seven years old. He was sent to jail and the smile never left his face! He couldn't agree to die peacefully in his bed if the world didn't change and become clean and pure.

HAIRA And young men are imitating

women, dressing like women, walking like women, behaving like women.

NOUAR And women in a faraway country called Vietnam plough the earth and reap the crops with one hand and carry a gun with the other. And thousands and thousands from the country of the new Hulagu are dying while he's laughing and drinking whiskey. Their land burns, but turns green the next day while the flames burn inside it to consume those who started the fire. Algeria's offered up a million martyrs. Systems of oppression are collapsing everywhere. The sun shall never set. They've planted the heart of one man in the chest of another. They'll find a cure for cancer. The freedom fighters in our homeland are laying the stones of the long road to liberty. New blossoms are opening and singing to the sun and the air. Black Africa has become as white as snow, the darkness has vanished away. The world has changed. In spite of all the stains and pain and bloodshed, the world will be a better place.

A period of silence.

HAIRAN (*After a little while*): Except that so far we don't know when it will be better.

THE GRANDFATHERS What's going to be better?

HAIRAN The world we live in.

THE GRANDFATHERS Your world's a strange place that we can't comprehend; we've understood very very little of what you've been telling us.

NOUAR Grandfathers, we're simply a new phenomenon, a different generation which looks ahead all the time. But there are others among us who care only for themselves and their immediate surroundings, and remain utterly involved in themselves alone.

HAIRA And we came asking for ... (*She stops.*) May ... May I speak?

THE 4th GRANDFATHER Of course you may speak. If woman has become a doctor and a ... of course you may speak.

HAIRA We came to you to consult with you, and ask for your help.

THE 5th GRANDFATHER Speak frankly!

HAIRA Hairan and I were married fourteen years ago, and we've had no children ...

THE 3rd GRANDFATHER In all those years?

HAIRA In all those years.

THE 2nd GRANDFATHER This is a great shame, I had four children when I was only twenty.

All THE GRANDFATHERS *laugh.*

HAIRA And now I'm twenty-seven years old.

HAIRAN (*Whispers*): Thirty.

HAIRA And still I have no child ...

THE 1st GRANDFATHER No boy and no girl?

HAIRA No boy and no girl.

THE GRANDFATHERS Why not, Hairan?

HAIRA He doesn't want any children.

THE GRANDFATHERS That's strange! Why don't you want any children?

HAIRAN I'd worry about the child. I want security for it.

THE GRANDFATHERS But that's a shame, you're already ...

HAIRAN Thirty eight years old.

HAIRA Forty.

THE GRANDFATHERS So you want to remain childless?

HAIRAN Can you guarantee security? We came for your help.

NOUAR *smiles sarcastically at the idea.* THE GRANDFATHERS *confer with each other, and after a little while* THE 7TH GRANDFATHER *speaks.*

THE 7th GRANDFATHER We'd like to help, but would our advice be suitable in the world you've been telling us about?

NOUAR No, it wouldn't.

THE 7th GRANDFATHER What did you say?

HAIRAN He didn't say anything. (*He signals to* NOUAR *to be quiet.*)

THE 7th GRANDFATHER We'll give you a robe and a cake . . . a robe and—

HAIRA —and a cake!

THE 3rd GRANDFATHER Because that's what the story says. Do you know the old story?

HAIRA Yes.

HAIRA *and* HAIRAN *begin to recite the story, and when they reach the cake and the robe they linger over the words.*

> Swing me, swing me to and fro,
> Take me where I long to go,
> Where my grandfathers live still,
> On the outskirts of Erbil.
> They'll give me a robe and cake—

They repeat this line three times.

THE GRANDFATHERS

> They'll give me a robe and cake,
> Both of which I'll proudly take,
> And store the cake inside the trunk.

HAIRA You mean *you*'ll keep the cake and the robe with you in *your* trunk?

THE 1st GRANDFATHER Don't you have a trunk then?

HAIRA and HAIRAN Yes, we've got one.

THE 1st GRANDFATHER You'll put the cake in the trunk.

THE 2nd GRANDFATHER And lock the trunk safely.

THE 3rd GRANDFATHER You'll lock it with the key.

THE 4th GRANDFATHER And the cake will last you for generation upon generation.

THE 5th GRANDFATHER And the robe will last you for all time.

THE 6th GRANDFATHER On one condition!

HAIRAN and HAIRA What?

THE 7th GRANDFATHER That you lock the trunk safely with the key and don't open it until you have a child.

HAIRA and HAIRAN We'll keep to your condition.

THE 7th GRANDFATHER Then take these two parcels.

THE 7TH GRANDFATHER *hands them to* THE 6TH GRANDFATHER *and they pass from one to the other until they reach* THE 1ST GRANDFATHER, *who gives them to* HAIRAN *and* HAIRA. *They take them.*

THE GRANDFATHERS May God protect you and be with you.

HAIRAN May God bless you and give you a long life.

NOUAR (*Laughs*): God provide long lives!

THE GRANDFATHERS *disappear with the rhythmic sound of the canes beating on the ground and repeating, "May God protect you".* HAIRA *and* HAIRAN *exit with* NOUAR, *repeating the same song, while its echo is heard in the far corners of the theater.*

> Swing me, swing me to and fro,
> Take me where I long to go,
> Where my grandfathers live still
> On the outskirts of Erbil.
> They'll give me a robe and cake,
> Both of which I'll proudly take,
> And store the cake in—store the
> cake—?
> I know! I know! Inside the trunk!

The song and the echo die out simultaneously.

THIRD SCENE

HAIRA *and* HAIRAN *and* NOUAR *are back at their village.* HAIRA *rushes out of her house carrying the trunk.*

HAIRA Here's the trunk. (*She opens it and places the cake and the robe in it, then closes it and looks at it—and suddenly screams:*) Hairan!

HAIRAN What?

HAIRA We haven't got a key.

HAIRAN Why do you want a key?

HAIRA A key for the trunk! If we can't lock it with a key, the cake and the robe are useless.

HAIRAN So where do we get a key from? (*He asks himself this question several times.*)

NOUAR The key's at the blacksmith's.

HAIRA Ha . . . Yes the key's at the blacksmith's . . . (*She repeats.*)

But!—the trunk will need a key
Which the blacksmith makes for me

That's right, the blacksmith's part of the story. Nouar, don't you know the story?

NOUAR No, but I know that the blacksmith makes the key, just as the carpenter makes the trunk, and the baker bakes the bread.

HAIRA Let's go to the blacksmith.

HAIRAN *does not answer.*

HAIRA Nouar, will you come with us?

NOUAR I'll go if you go.

HAIRAN But what about the trunk? Do we leave it open?

HAIRA I'll hide it, I'll hide it somewhere where no human and no genie will ever find it. (*To* HAIRAN:) Come with me. (*She exits with* HAIRAN).

NOUAR (*Laughs*): Let them try. Let me watch them try.

HAIRAN and HAIRA (*Reentering*): Come on . . .

ALL (*On their way to the blacksmith singing*):

Swing me, swing me to and fro,
Take me where I long to go,
Where my grandfathers live still,
On the outskirts of Erbil.
They'll give me a robe and cake,
Both of which I'll proudly take
And store the cake in—store the cake—?
I know! I know! Inside the trunk!
But!—the trunk will need a key
which the blacksmith makes for me.

These last two lines are repeated three times, then the sound dies out and the light dies down.

FOURTH SCENE

Beside THE BLACKSMITH*'s shop. The* NARRATOR *is standing to one side.* HAIRA, HAIRAN, *and* NOUAR *enter.* THE BLACKSMITH *mimes with his hands the words of the* NARRATOR.

NARRATOR By sweating and exhausting himself at his fire, the blacksmith turns the solid iron into a molten liquid, and then casts from it some instruments which are useful to people, and some which do them harm.

THE BLACKSMITH I make the sword, the sharp, cutting sword. In the hands of a tyrant this sword could be used for attack and assault: it could be used with an evil intention. But another person could use it to overthrow tyranny or to protect himself, and that would be to use it with a good intention. I make the scythe that the farmer uses to nurture his crop and to reap his harvest and take his reward after all his hard work. And I make the key.

HAIRA and HAIRAN The key!

THE BLACKSMITH The key that opens doors to let in the light and the sunshine and to allow people to walk out for some fresh air and a good time, and to meet those they love. But the key that opens doors is also the key that locks them; it locks up light and it suffocates it. In both cases it is called a key. A key is used by robbers to rob people and to carry off their money.

HAIRA Holy Protector!

THE BLACKSMITH And the same key protects people's money and preserves all they possess.

HAIRA That's absolutely true.

THE BLACKSMITH That's me, and that's the thing I make. I'm a father and a husband and brother. I've ten mouths to feed; they wait for me daily to bring them food to fill their stomachs. I melt the iron and change it to a red liquid, as red as blood.

NOUAR That's wonderful!

HAIRA (*Comes forward hesitantly*): Sir ... we need a key.

THE BLACKSMITH (*Notices them*): What?

HAIRA We need a key from you.

THE BLACKSMITH A door key? A prison key? A trunk key?

HAIRA Yes, a trunk key.

THE BLACKSMITH A small trunk or a big trunk?

HAIRA A medium-sized trunk. We're going to store in it a gift that was given to us by our grandfathers and it will last us for generation upon generation.

THE BLACKSMITH That's strange.

NOUAR (*To* THE BLACKSMITH): So what do you think of that?

THE BLACKSMITH Think of what?

NOUAR Of something that would last for generation upon generation?

THE BLACKSMITH All I've got to do is make the key. What remains remains, and what vanishes vanishes. Give me ...

HAIRAN Give you what?

THE BLACKSMITH Some money.

HAIRA What money? We've got no money. The story didn't mention any money ...

THE BLACKSMITH How far are you up to with the story?

HAIRA We're as far as:

But the trunk will need a key
Which the blacksmith makes for
me—

THE BLACKSMITH

And the blacksmith must be paid,
And the young bride, I'm afraid
Has the money he will want.

HAIRA The bride?

THE BLACKSMITH Yes, the bride! The bride that lives in the big castle over there ... far away over there.

HAIRA And how do we get to her?

THE BLACKSMITH You walk from here straight ahead on a straight line without turning at all. Just walk straight on.

NOUAR Straight on?

THE BLACKSMITH Straight on.

HAIRA Straight on?

THE BLACKSMITH Straight on.

NOUAR Straight on, then.

Their voices die out, the light dies down, and the song of the bridal procession is heard.

FIFTH SCENE

The walls of the castle where the bride lives. Her bridal procession, bearing all the ceremonial utensils for her bath, enters, and makes its way through a door into the castle, singing. The voices can still be heard inside the castle when HAIRAN, HAIRA, *and* NOUAR *appear. Then it dies down.*

SONG

Everyone, with happy voice,
At her marriage hour, rejoice!
On her full and lovely day
Tread the merry time away
Round and round in graceful
measure,
Urging her to joy and pleasure.
Let our bride sing, and express
With our song her happiness.

MAIDS and SERVANTS

We exist to serve you, hold
You safe from wind and cold
And sun and heat, and safely keep
You distant, as a bride and wife,
From envy's deep eye, all your life.

We shall banish every devil
From your house, and every evil
We shall cast out, all things vile
Will disappear, and all things ill
Will fly, and vanish.

ALL

Everyone, with happy voices,
At your marriage hour rejoices!
On your full and lovely day
Treads the merry time away
Round and round in graceful
measures,
Thinking of your joys and pleasures.
May your ritual bathing bless
You with health and happiness.

Ululations are heard in celebration.

HAIRA How can we get to see the bride?

HAIRAN We'll inquire about her.

HAIRA But who do we ask? There's no one here.

The BRIDESMAID *enters, dancing and singing parts of the song of the procession; after a little while she notices* HAIRAN, HAIRA, *and* NOUAR *and looks surprised.*

BRIDESMAID Who's this? Who are you?

HAIRAN We're from over there . . . We're . . .

BRIDESMAID You're *what?*

HAIRA We're . . .

HAIRAN We're . . . human beings . . .

NOUAR We're people just like you . . . we're . . .

BRIDESMAID No you're not, you're thieves.

HAIRAN Thieves?

BRIDESMAID Yes, thieves, I'll call the guards.

NOUAR We're not thieves. (*He takes hold of her. The* BRIDESMAID *looks at him closely, with some interest. Then she smiles at him*).

BRIDESMAID It seems to me that you're not like *them*. You're not one of *them*.

NOUAR I *am* one of them, and we're not thieves.

BRIDESMAID (*Talking flirtatiously and coyly*): Why have you come here?

HAIRAN (*Comes closer to her*): We came . . .

THE BRIDESMAID *is frightened of him and hides behind* NOUAR.

HAIRAN What's wrong with you? I'm not a demon.

NOUAR This is my brother Hairan, and this is his wife Haira.

BRIDESMAID Hairan and Haira. (*She looks at them*). Hello. Welcome.

NOUAR I'm Nouar.

BRIDESMAID (*Looking closely at him again*): Nouar's a beautiful name. Hello! Welcome!

HAIRAN Thank God . . .

HAIRA (*Smiles and comes closer to her*): Madam, we went to the blacksmith asking him for a key to our trunk, and he sent us to you.

BRIDESMAID To us?

HAIRAN He sent us to you personally.

BRIDESMAID To me?

HAIRA Yes, to you.

BRIDESMAID And what have I got to do with the key?

HAIRA That's what the story says:

> The trunk will need a key
> Which the blacksmith makes for me,
> And the blacksmith must be paid,
> And the young bride, I'm afraid,
> Has the money.

And you're the bride.

BRIDESMAID Oh, I see! You're looking for the bride.

THE THREE Yes.

The BRIDESMAID *bursts out laughing.*

HAIRAN Why are you laughing? (*To* NOUAR:) Why is she laughing?

NOUAR I don't know. (*Moves closer to her.*) Laughing for no reason is—

BRIDESMAID (*Flirtatiously*): Is a sign of bad manners. And laughing for a good reason is like the taste of dates.

HAIRAN It seems as though we won't get one penny, because the bride's gone straight to the top of the palm tree.

BRIDESMAID (*Still laughing*): I'm not the bride, I'm the bridesmaid.

HAIRA The bridesmaid?

BRIDESMAID Yes, the bridesmaid.

HAIRAN (*To himself*): If the bridesmaid looks like that, what must the bride look like?

HAIRA Madam, can we see the bride?

BRIDESMAID That's impossible.

NOUAR Why impossible? There's nothing impossible under the sun.

BRIDESMAID We're beyond the sun! Our bride is the one who makes the decisions, and we're the ones who do as she says. And today she's celebrating her seventh day.

HAIRA What do you mean—seventh day?

BRIDESMAID It means that seven days have passed since her marriage, so she must celebrate, and we must celebrate with her. Can't you hear the music and the singing?

NOUAR You go and tell her; maybe she'll agree.

BRIDESMAID (*After giving it some thought*): Very well, I'll go. (*She enters the castle humming the song.*)

HAIRA (*To herself*): Celebrating her seventh day! Not like me and my bad luck! Neither the seventh nor the eighth ... (*She looks at Hairan:*) Can you hear the music? Can you hear the singing and dancing? I didn't hear any music or singing at my wedding, and I didn't see any dancing. My trousseau consisted of no more than a rusty pan and a squeaky bed and a three-legged chair.

HAIRAN You've started digging up the past! Have you forgotten the henna and the fruit I bought you from the local market? Have you forgotten the candle I bought you from the cloth market?

HAIRA And you're boasting about that candle? Have you forgotten how it bent five seconds after I lit it?

NOUAR In any case, all those formalities depend entirely on a person's circumstances. I know someone from a town not too far away from ours who distributed gold pieces on his daughter's wedding day instead of handkerchiefs. And they brought the gateau to the palace in a huge van.

HAIRA "Gateau?" What's "gateau"?

HAIRAN It's a kind of bread eaten by the English. (NOUAR *laughs.*)

BRIDESMAID (*Coming out of the castle*): The bride sends her welcome to you.

HAIRA and HAIRAN Thank God.

BRIDESMAID (*Bringing glasses of juice*): Come on, drink up!

HAIRA (*Drinking the juice*): My God, this is nice. It's much nicer than the juice at poor people's weddings.

BRIDESMAID (*Coming closer to* NOUAR *and flirting with him*): Do you like it?

HAIRA It's too sweet . . .

BRIDESMAID Much better than bitterness . . .

NOUAR Meaning?

HAIRA Now that we've drunk the juice, can we meet the bride?

BRIDESMAID No, never. It's impossible to meet her. It's forbidden. If you want some food or water, I'm ready to make it available for you.

HAIRA But we need money . . .

BRIDESMAID The money's only provided by the bride, and the bride, as I've already told you, is in the bath today.

HAIRAN And what does it matter if she *is* in the bath?

HAIRA (*Nudges him*): Sh . . . sh . . . that's not the proper thing to say!

BRIDESMAID The bath needs a lamp. If you don't bring the lamp, then the bride won't provide you with the money.

HAIRAN (*Sits down on the ground floor*): We'll wait until she comes out of the bath.

BRIDESMAID The only thing that would do any good would be to bring the lamp.

HAIRA We'll come back tomorrow . . .

BRIDESMAID Tomorrow? Tomorrow means nothing to us. We live our lives without any notion of yesterday leading to today, or today leading to tomorrow, or any of that . . .

HAIRAN So how do you count the days and the months and the years?

BRIDESMAID We don't count them; we just let them pass by.

HAIRAN And what do your people do while the months and the years are passing by?

NOUAR They live as they please! They've got money, and they've got keys. Their keys are made of gold.

HAIRA Tell them to give us one.

NOUAR Their key wouldn't lock our trunk.

BRIDESMAID (*Watching* NOUAR *all the time*): Do you know you're very attractive and handsome and likable?

HAIRAN What's to be done? I'm fed up.

HAIRA The lamp, we've got to get the lamp.

HAIRAN Where will we find the lamp?

HAIRA And the young bride, I'm afraid,
Has the money he will want,
And she's in the bath and can't
Find the money, in the dark,
Without a lamp! (*Repeats line three times.*)

BRIDESMAID (*Still enjoying watching Nouar*): And the lamp fell down the well, so if you're clever, you can get the lamp out of the well, and come back here with it.

HAIRA Come on! Let's go to the well.

HAIRAN (*Gets up*): With the help of God.

HAIRA (*Walks behind him*): God, make it easier for us.

NOUAR *attempts to leave, but the bridesmaid runs after him.*

BRIDESMAID If they find the lamp, will you come back with them?

NOUAR I've told you, I'm one of them; if they come back, so will I . . . (*Exit*).

BRIDESMAID And I've already told you a while ago that you're very attractive, handsome, and likable. (*She laughs loudly.*)

NOUAR *follows them. The* BRIDESMAID *resumes her dancing and singing and moves back toward the castle. The sound dies down and the light dies out simultaneously.*

SIXTH SCENE

At the well. The three enter, looking exhausted. The most exhausted seems to be HAIRA, *yet she shows no outward signs of boredom or unease.* HAIRAN *is the only one who shows how bored he is.*

NOUAR We've reached the well.
HAIRA After *such* a long journey.

NOUAR *approaches the well.*

HAIRAN I told you I didn't want any children, but you insisted, and now we're all utterly dead tired.

HAIRA The worst part's over.

HAIRAN Only God knows what else we're going to see. My legs are swollen, and my mouth's dry, and still Nouar insists that I walk straight on, and keep on walking and all that happens is I walk myself into the ground.

NOUAR (*Smiling as usual*): The road's too long and our destination's too far away, so we've got to get tired if we're to reach the end.

HAIRAN Now we've arrived, where's the lamp?

HAIRA Let's ask someone where the lamp is.

HAIRAN Ask who? There's no one here.

NOUAR Let's ask the well.

HAIRAN Have you ever heard of a talking well?

A flickering of blue ripples from the well in the background. Music is heard, which gradually increases in volume.

NARRATOR Things hidden in the well will speak for us. The well is a vessel of secrets—secret upon secret upon secret: secrets of the heart, suppressed desires, lost truths. In the well there are all kinds of experience, every kind of lesson to learn, buried incidents, things too numerous to number and calculate, some of them funny and some tragic . . . Some of them are things we can still be proud of; others are a matter for shame. And the more the well tries to hide what it contains, the clearer these truths become. They appear to people to assert their presence, the good things and the evil things. But human beings are even stronger than the well, and they can remove a thousand and one veils to get what they want . . . Even so, the well remains reliable and loyal, even when it reveals what it hides in its depths.

THE WELL No . . . I won't tell . . . My name is "Well," a deep, deep well and I betray no one.

HAIRAN *and* HAIRA *are terrified on hearing this loud noise coming from the well and filling the stage.* NOUAR *listens carefully to what the well says.*

THE WELL Who is it that has made me talk after a long, long silence? Who is it?

NOUAR It's us.

THE WELL Who are you?

NOUAR I'm Nouar . . . and this is my brother Hairan and his wife, Haira.

THE WELL Nouar, Hairan, and Haira . . . Come closer, so I can hear you and you can hear me.

The three come closer. HAIRAN *leans over the parapet of the well, then screams, because he is nearly falling into it.*

HAIRA and NOUAR What's wrong with you?

HAIRAN (*Trembling*): Scorpions, snakes

and skeletons! Who's entangled us in this situation and brought us here?

NOUAR *approaches the well so as to put his head over the side and see what it contains.*

HAIRAN Nouar.

NOUAR *stands looking intently into the well.*

HAIRAN Hey . . . ? Nouar!
HAIRA What can you see?
NOUAR I see skeletons—and snakes.
HAIRAN Didn't I tell you?
NOUAR But I see beautiful faces as well, and clear water. I can hear soft, sweet music. (*The music is heard.*) Come here, both of you, come and look!

They both approach, and the music plays on.

HAIRAN (*To* HAIRA): Don't look too deeply into the well; you might get dizzy.

The three of them contemplate the well. The music, and the beautiful shadows and waves can still be heard and seen.

THE WELL (*After a pause*): Why have you come to me?
HAIRA (*Hesitantly*): We came to ask for the lamp.
THE WELL And who told you that I've got the lamp?
NOUAR The people living in that high castle over there . . . they told us.
THE WELL And why did they tell you?
HAIRA Because the bride is in the bath! . . . and . . .
THE WELL (*Interrupting*): What have I got to do with the bride? All those people living in the castle! They've got nothing to do but reveal my secrets, dig them out and reveal them. They live in a place with strong protection, surrounded by a high wall. Its doors are locked and its walls are thick, but they are vulnerable. Their own secrets are known, all the world knows the truth about them. They desire only to reveal other people's secrets and to distort those secrets. They realize that the well is open to the air and the sun, and yet in spite of that it remains closed; its secrets are well protected. But this truth disturbs them and troubles them, so they keep on digging and digging, looking for the secrets belonging to others . . . Go and tell them that the well won't yield up the lamp. The well doesn't care if their bride's in the bath or in the reception room . . . The lamp's here, and well protected, for those who need it, for those people who live in darkness.

None of the three have anything to say in answer to this.

THE WELL Go on, what are you waiting for? Go and tell them I won't give them the lamp.
NOUAR We're not asking for the lamp for them.
THE WELL For whom are you asking for it, then?
HAIRA We want it for ourselves.
THE WELL And what will you do with it?
HAIRAN The blacksmith must be paid—
HAIRA —And the young bride, I'm afraid,
Has the money he will want—
HAIRAN —And she's in the bath, and can't
Find the money, in the dark—
HAIRA —Without a lamp to throw a spark—
THE WELL —Of light, the lamp which fell,
Through some mishap down the well!

HAIRA (*After a pause*): We appeal to your chivalry.

THE WELL (*After a pause*): If the lamp is for you alone, then I'll give it to you.

HAIRA and HAIRAN May God give you long life and ensure you enjoy your youth.

NOUAR *smiles.*

THE WELL Come—take it.

HAIRAN How do we take it?

THE WELL Didn't you bring a rope with you?

HAIRAN *and* HAIRA *look at each other.*

THE WELL (*Hums*):

And the rope has gone! The rope
Is tied up tightly round (I hope)
The horns of the bull.

Go, and bring the rope from around the bull's horns and you'll get the lamp.

DARKNESS

SEVENTH SCENE

The sound of bulls bellowing.

NARRATOR The bull has served humanity. The bull has contributed to the prosperity of agriculture and industry and to civilization in general.

In the old legends the bull was a symbol of strength; and in some countries there are some people who fight the bull and enjoy killing it. Then flowers are distributed to the killer and medals and badges of honor are handed to him. They rear the bull and pamper him only to kill him, and if the bull defends himself and kills whoever wants to kill him, people object to that and take their revenge on him in the ugliest way. The important thing to remember is that the relationship of men to bulls is a *strange* relationship. The bull has even been used as a *bad* example. A heavy, blundering person is a bull in a china shop, and slow, ignorant people in the mass are said to behave like cattle.

Spotlights on the HERDSMAN *and the bull . . . and on* HAIRAN, HAIRA, *and* NOUAR, *standing close to them.*

HERDSMAN Meet my bulls . . . We don't care a jot for what people say. I rear my bulls, and I care for them. I treat them well so they'll benefit me. This herd here walks in a straight line. These bulls plough the land into furrows for planting; they dig canals so that the land may be irrigated; they defy the stubborn strength of the land and leave their mark on it; and they prepare it so that people may come and finish the task and enjoy the fruits. Now!—you see this other herd which goes round in circles.

HAIRAN But we . . .

HERDSMAN Let me finish . . . This herd is pathetic! It keeps going round and round without knowing what it wants and what's happening around it. Its eyes are covered up while it trudges round and round. It enables water to reach the thirsty land, and thus it increases wealth. But when it finishes its work it goes back thirsty and gets dizzy if it walks in a straight line, because turning round in circles has become its natural course. (HAIRAN, HAIRA, *and* NOUAR *remain quiet.*) As to this herd . . . (*He points to the large, energetic bulls.*) Come here and I'll tell you about it. (*He takes* NOUAR *aside*). It's not proper that I speak in front of the lady. (*He whispers something, then laughs*).

NOUAR We call it improving the stock: a symbol of perpetuity and survival.

HERDSMAN This is the most important of my herds. We have other herds, but I don't think you'll need them. They're available everywhere.

NOUAR The truth is that my brother Hairan needs . . . (*He calls him*:) Hairan!

HAIRA (*Nudges him*): Hairan!

HAIRAN (*Wakes up*): Ha?

HAIRA Mr., to put it in a few words:

> The blacksmith must be paid,
> And the young bride, I'm afraid,
> Has the money he will want,
> And she's in the bath and can't
> Find the money, in the dark,
> Without a lamp to throw a spark
> Of light, the lamp which fell,
> Through some mishap, down the well,
> And the rope has gone! The rope
> Is tied up tightly round (I hope!)
> The horns of the bull—

HERDSMAN That's right, the rope's around the bull's horns.

HAIRA We need the rope to get the lamp.

HERDSMAN So you need the rope and not the bull.

HAIRAN Yes, we only need the rope.

HERDSMAN But I won't be able to take the rope off the bull's horns unless I give him the grass.

NOUAR So you mean we can take the rope if we offer him some grass?

HERDSMAN Of course you can. Go and get the grass from the *garden*, then I'll give you the rope. (*He sings*:)

> . . . the lamp which fell,
> Through some mishap, down the well,
> And the rope has gone! The rope
> Is tied up tightly round (I hope!)
> the horns of the bull, and alas,
> The bull must have some grass
> From the garden where it grows . . .

Exit the HERDSMAN. *The others follow him.*

EIGHTH SCENE

NARRATOR And as the story tells, they kept on walking and walking, from land to land and from place to place until they came to the *garden*. But the garden they came to was a deserted garden with no people in it and no sign of life. The ravens were croaking, and the wild beasts were ravaging it. It had tried to preserve every fresh drop of water inside it; it had squeezed the sap of every living branch so that its earth remained fresh and fertile. But the days were rapidly passing by, and the rays of the sun were beating down, and the clouds passing over it, giving it nothing but shadow, then leaving it once more to the burning heat.

The garden kept stretching out its roots to reach the water—it was only asking for a *taste* of water—until its roots were tired out and they wilted and died. The garden was suffering from drought, while in other places the water was suffocating the earth and rending it apart, killing whatever was inside it, or lived on its surface. The overflowing river, the falling torrent, the bursting dams . . . But our garden only needed one downpour of rain.

NOUAR *and* HAIRA *and* HAIRAN *are in a barren empty land. As soon as the narrator finishes, we find the three of them very tired,* HAIRA *the most tired of all,* HAIRAN *the most dejected as usual, and* NOUAR *scrutinizing the state of the garden.*

HAIRAN (*Looks around at the place*): Do you call this a garden? It's a desert. If it were a garden, we would have found plums and pomegranates, palms and apples.

HAIRA (*About to be sick*): Hairan!

HAIRAN *runs to her.*

HAIRA Hairan, let me sit down and rest. I feel dizzy, as if I'm going to be sick. Hairan, help me.

HAIRAN I don't know what to do. Had we been in a real garden, I would have picked the best lemon for you and squeezed it for its juice, and freed you of the nausea.

HAIRA What I feel is worse than nausea. I'm going to die.

HAIRAN Don't say that. I've nothing in this world but you.

HAIRA And I have no one but you.

HAIRAN Didn't I tell you to get out of your mulish stubbornness and forget about having children?

HAIRA I won't forget about having children. It's my right. It's my right, Hairan.

HAIRAN OK, OK, then you'll have to put up with the suffering which goes with this right.

NOUAR (*He has been walking round the garden and now he returns*): No, you're wrong, I'm sure it is.

HAIRAN Sure what is?

NOUAR I'm sure this is a real garden.

HAIRAN A garden? You call this a garden? Oh, it's a kind of garden, but it's upside down. Otherwise, where's the lotus tree and where are the branches? Where are the palms and where are the fruits? And are they green, or hasn't it ripened yet? (*Haira seems about to be sick.*)

HAIRAN (*Rushes to her*): What's wrong with you?

HAIRA Nothing.

HAIRAN I hope not.

HAIRA Let me rest for a while.

HAIRAN By all means. Rest.

NOUAR (*Slapping the earth with his hand, then holding up a handful of soil*): It's a land with soil suitable for agriculture, and it could be improved to yield an excellent crop.

HAIRAN And we've only happened to choose this land that needs all this improvement, and you call it a garden . . . A garden! (*A sudden echo is heard.*)

THE ECHO A garden . . . a garden . . . a garden.

A cluster of branches and flowers appears suddenly at the back of the stage. HAIRAN *is bewildered, and* HAIRA*'s attention is caught by the echo.*

NOUAR (*After a pause*): Did you hear it?

HAIRAN I did hear it, but . . .

THE ECHO I am a garden . . . I am a garden . . .

NOUAR Do you believe me now?

HAIRAN OK, if this is a garden, where's the grass?

THE ECHO The grass grows if the rain falls, if the rain falls . . . the rain. (*A short pause.*)

HAIRAN And now? What do we do now?

HAIRA We wait for the rain. (HAIRAN *is silent.*)

HAIRA What do you say, Hairan?

HAIRAN As you wish, then. We'll wait for the rain.

NOUAR That's right, we'll wait for the rain. (*There is a period of silence and waiting.*)

HAIRA (*Sings, with a special tune, a song for the rain*):

God! Send, please, the fruitful rain
So the crops can grow again;
Cheat the cheats who hoard the
grain.

HAIRAN

My hair still grows and grows, and I
Feel no rain falling from the sky;
And still the land is parched and dry.

(*He stretches out his hand to check whether it might be raining, but there is no rain.*) It's not raining!

NOUAR

Our little tent gathered no rain,
She spread her sheets for it in vain.
God, send from your lovely heaven
Blessings of rain for our bright garden,
Grant to us those fruitful crops
Which spring up under rich raindrops.
Our neighbours need ten showers to thrive,
But one small shower keeps us alive
—And send rain for the young girls where
They tie the sweet braids in their hair.

HAIRA

God! Send, please the fruitful rain
So the crops can grow again . . .

Her voice recedes gradually. Darkness covers the stage for a while as the prayers for rain go in the background, then dawn comes up. And everyone is asleep. Then a sweet rhythmic voice is heard in the distance.

VOICE The sun shines down on the grave of Aisha, the Pasha's child. She plays with a rattle, and in the garden the cock crows, "May God protect the sultan!" Masters, let us go our ways now. We have run out of time, our sun has set, our souls have withered, and we are left in the cold and the dark. (*The voice dies down.*)

HAIRA

I climbed all the way up the mountain,
And found a dome on the mountain,
I climbed all the way up the mountain,
And found *another* dome.
And I wept a while on the mountain,
And I slept a while on the mountain,
I wept and I slept on the mountain, and—
God bless, I cried, this feathery place!
God bless, I cried, this heathery place!
And God grow green grass on its face,
And God grow green grass on its face,
Green grass, green grass, green grass! Hairan!

NOUAR (*Wakes up and approaches* HAIRA *as she repeats the word* grass): Haira.

HAIRAN (*Wakes up and repeats*): Grass, grass, where's the grass?

NOUAR There's no grass; Haira must have dreamt it.

HAIRAN Haira.

HAIRA (*Opens her eyes*): Where's the grass?

HAIRAN There's no grass, you've been dreaming.

HAIRA Hairan.

HAIRAN Yes.

HAIRA I am . . . I am . . . (*She bursts into tears.*)

HAIRAN Haira.

The wind is suddenly heard; a black cloud covers the place; there is lightning, then heavy rainfall. On the horizon a sail appears, a symbol of the rain.

HAIRA and HAIRAN (*Shouting*): Rain! It's raining!

NOUAR It's raining!

Haira ululates. She and Hairan dance and sing. The grass grows quickly while they are rejoicing.

CURTAIN

SECOND PART: THE RETURN

INTRODUCTION

In front of the curtain. NOUAR, HAIRAN, *and* HAIRA *are carrying grass in their hands, singing and dancing.*

We've brought the grass
And it's lighter than feathers,
We've come with the grass
And it's rich and green;
It's sweeter than sugar
And *nicer* than sugar,
The freshest grass
The world has seen.

The rain had fallen,
Tall grass had grown,
But when the rain stopped
The grass lay down.
We've brought the grass, etc.

There's one and a half, and another up there,
And one is cheap and the other one's dear,
And one has lost and the other has won,
And that's the truth when the day is done!

And all the time the world turns round,
And one day it's up and the next day it's down,
And if it's on your side it can't be on mine,
And if it's not dark then the sun might shine!
We've brought the grass, etc.

Some people are intelligent and other people ignorant,
And some of them are pious folks, and some are skeptical,
And some of them work very hard, while some of them just laze around
—And who would you say benefited mankind most of all?

And which of them has most deserved great fame and estimation?
The owl, the hen, the pigeon, or some other feathered thing?
The camel, or the donkey, or the steady, sturdy oxen?
Or some other happy beast which eats the fresh green grass we bring?
We've brought the grass, etc.

FIRST SCENE

Near the place where the HERDSMAN *lives. The area looks burned down and dilapidated, and much of it appears to be completely derelict. The three of them look round with astonishment.*

HAIRA What's happened here?

HAIRAN Perhaps something upset one of the bulls and it tore down the wall and the fence.

NOUAR (*Shouts*): Who's there?

HAIRAN Don't shout like that!

HAIRA There's no one there. What shall we do?

HAIRAN They might have gone somewhere else. They'll be back soon. (*He sings with* HAIRA:)

We've brought the grass
And it's lighter than feathers,
We've come with the grass
And it's rich and green;
It's sweeter than sugar
And *nicer* than sugar,
The freshest grass
The world has seen.

Suddenly the HERDSMAN *enters, obviously agitated. He carries a thick stick in one hand and shields half of his face with the other. It is clear that he has suffered burns on his face.*

HERDSMAN (*Shouts*): Hey! You've taken advantage of the storm! You criminals! (*He waves his stick.* HAIRA *is frightened and screams.* HAIRAN *draws closer, to hide with her.* NOUAR *also edges away from the* HERDSMAN).

HERDSMAN Where are you? Are you hiding, or are you beaten? You've tried to blind me so I can't see you, but you've forgotten that sight's only one of my senses, and I've got four senses left. I can still hear well, and smell everything far and near. I can still touch, and feel my way perfectly. Where are you hiding, you criminals?

HAIRA (*After a pause*): Hairan . . .

HAIRAN Ha?

HAIRA What are we going to do?

NOUAR Wait. Let's understand what the whole thing's about.

HERDSMAN (*Listens to the sounds*): Are you still there? Are you? (*He waves with his stick.*) You won't be able to get away from me and you can't escape . . . I've still got four senses, all fully active.

NOUAR But we're . . .

HERDSMAN You're here! (*He waves his stick.*) Criminals! Criminals!

HAIRAN (*Speaks quickly, then rushes back to hide again*): We've brought the grass.

HERDSMAN So you're not . . .

HAIRA Uncle—we've brought the grass.

HAIRAN We've brought it so we could take the rope.

HAIRA You told us to bring it. (*The three speak in a rapid, staccato fashion.*)

HAIRAN And we've got the grass with us now . . .

HERDSMAN (*Sits down exhausted*): Yes, I remember now, grass for the bulls . . . Where are the bulls now? I've got nothing left; everything's destroyed. All I've got left now is the wind whistling through the ruins.

NOUAR But where *are* the bulls?

HERDSMAN The bulls?

HAIRA Have they run away?

HERDSMAN The bulls have gone, but they didn't run away. The bulls, which turned round and round in circles to enable the water to reach the people and the crops, kept on turning and turning without knowing that while the noria was turning there wasn't one drop of water in the stream. The herd didn't know that the land was as hard as rock and that its owners had left it, and those who hadn't left had died of thirst. They kept on turning and turning until they died of fatigue and thirst and the sun and the cold. They turned into hard clods of earth. As to those who were ploughing the earth and opening it and walking on it in a straight line, they kept on walking and walking until the last drop of blood and sweat dried up in their veins and they too became part of this hard earth.

HAIRAN But didn't the rain fall here?

HERDSMAN Yes, but long after it was too late. It wetted the surface and swept away the soil and cast it into the sea.

NOUAR And the bulls that were kept in a safe place, aren't any of those left?

HERDSMAN They stole them.

HAIRAN Stole them?

HERDSMAN Yes they stole them . . . An evil gang, they came in dozens and hundreds, they came with the storm, they used the storm as their cover, they attacked us, they screamed like wild beasts, they wore big hats, and had different kinds of rifles, they dropped bombs, they burned the crops, and slaughtered the children . . . Napalm . . . napalm. (*The Zionist attacks in Palestine could be shown as a background to this scene, as a film projected on the back of the stage. Also scenes of imperialism and its agents in more than one of the liberated countries could be shown.*)

Flames have seared my face. I did try to push them back, all of us did, but they were better armed than us; they leaped on us with modern weapons. They hit me on the head and I passed out, they stole my herd and everything else I had. When I woke up I could see nothing, I was tired, exhausted for days and days . . . now I've recovered, so . . .

HAIRA And what will you do now all this has happened?

HERDSMAN I want to get back what they took away from me.

HAIRAN Everything?

HERDSMAN Everything! I've got to recover what's rightfully mine. As long as blood runs in my veins and as long as I breathe, I'll strive to recover what's mine.

HAIRAN Why don't you come with us? And live like us?

HAIRA We're going to find a security that will last us for one generation after another when we take the rope from you and go to the well.

HERDSMAN And you'll take the lamp?

HAIRA Yes, and take it to the bride.

HERDSMAN And you'll take the money? (*Now he speaks quietly.*) But my dear, I can't leave my land.

NOUAR So what will you do?

HERDSMAN I'll start again from the beginning.

NOUAR That's wonderful.

HAIRA (*After a short pause*): How about the rope? When will you give it to us?

HERDSMAN Give you the rope? Go and look, here, there and everywhere—I can't see anything.

HAIRAN *and* HAIRA *go in search of the rope.*

HERDSMAN I'll start again from the very beginning.

NOUAR *touches him on the shoulder, supportively.*

HERDSMAN Where's the grass?

NOUAR (*Brings the grass and hands it to him*): Here, take it.

HERDSMAN I'll plant the grass in my land. I'll water it. I'll plough it with my hands. I'll increase the crop, and as the days go by I'll be able to bring back the bulls that were stolen from me. I'll work as long as I live . . . (HAIRAN *and* HAIRA *reenter.*) We've looked everywhere. We can't find the rope. (*The* HERDSMAN *stands up and takes out a rope he has wrapped around his waist.*) Here, take it, this is the rope of the last bull that was taken away from me. I tried to pull it back but the rope was cut. Take it.

HAIRA Thank you.

HERDSMAN May you go safely. I've got to work; I have no time to waste. I'll start now.

The three watch him.

HERDSMAN (*Works and sings*):

All the land that's left to me,
I will keep it carefully.

And I'll plant it, day by day. It'll prosper, and then a new sun will shine. I'll see the light soon, for the darkness *will* vanish one day, as long as there's a sun to shine! (*His voice and the light die down simultaneously.*)

SECOND SCENE

On the way to their destination, the well, HAIRA *mimes the action of moving a crib with a baby in it, then cuddling a baby and singing lullabies to it. Then she catches up with* HAIRAN *and* NOUAR, *who have already reached the well.*

HAIRAN (*To Nouar*): How about singing a song to the well!

HAIRA Hairan, please, no singing this

time. We sang for the herdsman, and look what we found there.

HAIRAN Let's tease it then.

NOUAR (*Laughs*): How do you tease a well?

HAIRAN You'll see . . . (*He approaches the well and drops a length of the rope down inside it. Bubbling sounds are heard.*)

NOUAR What's that?

HAIRAN Maybe he's got . . . (*Points to his stomach.*)

HAIRA *gestures to him to be quiet. More bubbling sounds.* HAIRAN *draws back, scared. A voice booms up through the bubbling sounds, which continue throughout.*

THE WELL (*With an echo*): Hairan!

HAIRAN (*Hiding the rope, which is in his hand*): He's recognized me!

HAIRA And maybe he's heard your conversation about . . .

HAIRAN (*Approaches the well*): Yes? How are you? How do you feel?

THE WELL What's wrong, Hairan?

HAIRAN Nothing.

NOUAR We've come back and brought the rope.

THE WELL I know. And how is he?

HAIRA How's who?

THE WELL The herdsman.

NOUAR He's—not so bad.

THE WELL What do you say?

HAIRAN I say that he's in a very bad way, the hurricane, the attack, the napalm.

THE WELL The hurricane came on us all, but the assault that he had to suffer was brutal.

HAIRAN Have you suffered in the hurricane as well?

THE WELL Of course, but I'm used to hurricanes and storms. The rain was about to stop. It wanted me to lose all my most precious possessions. But I took my precautions; I carried them all away and stored them on the upper layers. Then I dug deeper to store all the excess water, trying to protect my things—though I'm sad to say I still lost some of them.

NOUAR What have you lost? Was it valuable?

THE WELL The thing is valued by the owners, not by me.

HAIRA Do you want us to provide you with a cover?

THE WELL A cover? How could I cover myself up, keep away from the air and the sun? Have you ever seen a well that stays clean without the sun and the air? The rain and the hurricane are little matters I can live with as long as I can see the sun and smell the clean fresh air. Without the sun and the fresh air, all my possessions will fall apart.

HAIRA May God preserve them.

THE WELL So please leave me without a cover.

HAIRA Hairan, ask him about the lamp. Is it lost?

HAIRAN The lamp. Is it lost?

THE WELL Hairan, you're selfish to ask only about that which concerns you alone.

HAIRAN No. But . . .!

THE WELL But what?

HAIRAN We don't really know what else you've got.

THE WELL Whether I'd lost it or still had it, I wouldn't utter one word about it. You've got to look for it. You'll either find it or you won't. Have you forgotten what I told you?

HAIRAN What did you tell us?

THE WELL That I won't reveal any of the secrets that are in my depth?

HAIRAN That's right. You did tell me that. My memory's playing tricks, it often gets that way when a person reaches forty.

HAIRA (*Laughs*): Reaches forty! (NOUAR *also laughs.*)

THE WELL You think forty's old?

HAIRA No, but he always insists that he's under forty. This is the first time he's admitted his real age.

THE WELL One thousand, two thousand, generation upon generation has come and gone while I'm counting their ages. But I've lost count of my own age. My age is a sum of numbers beyond calculation. Nouar! (NOUAR *looks at the well.*)

THE WELL Why don't you say anything?

NOUAR I'm listening . . . and trying to understand what I hear.

THE WELL The more a person talks, the more there is for him to learn.

HAIRA Hairan.

HAIRAN What?

HAIRA The lamp! We must find out about the lamp!

HAIRAN *You* ask him. Or do you keep your sharp tongue for me only? (*Approaches the well hesitantly and speaks to it.*)

THE WELL I know! You want the lamp. Come and take it, then, it's yours for the taking.

NOUAR Hairan, come here and throw down the rope.

HAIRAN *approaches the well and throws down the rope.*

THE WELL Where's the rope?

NOUAR (*Reaches deeper into the well*): Here . . .

THE WELL This rope's too short. This rope won't reach the lamp.

HAIRA If we all try together we'll be able to reach it.

THE WELL Well, try together, then. The lamp now belongs to you by right.

NOUAR Let me go down. (*He climbs into the well, gripping the rope.* HAIRAN, *holding on to it tightly, is halfway over the parapet of the well.* HAIRA *hangs on to* HAIRAN.)

HAIRAN Leave me alone. Don't hold on to me!

She releases him and sits down. HAIRAN *now feels he's being slowly sucked into the well, and that he can't stop this happening. He calls to Haira for help.*

HAIRAN Haira . . . Come on, help me! I'm going to fall into the well!

HAIRA (*Gets up, grabs hold of him, and pulls him out*): I offered to help you, but you refused.

HAIRAN I didn't know the lamp was so heavy.

NOUAR (*From inside the well*): I've fastened it to the rope!

HAIRA (*Ululating*): God bless the prophet Muhammad!

HAIRAN Wait! Let's see it with our own eyes before we start rejoicing.

After a little while NOUAR *emerges, holding the lamp.*

NOUAR I have it! I have the lamp!

HAIRAN Now you can rejoice!

HAIRA *takes the lamp in her hands and gives a great wail of rejoicing. As they all walk away, the music inside the well begins again and rises to a climax.*

THIRD SCENE

Back at the castle again. HAIRA *and* HAIRAN *are standing to one side,* NOUAR *with them.* HAIRA *and* HAIRAN *are singing.*

SONG

Sweets in the bag,
And money for the key,
We will enjoy ourselves; and we
Will rest when the day is through.

The lamp is ours
Without sorcery,
Now we'll enjoy ourselves; and we
Will rest when the day is through.

The lamp lights up
With candles five,
Each one radiantly
Flaming, alive
For one whole week; and we
Will rest when the day is through.

What can you give us,
And we give you?
We'll take you to Mecca
When the night is through!

HAIRA (*Sings alone*): Where are you, where are you? May God bless you.

HAIRAN Maybe they've changed their minds.

NOUAR *approaches the door and knocks, but the knocking produces no sound.*

NOUAR That's strange. Even the knocker doesn't make any sound.

HAIRA How's that? Perhaps something's happened to them.

NOUAR What could have happened?

HAIRA The rain . . . the hurricane . . .

NOUAR The rains and the hurricane don't affect their walls or their ceilings.

HAIRA Perhaps something happened to the bride . . .

HAIRAN Something like what?

HAIRA A fainting spell!

HAIRAN How would the bride get a fainting spell?

HAIRA From the brazier.

HAIRAN What brazier?

HAIRA They must have taken the brazier to her room to warm her after her bath. They must have shut the doors, and she must have become dizzy from the fumes.

NOUAR What brazier, Haira? They don't heat their homes as we do. They've got central heating. It's all automatic.

HAIRA (*Not understanding*): Automatic?

HAIRAN (*Joking*): Do you want me to open the door for you?

HAIRA Could you?

HAIRAN I can try . . . (*He approaches the castle door, sits down on the ground, places his hand on his right ear, and starts singing an old Iraqi song. The door of the castle opens and the bridesmaid emerges. Hairan is frightened: he doesn't believe that his singing could have opened the castle door.*)

BRIDESMAID Sh . . . sh . . . (*She calms him down.*)

HAIRA (*Rushing over to her*): I'm so relieved you're all right.

BRIDESMAID Shsh . . . shsh . . .

NOUAR What's happened to you?

BRIDESMAID It's forbidden . . .

NOUAR What's forbidden?

BRIDESMAID You're not allowed to speak so loudly.

HAIRA Has she got a fever?

BRIDESMAID No.

HAIRA Is she feeling ill?

BRIDESMAID No.

HAIRA Is she still in the bath?

BRIDESMAID What bath?

NOUAR That's strange. Look, will you just go ahead and explain things to us?

BRIDESMAID Shsh . . . (*She gathers them around.*) The bride is pregnant.

THE THREE Pregnant! (HAIRA *gives a wail of rejoicing.*)

BRIDESMAID Shsh . . . it's forbidden.

HAIRAN Even a cry of rejoicing is forbidden?

BRIDESMAID The doctors have forbidden every sound that might agitate her. They've forbidden any strangers to come near her. They've prescribed a special bed, special food, a special light, even a special perfume. They've even covered the walls with a material that's—

HAIRAN Some special material?

BRIDESMAID No, it's an insulator that prevents noise getting out from our castle to the outside world, and allows no noise to get inside it either. Our larynxes were examined very carefully by the doctors, and whoever was found to have an infected larynx had it removed. Whoever was healthy was given a special medicine to keep the voice clear. And as for the shoes . . .

HAIRA What about the shoes?

BRIDESMAID We threw away the old shoes and we now have rubber-soled shoes that don't produce any noise. You're forbidden to enter, because you're wearing such old, noisy shoes.

HAIRA But we didn't come here to walk round the castle. We came to bring the lamp for—

BRIDESMAID The lamp? What lamp?

HAIRA Didn't you say that the bride was in the bath and the bath needed a lamp? So we brought it here so that the bride can give us the money.

BRIDESMAID A lamp?

HAIRA Yes, a lamp.

BRIDESMAID (*Tries to remember*): The lamp, the bath, the money . . . Ah, I remember! (*She laughs.*)

HAIRAN *and* HAIRA *join in with her, pretending to see the joke.* NOUAR *watches them.*

HAIRA Doesn't the bride go to the bath any more?

BRIDESMAID No, the bath comes over to her now, and your lamp's become an old device that we don't use anymore, and we can't even speak to the bride, let alone ask her for anything. She does all the demanding, and we just supply her requests. (NOUAR *laughs sarcastically but* HAIRAN *just sits bored.*)

HAIRA And you accept this?

BRIDESMAID Accept what?

HAIRA That we've gone round and round looking for the lamp and then, at the end of it all, you refuse even to speak to the bride.

BRIDESMAID What am I supposed to do?

HAIRA Just tell her.

BRIDESMAID Tell her what?

HAIRA Tell her that there's a woman called Haira who wants to be a mother, who wants to have a child just like her. But Haira asks for no bed like hers, no food like hers, no perfume like hers; neither does she want the bath to come to her so as to take a bath. No, Haira goes to the public bath and bathes there with the others, with the simple, poor women. Tell her that Haira needs money for the key in order to secure her child's future and to rejoice in its birth. Just tell her that, and I'm sure her heart will soften and she'll give us the money. (*The* BRIDESMAID *looks at her for some time as if she has heard nothing*). It's forbidden . . . (NOUAR *attempts to say something to her but* HAIRAN *interrupts him.*)

HAIRAN Could you kindly please tell me why is everything forbidden? Forbidden! Is this the first time a woman became pregnant? And gave birth? I was born on a train going to Basra. There wasn't even a little dim light on; I was born in darkness. Nouar was born while my mother was separating the rice from the bran.

BRIDESMAID (*Remembers*): Nouar. (*Rushes over to him*:) Oh! I've remembered who you are! (NOUAR *looks at her*).

BRIDESMAID Dearest Nouar, you've

proved your loyalty to me and you came back with them. Oh dearest, was that how you were born? How you must have suffered!

NOUAR It was my mother who suffered, not me. Come on! Go and tell your mistress—who is to deliver her child electronically—that the lamp's here, and the people are asking for the money!

BRIDESMAID Nouar . . .

NOUAR Yes, it *is* Nouar. Can't you understand what I'm saying?

BRIDESMAID (*Grasps his hand and takes him aside*): Nouar . . . Don't bother yourself with them. Come with me.

NOUAR Where to?

BRIDESMAID Come inside here with me, we'll live together in the castle. Money and rank, maids and servants, we'll eat and drink and dance, and all joys will be within our reach. Come with me; don't worry yourself about them.

NOUAR I want their happiness.

BRIDESMAID Don't worry yourself about them! You'll live like a king. You'll give orders, and get whatever you wish. What a terrible shame it is that such a handsome, attractive man should live with this rabble.

NOUAR (*Angrily*): Be quiet, will you! These are my people, my origins. If I break away from them or abandon them, I'll be stranded, no place will be mine, and no person will protect me except them. No matter where I go or travel, or allow myself to mix in with others, I'll find no place for myself except with my own. My roots are with them and no one else.

BRIDESMAID I'll protect you and love you and cherish you. Say you'll agree, and come and see how you'll live.

NOUAR How about my family?

BRIDESMAID I'll arrange for them to have the money.

NOUAR But you just said that you couldn't ask for anything from her.

BRIDESMAID I'll steal it, I'll steal her money.

NOUAR You're despicable.

BRIDESMAID Nouar, you're insane! You call happiness despicable? Here we live to laugh and be happy. We do whatever we want to do, and no one knows about us.

NOUAR Everyone knows. Even the well had all your secrets registered.

BRIDESMAID So what? The important thing is that we live our life and that's enough. We don't care for the means; it's all the same for us. We've wiped out all that pride and honor people talked about so long ago. We've erased all that, and in its place we've written the words *joy*, *pleasure*, and *opportunism*! (*She laughs, and gestures coyly.*)

HAIRAN That's a great disaster.

HAIRA I understood nothing of what she said.

HAIRAN I understood only half of it!

BRIDESMAID Nouar, be realistic. Live like us. Throw your principles in the sea. Come. Come to us; you need us.

NOUAR Never.

BRIDESMAID If you didn't need us, you wouldn't have come back here.

NOUAR It's only necessity that's brought us here, and it's the story that led us to you.

BRIDESMAID (*Watches him angrily*): Nouar.

NOUAR Yes.

BRIDESMAID Is this your last word on the matter? (*Nouar does not answer.*) Are you coming with me or not?

NOUAR (*Looks at her sternly*): No, I'm not.

BRIDESMAID (*Screams*): Guards! Guards! Take them prisoner—they're robbers! Robbers! (*She rushes into the castle. Strange noises are heard; stones are thrown down on* HAIRAN, HAIRA, *and* NOUAR, *but they produce no sound.* NOUAR, HAIRAN, *and* HAIRA *throw the stones back and call out.*)

THE THREE You're the thieves! You're the robbers! (*They go off stage, and again sing, a loud song that echoes all round the theater.*

SONG

Sweets in the bag,
And money for the key.
It's not your money, it belongs to the
people!

The song is repeated several times, then the voices and the light die down simultaneously.

FOURTH SCENE

Back outside THE BLACKSMITH*'s shop. The door of the shop is closed, and a paper has been posted on it.* HAIRAN, HAIRA, *and* NOUAR *are standing in front of the shop.*

NARRATOR The Thirty-third Court of Justice has been set up, and the following decree issued on 13th March 1967:

The Plaintiff, Sultan ibn Rushdi Khan.

The Defendant, Khalaf ibn Abboud, the blacksmith.

The Verdict:

This decree issued by the office of the public prosecutor, wherein it is confirmed and proved by all the evidence presented by the plaintiff, Sultan ibn Rushdi Khan, that the defendant, Khalaf ibn Abboud, the blacksmith, has abstained from paying the rent of the shop he occupied to its owner, Sultan ibn Rushdi Khan in spite of repeated demands; And this being confirmed by the defendant, the said defendant is hereby instructed to vacate the shop No. 1081/68, which is located in the Ain Al Sabᶜ area in Ras Al-Nabᶜ, and to render the same back to Sultan ibn Rushdi Khan empty of all contents, all expenses of the transfer to be born by the defendant.

Publicly posted on 13th March 1967.

NOUAR Signed by the governor.

HAIRA What does that mean?

HAIRAN It means that the blacksmith's been declared bankrupt and has to hand the shop back to its owners.

NOUAR He wasn't informed, so they stuck the verdict on his door.

HAIRAN That completes our chain of bad luck!

HAIRA That's my luck. If I went to a river, its water would dry up. My evil luck! (*About to burst into tears.*)

HAIRAN Are we crying again?

HAIRA What am I supposed to do? Neither cry nor laugh? Leave me alone.

NOUAR Hairan?

HAIRAN Yes?

NOUAR We'll go and look for him.

HAIRAN Look for whom?

NOUAR The blacksmith.

HAIRAN What's the use? We've come back without any money.

NOUAR It doesn't matter.

HAIRAN What do you mean, it doesn't matter?

HAIRA We've got no money!

NOUAR We'll find him first.

HAIRA As you wish . . .

NOUAR (*To Hairan*): Come on. (HAIRAN *and* NOUAR *go out to look for* THE BLACKSMITH).

HAIRA (*Weeping, and repeating the words of a lamentation*):

I don't think my fate keeps any
hidden good fortune in store
for me.
I've roved the wilderness exhausted,
My stomach empty, my strength all
wasted.
A woman with no luck at the
beginning

Is more and more foolish to dream
of winning
When her lands are parched and
dry. She knows
They'll yield no fruit whatever she
grows;
And the man who held back, and
planted late,
Will reap no sympathy from fate

Someone appears wrapped up in a wide, black cloak, standing beside the shop. He points at HAIRA, *but she doesn't see him, so he has to call to her in a whisper.*

THE PERSON Psst . . . Psst!

At first she doesn't look toward him.

THE PERSON (*Repeats the call*): Psst . . . Psst!

HAIRA Are you calling me?

THE PERSON Yes.

HAIRA What is it? What do you want from me?

THE PERSON Come over here.

HAIRA (*With boredom*): Please! . . . Leave me alone.

THE PERSON Listen to me, for God's sake!

HAIRA And for God's sake leave me alone! Ask God to provide for you. A beggar begging from a beggar!

THE PERSON I'm not a beggar.

HAIRA (*Sarcastically*): No, you're a sultan. Go on, may God protect you.

THE PERSON I assure you I'm not a beggar; I'm the blacksmith.

HAIRA (*Ignores him, then realizes what she has heard*): What?

THE PERSON I'm the blacksmith . . .

HAIRA The *blacksmith*?

THE PERSON Yes, the blacksmith.

HAIRA Why don't you open your shop and . . .?

THE PERSON This is a complicated matter. Go and look for your companions and come back here.

HAIRA OK.

BLACKSMITH Listen! Don't tell anyone but them that you've seen me.

HAIRA No. (*She runs off.*)

THE BLACKSMITH *conceals himself in his cloak and moves aside. After a few moments,* HAIRAN, HAIRA, *and* NOUAR *enter.*

NOUAR Where is he?

HAIRA He was standing here.

HAIRAN Where's he gone then?

HAIRA I assure you he was here.

BLACKSMITH (*Whispers from the other side*): Psst . . . Psst!

HAIRA That's him . . . (*The three go forward toward him.*)

BLACKSMITH Speak quietly. They've thrown me out of the shop.

NOUAR I've read the court decree. Why don't you vacate the shop?

BLACKSMITH How should I vacate the shop! Everything in the shop's been confiscated. To transport it would mean extra expense. Let them empty the shop and bear the expense.

HAIRAN And what are you going to do now?

BLACKSMITH I'm on the run.

HAIRAN From whom?

BLACKSMITH From my creditors, from the people who are after me . . .

HAIRAN How about your work?

BLACKSMITH My work? The coal was the first thing they confiscated. How can a blacksmith work without coal?

HAIRAN Why have you done this to yourself?

BLACKSMITH I didn't. I was driven to it by poverty. I don't know what kind of a world this is! I work day and night, and this is the result. I used to borrow money so I could pay the rent, and work to pay the debt, and borrow again. As the days passed the debts accumulated, and the interest kept multiplying tenfold, so I wasn't able to pay the rent or the debt any more. I was hoping that things would improve, but I was only deceiving myself. I even deceived my own children. I gave them hot water with salt and told them that it was chicken broth!

HAIRA Poor souls!

BLACKSMITH In the end I lost everything. I was crushed by the world; I didn't do it to myself. The bloodsuckers of the world sucked all the blood out of my body.

NOUAR So what will you do to stop this happening again?

BLACKSMITH I don't know.

NOUAR Look for some other kind of work.

BLACKSMITH But I'm working now; I work away from the shop. I work at home, and I don't tell anyone. People used to come to me to ask for special jobs to be done. Now I go to them without their recognizing me. I work as much as I can, to satisfy basic needs.

HAIRA Does that mean you could make our key?

BLACKSMITH Of course I could.

HAIRA Thank God.

HAIRAN But . . .

BLACKSMITH But what? Give me the money and I'll make it as fast as I can. I'll make it to fit any trunk at all, but on one condition: please don't give it to any stranger; someone might abuse it and open others' trunks and rob them. I ask you to keep it in a safe place, and bring it back to me when you've no more need for it.

The three do not answer him.

BLACKSMITH Why don't you answer? I promise I won't charge you more than the labor costs.

NOUAR That's not the reason.

BLACKSMITH What then?

NOUAR We couldn't get the money.

BLACKSMITH Why?

HAIRAN The bride wouldn't give us any.

HAIRA They threw us out of the castle.

BLACKSMITH Threw you out? Why?

HAIRAN Just threw us out. Don't concern yourself with us; you've already got enough on your mind.

BLACKSMITH How about me?

HAIRAN You're only asking for your right. You want money to make the key. (*To Haira:*) Let's go back; we're out of luck.

HAIRA We'll give you the lamp.

BLACKSMITH (*Laughs*): And what would I do with it? I couldn't light it because it would make it easier to spot me. I go around in darkness. Even at home I use no light.

NOUAR You could sell the lamp.

BLACKSMITH I can only sell those things that I make myself. If I sell anything else I'll be considered a thief; though if they want to be lenient they'll call me a smuggler.

HAIRAN Let's go, then.

HAIRA (*Gets up, almost in tears*): It's our evil luck!

BLACKSMITH (*Looks at* HAIRA *and calls her after a little while*): Listen, wait for me! I'll be back in a moment.

NOUAR What are you going to do?

BLACKSMITH I'm going to make the key.

HAIRA The key?

BLACKSMITH Don't shout.

HAIRAN But the money?

BLACKSMITH Damn the money; let the bride sleep on it. Don't move from this spot. (*Exit*).

NOUAR (*To the audience*): We brought the lamp to the bride, but she wouldn't give us the money. We came to the blacksmith with no money, but he'll make us the key!

HAIRAN (*To himself*): If the world was empty of good people, it would have turned upside down.

The song "Sweets in the bag / And money for the key" is heard all around the theater ending with the words "It's not your money, it belongs to the people!"

BLACKSMITH (*Returning at speed*): Here's the key!

HAIRA (*Takes it*): May God bless you!

BLACKSMITH May God bless us all! Don't forget my warning. Don't give it to any person you don't trust.

THE THREE Never! (*They leave the blacksmith alone on the stage.*)

BLACKSMITH God be with you. (*He repeats, in a low voice that increases in volume:*) By sweating, and exhausting myself at my fire, I turn the solid iron into a molten liquid, and then cast from it some instruments which are useful to people and some which do them harm.

The sound of his voice and the light die down simultaneously.

FIFTH SCENE

Back again outside the house where all three of them live. HAIRAN *and* HAIRA *enter, holding each other's hands, their eyes closed as if looking for something they can't find, singing.*

HAIRA and HAIRAN Are we there?

NOUAR (*Looking ahead*): We'll be there soon now.

HAIRAN and HAIRA Are we there?

NOUAR Now we're there!

The three shout with joy and bend down to kiss the earth.

NOUAR The most beautiful thing in the world is one's home and country, land and family . . . Oh God . . . (*He smells the earth*).

HAIRA *gives a wail of rejoicing,* HAIRAN *dances, and accompanies* NOUAR *and* HAIRA *in their singing:*

This is our house, we play here, live here,
So why should strangers interfere?

HAIRA (*Suddenly remembers*): The trunk!

HAIRAN Bring it out here immediately, and lock it with the key, and let's sleep peacefully. (*He sits down and leans at the wall as if sleeping.*)

HAIRA *goes to fetch the trunk.*

HAIRAN And we'll have a child, and Haira will hold it and love it and rock it in its crib; that's happiness.

NOUAR *watches him.* HAIRA *enters and places the trunk in the middle of the stage, then gets the key out and locks it.*

HAIRA I've locked it. (*She wails with triumph and delight.*)

HAIRAN Haira, try the key. Check it to see if it unlocks the trunk or not?

NOUAR If it locked it, it must unlock it.

HAIRA How do you expect me to open it when the baby isn't here yet? Don't you remember what our grandfathers said?

HAIRAN We'll open it, but we won't take out the robe and the cake; we'll just try the key. Give it to me. (*He tries to open the trunk.*) Look, I've opened it. (*He looks inside the trunk and screams:*) Hey!

HAIRA and NOUAR (*Both looking at him*): What?

HAIRAN There's nothing in the trunk! No robe, and no cake either.

HAIRA But that's not possible.

HAIRAN There's nothing in the trunk.

HAIRA (*Comes forward and looks at the trunk*): But I put it there with my own hands. (*She turns the trunk upside down, then rushes out to look for the cake and the robe.* NOUAR *laughs.*)

HAIRAN Some have to struggle all the livelong day,
And others get it on a silver tray.

(*Then he looks at Nouar*:) Why are you laughing?

NOUAR All our troubles were in vain! We walked the road to nowhere, the story turned imagination into reality, it was no more than a delusion. Hairan, the secret isn't how much you try.

HAIRAN What is the secret, then?

NOUAR It's the motive with which one's trying.

HAIRAN And what was the motive? To deceive people, and cheat them?

NOUAR It was to obtain something that didn't exist.

HAIRAN How?

NOUAR We imagined it. What isn't obtained by work and effort remains valueless, nonexistent. And we remain worthless as well if we don't look for what's rightfully ours, and for the ingredient that completes our life and makes it beautiful, and settled, and luminous.

HAIRA (*Enters, scared*): Hairan, I haven't found anything.

NOUAR But of course you won't find anything. Don't think about it anymore.

HAIRA How can I not think about it? (*Screams*:) Hairan!

HAIRAN What?

HAIRA What shall we do?

HAIRAN We're back where we started.

NOUAR No, you can still attain the impossible.

HAIRA How?

NOUAR Not all the doors are closed yet, not all the roads are blocked. We can start again, start by changing ourselves from within. Not keep clinging to the story and following its course, and believing it. Not keep going round and round following nothing greater than a delusion.

HAIRAN I'm not moving out of here; I've already told Haira I want no child.

HAIRA But . . .

HAIRAN But what?

HAIRA I'm . . .

HAIRAN You, you want a child; we know that, and you know what happened to us. We've had no luck; there's no security, and it's no use looking for it!

NOUAR No use to search because our ways of searching were founded on a delusion—nothing greater than a delusion.

HAIRAN A delusion, or a fact? I want no children. (*Shouts*:) Can you hear? *I want no children!*

HAIRA Hairan.

HAIRAN Yes, Haira?

HAIRA Hairan, the baby's here.

HAIRAN *looks at her.*

HAIRA The baby's here. (*She points to her stomach.*)

HAIRAN When?

HAIRA I felt it when we were in the garden.

HAIRAN Why didn't you tell me?

HAIRA I wanted to tell you but the rain came, and I was so happy. Then I said I won't tell you the secret until we lock the trunk, then . . .

She is about to cry. NOUAR *leaps up quickly as if he is about to run.* HAIRAN *does not know what to do when he notices that* NOUAR *is moving. He stands bewildered.*

HAIRAN What's the matter with you?

NOUAR I've got to move. I've got to run; a new generation's about to be born. If I don't start running now, I won't catch up with it. We've all got to run. You've got to run. Leave the story, forget about the trunk, run so you'll catch up with those who've already beaten you in the race for the real key . . . Come on . . .

HAIRAN But we'll never catch up with them.

NOUAR Yes, you will!

HAIRA We can't.

NOUAR You can if you run, and if you keep on running on the right path. Hairan, this won't do you any good. Come on, run! Run forward!—Run!—Run!

HAIRAN (*Starts to run*): I will! I'll run!

HAIRA What about me?

HAIRAN Don't you run. You stay where you are.

NOUAR On the contrary, she mustn't stay here. Let her run like us.

HAIRA How about the baby? I'm worried that it might . . .

NOUAR Don't worry. Besides, the baby must get used to running from now on, so he won't lag behind the generation that follows his . . . Come on Haira, run!

She starts to move, and runs with them.

THE THREE All of us, run! All of us, run! Come on!

They are moving fast, running with their eyes looking straight ahead, running, running. Music is heard, growing louder. And then THE BLACKSMITH *and the owner of the bull, and everyone in the play joins them. All except the* BRIDESMAID, *who stands quite still and doesn't move at all.*

CURTAIN

SALAH ʿABD AL-SABUR

Night Traveler

Translated by
Mohammed Inani
and Anselm Hollo

Salah ᶜAbd al-Sabur's verse play *Night Traveler* (*Musafir Layl*) was written at a period when the notion of absurdist drama was very much in vogue in Egypt, and the playwright admits to having been influenced by the plays of Eugène Ionesco. He designates his work a black comedy. Of the three characters, the Narrator fulfills a role similar to that of the chorus in Greek drama, as the playwright notes in a postscript to the play. The Narrator introduces and comments on the actions but does not get involved. The play opens with a Passenger traveling late at night; to while away the time, he is fiddling with his rosary and recalling the names of famous historical figures. His mention of Alexander the Great is the cue for the entry of a Ticket Collector, who claims to be Alexander. When the Passenger scoffs at him, the Conductor produces a terrifying array of instruments of terror. The Passenger becomes more and more frightened and amazed as the Conductor demands his ticket, eats it, then demands it again, asks for his identification card and devours that, too. Pinning the badge of a marshall from a cowboy film on his chest, the Conductor conducts a "trial" of the Passenger on a charge of killing God. Convinced of his guilt, the Ticket Collector discusses the most appropriate mode of death: whipping, poison, shooting, or stabbing. Invoking once again the name of Alexander, he stabs the Passenger to death. Addressing the audience, the Narrator points out that, being unarmed, there was nothing he could do to change things. The clever interplay here between the figure of the Narrator and the two other characters, expressed through a poetry of great subtlety, lends support to the author's view that the play can allow for a variety of stagings to explore its theme of the helplessness of the individual faced with tyrannical authority.

R.A.

NIGHT TRAVELER

SCENE

Train carriage in motion. The noise of the engine provides the only background music.

TIME

Just after midnight.

CHARACTERS

NARRATOR

PASSENGER

CONDUCTOR

NIGHT TRAVELER

To one side of the stage, at the end of the carriage, the NARRATOR *stands. He is wearing either a very elegant modern suit, a boutonniere, a fashionable tie, a striped waistcoat, or a gold watch with a gold strap. He could be wearing all of these. His facial expression is one of tepid serenity, his voice metallic with a hint of shrewd indifference.*

The PASSENGER *sits on a seat somewhere in the carriage. He is a nondimensional man, a man who can be described only from the outside, as fat or thin, tall or squat, dark or fair, though it all amounts, in fact, to the same thing.*

The CONDUCTOR, *who will soon appear, has a round face and a round body. He looks suspiciously innocent.*

NARRATOR

The hero, the clown of our play is a man called . . .
Well, he's called what he's called.
"What's in a name? A rose
By any other name would smell as sweet."
And a hedgehog by any other name
Would roll itself up . . . all the same!

His line of business . . . any line of business!
We can judge, from his appearance and his attire, that . . .

But really, it's of no consequence!
Let's leave it at that, then . . . any line of business!
He's going somewhere by train, at night,
(Managed to catch the last train, in fact)
And now is counting the telegraph poles, one, two,
Three, five, a hundred . . .
He fidgets in boredom: the game has no appeal!
He tries instead to toy with his memories;
He digs up rusty ones and tries to polish them.
But how unfortunate! His memories do not shine;
So now he knows it: his life's been colorless!
From his eyes, he drops his days,
They vanish in ever-widening circles on the metal floor
But they don't break up or splinter;
There's nothing *solid* there, to fall;
Tick-tock, tick-tock, tick-tock!

He remembers his rosary
Takes it out from the righthand pocket of his trousers
But the beads fall down, and his fingers reach out for them.
They escape and settle in a gap between two seats;
He tries hard to recover them, but the string breaks, and they sink deeper and deeper still,
Until, chased by his fumbling fingers, they scatter all over the floor,
Falling down, tick-tock, tick-tock, tick-tock!

And now he takes a parchment from
his coat,
Wherein history has been recorded in a
mere ten lines.

A few names arrest his attention,
The black, embossed letters
Shine on the wrinkled leather.

PASSENGER

Alexander
Tick-tock!
Hannibal
Tick-tock!
Tamerlane
Tick-Tock!
Hitler, Mitler; Johnson, Monson;
Tick-tock, tick-tock!
Alexander, Alexander, Alexander!

NARRATOR

Excuse me! A man is one with his
name!
Great men can come back if you
summon them from the memory of
history
To impose their greatness and
dominate the humble
And the humble can come back, if you
summon them from your memory
To be trampled underfoot by the great!
It is better, therefore, to forget the past
So that it won't deceive us and repeat
itself!

PASSENGER

Alexander-tick-tock
Alexander—tick-tock, tick-tock!

Raises his voice, as if relishing the tune; meanwhile, a spotlight on the other corner of the carriage, opposite the NARRATOR, *reveals the* CONDUCTOR *wearing his traditional khaki uniform.*

CONDUCTOR

Who's shouting out my name? Who's
calling me?
Who has disturbed my sleep here in
the corner?
You?

PASSENGER

I beg your pardon! Who are you?

CONDUCTOR

Alexander the Great!
As a boy I broke in wild colts,
In my prime, I broke Aristotle in,
When I came of age, I broke the world
in!

NARRATOR

The passenger is astonished—
Open mouth, raised eyebrows—
Like a painted face on a poster!
He is even afraid,
Though, to be fair, just a little.
He says to himself:

PASSENGER

That swarthy barrel in that khaki sack
. . . Alexander
Oh, no!

NARRATOR

The passenger's heart is divided
As the scales of a balance,
And he moves only to help his
suspicion
Outweigh his fear—

PASSENGER

Welcome Alexander! Been drinking,
haven't you?
Had one too many, I bet!

CONDUCTOR

Idiot! Don't you know who I am?
I'll break you in, I swear, as I broke in
the wild colts!

NARRATOR

Alexander's hand goes into his
righthand pocket:
Takes out a folded whip;
Alexander's hand goes into his
lefthand pocket:
Takes out a dagger;
Alexander's hand goes to his belt:

Takes out a revolver;
Alexander's hand goes to his throat:
Takes out a vial of poison;
Alexander's hand goes into a back pocket:
Takes out a rope;
This, however, he notices with embarrassment, and says:

CONDUCTOR
Forgive me! This has killed my dearest friend!
I gave the rope to my friend, just to play with it, you know,
But he misused it!
Do you know? The tribute I paid him on his death
Was acclaimed as a literary masterpiece;
I didn't write the tribute myself, mind you,
But I watched my minister do it;
I ordered bread and wine for him until he finished it,
And until he taught me to deliver it tragically
And grammatically;
Grammar is not my strong point, you see;
My minister was ambitious, however, and asked for a province
In return for my going down in history as a writer.
Well, I gave him the whole earth wherein he lies:
Ashes to ashes, dust to dust.

The Conductor hides the rope inside his cap.

NARRATOR
The scene may be summed up as follows;
The passenger is feverish with fear;
The expression on his face changes like traffic lights
Alexander has mobilized his army
Righthand flank: the whip and the vial of poison
Lefthand flank: the revolver and the dagger;
We daren't, of course, mention what's in his cap:
It could upset him.

CONDUCTOR
Nobody dares disobey my orders, do you?

PASSENGER
No, my Lord!
Give me your orders
And I'll be quicker than your echo!

NARRATOR
Who knows, the passenger thought,
The man may indeed be Alexander the Great!
Great men, though dead,
May still be alive!
These are funny days, anyway,
And it is wiser to be cautious.
Perhaps if I give way he'll leave me alone,
The passenger said to himself,
Let me humble myself to him.

PASSENGER
What do you want from me, my Lord?
I beg your pardon, people like you can't want anything
From people like me!
What I mean is: which way is your kindness inclined?
How would you honor me?
Would you have me make a saddle for your horse?

CONDUCTOR
I'm bored with riding.

PASSENGER
How about an insole for your shoe?

CONDUCTOR
I rarely walk now; I suffer from lumbago;
Sometimes I bask in the sun, and I take a steam bath every morning

PASSENGER

Let me heat the water for your bath
Let me take care of your rosy towels
Let me fetch your golden slippers
But don't kill me . . . please!

NARRATOR

Irritably, the Conductor drops his weapons,
Lazily stretches his empty hands
Toward the Passenger.

PASSENGER

Kill me with your bare hands. Oh, no!
Please! try me at anything!
Give me the meanest job,
Trust me with the greatest,
Do what you like with me,
But don't kill me!

CONDUCTOR

What's the matter with you?
What are you screaming about, Mister . . .
Having a bad dream, are you?
Why are you cowering like a frightened mouse?
Haven't you ever been on a train before?
Goodness! Why do you grow so white when I put out my hand to you!
Don't you know what I want?
Can't you think who I am?

PASSENGER

You're Alexander the Great!

CONDUCTOR

My name is not Alexander;
My name is Zahwan.*

PASSENGER

What are your orders my Lord . . . the Zahwan?

CONDUCTOR

You're cowardly *and* stupid!
Can't you tell from my uniform what I want?
Your ticket, please!

*Literally, "vainglorious."

This is my job, hard work;
It drags me out of my bed in the middle of the night,
It deprives me of sleep, the most delicious bread on God's table!
Sometimes there are only a handful of passengers
Scattered about the carriage like cotton sacks in a deserted warehouse;
Sometimes only a man or two,
And the carriage is dark, cold and airless,
Like the inside of a dead whale!
I know this when, standing on the platform,
I hear the rumbling of the train pulling in,
The lights off, and the frosted window panes revealing no human head!
I get on all the same and search all carriages;
It's my duty, you see!
I feel all the seats and stare in the dark;
Sometimes I turn a seat upside down,
Sometimes I kneel down to see what's under it,
Sometimes I plunge my penknife into the seat!
Indeed! I can't allow anyone to be on this train without a ticket!
Now have you calmed down?
Your ticket, please!

Passenger forgets where he has put his ticket. He searches his pockets, one after another, but finally finds it in his hand.

PASSENGER

Here!

CONDUCTOR

Thank you. It's a green ticket
And almost square,
And soft,

That means you're a good man
Do you know? After my evening
prayer I had a nap!
I was properly dressed,
Ready to go to bed, I mean,
When a bell rang in my head;
I jumped out of bed,
Having had nothing to eat.
Green; thank you.
You embarrass me by putting me
above yourself.
Good manners win me over, thank you!

NARRATOR
Attention, please!
A most fantastic thing will happen:
The Conductor opens his mouth,
wipes the ticket clean,
Tastes it with the tip of his tongue,
Finds it delicious, takes bite after bite,
Chews, swallows and belches.
His hand rubs his stomach and,
Gratified, both hands feel his belly;
He says a little prayer
And kisses the palm of his hand, as a
sign of gratitude.
In shocked surprise, the Passenger's
unable to think;
He doesn't know what to think.

CONDUCTOR
Your ticket, please!

PASSENGER
I gave it to you!

CONDUCTOR
And where may I ask is it now?

PASSENGER
In your stomach!

CONDUCTOR
Ceremony is waived only between
friends
Now! know your limits!
You're being sarcastic, I'm sure,
But sarcasm will do you no good;
Your sense of humor may amuse me,
indeed,
But within limits.
Duty will always be duty.

PASSENGER
But I gave it to you, I swear.

CONDUCTOR
And I threw it out of the window?

PASSENGER
No, indeed! You are—

CONDUCTOR
What? I am what?
Well, I'm too old to lose my temper,
Old enough to let reason rule my
emotion,
But I can never allow my reason to
break the law!
So now! Will you listen, Mister.

PASSENGER
Abduh.*

CONDUCTOR
Listen, Abduh,
Let's discuss this thorny subject
As friends
As fellow travelers
And not as opponents
Well, then, move over and I'll sit by you
But let me take off my coat first
So that you won't be afraid of me.
Some people, I know, are allergic to
yellow,
Take my advice as a friend
Don't talk of anything against your will;
Weigh your words carefully, as in a
balance;
Think a dozen times of each question,
And a hundred times of each answer;
Beware of tangles of speech: words
unclear
Can turn into ropes around your neck;
But wait until I have taken off this
uniform.

*Literally, "servant of God."

NARRATOR

The Conductor takes off his coat;
There is another one under it;
The Conductor takes off his second coat,
But another one appears:
We still see yellow!
Which reminds me: I must comment on this color!
Views on this are divided:
Some believe it is the color of glittering gold;
Others believe it is the color of sickness,
Of a sallow complexion,
The color of death.

CONDUCTOR (*Seating himself by the Passenger*):

That's better!
Now, without this uniform
We can talk as friends.
What did you say your name was?

PASSENGER

Abduh.

CONDUCTOR

Mine is Sultan.

PASSENGER

Zahwan you said it was!

CONDUCTOR

Me? Zahwan? Goodness, no!
That's my superior's name;
His rank is four-coats
I often dream that I've killed him and taken his place.
His wife has a white complexion and plump thighs,
Mine is old and bony.
He lives in the sunny part, west of the rosy district,
My home is alright, though I'm sometimes bothered by the shouting pedestrians and howling cars.
What's your line of business?

PASSENGER

I am a craftsman.

CONDUCTOR

A craftsman?
My parents never bothered; I could never be apprenticed
As a craftsman! All I can do is search the cars!
Haven't missed much, anyway; the pay is good and the grading
Goes up to the ten-coat rank.
What was your name you said?

PASSENGER

Abduh.

CONDUCTOR

Your name is not Abduh! You're lying!

PASSENGER

But I am Abduh! I swear!
My father is Abdullah, my eldest son Abed,
My youngest Abbad, and family name Abdoon!*

CONDUCTOR

Do you have an identity card?

PASSENGER

I always keep it in my righthand pocket;
It's easier to reach for there,
When they want to see it
A dozen times a day! One day I was asked for it eighty-six times!
Seventy on another day.

CONDUCTOR

No more than ninety, by law!
One has to be crystal clear,
To reveal oneself unequivocally!
For every question, we must be ready with an answer
That doesn't lead to another question!
The sound fruit in the basket are not disturbed

*The names are symbolic, being variations on the root verb *abada*, "to serve." The derivatives are puns on the meaning of "servant," "slave," etc.

By the hands which remove the bad
ones!
You seem to be a good man;
Keep this card always close to your
right hand;
It is your identity card,
Your most precious possession.
Show it to me for a second, please.
Thank you. Green and almost square.
But dry!
Quite all right, though.
Do you know, after my evening prayer
I had a nap,
I was properly dressed, ready to go to
bed, I mean,
When a bell rang in my head,
I jumped out of bed, having had
nothing to eat.
Green; thank you. Quite all right.

CONDUCTOR *raises the card to his lips;* PASSENGER *shakes with terror.*

PASSENGER
Please! Don't eat it, please!

CONDUCTOR
Eat it?
I thought you were a man who, well,
who had some sense?
Eat it! Goodness gracious me! Eat it?
Can anyone eat a card?
This is unheard of!
We've heard of eating horsemeat,
locusts, frogs' legs,
Seaweed, and, sometimes, how cruel,
of eating the flesh of the living
dead,
But we never heard of eating paper!

NARRATOR
This is not true.
Sorry to interrupt you
But I have to say this:
The most delicious food for man, as
yet, is paper!
And the most appetizing part of paper
is history;
We devour it all the time and
everywhere,
Only to rewrite it on different paper,
Still to devour it later on.

CONDUCTOR
You surprise me;
I thought you had better
understanding;
But I shan't be hard on you,
Shan't censure you much
For the friendship you so cheaply
threw away before it had even taken
shape!
I am forced, dear sir,
To be formal with you.
However, as a responsible official,
Of the three-coat rank,
I have to abide by the words of our
superior,
Of the ten-coat rank;
I remember his words to us when he
handed each his appointment
papers.

NARRATOR
I know these words by heart
Among other pearls of wisdom,
Such as:
"Keep thy dog hungry: he'll follow
thee"
—Master Nu'man Ibn al-Mundhir
"When I hear the word *culture* I reach
for my revolver"
—Master Hermann Ibn Göring
"Teach them democracy, even if you
have to kill them all"
—Master Lyndon Ibn Johnson
"I can see heads that are ripe and ready
for the picking"
—Al-Hajjaj Ibn Yusuf
The words of the ten-coat man
himself, however, were "Investigate
leniently, castigate severely."

CONDUCTOR (*Raising his hand in salute*):
Here am I, your ten-coat highness,
The soul of leniency, the milk of human kindness!
To this man, ill-disguised
By a transparent mask of stupidity,
Let me say:
I had no intention of eating your card
When I raised it to my face;
I was just staring at it,
Am still staring at it,
Still staring at it,
Hell and damnation! What is this?

NARRATOR
There's a mystery somewhere,
There's a mystery somewhere,
The Conductor has thrown the card on the floor,
Panicking, or in apparent panic!

CONDUCTOR
This is a blank piece of paper!
Only one individual
Can have such blank papers;
An individual who has existed from time immemorial,
Hasn't existed as yet,
Or never, indeed, existed,
Though we hear of him everywhere!
Some people have seen him,
Or think they have seen him;
Some have spoken to him the way I speak to you now,
Some claim to have, one day, spoken to him.

PASSENGER (*Picks the paper up from the floor and points at it as he talks*):
But my papers are not blank:
This is my name;
And this is what I look like!

CONDUCTOR
Oh, no! Your papers are blank! Look!
Perfectly blank, look!
Can't you recognize your own papers?
Oh, I see now!
These are NOT your papers!
You've stolen them—just a minute—
This is serious!

NARRATOR
The conductor takes out from one of his pockets
The badge of an American sheriff and pins it to his chest;
He turns his seat round to face the passenger,
Pulls out a shelf from under the seat
And turns it into a table.
He puts some papers on it.
He takes out a few pens from the back pocket of his trousers,
Lights a cigarette, and twirls his mustache,
Wetting it or using a little ointment from a bottle
Which he takes out of his back pocket.
He clears his throat haughtily and says:

CONDUCTOR
Abduh!
Stand up and listen to the charge!
You have killed God
And stolen his identity card,
And I, Ulwan Ibn Zahwan Ibn Sultan,
Chief law-enforcing officer
In this part of the world,
In your name, O Ten-Coat Man,
I declare the court in session.

PASSENGER
Oh, no! I haven't!
I plead not guilty!
I appeal to the Ten-coat Man himself,
I want his Justice!

CONDUCTOR
Just a minute!
For justice to be done,
Certain formalities have to be observed!

NARRATOR
That is right!
Justice without formalities
Is like a woman unpainted,

Like a stage (even like this one of ours) without curtains!
And this is why the conductor jumps up to sit on the luggage net
Hangs down his legs, and swings his boots over the passenger's head
Don't be surprised; this too is right;
It has been said that the law is above the heads of individuals.

PASSENGER
Innocent, I swear! Innocent, innocent!
Never killed anybody or stole anything!
Help me, Ten-Coat Man!

CONDUCTOR
Are you calling the Ten-Coat Man himself?

PASSENGER
I'm innocent! Innocent!

CONDUCTOR
I am the Ten-Coat Man! Look!

NARRATOR
The Conductor unbuttons his coat—
Once, twice . . . seven times over!
The buttons shine through right up to his skin!

PASSENGER
Justice! Ten-Coat Man!

CONDUCTOR
So you want my justice?
What do you know of my justice?

PASSENGER
Your justice is unequaled on this earth!

CONDUCTOR
Not bad!
Speak of my kindness to the weak!

PASSENGER
"You're as kind as a mother or a father,
Such indeed is real kindness!"

CONDUCTOR
That's even better;
Speak of my knowledge!

PASSENGER
"He knows the secrets of languages and religions;
His meditation puts all to shame, both men and books."

CONDUCTOR
Good . . . Good!
What about my generosity?

PASSENGER
"If he had nothing left to give away but his life,
He would gladly do it! So fear the Lord when ye approach him!"

CONDUCTOR
Oh, no! This is reckless!
I can't give away my life! Not to anyone!
Not because I'm not generous, but I just wouldn't want
To upset the cosmic order!
Keeping it, my friend, is quite a responsibility!
Was that your verse?

PASSENGER
No, by the Majesty of your Glory!
Those were lines of dull and insipid doggerel
Which survived in my memory from boyhood!

CONDUCTOR
You know the author?

PASSENGER
Al-Mutanabbi, if I remember rightly!

CONDUCTOR
Certainly not! My intuition never fails me!
They sound like al-Aaᶜim!
Shaᶜbaan Ibn al-Aaᶜim!

NARRATOR
The Passenger proves tactful;
He picks up one of the Conductor's pens,
Pretends to be fascinated by this information,
And asks in fawning tones:

PASSENGER
Who, my Lord?

CONDUCTOR

Sha^c^baan Al-Aa^c^im!
A journalist of my entourage.
Good for nothing except that hollow prattle,
But it amuses me.
Do you know . . . I am not happy!
Some fools think I am lucky
When they go back in the evening
To their shacks and sheds;
They often wonder:
"What is it that the Ten-Coat Man does?
"He receives the highest salary,
"Lives in a palace
"Controls the destinies of people . . . etc."
They don't know that I bear the heaviest burden,
That I jump out of bed in the middle of the night
If something happens,
I leave my palace to find out for myself how things are!
I retain in my mind the names of killers and murderers,
And those who have wicked ideas which are more dangerous
Than the most dangerous killers and murderers!
I receive the strangers who visit our country,
I suffer their dumb malicious looks;
I have coffee with every caller,
Even with my enemies,
I have two hundred cups a day;
My digestion is ruined: I live on a diet of boiled vegetables!
Do you know that sometimes
I have to go without sleep, except for a few hours a week!
Oh, I don't want you to think I'm afraid of being killed in bed!
I am not afraid of death,
But one must be careful;
And that is why I kill my enemies or buy them off!
Indeed, I'm not afraid of my enemies;
I'm afraid of my friends,
Their hearts are gnawed by envy,
They may smile in my face
But there is black spite in their hearts.
I am lonely;
It's a lonely life,
I am lonely!

PASSENGER

Don't be sorry for yourself, my lord!

CONDUCTOR

Oh! I am not sorry for myself!
I am sorry for the envious who have lost their souls!
I deplore their black hearts
And wish they could see the light, know the light!
If only they knew what it means for a heart to be pure,
To be purified by love!

PASSENGER

Cheer up, my lord!
Your tears are too precious
To be shed in pity for bad people!

CONDUCTOR

That's right
You seem to be a good man;
Just a minute.

NARRATOR

The Conductor gets down from the shelf
And sits beside the Passenger;
The Passenger believes this is a hopeful sign,
Believes that his humility is saving his neck!

CONDUCTOR

Let's talk as friends!
Perhaps you'll forgive my looking so closely into your case.
My telling you of a rumor

The veracity of which I cannot determine.

PASSENGER

Ascertain its veracity, my Lord!
You are so shrewd, so very clever!

CONDUCTOR

This is precisely what I am doing!
Now look! Try to appreciate my position!
I am responsible for this entire valley,
And the rumor says that one valley dweller
Has killed God and stolen his identity card!

PASSENGER

This is the most awful thing anybody's ever heard!
The rumor is false, no doubt, my lord!

CONDUCTOR

Well, unfortunately it isn't!
It is quite true, though indirectly so!

PASSENGER

But how? If you'll pardon my poor understanding!
What do you mean, my lord?

CONDUCTOR

I appreciate your interest in the case;
Let me clarify the matter to you.

PASSENGER

Thanks, my lord.

CONDUCTOR

Don't mention it!
Well, now! Do you know what it means to lose your identity card?
It means that you don't exist!
Whoever steals it kills you
By depriving you of your specific individuality!

PASSENGER

Forgive my ignorance, my lord!
What is the meaning of that expression?

CONDUCTOR

Your very existence! It means depriving you of your existence!
Understand?
Now when I say "You have killed God" I do not mean, of course,
That (may God forgive me!) you have . . .
Certainly not! What I mean, rather, is that you have stolen
His identity card—which amounts to the same thing!

PASSENGER

But I never did anything of the sort!

CONDUCTOR

Ah, well! That's another story!
We'll discuss it later on!
The point now is, however,
That God has forsaken this part of the universe!
He never looks this way now as He used to do
He never gives us anything now!
We've been wondering what has happened,
And the answer is: someone has killed God in these parts!
That is why He has abandoned us!
What I mean, of course, is that someone
Has stolen his card and assumed His identity!
We decided first to investigate the matter in secret;
We did.
We examined every file,
Tapped all telephone conversations,
Photocopied all letters,
Held thousands.
Tortured twenty until they were dead,
Tortured thirty until they were maimed,
Tortured eighty until they fainted,
To no avail!

PASSENGER

Were there any confessions?

CONDUCTOR

A few. A hundred, as far as I remember,
To no avail.

PASSENGER
But how? I mean, why not?
CONDUCTOR
Well, God is still abandoning us!
It is serious indeed!
So much so, in fact, that I, the
Ten-Coat Man, no less,
Have disguised myself in workers' overalls,
Or in peasant rags,
Walked down the valleys
Or sunk into the depth of alleys
Reached the top floors by back stairs
Eavesdropped on people behind walls,
Painted my face white and played
At firewalking at hashish-takers' dens,
In the hope of overhearing
A telltale word, or getting a clue
Which might unravel the mystery!
I hoped a door might open, even a secret passage,
Leading to the unknown!
Look! Here we are! Such a pair!
A common plebe of the valley,
And the Ten-Coat Man himself,
Sitting side by side,
Shoulder to shoulder,
Talking like old friends—
Who knows? Perhaps you'll reveal the secret to me.
Do you realize how serious this is?
How it calls for self-abnegation?
PASSENGER
Very much, my lord!
CONDUCTOR
Are you willing to do something for me, then?
For the whole of the valley, rather?
PASSENGER
Indeed! Anything for you, my lord!
Let me join you in the search!
CONDUCTOR
Join me in the search?
PASSENGER
If you'll allow me, my lord!
CONDUCTOR
But we've found him already!
Here he is!
PASSENGER
Who, my lord?
CONDUCTOR
You! But, please! Wait! I'd like you to get my meaning in full;
The whole question had been a carefully guarded secret,
Strictly confined to a number of my closest associates,
But it soon got out!
The grievous thing was reported to my enemies,
My enemies spread it far and wide,
And everybody came to know about it!
That is why we hardly have time to distinguish
Those who tell the truth from the liars!
We have to be decisive,
Otherwise the order of the valley will be upset;
I know what I am doing;
I'll tell everybody in tomorrow's papers
That I myself have caught the culprit
And killed him!
Your photograph will be published
And your body will lie in state
You're a good man,
You're of the noblest quality
Worthy of the great sacrifice
You're willing to do something for me, remember?
Let us forget about it now;
We'll discuss it later on!
Let me ask you a question
Your answer will show your taste!
Let us suppose then that you have a choice
Between four methods, or instruments, of death:
The whip . . .
PASSENGER
Oh, no!

CONDUCTOR
You have no taste for it?
You're quite right!
It's barbarian, even backward,
Ah, Tamarlane, the barbarian!
What do you think of poison?

PASSENGER
Oh, no!

CONDUCTOR
Doesn't agree with you, either?
You're right!
It is a method tinged with meanness and treachery
The Medici method
What about the revolver?
No, no! I don't like it myself;
It's killing from a distance; lacks the warmth or touch!
A vulgar modern method,
A game for the young and cowardly!
What we need is a classical method,
If death is to retain its splendor, its grandeur.
Ah! The dagger!
Alexander!
I am sorry Abduh!
O most noble,
Let the dagger touch thee,
Let the dagger pierce thee!

(*Stabs him with a dagger.*)

NARRATOR
I have no power to talk
And I advise you too to be silent
Perfectly silent.

PASSENGER
But we haven't discussed it yet.

CONDUCTOR
Oh, we'll discuss it later on.

PASSENGER
I swear I never killed anybody, never stole anything,
I swear, I swear . . .

CONDUCTOR
I know that, oh noblest and purest!
Do you know who killed God and stole his identity card?
Well, I can't reveal his name, though I could, I believe.
Well! Open your eyes for the last time,
Cast a look for the last time!

The CONDUCTOR *unbuttons his undercoat; from a pocket closest to his bare chest he takes out a blank card and waves it before the eyes of the dying man. The* PASSENGER *looks at it once and drops dead.*

CONDUCTOR
Ah well! How am I going to lift the heavy body of this man?
(*Approaching the* NARRATOR.)
You there! Could you lend a hand?
Come on, let's carry him together!

NARRATOR (*To the audience*):
What should I do?
What can I do?
He holds a dagger;
But I am unarmed, like you;
I have nothing but my commentary;
What should I do?
What can I do?

ALFRED FARAG

ᶜAli Janah al-Tabrizi and His Servant Quffa

Translated by
Rasheed el-Enany
and Charles Doria

In ʿ*Ali Janah al-Tabrizi and His Servant Quffah* (ʿ*Ali Janah al-Tabrizi wa Tabiʿuhu Quffa*), Alfred Farag successfully transfers to the modern comic stage a famous motif from the *Thousand and One Nights*, the "caravan bluff" found in such tales as "Merchant ʿAli from Cairo" and "Maʿruf the Cobbler," whereby all sorts of credit are placed at the disposal of a merchant in anticipation of the arrival of a delayed caravan bringing fabulous riches. The merchants in the city where ʿAli and his henchman arrive are only too pleased to lend ʿAli money, all of which he disburses to the city's poor. The King himself is brought into the business; he not only lends ʿAli money from the treasury but also allows him to marry the King's daughter. The chicanery involved in all these dealings and the suspicions of the King's vizier about ʿAli's probity provide plenty of opportunities for comic situations on stage: various groups rushing in and out, and characters hiding behind screens to eavesdrop on conversations. Beyond the fun, however, the play has a serious message to impart. Quffah, the absolute pragmatist who wants to deal with the realities of the present, serves as a perfect foil to ʿAli, the dreamer who aspires to a better future and endeavors through his munificence with other people's money to bring about social change. The links between the implications of this play and the vicissitudes in the recent history of many nations in the Arab world and that of Egypt in particular are clear enough.

R.A.

ʿALI JANAH AL-TABRIZI AND HIS SERVANT QUFFA

CHARACTERS

ʿALI JANAH AL-TABRIZI
A wealthy man who has lost his fortune

QUFFA
A shoemaker who becomes AL-TABRIZI*'s servant*

SAWAB
AL-TABRIZI*'s first servant*

PROPRIETOR

MERCHANT

CHIEF MERCHANT

INNKEEPER

PRINCESS

MAID

KING

VIZIER

EXECUTIONER

BEGGARS, SERVANTS, SOLDIERS, and others

JUDGE

TWO LITIGANTS before the JUDGE

Time: One night

Place: The world of the *Thousand and One Nights*

ᶜALI JANAH AL-TABRIZI AND HIS SERVANT QUFFA

ACT ONE

SCENE ONE

A beautiful orchard. A tree stands upstage. To the left appears part of a magnificent mansion and a door which leads to the inside of the mansion. Downstage right is the orchard gate in front of which is a step. The street where the mansion stands is partially visible so that anyone approaching can be seen before they enter the orchard. The orchard gate stands half open; inside can be seen ᶜALI JANAH AL-TABRIZI *and his servant* SAWAB.

ᶜALI What do you mean, Sawab?

SAWAB I mean, master, that there's only one more hour left for you in this mansion before the new proprietor comes to take over.

ᶜALI Wrong! You mean I've *still* got one more hour in this mansion.

SAWAB However you put it, it means I've still got one more hour in your service before the proprietor comes who'll be my new master.

ᶜALI Wrong! There's *only* one more hour left for you in my service.

SAWAB Whichever way I say it, you turn it round.

ᶜALI I only meant to express my delight at having yet another hour to enjoy as master of this mansion and your misery because there's only one hour left for you as my servant, after which . . . (*He pats him on the shoulder in a genuine show of sympathy.*)

SAWAB It makes no difference.

ᶜALI The trouble with you, Sawab, is that you always see things upside down.

SAWAB Me?

ᶜALI You've got no imagination . . .

SAWAB I'm no romantic.

ᶜALI (*Goes on*): You've got no dreams, no perception, no vision . . .

SAWAB But I foresaw all that's happened to us, and I always gave you good advice as you squandered your father's inheritance—and it wasn't a small one—here and there, on your friends, your banquets and . . . your imagination. I warned you, and now what I was afraid of has happened. You've lost everything: the shop, the mansion, the furniture, the servants, and even me . . .

ᶜALI (*Very touched*): God help you, Sawab; you've lost a master.

SAWAB And you, master, was your loss a small one?

ᶜALI (*Uncertainly*): Well . . .

SAWAB And your friends . . . They ate away at your fortune; then, when we fell on hard times, all we got from them was (*Mimicking someone*:) "I'm afraid my wife's ill, and the doctor's prescribed such expensive treatment for her. Pay my respects to your master." (*Mimicking some-*

one else:) "The fact is my sister-in-law's aunt has passed away, and I'll have to take care of the funeral expenses, as I'm the head of the family. Pay my respects to your master." (*Mimicking a maidservant*:) "My master? I swear he isn't at home. He received a letter from a sick relative who lives a long way away, and he went off to see him."

ʿALI "When sorrows come, they come not single spies."

SAWAB Sorrows! I'll be damned if at this minute they aren't eating and drinking and making merry, *and* laughing at you.

ʿALI And us? Aren't we eating and drinking and laughing at them?

SAWAB Rather at ourselves, since we eat air and drink memories.

ʿALI How's that? Don't you cook any more?

SAWAB Are you quite well, master? Have you forgotten that we sold the stove, the pans, the spoons, the copper dishes, and then the glasses?

ʿALI (*Aside*): He's off again. (*Gently*:) How do you serve me then, Sawab?

SAWAB (*Aside*): He insists on making fun of me. (*To* ʿALI:) Please, master, don't go back to saying such things. You make me worry about you.

ʿALI (*Gently trying to remind him*): Don't I order my meals on time? And you, don't you . . .

SAWAB (*Impatiently*): Yes, you order them.

ʿALI And *you*, what do you do?

SAWAB I run inside like an idiot and come back, with my arms stretched out as though I were carrying the large copper tray with your favorite foods on it, and then lay them in front of you.

ʿALI Ah! Now you remember. The large copper tray.

SAWAB Yes, the large copper tray.

ʿALI With my favorite foods on it.

SAWAB (*Correcting him*): You mean as *though* your favorite foods were on it.

ʿALI And what is there on it then?

SAWAB Where *is* the tray?

ʿALI What do you carry the food on then?

SAWAB But where's the money to buy the food?

ʿALI What have we been eating, then?

SAWAB Eating, master? God keep you. (*He wistfully pats his own stomach.*)

ʿALI What was it then, Sawab, you used to see me hold in my hands, put in my mouth and chew?

SAWAB But *you* know, master. As soon as I put the tray down . . . (*Correcting himself*:) I mean as soon as I pretended to put the tray down, I'd run away from your eating and enjoyment, fearing for my sanity . . .

Quffa appears outside the orchard gate. He looks shabby, and his head is bandaged. From his shoulder ten pairs of shoes are hanging, all tied together with one string. He moans with fatigue and sits on the step, then he moans again and wipes his perspiration.

ʿALI And what did I praise your cooking for, then? And what was it you carried away from me after the meal?

QUFFA (*Suddenly turning his ear in their direction; speaking aside*): They're talking about food. (*He smacks his lips.*)

SAWAB (*Aside*): I no longer know which of us has gone out of his mind.

QUFFA (*Aside*): A pretty orchard. Its paths are covered with marble. (*He wipes his perspiration.*) How lucky they are; they have food to eat, and they can feel cool.

ʿALI What are you thinking? Have you thought about what I said?

QUFFA (*Aside*): The master's threatening his servant.

SAWAB (*Aside*): He may well have gone out of his mind; he hasn't eaten for four days.

ʿALI You remember now?

SAWAB (*Aside*): I'd better humor him for another hour. It'll be over soon. (*To* ʿALI:) Yes, master.

ʿALI Go back to your work, then. Who knows, we might have a visitor to show our generosity to . . .

QUFFA (*Aside*): A visitor? The master says a visitor! I'll pretend to be blind and flatter him; maybe he'll ask me in. (*He lowers the bandage over his eyes.*) Is there no hospitable man in this city to invite a shoemaker whose feet are worn with travel and who's in pain?

ʿALI Who's at the gate?

QUFFA (*Enters the middle of the orchard*): It's me, master. Quffa. My name's Quffa; I make shoes. I've been going round the streets to sell my shoes, but no one will buy any. The sun's glare has hurt my eyes, and I fear I may have lost my sight from weakness and hunger. Won't you try a pair, master?

ʿALI Lay down your burden, poor man! Sawab! Bring lunch for me and my guest, and hurry!

SAWAB (*Hesitating*): Master . . .

QUFFA (*Aside*): The servant doesn't like the idea of serving me . . .

ʿALI (*To* SAWAB): Hurry!

QUFFA (*Aside*): But the master rebukes him.

SAWAB (*Decidedly*): As you wish, master.

Exit Sawab

ʿALI Tell me your grievance, my friend. Don't be shy. What's the matter with you? What's your complaint?

QUFFA What shall I tell you, master? God give you health! I make the best shoes in the world, but where's the money to open a shop? I spent all night making shoes and went out at daybreak roaming the city until I got swollen feet, without selling a single pair.

ʿALI Poor man! Not one?

QUFFA Not one, master. I swear it. The shopkeepers drove me away from the market when they saw me offer my shoes to their customers; and when I tried to sell them outside the market, I got kicked out by the policeman.

ʿALI How awful! All that with nothing to eat!

QUFFA (*Aside*): The more I exaggerate my troubles, the more he'll feed me. (*To* ʿALI:) And you know what hunger's like, master. I walked along thinking about the children I left crying and the wife I left wailing, about my aching eyes and my life of poverty . . .

ʿALI Oh! Oh! Oh! Shame on me for living unaware of so much suffering!

QUFFA I walk from one end of the city to the other just to keep a roof over my head. (*He sniffs, then leans over* ʿALI *and asks timidly*:) Grilled meat?

ʿALI How you've been grilled, poor man!

QUFFA (*Almost crying*): Nowhere to go and no way to make ends meet, master . . . (*He sniffs again and asks* ʿALI *in a low voice*:) Or is it fried? (*Wailing*:) How I've suffered, master!

ʿALI No. No. This is too much to bear. (*He makes as if to pull his garment apart.*)

QUFFA (*Stopping him*): Calm down, master! Calm down! Don't rip your clothes, for God's sake. (*Aside*:) He gets a kick out of wailing. (*To* ʿALI:) Take it easy!

ʿALI (*He clutches Quffa's hand* ￿rmly): From now on, have no fear. Be my companion; everything will be all right.

QUFFA (*Elated*): I'll be your companion

and follow you like your shadow . . . (*Aside*:) This man's either nobility itself or stupidity personified. (*He sniffs, overcome by his hunger.*) Is it braised meat?

ᶜALI Let this be a pledge between us!

QUFFA (*At the top of his voice*): Let God be my witness! May He give you in plenty and grant all your wishes.

Enter Sawab, as though carrying the copper serving tray.

ᶜALI Hurry up, Sawab! My friend's hungry.

QUFFA Down here. Down here. God reward you!

Sawab lays the imaginary tray in front of them, while Quffa adjusts his position and rolls up his sleeves. His eyes are still bandaged.

ᶜALI Eat, my friend; don't be shy. (*As though putting something in his mouth*:) Delicious!

Quffa puts out his hand confidently, but touches nothing. He moves it to the right and to the left but to no avail. He gropes violently in every direction and then freezes. He removes the bandage from his eyes quickly and is taken aback. He jumps to his feet and moves away, trembling.

ᶜALI What's the matter with you? Are you all right?

QUFFA (*Cautiously*): Nothing . . . only sometimes I see visions . . .

ᶜALI And what have you just seen?

QUFFA (*He stretches out his neck, looking fearfully at the imaginary food*): I saw food.

ᶜALI Sit down and help yourself then.

QUFFA (*Aside*): If he's mad, then I shouldn't contradict him in case he harms me. I'd better go along with him; maybe food will come after all. (*He makes up his mind and walks towards* ᶜALI, *trying to control his fear.*) Forgive me, Master, if I was so confused at the sight of food; it's only because I haven't had any for so long.

ᶜALI (*Taking him by the arm*): Come and sit here at the middle of the table and help yourself to any dish you fancy; don't be shy! I know how hungry you are. Look at this nice white bread . . . (*He makes as though he offered him bread.*)

QUFFA (*As though taking the bread and still trying to overcome his fear*): Fabulous! By God I've never seen bread as white as that, master. (*As though cutting a piece and eating*:) Or that tastes half as good. (*Aside*:) Bread indeed!

ᶜALI This bread, my friend, was baked by a maid I bought for five hundred dinars. Try this kebab; it's too good even for a king's table.

QUFFA (*As though eating*): Delectable, indeed.

ᶜALI Do eat, my guest. You're weak; you need nourishment. Try this chicken stuffed with pistachios.

QUFFA (*As though tasting it, and beginning to enjoy the game*): Yum-yum! By God, master, this food's the best I've ever eaten. (*As though offering him food*:) Take this chicken breast from me; don't say no. (*Aside*:) A nice chap he is. If he's having a joke at my expense, I ought to humor him; maybe he'll reward me later. (*Ecstatically*:) How delicious!

ᶜALI Eat! Have some more, don't be shy! Tell me honestly, have you ever tasted better gravy than this?

QUFFA Never! (*He laughs boisterously, his fear completely gone now.*)

ᶜALI I only keep this cook because he's so clever. Otherwise I'd sooner give him the sack, because he's rude and contradicts everything I say.

QUFFA (*Acts as if he were frantically gobbling different foods from all the dishes near and far, picking up what he drops and wiping off what dribbles from his mouth or falls on his clothes*): God bless his rudeness!

ʿALI Eat, eat!

QUFFA (*Writhing on the ground*): My stomach! I can't, master.

ʿALI It's time for dessert. Sawab, the sweets!

QUFFA (*Aside*): He's made my mouth water and stirred up my hunger. Damn him! Still, there may be hope yet.

ʿALI Try these pancakes, my friend. (*As though offering him one*:) Take this one; watch out for the dripping honey.

QUFFA (*As though eating it*): Thank you, master. (*Chews enjoyably.*) Yum-yum! There's so much musk in it. How on earth can you afford so much musk? (*Smacks his lips.*)

ʿALI This is how I like it made in my house. I instruct them to put a measure of musk and half of ambergris in every pancake. Have some nuts, my friend.

QUFFA Oh, how big these walnuts are, and how delicious these almonds are! Gosh! These sultanas, they're as big as apricots. (*As though cracking and eating.*)

ʿALI Eat, my friend. Don't be shy!

QUFFA To hell with shyness! We're friends now! (*Claps* ʿALI *heartily on the shoulder.*)

ʿALI (*Laughs and hits* QUFFA *forcefully on the chest*): You should see what we'll be like in two days' time.

QUFFA (*Writhing on the ground*): We'll be like two brothers! Oh, my stomach!

ʿALI Eat—tell your stomach to put up with it! You're enjoying the hospitality of the famous ʿAli Janah al-Tabrizi, praise be to his food caravans! . . .

QUFFA I've heard of it everywhere. (*Gets up on his knees and makes as though he was snatching food from the table in a frenzy.*)

ʿALI Hearing isn't like seeing and tasting.

QUFFA Oh, it's so delicious. I don't have the patience to munch properly . . . (*Hiccups.*)

ʿALI What's the matter?

QUFFA (*Hiccups*): Water! (*Hiccup.*) I need to drink. (*Hiccup.*)

ʿALI Water? There's none in my house; I only drink the best wine. Sawab, the wine and be quick! (*Clapping.*)

Enter Sawab, as though carrying the wine and the glasses. He sees Quffa hiccuping and is terrified. He puts down the tray and runs away.

ʿALI (*As though pouring for his friend*): You'll like this wine.

QUFFA (*Makes as though he was drinking with obvious enjoyment*): What is this, master?

ʿALI Do you like it?

QUFFA Very much.

ʿALI (*Offering him another imaginary glass*): Have another. Here's to your health.

QUFFA (*As though drinking*): It's very strong.

ʿALI Drink and be merry!

QUFFA This is vintage wine . . . At least a thousand years old.

ʿALI (*Bending down and whispering to him*): Shall I let you into a secret? This wine's stolen from the very cellar of Omar Khayyam.

QUFFA Oh! I never thought you could do such a thing. (*Slaps* ʿALI *on the face.*)

ʿALI (*Dumbfounded and angry; jumps to his feet*): How dare you, you miserable creature?

QUFFA (*Jumps up too and moves away from* ʿALI*; staggers to the right and left, nearly falling*): Drunk, my friend. Completely drunk. I don't know what I'm saying or doing. Drunk as a sponge. Please forgive me.

ʿALI You'll pay with your very life for this. Come here!

QUFFA (*Drops on the ground with fear and shakes violently*): I'm lost. Master, I'm only your slave to whom you've been so kind. You've fed me and gotten me drunk, and if I've taken a liberty with you, your station in life is far too exalted to let you hold me accountable for my stupidity.

ʿALI: Sawab! Fetch me the whip!

Enter SAWAB. *He hesitates, then hands him an imaginary whip.*

ʿALI (*Stands over* QUFFA *and makes as though he was whipping him.*) Here, for your impudence. Take this.

QUFFA (*Jumps away as if stung; feels his back in terror. Aside*): I swear I could hear the whip with my own ears, swishing in the air. I've been whipped. (*He cries and feels his body in pain.*) Oh! My back, my back!

ʿALI Come here!

QUFFA Mercy! Help! Help! (*Aside, astonished*:) I swear I can feel the pain where the whip hit me.

ʿALI Come!

QUFFA: Forgive, O master, an insolent man! A laughingstock! A man who loses his senses after the first glass . . .

Enter the PROPRIETOR *and his* SERVANT.

SAWAB (*Trying to alert* ʿALI *to the arrival of the proprietor*): Master . . .

ʿALI (*As though whipping* QUFFA, *to* SAWAB): This is none of your business.

SAWAB (*He jumps away and feels his body. Aside*): Good heavens! What am I frightened of? Could I have been hit? (*Feeling his shoulder*:) My God! Ouch! (*Runs in terror into the house and peeps with his head through the doorway.*)

PROPRIETOR What's going on here?

QUFFA (*Throwing himself at the* PROPRIETOR'*s feet*): Help me! (*Wipes the proprietor's shoes with his sleeve and looks intently at them.*) Master Tabrizi, there's a stranger in the orchard. Shall I tell you what sort of man he is? Or read his fortune for you?

PROPRIETOR (*He draws back as he kicks* QUFFA): Who's this buffoon?

SAWAB (*Peeping through the doorway*): The new proprietor's here, master . . .

ʿALI (*As though flinging the whip away; to the proprietor*): Welcome! Won't you join us for lunch?

PROPRIETOR I really don't know who's the host and who's the guest . . .

QUFFA (*Hurling himself at the* PROPRIETOR'*s shoes to look at them*): I can tell you.

PROPRIETOR (*Draws back as he kicks* QUFFA): This is a painful occasion. I was a friend of your father's . . .

ʿALI You take over the house. We're traveling, my servant and I.

PROPRIETOR (*Sighing in relief*): God be with you.

SAWAB (*Peeping through the doorway*): Me?

ʿALI I no longer like Sawab. I'll travel with my servant Kafur. (*Pointing at Quffa.*)

QUFFA (*Correcting him*): Quffa, master.

PROPRIETOR And where will you go?

ʿALI To the mountain of Qaf. (*Pronounces the "a" as in "father"*)

QUFFA Kaf. (*Pronounces the "a" as in "fat"*)

ʿALI Qaf.

PROPRIETOR (*Amused*): But that's a fictitious place . . . How are you going to travel?

ʿALI By sea.

QUFFA No. It made me sick last time. The magic carpet's better.

PROPRIETOR (*Draws back toward the door of the house; asks Sawab with concern*): Is he mad?

SAWAB Drunk.

PROPRIETOR But where's the wine?

SAWAB (*Puzzled*): I don't know.

PROPRIETOR (*To* ʿALI): Permit me to have a look at the house.

ʿALI Certainly, and please take your time . . . with you.

QUFFA But don't take it all, or you'll have none left.

The PROPRIETOR *and his* SERVANT *enter the mansion.*

QUFFA (*Laughing and mimicking his gait*): Who's he? He's very straightfaced.

ʿALI I sold him the house and its contents, Kafur.

QUFFA And where's the money?

ʿALI All gone on drink.

QUFFA When?

ʿALI In times past.

QUFFA (*Slapping his leg*): Oh dear me! And what about lunch, master? (*Aside:*) I cast my net, and it brought me up a destitute prince, and he cast his net and it brought him up a downright pauper. But I like him. It's as if I've been looking for him all my life. He's charmed me with his frivolity and his eccentricity, his madness and his sanity. He's like me. It's as if he were me.

ʿALI Sawab! (*Enter Sawab slackly.*) Fetch your elegant suit and give it to my friend here.

SAWAB (*Stuttering*): But . . . master . . . the thing is . . . my wages . . .

QUFFA (*Yelling*): He told you to fetch the suit. The elegant one. Don't you understand?

ʿALI (*He flings* QUFFA*'s bundle of shoes at* SAWAB): Here's the balance of your wages! Now go and bring the suit!

QUFFA (*He rushes to salvage the shoes, but* ʿALI *holds him back*): Master!

SAWAB (*Looking at the shoes*): How much are they worth, anyway?

QUFFA My shoes, master! My capital! What will I do with a suit?

ʿALI You'll need the suit, not the shoes. I've changed your profession. (*The suit is thrown to* QUFFA *through the doorway.*) Try it on.

QUFFA (*Wears it on top of his clothes*): How much is it worth anyway? (*Shouting with sudden realization:*) Who's changed my profession?

ʿALI Your friend. Your master. Have another glass of wine.

QUFFA What can I say to you? First you starve me and then you whip me . . . What about lunch, master?

ʿALI Have you got any property in Baghdad?

QUFFA All my property's on me.

ʿALI Me, too. Do you have anything to hope for from roaming its streets?

QUFFA My hope's in my hand.

ʿALI We're agreed then. (*Grabbing him:*) You and I shall travel drunk and without fear. Have something to eat before we set off!

QUFFA Will nothing exhaust this table of yours?

ʿALI Let's travel until we reach its far end.

QUFFA I'll find out where it ends. (*Makes as though he were tracing the edge of the table with his hand, until he disappears behind the scenes. He then returns, fumbling in his clothes.*) It's endless.

ʿALI What are you looking for? A flea?

QUFFA (*Still fumbling*): Here they are! Two pieces of silver. I've kept them for my lunch. One piece will buy us four loaves of bread and the other a quarter of a pound of halva. You invited me to your table in good faith, and it would be mean of me not to return your hospitality.

ᶜALI Have you got more?

QUFFA No, master. This is all I have.

ᶜALI Give them to me. (*Seizes the two coins.*) Each shall give according to his wealth. Now let's drink one last toast to our friendship.

QUFFA *offers* ᶜALI *an imaginary glass and picks up another for himself. Laughs hysterically.*

ᶜALI What's the joke?

QUFFA You know, this table of yours is very much like the "table" of wrongs which I laid before you when I first arrived. And my feasting at your table's no different from your sympathy for me when you listened to my moaning—and even if I had no wife and no children, and my eyes were healthy, and no policeman had kicked me, you would still have wept for the situation I was in.

ᶜALI No. I wouldn't have wept for you, but for another shoemaker who suffers from all that.

QUFFA But you haven't seen that *other* shoemaker!

ᶜALI Do I have to see him to weep for him? I know that he's walking at this very minute in one of the streets of Baghdad, carrying his shoes on his shoulders and starving.

QUFFA Amazing! That should mean that I've been enjoying food that I don't see, but which I know is laid on some other table in the city.

ᶜALI You can't have been enjoying thin air.

QUFFA I wonder.

CURTAIN

SCENE TWO

A marketplace at dawn. In the background are shops, still closed, and an inn with a signboard above it. Enter ᶜALI *and* QUFFA; *the latter wears* SAWAB*'s suit over his original clothes.*

QUFFA Oh, my feet! My back! My stomach! My eyes!

ᶜALI Why on earth are you hawking parts of your body like that? Do you want to sell them?

QUFFA It's tiredness, master.

ᶜALI And why are you tired?

QUFFA Haven't we walked from Baghdad to the borders of China?

ᶜALI We traveled with the caravan.

QUFFA Yes, but only the rich had mounts . . . For our two dinars we were only allowed to walk with the caravan.

ᶜALI You got your money's worth.

QUFFA And you? Don't you have any money? I can't believe this: here I am, traveling in the service of a prince and paying everything out of my pocket.

ᶜALI You'd also better not forget how you were made to pay.

QUFFA How can I forget the two kicks in my ribs?

ᶜALI Always remember that when it's time to pay.

QUFFA Too late now. You've made me broke already.

ᶜALI All the better for your ribs!

QUFFA I was only hoping for a free lunch; that was how it all started.

ᶜALI Your hope brought you on foot to the borders of China.

QUFFA But, master, you've made me pay for the expenses of the journey even though I'm only your servant.

ᶜALI I'm *your* servant.

QUFFA I'm only a poor shoemaker, but you're a gentleman of the nobility . . .

ʿALI I serve you in my capacity as your master.

QUFFA But I'm *the* servant.

ʿALI And I'm the master who serves you.

QUFFA I'm only like a hand or a foot to you . . .

ʿALI Tell me, shoemaker, which serves the other: your mind your hand, or your hand your mind?

QUFFA God! Isn't he convincing? Oh, my stomach! Oh, my brains! Oh, his hand and his foot! (*Fumbles in his clothes.*)

ʿALI What are you looking for in your clothes?

QUFFA I'm trying to see if my bowels have come out of my body . . .

ʿALI Moaning won't bring you food.

QUFFA How long have we been without food?

ʿALI Not as long as you imagine.

QUFFA You can say what you like, but I know we haven't eaten a thing since the meal we had in your orchard . . . (*Aside*:) There they are.

ʿALI Are you hiding something from me?

QUFFA Only my helplessness.

ʿALI That's something you never hide. You're a born beggar. Show me what's in your hand.

QUFFA I'll speak, but on condition you let me do what I suggest at once.

ʿALI Come here! What have you got in your hand?

QUFFA Here they are. I've another pocket apart from the one you've searched and there were two coins in it. Let's buy four loaves of bread and a quarter pound of halva this minute.

ʿALI Another pocket? You liar! Show me!

QUFFA (*Moves away*): No. Here they are. I'll go and buy the food now. Wait for me here. (*Exits running and then comes back shuddering.*) It's pitch dark and all the streets are littered with sleeping beggars . . . What sort of city is this? It's very poor. I'll wait for the morning. How horrible!

ʿALI I think it's a very rich city.

QUFFA And these? (*Pointing at the beggars.*)

ʿALI Learn, Kafur, that . . .

QUFFA My name is Quffa, master.

ʿALI Learn, Kafur, that the richer a city is, the more beggars it has. That's because great wealth ignites rivalry and conflict; as a result, the weak fall in abundance, while the greed of the rich flares up as the circle of rivals becomes smaller. I believe this is the richest city I've seen in my life, judging by the number of its beggars, and their nakedness.

QUFFA And their bare feet.

ʿALI And their bare feet.

QUFFA A shoemaker can't even earn a living here.

ʿALI Haven't you done anything else in your life?

QUFFA I have.

ʿALI What?

QUFFA Medicine.

ʿALI You worked as a doctor?

QUFFA Not exactly. I'd go to the market and place a number of big baskets all round me, covered with material, with the heads of terrible snakes seeming to stick out of them. I carried small boxes too, and I used to stand up and cry out: "I'm Hawis, the sorcerer and snake-charmer. In this basket is the life-snatcher. He that slowly unfolds and is as deadly as a raging lion. He that swiftly strikes and swiftly retreats. The very death incarnate whose name is viper. Woe betide the man who meets him in the wilderness and sees him raise his crested head like a sail, before he bites into the vein. And in this basket, my good folk, is the stealthy destroyer sometimes known as the queen of death, sometimes as the flying one and the darter, she who lives in the barren wastes, whose breath sets fire to the green grass. Praise Him who conquered her with this antidote. (*As though showing the boxes*:) and through it spread far and wide the fame of Andromachus. (*Holding up another box*:) Here is the healer of tears, fractures, bites, ailments, and diseases. I brewed it from mouse-ear, sea-onion, counter-poison, by adding white pepper, opium, and ginger, as well as galabanta dinka, varonitus sanitatum, and catadumus actatatum."

ʿALI (*Laughing*): I know doctors' writing's illegible, but I didn't know their speech was garbled too.

QUFFA Those are just words I made up to impress people with the power of the medicine.

ʿALI What about the snakes? Did you buy them?

QUFFA There weren't any. The baskets only had rags and stones in them, but if I could make people think there were snakes inside, they were afraid, and that gave them faith in the treatment. It's a real art. Why don't you try your hand at it?

ʿALI Never. If I were to enter the medical profession, I'd accept nothing less than being the chief of physicians, not a street-seller chased by the police.

QUFFA Do you know how doctors advertise themselves?

ʿALI "I am Valiant the healer, master of scalpel and blade. I am the cutter and piercer who chases away spirits and heals wounds. Bring unto me the man who cannot hear, and he who has not seen for a year. Show me the doctor who can handle my clamps or lance the abscess in the eyelid as well as I do. Show me the man who can cut or slice like me. Let him look me in the eye and say he's as bold as I!"

QUFFA A fine speech, master, but what about treatment?

ʿALI Don't you know that the best doctors are the ones who are best at talking?

QUFFA But what about treatment?

ʿALI Words which inspire confidence strengthen the patient's faith in his doctor, and that's halfway to recovery.

QUFFA Half a recovery won't save a patient's life. What if he dies?

ʿALI Nothing. The executioner, the doctor, and the soldier: they all inflict legitimate death.

QUFFA He's really convincing, this fellow.

ʿALI But listen, Kafur . . .

QUFFA Quffa, master. Quffa.

ʿALI Listen, Kafur, no matter what craft you choose to work at, as a stranger in the city you'll need to bribe the chief of the craft to let you join. Then customers will argue with you and belittle your skills to reduce your fees. And apart from that, the other craftsmen in the city will try and provoke you; you may lose your temper and insult one of them, in which case they'll join together and beat you up and kick you out. And if, instead, you open a shop, people will be curious and come to see if you're selling cheaper than the other merchants. And if you actually are, you'll arouse their hatred; merchants, as you know, are always friends with the police and the authorities, which means charges will be drawn up against you and you'll end up in prison. On the other hand, if you decide to play it safe and stand on a street corner begging, you'll only meet scorn; the beggars of the area will beat you up and you'll become the laughingstock of street children.

QUFFA If that's how things are, why did you bring us to China?

ʿALI As strangers we must adopt the

most suitable profession for a foreigner in a country where nobody knows him.

QUFFA And what's that?

ʿALI Sightseeing. Tourists . . . We're tourists.

QUFFA Tramps, you mean.

ʿALI (*Not listening to him*): And the best-liked tourists are the rich.

QUFFA Rich? Us?

ʿALI Yes. No need to pretend to be tradesmen or pretend we have skills.

QUFFA (*Sarcastically*): We must be honest.

ʿALI Exactly. I'm ʿAli Janah al-Tabrizi, the richest man in Baghdad, or anywhere else between China and Andalusia, and you're my servant Kafur.

QUFFA And what's wrong with being Quffa?

ʿALI Then you'll see the respect, the veneration they'll show us.

QUFFA And how, master, are you going to show them your wealth?

ʿALI Ah! That's where you come in.

QUFFA Me?

ʿALI You must sell me as you would a precious stone, and you must do it like a good salesman.

QUFFA What shall I say?

ʿALI Say anything that comes to your mind as long as you play your part well. Act naturally.

QUFFA Naturally?

ʿALI Yes. Give free rein to your imagination.

QUFFA I won't know what to say.

ʿALI Come, come! You know how to go on about being poor and hungry, with unfed children and diseased eyes, and so on . . .

QUFFA I know that very well.

ʿALI Those are the things that belong to misery and suffering. Why don't you try the things of happiness and power? Why not say: "I'm rich and generous; my children are strong and healthy?"

QUFFA Oh, I see. You mean, beg the way the rich do. Go on about the kebab worthy of a king's table and the chicken stuffed with pistachios . . . as long as someone pays in the end, as I did for the caravan.

ʿALI Try to describe me. Who am I?

QUFFA Chief merchant of all chief merchants under the sun. ʿAli Janah al-Tabrizi, the owner of countless caravans that travel the world, master of innumerable ships sailing the seven seas; in his coffers there are mountains of pearls high enough to block the sun's light from the earth!

ʿALI Superb. But always make sure you say the right thing at the right time. And don't overdo it.

QUFFA Why not?

ʿALI To ward off the evil eye.

QUFFA The evil eye!

ʿALI Make sure you don't sound like a braggart, or people will hate us.

QUFFA Don't brag.

ʿALI Do it in an honest, straightforward manner.

QUFFA If only you'd help me with some details; I don't know what it means to be wealthy.

ʿALI Never mind the details. Give free rein to your imagination and you'll find me at the farthest limit it can reach. Learn that people's dreams will help because they outstrip you, and no matter what you do, you'll never be able to catch up with them.

QUFFA (*Shuddering suddenly*): What if we're found out? I'll lose my head . . .

ʿALI What's it worth?

QUFFA Less than a loaf of bread.

ʿALI Don't be nervous. Straighten your back, lift your head, and step out firmly on the ground.

QUFFA Will words alone do, master?

ʿALI If they can be supported by action.

QUFFA What kind of action?

ʿALI Liberal spending.

QUFFA If only we had the money!

ʿALI (*Walking toward him*): Yes, if only . . .

QUFFA No. Stay where you are! I've only got two coins. One for four loaves of bread and the other for a quarter pound of . . . Stop! What do you want?

ʿALI (*Grabbing him and searching his clothes*): The fourth pocket!

QUFFA (*Trying to wriggle out*): No. I haven't got anything. There isn't a fourth pocket. Help! Thief! Help!

ʿALI This man struggles to save his money more desperately than he'd fight for his very life.

QUFFA Help! I'm done for.

ʿALI God almighty! You have all this money, and you walked all the way from Baghdad to China.

QUFFA (*Kicking*): Something I keep for life's ups and downs, master.

ʿALI How can you treat yourself so meanly?

QUFFA This is my capital; I've been saving up to buy myself a respectable shop.

ʿALI Then why did you travel with me to the end of the world? I can't understand your attitude toward money.

QUFFA Wait! (*Produces a small notebook from his pocket.*)

ʿALI What's that?

QUFFA The debt book. I must write down everything. You owe three hundred dinars now and two from before for the caravan . . . and . . . let me see now, how much did we spend on food?

ʿALI I see someone coming. Let's hide until we find out who they are.

They hide in the wings. Enter the MERCHANT *from the right. He wakes up a beggar sleeping on the ground.*

MERCHANT (*To the* BEGGAR): Get up, boy! Here! Take this coin and go and delay the Chief Merchant. Don't let him open his shop until I've opened mine.

The MERCHANT *opens his shop and brings out rolls of material and other goods, while the* BEGGAR *is watching the road and waiting for the* CHIEF MERCHANT.

MERCHANT Just you wait, Chief Merchant. One of these days you'll go broke, and all because of me . . .

Enter the CHIEF MERCHANT *from the left. He is fat and walks fast. He wakes up the first sleeping beggar he comes across.*

C. MERCHANT Boy! Take this coin and go and pester the Merchant. Make him lose his temper and quarrel with his customers. I don't want him to sell a thing all day.

The second BEGGAR *hurries to the* MERCHANT, *begging from him and annoying him, while* BEGGAR 1 *catches up with the* CHIEF MERCHANT.)

BEGGAR 1 (*Obstructing the path of the* CHIEF MERCHANT): Give me alms, master, for the Lord's sake. May God keep your children! And bless this day for you!

C. MERCHANT Go away, boy! Go away!

BEGGAR 1 (*To the* MERCHANT): What sort of treatment's this? Have you no fear of God? He won't bless the unjust . . . How dare you beat me! I'll get the police to haul you away like a common criminal. Bastard!

The INNKEEPER *opens his inn and yawns. Beggars approach him from the right and the left and watch.*

INNKEEPER This hullabaloo every morning is getting just too much. These aren't beggars, they're invading Tartars! I'll petition the King to ban them from the market. (*To the beggars:*) I'll slaughter you and serve you to the customers free. Get me the kitchen knife, boy!

ᶜALI *and* QUFFA *peep out from the wings.*

ᶜALI The inn's open now. Go on. (*Pushes him.*)

QUFFA (*Retreating*): Let me get ready first.

ᶜALI (*Pushing him*): Don't be frightened.

QUFFA (*Assumes a grandiose air and approaches the innkeeper*): You there . . . come here! I want to talk to you.

INNKEEPER What? Now who is it?

QUFFA Have you got a soft chair upholstered with the best red silk, with two cushions brocaded with gold? A chair fit for a king or a prince to sit on?

INNKEEPER What for?

QUFFA For my master to sit on.

INNKEEPER Who is he?

QUFFA (*Shocked at the boldness of the question*): What? How dare you ask, you vile creature! I could kill you on the spot for this, and pay whatever your blood money is.

INNKEEPER Clear off!

QUFFA You asked for it! (*Rushes at* ᶜALI, *snatches his sword from its sheath, and charges the inn. Exit the Innkeeper in a rush.* QUFFA *walks backwards until he collides with* ᶜALI.) He's gone to get the kitchen knife.

ᶜALI Don't panic. Step forward.

QUFFA (*Advances hesitantly; the effect of seeing the chair shows on him before the* INNKEEPER *appears carrying it*): Put it here. No, no. Here. (*To* ᶜALI, *pointing at the chair*:) Your highness!

ᶜALI (*Grabs his sword from* QUFFA *and begins to beat him with its side*): How dare you draw my sword at people! (*Aside*:) Cry out very loud. (*At the top of his voice*:) This time I'm going to kill you. Apologize to the keeper of this inn and kiss his hand. At once!

QUFFA Help! (*To the* INNKEEPER:) Forgive me please, sir. Say a good word on my behalf. (*Aside, to the innkeeper*:) My master's a terrible tyrant, but he's *so rich* . . . He thinks he can kill and cut and maim because he's *so rich*. Mercy!

INNKEEPER (*Bows to* ᶜALI *several times*): Forgive him, master. Don't upset yourself. I beseech you, master! (*Aside*:) The servant's a scoundrel, but his master's an important prince.

ᶜALI (*To* QUFFA): Stand still! (QUFFA *straightens up and shuts his mouth at once.*)

INNKEEPER (*Aside*): A real tyrant. I'll serve him well; maybe he'll reward me generously. (*To* ᶜALI:) Good morning to you, master.

ᶜALI (*Takes a handful of coins from* QUFFA*'s purse and gives it to the* INNKEEPER): Here. Take this to make up for the boy's rudeness to you. (QUFFA *gasps as he gazes at his money in the hand of the* INNKEEPER. ᶜALI *silences him.*) Shush!

INNKEEPER (*Coming to*): To make up?

ᶜALI For my servant's rudeness to you.

INNKEEPER O Prince of all time! O Patron of bounty and charity! (*Pulls one of the inn servants to him*:) Call all the servants. Leave all the residents and gather round this prince to serve him. Hurry! (*To* ᶜALI:) Master, I'm at your beck and call.

(*To the beggars drawing nearer curiously and cautiously*:) Be gone with you! Out! Out! Leave the market!

ʿALI No. Let them come, Innkeeper. (*To the beggars*:) Come to me, my poor friends. How unhappy you are! Take this. (*Takes a handful of gold from* QUFFA*'s purse, and they rush to his hand.* QUFFA *pushes and shoves with them, but* ʿALI*'s fist stops him.*) Leave them! They'll do me no harm.

QUFFA (*Aside*): My life's savings!

ʿALI (*Giving the beggars a handful of coins each*): Don't jostle. Each will have his share.

The beggars stare, each at the contents of his hand, in disbelief.

INNKEEPER (*Aside, to* QUFFA): He gives like a king. He's giving them gold.

QUFFA (*Heartbroken and emphatic*): I know. I know.

BEGGAR 1 He gives without counting.

BEGGAR 2 Without counting.

INNKEEPER'S SERVANT (*Aside*): He's fabulously open-handed.

QUFFA (*Heartbroken and emphatic*): Open-handed indeed!

ʿALI Don't jostle. Each will get his share.

BEGGAR 3 His share.

INNKEEPER (*Aside*): He must be a man of enormous wealth . . .

QUFFA (*Heartbroken and emphatic*): Enormous indeed!

INNKEEPER Or he wouldn't give so lavishly.

WOMAN BEGGAR A man of wealth!

INNKEEPER'S SERVANT (*Aside*): A man of enormous wealth.

QUFFA Enormous!

ʿALI Don't push and shove. Come to me.

INNKEEPER (*Aside, to* QUFFA): He still says "come to me?"

QUFFA (*Genuinely heartbroken*): You can hear him with your own ears, can't you?

Drums. Enter a group of soldiers who scatter the beggars with their whips.

SOLDIERS Move on! Make way! Move on! Make way!

The beggars disperse.

QUFFA (*Aside, to* ʿALI): We're done for. (*Trembling*:) They've come to arrest us.

ʿALI (*Aside, to* QUFFA): Don't be a coward. We've done nothing wrong yet.

QUFFA (*Aside, to* ʿALI): Perhaps it's against the law to distribute money. Do you know what city this is?

ʿALI (*Aside, to* QUFFA): Look! She must be a princess. How beautiful she is!

Enter the PRINCESS *followed by her maid and a young boy servant.*

QUFFA (*Turning round himself*): What a vision!

ʿALI (*Beckons to the* INNKEEPER, *who goes and bends over him*): Who is she?

INNKEEPER The King's daughter, master. (*Withdraws to stand politely in attendance.*)

ʿALI (*Aside, to* QUFFA): The King's daughter.

QUFFA My head's spinning.

The PRINCESS *enters the* CHIEF MERCHANT*'s shop.*

ʿALI (*Beckons to the* INNKEEPER, *who comes and bends over him*): Where did she go?

INNKEEPER Into the Chief Merchant's shop, master. (*Goes back to where he was standing.*)

ʿALI (*Aside, to* QUFFA): Into the Chief Merchant's shop.

QUFFA I can no longer see . . .

ʿALI Let's go.

QUFFA Where?

AL-TABRIZI *makes his way to the* CHIEF MERCHANT*'s shop followed by* QUFFA *and the* INNKEEPER. *The* PRINCESS *comes out of the shop followed by the* CHIEF MERCHANT, *the maid, and the boy carrying a variety of dresses and rolls of material and frills, whose colors the* PRINCESS *wishes to examine in the daylight. Meanwhile the soldiers have evacuated the beggars from the market and encircled it.*

PRINCESS No. I don't like the color, or the cut.

C. MERCHANT I've got it in every color. Look at this one . . .

ʿALI (*Holding the dress*): How dare you offer the Princess something that's not even fit for her kitchen maid?

C. MERCHANT I beg your pardon!

ʿALI Come, come! You're not really that surprised. Don't you know that material worthy of a princess won't tear like this . . . (*Rends the dress*) or like this? (*Rends it again.*)

C. MERCHANT What have you done?

ʿALI I'll pay you for it. Kafur, take this dress and give it to a beggar woman.

C. MERCHANT But, sir . . .

The MERCHANT *is watching with delight from a distance.*

ʿALI And these frills, they tear. (*Tears them and throws them to* QUFFA.) And this brocade . . . (*Tearing it*:) you'd better give it to the poor . . . charge it to me.

C. MERCHANT No!

The PRINCESS *laughs into her* MAID*'s bosom, while the* INNKEEPER *pulls the* CHIEF MERCHANT *by the arm and reassures him about his money.*

ʿALI Kafur! Show me what he's got inside the shop, too.

C. MERCHANT (*Imploringly*): I beg you, sir . . .

PRINCESS (*To* ʿALI) Young man!

ʿALI (*Bowing to her*): A stranger, Your Highness, who wishes to serve you with his heart, sword, and fortune.

PRINCESS Do you know me, young man?

ʿALI Yes. You are the rising sun for him who can see. The flower's scent for the enamored. The nightingale's song for the melancholy.

PRINCESS (*Nearly swooning, to her maid*): Take us home.

Exit from the same way they entered, followed by the soldiers. The beggars return.

SOLDIERS Make way! Move off!

QUFFA (*Emerges from the* CHIEF MERCHANT*'s shop carrying clothes*): Did she leave, master?

ʿALI Give these clothes to the poor, Kafur.

QUFFA (*Looking in the direction of the* PRINCESS*'s train*): How beautiful she is!

ʿALI (*Aside, to* QUFFA): Wake up!

QUFFA (*To the beggars*): Come to me. Don't shove. Each will have his share. (*The* INNKEEPER *and his staff, the* MERCHANT *and the* CHIEF MERCHANT *and their staffs, as well as the beggars, all gather round him, with the pile of clothes in front of him.*) Shush! (*He moves downstage right followed by them in one mass.*) My master's the richest man of all time. (*He moves downstage center followed by them in one mass.*) His name is ʿAli Janah al-Tabrizi.

PERSON 1 (*Standing next to* QUFFA, *he*

communicates the name to the next person in a whisper and so on until the name reaches the farthest person): ᶜAli . . . Janah . . . al-Tabrizi . . .

QUFFA (*Moving left*): All cities and ports of the world know of his wealth. There is no man under the sun richer than he. He has partners in India. In Sind. In Yemen. In Egypt. In Persia and in Byzantium.

PERSON 2 (*As with* PERSON 1): He has partners in India and Byzantium.

QUFFA (*Moves right and then changes his mind while they follow him in one mass*): His generosity knows no bounds. So know his worth, lift him high, and serve him well.

PERSON 3 (*As with* PERSON 1): He's very generous.

QUFFA And learn that his arrival in your city isn't for business. He's only here as a tourist. Because he doesn't need to do business.

PERSON 1 (*As before*): He's a tourist. He's not here for business.

QUFFA He doesn't need to travel to foreign lands for profit because his possessions . . . (*Pauses for a second, then moves quickly to the right, followed by them.*)

PERSON 2 (*As before*): He'll tell us about his possessions.

QUFFA My master wanted to see the world, so he took from his possessions just enough to cover his travel expenses and loaded the money onto a caravan of three hundred mules, each led by a special slave and bearing a chest packed with gold and precious stones. Behind the mules came the camels. Five hundred of them, each hundred laden with a hundred different fabrics: Egyptian, Syrian, Persian, Indian, Byzantine. All around them rode three hundred guards, the best to be seen on horseback. But my master was bored with the slow pace of the heavily laden caravan, so he took me along with him and we galloped fast to wait for its arrival in your city. My master has in his possession . . . (*Pauses for a little.*)

PERSON 2 (*As before*): He'll tell us about his master's possessions.

QUFFA A fortune that no fire can consume, and I am but his humblest servant.

PERSON 3 (*As before*): He's his humblest servant.

QUFFA You're suffocating my master. Move off a little.

A circle forms round ᶜALI. *The* MERCHANT *and the* CHIEF MERCHANT *draw near him, followed by the* INNKEEPER *and his staff. Meanwhile* QUFFA *distributes the clothes among the beggars, who put them on.*

MERCHANT Sir, do you have any silk from Mosul in your caravan?

ᶜALI Plenty.

C. MERCHANT Is there any velvet from Aleppo in your caravan, sir?

ᶜALI Plenty.

C. MERCHANT Red and maroon?

ᶜALI Plenty.

INNKEEPER His Highness has brought loads and loads of expensive fabrics with him.

QUFFA (*Aside, to those around him*): All this is only a tiny fraction of the revenue of one of his estates.

Enter new beggars jostling and shouting.

BEGGAR 5 We've had nothing, master.

ᶜALI Come to me. (*Takes a handful of coins and gives it to him.*) Don't push. Come to me.

WOMAN BEGGAR 6 (*Shouts into the wings*): Bahana! There's a stranger in the market, a real prince, giving away gold.

BEGGAR 7 (*Shouts facing the wings*): Woman! Follow me to the market!

QUFFA, *having finished distributing the clothes, joins his master.*

QUFFA (*Horrified at the depletion of his money, aside to* ʿALI): Master, keep something for us.

ʿALI (*Aside to* QUFFA *as he still takes handfuls of coins and gives them away*): It'll all be stored up for you in Heaven.

QUFFA (*Aside to* ʿALI): By the look of it we'll be *in* Heaven before the day's over.

VOICES His caravan's so long, it' s vanguard's here while its tail's still in Baghdad.

QUFFA (*Aside to* ʿALI.) I haven't got a fifth pocket.

ʿALI (*Still giving away money, aside to* QUFFA): God's mercy is vaster than your pockets.

VOICES He travels from one city to another, and the one he likes, he buys.

QUFFA (*Aside to* ʿALI): All my life's savings! How could you!

ʿALI (*Aside to* QUFFA, *while still giving away handfuls of money*): A cheap life, yours has been!

VOICES When God saw how poor we are, He sent him to us.

The gold is finished, and ʿALI *rests his head between his hands, looking upset.*

INNKEEPER (*To* QUFFA): What's wrong with your master? Is he ill?

QUFFA (*Aside, very alarmed*): Perhaps his heart's stopped beating like mine.

C. MERCHANT You're suffocating him. Damn you! Move off!

MERCHANT (*To one of the servants*): Get moving! Bring some rose water.

ʿALI (*Raising his head and two hands to the sky in a supplicatory movement*): God is my succor! He will help me!

BEGGAR 5 God keep you from evil, Your Highness!

BEGGAR 6 God's name protect you, holy man!

INNKEEPER Are you in pain, master?

ʿALI I've found most people in this city are poor and unhappy. If I'd known that, I'd have brought sackfuls of money for them. Now I'm afraid I may have to wait a long time for my caravan, and it's not in my nature to turn away a beggar, yet my gold's finished.

MERCHANT Tell them who ask: "God will provide."

ʿALI I've never done that, and I never thought the day would come when I did, *and* in a foreign land.

INNKEEPER Take it easy, master. Here's some money you've given me. Take it until your caravan arrives, and don't be sad.

MERCHANT (*Interrupting with a pouch of money in his hand*): Master, do your humble servant who stands before you the honor of accepting this loan until the caravan arrives.

ʿALI (*Stands up, overjoyed, and takes the pouch. Places his hand on the* MERCHANT*'s shoulder*): I won't forget this favor for as long as I live.

VOICES He won't forget.

ʿALI You're a good man.

VOICES A good man.

ʿALI A friend.

VOICES A friend.

ʿALI A brother.

VOICES A brother.

ʿALI *scatters the contents of the pouch over the heads of the crowd. The beggars fight over it, while the* MERCHANT *slips among them in horror and fights with them over his money.*

QUFFA (*Aside, covering his eyes with his hands*): Oh no!

C. MERCHANT (*Bringing along two pouches*): Master, don't take money from this merchant; he's poor. Take from me.

MERCHANT (*Getting up*): Don't believe him, master; he's my rival. I'm richer than he is. I was only helping my friends, the poor, pick up the money. (*As though lending them a hand*:) Here, take this, my friend. Take this, my good man. Here, here . . .

VOICES He says "my friend"! He says "my good man"! I can't believe my ears.

*ᶜ*ALI *takes the* CHIEF MERCHANT*'s pouches and scatters their contents over the beggars' heads.*

C. MERCHANT (*Aside, out of breath with disbelief*): He must be a king of some country. Maybe he's the Caliph of Baghdad himself. (*To* ᶜALI:) Master, this inn is far too humble for a prince like you. I have a beautiful house . . . if you will be so kind as to do me the great honor . . .

MERCHANT (*Pushing him*): No. He's going to stay in *my* house. I lent him money first. (*They grab each other.*)

QUFFA (*Upstage, as though delivering a speech*): Gentlemen, instead of quarreling, serve us breakfast, and hurry; my master's hungry and faint from traveling. Bring us soft white bread; real bread which the eye can see. Eggs fried in cream whose hissing and spitting the ear can hear. Grilled pigeons whose meat the hand can feel. And dessert . . . don't forget the pancakes. My master likes them stuffed with pistachios; which, when crushed with the teeth, proclaim their reality beyond any doubt. (*He shouts louder.*) And doughnuts soaked in honey.

CURTAIN

SCENE THREE

The KING*'s court. Behind the throne is a curtain which separates the court from the women's apartments. The* PRINCESS *and her maid watch what goes on from behind the curtain. In the court are the* KING*, the* VIZIER*, the* EXECUTIONER*, the* MERCHANT*, and the* CHIEF MERCHANT.

KING How could you two, of all people, fall into his trap?

C. MERCHANT If only you'd heard him talk, Your Majesty . . .

KING What's happened to your brains? Your caution? Your experience?

MERCHANT There's no escaping fate.

KING Just a young man! You say he's a young man?

C. MERCHANT He took my house. I spend my nights in the inn while he carouses with the riffraff in my garden.

KING How did he take your house?

C. MERCHANT I invited him to stay there.

MERCHANT And I fought with him (*Pointing at the* CHIEF MERCHANT) over it. Now I've lost everything. Thank God, at least I still have my house.

MERCHANT But we're not quite sure yet, Your Majesty.

MERCHANT Are you still looking on the bright side, Chief Merchant?

C. MERCHANT I still have hope.

VIZIER I think he's a liar and an imposter.

MERCHANT He shook the city. It's as if he was redistributing the wealth just as he liked.

C. MERCHANT He's given sixty thousand dinars in a matter of a few days.

MERCHANT Vermin, beggars, and thieves are now competing with us in the market, opening shops and going into business.

They have capital now, and talk about imports and exports.

C. MERCHANT I'm completely lost; I don't know what's right from what's wrong any more.

KING I've never seen any merchant as foolish as you two. Anyway, he'll soon be here, and then we'll see.

VIZIER I think we should execute him on the spot.

C. MERCHANT But we're not sure. Perhaps he *has* a caravan after all.

MERCHANT He still hasn't lost hope!

PRINCESS (*Puts out her hand from behind the curtain and beckons to her father*): Psst! Psst! Psst!

Everybody looks at her hand as it is pulled back inside. The VIZIER *seems particularly enamored of her. The* KING *enters her apartment.*

KING What's this nonsense? Psst, psst? Can't you see I'm busy dealing with the affairs of the kingdom.

PRINCESS You were going to make a mistake, father.

KING What mistake?

PRINCESS I mean about that young man.

KING What about him?

PRINCESS He's better than all of them; he's the son of a great king. And he's handsome . . . in his manners, I mean.

KING How do you know that?

PRINCESS I met him in the market.

KING Oh, marvelous! That's all we needed!

PRINCESS (*Breaks into tears at once*): I only saw him.

KING You're not to go out to the market again. You understand?

PRINCESS You'll see for yourself that he's a noble man. And I'm *not* going to marry the Vizier.

KING Nobody's forcing you.

PRINCESS Every time I try and help you, you tell me off.

KING That's enough now! We'll talk about it some other time. (*Goes back to the throne, and everybody rises for him. To the merchants*:) Don't worry. I'll test him and find out if he's an imposter or an honest man, and whether he was raised in a house of honor and wealth.

VIZIER If we ask him, he won't tell us the truth.

KING Do you think I'm going to ask him? I'll show him the gem in my turban. (*Pulls out the gem and shows it to them in the palm of his hand.*) My grandfather bought it for a thousand dinars from an African merchant. It's the most precious stone in my collection and a real work of art. If he knows its true worth, he'll prove himself a man of noble lineage and great wealth. But if he doesn't, he'll act like an upstart and a cheat, and we'll have to inflict an exemplary death on him.

C. MERCHANT Please, God, let my enemy be a man of wealth, the owner of a caravan, loaded with all the treasures of the earth. By God, I'd sooner have my money back than see his head cut off, and I'd much rather wait a whole year for his caravan to arrive than give up hope.

Enter the USHER.

USHER Master ᶜAli Janah al-Tabrizi.

The KING *signals to the* USHER *with a wave of his hand to let* ᶜALI *in. Exit the* USHER; *enter* ᶜALI *and* QUFFA. *They greet the* KING, *who gestures with his hand to ask them to sit down.*

QUFFA (*Aside to* ᶜALI): A trap, master.

KING Are you ᶜAli Janah al-Tabrizi, the merchant?

ALI I am, Your Majesty, but I'm not a

merchant. I only travel with my caravan to see the world.

QUFFA (*Aside*): Are you going to sell that to the King, too?

ᶜALI (*Pinching his arm*): And this is my servant, Kafur.

KING These merchants say that you owe them sixty thousand dinars, is that right?

ᶜALI As a matter of fact, I don't count what I borrow or spend, but I'm sure they're right.

KING Why haven't you paid them back their money?

ᶜALI If they'll just wait until my caravan arrives, I'll give them twice that amount. If they want gold, I'll give them gold; if they want silver, I'll give them silver, and if they prefer merchandise, that will be all right with me, too. And whoever I owe one thousand, I'll pay him back two thousand to show my gratitude for saving my face before the needy.

KING Hmm! Would you take a look at this gem, ᶜAli Janah, and value it for me? I found it in my grandfather's collection and I can't tell what it's worth.

The gem moves from one hand to another until it reaches ᶜALI. *He takes one look at it, then puts it on the floor and with the handle of his sword smashes it.* QUFFA *stifles a cry of horror and shrinks behind* ᶜALI.

KING (*Dumbfounded*): Why did you smash it?

ᶜALI Your Majesty, this is no gem. It's a stone worth no more than a thousand dinars, and in Africa there are thousands and thousands like it, and better. Indeed, your grandfather should never have included it in his collection; it would only be a suitable ornament for one of his minor servants.

KING (*Very concerned*): And what, in your opinion, is a gem?

ᶜALI I'll only call a gem by that name if it's worth seventy thousand dinars and above.

KING And what would such a gem look like?

ᶜALI It should glow from within like a glaring lamp. If it doesn't, then it's worth nothing and I wouldn't wear it. How can you be a king and call that thing a gem?

KING Ahem! Ahem!

PRINCESS (*Puts out her hand from behind the curtain and beckons to her father*): Psst! Psst! Psst!

The KING *goes to her.*

QUFFA (*Aside*): I'm done for. She's pointing at me. They'll kill me for *your* crime. First you smash his gem and than you insult him.

ᶜALI (*Aside*): Shut up!

KING (*As though talking to himself*): This man is either a very sophisticated thief or the very cousin of the Caliph of Baghdad.

PRINCESS Marry me off to him . . . I want to marry him . . . I want to marry him.

KING What did you say?

PRINCESS (*Beginning to cry*): I will *not* marry the Vizier . . . I want to marry Tabrizi . . . I want to marry him.

KING Excellent! Just what I needed for my disasters to be complete!

PRINCESS You tested him, and he passed. I love him!

KING You've gone too far.

PRINCESS The Chief Merchant will marry his daughter off to him; he's given him his house.

KING Shut up! It's none of your business. Shush!

Exit the PRINCESS *crying, followed by her maid. The* KING *returns to his court and sits on the throne in a preoccupied manner.*

KING Do you have jewels like the one you described?

ᶜALI Plenty.

KING I mean ones worth seventy thousand or more each.

ᶜALI Plenty.

KING Do you carry them in your caravan?

ᶜALI Yes. No matter how many you ask for, they'll all be yours, as a present from me.

KING (*Feeling his turban sadly*): But when?

ᶜALI When my caravan arrives, God willing.

KING (*Aside, still feeling his turban and looking at those of the Vizier, the Merchant, and the Chief Merchant*): I feel naked without my gem. The bastard! But it was stupid of me to test him with my own gem. (*He plucks out the gem in the* VIZIER*'s turban and throws it to* ᶜALI:) Tell us how much this one's worth. (*He does the same to the other two.*) And this one. And this.

The three men are struck dumb. Their arms automatically try to reach after the gems. The KING *gloats over their plight.*

ᶜALI (*Looking at the* VIZIER*'s gem*): Five hundred dinars. Made in Persia. (*Smashes it.*)

VIZIER (*Aside*): True! What a pity!

ᶜALI (*Looking at the* CHIEF MERCHANT*'s gem*): Seven hundred. Made in China.

C. MERCHANT You're right, but spare it, please.

ᶜALI I remember giving one like it to Kafur. (*Smashes it.*)

QUFFA And I threw it away.

ᶜALI (*Looking at the* MERCHANT*'s gem*): Three hundred. I've seen children in Syria play with these. (*Smashes it.*)

MERCHANT (*To the* KING): Your Majesty, I would have liked my friend to hit the truth without hitting my gem.

KING (*To the merchants*): Go now, and be patient with my guest until his caravan arrives; then come to me and I'll make up for your jewels from my own money; I'll even give you more.

The two merchants make as if to leave in a rush, but halt at the door for a while.

MERCHANT (*Aside, to* CHIEF MERCHANT): He wants to keep him all to himself.

C. MERCHANT Didn't I tell you to be patient and keep the greedy King from meddling in our affairs?

Exeunt the two men. The KING *goes into the women's apartments, now empty, not knowing what to do.*

KING (*Aside*): Thank God for sending him our way. I must keep the whole caravan for myself. Those merchants are very cunning; they think they can hog him for sixty thousand and a house. *I* shall give him my daughter in marriage. (*Mimicking* ᶜALI:) *He doesn't count what he borrows or spends.* Well, I'll count for him! I'll hold him captive in wedlock. (*Looking outside*:) The girl's angry. I must find her and make it up to her. (*Exit.*)

QUFFA (*Aside to* ᶜALI): All clear?

ᶜALI (*Aside to* QUFFA): All clear.

QUFFA (*At his ease*): Shall I tell you how much this curtain's worth? Or this throne? Or this vizier? (*Aside*:) Oh dear me! (*To the* VIZIER:) Hollow!

The VIZIER *looks sharply at* ᶜALI *and* QUFFA, *while they look back defiantly.*

VIZIER You've smashed a fortune.

ʿALI Look here, Your Excellency, what do you see on my finger?

VIZIER I can't see anything.

ʿALI This is the smallest particle of the King's gem.

VIZIER You mean what *was* his gem.

ʿALI No. The smallest particle of it is more precious than all of it.

VIZIER Yes, yes, if only because it's the part of it which is indivisible and can't be smashed.

ʿALI It's like a tiny bottle, tightly sealed; and inside it there's a dangerous jinn.

VIZIER God protect us!

ʿALI And this jinn has at his command seventy-two thousand tribes, each tribe numbering seventy-two thousand men, and each one of those men has at his command a thousand giants who each have a thousand servants; *all* in the service of one jinn.

QUFFA No! Show me!

VIZIER Are you a sorcerer? (*Aside*:) Maybe he's charmed the king. (*To* ʿALI:) And this jinn, how can he be set free?

ʿALI With a little charm.

VIZIER A talisman?

ʿALI Yes, such as TR + TH = S + THG

VIZIER Is that a magic charm or a mathematical equation?

ʿALI They're the same.

VIZIER (*Frightened*): And can . . . you . . .

ʿALI No. It will take seven hundred mathematicians seven hundred years to arrive at the right clue to set him free.

QUFFA Just imagine! As the Prophet says, "Go after knowledge, even as far as China!"

VIZIER And this *jinn*, is he good or evil?

ʿALI The *jinn* is the servant of the man who sets him free; if in the end he's freed by a virtuous scientist, he'll sow and reap, raise buildings and dig rivers; he'll abolish distances and bring prosperity to the whole world. *But* if he's released by a wicked scientist, he'll go berserk, destroying and burning, killing and exterminating . . .

VIZIER God protect us! But how do you know these things?

ʿALI I contemplate the sky like an astronomer.

QUFFA As for me, I know things by looking at the ground. (*He swoops on the* VIZIER'*s shoes.*) Master Tabrizi, shall I read his character for you? Oh dear! (*The* VIZIER *tries to break loose from his grip.*)

QUFFA He's *very* deep.

VIZIER How do you know I'm deep?

QUFFA From the way you tighten the strings; a bandit would sooner make off with your ghost than your shoes.

VIZIER Watch your language, man! Are you a shoemaker?

QUFFA (*With hidden mockery*): How does Your Excellency know these things?

Enter the KING *and the* PRINCESS *into the women's apartments. The* PRINCESS *is arguing and crying childishly.*

KING All right. I will let you marry him, but what if he turns out to be a thief?

PRINCESS No, no, no, he can't be a thief.

KING All right, all right. Pretend you don't know he's in the room when you come in for something or other, and when he's seen you, hurry back to your apartment, and leave the rest to me.

PRINCESS I can't, I'm so shy.

KING What about the market? You weren't so shy there.

She shrugs her shoulders girlishly, then enters the main room, feigns surprise, stops and goes out. Enter the KING *and sits down.*

KING (*Aside to the* VIZIER): Vizier, my daughter entered the room unintentionally and saw this stranger just as he must have seen her. He must be under the influence of her charm now; I want you to be nice to him, and speak to him, and let him know I like him and that I'll accept him as my daughter's husband.

VIZIER (*Aside*): My King, I don't like this man, I still think he's an impostor and a liar. Don't give your daughter away for nothing.

KING (*Aside*): Traitor! You wish no good to come to me. You've made a deal with the merchants against me, haven't you? Just because you wanted to marry the girl yourself and I refused; now you want to stand in her way until she's unmarriageable and you can have her for yourself!

VIZIER (*Aside*): Your Majesty . . .

KING (*Aside*): How on earth can he be an impostor or a liar when he could value all our jewels and tell where we bought them, and smashed them in the end because he found them too cheap for his taste? He has riches beyond count; when he's married to my daughter, he'll shower her with jewels and things and he'll place his wealth at my disposal . . .

VIZIER (*Aside*): I'll do as you wish.

KING (*Aside*): Be quick, then!

VIZIER (*Goes to* ᶜALI *and* QUFFA): Sir, His Majesty the King has noticed that his daughter came into this room unaware of your presence, and that she saw you and you saw her. His Majesty has taken a liking to you and he won't say no if you ask her hand in marriage. What do you say?

QUFFA (*Pulling* ᶜALI *to a corner, aside*): I saw her too, maybe even before you did. *I* want to marry her.

ᶜALI (*Aside*): But the King wants to marry her to *me*.

QUFFA (*Aside*): No, no, no. We're operating with *my* capital. (*Wagging his notebook at him.*) She'll be *my* wife.

ᶜALI (*Aside*): By all means. Tell the Vizier that.

QUFFA (*Aside, undecidedly*): *You* tell him.

ᶜALI (*Aside*): If I say that to him, he'll kill me.

QUFFA (*Aside*): Just think what he'll do to *me* if I tell him.

ᶜALI (*Aside*): I hate to think.

QUFFA (*Aside*): Why did you call yourself "master" and me "servant"?

ᶜALI (*Aside*): It's the nature of things.

QUFFA (*Aside*): No. I beg to differ . . .

ᶜALI (*Aside*): Listen, why don't you marry her maid? She's pretty.

QUFFA (*Aside*): Why don't you?

ᶜALI (*Aside*): Because those are the rules: the master marries the mistress, and the valet marries the maid. It's always been like that. Look at books and traditions anywhere in the world.

QUFFA (*Aside*): It's *my* capital. *You're* the servant.

ᶜALI (*Aside*): You tell the Vizier that and I won't contradict you.

QUFFA (*Aside*): Do you want me killed? Listen, you marry her and then let's share her between us.

ᶜALI (*Aside*): You know, you're frightened of your own shadow, but you think you can be rude to me.

QUFFA (*Aside*): That's because I know you.

ᶜALI (*Aside*): You don't know me yet. Look, I'm not going to marry her.

QUFFA (*Aside*): Just as well.

ᶜALI (*In a loud voice to the* VIZIER): Your Excellency, be so good as to convey to the King my gratitude for his kindness. It will be an honor for me to marry his daughter, but let His Majesty bear with me until my caravan arrives.

QUFFA Yes. When his caravan arrives.

KING (*Aside to the* VIZIER): If we agree to delay the marriage, he'll just pay off his debts when the caravan arrives and carry on with his journey. Now!

VIZIER (*Aside to* ʿALI): The King can see no reason for waiting. Why wait?

ʿALI (*Loudly*): Because the dowry of a King's daughter is huge. A King's daughter should only be paid a dowry proportionate to her high position, but at the moment I have no money. Let's just wait until my caravan arrives; there'll be no problem then. I really can't pay her less than five thousand bags of money for her dowry, and I shall need a thousand more to distribute among the poor on the wedding night, and still another thousand to give to those who walk in the wedding procession, not to mention a thousand more for the banquet I'll give for my guests. And naturally I shall need a hundred jewels to present to my mother-in-law on the wedding morning, and another hundred to distribute among the bridesmaids—each shall have one as a token of her mistress's elevated status. I shall also need to clothe a thousand beggars and give them alms. I can't do any of this until my caravan arrives. But once it's here, all this will seem nothing, because this is only a fraction of what it carries.

KING (*Aside, to the* VIZIER): My oh my! This *is* the Baghdad we've heard of, with rivers of riches! How could you say such a man's an impostor and a liar! By God, if it weren't for our long friendship, I would have thrown you out of my palace.

QUFFA (*Aside to* ʿALI): Good Heavens! You put the state coffers to shame.

ʿALI (*Aside*): I'm only trying to put obstacles in the way of the marriage, for your sake.

QUFFA (*Aside*): If I hadn't fallen in love with her myself, I would've let you marry her.

ʿALI (*Aside*): I understand. It's only natural that we both fell in love with her at the same time.

VIZIER (*Aside to the* KING): It's *because* of our long friendship, Your Majesty, that I insist on giving you good counsel instead of just going along with what you want.

KING (*Aside to the* VIZIER): Stop accusing him, or you're a dead man. I swear it! I know what you're thinking, but you will *not* marry my daughter. (*To* ʿALI:) Listen, my son! Don't make such excuses. Approach! (*Unfastens keys from his belt.*) These are the keys of my safe, which is full. Take them and open it yourself. Spend as much as you like . . . give anybody you please as much as you like . . . just do as you like. As for the girl and her mother, you shouldn't really worry because we're one family now. They'll wait until your caravan arrives, and then you can be as open-handed with them as you wish. Don't worry about the dowry either; I'm not rushing you; I'll happily wait until the caravan arrives. Remember, you and I are one now.

The KING*'s hand is still stretched out with the keys.* ʿALI *is at a loss as to what to do. He looks at* QUFFA, *whose eyes nearly pop out with surprise. He nudges* ʿALI *with the elbow to take the keys.*

QUFFA (*Aside to* ʿALI): Take them, take them.

ʿALI (*To the* KING): I accept. (*Takes the keys with both hands and kisses the* KING*'s hand.*)

KING Congratulations!

The KING *claps his hands. From inside, Arabic music can be heard. Enter dancing girls.*

CURTAIN

INTERLUDE

The action takes place before a center stage curtain. The USHER *stands behind the seated* JUDGE. *In front of him stand, one on the right and the other one on the left, the two* LITIGANTS. *All are masked.*

USHER The court is in session!

JUDGE Why are you here? What's your quarrel? Who's the defendant?

LITIGANT 1 May the Lord help you, Your Honor! This bag is mine; everything in it is my own property. I lost it yesterday; since then I haven't slept or eaten or stopped for a drink until I found it today with this man in the market.

JUDGE (*To* LITIGANT 2): What do you plead?

LITIGANT 2 Your Honor, I went to the market this morning accompanied by my servant, whom I made carry this bag to hold the things we buy, when all of a sudden this fraud attacked us in front of everybody and snatched the bag from me with the words: "This is mine and everything in it's mine." So I called on good folk to save me from him, and here we are standing before Your Honor.

JUDGE (*To* LITIGANT 1): If you claim the bag's yours, describe its contents.

LITIGANT 1 Sir, in this bag of mine are a gold container for kohl, and two silver sticks to put it on with; a handkerchief; two golden tassels; two candlesticks; two spoons; one dish; one pillow; two pitchers; one tray; one washtub; two earthen jars; one ladle; two bowls; one crippled woman I give one meal a day to; a cow with two calves; one camel and two she-camels; a buffalo; two bulls; one lion; two foxes; a mattress and two beds; a palace with two halls; a kitchen with two doors, and a bunch of friends and a usurer who will all testify that the bag's mine.

JUDGE Whatever you say, we must also listen to your opponent.

LITIGANT 2 (*Resentful*): May God give you health and strength, Your Honor! In this bag of mine, there's nothing but a deserted palace; a house without a door; a kennel for dogs; a school for boys; young men playing football; tents for soldiers; the palace of Shaddad son of ʿAd; a blacksmith's forge; a fisherman's net; a sad girl; and a thousand knights, friends of mine who'll testify that the bag's mine.

LITIGANT 1 (*Crying out*): Your Honor, this bag of mine's known to everyone; and nothing in it's a secret to anyone. In this bag of mine there are forts and citadels; birds and lions; men playing chess; one room; two ponies; two long spears; one tiger and two rabbits; one city and two villages; one blind man and two who can see; one priest and two deacons; one open-eyed judge and two witnesses who'll testify that the bag's mine.

JUDGE (*To the second* LITIGANT): Do *you* have anything to add?

LITIGANT 2 (*More resentful*): The Lord give you His aid, Your Honor! In this bag of mine there are coats of mail; armor plates and storerooms for arms; grazing land for sheep; orchards; vineyards, flower beds; fig and apple trees; shades and ghosts; bottles and glasses; brides, singing and weddings; noise and loud calls; friends, pals and lovers; prisons for punishment; mates to drink with; mandolins and flutes; flags and banners; boys and girls; singing women; a flint and a fire steel; Iram, the City of Colonnades;* a piece of wood and a nail; a vanguard and an army on horseback; a hundred thousand dinars; the audience hall of the mighty Persian King Anushirwan; the Egyptian city of Aswan and the Persian province of Khurasan; *and*, God save Your Honor, a thousand sharpened blades to slaughter those who make false claims.

JUDGE (*Stands up, steps forward, picks up the bag and examines it from the outside*): An ill-fated case and a pair of godless plaintiffs. Is this bag a bottomless sea? Or a new planet traveling through space? (*Dips his hand into the bag and brings out two things in succession, naming them as he does so*:) A piece of bread . . . and an olive.

CURTAIN

ACT TWO

SCENE ONE

An inner room in AL-TABRIZI*'s house. A door on the right leads to a hall, and another on the left leads outside the house. In the center there is a window with the curtain down. Upstage left is a wide sofa in front of which stands a small table with a plate on it. Upstage right stands a wardrobe, and near the window hangs a waterskin and a shelf with a few tumblers on it. Downstage right stands an Arabic folding screen; the room is generally decorated in lavish Arabic style.* ᶜALI *and* QUFFA *stand facing each other.*

QUFFA Let's settle our accounts.

ᶜALI Let's.

QUFFA How much have we gained from the merchants? How much from the King's coffers and all the rest? And what's my share of all that?

ᶜALI (*Satirically*): How much this and how much that . . . and you can't even count from one to a hundred.

QUFFA Of course I can. (*Counting on his fingers*:) One, two, three, four, five, six . . .

ᶜALI He's counting his fingers!

QUFFA To show you that I can bring you to account.

ᶜALI Show me!

QUFFA Fifty-fifty.

ᶜALI I accept. Come and share my dinner with me. (*Uncovers his plate.*)

QUFFA (*Mockingly*): Your dinner!

ᶜALI Come on, have a bite!

QUFFA No, thank you. You can have it all. I know what you eat for lunch and dinner: a piece of bread and an olive.

ᶜALI Don't belittle the beginning and the end of the world.

QUFFA (*Mockingly*): Yes, yes, I know. It starts with a piece of bread and ends with an olive.

ᶜALI An olive in the ground grows into an olive tree.

QUFFA Yes, but it won't grow into one in my stomach.

ᶜALI Because your stomach's like marshy land and your mind's like rocky ground.

QUFFA I'm happy with my mind.

ᶜALI This olive, in the stomach of Omar Khayyam, turns into blood which flows into his great heart and makes it beat with noble sentiments; and through the stom-

*Iram is a legendary Arabian figure from ancient pre-Islamic times. One story associated with him tells of how he built Iram, the City of Colonnades, near Aden as an imitation of Paradise, and how he was then, as a punishment for his pride, destroyed by a tornado and his city buried in sand. Both Iram and ᶜAd (referred to earlier) are mentioned in pre-Islamic poetry and in the Qurʾan.

ach of the illustrious Avicenna it gets woven into the very texture of his brain and inspires him with brilliant ideas. This is the way the world began and the way it ends, its starting point and its ultimate destination: an olive and a piece of bread. On them, civilization was built and over them nations have fought.

QUFFA Just keep the preaching for yourself, will you, and tell me about the money.

ʿALI Fools will always be fools! As you like! Ask what you want. (*He begins to eat.*)

QUFFA (*Bursting forth*): I want . . . a hundred thousand . . . two . . . three hundred thousand dinars, and twenty hundred thousand whole rolls of expensive material . . . silk! And ten thousand thirty . . .

ʿALI He's counting on his fingers again.

QUFFA Let's settle accounts!

ʿALI Alright, alright! Don't lose your temper.

QUFFA And one thousand five hundred twenty-one hundred . . .

ʿALI Anything you say.

QUFFA (*Panting*): And ten two hundred two thousand seventy . . .

ʿALI You'll have all that and more when my caravan arrives.

QUFFA (*Freezes for a moment, unable to believe his ears; shakes his head*): What did I hear you say?

ʿALI When my caravan arrives.

QUFFA (*Rubbing his ears*): Say that again.

ʿALI When my caravan arrives.

QUFFA What did you say?

ʿALI When my caravan arrives.

QUFFA (*Beginning to relish the joke, he shouts*): Encore! Encore!

ʿALI (*Louder still*): Wheeeen myyyy . . .

QUFFA Thief of thieves! You think you have a caravan?

ʿALI Why, didn't you know that?

QUFFA (*Incredulously*): Do you really have a caravan?

ʿALI Isn't that what we tell everybody?

QUFFA You're trying to tell *me* that now?

ʿALI Don't you believe me?

QUFFA Are you trying to tell me you have a caravan I don't know about?

ʿALI I don't know what you know, but yes, I have a caravan.

QUFFA You dare say yes! You think you can fool me, too?

ʿALI Don't you believe me?

QUFFA He wants me to lose my mind, this crazy fellow. Have you forgotten it's all a lie?

ʿALI Even *you* say I have a caravan.

QUFFA I'm a liar.

ʿALI It can't be.

QUFFA Yes, I'm a liar and the son of a liar.

ʿALI It can't be.

QUFFA But why not?

ʿALI Because it's preposterous. Think about it yourself.

QUFFA What do you mean, "preposterous?"

ʿALI "I'm a liar" is a rare sentence, because although it appears to be affirmative, it is in fact negative, as it negates truth from the speaker. You say "I'm a liar" and want the person you're speaking to to believe you and accept the fact that you're a liar. On the other hand, your statement tells him that you *are* untruthful and invites him *not* to believe you, that is, not to believe your statement that you're a liar, which means that you *are* truthful. Thus your statement "I'm a liar" can't mean that you're truthful, nor can it establish that you're a liar.

QUFFA What does that mean? That there's no money.

ᶜALI It's all written down in Aristotle.

QUFFA Iris who?

ᶜALI A great man, my friend, who stands against you.

QUFFA (*Unimpressed*): Against me? Me?

ᶜALI Yes. Do you know him?

QUFFA I've never supplied his shoes.

ᶜALI Yet the world lives by his logic.

QUFFA I've never even tasted it.

ᶜALI And runs on his laws.

QUFFA I've never bumped into them.

ᶜALI And stands firm by his ideas.

QUFFA I've never stood or sat by one.

ᶜALI No matter. Whatever you do, you have to submit to his opinion.

QUFFA He hasn't bought me as a slave.

ᶜALI And follow the dictates of his thought.

QUFFA Or even hired me.

ᶜALI But you lost your case to him.

QUFFA I know who I lost to.

ᶜALI Tell me.

QUFFA Three. The first is the judge who took away the license of my brother Abu al-Fudul, the barber, and so I had to provide for him. The second is another good-for-nothing, idle, arrogant brother, called Buqbuq; I have to provide for him too.* I ran away from the two of them only to bump into the third, you, the worst of the three.

ᶜALI No, no. You lost your case to Aristotle, who's a Greek.

QUFFA Let's settle the accounts, even if we do it in Greek!

ᶜALI It hurts me that I can't afford what you want, Kafur.

QUFFA Quffa!

ᶜALI What can I do to satisfy you?

QUFFA What did we shake the town for?

ᶜALI For its fruit to fall.

QUFFA Nothing's fallen in my lap. We had a fortune, which you in your madness gave away.

ᶜALI Why don't you start a shoemaker's shop? I'll find the money for you.

QUFFA You want me to live like a shoemaker while you live like a king?

ᶜALI Don't we share everything?

QUFFA I don't want to be your guest all my life. I want to have something of my own to do what I like with.

ᶜALI I'll give you everything you want when . . .

QUFFA Don't you dare say "the caravan." You've driven the whole city mad and now you want me to lose my wits, too.

ᶜALI Listen, Kafur, it's all my fault and I must apologize to you. The truth is I've hidden something from you until today and I want to come clean now.

QUFFA What is it?

ᶜALI I *have* a caravan.

QUFFA Liar! I invented the whole caravan thing before it even occurred to you.

ᶜALI I admit the credit is yours.

QUFFA O, dear God, please don't let me go mad!

ᶜALI Watch out for your sanity!

QUFFA Look who's talking!

ᶜALI (*Aside*): I don't know what's happened to him.

QUFFA (*Aside*): It seems I won't get anywhere with this man unless I blackmail him. (*To* ᶜALI:) So you don't want to pay? Alright! Just you wait! (*Aside*:) I'd better have a couple of drinks first. (*Leaves through the left door while watched by* ᶜALI.)

ᶜALI The man's gone out of his mind. Drink indeed! Omar Khayyam used to drink to rise high above the world, and

*"Abu al-Fudul" and "Buqbuq" are references to two other plays of Alfred Farag: *Hallaq Baghdad* (The barber of Baghdad, 1964) and *Buqbuq al-Kaslan* (Lady Buqbuq, 1965).

mystics drink to soar aloft with their spirits, but I've never seen a man like Kafur who drinks to become even more tied down to the ground. What does he drink? Something lousy, I'm sure. What really amazes me is that this shoemaker doesn't believe in philosophy, in the fact that the mind can't create something out of nothing, just as a shoemaker can't make a shoe without leather. Hasn't he seen for himself that this caravan's brought prosperity to the town before it's even arrived? Prosperity which can be seen and touched. Hasn't it created jobs with concrete results for the people: food and drink and clothes? It's like a consummated marriage which has produced real children. How on earth can nothing make something? How can that which doesn't exist give rise to material existence which the eye can see, the ear hear, and the hand touch? All this even before the caravan arrives; what will happen when it does? Believe it or not! I believe it. I must join my friends now.

He leaves through the door on the right while the PRINCESS *and her* MAID *enter from the left. They appear to carry on with a conversation begun offstage.*

PRINCESS ... And sometimes I find him strange, as if he were the king of a city I never heard of, or an amiable jinn in human form.

MAID God protect us! Are you frightened of him?

PRINCESS (*Taking no notice of her maid's words, looks through the door on the right and then resumes her speech as if under a spell*): No, no, he's rather like a mystic who sees visions. No, not that either. I feel he's a mighty prince from Baghdad, a relation of the Caliph himself.

MAID This is amazing! Do you think he changes color on purpose just to bewitch you?

PRINCESS (*Taking no notice of her maid, goes and looks through the door on the right again and then resumes her speech as if under a spell*): No, he's more like a beggar at the gate of a great city; a beggar who was once a philosopher, but because he made the king angry was forced to escape in disguise.

MAID Oh, my darling princess, you *are* head over heels in love with him. If only he *is* real!

PRINCESS (*Takes no notice of her, glances at the right door and carries on as before*): No, no, it's as if he weren't flesh and blood; as if he came from a different age, or descended from ancestors different than Adam and Eve.

MAID God save you, child! What are you saying?

PRINCESS That's why I love him, nanny. I love him for all his ways, his warmth, his trueness, his gentleness, his common sense ... for everything in him. I love him!

Enter the PRINCESS*'s* SERVANT *panting.*

SERVANT The King, Your Highness.

PRINCESS (*Preparing to receive him*): My father! (*Enter the* KING *and the* VIZIER *covering their faces with their cloaks. They uncover themselves and the* PRINCESS *throws herself into her father's arms.*) I missed you.

KING Thank you, thank you. We've come at an unsuitable time. I want this visit to remain a secret; no one should know. Can we talk privately?

The PRINCESS *waves her hand to her* MAID *and boy* SERVANT*, who leave through the door on the left.*

PRINCESS (*Fills a glass of water for her father from the waterskin*): What's the matter, father? You've made me worried. I've never seen you like this. (*Gives him the glass.*)

KING (*Drinking*): Where's your husband?

PRINCESS (*Putting the glass on the table*): In the hall playing chess with his friends.

KING Can he come in here unannounced?

PRINCESS Do you want to see him? Shall I call him?

KING No. I particularly don't want him to know I'm here. If we close the door . . .

PRINCESS Yes, if we close the door, he can't come in here unless we open for him. But why? You frighten me.

KING Close the door first and lock it with the key.

PRINCESS (*Locks the door and comes back quickly*): What's the matter, father? (*Cries on his shoulder.*)

KING Don't be upset. Speak, Minister!

VIZIER We want to learn something from you, Your Highness. Does your husband have a caravan?

PRINCESS (*Wiping her eyes*): What sort of question's that?

KING You saw me with your own eyes give him the keys to my coffers. He's spent an awful lot on the wedding; we all know that. And yet he hasn't paid me your dowry yet. He didn't give you a present on the wedding night, and he didn't give anything to your mother next morning. All the money's gone, I don't know where: alms, grants, gifts, and suchlike. Anyway, this boy's drained my coffers down to the last penny; there's nothing left. As for the caravan, we hear about it but it never turns up. We've waited long enough.

VIZIER He took everything! Everything!

PRINCESS (*Gasping*): And my dowry?

KING Your dowry indeed! What about me? How can I rule my kingdom now that I've become poorer than my subjects?

PRINCESS I don't know if I should cry or laugh.

VIZIER No one understands a man better than his wife.

KING What matters is to know.

VIZIER We want to know.

KING We must.

PRINCESS Me, too!

KING But he mustn't know we're making inquiries behind his back. We don't want to make him angry in case there *is* a caravan.

PRINCESS (*Passionately*): Father! Maybe he *is* a beggar.

KING It's not funny!

VIZIER Did you notice anything about him that made you think he might be?

PRINCESS (*With gusto*): Or maybe he's a king from Baghdad or an angel from heaven come down to test us.

KING An inspector?

VIZIER Did you notice anything to make you think he might be?

PRINCESS (*Very excited*): I feel ecstatic, yet my tears are running down. I don't know if I'm miserable or happy. I don't understand what's happened to me.

VIZIER Take it easy, Your Highness.

KING What's the matter? Did he cast a spell on her?

VIZIER Try to think with us, Your Highness. We're in a difficult situation.

KING A disaster!

VIZIER And no one but you . . .

KING Help us!

PRINCESS What can I do?

VIZIER His Majesty and I will hide somewhere . . . (*Looking around:*) Behind this curtain, on the windowsill. Call and ask him, try to pull his leg.

KING (*Aside to the* VIZIER): Why don't we go home and let the girl talk to him?

VIZIER (*Aside to the* KING): I'm not sure she isn't already in love with him. She might want to hide the truth from us.

KING What do you say to that? What are you sniggering at?

PRINCESS I'm trying to imagine you behind the curtain.

KING Really, you ought to be ashamed of yourself! Let's begin, Minister.

VIZIER Say to him . . .

PRINCESS I know what to say.

The KING *and the* MINISTER *hide behind the curtain while the* PRINCESS *opens the door and beckons to* ʿALI *with her finger.*

PRINCESS Psst! Psst! Psst! (*Sits on the sofa. Aside*:) Can it be true? (*Enter* ʿALI. *She stretches out her arms to him*:) I missed you, darling.

ʿALI (*In her arms*): And I missed your eyes.

PRINCESS You've made me forget my own parents and the whole world. You only have to say so, and I'll follow you barefoot to the farthest corner of the earth.

ʿALI I love you barefoot.

PRINCESS I would have loved you even if you were a beggar sticking out your hand outside my father's palace. I would have thrown you my handkerchief instead of alms.

ʿALI I would have raised my eyes to your window begging a glance.

PRINCESS Now that I'm your wife, I won't exchange you for the world, no matter what they say about you.

ʿALI Let them say what they like.

PRINCESS But I'm afraid.

ʿALI Do they say I don't love you?

PRINCESS They say that you're poor, that you don't have a caravan. I'm afraid.

ʿALI What are you afraid of, my love?

PRINCESS Of the merchants . . . my father . . . those who envy you . . .

ʿALI Don't be afraid.

PRINCESS If you're poor, my darling, don't hide it from me; I'm your wife. Tell me, so I can think of something to save us both. Don't worry, just tell me.

ʿALI (*He surveys the room with a hesitant look*): I don't want to hide anything from you. Yes, madame, I admit I used to be a beggar in my country. But one day, destiny led me to a house of many stories. I knocked at the door (*Begins to act the scene and the* PRINCESS *looks very amused*) and heard the landlord shout from the top floor, "Who's there?" but I didn't answer. So he came down, opened the door and asked, "What do you want?" "A favor," I said. "Follow me," he said. He kept climbing one flight of stairs after another while I panted behind until he got to the top floor. Then he said, "Why didn't you answer when I asked who was at the door?" "I was afraid you might think it wasn't worth your trouble to come down, and you'd tell me to go away," I said. "Well done!" said he. And with a broomstick (*Draws his sword and holds it by the blade*) he charged me (*Strikes with his sword, in the air and over things until he hits the curtain*) shouting, "Here's a favor, you bastard. Here's a kindness for you."

KING (*From behind the curtain*): Mmm!

The PRINCESS *gasps and raises her hand to her mouth.*

ʿALI Oh, the curtains are alive! They can feel pain! (*Puts his sword back in its sheath.*) And you feel pity for them, darling. I love you for the tenderness of your heart, for your belief that all things are alive, which is the creed of the great master, Omar Khayyam. It's something I've believed in myself since I was a boy. Yet some people think that man himself feels no pain . . . If you'll allow me, madame, I'll go back to my friends and finish that game of chess.

Exit ʿALI *waving his hand to her. The* KING *and the* VIZIER *emerge from behind the curtain, each feeling one part or another of his body. The* PRINCESS *muffles a laugh.*

KING Aaaah! I nearly let out a cry which would have betrayed us. Thank God I was able to stifle it. I don't want to make him angry in case he really has a caravan. Aaaah!

PRINCESS Dear father! You wanted me to ask him and you heard the answer.

KING What was he ranting about, Minister?

VIZIER I couldn't tell whether he was serious or joking.

PRINCESS (*Enthusiastically*): He's very entertaining, father, don't you think?

KING Shut up! Can't you see I've been beaten by your husband?

PRINCESS Don't get mad, father; it was all your minister's plan!

KING (*To the* VIZIER): What do we do now?

VIZIER Perhaps the Princess will be so kind as to ask him again.

KING No, no. I've had enough!

PRINCESS Poor father!

KING It's all your doing.

VIZIER Don't be afraid, Your Majesty. Let's hide behind the sofa this time; it should be safer.

KING (*Aside to the* VIZIER): Don't you think it would be better if we left and let her ask him?

VIZIER (*Aside to the* KING): Don't you see how infatuated she is with him?

KING (*Aside to the* VIZIER): Do you think she really loves him? I mean did *you* truly feel jealous? (*The* VIZIER *does not answer.*) That would be still another disaster. (*Crying out*:) And worst of all is the fact that now I've become poorer than my subjects. (*Pointing at the sofa*:) I'll go along with you once more.

PRINCESS If he attacks you again, I'll stop him.

KING No, my child; he'll discover our presence.

PRINCESS But I'm worried for you.

VIZIER Don't worry, I'll shield His Majesty with my own body.

KING *and* VIZIER *hide between the sofa and the wall. The* PRINCESS *beckons to* ᶜALI *through the door on the right.*

PRINCESS Psst! Psst! Psst! (*She sits on a cushion on the floor to the right of the window and waits there.*) I can't believe it. Can it . . .

Enter ᶜALI. *He goes to her cheerfully.*

ᶜALI I was nearly beaten. What's the matter, sweetheart?

PRINCESS You left too soon; already I miss talking to you. Never stay away from me, my love; never let time separate us. Oh, my heart's so full with love for you!

ᶜALI (*Sits by her on the floor*): How sweet you are!

PRINCESS I asked you a question, my darling, because I was worried about you, but you only answered in your lovely joking manner.

ᶜALI I love you when you smile and when you frown, too.

PRINCESS I want to know the truth so I can do something to protect you; I fear for your safety. Darling, are you rich or poor?

ᶜALI (*He acts out the scene while the* PRINCESS *watches enraptured*): Poor, my lady. I admit that I used to be a water carrier in the back streets of my country. I used to stagger all day long under the weight of my waterskin; on a good day I made no more than a dirham. One day when I was standing in the scorching heat crying my water to passersby, a man from Persia approached. "Give me a drink!" he says, so I fill the jug and serve him. He takes one look, shakes it, and spills it on the ground. "Give me a drink!" he says again; I fill the jug and serve him again. He takes one look, shakes it, and spills it on the ground. "Give me a drink!" he says for the third time, and for the third time I serve him and he spills the water on the ground. At that point I felt I could take no more, so I raise the waterskin above my head (*Lifts the waterskin hanging near the window*), shake it, and spill it over his head. (*Spills the water behind the sofa and flings the empty skin there.*)

KING (*From behind the sofa*): Mmm!

The PRINCESS *gasps, covering her mouth with the palm of her hand.*

ʿALI Oh my tender-hearted love! Your heart goes out for the sofa because you know it's alive and it can feel. You're a true follower of Omar Khayyam; I love you for that. Give me just one hour, my pretty one, to finish that game of chess with my friend!

Exit ʿALI *while the* KING *and the* VIZIER *emerge from behind the sofa soaking wet. The* KING *is feeling his back and moaning.*

KING Oh my back! Oh my ribs! What was he ranting about, Minister?

VIZIER To be honest, I'm still trying to make sense of what I heard.

KING I did try, Your Majesty, but it's as if he was aiming at you. Wasn't this your plan, Minister?

VIZIER If we could only have waited . . .

KING Waited! It's all right for you to say that: you didn't have your ribs smashed like me.

VIZIER Let's try again, just once more.

KING This time it'll be the death of me.

VIZIER If we hide in the closet, we should be safe.

PRINCESS The closet!

KING (*To* PRINCESS): Does that fellow never talk seriously?

PRINCESS I'll try my best, father.

KING (*As though talking to himself*): What's happening to us? (*To Vizier*:) This is the last time. (*As though to himself again*:) What sort of trap have we fallen into?

The KING *and the* VIZIER *hide inside the closet, while the* PRINCESS *beckons to* ʿALI *through the door on the right.*

PRINCESS Psst! Psst! Psst! (*Sits on a cushion below the sofa. Aside*:) I wouldn't be surprised if he can hear everything that goes on here from the other room. Perhaps he really is a nice *jinn* driven here by fate to take my father's money and give it away to the people. (*Muffles her laughter.*)

Enter ʿALI *merrily.*

ʿALI I admit to you, my lady, that I used to be the executioner of the Vizier Zafir Bihram himself. (*Draws out his sword to the* PRINCESS*'s consternation.*) I'm a soft-hearted man really, but I had to make a living. I used to stand at his door like this, and every now and then he'd shout to me, pointing at one man or another, "Off with his head!" Then I'd shut my eyes, feeling my head spinning, and run berserk, striking with my sword here and there while he watched me laughing. (*Waves the sword in the direction of the closet and the* PRINCESS *screams out.*) Darling! You fear for the closet! Now I know that I love you for the softness of your heart and your belief that even wood's alive. I was on the point of winning that game of chess, so allow me, queen of my heart, to go and do just that.

Exit ʿALI *hurriedly. The wardrobe opens and the* KING *comes out, his hand on his belly, the* VIZIER *following.*

KING The toilet! Where's the toilet?

PRINCESS Are you all right, father?

KING It's all because of you. The toilet!

PRINCESS This way, father.

VIZIER Didn't I tell you, Your Majesty?

KING Not one more word. Don't make me feel any worse than I already do. The toilet, girl!

Exeunt all three in a hurry. Enter QUFFA *after a while, staggering. He shades his eyes with his hand and scans the room before walking in.*

QUFFA I saw the King himself stealing away from this room followed by his daughter and minister. The King was running in an undignified way. Why should he want to come here secretly? I bet he's beginning to have doubts; I know I'm not going to have what's mine from my despotic master unless I threaten him with telling the King. I must find him now and strike terror in his heart. Ha! I'll make him pass everything on to me and thank me for it. Everything, even the girl. Where is he? (*Shades his eyes with his hand and scans the room.*) Not here. (*Takes out of his pocket a Punch and Judy puppet, which he manipulates and speaks to in a Punch and Judy voice:*) Tabriiiiiizi! (*Mimicking* ᶜALI*'s voice:*) What do you want, Kafur? (*In puppet's voice:*) My name's Quffa. (*In* ᶜALI*'s voice:*) No, your name's Kafur. (*In puppet's voice:*) Quffa, I said. (*In* ᶜALI*'s voice:*) Kafur! (*Puppet:*) Take this then. (*Smacks the puppet.*) Aah! You dare beat me! Just you wait! (*Laughs.*) I'll drive him mad. Where is he? I must go and find him. (*Puppet:*) Tabriiiiiizi!

He leaves through the door on the right, while the PRINCESS *and her* MAID *enter through the left.*

PRINCESS (*Mirthful and excited*): I'm going to tell you a very important secret, nanny, but you must swear never to tell anybody, not even in your last words to your children on your deathbed.

MAID God protect us! What is it, mistress?

PRINCESS Swear!

MAID As God is my witness, mistress, your secret will be safe with me. I'd sooner die than tell anybody.

PRINCESS (*Elatedly*): My husband, ᶜAli Janah al-Tabrizi . . . isn't rich.

MAID How come, mistress? He gives like a king.

PRINCESS (*Overjoyed*): No, no, no. He only pretends to be rich.

MAID Dear oh dear! And the caravan?

PRINCESS (*Laughing with the abandon of a child*): He hasn't got a caravan.

MAID God almighty! But . . . your father's money and the merchants' . . .

PRINCESS (*At the peak of her excitement*): They won't get one dirham back.

MAID What a disaster! If they found out . . .

PRINCESS They won't find out. I listened to him just as they did, but I understood what they couldn't understand, what they won't in their hopeful bankruptcy! Let them wait and hope. (*Bursts out laughing.*) It won't do them any harm.

MAID But they might hurt him.

PRINCESS They'll never be able to face up to their loss and give up hope.

MAID Amazing! This is even stranger than fiction.

PRINCESS Didn't I tell you? It is like a story, lovelier than a story.

MAID Unbelievable! They'll write about this in books, mistress, and poets will sing of these happenings to men in coffeehouses.

PRINCESS (*Anxiously*): Will they mention my name in the story, nanny?

MAID Your name, your father's name, your . . .

PRINCESS (*Worriedly, as she sits on the sofa*): What if they just call me "the princess" and forget my real name?

MAID No, no, no. Poets mention everybody's name. Those are the rules.

PRINCESS (*Rolls gleefully on the sofa*): My darling's name . . .

MAID Someone's coming.

PRINCESS Shush!

MAID (*Her finger on her mouth*): Shhh!

The PRINCESS *falls into the arms of her* MAID *laughing. Enter* QUFFA *staggering. They watch him with alarm. He shades his eyes with his hand and scans the room until he sees them.*

QUFFA (*Aside*): There's the master. I'm going to blackmail him now. I used to be a shoemaker and a tramp, never certain where my day's dinner was coming from, but I never resented it. Now I'm wallowing in the luxury of this palace like a lord, but I'm full of resentment. I haven't got a single dirham in my pocket. I must become the richest man in this city; I won't settle for less. (*Loudly*:) Tabrizi! (*Shades his eyes again, trying to locate the two alarmed women. Points his finger at them*:) You! Master!

MAID (*Pounding her chest*): He's drunk!

QUFFA (*Rubs his ears in bewilderment*): Isn't this the mistress? (*Shades his eyes again and draws near them. They scream.*) Aha! It's the mistress and her maid. Never mind. I'm going to sit here. (*Sits on the floor.*)

PRINCESS Get out, Kafur! What are you doing here?

QUFFA Even my mistress won't call me by my name!

PRINCESS What do you want?

QUFFA I want my due. I've come to demand my due from the master.

PRINCESS Go to him in the hall.

QUFFA No. What I want is here, and here I'll stay to protect it until the master comes.

PRINCESS And what is it?

QUFFA Half of you! (*Laughs wantonly.*)

The PRINCESS *and her* MAID *run away in horror: one leaving by the right door and the other by the left door.*

QUFFA (*Regaining his self-control*): Where did they go? (*Shades his eyes and looks around for them.*) Where did they hide? I hope they haven't gone for help. I'm going to hide myself behind the screen. Where's it gone?

He staggers his way to the screen. Enter the PRINCESS *and* ʿALI.

PRINCESS He was here. He was very rude to me. He must be killed . . . killed . . . killed.

QUFFA (*Aside, still behind the screen*): I'm done for.

ʿALI Calm down, my darling.

PRINCESS Is this the man you call a brother and more than a brother?

ʿALI What can I do now? Maybe he's gone. Calm down.

PRINCESS (*Crying*): I've always been so good to him for your sake.

ʿALI (*Comforting her*): Take it easy, my love.

QUFFA (*Showing the puppet from behind the screen and talking in its voice*): I'm here.

The PRINCESS *starts and then laughs.*

ʿALI What are you doing there, Kafur?

QUFFA (*In puppet's voice*): Eating bread and olives.

ʿALI Come out, Kafur.

QUFFA (*In puppet's voice*): Maaaster!

I'm reduced in size now. Will you give me one fourth of what you owe me?

ᶜALI *throws a cushion at the puppet. It hits* QUFFA, *and he falls.*

QUFFA Oh my head!

PRINCESS Kafur, are you angry or something?

QUFFA What a question!

PRINCESS Did you cross him, ᶜAli?

ᶜALI What is it you want?

QUFFA I want to know how it all began, how I've come to this pretty state of affairs.

ᶜALI Don't you remember? You called me.

QUFFA I?

ᶜALI Yes. You said, "Is there no hospitable man in this city to invite a shoemaker whose feet are worn with travel and who's in pain?" I asked who was at the gate; there you were, standing in front of me.

QUFFA I stepped with my own feet into the trap.

ᶜALI Don't be ungrateful, Kafur.

QUFFA What is there to be grateful for? What did I get out of this spree? Nothing. It's all been like the table in your garden.

ᶜALI What do you want now?

QUFFA I want you to appoint me king of this city. There.

ᶜALI You're a shoemaker. What do you know about a king's job?

QUFFA Alright, make it a chief merchant. Look, either king or chief merchant. Or a prince. Make me a prince. Is that too much for me?

PRINCESS How can he make you a prince, Kafur? He doesn't have the power to do that.

QUFFA Let him name me ᶜAli Janah al-Tabrizi or Muhammad Janah al-Tabrizi, or even Hasan Janah al-Asfahani . . .

ᶜALI Call yourself whatever you like. What have I got to do with it?

QUFFA Don't call me Kafur. *You* called me Kafur.

ᶜALI Is that what you want?

QUFFA No.

ᶜALI What do you want?

QUFFA To get drunk.

ᶜALI You're going to ruin your health drinking too much.

QUFFA (*Aside*): He's trying to squelch me again indirectly. He's pretending to be master of the situation. (*To* ᶜALI:) Will you please get out of my way, Master? I want to go to the inn.

ᶜALI Nobody's standing in your way.

QUFFA Light the way for me please, master, will you?

ᶜALI Come on. (*Takes down a hanging lantern and leads the way.*)

PRINCESS Don't let him drink too much. Poor Kafur!

CURTAIN

SCENE TWO

The empty marketplace at night. QUFFA *is alone.*

QUFFA It's not yet midnight and the inns are already closed. I've hardly had two or three drinks. What sort of city is this? Come back, Baghdad! I miss you, city of Harun al-Rashid, you who glitter in the night. What brought us here? Ah, the flying horse! The Rakhkh* of Tabrizi son of Sinbad, my master. The master I bought with my own capital! The giver of great banquets! (*Raises the puppet and*

*A huge fictitious bird from the *Thousand and One Nights.*

speaks in its voice:) "Try this kebab, which is too good even for a king's table." (*In his own voice*:) Not to mention Khayyam's wine! (*Laughs wantonly. In puppet's voice*:) "Drink and don't be shy!" (*In his own voice*:) What a nightmare! To think I followed him all the way, as though sleep-walking, from Baghdad to China! How could this happen to me? But it's not too late yet. He may have fooled the King, the Vizier, the Chief Merchant, and the Princess, but not me. Not Quffa! He'll find me awake to his tricks. Wake up, Quffa! (*Slaps himself.*) Wake up! You've slept for two months. What a fool, the Chief Merchant! (*Laughing wantonly.*) He lost his fortune down to the last dirham, and his house too. He's been reduced to nothing, but he still has hope, the idiot, and he's still (*Laughing more boisterously*) waiting for the cara . . . cara . . . caravan. Wake up, Chief Merchant! Chief Meeerchaant! Get up, have dinner with me! You must be hungry, now that you're bankrupt. Come to my table. Here kebab's served whose likes no royal table has seen. Don't forget the pancakes with ambergris. (*In puppet's voice*:) "Take this one from me, don't say no." (*In his own voice*:) Eat and don't be shy because next we're going to drink wine (*Whispering in puppet's voice as though revealing an important secret*) "stolen from the cellar of Omar Khayyam himself."

Enter a POLICEMAN. *He stands on one side watching* QUFFA *hesitantly.*

POLICEMAN (*Aside*): Is he mad or drunk?

QUFFA Wake up, Tabrizi! Come and eat! You've eaten everyone up, but *not* me. I'm not going to be a shoemaker again. Either I become the richest man in this city or I'll ruin you.

POLICEMAN (*Aside*): Drunk or mad?

QUFFA The idea makes the mind boggle! The city's bustling with new business; everybody's opened up a shop except me, even though it was *my* money which started all this. Where's the debt notebook? (*Searches in his clothes.*)

POLICEMAN (*Aside*): He frightens me. But he's in my area; if he does wake people up, they'll complain; I'll be held responsible.

QUFFA I can't find it. It doesn't matter. My four pockets all testify that it was my money which started everything. I'll be your ruin, Tabrizi! (*Calling at the top of his voice*:) Tabrizi! (*Raising his hand with the puppet and speaking in its voice*:) Tabriiizi! (*Laughs. The* POLICEMAN *walks up to him. They collide;* QUFFA *falls. He looks keenly at the* POLICEMAN*'s shoes. In his own voice*:) Who are you? Ah! You must be the Aristotle who stands against me!

POLICEMAN (*Aside, trembling*): He *is* mad.

QUFFA (*Making another guess*): No, no. You must be the jinn imprisoned in that indivisible particle of the King's gem, the servant of anyone who sets you free.

POLICEMAN (*Alarmed*): God protect us!

QUFFA (*Reading the* POLICEMAN*'s shoes more closely*): No, no, no. You're the night patrol. Now I know you. Come on, let's wreak havoc together. (*Jumps to his feet and pulls the policeman away by the hand.*) Take me to your boss. I've got an important confession to make. It's a confession that will immediately be brought to the King's notice, and you'll be rewarded. (*Raises the puppet and assumes its voice*:) Quiiiickly! (*Exeunt.*)

CURTAIN

SCENE THREE

The market. Upstage left stand two poles to which ʿALI *is tied by the wrists. The executioner, who is sitting on the ground with his sword across his knees, is fast asleep. Around the stage are some guardsmen. Enter* QUFFA. *He looks at* ʿALI *and goes out again as though unable to see his friend in his predicament. He enters again and stands there not knowing what to do.*

ʿALI Kafur?

QUFFA Quffa, master! Do remember, please.

ʿALI You went out last night without dinner. Where did you have your dinner?

QUFFA (*Very touched*): At the King's, master.

ʿALI What did he give you for dinner?

QUFFA Thirty dirhams, master.

ʿALI And did you eat them?

QUFFA No. I betrayed you. The money was your price.

ʿALI Only thirty?

QUFFA (*Protesting*): They kept saying to me, "You've taken a lot already. Consider yourself lucky."

ʿALI And you didn't have dinner?

QUFFA It breaks my heart, master, that I betrayed you. I sold you; now your blood will be on me.

ʿALI Kafur, didn't you always accuse me of not sharing with you?

QUFFA Don't remind me, master.

ʿALI Didn't you ask the King to give you what was due to you and divide everything between us?

QUFFA (*Excitedly*): Insult me, master, spit on me, do anything, but don't add to my misery with those words.

ʿALI Why should I insult you?

QUFFA Because I've been your death.

ʿALI It wasn't you exactly.

QUFFA Yes, it was. I was totally drunk.

ʿALI No, it was *they* who decided to give up hope.

QUFFA But I was the one who told. They even sent for the Minister and the Chief Merchant in the middle of the night. They questioned me for hours; I told them everything, from the very beginning and at great length, from the moment we had lunch at your mansion in Baghdad . . .

ʿALI (*Reminding him*): And got drunk.

QUFFA And got drunk.

ʿALI Did you tell them you got drunk after only two glasses?

QUFFA Yes, the King was very surprised.

ʿALI Why?

QUFFA That I got drunk.

ʿALI He doesn't know what it's like. I can assure you one glass of my wine would've got him drunk.

QUFFA Amazing! Must everyone who tastes it get drunk?

ʿALI Where are the workers and shopkeepers, Kafur? It's opening time, but no one's turned up.

QUFFA Don't you see the soldiers? Today all workers and poor people are to stay indoors on the King's orders. Because they love you.

ʿALI But you're free to go around, Kafur!

QUFFA I'm the one who sold you. Everywhere I go they smile at me.

ʿALI Listen, Kafur. Will you do me a favor?

QUFFA At your service, master.

ʿALI There are a few things I want you to do for me.

QUFFA You only have to ask.

ʿALI Go to the sculptor, and ask him to build a marble mausoleum for me . . .

QUFFA A marble mausoleum.

ʿALI It must be expensive and inlaid. Something suitable, you know . . .

QUFFA I'll make sure of it myself.

ʿALI Then go to the engraver . . .

QUFFA The engraver.

ʿALI Tell him to carve in gold, on the mausoleum . . .

QUFFA Yes?

ʿALI "An olive tree grows from one olive."

QUFFA "An olive tree" . . . (*Searching in his pockets.*) Wait until I write it down, master, I might forget. There! (*Takes out his notebook and leafs through it. Looks at* ʿALI *and at the notebook alternately and undecidedly, and finally makes up his mind.*) What about your account, master? Three hundred and two dinars, and some change . . . If you remember . . .

ʿALI Write down that sentence first.

QUFFA (*Writing*): "An olive tree" . . .

ʿALI Next go to the judge.

QUFFA The judge.

ʿALI Ask him to come here and bring two witnesses.

QUFFA Two witnesses! What do you want the judge and two witnesses for, master?

ʿALI To make a will.

QUFFA No need. They've stripped you of everything.

ʿALI I want to tell you, but I'm afraid you'll be angry.

QUFFA Nothing can make me angry with you now, my friend.

ʿALI Swear first that you won't be angry.

QUFFA I swear by almighty God that I won't be angry. Now tell me.

ʿALI I want to bequeath my caravan.

QUFFA (*Dumbfounded; spins round himself and hits his head with his two fists*): This guy's driven me out of my mind. Help me, O God!

ʿALI You see, didn't I say you'd be angry?

QUFFA (*Exercising self-control*): No, no, it's all right.

ʿALI Go, and do as I said.

QUFFA I'm going. (*Leaves hurriedly, then returns walking very slowly. Looks touched.*) It hurts me to leave you like this, master. Are you sad like me?

ʿALI Yes.

QUFFA Feeling sorry for yourself?

ʿALI No. I feel sorry because they're killing hope in you, poor man.

QUFFA I hate to think what's going to happen to me after you leave, master. I'll regret this for the rest of my life. There must be a solution. I loved this man. Very much. What can I do? What can I do? (*Exit.*)

Enter the PRINCESS *and the* MAID. *The* PRINCESS *immediately turns her back on* ʿALI.

PRINCESS You talk to him, nanny. I can't bear to look at him like this.

MAID What shall I say to him?

PRINCESS Ask him how he feels, if he's sad.

ʿALI I never asked anybody for anything. They all gave of their own free will.

PRINCESS (*Crying*): This must be a practical joke. I'll go to my father and ask him to stop it. How can they kill my husband without asking me first?

ʿALI Remind him that he gave me the keys to his coffers of his own free will.

PRINCESS I declare here and now, my darling, that I waive my right to a dowry and a wedding present.

ʿALI As a matter of fact, I'm waiting for the judge to come, to bequeath part of my caravan to you.

MAID (*Aside to the* PRINCESS): He still hasn't repented.

PRINCESS Yes, yes. There's no doubt that everything in the world is alive and can feel pain, that the indivisible particle of anything is just a small jar containing a dangerous jinn, and that ᶜAli Janah al-Tabrizi has a caravan.

MAID (*Aside to the* PRINCESS): God preserve your mind, mistress!

PRINCESS Yes, everything he says is true, but we're narrow-minded. We can't understand him. (*Facing* ᶜALI:) I believe you, ᶜAli.

ᶜALI This gives meaning to everything.

MAID (*Aside to the* PRINCESS): Yesterday didn't you say he was poor?

PRINCESS Yes. That was yesterday, today is today. Just this once, let imagination rule the city!

MAID (*Aside to the* PRINCESS): I never thought imagination and reality were the same!

PRINCESS That's because you're stupid . . . like my father. I'll go to him . . . I'll scream at him . . .

Exit followed by the MAID. *She nearly collides with the* CHIEF MERCHANT *and the* MERCHANT *as they enter.*

CHIEF MERCHANT (*Aside to the* MERCHANT): Do you think it would be right to end what little hope we still have by killing this man, just for revenge?

MERCHANT (*Firmly*): Yes.

CHIEF MERCHANT Isn't it possible, my friend . . .

MERCHANT (*Interrupting him* ◻*rmly*): No, it isn't. We've made certain of that; it's all over.

CHIEF MERCHANT Shouldn't we wait?

MERCHANT And give him another chance to make fun of us?

CHIEF MERCHANT I've lost my money; now you want me to lose hope as well. Can't you understand?

MERCHANT Watch your language!

CHIEF MERCHANT (*Bewildered*): How can I explain it to you?

MERCHANT (*Aside, pointing at the* EXECUTIONER): And this bastard sleeps! On your feet, boy! (*Pokes him. The* EXECUTIONER *rises, alarmed.*) How dare you sleep! Do you want one of his friends to come and set him free?

EXECUTIONER Nobody came this way, sir. I'm awake.

MERCHANT If you don't want to lose them, keep your eyes open!

Enter QUFFA *in disguise, wearing a cloak, a beard, and a huge turban.*

QUFFA (*Aside, adjusting the beard round his chin*): This is the solution. I must take a risk to save my master. (*In a coarse, authoritative voice*:) Citizens of the city, is there with you a royal personage who's come sightseeing to your city, whose name is Prince ᶜAli Janah al-Tabrizi?

CHIEF MERCHANT (*Anxiously*): Yes, yes. Who are you?

QUFFA I'm the custodian of his caravan that's traveling behind him.

CHIEF MERCHANT and MERCHANT (*In the same breath*): Who?

QUFFA (*Startled by their scream, he leaps away from them. Continues in the same coarse voice*): What crazy city is this? Didn't he tell you about his caravan?

CHIEF MERCHANT and MERCHANT Yes, but we didn't believe it.

QUFFA (*In his coarse voice*): Because you're mean-minded. Show me the way to his mansion.

CHIEF MERCHANT, MERCHANT, and EXECUTIONER (*In the same breath*): His mansion!

QUFFA (*Startled by their scream, he leaps aside. Continues in his affected voice*): Why do they just repeat my words like madmen? Where's your King? I'll ask him. (*Aside, in his natural voice*:) I must frighten them some more . . .

CHIEF MERCHANT (*Aside to the* MERCHANT): What shall we do?

MERCHANT (*Aside to the* CHIEF MERCHANT, *bewildered*): We must make sure . . .

CHIEF MERCHANT How thick-headed you are! (*Hitting the* EXECUTIONER *with his fist*:) Hurry, idiot! Set the master free! (*Both the* EXECUTIONER *and the* CHIEF MERCHANT *race to* ʿALI. *The first cuts him loose with his sword, while the latter prostrates himself at his feet.*) O great master, I bring you good news and hope for a good reward . . .

MERCHANT (*Catches up with them; hits the* EXECUTIONER *with his fist*): Hurry up, idiot! (*To* ʿALI:) O, master! Your Highness! Your Majesty . . .

QUFFA (*Joins them and pretends to be shocked at the sight of* ʿALI. *Speaks in his affected coarse voice*): What do I see? Is that you, master? Who did this to you? The Chief Merchant? The Minister? The King? No matter who, this city must be razed to the ground. Oh, master, master! Don't you know, scum of the earth, that my name is Hasan the-Evil-on-the-Road, my master's servant, and that I'm called that because I strike sooner than I speak?

CHIEF MERCHANT (*Imploringly*): No, please, no. Nobody did anything. Please, try to understand.

MERCHANT (*Goes to* QUFFA *and tries to placate him*): Don't upset yourself, please, sir. We've all been his servants and even less than his servants. You say the caravan is . . .

QUFFA (*Harshly*): My master!

EXECUTIONER Don't fret, Your Honor. His Highness only wanted to have some fresh air, and there he is enjoying the highest respect from everyone.

*ʿ*ALI *comes forward rubbing his wrists. They all bow to him repeatedly.* QUFFA *takes him aside.*

CHIEF MERCHANT And the caravan . . . is it on its way?

QUFFA (*Signals him to stay where he is; in his affected voice*:) You stay where you are! (*In his natural voice, aside to* ʿALI:) Master, we must escape at once. I'm Quffa.

ʿALI (*Aside to* QUFFA): What's delayed the caravan?

QUFFA (*He looks around making sure that no one is too near; aside*): What can I say to him? (*Aside to* ʿALI:) Listen, my friend, if we hang around for one minute longer, bandits will get to the caravan before we do. Hurry!

ʿALI Bandits?

QUFFA Yes. Don't hold us back, please. (*To the* CHIEF MERCHANT *in his coarse voice*:) Two strong horses right away!

CHIEF MERCHANT The police have the best. Hey, soldier! Fetch three horses quickly! And you! Go to His Majesty at once, wake him up and tell him the good news. (*Exeunt two soldiers, running. Enter the* PRINCESS *and her* MAID. *To the* PRINCESS:) The caravan is here, Your Highness; we're going to meet it.

QUFFA (*In his affected voice*): Not you. Only the two of us. The master must meet his caravan alone first and make sure everything's all right.

PRINCESS (*Excited*): My husband! (*Throwing herself in his arms*:) Take me with you.

ʿALI Yes, we must go together, all three of us.

MERCHANT Would you mind if we follow at a distance?

QUFFA (*In his harsh, affected voice*): Not one!

PRINCESS (*To her* MAID): Hurry to the palace and tell my father.

MAID If only someone could explain to me what's going on.

Enter a SOLDIER.

SOLDIER The horses are ready, Your Highness.

They prepare to leave. The people of the city flood the stage, waving their hands to the three riders. The scene suddenly freezes into a painting.

CURTAIN

AN AFTERWORD BY THE PLAYWRIGHT

I derived the story of al-Tabrizi and Quffa from three separate tales in the *Thousand and One Nights*, "The Imaginary Table," "The Bag," and "Maᶜruf the Shoemaker." The first portrays a rich youth who plays a prank on a guest of his who had set much store by his generosity, while the second shows a man who fell prey to the fantastic illusion that the whole world had so shrunk that it was contained in a small bag whose owner he was. As for the third tale, it centers on a poor shoemaker who, traveling in a foreign land, seeks to save himself the humiliation of begging by posing as a wealthy and generous man, with the result that he is showered with presents and loans from those who place their hopes in his so-called wealth and generosity.

Although the three tales are widely spaced in the *Nights* and seemingly different in their appeal and purpose, yet the thought haunted me that they were in fact connected. For each of the three protagonists was naturally inclined to delude himself and others, in a very convincing manner, into believing a total fiction. Now delusion is an act which emanates from a great human faculty, amazing in its intense diversity: imagination. With this faculty, people can deal with a mere symbol as though it were the thing itself. Maps become lands, seas, and mountains; figures and equations are transformed into the very objects they stand for; and the creations of art affect us as if they were real life, thanks to imagination. Yet this delusion, which people practice so naturally and without thinking in their daily life, is in fact multifaceted. We sometimes describe it as an artistic talent, sometimes as deception, or even madness, according to the intention of its practitioner, or rather what we make out to be the intention of its practitioner. It may be appropriate to remark here that some people consider acting an art, while others can see nothing in it but frivolity. Others still think it is a kind of deception.

Let us, however, begin at the beginning. Who is ᶜAli Janah al-Tabrizi? And who is Quffa? I could never picture either of them living in a particular city at a specific time, as dramatis personae, whether fictitious or historical, are normally represented. In this they are probably even different from their cousin, Abu al-Fudul, in *The Barber of Baghdad*, as I have made him myself, and it seems to me that if we wished to issue an identity card to either ᶜAli or Quffa, we would have to record their place of birth as the *Thousand and One Nights*, and their date of birth as "one night." By doing so, we should be able as actors, producers, viewers or readers to avoid picturing either character in a realistic way.

For how I see them on the stage is devoid of any realistic projection. Nor should this conflict with their being "real" characters. Just as a dream is real, even though it never happened in reality, fantasies and feelings are real in spite of never existing.

So it appears appropriate that the atmosphere for this play should be drawn from the world of folktales, whether for presentation of character, movement, decor, costumes, or anything else. For a realistically inspired production will, to my mind, inevitably bring the play from its soaring heights, back down to earth. In that case, this charming fiction which derives beauty from its folktale character will turn into a realistic and tawdry story about a confidence trickster.

Allow me to say a few things here about the caravan, inappropriate as it is to slit open the chest of a beautiful tropical bird to dissect its heart. What encourages me to perpetrate this monstrosity is the way we have become accustomed to subject everything to analysis and interpretation, to such an extent that all the poets' beautiful creations have been driven into bleak laboratories and killed with explication and exegesis. And not even painting and music have been spared this.

Tabrizi's caravan and the expectations of those who believed him were, to my mind, nothing but a mould in which they cast old and pressing longings; a hope to which their hearts clung. One might argue that it is similar to the expectations of scientists in modern times vis-à-vis technological advance, or the hopes of ordinary people for the achievement of permanent world peace which will lead to the money lavished on defense and war being used instead to provide welfare for all humanity. Yes, the caravan will come; it will be man's fair reward for his arduous struggles in war and peace. It is the lush oasis behind the mountain; it is hope.

Possibly al-Tabrizi exploited this hope in an unscrupulous manner or Quffa capitalized on it with the cleverness and unrestrained license typical of a folk entertainer who seeks to punish the rich and help the poor, poking fun all the time, together with ʿAli, at those around them, until they finally fall victim to their own intrigues. For after a while we find Tabrizi beginning to believe the very illusions he had created to delude others with; he always had the propensity anyway. He thus joins wholeheartedly the ranks of his "poor friends," and it is this which turns Quffa against him.

Perhaps I am not the most suited or indeed the person most entitled to draw the line between the reformer and the trickster, or the actor and the madman, in al-Tabrizi's character, but if I may be forgiven the observation, I would like to record that I have noticed, with no small astonishment, that we normally forgive fabrications of the imagination when they assume the mantle of art or humor; we even delight in them. However, our delight suddenly evaporates when the prank touches our purse. Take, for instance, the street entertainer. Does he not see cheerful, laughing faces while he performs? Doesn't this encourage him to stick out his hat, only to be shocked at the sudden and unjustified fading of his audience's smiles?

Let us at any rate bring an end to this digression which I let myself be lured into. It is my belief that any analysis or interpretation given above is but a tentative attempt at measuring imagination, which is essentially immeasurable. These two, al-Tabrizi and Quffa, and their adventures with life, both in their folk origins and with my humble additions, are a beautiful dream which thrilled me, and which I wanted others to be thrilled by. The tale lifted me up, I wanted it to lift others up. It is a vision sprung from a childish whim in my soul; I wanted to stir up the child in other souls, because of its sweetness, its wild imagination, and the love, gaiety, and beauty that shine from it. It was also my intention to cast their story in a folkloric mould and preserve their purely Arab character.

If I may raise one last point: a thousand years ago when the human mind conceived the tales of the *Nights*, and even earlier, thousands of years before the birth of socialist thought, man had always dreamed, in his playful and sober moments alike, of social justice. How can the hungry not dream of abundant food? How can the deprived not imagine a world free of deprivation? Man's conscience has always been awake to the lack of equilibrium in reality and always sought to register his protest in the fashion of his times. It is my contention that the folk author of these tales from the *Nights* must have dreamed of justice, just as the author of the adventures of Robin Hood did, since both story cycles are fiction, but desirable in reality.

Thus the folk author created the many threads from which al-Tabrizi's character is woven: adventurer, tramp, wealthy man, intelligent, daring, mirthful, wasteful, smart, imaginative, actor, man absorbed in his own world, lover of life and beauty, and seeker after justice. In a similar fashion he must also have made the other threads from which the characters of the many craftsmen in the *Nights* are spun, including that of Quffa, who figures as a satirist, tramp, worldly wise man, realist, lover of life and merriment, and owner of a great heart and simple dreams.

This is an admission of my artistic indebtedness to the author of the *Thousand and One Nights*. It is he who should be credited for any love that this strange pair inspires in the reader. It is also he who is responsible for the princess's tender heart opening up to her gallant knight.

ᶜALI SALIM

The Comedy of Oedipus

YOU'RE THE ONE WHO KILLED THE BEAST

Translated by
Pierre Cachia
and Desmond O'Grady

ʿAli Salim is well known in Egypt as the author of a number of extremely popular comedies. In such a context, the title *The Comedy of Oedipus: You're the One Who Killed the Beast* (*Inta 'l-li Qatalt al-Wahsh*) is intentionally ironic, not only because the work is really more akin to a tragicomedy but also because the Greek version of the Oedipus story is not utilized. The site of the play is Egyptian Thebes, and at the beginning of the play Oedipus is an ordinary citizen. He volunteers to solve the riddle of the Sphinx, the beast that is besetting the city, provided he is made king and can marry Queen Jocasta. Having solved the riddle, become King, and married the Queen, he finds himself beset by all the propaganda and publicity apparatus of the modern ruler. Officials miraculously discover that he is no mere mortal; radio songs and television miniseries recount the story of his "killing the beast," a slogan that becomes a rallying cry for the entire city. All of this allows the play's director to inject some fast-paced multimedia presentations into the action. Furthermore, the implications of these developments within the play would clearly not have been lost on an Egyptian audience that had become inured to the public security measures of the government during President Nasser's era. The Queen, however, is far from satisfied with her new husband and plots to get rid of him. The chance comes with the appearance of a second beast. Oedipus tells the people that they must learn to be self-reliant, since he will not be with them forever. When the beast kills all those who go out to fight it and a thwarted Oedipus comes to realize that his people will not acknowledge his mortality, he shuffles off the stage to fight this second beast alone. President Nasser died in 1970, the year this play was published. The total reliance of "the city" on the "King," the callous way in which the needs of the people are manipulated by the "King's" officials, the resulting disillusion and failure to accept responsibility, and other themes in this intensely political play present a telling commentary on the course of the Egyptian revolution.

R. A.

THE COMEDY OF OEDIPUS

You're the One Who Killed the Beast

CHARACTERS

OEDIPUS
A young man whose precise provenance is unknown, living in Thebes

JOCASTA
The Queen of Thebes

HORIMHEB
High Priest of Amon and President of the University of Thebes

ONAH
President of the Chamber of Commerce and of the Municipal Council of Thebes

AWALIH
Chief of Police in Thebes

CREON
Commander of the Guard in Thebes

TIRESIAS
The same personage, with the same well-known characteristics, as in ancient Greek literature

CHORUS
Of Theban inhabitants

EXTRAS

THE COMEDY OF OEDIPUS

You're the One Who Killed the Beast

ACT 1

The Scene: *Thebes—the Egyptian, not the Greek Thebes. Its high ramparts, on to which the populace has climbed to watch in great apprehension something taking place at a distance. On the left is the balcony of the pharaonic temple of Thebes, around which are some ram-headed sphinxes, as if guarding the access to it. All around the place are semicircular gradated stone benches, and in the center is a round stone table with four seats round it—these are reserved for sessions of the Municipal Council, the stone benches being for the inhabitants of Thebes. To the right and at the front sit two persons,* OEDIPUS *and his friend* KAMI, *engrossed in a peaceful game of chess. From the depths of the stage, which is bathed in soft lights, comes* TIRESIAS *leaning on a stick. He advances to the front of the stage, where he becomes clearly visible.*

The Time: *A long time, a very long time ago.*

TIRESIAS Gentlemen—you who live in this city, let me tell you the story of another city. The story of Thebes—Thebes, the bride of the Nile, the capital of the ancient world; Thebes of the great temples, of flourishing trade . . . The Thebes of today is wretched and sad. For the first time in its long life, poverty and misery have cramped my beautiful city. (*After a moment of silence*:) At a spot not far from Thebes, on the only way to the lands of the North, there has appeared a strange beast. It is said to have the head of a beautiful woman and the body of an enormous animal. They call it "The Sphinx." This beast poses a riddle to travelers and kills those who do not know the answer. During the last three months, it has done away with all the men in the caravans coming to Thebes by land, and those coming by way of the mighty Nile. Many have ventured out to solve the riddle and earn the prize, but none have returned. Now, at last, Professor Ptah has gone—the Professor of Creative Rational Studies and Surgeon to the Royal Skull . . . (*At the other end of the stage,* OEDIPUS *is speaking with his friend.*)

OEDIPUS And the Municipal Council has set the prize at . . . how much?

TIRESIAS (*Continuing*): Fifty thousand gold Theban pounds is what Professor Ptah will get if he solves the riddle. (TIRESIAS *exits quietly. At the same time the Queen,* JOCASTA, *appears on the balcony.*)

JOCASTA (*Calling*): Creon!

CREON (*Answering from his place on the ramparts*): Yes, my Lady?

JOCASTA Has he got there?

CREON He's on his way, my Lady. (*Voices rise among the populace: "He's there! He's there!"*)

ONAH (*Raising his voice*): He's there, my Lady, he's there! He's standing before the beast thinking, clutching his head . . .

OEDIPUS (*Quietly*): Can't he think unless he's clutching his head?

Voices are raised among the people to encourage Professor Ptah.

VOICES Speak, Ptah, speak! Talk! Solve the riddle! He's about to speak! He's going to talk! (*There is a sudden wild shout among the people, then a deep silence.*)

A MAN (*Wailing*): The beast has got him by the neck!

CREON He's dragged him behind the hill . . . We can't see him.

A MAN An arm! An arm was thrown in the air!

ANOTHER A leg!

A MAN Maybe it's not the Professor's leg . . . Maybe it's the leg of someone else before him.

ANOTHER Oh, it's his alright! I know it well. He's used it many a time to kick me to study.

A MAN (*Loudly, in a weeping voice*): Oh God! The man's been torn to bits!

The people climb down from the ramparts, obviously in deep sorrow. They take their places on the stone benches, while members of the Municipal Council make for the round table.

OEDIPUS Listen! Do you hear that?

KAMI What?

OEDIPUS Like someone chewing something, crunching something . . .

KAMI (*Straining to hear*): Something like what?

OEDIPUS To be precise, a University Professor. Now then, my good man: check! Checkmate! He could have solved the riddle, *if* he'd gone out to solve the riddle.

KAMI What did he go for then? A walk? You do have some strange notions, Oedipus.

OEDIPUS Not at all. He went out thinking of the prize. One cannot think of the prize and the riddle at the same time.

By the time OEDIPUS *and his friend end their dialogue, the members of the Municipal Council have taken their places at the table, and the citizens theirs on the stone benches.*

OEDIPUS Come on, let's sit among the people. (*They do so.*)

HORIMHEB I told you from the start. It's a plot to do away with the scientific wealth of Thebes—a beast that first eats the Professor of Mathematics, then the Professor of Rational Creativity. This is why (*Assuming an oratorical stance*) I, Horimheb, High Priest of Amon and President of the University of Thebes, proclaim that I will not allow any professor in the University to go and solve the riddle. You may take this to be a decree.

ONAH Who, then, is to go?

HORIMHEB (*Angrily*): I don't know, Onah, I don't know. It's not my responsibility . . .

AWALIH But it *is* your responsibility. Riddles and conundrums and equations and things of that sort, they can be solved only by people who are good at thinking, and the people who are good at thinking are the university professors.

HORIMHEB That's true; but I cannot lower the status of my professors. If the beast wants to challenge us over lectures, over M.A.s and Ph.D.s, I would have no objection; but riddles and trivialities of this kind—I refuse.

ONAH Well, then, go on refusing—until everybody dies of hunger. Not one relief supply has gotten through in three months.

HORIMHEB So that's what's worrying you. You, as President of the Chamber of Commerce, are concerned that trade should revive and your capital be enlarged. (*The Queen comes forward on the balcony.*)

JOCASTA Are you going to quarrel? Have I summoned you to think and relieve the people of the trouble they're in, or to spread out your dirty washing and make a display of yourselves?

AWALIH We are exchanging points of view, my Lady.

JOCASTA And do you, Chief of Police, have the nerve to speak out?

AWALIH Why not, my Lady?

JOCASTA Don't you know why not? Where is His Majesty the King? Where is your Lord and the creator of your prosperity, the King of Thebes? If he were here, he would have solved the riddle in a minute.

ONE OF THE PEOPLE May God have mercy on his soul—he was another moron.

The people burst out laughing. The Chief of Police gives them a threatening look, and they stop.

JOCASTA He was killed at the crossroads a mere five leagues from Thebes. Right? Who are the killers? Where are the killers? Have you looked for them, Mr. Chief of Police? Answer me.

AWALIH (*Stuttering*): My Lady . . . the investigations . . . I mean . . . the confidentiality of investigations . . .

JOCASTA Answer! I command you to answer.

AWALIH There are certain secrets, my Lady, that I cannot reveal in public . . .

JOCASTA Please go ahead and answer in public. Have you looked for the murderers?

AWALIH (*Looks around with embarrassment, then leaves the meeting and approaches her. In an aside to the Queen, nervously and in a low voice*): What is all this, my Lady? Didn't you tell me *not* to look?

JOCASTA I said that?

AWALIH Yes. You told me not to look—not very hard, that is. That was his fate, you said, and we're all destined to die . . .

JOCASTA Well, then, I'm sorry, Awalih. I wasn't being quite alert.

AWALIH Won't you please make a point of it, my Lady? You nearly cooked my goose. (*Resumes his seat at the meeting.*)

OEDIPUS (*Rises among the people and shouts in a firm voice*): Awalih—the Chief of Police. He's the one to go and solve the riddle.

THE PEOPLE (*In a voice like thunder*): Yes. He's the one to go and solve the riddle.

AWALIH (*Thunderstruck*): Me? Why me?

OEDIPUS You're the Chief of Police, and you're supposed to be the cleverest man in the land. (*Addressing the people, in order to persuade them*:) When any crime takes place, the Chief of Police applies his mind to it, and thanks to his cleverness he finds out who the criminal is. Any such case may be looked on as a riddle. The Chief of Police is expected to know how to solve any riddle.

CREON That's sound talk. You're the Chief of Police because you're the cleverest man in Thebes.

THE PEOPLE Hear! Hear! That's right!

AWALIH (*Sensing that the noose is tightening around his neck*): What's right? Are you trying to get rid of me? What riddles and what crimes am I supposed to apply my mind to? In that kind of thing I'm the most thick-headed man in town.

HORIMHEB What kind of talk is this?

AWALIH That's how it is.

OEDIPUS (*Challenging him*): If that's how it is, then how do you catch the criminals?

AWALIH I just arrest them. I'm a very arresting man. His Majesty the King—God rest his soul—he's the one who knew them one by one. He used to give me lists of names and addresses: "Arrest these, let those go." So I used to let those go and arrest these. Simple. (*Shouting, pleadingly*:) Does that make me a clever man?

THE PEOPLE It makes you a dummy.

AWALIH (*Resuming his seat, muttering*): A dummy let it be—just let me live.

KAMI I say, the son of a . . .

JOCASTA Please go on. This problem has to be solved tonight!

AWALIH Good people, I want to warn you of something serious: the food available in Thebes will last us only a week. After that . . .

A VOICE AMONG THE PEOPLE After that you'll eat us! (*Loud laughter among the people*).

TIRESIAS *appears, calling out from some spot on the stage—it will be noticed that* TIRESIAS *appears and disappears at any time that suits.*

TIRESIAS Good people, a little seriousness. Merriment is a great thing, but the temples and mausoleums and great ramparts about you were not built by merriment. It is admirable that one should face up to calamities laughing, but when laughter becomes a tomb in which to bury the future of the land, when jokes become demands that devour your sense of responsibility, when merriment becomes a shroud, when wretchedness and misery are called great fun—what is there left to link you with life? All is lost then, and what remains is sure to be lost too.

ONE OF THE PEOPLE So what do you want us to do, Uncle Tiresias? Sit down and weep?

TIRESIAS You are in fact sitting down and weeping, and even slapping your faces like women at a funeral. What do you think weeping is? Tears running down one's cheeks? Do you understand what despair is? (*Wanders among them as if trying to implant his words into their depths.*) Despair is empty laughter. It is naive optimism. It is senseless mockery of all things. This is the stupidity you have concocted in order not to get to know the truth. Senefru . . . Senekht . . . Aton . . . Kaʿit . . . and others . . . and others. Not a household in Thebes but one of its children has been devoured. What are you waiting for?

HORIMHEB Lord Tiresias, such emotional outbursts never solve any problems. There is no reason for resignation—or for anger. What is needed is calm thinking.

ONAH The basic problem, Lord Tiresias, is that there is a riddle, and someone is needed to solve it.

AWALIH That's right—not a lot of talk about jokes and fun and mockery. Are you trying to depress people? Leave people to their own ways, brother.

HORIMHEB And if we find someone to solve this riddle, the beast will go away and leave us alone. That's the problem.

TIRESIAS That's a lie! Nonsense! That is *not* the problem!

AWALIH What do you mean? That there's no beast and no riddle?

TIRESIAS There *is* a beast, and there *is* a riddle—not the riddle that you think, but another riddle that not one of you has mentioned. Good people: riddles are made up by philosophers and thinkers and the types of people who muse at night by the light of the moon. Why should beasts pose riddles? Why should beasts exercise their brains? Beasts use their muscles and their fangs; they use their talons and their claws. Have you ever heard of a serpent appearing to someone to pose him a riddle? Have you ever heard of a lion intercepting someone to challenge him at hopscotch? Good people, use your brains! This riddle is just an excuse. The aim of the beast is very clear. I am surprised that you cannot see it.

AWALIH (*Sarcastically*): So we can't see it, and you're the one who can?

TIRESIAS I am blind in the eyes only, Awalih. The tables are turned on you, you who are blind in perception. People of Thebes, listen! The beast's purpose is very clear. It is to devour all the clever people in the land one by one. After that, the remaining foolish ones won't give him any trouble—he'll gobble them up wholesale.

OEDIPUS So what is the solution, Tiresias?

TIRESIAS Go out to meet the beast all together. If the story of the riddle is true, surely one of you will be able to solve it. And if it is a lie, then it is you who will be able to devour the beast.

A VOICE AMONG THE PEOPLE But what if he devours *us*?

TIRESIAS Let him, my good man! Are you any better than those he has devoured already? And in either case—whether he eats you or you eat him—your problem will be solved. (*Silence engulfs them all.*) What have you to say? Of course my words don't please you. You don't like to hear talk of this kind. You want somebody who will stand and tell you jokes, who will amuse you. (*With bitter sarcasm*:) O brave men of Thebes: every one among you is ready to cross many seas . . . to face up to crocodiles at the height of the flood . . . to wrestle with the gods . . . to sacrifice his life—all for the sake of hearing a new joke. May you wallow in a worse mess than you are in already! (*There are bursts of laughter among the people as* TIRESIAS *calmly exits.*)

AWALIH This man has no right to come and humiliate the people in the presence of the Municipal Council. We've let him get away with too much all along; but the difficulties we're going through won't allow us to let anyone disturb our thoughts or break our resolve. Having said that, I request that the Council allow me to arrest him.

CREON (*Rising and shouting*): I object! In my capacity as Commander of the Guard in Thebes, I will not allow anyone to be put under arrest merely because of his opinions. Regarding Tiresias in particular, no one can doubt his great love for the City. Tiresias was born with Thebes. Tiresias *is* Thebes.

PERSON NO. 1 At the time we were born, he was already there.

PERSON NO. 2 My father told me he existed even before he himself was born.

PERSON NO. 3 My great-great-grandfather heard from his great-great-grandfather that he existed before any of them were born.

CREON If you imprison Tiresias, you'll be imprisoning the whole of Thebes. If you stop him talking, you'll be gagging the entire population of Thebes.

HORIMHEB We've strayed from the subject.

ONAH True. That is *not* the subject.

OEDIPUS Yes, it *is* the subject.

AWALIH *rises, blazing with anger. He moves toward* OEDIPUS.

AWALIH What do you mean? What are you hinting at? Speak out plainly!

OEDIPUS You know what I mean.

AWALIH You mean that I'm placing freedom of speech under sequestration. You mean that I'm preventing people from speaking their minds.

HORIMHEB That's enough, Awalih. Are you going to blow this up into a quarrel?

AWALIH Oh, no! I can't let this pass without clarification. (*Turning to the populace, and shouting menacingly*:) Have I prevented any of you from speaking? (*Some of the policemen standing by move as if to encircle the public.*) Speak out! Is there anyone who has something to say and doesn't know how to go about it? (*Stretches out his hand, gets hold of one of those sitting, and pulls him up*:) Senefru—speak! You're a playwright, and every year one of your plays is staged in the temple yard. (*In a changed tone*:) It could have happened that nothing of yours was presented, couldn't it?

SENEFRU Yes.

AWALIH And yet all your plays have been presented and you say whatever you want to say—isn't that so?

SENEFRU Yes.

AWALIH And what was it you said in your last play? Go ahead and speak so that Mr. Oedipus should know that we have freedom of speech here.

SENEFRU (*Whispering*): Which play? The one you banned . . .?

AWALIH (*In a low but rancorous voice*): The one that was produced, you fool! (SENEFRU *speaks out with confidence and assurance, with* AWALIH'S *hand still on his shoulder.*)

SENEFRU In my last play I sai . . . er . . . I said the boldest things it's possible to say . . . I don't use symbols or project things back in history . . . I write with great daring, and I'm prepared to lay down my life for the sake of writing what I choose to write . . . In my last play, I demanded that we try studying anew the myth of Isis in the light of the real needs of the people, and this without going too far, as some do, by disrupting the methods which are incompatible with our ability to bring civilization to fruition, especially in the period immediately following the flood of the Nile . . .

AWALIH (*Shouting*): Is there anything more daring than that, brothers? Is there any country in the whole world that allows such words to be spoken on its stages? Well, we do, with the sole restriction that they be spoken within an artistic framework. Now there are things that are *not* spoken in a good artistic framework. We're not the ones who ban these. It's the responsible artists who ban them. (*Addressing himself to a section of the public dressed in bright clothes*:) Isn't that so, responsible artists?

THE GROUP (*Rising*): Yes!

AWALIH Sit down! (*Addressing* OEDIPUS:) You must understand, brother Oedipus, that we're not savages. We're civilized. In fact, more civilized than the country you come from.

CREON (*Very angry*): That's enough—enough demagoguery. Thebes is facing a calamity, and our Lord Awalih can think of nothing better than defending himself and displaying his oratorical skills. Who will rid us of the beast?

AWALIH Why don't *you*? You go and solve the riddle. You're the Commander of the Guard, and you're responsible for repelling all outside threats. You go and repel the beast!

CREON I'm a warrior. I can make myself understood with the sword. I know how to die below the walls of Thebes, facing any enemy that attempts to approach my city. But riddles are something I know nothing about. (*The Queen comes out on the balcony*).

JOCASTA Are you still squabbling? Haven't you found somebody yet with enough brains to solve the riddle? When there are positions vacant that call for brains, you all come forward; but when there's a calamity to face, you all act stupid. If within a quarter of an hour by the sandglass no one has come forward to solve the riddle, let the Municipal Council consider itself dissolved. (*Addressing the populace*:) People of Thebes: let the wisest among you, the sharpest in understanding, the greatest in intellect, the widest in experience come forward to solve the riddle.

OEDIPUS Here am I, my Lady.

OEDIPUS *steps out of the ranks of the common people and makes for the balcony on which the Queen is standing; he takes up position where he can be seen by all. Among the people, his name is echoed and reechoed: "Oedipus . . . Oedipus . . .")*

JOCASTA Where are you from, Oedipus?

OEDIPUS It doesn't matter, my Lady, whether I'm from Methana or Babylon or any other place on earth. All that matters to you is that I rid you of the beast.

JOCASTA Chief of Police! What do you know of Oedipus?

AWALIH (*To one of his men*): The Oedipus file! (*He is given the* ﬁ*le, opens it and reads*:) Oedipus: color of eyes—brown. Complexion—darkish. Distinguishing marks—swollen fee . . .

JOCASTA Are you about to describe him when he's standing right here before me? All right, go on!

AWALIH There are many rumors about him. One is that he escaped from Methana after killing his father or having caused his death. Another is that he is running away from a case involving alimony. Mental ability—enjoys great mental powers; within one month of taking up residence in Thebes, was able to defeat all chess experts. Degree of dangerousness—not involved in dangerous political activity. Occasionally visits the temple of Amon before important chess matches . . .

OEDIPUS None of that is of any importance. What is important is that I be able to solve the riddle. What will you give me?

ONAH Solve the riddle and you will get fifty thousand pieces of gold. And as President of the Chamber of Commerce, I undertake to pay you another fifty thousand out of its funds.

OEDIPUS O-ho!

HORIMHEB And we'll appoint you an assistant priest—that will be another hundred gold pieces a month, to say nothing of an allowance for acting. And we'll promote you to full priesthood after two years.

OEDIPUS I didn't ask how much you'd pay me or what position you'd give me. I'm asking: *What* will you give me?

HORIMHEB What do you want?

OEDIPUS Thebes!

THE PUBLIC (*In astonishment*): Thebes . . .

OEDIPUS Yes. You have a King's position vacant. Let me be appointed King.

THE PUBLIC King?

OEDIPUS Yes. That's the only position I'm good for.

HORIMHEB What do you say?

AWALIH I say we agree.

ONAH And if he causes us trouble?

AWALIH No problem! We'll make out that he's anti-Amon and bring about a coup d' état.

JOCASTA Why do you want to be King, Oedipus? What are your qualifications for such an important position?

OEDIPUS My brilliance! My genius!

CREON If only your qualification was love of Thebes . . .

OEDIPUS I have no love for anything that can be grasped by the hand. I love principles, ideals, conceptions . . .

JOCASTA And if you succeed in solving the riddle, what do you intend to do for Thebes?

OEDIPUS I'll put it forward by five thousand years. I shall realize for it all the inventions that Man is due to bring about over the next five thousand years. To put it very briefly: I shall create civilization. Civilization: printing presses, motor cars, airplanes, electricity, electronics, the telephone, television . . .

ALL (*Cries of inquiry arise from all present*): What does it mean? . . . What does it mean? . . .

OEDIPUS It means one thing: let's not waste our time. If I solve the riddle, I become the King of Thebes. Do you agree?

AWALIH We agree.

OEDIPUS And the people?

AWALIH What have the people to do with it? We are the authority.

OEDIPUS It must be the people who agree to my appointment. You're capable of appointing me today and dismissing me tomorrow; but if the people appoint me, no one will know how to dismiss me. People of Thebes, do you agree?

PEOPLE We agree.

OEDIPUS One thing more.

PEOPLE What?

OEDIPUS I shall marry the Queen. (*There is a moment of silence*).

JOCASTA The impudence! How dare you ask for union with a descendant of Amon?

OEDIPUS To me, my Lady, you are neither Queen nor a descendant of the gods. To me, you are the most beautiful woman ever created by the gods. (JOCASTA *hides her face in embarrassment as he continues*:) For many years, my Lady, I have been wandering over hill and dale; I have sailed the seas, I have crossed the ocean even to Mexico; all in search of the mistress of this universe, the fairest of the fair, the princess of princesses, the queen of queens. Now I have found you, my Lady.

JOCASTA I respect your point of view, and I can see that it's worthy of discussion. All the same, it doesn't give you the right to marry a queen. Don't forget that you're an ordinary man, a son neither of Amon nor of Ra.

OEDIPUS So be it, my Lady. I am at your command. By the same token, it had better be one of the sons of Amon or of Ra who solves the riddle.

He moves away, but from the people rise shouts of protest and anger. AWALIH *approaches the Queen and speaks with her in asides.*

AWALIH Consent, my Lady, consent! Oedipus is a lad who'll please you very much . . .

JOCASTA How do you know?

AWALIH My investigations . . .

JOCASTA And if he proves a dud?

AWALIH Impossible, my Lady. I am answerable for what I say . . . (*Resumes his place.*)

JOCASTA People of Thebes! For the sake of Thebes, and only for the sake of Thebes, I shall sacrifice all our sacred traditions. More than that: I sacrifice myself in order to save Thebes. Oedipus, sir, I consent. (*The people break out in uproar and confusion.*)

HORIMHEB A little order . . .

ONAH There's no time for that. Do us the honor, Oedipus, sir!

CREON Guard! Open the gate! Do us the honor, Oedipus, sir!

OEDIPUS *advances among the populace as they shout and cheer. Suddenly* TIRESIAS *appears, barring their way.*

TIRESIAS (*Shouting in apprehension*): People! Good people! Good people! Wait! What is this you're doing? What are you doing? It may well be that Oedipus will solve the riddle and settle the problem of the beast. But what of the beast within you? Who is going to kill that—that stupid beast that makes you forever wait for the one who will solve your problems for you, in return for which you will concede him anything? Have you ever read before of someone who became king merely because he found the answer to a riddle-meree? Think again, I beg you! Think once and think twice before you do what you are about to do. Suppose that Oedipus was not among you—what would you do then?

ONE OF THE PEOPLE He's at it—philosophizing! Why should we suppose, when the man's right here and about to solve the riddle?

ANOTHER Why indeed? He just likes to hear himself spouting.

TIRESIAS Good people, do stop making a joke of everything.

JOCASTA What's the matter, Tiresias? Are you trying to convince us that we're all wrong and only you are right?

TIRESIAS Is it a matter of numbers, my Lady? What is right is right because it is right. What is true is true because it is true. If the entire population of Thebes were to stand up and say that the Nile does not exist, would it indeed be nonexistent?

SOMEONE Take it easy, old man—and spare us the noise!

The populace take no heed, but resume their rhythmic, modulated cheering: "Off you go, Oedipus! On you go Oedipus! Out you come, beast of beasts! . . ."

TIRESIAS (*In utter misery*): Oh, people! Good people! Good people! . . . (*Exits.*)

OEDIPUS *goes out of the city gate, and the populace crowds onto the wall watching him, still shouting and cheering.*

SOMEONE The beast's behind the hill!

ANOTHER Can't see it!

ANOTHER Oedipus is still advancing . . . Come out, beast!

ANOTHER Beast of beasts . . . Oedipus has got to the hill!

ANOTHER What a man! He walks on without a care!

ANOTHER Behind the hill . . . Out of sight . . . can't see . . .

THE POPULACE (*All together*): May God shield him!

SOMEONE Oedipus . . . He's reappeared . . . He's holding his hand high . . . He's running back . . .

ANOTHER (*In great joy*): Oedipus has solved the riddle . . . Oedipus has killed the beast!

Shouts of joy burst out all over the stage. The people dance with joy and exchange kisses. They meet OEDIPUS *at the gate and carry him shoulder high. Flowers are showered on him from all sides.*

OEDIPUS (*Trying to raise his voice above the din*): Sons of Thebes! . . . My children! . . . (*His voice is drowned by the crowd.*)

THE PEOPLE (*Modulating their cheers*): You're the one who killed the beast . . .

OEDIPUS Listen to me!

THE PEOPLE You're the one who killed the beast! . . .

OEDIPUS *loses control over the populace.* TIRESIAS *appears from the wings, and he also shouts in despair.*

TIRESIAS Listen to him . . . Let him speak . . . Let him speak . . . Good people . . .

The lighting is dimmed, and the shouting abates. The stage sinks into complete darkness. Then the lights come on again, gradually, revealing the throne room in the pharaonic palace. OEDIPUS *is on the throne, wearing the royal mantle and the crown.* HORIMHEB *comes in and bows at great length.*

HORIMHEB Good morning, my Lord!

OEDIPUS Good morning, Hõr!

HORIMHEB The Supreme Council of the Priests of Thebes awaits your directions.

OEDIPUS Call a meeting for today, after sunset. I want to talk to you about the new temple ritual, and about the new educational system I want to introduce.

HORIMHEB Yes, my Lord.

OEDIPUS Is there something else?

HORIMHEB Last night, as I was looking through the Amon and Ra documents that we keep in the Temple archives, I noticed that the name "Oedipus" occurred in seven papyri. I was greatly surprised, my Lord, because these documents record only the names of the gods and of humans descended from the gods.

OEDIPUS What I'm driving at?

HORIMHEB What I'm driving at, my Lord, is that you are without doubt a descendant of the gods.

OEDIPUS (*Weighing his words*): So— I'm a descendant of the gods, am I? And this business is something you've discovered during the night?

HORIMHEB Yes, my Lord.

OEDIPUS What a wonderful man you are—you don't waste any time, do you? Anyway, you may go now, and I shall give thought to this matter later on.

HORIMHEB We don't want to delay publicizing this matter too long, my Lord. Scholarly integrity makes it incumbent upon me that I make it known.

OEDIPUS Scholarly integrity, is it? A charlatan and a hypocrite—must you be a braggart as well? Off you go! And don't you dare raise this topic at present.

HORIMHEB As my Lord commands. (*Bows and exits. Enter* AWALIH).

AWALIH May your morning be like a river in spate, my Lord.

OEDIPUS Welcome, Awalih!

AWALIH My appointment with your Majesty is at noon, but there is a matter I discovered last night which I had to come and lay before your Majesty.

OEDIPUS It seems that lots of people made important discoveries last night. So what is it, sir?

AWALIH The moment your Majesty demanded to be king, I sent out my detectives to investigate your origins. Forgive me, my Lord; this was something I had to do. It is my personal responsibility . . .

OEDIPUS All right, all right! Go on!

AWALIH The investigations made and the reports received, my Lord, prove that you are directly descended from divine loins . . .

OEDIPUS You don't say?

AWALIH I swear it by the life of Horus, my Lord, by whom I have never sworn but . . .

OEDIPUS And what is Horus god of?

AWALIH He is the god of police, my Lord.

OEDIPUS *rises from his seat, gets hold of* AWALIH *and addresses him coldly.*

OEDIPUS Listen, Awalih, I am a human, and the son of a human. Understand? The true secret of my greatness is that I'm a man, the first human to rule over Thebes. Understand? Get that into your colleagues' skulls, and all of you try to help me realize the dreams of Thebes. Understand?

AWALIH Why blame me? This is what the investigations have yielded.

OEDIPUS Do you take me for a fool? The investigations always yield what you want yielded.

AWALIH I'm sorry, my Lord.

OEDIPUS All right! Off you go and see to your business.

AWALIH If your Majesty will be so good as to give me the lists of criminals . . .

OEDIPUS What criminals?

AWALIH Those who are opposed to your rule, my Lord.

OEDIPUS My rule? Have I had the time yet? I was appointed only yesterday.

AWALIH And is that a short interval, my Lord? By now, half the city is against you—the envious, the resentful, the adventurers, the madmen—these are the ones that we term enemies of the regime. If your majesty will have the kindness to give me the lists of their names and addresses, so we may arrest them . . .

OEDIPUS I know of nothing that may be termed "enemies of the regime," but there is something that may be termed "enemies of Thebes." Those are your concern. If anybody does anything against Thebes, it's your responsibility to stop him in his tracks.

AWALIH I see: each to his own style. His Majesty the King who preceded your Majesty handed me his lists three days before he ascended the throne. That's why he went on ruling for fifteen years without any enemies. He was greatly loved.

OEDIPUS And that's why when he was murdered no one took the trouble to find out who killed him. Isn't that so, Chief of Police?

AWALIH His fate will be known, my Lord. Anyway, my Lord, I shall go on operating on the basis of the old lists.

OEDIPUS The old lists?

AWALIH Look here, my Lord. Our family—the Awalih family—has held the post of Chief of Police for four hundred years. I've noticed a strange thing: the lists of names of enemies of the regime are always the same. They've been passed on from father to son—sometimes one or two names more, sometimes one or two names less. But the lists have always been the same.

OEDIPUS Awalih, I have no time for this sort of thing. You're supposed to know your business and your business is the maintenance of Thebes' internal security. Out with you!

AWALIH *bows and goes. In comes* KAMI, *the friend of* OEDIPUS *who was playing chess with him in the first scene.*

KAMI (*In a carefree, jocular mood*): My, my! What magnificence!

OEDIPUS Welcome, Kami.

KAMI (*Laughing full tilt*): Who would have believed it? Give me a promise too, O Ra! Now tell me, buddy—what job are you going to give me?

OEDIPUS (*Perturbed*): Kami, be serious!

KAMI (*Still laughing heartily*): Ho, ho! (*Chanting*:) You're the one who killed the beast! You know, when you ran out to solve the riddle, I was running behind you. I hid behind the hill to see how you were going to handle it.

OEDIPUS What are you driving at?

KAMI Nothing!

OEDIPUS Kami, that's enough clowning. You are now standing in the Royal Hall. You'd better not speak this way.

KAMI *bursts out laughing again. At that moment, an arm stretches out from behind the throne, seizes him by the throat, and drags him away.* OEDIPUS *stares in amazement.* AWALIH *appears from behind the throne.*

OEDIPUS What's brought you here, Awalih? Where did you come from? How? What's happening?

AWALIH (*Coldly*): These are inevitable measures, my Lord. It's true they're not very pleasant, but they're necessary.

OEDIPUS Necessary?

AWALIH You'll find out later on that they are necessary. Excuse me, my Lord. This is my personal responsibility.

AWALIH *bows and exits. The lighting diminishes, except on* OEDIPUS, *who looks fixedly ahead, in bafflement and confusion.* TIRESIAS *appears in a corner of the stage.*

TIRESIAS The worst horrors and most intractable calamities always begin thus: as the lord Awalih said, with things that are unpleasant but necessary. Only he hasn't told us why they are unpleasant, or why they are also necessary.

The lighting fades as the curtain falls.

ACT II

The second act is made up of numerous quick scenes. This places a greater burden than usual on the producer and the stage manager. To ease the problem of quick changes, the producer had better resort to the puppet show technique: blackened stage, ultraviolet rays, projected shadows. It may be necessary to use actual puppets in the staging of parts of some scenes.

SCENE I

In the living room of SENEFRU'*s house. The furniture is semimodern, but with a pharaonic flavor. The same is true of the clothes worn by the characters.* SENEFRU *is sitting reading a magazine, turning the pages in a way that reveals annoyance. A small* CHILD *is playing with a toy.* SENEFRU'*s wife,* NEFER, *is plucking at a large harp. In the living room is a large television set, a radio, and a telephone. The telephone rings.*

SENEFRU Hello . . . Yes, this is Senefru . . . Listen to me, Kaʿit . . . Later, later . . . We'll meet at night . . . Goodbye! (*Puts the receiver down with some violence*).

NEFER Be careful with the phone—you'll break it!

SENEFRU Kaʿit's a fool! I've told him a thousand times there are things not to be said on the telephone. And yet whenever he gets on the line he prattles on. I've told him a thousand times I have a household to look after, a son to bring up. The fool!

CHILD (*Holding up his toy*): Daddy, please mend my toy.

SENEFRU Bring it over, my pet; I'll mend it for you. You go and do your homework, and by the tine you've finished that, this will be mended. (*The* CHILD *gets hold of a large book and settles down in a corner*).

SENEFRU What's this, Nefer? Couldn't you find any toy but this for the boy? Does it have to be a beast with Oedipus killing it?

NEFER Where am I to get anything else? All the toys on the market are like this: a beast riding a bicycle with Oedipus killing it; a beast on a plane with Oedipus killing it; a beast playing ball with Oedipus killing it . . . (SENEFRU *reacts with annoyance*).

THE CHILD B-e-a-s-t beast; k-i-l-l kill.

Rameses, did you see the beast? Yes, Kamis, I saw it.

SENEFRU Ahmis, my darling, what are you doing? What book is this?

THE CHILD It's the beastly reading book, Dad!

SENEFRU All right! Go and do your studying in your room. (*The* CHILD *goes.*) Even the children . . .

NEFER What's the matter with you? Your nerves are frayed. Is anything wrong?

SENEFRU No, nothing at all. We could do without the piece you're playing just now. (*This brings out the fact that what she has been playing is "You're the One Who Killed the Beast."* SENEFRU *gets up to turn on the radio.*)

FEMALE BROADCASTER'S VOICE You will now hear a selection of sentimental songs, beginning with "You're the One Who Killed the Beast" from the album of the same name. This will be followed by "Beastly Is My Loneliness" and "Bei mir Bist du Schön." You will then hear that moving artist, Camille Hoarse, in a rendering of a new song, "My Love Is a Beast in His Passions." The closing item will be "If Thou Be-est My Love." (SENEFRU *switches off.*)

NEFER Why did you switch off? Those are lovely songs.

SENEFRU I'd rather we looked at television. There's a literary program on about now. (*Switches on and a woman* BROADCASTER *appears*).

THE BROADCASTER Hello, we've received thousands of letters requesting a repeat of the comedy "Don't Be a Beast to Me and I Shan't Be a Beast to You." We're pleased to tell our viewers that we shall be showing it at the end of this evening's transmission.

NEFER That'll be good this evening. It's a wonderful play. Don't go out tonight. (SENEFRU *looks at her with distaste*).

THE BROADCASTER Just now, we're in the company of the eminent critic Mahi Kah, in the program entitled "Questions and Answers." (*Professor* MAHI KAH *appears on the screen.*)

MAHI KAH The fateful and beastly struggle between Man and Beast, which is the subject of certain artistic works, besets us with sentiments best described as atavistic toward this bestial contest. I say this in connection with the publication this week of a book by Abwakh Kalt, to which he has given the title *Views on the Slain Beast.* (SENEFRU *rises and switches off the television.*)

NEFER What are you doing? What's wrong with you? Why are you so upset? You want to smash the television, smash the radio, smash the telephone! Perhaps there is some sense in it. After all *you* don't have to worry about anything. I'm the one who has to go to all sorts of trouble over the installments . . .

SENEFRU (*Almost in tears*): Please, Nefer; please shut up and leave me alone.

NEFER Have I come anywhere near you? What's the matter with you?

SENEFRU Nothing's the matter with me. It's just that everything has turned beastly . . . (*Correcting himself*:) I mean, objectionable.

The lights are gradually dimmed.

SCENE 2

Lecture hall in the University of Thebes. Dozens of students are sitting in the auditorium, only their heads showing. Before them stands HORIMHEB.

HORIMHEB We dealt in the previous lecture with conditions in Thebes before the appearance of the beast. In today's lecture, we shall give details of the main reference works relevant to this subject, wherefrom it will be definitively established that under no circumstances is it possible for man to solve the riddle posed by the Sphinx. I say that no human could solve the riddle unless he was descended from the gods. This is why Oedipus was able to do it. I refer you to pages 15 to 340 of our own doctoral dissertation, in which we spoke at length of the divine origins of His Majesty Oedipus-Ra. Let me return to the main theme of the lecture. This is how Oedipus did away with the beast and brought about in Thebes such efflorescence, such wealth, and such modern inventions as we enjoy today; this is how Oedipus made ours the greatest city in the world.

Gradual dimming of lights, as a large screen lights up, and on it appears the shadow of OEDIPUS, *gigantic in stature, with tens of thousands cheering around him.*

OEDIPUS My sons, sons of Thebes! Today we celebrate the fifth anniversary of the slaying of the beast.

PEOPLE (*Cheering in modulated fashion*): You're the one who killed the beast ... (*Gradual dimming of lights.*)

SCENE 3

In a narrow tomb inside a temple. AWALIH *is interrogating* KAᶜIT, *one of the citizens of Thebes.* KAᶜIT *is tied to a stone pillar; beside him is a very young* POLICEMAN.

AWALIH Our inquiries have established that you are spreading rumors to the effect that Oedipus did not solve the riddle and did not kill the beast. There isn't a place where you haven't said such things—in cafés, bars, graveyards, on the telephone ...

KAᶜIT I said no such thing.

AWALIH What did you say, then?

KAᶜIT I asked just one question: what was the riddle?

AWALIH What business is it of yours? *Why* did you ask?

KAᶜIT I want to know; and I believe there are many people who want to know.

AWALIH Very good! We're getting to the point. Who, then, my dear sir, are those who want to know?

KAᶜIT I swear by Horus ...

AWALIH *Don't!* Don't swear by Horus. Don't cut your own throat!

KAᶜIT I swear by all the gods that I know of no one particular person ...

AWALIH Liar! How else would you learn that there are people who want to know? Is your Lordship a fortune teller?

KAᶜIT (*In great weariness, speaking with immense difficulty*): Listen, Awalih. I'm tired of this game. Every time a new king is enthroned, you get hold of me, beat me in the same way, and ask me the same damned questions. I want to know, good people; I want to know! I'm losing all faith—or perhaps one is better off dying ... (*His head sinks to his chest.*)

AWALIH Don't try to evade the question! Let's have no twisting and turning. How did you find out that there were people who wanted to know? Answer!

KAᶜIT *does not answer.* AWALIH *repeats the question. The young* POLICEMAN *raises* KAᶜIT*'s head and then lets go, whereupon it again sinks to his chest.*

POLICEMAN (*Distressed*): He's dead!

AWALIH (*Calmly*): So ... And why are you so upset?

POLICEMAN (*Greatly perturbed*): It's just that ... he's dead ... dead!

AWALIH It's his choice, my man! Each one is free to do whatever he pleases. Tell me, how long is it since you were admitted to the force?

POLICEMAN One week.

AWALIH That's why. You'll get used to it tomorrow. Sit down and write the report.

The POLICEMAN *gets hold of paper and pencil and writes, with a markedly trembling hand.*

AWALIH (*Continuing*): . . . and when the accused was confronted with irrefutable proof of his theft of the treasures of Ra . . . (*The young man stops and stares at* AWALIH *in amazement.*) Go on writing, young man—why do you stop? . . . his theft of the treasures of Ra stored in the temple . . . when confronted with proof . . . his resistance collapsed and he committed suicide by throwing himself out of the window on the fourth floor . . .

POLICEMAN But there are no windows on the fourth floor!

AWALIH So make it the fifth.

POLICEMAN There are none on the fifth floor either.

AWALIH Go on writing. Don't bore me. It's just a technical term.

POLICEMAN A technical term?

AWALIH It's not a window in the factual sense. It's a symbolic one. When you're a little more advanced you'll understand—and you'll get used to it. Oh, that's enough. Close the report! I have to go now. An appointment for the cinema. (*He looks at his watch*:) Who-a! I'm half an hour late. (*He looks at the corpse*:) Damn you! Damn you! I suppose you're pleased with this delay. What will I tell my wife? Well, by your leave . . .

POLICEMAN What will I do with this?

AWALIH He's not very heavy. Take him and throw him off the roof.

POLICEMAN (*In great terror*): Off the roof?

AWALIH Didn't you say there were no windows on the fourth and fifth floors? (*Very angrily*:) Why do you have to complicate things for me? Where else are you to throw him from? How stupid can you get?

POLICEMAN (*Totally rattled*): I'm sorry. Do go, Your Honor! Please go on to the cinema—or you might miss the Mickey Mouse cartoon . . .

Gradual dimming of lights.

SCENE 4

The Royal Throne Room. JOCASTA *is pacing angrily;* AWALIH *stands silent.*

JOCASTA In his laboratory all day long and all night long. His Lordship is busy with his inventions. Since the day I married him, I haven't seen him more than four times. It's true I'm a Queen, and a descendant of the gods as well. But I'm also flesh and blood.

AWALIH How am I responsible for all this, my Lady?

JOCASTA Your responsibility is that you made me agree to marry him. You're the one who advised me to consent.

AWALIH But, my Lady, I didn't know that this was how he was going to respond.

JOCASTA And since you're an ignoramus and know nothing, why did you make me agree? (*Imitating him*:) "Consent, my Lady. Oedipus is a lad who'll please you very much." "And if he proves a dud?" "I am answerable, my Lady . . . " Well now, sir—discharge your responsibility.

AWALIH What am I to do, my Lady?

JOCASTA You know, Awalih. Do you

want me to teach you your job as well? You know what to do—the same as you did with his predecessor and the predecessor's predecessor. An accident of the kind that takes place every day. Who can be sure of his own life?

AWALIH I can't do it this time, my Lady.

JOCASTA What's different about this time? You always managed before.

AWALIH Before now, people used not to ask. The King is dead, long live the King. Goodbye Ahmes, hello Rameses. Goodbye Mena, hello Thotmes. It was no concern of theirs. But with Oedipus, the situation's different. The people are the ones who appointed him. Besides, he's made all these inventions for them. And even if we could cope with the people, there's a very large group of Theban citizens who make a living out of all this, and this group's very powerful and influential. The clearest examples are Brother Onah and Brother Horimheb. The moment Oedipus invents something, they get hold of it, manufacture it, and sell it. An awful lot of people are benefiting. If anything happened to Oedipus, they wouldn't keep quiet, and we, my Lady, would be exposed.

JOCASTA And the solution? There has to be a solution.

AWALIH Your arsenal, my Lady—a woman's arsenal. It's more powerful than the atomic bomb, which Oedipus is intent on inventing. See to your beauty, my Lady. Certain essences have come on the market these days that can turn the head of the ablest of men; there are perfumes that can turn the head of a monk, my Lady.

JOCASTA Perfumes, oils, ointments, powders—there isn't one I haven't tried. And still it's no use. He's busy with his inventions.

AWALIH All right, then. Nothing's left but the traditional method, the method our family's specialized in. It's true it takes time, but in the long run the results are guaranteed.

JOCASTA And what is the traditional method?

AWALIH Whenever he does something beneficial, he adds to the number of people who love him. So my task will be to add to the number of people who hate him. Of course you know the rest.

JOCASTA How are you going to make people hate him?

AWALIH Nothing to it; it's very simple. I shall make them love him . . . (*Pause*) by force! That's our business, my Lady. Don't you worry. I only beg you by Isis that you intercede for me so that Horus may be at my right hand.

JOCASTA I'll go this very night to pray in the Temple of Amon and to call down blessings on you.

The Queen leaves the stage. ONAH *appears from the inner galleries, holding some modern devices.*

AWALIH Well, well, my good man! You *are* busy! All these inventions are to be transmuted into gold. And in the end the gold will pour into the Municipal Council and the Chamber of Commerce.

ONAH So what, brother? You're a member . . .

AWALIH A fat lot I get out of it, worse luck!

ONAH You got an automobile, a yacht, and a helicopter. Every one of your children got a toy car. And every month you get you-know-what. What more do you want?

AWALIH Nothing—but just keep an open mind. All you've mentioned amounts to crumbs in comparison with what you get.

ONAH Is that all that's worrying you? I'm at your service. How many Awalihs have we got? You have only to say . . .

AWALIH It's no skin off your nose. Our good friend invents, and you make a profit.

ONAH You mean *we* do. (*They chant together*:) We're the ones who killed the beast!

Both burst out laughing. Gradual dimming of lights.

SCENE 5

On the large screen: the PEOPLE *of Thebes in silhouette are kneeling and chanting in voices filled with awe and devotion, as if praying.* OEDIPUS *stands before them.*

PEOPLE Oedipus-Ra . . . You're the one who killed the beast . . . Oedipus-Ra!

Gradual dimming of lights.

SCENE 6

The Throne Room. OEDIPUS *is sitting on the throne, and before him are* AWALIH, HORIMHEB, CREON, *and* ONAH. OEDIPUS *is greatly worked up.*

OEDIPUS What's happening behind my back? How did all this business develop? I want to know.

HORIMHEB Calm down, my Lord. We're the ones who want to know.

OEDIPUS The people today were kneeling before me as the pharaonic bark sailed on. The people today prostrated themselves before me in the temple as I prayed.

ONAH They respect you, my Lord.

OEDIPUS And didn't they respect me before? Yet before today they used not to kneel before me. Before today they addressed me as Oedipus, plain Oedipus. Now I have become Oedipus-Ra. Awalih, have you issued a declaration saying I am a god?

AWALIH I have not, my Lord. But it may be that the news leaked out.

OEDIPUS Leaked out?

AWALIH Nothing can remain hidden, my Lord. Isn't it so, Horimheb? Speak out! Why do you stand silent?

HORIMHEB In reality, my Lord . . . The truth is . . . As I see it . . . I mean, my point of view . . . I would contend . . .

OEDIPUS That means you're about to tell a lie. Since you mention reality and truth, it means you intend to tell a lie.

HORIMHEB No, my Lord. I'm not about to tell a lie. By now everybody knows that your Majesty is descended from the gods.

OEDIPUS I warned you not to tell this tale.

HORIMHEB We're not telling it, my Lord. We're studying it.

OEDIPUS Studying it, are you?

HORIMHEB Yes, in the various stages of the educational system.

OEDIPUS I issued no orders to this effect.

HORIMHEB Excuse me, my Lord. With all due respect to your Majesty, this does not come within your Majesty's competence. This is a scientific fact, and scientific facts must be made known. Integrity makes it incumbent . . .

OEDIPUS (*Rising from the throne and shouting*): Integrity? Is it integrity that you should lie?

HORIMHEB I'm no liar, my Lord. It's not fitting that you should say such a thing to someone who is your father's age; nor is it fitting that you should shout in the presence of your elders. This matter is no lie; it's a fact. Isn't that so, Awalih?

AWALIH Indeed.

OEDIPUS Fact, is it? So you two know that I'm a god while I don't—and you don't want me to shout? Creon, why don't you speak?

CREON Sorry, my Lord. I'd better remain detached from any political currents. If the guard should interfere in domestic or foreign policy, the outcome wouldn't be desirable. I'm under your orders, my Lord, in anything that relates to the security of Thebes.

OEDIPUS So it doesn't matter to you whether the King of Thebes be man or god?

CREON It makes no difference to me, my Lord. And I have no time. I'm responsible for the training of the Guard in relation to the defense of Thebes. I have no time for anything else.

OEDIPUS (*With genuine sorrow*): Thank you, Creon. You may go. Goodbye!

CREON *stiffens in a military salute and goes.*

OEDIPUS Creon's an earnest fellow. All he cares about is the defense of Thebes.

HORIMHEB We too, my Lord; we care about the defense of Thebes.

OEDIPUS That leaves one function unfulfilled. I need someone to protect me from you.

ONAH My Lord, you're looking at this matter in a very romantic way. You need to look at it from a realistic point of view. The people of Thebes have been ruled by gods for thousands of years. The worship of Pharaoh isn't merely a pious custom; it's a national tradition. We can't all of a sudden come and tell people that the king's an ordinary man.

HORIMHEB Besides, the educational curricula at all stages assert this. We can't change them. The prayers also assert this. All our customs and traditions, our songs and tales, say the same thing. It's a pyramid, my Lord, a pyramid of beliefs and concepts—and a very big pyramid. This pyramid is erected on a very sound base. This base says that Pharaoh is a god. If now we come and say that Pharaoh is an ordinary man, everything will be confusion and chaos, and we'll all go down the drain—especially the priests of Amon.

OEDIPUS I have a different point of view. We must make the people understand that there's something called the Law of Evolution. You need to study this subject. It's true that there were once kings who were gods, or the sons of gods . . .

HORIMHEB (*Interrupting*): Do you believe that, my Lord? Do you still believe that there were kings who were gods? They were all wretched human beings like ourselves, and some of them, even, were beggars. But we had to make them into gods.

OEDIPUS Why did we have to do that? I don't see any necessity at all.

ONAH My Lord, you seem to think that this matter concerns you alone.

OEDIPUS Of course it concerns me alone.

ONAH Not at all. It concerns us even more than it concerns you.

OEDIPUS How so?

ONAH All the organizations, the directorates, the departments, the institutions that function under the aegis of the Municipal Council, and which we are required to operate in the best possible manner—people respect us more when they know that at our head there's a god. But if they knew that what makes us tick is a human, they'd become insolent toward us, and we wouldn't know how to make them function.

HORIMHEB It's a matter of prestige, my Lord.

ONAH Of course. Do you think that if people knew that Cheops wasn't a god, they would still have built him this pyramid? They would scarcely have placed one slab above another.

AWALIH The truth is that your Majesty is still new at this trade and has no experience of pharaonic problems. We're sparing your Majesty a great many calamities.

OEDIPUS Calamities?

AWALIH Of course. For example, there are people who are skeptical about the story of the beast and the riddle. They want to know what the riddle was. What they're after is the riddle. Their only concern is to demolish. Just imagine: if people knew that you're just an ordinary man, they'd become insolent. I tell your Majesty that we're sparing you a great many disasters, only one is reluctant to talk . . .

OEDIPUS What's so frightening about the riddle? I'll tell you what it is, sir. (*After a moment's consideration*:) What is it that walks on four in the morning, on two at noon, and on three at sunset?

AWALIH (*With exaggerated wonder*): My, my! It would be impossible for anyone in Thebes ever to solve this, my Lord.

HORIMHEB And what is the answer, my Lord?

OEDIPUS Man.

AWALIH Wonderful . . . Wonderful. Bravo, my Lord, bravo!

ONAH And does your Majesty want to convince us that you are an ordinary man? There's no way an ordinary human can solve this riddle. It's certain that your Majesty is of divine descent, or at least that the spirit of the gods is being incarnated in you.

OEDIPUS Do you think so?

ONAH Certainly.

OEDIPUS (*Pleased*): Thank you.

As he rises to leave, they bow to him.

HORIMHEB (*Sarcastically*): Ha! Is that the riddle?

ONAH Isn't that the riddle that was part of our curriculum in elementary school? So why is it that no one could solve it?

AWALIH Any child in Thebes knows this riddle, and the answer.

HORIMHEB So how did the beast die?

AWALIH (*Chanting*): He's the one who killed the beast! Why should we care, brother? Our task now is to think up a somewhat difficult riddle to give out to the people, since some of them are beginning to ask.

HORIMHEB I'll tell you. (*He thinks.*) What is it that walks on four in the morning, on two at noon, on three at sunset, on five at twilight, and that crawls on its belly at dawn?

ONAH And the answer?

AWALIH It's still Man. (*Suppressing laughter*:) Is anyone going to contradict us?

They burst out laughing as the lights are gradually dimmed.

SCENE 7

The great courtyard before Pharaoh's Palace, but with altered features: there is a multitude of shops before which people stand, selling the most modern devices, advertising them in modulated phrases. TIRESIAS *appears, and the noise of the crowd abates.*

TIRESIAS The common voice now is Oedipus and the beast that was killed. Everyone sings the same song to the new Pharaoh who has shortened the span of time by five thousand years. The people of Thebes are benefiting from inventions which no one else shall see for a long, long time. The Municipal Council has made good use of these inventions to implant the desired tunes in the minds of the people—and, at the same time, to fill certain accounts with money. Nor did the Municipal Council omit to put out a proclamation setting out the riddle and the solution which Oedipus offered to the beast. The answer was: Man! Strange that Man has remained for thousands of years, and shall forever remain, the only answer to all riddles. And man shall remain the correct tune, the one true, clear tune among all the bad tunes as age follows age. Strange also that this truth, clear as the sun in a Theban day, often escapes the minds of many of the composers who make up the various peoples' music . . .

TIRESIAS *disappears as* OEDIPUS *appears on the palace balcony, whereupon the* PEOPLE *in the courtyard crowd before it.*

OEDIPUS Sons of Thebes, my sons! . . . Today we celebrate the killing of the beast . . .

PEOPLE (*Chanting*): You're the one who killed the beast!

OEDIPUS I still remember that day as if it had happened yesterday, when I went out to the beast . . .

PEOPLE You're the one who killed the beast!

OEDIPUS One thought was dominant in me, pervading all my perceptions. It was a supreme faith that this beast . . .

PEOPLE You're the one who killed the beast!

AWALIH, *holding on to* SENEFRU, *detaches himself from the masses and stands away from the crowd, at the front of the stage.* OEDIPUS *is still delivering his speech, but we no longer hear him.*

AWALIH (*With murderous gentleness*): Senefru, why aren't you singing? I've been watching you. You've been standing there for an hour, not chanting.

SENEFRU (*Picking up some courage*): You, sir, weren't singing either.

AWALIH Senefru, I am the composer.

SENEFRU (*Trying to make his voice sound hoarse*): It's just that my voice has gone hoarse today.

AWALIH You don't say? Hoarse, eh? Well then, whistle, or hum, show some response to the music! What are you made of—stone?

SENEFRU To be frank . . .

AWALIH Ah, yes! Do be frank!

SENEFRU It's just that I haven't a musical ear.

AWALIH I beg your pardon, Mr. Senefru, sir. The fact is that your ear is very musical indeed. It's just that it isn't clean, and I am going to clean it up for you.

SENEFRU (*Pleading, in a low voice*): Awalih, I place myself under the protection of Amon . . .

AWALIH (*Whispering*): Come with me, quietly—or do you want people to know that your ear isn't clean? It would be a scandal . . .

SENEFRU I'll go home, wash my ears, and come back immediately to sing.

AWALIH You won't know how. This is a matter for a specialist. It will take just one minute. Come with me!

He goes out into the wings. OEDIPUS*'s voice becomes audible.*

OEDIPUS I thought of only one thing: Thebes must become the greatest city in this world. And for Thebes to become great, what is needed . . .

SENEFRU *dashes in, singing loudly and enthusiastically, and with true harmony.*

SENEFRU You're the one who killed the beast!

OEDIPUS *stops, and the people look in amazement at* SENEFRU, *who goes on singing with enthusiasm, but his wholeheartedness and enthusiasm gradually change to bitter weeping. He takes refuge in a corner at the front of the stage, drops into sitting position, and weeps quietly.*

OEDIPUS So it was, my children, that the beast died.

PEOPLE You're the one who killed the beast!

OEDIPUS *responds with a wave of his arms, and disappears inside the palace. At the same time, a huge howl rises of a man in torment.* THE PEOPLE *freeze where they stand in horror. A man rushes in from the gate in the wall, his face and body covered with blood.* THE MAN *is still uttering dreadful cries, then he drops to the floor among* THE PEOPLE.

THE MAN A beast . . . A very great beast! . . . By the wall . . . It devoured my leg . . . Ah! . . . I'm dying! . . .

THE PEOPLE A beast! . . .

THE MAN'S *movements cease.* THE PEOPLE, *speechless, exchange glances.*

SENEFRU (*Through his tears*): So the beast has come back!

AWALIH *springs on* SENEFRU.

AWALIH You wretch! What beast has come back? Weren't you singing a moment ago that Oedipus had killed the beast?

SENEFRU (*Seized with terror*): Yes, yes . . . It must be another beast . . . a different beast . . . The first beast was killed by Oedipus . . . Oedipus killed . . .

He tries to sing but cannot. He goes on weeping silently, his whole body shaking in utter misery as down comes . . .

CURTAIN

ACT III

SCENE I

The same as at the beginning of the play: THE PEOPLE *of Thebes are sitting on the stone benches, but they are now in gloomy silence. The members of the Municipal Council sit in the middle.* AWALIH *stands, holding a large sheet of paper from which he reads to* THE PEOPLE.

AWALIH People of Thebes! The Municipal Council has entrusted me with the presentation of a report setting out the dimensions of the present situation regarding the beast's assault on the walls of the city.

Item One: The Municipal Council asserts that this beast is a new one. It also is in the semblance of a sphinx, but it is smaller in size than the previous one which was killed by Oedipus. Such is the assertion of the experts in beasts, authenticated by Professor Horimheb.

Item Two: The beast has attacked thirty-five persons, of whom thirty were devoured, and five have suffered lethal injuries from which they have since died. Their consignment to the afterlife was carried out with due honors, this by debiting the account of the Chamber of Commerce—in consideration whereof the Municipal Council offers thanks to Brother Onah for this generous gesture.

Item Three: We have no certain indication that the beast is posing riddles. However, by analogy with the previous beast and in view of the fact that the new beast is of the same species and genus as the previous one, it is held to be almost certain that the new beast also poses riddles to travelers and demands solutions.

It has been decided to hold this plenary meeting of the inhabitants of Thebes to discuss the problem and arrive at a solution. Long live Thebes! Long live the people of Thebes, always and ever capable of killing beasts wherever they may be! Long live Oedipus! . . .

PEOPLE (*Chanting*): He's the one who killed the beast.

AWALIH Promulgated at the permanent seat of the Municipal Council within the Temple of Amon. Signed on behalf of the President of the Municipal Council: er . . . hmmm . . . Awalih.

Honored citizens of Thebes, in accordance with true democracy, we meet today in order to seek your views. How are we to get rid of the beast?

A member of the public speaks out, but we cannot spot him or ascertain the source of the voice.

VOICE Oh, brother, what cheek! What business is it of ours? You've always decided matters on your own—why the sudden change today? What do you take us Thebans for—fools to be left out of every party and invited to every funeral?

AWALIH (*Angrily*): Who is it who spoke? . . . Let the speaker stand up . . . (*Even more angrily*:) Let the speaker stand up! (*Then, trying to conceal his anger and to speak softly*:) What need is there for anyone who speaks to be afraid? Let him give his name so it may be recorded in the minutes . . . (*Leaves his place and wanders among the people.*) Who was it who was speaking? The voice came from over here . . . Who spoke? Anyone who wants to speak should put up his hand, ask for the floor, and give his name . . . Ever heard of something called democracy, you cattle? . . . (*Turns his back on the people and returns to his place*). A sorry lot without any feeling for democracy . . .

VOICE That's enough from you, Awalih, enough! (*In a muffled voice*:) A curse upon your father's soul.

AWALIH (*Springing up in horror and turning toward the people*): Who is it who used insulting words just now? Who is it being rude? (*Exploding*:) Oh, no! I'm not going to be insulted by any of you! Let him who was abusive stand up at once! You don't want to tell? (*Turning to the policemen*:) Seize Thebes!

POLICEMAN Thebes?

AWALIH Yes, Thebes. All of it! The people, the Municipal Council, Oedipus, Jocasta . . . Everyone's under arrest. Let no one move from his place. Everyone's under arrest until you produce the man who insulted me. (*In highly emotional tones, almost weeping*:) Am I . . . Awalih . . . Am I to be insulted?

HORIMHEB Calm down, Awalih.

AWALIH (*Savagely*): Don't you open your mouth, sir! You are now under arrest. Such matters are not to be treated lightly. Don't utter a word until I bid you to. (*Facing the people*:) Am I to have my father's soul cursed? A curse on the soul of the father of every one of you, no matter how big a mob! Who was it who uttered that insult? You don't want to talk? All right, here we stay. (*He squats down on the ground.*) There's no business to call us away, is there? No one's going home today. (*To the policemen*:) Listen, my boys: if anybody moves, shoot—even if it's me. We'll see how I can be insulted. (*In a voice choking with emotion*:) So, you tinkers, after all my services to you, you turn round and insult me. For years I've been working for you, day and night—and in the end I get abused. All right, I'm going to teach you a lesson.

TIRESIAS (*From among the crowd*): It's me, Awalih. (*It is clear that* TIRESIAS *was not the one who cursed*).

AWALIH Come on! Come up to me! Show yourself to me. Who are you? (TIRESIAS *stands up.*) Tiresias . . . Take him! (*Not one of the policemen makes a move; instead they stand in confusion.*) Men, obey your orders, one and all!

TIRESIAS Don't be silly, Awalih. It's no good arresting Tiresias, my son. Have you forgotten? It's the first lesson you were taught when you were small. Have you forgotten? If you have, your policemen haven't.

AWALIH (*Confounded*): Isn't it shameful of you to insult me, Uncle Tiresias? I swear by Horus, if it wasn't that you're an old man, this day wouldn't have ended well.

TIRESIAS Sorry, Awalih. It slipped out in spite of me. You know that I utter insults only once every hundred years. Never mind; you just happened to be the butt this time.

AWALIH Only the last person you insulted did happen to be my grandfather, Uncle Tiresias.

TIRESIAS That's how your luck runs. I'm sorry.

ONAH Reconciliation is a blessing. He's like your father, Awalih.

AWALIH All right: an amnesty. An amnesty for Thebes. I beg you, good people: there are traditions we ought to maintain. If there's anything anybody wants, let them speak out. Only let him say his name first. We must have the name of anyone who wishes to speak. Otherwise our democracy would crumble at the base, and the beast would eat us up. Do you want the beast to devour us? Of course not. All right, then. No one is to speak a word until he's given his name. If he doesn't, it's up to anyone of you to give him away. That's settled, then. Just allow me a word. In my view, the person responsible for doing away with the beast must be the Lord Creon, since he's the person answerable for guarding and defending Thebes. Therefore I suggest he be entrusted with doing away with the beast.

CREON If the purpose of the Lord Awalih is to do away with me and with the Theban Guard, so be it; let's go and meet the beast. But if the aim is to kill a beast the size of which by your own accounts is that of a pyramid, that has the face of a woman and the body of an animal, then that will take me a long time.

HORIMHEB What we understand from this is that you are afraid to join battle with him at the present time.

CREON Understand me well, Horimheb. I don't know the meaning of fear. But all the lessons and drills known to the Theban Guard are based on the assumption that the warrior is to encounter a warrior of his own ilk. The Theban Guard is capable of fighting with arrows and spears and war chariots. It can fence. It can wrestle. But the Theban Guard has never learned how to face up to a beast.

AWALIH Attack him as if he was an army.

CREON A brawl—is that what you want? There is a difference between warfare and brawling. What you're calling for is an act of collective suicide. To fight such a beast as this, we need to know what size he is; we need to know how thick his skin is, his range of vision, the parts of his body that are vulnerable; how he moves; how fast he can be; when he sleeps, and for how long. When we have all these data, we shall modify our training on the basis that our enemy is a particular beast whose characteristics are such-and-such, whose strong points are so-and-so and his weaknesses thus-and-thus. That is warfare. One might have expected the intelligence services run by the Lord Awalih to have supplied us with all this information, but it seems they were busy with other things. Such are the ways that I know. But then there is another, an easier way. It is that His Majesty Oedipus-Ra, just as he rid us of the first beast, should rid us of the second, and no one else need trouble himself. (*This last sentence is spoken with bitterness mingled with sarcasm*).

HORIMHEB Pharaonic traditions forbid that Pharaoh be exposed to any possibility of danger.

CREON But he did expose himself once before.

HORIMHEB He hadn't become Pharaoh at that time.

ONAH Pharaonic traditions must be respected no matter what dangers threaten Thebes. Traditions are our very life.

CREON Pharaonic traditions are your very life, are they, Mr. Onah, President of the Chamber of Commerce, sir? Why don't you tell the truth just once in your life? The truth is that you're afraid something may happen to Oedipus—you're afraid for the goose that lays the golden eggs. If anything happened to him, the string of inventions would come to an end, and you would have to shut up shop.

HORIMHEB (*Protesting*): I will not allow such demeaning words to be spoken in the Municipal Council.

ONAH Nor I.

AWALIH Nor I.

CREON You don't say? Why don't you arrest me, while you're at it? Not so long ago, you had the whole of Thebes under arrest.

JOCASTA *appears on the balcony.*

JOCASTA What is this? What's going on? What's this gathering for?

CREON The beast has reappeared, my Lady.

AWALIH A different beast, my Lady; another one.

JOCASTA Have you alerted Oedipus?

ONAH The Lord Oedipus is in his laboratory, working on the most important of his inventions, my Lady.

JOCASTA Nevertheless, you ought to notify him. He's the one who specialized in solving beasts' riddles and in killing them.

AWALIH Just so, my Lady. That's sound talk. Oedipus-Ra—he's the specialist.

HORIMHEB But pharaonic traditions, my Lady . . .

JOCASTA Forget about traditions. The whole set of pharaonic traditions shrinks to nothing and becomes valueless when Thebes is exposed to danger. (*Addressing the people*:) People of Thebes! Experience has proved that Oedipus is the cleverest of men. Therefore it is Oedipus who shall solve the riddle.

PEOPLE Yes . . . He's the one to solve the riddle!

A VOICE What do you make of that dame, brother? She wants to do the fellow in!

AWALIH *turns to face the people.*

AWALIH Didn't we say that whoever wants to speak must give his name? Why are you trying to annoy me? Who was it that spoke?

PEOPLE We don't know.

OEDIPUS *appears on the balcony, whereupon the people take to chanting.*

PEOPLE You're the one to kill the beast!

OEDIPUS What's this? What's up with you? Is something the matter?

JOCASTA A second beast has appeared, my Lord; and the people have commissioned me to convey to your Majesty their wish that you go forth to solve the riddle and kill the beast.

OEDIPUS (*Facing the people*): You want me to kill the beast?

PEOPLE Yes.

OEDIPUS So be it! I shall go and solve the riddle and kill the beast. And if yet another beast appears, I shall go and solve its riddle and kill it. But what then? What will you do when I'm dead?

PEOPLE Dead? . . . Can Oedipus die?

OEDIPUS Yes, Oedipus shall die.

PEOPLE Oedipus is a god.

OEDIPUS No! Oedipus is a human.

HORIMHEB *intervenes in the exchange.*

HORIMHEB It's true that Oedipus is human, but he's descended from the gods; and men descended from the gods don't die, but merely transfer to the other world, to rule there too. You are well aware that Pharaoh rules over this world and the next. This is what my Lord means. (*Firmly to Oedipus*:) This is what you mean, my Lord.

OEDIPUS Listen to me! We mustn't allow theories to impede our thinking. We don't want words to tie us up in knots. Whether Pharaoh dies or transfers to the other world, whether he goes on to rule there or not—none of that matters to us. We need to take heed of fact, of reality and its practicalities. And the fact is that some day my heart will cease to beat; my lungs cease to breathe; my brain stop thinking; my blood stop flowing. At that point, my existence comes to an end. At that point, I shall be embalmed in the House of Death like any human among you.

AWALIH May you be spared, my Lord!

OEDIPUS Shut up, Awalih! (*Turning again to the people*:) When that happens, what will you do? What will happen to the entire civilization I've brought about? To the paved roads? To the electric devices? To the electronics? To the motor cars and the airplanes? The five thousand years that we've compressed into a few? What will happen to all that? Is all of this civilization to be demolished by some beast coming out of the desert? I begin to feel that this massive edifice of civilization is a frail structure that any beast can destroy once I have passed to the other world. I fear I shall be subjected to torment because I've bequeathed this civilization to those who are incapable of defending it. People of Thebes! In the name of life I ask you to go out and confront the beast and do away with it—for your own sakes, for the sakes of those who will follow, for the sake of Thebes.

TIRESIAS (*Springing up from among the people*): At last we are back to our starting point. This is what I said at the beginning. The people must undertake their own defense against the beast. If there is to be a struggle, let the people go out and fight in its own defense. Did we have to go through all that we have gone through so you should understand this plain truth? Beasts do not pose riddles for their amusement. Beasts attack cities in order to devour them. There are small animals—like snakes and wolves—that confront men individually, and there are beasts that attack entire societies. And then there is the Sphinx. Now the Sphinx—understand this well, people of Thebes—devours whole countries and cities. Should he leave Thebes alone now, he would return to it later, and then turn his attention to the remaining cities of the world. People of Thebes, not for the sake of Thebes alone but for the sake of all cities, let us go out to encounter the beast. The outcome, no matter what, will be a victory. If we do away with the beast, we shall sing. We shall rejoice for ourselves. The people will sing for themselves alone. And if the beast destroys us, it will mean that we do not deserve life, but deserve our destruction. A new age shall be born marking the end of humankind and the victory of the beasts. People of Thebes . . . all together . . . to the beast!

PEOPLE (*Thundering*): To the beast! . . . To the beast! . . .

They rush all together to the wall. JOCASTA *leaves the balcony.* OEDIPUS *remains standing, looking proudly upon the people of Thebes who are leaving the stage with great enthusiasm, with only Awalih remaining behind.*

OEDIPUS Why didn't you go with them, Awalih?

AWALIH And Thebes' Internal Security, my Lord? Who would maintain security in Thebes?

OEDIPUS As I see it, the city's deserted.

AWALIH On the contrary, you will find it filled with the beast's supporters.

OEDIPUS I perceive no one but you and me . . . So it must be one of us.

Loud shouts are heard. Dust is stirred, reaching across the walls. There is fearsome roaring from the beast. The sounds of battle rise. Lights are gradually dimmed.

SCENE 2

OEDIPUS *is prostrate upon the throne, his head thrown back, his eyes closed—the very picture of wretchedness.* CREON *stands before him, with spots of blood and mud on his clothing and face.*

OEDIPUS How could it be, Creon? What exactly happened?

CREON I don't know, my Lord, nor is there anyone who knows. All I do know is that we were defeated. The Sphinx defeated the people of Thebes. We couldn't stand up to him. We didn't know precisely who or what we were fighting. For the first time in Thebes' history, its people were unable to stand their ground in battle. Thebes the magnificent, mother of heroes and of civilizations, could not stand firm in its struggle against the beast.

OEDIPUS It's your responsibility, Creon, the Guard's responsibility. The Guard was in the forefront. Surely there must have been some deficiency in the equipment, in the training of the Guard.

CREON Quite so, my Lord. I am responsible for the defeat, as indeed every commander is for victory or defeat. But why is it that I was defeated?

OEDIPUS Nothing can justify this defeat.

CREON I'm not trying to justify the defeat. I'm carrying the full burden of my responsibility. The question is of another kind; amid the cries of the wounded and the dying, in the thick of battle, before the terrifying roaring of the beast, I suddenly felt my mind calm and clear. It's true that I'm answerable for weapon training; but weapons aren't what a man fights with. Who trains the man?

OEDIPUS Trains him for what?

CREON For being a man. To put it more clearly: who's responsible for the making of human beings in this city? We deployed our forces correctly. We took up the correct positions. Our weapons were powerful and sure. Our zeal was great. Our faith was strong. Yet there was something wrong, and I don't know what it was. I know the Thebans well. The Thebans are very bold people. They have no fear of death—to them death is merely a passing into another, a better life. Why, then, were there so many who didn't hold their ground until either they died or we destroyed the beast? Is it because we know nothing about this beast? That's possible, but that's not sufficient reason. Some pestilence has infected the people of Thebes, some strange disease. What is it? I don't know. Who's responsible for it? I don't know. Something's wrong with the species of man in this place, and whoever's responsible for that flaw is necessarily responsible for the formation of man here.

OEDIPUS Defeat's turned you into a poet, Creon. Thebes has lost a commander and gained a poet.

CREON If your intention is to humiliate me, my Lord I'm now insensible to everything. I can't feel shame. There's something wrong within me. I also have been penetrated by the pestilence to my very depths.

OEDIPUS So far as my responsibility goes for the making of Theban man, you know what I've done, Creon. I've done the utmost that could be done. I've hurried the evolution of Thebes by thousands of years. I've invented for people what Man is yet to make in the future.

TIRESIAS *appears.*

TIRESIAS You are also, my Lord, the author of the worst invention in history—fear! It is the one invention that ruins the effect of all other inventions. It is the most horrific of human afflictions, more horrendous even than plague. It is the one disease that turns men into things. All the afflictions we know have clear and evident symptoms, but the symptoms of fear are deceiving and misleading. Let fear worm its way into the heart of man and it mingles with his blood, his intellect, his dreams. Man and fear become one and the same thing. Man himself becomes fear itself walking on two legs. At that point, man is no longer man. He becomes something brittle, and what's brittle easily crumbles.

OEDIPUS Tiresias, what you are saying is momentous—and ugly. My one concern was the happiness of man in Thebes. My one concern was to free him from fear.

TIRESIAS You were liberating him on the one hand, and others were imprisoning him in fear on the other. To all appearances, your Majesty . . . What is that Awalih up to?

OEDIPUS I don't know.

TIRESIAS It's your business to know!

OEDIPUS Even if Awalih was spreading fear through the land—and this I don't know for a fact—it still wouldn't be my responsibility. Awalih was here before I became King.

TIRESIAS But you allowed him to operate, and by the same method his family has been operating for four hundred years.

OEDIPUS (*In great torment and regret*): What method? I don't understand anything. It's becoming evident to me at last that I've been blind. (*Calling out:*) Awalih!

AWALIH *immediately appears from behind a curtain.*

AWALIH Yes, my Lord.

TIRESIAS Awalih's like the air—always to be found everywhere.

OEDIPUS What have you been doing to the people, Awalih?

AWALIH Nothing, my Lord. You may ask them.

TIRESIAS (*Sarcastically*): Ha! They'll say nothing happened. The fearful always give the answer you want.

AWALIH If what you're driving at is that some individuals exposed themselves to . . . to . . . (*He fishes for the right word*) to less than pleasant treatment, that involves only some individuals, not the people of Thebes. And that *had* to take place.

OEDIPUS Why?

AWALIH For the protection of Thebes, my Lord.

TIRESIAS We are not speaking of traitors, evil-doers, thieves, criminals. These are all corrupt elements in the body politic. What we are driving at is something else, Awalih. You know what we mean ...

AWALIH I don't know what you're driving at. There are people who say that your Majesty didn't solve the riddle, and some who raise doubts about the solution. Yet no one was with your Majesty when you encountered the beast. There are also people who say that the second beast and the first were one and the same. So we may have gone a little beyond the score with some. It was necessary to stop people from saying such things, in order to preserve the dignity of the pharaonic system.

OEDIPUS And how did you stop them, Awalih?

AWALIH By all possible means, my Lord.

TIRESIAS All possible means . . . That means just one thing: torture—the crushing of everything within them, beautiful or ugly, then the wakening of the most repulsive thing in Man—rancor, the hatred of all things ...

AWALIH It's clear that you want to get rid of me. It's not as bad as all that. If three or four expose themselves to treatment that is ... that is ...

OEDIPUS ... less than pleasant ...

AWALIH That's right—less than pleasant. That doesn't mean that the entire population of Thebes was affected.

TIRESIAS Fear is not divisible, Awalih. Fear is a common ill. The people of Thebes is not a collection of individuals. It is a living, self-consistent body, like any other society on the face of the earth. And anything that happens to any part of this body affects the body of the society in its entirety.

AWALIH All right, then! Sorry!

OEDIPUS What do you mean, "sorry"?

AWALIH I'm apologizing for my mistake. It's just that I wasn't aware of this business of the social body. The fact is that we've been operating all along by the same method and things were working out well. No one ever complained about us. Why suddenly now?

TIRESIAS You'll never understand, Awalih. You belong to another world.

OEDIPUS Awalih, you'll have to be outside the city walls by sunrise.

AWALIH So be it, my Lord. I'd anticipated something of the kind. That's why I got myself a contract of employment in Babylon. (*Brings a sheaf of papers out of his pocket.*) To whom shall I pass on the trust, my Lord?

OEDIPUS What trust?

AWALIH The list of criminals ...

OEDIPUS Take them with you.

TIRESIAS You know now, Awalih, that fear is a social ill, don't you? You too were afraid. This is why you had in reserve a contract of employment in another country.

OEDIPUS If you stay one moment longer, I shall be giving out less than pleasant treatment.

AWALIH (*Muttering angrily as he leaves*): We've been operating all along in this manner, and nobody ever brought up this business of the social body. Why now? (*Exits*).

OEDIPUS (*In extreme despair*): Creon!

CREON My Lord! Command me as you will. I am prepared to sacrifice anything for the sake of Thebes; and for your sake, my Lord.

OEDIPUS Tiresias . . . Creon . . . The two persons dearest to me . . . Don't abandon me. I don't know what to do. For the first time, I feel that I'm blind. You are now the eyes by which I see. What are we to do?

CREON From a military point of view, we need to find out everything about the Sphinx, and we must remake Theban man. Provide me with a well-made man, and I shall provide you with victory.

OEDIPUS Where are Horimheb and Onah?

CREON I never saw them during the battle.

TIRESIAS They aren't the kind to appear in battle. But let there be some profit-making, and they'll soon appear and jump to action.

OEDIPUS And how are we to remake man, Tiresias?

TIRESIAS The people of Thebes love you, my Lord. Let this be the starting point. Let us preserve this love and foster it. Whenever an attempt is made to hide the truth, people have to pay the price in the long run. I don't know whether or not your Majesty killed the beast the first time around. Whatever the truth of that may be, there is a truth that Thebes must understand. You must make the Thebans understand that no matter how great the power or genius of an individual, he cannot forever be killing beasts on his own—even if you did solve the riddle, and even if you did kill the beast. Come on, Oedipus. We have no time to waste . . .

OEDIPUS goes out to the balcony, together with CREON and TIRESIAS.

OEDIPUS People of Thebes . . . My children . . .

The people assemble.

OEDIPUS We've lost a battle, but a whole war still lies ahead of us. And there are some truths I want to proclaim to you. Awalih has been banished from Thebes. That means that there will no longer be a place for fear among us. There will no longer be anything in Thebes to hinder the growth of Man's greatness and creativity. And there is another truth which you must fully comprehend if victory over the Sphinx is to be won. That is, no individual on his own can kill the beasts that attack cities. I did not, on that first occasion, kill the beast . . .

PEOPLE (*Chanting*): You're the one who killed the beast!

OEDIPUS It's you who have asserted this. I didn't say, on my return . . .

PEOPLE (*Chanting*): You're the one who killed the beast!

OEDIPUS The truth was not quite that . . .

PEOPLE (*Chanting*): You're the one who killed the beast!

OEDIPUS Please . . .

PEOPLE (*Chanting*): You're the one who killed the beast! . . .

His voice is drowned by the chanting. The lights are gradually dimmed.

SCENE 3

Gradual intensification of light on a single spot near the front of the stage, in which TIRESIAS appears. The rest of the stage is in darkness.

TIRESIAS It's easy to banish Awalih from Thebes, but it's impossible to expel him immediately from the hearts of the people. I was well aware of this sad outcome, but it was essential that Oedipus see for himself what fear does to people. It becomes possible for them to sing in celebration of error. It becomes possible for them to develop a zeal for fakery. It becomes possible for the truth to be dispersed among them. Even the noblest impulses and traits, such as enthusiasm, daring, courage, can take shape as symptoms of this pestilence that is fear. The true starting point to the remaking of Man in a way that will release the creative potential within him is to free him of fear, free him from anxiety, and from doubt . . .

The lighting is gradually extended, revealing OEDIPUS *and* CREON *in the throne room.*

OEDIPUS But how, Tiresias, how?

TIRESIAS I know millions of answers to millions of questions, but this one question is the one that has confounded all philosophers. This is the true riddle. Whoever knows the answer shall create the greatest civilization on earth. The one who knows how to liberate Man from fear deserves to be recognized as the father of sages and philosophers. To put it simply, my Lord, he is the one who deserves the title of Ruler.

OEDIPUS How faint the light is in the palace tonight. I can't see very well. (CREON *looks at him in puzzlement.*)

CREON Indeed, my Lord . . . The torches are not at full strength.

OEDIPUS It's strange. I can't see well at all . . .

CREON There is the first glimmer of a solution in my mind, my Lord.

OEDIPUS Don't talk about it, Creon! Carry it out with all the zeal of youth. You have Tiresias with you.

CREON And you, my Lord?

OEDIPUS (*Rises from the throne*): I shall go in search of the solution alone. I've discovered at the peak of my glory that there are still things I don't know. I shall leave . . . I shall set off on a long journey, in order to learn. Take my hand, Creon; show me the door. I thought it was the light that was faint . . . (*In distress:*) Ha! . . . I didn't know the world could hold so much darkness . . . You go back, Creon.

CREON My Lord . . .

OEDIPUS That's an order—the last order given by Oedipus. (*Exits.*)

CREON Everyone in Thebes will have to pay a heavy price. With that price we shall buy Thebes . . . we shall buy life for Thebes—someone of great standing . . .

TIRESIAS Explain that.

CREON I shall explain in a practical way.

CREON *goes out into the square, to which the light is gradually extended. Proudly he marches through the square, and with his head held high, he goes out of the gate. The people climb on to the wall.*

ONE PERSON Creon's going out to meet the beast on his own . . .

PEOPLE On his own? Alone?

ANOTHER PERSON Come back! Creon, come back!

A THIRD He's approaching the beast sword in hand, his hand held high . . .

PEOPLE On his own . . .

SOMEONE He's getting information about the beast . . .

FIRST PERSON We must follow him!

A shout is uttered by the people. Some jump off the wall, and return carrying CREON *on their shoulders, dead. The people gather round the corpse as the lighting is gradually restricted to a spotlight on* TIRESIAS, *at the front of the stage.*

TIRESIAS Creon has paid the great price—the price of making people in Thebes understand that death must be met for the sake of life, that in death Man loses nothing except his fear, that annihilation is preferable to a life threatened by the Sphinx. It is not important that we know what has happened to Oedipus. He has become—someone said—a King of Poets. Now Thebes will belong forever to its people, a people which has truly begun to know the solution. Thousands of years hence, any one of you who comes to visit Thebes, my beautiful city, shall see the great temples and other things that Man has made to endure, in defiance of Time, in defiance of the beasts of the desert. And you people who live in this city and to whom I have told the story of my city, know that although you were provoked to some laughter as you listened to this story, I swear to you by all the gods that that was not my intention.

CURTAIN

MAHMUD DIYAB

Strangers Don't Drink Coffee

Translated by
Owen Wright
and Alan Brownjohn

Mahmud Diyab's *Strangers Don't Drink Coffee* (*Al-Ghuraba' la Yashrabun al-Qahwa*) is one of a number of plays in contemporary Arabic drama that deal with the subject of the ordinary citizen faced with anonymous authority. Diyab's work manages to create a frightening atmosphere, as an apparently typical, harmless individual is terrorized by a series of strange men whose appearance is made all the more sinister by the similarity of their clothing. The horoscope that this man reads out to his wife at the beginning of the play proves to be horribly wrong: instead of making a good business deal, he is informed by the men that his house does not belong to him. They tear to pieces all his documents and photographs, the record of his life and individuality. Retreating inside his house, the Man decides to resist, but as the door closes and the play ends, there is surely a symbolic gesture when a gust of wind blows his papers across the stage. The oppressive atmosphere created by this play provides a powerful picture of the authoritarianism and quashing of civil liberties that was typical of many countries in the Arab world during the 1960s, a topic that was much discussed in the wake of the June 1967 defeat.

R.A.

STRANGERS DON'T DRINK COFFEE

CHARACTERS

MAN
Good-natured, nearly sixty years old.

STRANGERS
A group of strangers, none over forty, apart from their leader, who is distinguished from the others solely by his age.

NEIGHBOR
A drunkard—one of the locals.

STRANGERS DON'T DRINK COFFEE

The scene: The façade of an old house. The paint has peeled off in places, and one can see where some of the cracks have been repaired. But the entrance, with its echoes of Arab architecture that still preserve something of a former beauty, suggests nevertheless that the house was built in a time of prosperity.

It is a one-story house in a peaceful road in an old residential quarter. Three worn marble steps lead up to the entrance, which is separated from the street by a wooden fence no more than five feet high. To the left of the entrance is an ancient tree, with no leaves.

The front door is ajar, the windows shut except for one, to the right of the door, which is opened only a little way so as not to reveal what is behind it. The MAN *sits to the right of the gate and in front of the fence, on a cane chair, wearing a loose white cloak and slippers, his head buried in the daily paper. To his right is a small table.*

MAN (*Suddenly raising his head from behind the newspaper*): Good heavens! (*He ponders for a moment, then buries his head in the newspaper again, then raises it once more and turns toward the open window, making you imagine there is someone behind it . . . To the window*:) What do you think of that? . . . I've got a most peculiar horoscope today . . . (*Pondering*:) That can't be under Aries . . . (*He looks intently at the paper.*) No, it really is Aries. (*Thinking*:) There must be some mistake . . . the printers often make mistakes . . . (*To the window*:) Listen! . . . Listen to what it says! (*He reads*:) You will meet an old friend . . . pull off a good business deal . . . divine providence will protect you . . . (*As if talking to himself*:) Well, there's no arguing about divine providence, but what I don't understand is the bit about a deal . . . How could I pull off a deal when I'm in the civil service, not business? It must have slipped down from Pisces without anyone noticing . . . the printers often make mistakes like that. (*He ponders for a moment.*) But I don't understand the bit about meeting an old friend, either. My friends are the neighbors here. New and old, they all live on the same street, so who could this old friend be? (*To the window*:) Who do you think, Saniyya? (*He ponders.*) There's one old friend I haven't seen for two or three years, though . . . Abd al-Quddus. Only he's dead . . . (*Uneasily*:) Does that mean that I'm . . . (*He banishes, with a forced smile, the unpleasant thought that has just come to him.*) No, no, you can't die just because a newspaper expects you to. Newspaper predictions are usually wrong. In any case, I've got my health. I know I'll be sixty in a few months' time, but I'm still in pretty good shape. (*He ponders.*) Anyway it doesn't make sense, one of my friends who live in this street appearing in the horoscope—you never see them away from their own front doors! (*Confused*:) That only leaves Abd al-Quddus. But how could I meet him when he's dead? (*Banishing the unpleasant thought.*) The zodiac signs must have got mixed up in the paper, so that what they say is all confused. I suppose Virgo fell into Aquarius . . . (*He gives a little laugh*) Cancer crept into Leo, Pisces invaded Aries . . . (*He is suddenly silent. He looks worried.*) Never mind, divine providence will sort it all out. (*A short pause.*) Saniyya, where's my coffee? It's almost evening and I haven't had my coffee yet.

The window is quietly shut, and at the same moment the first STRANGER *enters from the right of the stage. Meanwhile, the* MAN *is still preoccupied with the paper. He gives it a last look, folds it and throws it on the table. At that moment he notices the* STRANGER, *who is neatly dressed, strongly built, grim in demeanor, moving deliberately, and with extreme self-confidence. The moment he appears on stage his gaze focuses on the* MAN'*s house. He pays no attention to the* MAN *himself, as if denying his very existence. It is obvious that he has come solely on account of the house: he moves right and left, back and forth, studying the facade and its surrounds carefully, paying attention to the slightest details, then recording his observations in a small notebook. The* MAN *follows the* STRANGER'*s movements in utter amazement, confused, not knowing how to react. He is even more taken aback when the* STRANGER *goes up to the wooden fence and shakes it as if to see how strong it is. The* MAN *gets up and cautiously sidles up behind the* STRANGER.

MAN (*Gives a hesitant greeting*): Hello! (*And an apprehensive smile, while offering to shake his hand.*)

The STRANGER *gives him a quick cold look and then goes on with his work, ignoring the outstretched hand.*

MAN I own this house . . . it's my home, you see. (*Smiles.*)

The STRANGER *pauses in his work, turns toward the man and coolly sizes him up.*

MAN Is there anything I can do for you?

The STRANGER *fixes his gaze on the* MAN'*s cloak.*

MAN (*Embarrassed*): Oh . . . that. Well, when I'm at home I like to be casual . . . otherwise how would I feel at home? (*A small forced smile.*) I hope you don't mind my interrupting—I didn't mean to bother you. Actually I just wanted to ask whether you liked the house. It's a bit of a historic monument. That's what I like about it. Perhaps that's what caught your eye.

The STRANGER *silently looks away from the man and continues his work. He goes over to the old tree, stops, examines it, and then walks round it, looking closely at it as he does so.*

MAN (*Trying to catch up with the* STRANGER *as he goes round the tree*): Perhaps you've got the wrong address. This is my house.

The STRANGER *stops and turns to look sharply at the man.*

MAN (*Confused, he pretends to laugh a little*): I suppose my clothes and my sitting there on the chair like that made you think I was the caretaker. But actually I'm not the doorman, I'm the owner.

The STRANGER *continues, studying the windows.*

MAN (*Following the stranger*):In any case people round here don't generally have doormen, and as for my sitting on this chair, well that's just an old habit of mine . . . I can remember when the neighbors would all come here for a get-together in the afternoon. We'd chat, have coffee. They'd hardly ever fail to turn up. It's not like that now.

The STRANGER *stops at the front door and examines it.*

MAN Forgive me asking, but what exactly do you want? (*Correcting himself:*) I mean, can I help you?

The STRANGER *does not seem to have heard.*

MAN (*Summoning up his courage*): Would you mind telling me . . . who you are and what you want?

Silence. The STRANGER *looks sternly at the man, then puts his hand in his pocket and takes out a yellow card, which he unfolds immediately in front of the man's eyes, then quickly folds up again and puts back in his pocket, turning his attention to the house.*

MAN Oh, I get it . . . thanks. (*He hasn't actually understood at all, only become more confused.*) In any case, please feel at home . . . I'm glad you like the place.

The STRANGER *makes an entry in his notebook. The man tries to steal a glance at what he is writing, only to be caught in the act by the stranger.*

MAN (*Gives an embarrassed laugh*): I just wanted to know what language you're writing in.

STRANGER (*Stonily*): That's strange.

MAN (*Taken aback*): You can speak! . . . I mean, you can speak Arabic . . . for a moment I thought you were a foreigner . . . one of those historic monuments enthusiasts. (*He laughs.*) How silly of me!

STRANGER (*Coldly*): You talk too much.

MAN (*Taken aback*): Pardon?

The STRANGER, *annoyed, puts his notebook back in his pocket.*

MAN (*Feeling insulted*): I didn't mean to annoy you at all, and yet you insult me. I'm sure you appreciate that I have a right, as the owner of this house, to ask . . .

STRANGER (*Interrupts*): You keep on asking questions. It won't do you any good. (*A brief silence.*) But you seem to be a good fellow.

MAN (*Looks more cheerful*): Thank you! Look, why don't we sit down for a bit? (*Gesturing toward the chair:*) Please, sit down and I'll get you some coffee. It'll give us a chance to get to know one another. To tell you the truth it's boring sitting here by myself now that the neighbors don't want to know . . . they've all got other things to do. We could become friends.

STRANGER (*Stonily*): You really are a decent chap.

MAN (*Shouts toward the window*): Another coffee, Saniyya . . . we have a guest! (*To the* STRANGER:) How do you like it? With sugar? One spoonful or two? I just take half a spoonful myself.

STRANGER I don't drink coffee.

MAN You'll like my wife's coffee . . . you really ought to try it.

STRANGER I don't drink coffee.

He happens to turn round and see the paper. He picks it up to check which one it is.

MAN That's the one I like best. It was my father's favorite too. I don't know about my son, though . . . he's working abroad.

The STRANGER *turns away from the paper and looks at the* MAN.

MAN I'll tell you something funny . . . In my horoscope today it said I'd meet an old friend. And I was racking my brains as to who this friend might be when I caught sight of you. You're not an old friend of course, but still, we might become friends, mightn't we? It just proves there was a mistake in the paper . . . only a little one, old friend instead of new friend, but it turned everything the wrong way round. (*He gives a little laugh.*) What sign are you?

The STRANGER *takes out his notebook and makes an entry. The* MAN *cranes his neck to see what the* STRANGER *is writing, only to be caught in the act again.*

MAN What are you writing? . . . Well? Is it something to do with me?

STRANGER You've started asking questions again.

MAN Well, if it's something to do with me I've a right . . .

STRANGER (*Interrupting*): Just make sure you don't get on my nerves. (*Pause.*) In any case, my job's finished.

MAN So soon? But you haven't explained to me what your job is.

The window is pushed open and a woman's hand holds out a tray with a large coffeepot and two cups. At the same time the stranger slips his notebook into his pocket and steps con□*dently over to the left of the stage.*

MAN (*Scratching his head in confusion*): I wonder what his job can be? (*notices the proffered coffee tray and calls the* STRANGER:) Excuse me! . . . You haven't had your coffee. (*But the* STRANGER *goes off without turning round.*) He's gone. Well, I'll drink it all myself . . . I could really do with a potful. (*He takes the tray.*) What a strange fellow! (*Addressing the window*:) He turns up out of the blue and then disappears without even saying who he is. I imagine there's something wrong with him . . . something not quite right in the head. (*He gives a small laugh.*) He hardly opens his mouth, just stares at the house and writes things down. I reckon he got lost on his way to the museum.

He goes over to the chair, head down, pondering. He keeps shaking his head and smiling at his thoughts. He sits down and pours coffee.

MAN I really ought to have caught what was written on that yellow card of his . . . but his hand was quicker than my eyes. (*To the window*:) Do you think he was some kind of policeman, Saniyya? (*Ponders.*) But I haven't done anyone any harm, so why should the police be interested in me? (*Putting an end to these musings*:) Oh, he's just some crazy fellow, that's all. He came, he went. He might as well have never existed, so the most sensible thing would be to forget all about him.

He raises the coffeecup, only for it to freeze on his lips when he sees two further STRANGERS, *replicas of the first. They enter left, eyes fixed on the house, which they examine with the same care and attention as the first* STRANGER.

MAN (*Taken aback, to himself*): I must be dreaming.

He puts the cup down on the table, looks at the window as if seeking help, then anxiously observes the strangers.

MAN (*To himself*): I just wish I knew what brings them here. (*He gives the house a quick look.*)

The two STRANGERS *halt in front of the house. Each one takes out a notebook and records his observations about the house and its surroundings, paying no attention to the man himself.*

MAN (*Looking about him*): What's

happened to the neighbors? (*To the window*:) Why is the street so empty, Saniyya? It feels like a graveyard out here.

The STRANGERS *advance slowly toward the entrance. The man rushes over and stands in front of the gate as if to prevent their going in.*

MAN Is there anything I can do for you?

The second STRANGER *calmly pushes the man out of the way.*

MAN But I'm the owner of this house.

The STRANGERS *exchange a glance and laugh, very briefly and mechanically.*

MAN (*Observes them in amazement*): Thank God you can laugh! The other one didn't laugh at all.

The STRANGERS *observe him, then let out a similar laugh, but longer. The* MAN *laughs along with them, feeling more at ease now.*

MAN (*Stops laughing*): Just imagine . . . a man who doesn't laugh. He stared at this and that, wrote things down, but he didn't laugh. He didn't even smile. His face was like a piece of granite. (*He alters his features to mimic the stony expression on the first* STRANGER*'s face. The* STRANGERS *laugh at length, the* MAN *with them.*)

MAN (*Continues*): I offered him coffee and friendship, but he couldn't even take the trouble to smile. (*He catches his breath.*) I always say that laughter's what makes you human . . . it shows you're good-hearted. You two are really good fellows; I'm sure we'll find it easy to get along. (*The* STRANGERS *give him a stony look.*) Let's all have some coffee! (*To the window*:) Saniyya, coffee for one more! (*The window is softly closed.*) There's coffee for two already here. I would have drunk it all myself if you hadn't done me the honor. (*With sudden awareness*:) How do you like it? Sugar? No sugar? (*He looks at their stony faces.*) I take just half a spoonful myself.

STRANGERS (*Together*): We don't drink coffee.

MAN (*Vexed*): You too! You don't drink coffee either!

STRANGERS We don't drink coffee.

MAN Isn't that strange? . . . (*The* STRANGERS *remain silent.*) Well, at least let's sit down together. That can't do you any harm. (*He takes the third* STRANGER *by the arm.*) Please, do sit down!

The STRANGER *removes his hand from his arm, takes a tape measure out of his pocket and gives the end to the second* STRANGER, *who takes it over to the front door. It is clear that they are going to measure the distance between door and gate.*

MAN (*Finds it difficult to understand what is going on, and is incapable of stopping them*): What exactly are you up to? Well? Why are you measuring my house? If I knew what was going on I'd be able to help you better.

The STRANGERS *are absorbed in their work.*

MAN Don't waste your time . . . it's about two meters . . . tell me . . .

STRANGER 3 (*Interrupting*): Two meters, five and a half centimeters . . .

Stranger 2 makes an entry in his notebook.

MAN (*Forces a smile*): Good heavens, what do five and a half centimeters of land matter? It never occurred to me to measure the distance. I never imagined that anyone would actually bother about measuring it. (*Looking round anxiously*): Where have the neighbors got to?

The STRANGERS *begin to measure the width of the gate. The* MAN *stands between them not knowing what to do.*

MAN Please, why don't we have the coffee . . . it'll be cold. (*The* STRANGERS *look at him sharply.*) I know, I know, you don't drink coffee . . . I just forgot. (*As if to himself*:) You and the other man, you're all the same. You concern yourselves with my house for no reason, and write things in your notebooks, and you won't share my coffee with me. God alone knows who you are. (*Suddenly shouting*:) Who are you? What do you want? (*The* STRANGERS *turn round toward him.*) I haven't put my house on the market: I've never thought of selling it. And I haven't done anyone any harm . . . so who could you be?

Silence. The STRANGERS *exchange looks, then each pulls out a yellow card, holds it up in front of the man's eyes, and immediately puts it back in his pocket before he can recover from his astonishment.*

MAN (*In resignation*): I understand . . . you all work together in the same place. Are you from the highways department? You must be from the Council. (*The* STRANGERS *don't answer.*) But I haven't done anything against the regulations. In any case this house was built a long time ago—long before I was born. The only thing I've done is to restore the front. I repaired the cracks and repainted it, but that was some years ago, thirty maybe . . . Why don't we sit down a bit and sort things out? Well? Why don't we sit down? What harm can it do?

STRANGER 3 One meter and fifty centimeters and a half. (STRANGER 2 *makes an entry in his notebook.*)

MAN And half a centimeter?. . . . . . . What's the point of half a centimeter? You're making things too complicated. When I put up this fence I didn't use any precise measurements; I did everything by rule of thumb. I'm the one who put up this fence, you know. I wanted to protect my flowerbeds, and I thought it would make the house look nicer, so I put it up, without any measurements. (*He puts on a little smile.*) What's the value of half a centimeter of land ?

The STRANGERS *pay no attention to what he is saying.* STRANGER 2 *has pulled the end of the tape measure to the righthand end of the wooden fence, while* STRANGER 3 *has taken the other end to the far left.*

MAN (*Fatigued*): Don't trouble yourselves—it's fifty meters! (*Adds mockingly*:) And half a centimeter . . . Fifty meters and half a centimeter . . . ! (*A forced laugh which ends in a sigh.*) I'm beginning to feel tired . . . All this arguing is too much of an effort . . . And I haven't even had my coffee yet.

He goes over to the chair, exhausted, but as the STRANGERS' *tape measure has become tangled up with the back of the chair, he quietly frees it and straightens it out for them alongside the fence, then sits down.*

MAN (*Continues*): I can't stand the strain any longer. I'm getting old. Just a few more months and I'll be retiring. I'd better take a holiday before then; I need the rest. (*He feels the coffeepot.*) It's cold; I don't like cold coffee. (*Short pause: he happens to glance at the paper.*) No old friend's appeared yet. (*He looks round, distressed.*) How nice it is to drink hot coffee among friends. (*He sighs.*) But still, divine providence . . .

STRANGER 3 (*Interrupting*): Forty-nine meters, and ninety-five centimeters . . .

MAN (*Alerted by the figure and turns round in alarm to* STRANGER 3): What? What did you say? Forty-nine meters and *how* many centimeters? (*He jumps up.*) That's impossible: you've got it wrong.

(*Shouting at* STRANGER 2:) Don't write that number down! It's wrong! The front is exactly fifty meters wide . . . maybe a fraction more, depending on your measurements. But not any less, not by as much as a half centimeter. I won't have it, do you hear? Don't write that down! I've put up with more than I can stand from you two—I won't have you play around with the measurements of my house.

STRANGER 3 Forty-nine meters and five . . .

MAN It's a lie, I tell you! (STRANGER 2 *records this number while* STRANGER 3 *folds up the tape.*) Listen to me! I don't know who you are or where you've come from. I don't care about your yellow cards. It doesn't matter to me what color they are . . . All I know is that this is my house, and that the front is fifty meters across. If I haven't thought about remeasuring it for a long time that's because the earth can't shrink with the passage of time. (*To* STRANGER 2:) Write that observation down in your notebook, and I'll sign it myself if you like . . . the earth can't shrink with the passage of time . . . there, you see, I've said it again. I insist it's true.

The STRANGERS *exchange looks and give a short mechanical laugh.*

MAN You can laugh . . . you play about with the measurements of my house and laugh . . . but I'm not going to laugh with you . . . there's no warmth in your laughter.

The STRANGERS *suddenly turn toward the front door as if intending to burst in.*

MAN (*Rushes to the door to barricade it*): You're not going into my house! You're not! Look at the front as much as you like, but you're not going in!

STRANGER 3 *exchanges a quick look with* STRANGER 2, *then walks purposefully toward the door.*

MAN You'd better stand back. A house is private . . . something sacred. I'm not going to let you into my home, you're not a friend of mine. Don't make me do something I might regret. I might get angry and hurt you.

STRANGER 3 *calmly pushes the man away from the door.*

MAN (*Steps aside, unable to resist*): I shan't take this lying down. I'll inform the authorities. I'll take you to court. I'm not going to give up my rights. Never mind about your yellow cards, I'm not going to let you insult me and get away with it.

STRANGER 3 *pokes his head inside the door and comes out with an expression of disgust on his face.*

STRANGER 3 The entrance is damp. No natural light.

STRANGER 2 *writes.*

MAN (*Shouting*): There's light inside. No one's going to make me have a window put in the entrance. In any case, it's my house—I know my way around every inch of it with my eyes closed or in the dark. I reject your observation . . . I reject it. (*Silence.*)

STRANGER 2 (*Calmly to* STRANGER 3): Our job's finished.

STRANGER 3 Our job's finished.

They turn and exit right while the man drops into the chair, exhausted.

MAN Forty-nine meters and ninety-five centimeters . . . What a lie! (*Sarcastically:*) Perhaps the earth's grown old too, and shrunk . . . idiots! (*Silence.*)

The window is opened and a woman's hand holds out a tray with a small coffeepot and one cup.

MAN (*Feebly looking toward the window*): Where have the neighbors gone, Saniyya? The coffee's got cold—there's no one to drink it.

He makes a great effort to get up, and shakes out his cloak.

MAN I'm confused ... first a man like a lump of stone, and then two more, and none of them drink coffee ... all carrying yellow cards . . . interested in my house, peering everywhere measuring and writing things down, and then they vanish. (*He takes the tray.*) Who do you think they could be, Saniyya? (*Without waiting for an answer*:) Just imagine, one of them tried to burst into the house ... Don't be alarmed! . . . He retreated straight away ... divine providence arranged something to keep him away. He couldn't stand the damp and the dark in the entrance, so he went straight back. It's all very confusing. (*He continues asking himself questions as he goes back to his chair.*) What is it they're after? Why do they measure the gate and the front of the house, worrying about every half a centimeter . . . (*Silence while he pours coffee.*) To tell you the truth, we shouldn't have let the boy go and live so far away. I should have told you long ago what I've been keeping to myself . . . The house is too big and lonely, Saniyya. Its old splendor has gone. Damp's eating away the walls. You know, before I fall asleep I spend hours every night listening to the scurrying of the mice as they race each other in the dark. I'm always afraid to turn the light on in case I see them . . . so I just listen to them moving about until I fall asleep . . . I'm often wakened by ghosts . . . Don't be scared! They're probably just nightmares . . . I have dinner and then go to bed without even taking a walk first. (*Short pause.*) If only the boy had stayed with us, he might have thought of pulling the house down one day and rebuilding it—or at least he would have dealt with the mice ... and we wouldn't have been so lonely. (*Silence*). There's nothing nice left in life, Saniyya . . . even the flowers don't grow in the flowerbeds anymore, and the neighbors aren't friendly as they used to be . . . It's got to the stage where I have to drink my coffee by myself . . . They're all too busy to bother ... and those who aren't working have taken to the bottle and can't stand coffee any more . . . The best one was Abd al-Quddus. (*He sighs.*) Why has life changed so? It loses its savor more with each passing day . . . (*He lets his head fall, musing absentmindedly for a while.*) Forty-nine meters and ninety-five centimeters . . . They're mad. Can the earth shrink, Saniyya? I told them it can't shrink. I said it twice; I insisted. I was right. Either they were joking or there was something wrong with their tape measure. The earth can't grow old, whatever its age. Thank heaven they've gone! They came and went, and it's as if they never existed . . . I'd best forget all about them; that's the most sensible thing to do.

He raises the cup, but it freezes on his lips as he sees three men who appear simultaneously on the right. They are replicas of the first STRANGER, *although one is clearly older than the others. At the same moment a further three appear on the left. They all approach with short heavy steps, looking straight ahead as if the house was of no concern to them.*

MAN (*Terrified, he trembles as he puts the cup back down on the table*): What on earth is happening to me? . . . God help me! (*He looks back and forth between the two advancing groups.*) They've multiplied . . . First one, then two, then six . . . and God knows how many more. They must all have come for the same reason . . . These look just like the others . . . but they're not bothering about the house . . . perhaps my house isn't what they're after . . . I'll pretend to be occupied so as not to arouse their interest. (*He picks up the paper and holds it open in front of his face, then whispers to the window.*) Saniyya, shut the window! Don't attract their attention! (*The window closes. His face stays buried in the paper. He holds his breath.*)

Step by step the STRANGERS *approach from both sides . . . slowly . . . slowly . . . the closer they come the tighter the man's grasp on the paper, until finally the steps come to a halt beside him. Silence reigns . . . The* STRANGERS' *eyes are all trained on him. The paper soon falls away from his face in a gesture of resignation. He looks round their faces, his gaze resting for a moment on the leader.*

MAN (*Attempts unsuccessfully to smile*): Welcome! (*The* STRANGERS' *faces retain their fixed expression.*) Is there anything I can do for you? (*Silence.*) Are you looking for someone? or somewhere? (*Silence.*) Perhaps I could direct you. (*Shouting, still glued to his chair*:) Why are you staring at me like that? If it's the house you're after you can go and stare at that as much as you like. (*He stands up and goes toward the leader.*) I haven't broken any regulations . . . I've never done anyone any harm . . . I live alone with my wife in this house . . . we wouldn't hurt a fly . . . we keep ourselves to ourselves . . . we haven't got anything to do with anyone outside our street, and even the neighbors leave us alone. (*He scans their faces, looking for a reaction.*) Why don't you say anything? Well, why? (*Softening his tone*:) I'm sorry I shouted . . . I'm a bit worked up . . . Look, why don't we sit down and sort things out? (*Realizing how many they are*:) Perhaps you'd like to come inside. (*Correcting himself*:) No, wait here, I'll go and get some chairs for you and we can sit together, just as we used to, my old friends and I.

STRANGERS (*In unison*): We don't drink coffee.

MAN (*For whom this is the last straw*): So who said anything about coffee? (*To one of them*:) Did you hear me mention coffee? (*To them all*:) I know you don't drink coffee . . . I knew all about you the moment I set eyes on you . . . you've got yellow cards in your pockets, and when I ask you who you are you'll get them out.

The STRANGERS *put their hands in their pockets to get their cards out.*

MAN (*Puts his hands over his eyes*): No . . . don't get them out . . . I know them; they frighten me.

But the cards appear and stay displayed until he takes his hands away, whereupon they are immediately slipped back into their pockets. Silence.

MAN (*In despair and resignation*): Alright, the front can be forty-nine meters . . . and ninety-five centimeters wide and the gate so many centimeters wide . . . plus a half a centimeter . . . Let's accept that the earth can shrink with the passage of time and that I was wrong to measure things by rule of thumb and not pay attention to the half of a centimeter . . . What do you want? What are you going to do to my house?

LEADER OF THE STRANGERS We'll do the asking, not you.

MAN All right . . . as you wish . . . go ahead, ask. (*Short pause.*) Why don't you ask your questions, I'm waiting. (*Silence.*)

LEADER Who are you?

MAN Who am I? (*Angrily*:) Who on earth are *you*? (*Correcting himself*:) I take that back . . . I've seen your cards . . . thank you.

LEADER (*Insistently*): Who are you?

MAN Is your business with me, or my house? (*Short pause.*) In any case, my name's . . .

LEADER We don't want to know your name.

MAN I thought you were asking me for my name.

STRANGERS (*Together*): We don't want to know your name.

MAN (*Nervously*): How can I let you know who I am?

LEADER Answer the question.

MAN I'm . . . I'm the owner of this house.

The STRANGERS *exchange looks with their leader and then all give a short mechanical laugh.*

MAN (*Annoyed*): There's no warmth in your laughter . . . I'm an expert on laughter . . . yours doesn't come from the heart.

LEADER (*To one of the* STRANGERS *holding a notebook and pen*): Write that remark down.

MAN (*Agitated, to the same* STRANGER): And also write down . . . that I don't like this whole business.

LEADER Write that too.

MAN (*In the depths of despair*): And note too . . . that there's nothing funny about my being the owner of this house.

LEADER Write . . .

MAN (*Impetuously*): And don't forget to add that I said . . . that it's you who are funny . . . with your stony faces . . . you're like statues (*He is nearly laughing*) and those ridiculous yellow cards (*He laughs*) and your "we don't drink coffee," like a school recitation (*He laughs louder*) and the way you walk about as if you were a lot of clockwork toys. (*He continues to laugh, with great agitation, while the strangers observe him stonily.*) Clockwork . . . they run on clockwork . . . (*With the action of someone winding up clockwork*:) tick . . . tick . . . tick, and they move. (*He keeps on laughing.*) The earth shrinks with the passage of time . . . shrinks in winter and expands in summer . . . (*He laughs.*) Do you hear me laughing? . . . That's genuine laughter . . . I haven't laughed so much for years. (*Noticing that the window has opened*:) Shut the window, Saniyya . . . I've got people with me . . . I'm all right, I'm not afraid any more . . . I can laugh! (*To the* STRANGERS:) You've made me laugh . . . I'm grateful.

His laughing has exhausted him and made his eyes water—he wipes away the tears with his hands and gasps, trying to regain his composure.

MAN Yes . . . go ahead . . . ask away . . . give me something to laugh at! (*Silence.*)

LEADER You talk too much.

A STRANGER You're senile.

ANOTHER Decrepit.

ANOTHER Not right in the head.

ANOTHER Idle.

ANOTHER Feeble.

ANOTHER Living in the dark.

ANOTHER With your ghosts.

ANOTHER One stroke of the pen and you're dead.

LEADER (*Decisively*): This house isn't yours.

Silence. The last blow seems to have stunned the man.

MAN What? . . . What did you say? . . . Did you say that this house . . . ? (*He is unable to finish the sentence.*) Can you back that up? (*He clenches his fists.*) Would you dare to repeat what you just said?

LEADER (*Matter-of-factly*): This house . . . isn't yours.

MAN (*Seething with fury*): I dare you to repeat that!

STRANGERS (*Together*): This house isn't yours.

MAN (*Shouting*): Clockwork! You've got clockwork inside you! Tick . . . tick . . . tick, and you move . . . I've found out who you are, and the malicious secret that brought you here. No, no, it's not as simple as you think . . . This house is mine . . . I inherited it from my father, as he did from his . . . it's been passed down in the family from one generation to the next. I belong here; my ownership of the house is firmly established. I've lived my whole life here: the house belongs to me as much as my own soul . . . and I have a thousand and one proofs.

LEADER (*In dry jest*): You remind us of a thousand and one . . .

STRANGERS Nights. (*They give a short scornful laugh.*)

MAN There's nothing friendly about you, however many jokes you make. There's no warmth in your laughter . . . But you won't frighten me . . . the time for fear is over.

A STRANGER You? Fearless?

ANOTHER You're spineless.

ANOTHER Useless.

ANOTHER Feckless.

ANOTHER Faithless.

ANOTHER One stroke of the pen and you're dead.

LEADER This house isn't yours.

Silence.

MAN I almost believe you're serious . . . this isn't some joke . . . it's a real-life farce. You want to tear me away from the house . . . tear the house away from me. You want to wipe out the truth, but you won't be able to. I belong here, and my ownership is firmly established. I'm not going to die at the stroke of a pen . . . not even at the blow of an ax. Do you hear? . . . not even if you used axes. Why are you silent? Why don't you speak?

He is suddenly silent as his gaze falls upon two further STRANGERS *who have appeared on the left and another two who have appeared on the right. All advance a few steps, then stop, observing the situation.*

MAN (*Bewildered*): One, then two, then six, and now ten. You must multiply by spontaneous division. How many of you are there? Tens? Hundreds of thousands? A million? Two? Well? How many of you are there? (*Short silence.*) Of course you're not really serious when you claim I'm not the owner of this house, are you? It's just a joke, isn't it?

LEADER We're completely serious.

STRANGERS (*Together*): Completely serious.

MAN (*Shouting*): Lies! I've got official documents to prove it's a lie! I've got a thousand and one proofs which will silence you. I never thought that one day I'd have to prove I owned my own house . . . I never imagined that anyone would come along and dispute that. (*The new* STRANGERS *advance a few steps, then stop.*) Still . . . never mind. (*In a confident tone:*) You can consult the maps at the land registry office.

LEADER (*Scornfully*): Land registry office?

The STRANGERS *give a slight mocking laugh.*

MAN (*Anxious*): What is there to laugh about? Those maps clearly show that it's my property.

LEADER We called in at the land registry office.

MAN And you found my house on all the maps?

LEADER We couldn't find any maps.

The STRANGERS *give their mocking laugh.*

MAN (*Even more anxious*): What about the deeds then?

LEADER (*Dismissively*): Deeds?

STRANGERS We couldn't find any deeds. (*They give their mocking laugh.*)

MAN (*Feeling that he is losing the battle*): What about the rates department?

LEADER (*Derisively*): The rates?

The STRANGERS *give their mocking laugh.*

MAN (*Shouting*): I've got my documents here! It's a lucky thing I've kept my own papers . . . Divine providence is on my side . . . I'm under no obligation to let you see my papers, mind, but I will . . . I'll let you see them so that you can convince yourselves that what you're saying is laughable, just a joke. (*He rushes to the window and bangs violently on the pane.*) Fetch me the box of papers, Saniyya! Hurry! (*To the* STRANGERS:) You'll be able to see with your own eyes, touch with your own hands . . . It's a lucky thing I've kept my own papers. (*To the window*:) Come on, Saniyya, quickly!

The window opens and a woman's hand holds out a tin box that must originally have contained sweets of some sort. The man takes it.

MAN (*Feebly*): Shut the window, Saniyya . . . I'm all right . . . I'm not afraid any more . . . I've got a small matter to settle with these many gentlemen, then I'll be in . . . You can get the cat's dinner ready while you're waiting for me to come.

The window closes. The man turns toward the STRANGERS, *hugging the box to him.*

MAN Here they are, gentlemen . . . My documents are all here. (*He taps the box.*) I'll show them to you one at a time so we can get through things quickly . . . my wife's waiting for me.

He starts to lift the lid of the box himself, but the LEADER *silently stretches out his hand to take it. The man recoils, protecting the box with his arms.*

MAN (*With a frightened laugh*): No, I'll open it myself if you don't mind.

The STRANGERS *advance in a heavy, threatening manner and surround him. He is terrified.*

MAN What are you going to do? . . . I can see you're angry, but what have I done? My papers are genuine; you'll be convinced they're authentic. I'll show them to you; you'll have enough time to check them. I'll only fold them away again when you say so. (*The four new* STRANGERS *advance still further.*) Look, I won't cheat . . . I haven't the slightest intention of cheating you . . . it's not in my nature. (*The* STRANGERS *press closer.*) All right, then, I'll hand them over and you can look for yourselves, but you must give me your word of honor. I like to trust a man's word. . . . ..You are men of honor, aren't you?

He puts the box in the LEADER*'s hands, as if surrendering his own heart.*

MAN I hope you'll handle them carefully . . . most of them are very old . . . and too fragile for . . .

The LEADER *goes back a few paces with the box . . . The man starts to follow, but three* STRANGERS *stand in his way. The* LEADER *lifts the lid of the box and starts to rummage around among the papers. The man's whole being is concentrated on* THE LEADER*'s hands.*

MAN (*Imploring*): Please be careful . . . please . . . one of the papers might get damaged . . . and who knows, there's enough evil in the world; some malicious person might come along and dispute my ownership of the house.

LEADER (*Picks up some old papers and examines them*): What's this?

MAN (*Anxiously examines what he can see of the papers between the shoulders of the* STRANGERS *surrounding him*): Oh . . . those are some school papers belonging to me . . . essays I wrote when I was young . . . I used to get top marks in composition . . . and those are my best . . .

The LEADER *passes the school papers over to one of the* STRANGERS, *who tears them into small pieces without even deigning to look at them and throws them on the ground. Meanwhile the man tries to escape from the arms that hem him in.*

MAN (*Shouting*): Why are you tearing them up? What crime have I committed? . . . Please don't tear them up . . . they're . . .

LEADER (*Interrupting*): And what's this? (*He turns over an old photo.*)

MAN (*Frightened*): No, don't bother about that . . . it's just an unimportant old photo . . . in any case it's not evidence that could be used against you.

LEADER A woman and a child.

MAN Quite right . . . the woman's my mother . . . she's been dead for a long time now. No one remembers her anymore . . . Dust to dust . . . The child's me . . . I was about eight, or maybe seven . . . not old enough to frighten a chicken . . .

The LEADER *hands the photo to one of his companions to be torn into little pieces.*

MAN But why? . . . Did the child do anything wrong? We didn't agree to that. That's not an honorable thing to do. The boy wouldn't have frightened a chicken . . . He was as innocent as a dove . . . Doesn't his white cloak prove it? . . . Why did you tear it up? What harm would it have done you to leave it?

The LEADER *considers another old sheet of paper.*

MAN (*Shouting*): At least leave that alone! It's my last letter from Abd al-Quddus . . . my friend Abd al-Quddus . . . he's dead now. You could at least spare *that*!

But the sheet is handed over to one of the STRANGERS *to be torn up. Other papers follow. Unable to move, the man can only suffer and avert his gaze.*

MAN Have I committed any crime against you? . . . Leave my papers alone . . . leave me alone . . . why do you torture me? It's unjust.

LEADER (*Mockingly*): Poetry? . . . Did this man write poetry? (*The* STRANGERS *give a scornful laugh.*)

MAN (*Gives a frightened look at the* LEADER*'s hand*): Yes . . . those are my first attempts at writing verse . . . my own poems . . . I was just a lad when I wrote them

. . . I didn't try to write any more after that . . . I'm quite proud of them. Please don't destroy them, I've forgotten the words . . . Don't destroy them!

But the sheet is torn up, followed by others. The man is still unable to break free from the arms that surround him.

MAN That's a school certificate . . . what have you to fear from a school certificate? (*The certificate is torn up.*) My son's birth certificate . . . How am I going to prove I've got a son when he lives abroad? . . . God help me! . . . My marriage certificate . . . that's my marriage certificate . . . my wife's indoors and that's her certificate . . . She hasn't done you any harm . . . It's that terrible horoscope . . . What a terrible deal I've had forced on me . . . I'll sue that paper! (*Points to the paper he was reading.*) It peddles lies. To hell with its predictions! To hell with Aries! . . . and Pisces! . . . and all the other signs . . . Please tear this paper up! . . . or let me tear it up! Let me . . . you're choking me! I can't breathe!

He half faints, and rests his head on the hand of one of the STRANGERS *holding him . . . Silence . . . while the* LEADER *goes on disposing of the papers.*

LEADER (*Looking at an old piece of paper*): This man was in love once.

The STRANGERS *give their scornful laugh.*

MAN (*Comes to, as if in a dream*): Yes, I was in love with my wife . . . Before we got married . . . she was just a girl and I was only a lad . . . What you're holding is a letter from her to me . . . the first love letter I ever received. Are you going to destroy it? . . . My wife would be upset if it was destroyed . . . and I respect her feelings. I'm proud of it too, so don't destroy it. (*But the sheet is torn up. Another piece of paper emerges which restores the man to full consciousness.*) The notification of inheritance! That's the notification of inheritance, my most important document. Listen, all of you . . . I hold you to your word of honor . . . I've trusted you . . . Don't destroy this paper . . . It's my one remaining document. (*But the paper is torn up. The* MAN *shouts madly*:) Murderers! . . . killers! . . . You're inhuman! . . . Clockwork toys! You won't kill me with the stroke of a pen . . . not even with an axe . . . I'm still alive in spite of you . . . and I'm going to go on living in spite of all your pens and axes. I hate you . . . I hate your cards . . . I hate the way you walk, the way you laugh. If you want to know the truth, I'm glad you didn't drink my coffee.

He is unable to add another word. He has reached a stage of exhaustion that renders him speechless. While he takes one breath after another the box is emptied of its contents and the LEADER *throws it away . . . Silence.*

The STRANGERS *surrounding the* MAN *let him go. He collapses to the ground. The window opens again.*

LEADER Our job's finished.
STRANGERS Our job's finished.

Silence. The STRANGERS *disperse to the sides of the stage and exit with a firm and confident tread . . . Their footfalls fade into the distance . . . Silence.*

MAN (*Takes a handful of scraps of paper, contemplates them sorrowfully, then throws them away and turns his head to the window*): They've torn up all our papers, Saniyya . . . They didn't spare any of them . . . They even tore up my poems, and your first letter to me . . . and the boy's birth certificate . . . They didn't leave a single document proving my ownership. You're crying . . . (*He goes over to the window.*) Stop crying! Your crying makes me feel done for . . . (*Summoning the remnants of his courage*:) Do you think I'm done for? They'll come back, of course, but you don't think I'm done for, do you? (*Trying to convince himself as well as her*:) I'm staying, Saniyya . . . I'm not some insect that can be squashed just like that. I'm standing in front of you, rock solid. (*As if letting her in on a secret*:) I deceived them. (*Putting on a little smile*:) Yes, I deceived them . . . I strung them along. It was obvious they were going to get at the papers, if not today then tomorrow, and that they were going to tear them up, if not today then tomorrow . . . But (*Suddenly turning to the tree*) have they uprooted this tree? (*He gives a small triumphant laugh.*) The tree's still standing firm, its roots are deep . . . its roots go many many meters deep . . . And do you remember what's on it, Saniyya? What we carved when we were young? Our simple love story, the heart with the arrow, and our names . . . do you remember? I'm going to see if it's still carved there. (*He goes toward the tree.*) I'm sure it's still carved there, but where? (*Worried and agitated, he runs his hands over the tree . . . and goes round it looking for the carving.*) It was on this side . . . no, this side . . . Where did we carve it, Saniyya? Don't you remember any longer? . . . I'm sure it was here (*Pointing to a spot head high*) but where's it gone? (*He looks higher.*) Either I've shrunk as I've got older or the tree's grown, taking the heart up with it. (*He hurries over to the chair and carries it to the tree.*) It can't have disappeared, it was cut too deeply just to vanish. (*He climbs onto the chair to look for the carving . . . and is suddenly jubilant*:) I've found it, Saniyya . . . Here it is! The heart with the arrow and our names, that's real proof. (*He gets down from the chair.*) There it is, proof they weren't aware of . . . and it will stay there. And inside the house . . . in the rooms and corridors . . . are the tiny nail marks I made on the walls when I clung to them as I learned to walk . . . . . . And the first letters I learned to write . . . the letters of my name . . . written large and bold . . . They're still there too . . . and the multiplication table carved into the wall of the boy's room. I'm the one who carved it there, to help him memorize it . . . And there are still spots of blood on the bathroom wall from when I slipped and hurt my head having a bath on our wedding day. Have they destroyed any of that, Saniyya? . . . It's all still there . . . They're all solid, incontestable proof. Why do you think I'm still as firm as a rock? Dry your tears . . . you don't have to be frightened of anything. If all these proofs aren't sufficient to convince the judges of the justice of our case, at least they're enough for us . . . and there's still a way for us to keep the house . . . We'll lock ourselves inside . . . you and me . . . you take a knife and I'll take a cleaver . . . and we'll put up barricades, and we won't let anyone in apart from our friends. I'm not finished yet, not by a long shot. You don't think I'm done for, do you? No, of course not. I'm standing here, still alive . . . so dry your tears . . . I'm coming in straightaway, try and meet me with a smile on your lips.

He turns to go in, but notices a NEIGHBOR, *who has appeared on the left. A broad smile spreads over his face, but swiftly vanishes: the* NEIGHBOR *is drunk . . . He walks along cautiously, afraid of falling . . . softly singing a mangled version of an old song. From the top of the front doorsteps the* MAN *watches him go by, but the* NEIGHBOR *doesn't notice him.*

NEIGHBOR (*Stops by the table and looks at the coffee things and the newspaper*): The table's all alone . . . no seat . . . no one sitting there . . . can't have been very enjoyable . . . can it? (*Looks intently at the coffee pots and cups*:) And coffee that hasn't been drunk . . . Looking for someone to drink it . . . (*Nauseated.*) But I don't drink coffee. (*He goes on his way.*) Never touch the stuff. (*He goes off, singing.*)

Silence.

MAN (*To the window*): Tomorrow, Saniyya . . . At the first crack of dawn I'll send the boy a telegram telling him to come back. Come back and live with us! Your mother and I and the house all need you; there are a lot of strangers . . . (*Ponders.*) Perhaps it might be best not to mention the strangers in the telegram; no, I don't need to mention all that, I just have to say: Come at once, and when you come don't forget to bring your rifle. He's sure to understand what I mean when I mention the rifle.

A moment's silence.

He goes in, head bowed, and shuts the door. The window is gently closed. As darkness envelops the stage, a light breeze rustles among the shreds of paper, scattering them about.

CURTAIN

NOTES ON AUTHORS, TRANSLATORS, AND EDITORS

Authors

SALAH ᶜABD AL-SABUR (1931–81)

One of Egypt's most illustrious poets and dramatists. Educated at the University of Cairo, Salah ᶜAbd al-Sabur held a number of administrative posts within the cultural sector of his homeland; at the time of his tragically early death, he was Undersecretary of State for Culture and Head of the General Egyptian Book Organization. He first came to prominence with his poetry collection, *The People of My Country* (1957), and his poetic gifts were also much in evidence in his verse play, *The Tragedy of al-Hallaj* (1964), which was awarded the State Prize for Literature. Besides several other collections of poetry, he wrote a number of plays, among which are *Night Traveler* (1969), *The Princess Is Waiting* (1969), *Layla and the Madman* (1970), and *Now the King Is Dead* (1971). ᶜAbd al-Sabur's plays were notable additions to the Egyptian dramatic tradition and have been successfully performed on stage.

YUSUF AL-ᶜANI (born 1927)

An Iraqi actor and dramatist. Born in Baghdad, Yusuf al-ᶜAni studied law before transferring to the course in drama at the Institute of Fine Arts in Baghdad. He has visited many drama centers in Eastern Europe and Austria and works as a drama critic. Having served for many years as Director-General of the Cinema and Theater Authority, he is now a Counselor at the General Institute of Radio and Television. He began his writing career in drama with a series of one-act plays but moved on to produce a number of full-length works, of which *The Key* (1968) is the most famous. Other works include *I'm Your Mother, Shakir* (1958), *Wel-*

come to Life (1960), *The Ruin* (1970), *The Inn* (1976), and *Yesterday He Came Back as New* (1983).

MAHMUD DIYAB (1932–83)

An Egyptian writer of fiction and drama. Born in Ismaʿiliyyah, Mahmud Diyab studied law at the University of Cairo before embarking upon a career in literature. He wrote in both the novel and short story forms, but his literary reputation rests primarily on his major contributions to the drama, most especially *The Storm* (1964) and *Harvest Nights* (1967), both of which depict in graphic fashion the tensions of village life. Later in his career he wrote a number of one-act plays, including *Strangers Don't Drink Coffee*, and a lengthy work reflecting on the 1967 defeat, *Bab al-Futuh* (The futuh gate, 1971), in which a mingling of past and present is used to suggest that the former provides a model that can be used in the context of the failures of the latter. His early death deprived Arabic drama of one of its foremost experimental figures.

ALFRED FARAG (born 1929)

Among the most prominent members of the generation of dramatists who contributed to the richest period in modern Egyptian drama in the 1950s and '60s. Born and educated in Alexandria, Alfred Farag served during the 1960s as both a journalist and adviser to the Theater Administration. Following the June War of 1967 he spent several years in exile in England. Farag's most successful plays find their basic plots in the Arabic heritage of the past: *The Barber of Baghdad* (1963) and the play translated here, *ʿAli Janah al-Tabrizi and His Servant Quffah* (1968), from the tales of the *Thousand and One Nights*; *Sulayman al-Halabi* (1964), from accounts of the French invasion of Egypt in 1798; and *Prince Salim* (1967), from accounts of tribal conflicts in the pre-Islamic period. While Farag has written some short plays in the colloquial dialect of Cairo, the language of his longer works represents one of the most successful attempts to produce a dramatic discourse in literary Arabic that can communicate effectively with a contemporary audience.

WALID IKHLASI (born 1935)

A novelist, playwright, and short story writer. Walid Ikhlasi, one of Syria's most distinguished authors, was born in Alexandretta. He obtained a degree in Agricultural Science and works with a cotton-trading company. He has made a number of significant contributions to Syrian and Arab letters. His novel *The Jamr Gate* (1984) won immediate fame. Among his short story collections are *Surprise in Cruel Eyes* (1972), *Black Grasses* (1980), and *The Rose Inn* (1983). In addition to his play *The Path* (1976), which has launched him as a dramatist, he has published *Democratic Evening on Stage* (1979), *Oedipus* (1981), and *Who's Killing the Widow?* (1986).

ʿIZZ AL-DIN AL-MADANI (born 1938)

One of the most important cultural figures in contemporary Tunisia. ʿIzz-al-din al-Madani has written several dramas and works of criticism focusing particularly on the literary production in his homeland. The play translated in this collection, *The Zanj Revolution* (1973), is one of his most famous and popular contributions to contemporary Arabic drama, but a number of other works show both his profound familiarity with the theatrical medium and his continuing desire to experiment. These include *Revolt of the Donkey Owner* (1970), *His Excellency Sultan al-Hasan the Hafsid* (1977), and *The Porter and the Girls* (1988).

ᶜISAM MAHFUZ (born 1939)

Lebanese poet, playwright, and critic. After studying at the Ecole des Haute Etudes in Paris, ᶜIsam Mahfuz returned home, where he now serves as literary editor of the prestigious *Al-Nahar* paper and as Professor of Dramatic Arts at the Lebanese University in Beirut. He has published several collections of poetry, including *Summer Grass* (1961) and *Virgo and the Sword* (1963). The latter produced an immediate impact on avant-garde circles in Beirut. He has also published several works of criticism and a number of plays published in the collection *Short Plays* (1984).

ᶜALI SALIM (born 1936)

One of Egypt's most prominent satirists and comic dramatists. Coming to the drama composition from a career as an actor, ᶜAli Salim has written a number of serious dramatic works about the dilemmas of modern man and pointingly critical comedies that expose the foibles of contemporary society, especially its bureaucracies. The play translated here is a tragicomedy, *The Comedy of Oedipus: You're the One Who Killed the Beast* (1970); it takes up the issue of the nature of tyranny. The same spirit pervades *Four Plays to Laugh from Such Intense Sorrow* (1979). More directly farcical in approach are such works as *People in the Eighth Heaven* (1965), *The Wheat Well* (1968), and *Our Children in London* (1975).

ᶜABD AL-ᶜAZIZ AL-SURAYYIᶜ (born 1939)

One of Kuwait's most distinguished litterateurs. ᶜAbd al-ᶜAziz al-Surayyiᶜ is at the forefront of the dramatic art in Kuwait. Early in his career, he cooperated with the prominent Kuwaiti dramatist Saqr al-Rushud, whose most promising career was ended by his untimely death. Al-Surayyiᶜ persisted in his dramatic experimentation and succeeded in reflecting the social and psychological changes that have taken place in a society trying to accommodate the advent of sudden oil wealth to a traditional and simple cultural background. Al-Surayyiᶜ was an official at Kuwait's prestigious Higher Council for Culture, Literature, and Art but recently accepted the post of Secretary General of the ᶜAbd al-ᶜAziz al-Babitain Prize for Poetry and Poetic Criticism and dedicates much of his time to the service of poetry and culture within the Arab world.

MAMDUH ᶜUDWAN (born 1941)

Prominent Syrian playwright and poet from Hama. Mamduh ᶜUdwan was educated in Damascus and worked in journalism for many years before joining the personnel of the Syrian Ministry of Information. A prolific poet and writer, he has published over eight collections of poetry, among which are *The Green Shadows* (1962), *The Impossible Time Has Come* (1982), *My Mother Chooses Her Murderer* (1982), and *The Waving of the Tired Hands* (1982). He has also published several plays, among which are the *Queen's Visit* (1984) and *Stories of Kings* (1989). In his play *That's Life* (1986), chosen for this anthology, he exhibits great creative audacity by choosing a villain as his main character, showing with subtlety and a poignant underlying irony the intricacies of the evil mind at work. The play, a skillful exposé of hypocrisy and deviance written in a matter-of-fact tone to give the appearance of a justified cause while in fact indicting it, was greatly successful on stage.

SAᶜDALLAH WANNUS (born 1941)

A Syrian dramatist, theater producer, and critic. Following education in Syria, France, and Egypt, Saᶜdallah Wannus has made major contributions to the Arabic theater tradition through a whole series of plays, of which the best known are *Soirée for June 5th* (1968), *The Adventure of Mamluke Jabir's Head* (1972), and the work translated here, *The King Is the King* (1977). These plays and others reflect Wannus's insistence that the performance of plays must involve the audience in an active way. His stage directions often invite the producer to adapt and adjust the language, decor, and musical accompaniment of the performance to local circumstances and tastes.

First Translators

NAZEER EL-AZMEH

Nazeer el-Azmeh is a poet, scholar, and dramatist. A Syrian-American, he was born in Damascus in 1930 and received his Ph.D. degree from Indiana University in 1969. From 1963 to 1982 he served as Professor of Literature at Portland State University in Oregon. Currently he teaches at King Saᶜud University in Al-Riyad, Saudi Arabia. He has published eight collections of verse, five books of criticism, and four plays. His play *The Son of the Earth* was produced by the Voice of America radio station in 1952. *Sisyphus the Andalusian* was performed on stage in both Rabat, Morocco, and Damascus, Syria (1975–76), under the sponsorship of the Ministry of Culture of each country.

AIDA BAMIA

A Palestinian by birth, Dr. Bamia obtained her Ph.D. degree in Arabic literature in 1971 from the School of Oriental and African Studies at the University of London. Her dissertation discussed the evolution of the novel and short story in modern Algerian fiction. After receiving her Ph.D. she taught at the Universities of Oran, Constantine, and Annaba in Algeria before coming to the United States to take an appointment in Arabic at the University of Florida at Gainesville. Now Associate Professor there, she is one of relatively few specialists working in the field of North African literature who write in English. She is also an editor of *IJMES*, a member of the editorial board of *Al-ᶜArabiyya*, and has contributed articles on Algerian literature and Maghribi authors to the *Encyclopedia of World Literature in the Twentieth Century*. She has published (in Arabic) *The Evolution of the Algerian Short Story 1925–1967* (1982).

PIERRE CACHIA

Professor Cachia recently retired after a distinguished career as scholar and professor in Arabic literature. Both through his teaching and his editorship of the *Journal of Arabic Literature*, he has considerably enhanced the development of modern Arabic literature studies in the English-speaking world during recent decades. After many years as Lecturer in Arabic at Edinburgh University, he came to the United States to take up the post of Professor of Arabic at Columbia University in New York. His study of Taha Husayn published in 1956 was the first study in English devoted to a single figure in modern Arabic literature. Since that time, he has produced a large number of articles on a wide variety of subjects within the field of Arabic literature. Most recently, his primary interest has been the tradition of popular poetic genres in Egypt, with particular attention to the *mawwal*. His major study of the genre, *Popular Narrative Ballads of Modern Egypt*, was published in 1989, and a collection of his articles, *An Overview of Modern Arabic Literature*, appeared in 1990.

SHARIF S. ELMUSA

After a childhood spent in the refugee camp at Nuaway^cimeh near Jericho, Dr. Elmusa took a degree in engineering from Cairo University before moving to Boston in 1971. He obtained a doctorate in urban studies from the Massachusetts Institute of Technology in 1986 and, after working as an Adjunct Professor at Georgetown University, moved to the Institute for Palestine Studies. There he has undertaken research on the fate of over four hundred Palestinian villages, including his own, that were depopulated in 1948 and have been largely destroyed by the Israelis. He is coediting a reference book on these villages entitled *All That Remains*. His research (with a Ford Foundation grant) concerns the question of water as a strategic resource in the Arab-Israeli conflict. His poetry has appeared in *Poetry East, Paintbrush*, and the *Christian Science Monitor*, and he has served as reader, reviewer, and translator for a number of PROTA anthologies, including *Modern Arabic Poetry* (1987), *Literature of Modern Arabia* (1988), and *Modern Palestinian Literature* (1992). He lives in Washington, D.C., with his wife, Judith Tucker, a Middle East historian, and their two children, Karmah and Layth.

RASHEED EL-ENANY

A lecturer in Arabic and Islamic Studies at the University of Exeter, he is the translator in English of Naguib Mahfouz's novel *Respected Sir* (1986), and his study of Mahfouz's novels, *Naguib Mahfouz: The Quest for Meaning*, was published in 1993. He has published articles in both Arabic and English on issues in modern Arabic literature.

MOHAMMED INANI

Mohammed Inani is Professor of English at the University of Cairo. In addition, he serves as an adviser to the Ministry of Culture on matters relating to books and publication, and, most particularly, as General Editor of the Contemporary Arabic Literature Series published by the General Egyptian Book Organization, a distinguished series of English translations of works by contemporary Egyptian writers in a variety of literary genres. In this latter capacity he has provided for Western readers a large number of perceptive introductions to the works published in this important series. He is a distinguished translator of English literature into Arabic. Among his more recent publications in this area are Milton's *Paradise Lost* (2 vols., 1982 and 1986) and Shakespeare's *Merchant of Venice* (1988).

SALWA JABSHEH

Salwa Jabsheh, a Palestinian by birth, has specialized as a dietician, obtaining the degree of Master of Science in nutrition from King's College, London, after previous study at Beirut University College. She has lived in the Gulf for a number of years, during which time she became well acquainted with the culture and dialect of the region. She now resides with her husband and two children, Shireen and Omar, in London.

OLIVE KENNY

Olive Kenny spent many years in Egypt, where she taught English and studied Arabic at the School of Oriental Studies at the American University of Cairo. This experience gave her a unique opportunity to absorb the multifarious aspects of Arabic culture and to understand the Egyptian scene in particular. She is the translator of the first two volumes of Najib Mahfouz's famous trilogy, *Palace Walk* (1990) and *Palace of Desire* (1991), both with William M. Hutchins. She has been involved in the work of PROTA for many years, translating many selections for the project's large anthologies: *The Literature of Modern Arabia, Anthology of Modern Palestinian Literature*, and *Modern Arabic Fiction*, as well as several of PROTA's single-author works: Fadwa Tuqan's autobiography, *A Mountainous Journey* (1991), and, in conjunction with her husband, M. Yusuf al-Qaᶜid's *War in the Land of Egypt* (1986), Hamza Bogary's *Sheltered Quarter* (1992), and Hanna Mina's *Fragments of Memory* (1993). They are both working on the translations of sections from Khalil al-Sakakini's diaries, *Thus Am I, O World.*

GHASSAN MALEH

One of Syria's most distinguished literary personalities, Ghassan Maleh (B.A. [Leeds University], Ph.D. [Birmingham University]) is Professor of English at the University of Damascus and Dean of the Syrian Academy of Dramatic Arts. He is the Arab World Editor of UNESCO's *World Encyclopedia of Contemporary Theatre*, author of *Renaissance Prose Fiction* (1974), and translator of various works from English, among which is Richard Wright's autobiography, *Black Boy*. He has taught drama and translation at several universities in the Arab world and participated in many international literary conferences.

ROBIN OSTLE

Dr. Ostle is Lecturer in Arabic at Oxford University and Fellow of St. John's College. Specializing in modern Arabic literature, he has published numerous studies of writers in the romantic tradition in modern Arabic literature, including Khalil Mutran, Iliyya Abu Madi, and Mahmud al-Masᶜadi. He has also served as editor of *Studies in Modern Arabic Literature* (1975) and *Modern Literature in the Near and Middle East: 1850–1970* (1991). He is a member of the editorial board of the *Journal of Arabic Literature*.

OWEN WRIGHT

Dr. Wright is Reader in Arabic at the University of London and serves as head of the Near and Middle East Department in the School of Oriental and African Studies. His principal interests lie in two separate fields. First, as teacher of Arabic, his interest lies in the areas of the teaching of

Arabic literature and of the Arabic language, and he has amassed an impressive corpus of material on the latter, targeted to enhance the learning of Arabic by foreign students. Second, as a scholar, he is constantly involved in research and publication on the history of music in the Islamic Middle East (including Muslim Spain), on which he is one of the major specialists in the West. Two of his published works are dedicated to this subject: *The Modal System of Arabic and Persian Music 1250–1300* (1978) and *Words without Songs* (1992). He has also contributed the specialized chapters on music both in volume I of *The Cambridge History of Arabic Literature* (1981) and in PROTA's volume, *The Legacy of Muslim Spain* (1992).

Second Translators

ALAN BROWNJOHN

Alan Brownjohn was born in southeast London and educated in elementary and grammar schools there and at Oxford, where he took a degree in Modern History. He taught at various schools and has been a lecturer in English in a College of Education and a Polytechnic. Since 1979 he has been a full-time writer. He is the author of several volumes of poetry, the most recent of which is *The Observation Car* (1990). His *Collected Poems* appeared in 1988, and his first novel, *The Way You Tell Them*, which takes a satirical look at the role of the artist in Britain near the beginning of the twenty-first century, appeared in 1990, winning the Authors' Club prize for the most promising first novel. His other work includes editing three anthologies of poetry: *First I Say This* (poems for speaking aloud), *New Poems 1970–71* (with Seamus Heaney and John Stallworthy) and *New Poetry 2* (with Maureen Duffy); as well as editing, with Sandy Brownjohn, three teaching anthologies for secondary schools, titled *Meet and Write*. Also with her he translated Goethe's *Torquato Tasso*, which was broadcast on the BBC Radio 3 in 1982 and published in 1985. For six years (1982–1988) he was Chairman of the Poetry Society. He received a Cholmondeley Award for Poetry in 1979 and a Traveling Scholarship from the Society of Authors in 1985.

RICHARD DAVIES

Dick Davies read English at Cambridge University and lived for eight years in Iran. He obtained the Ph.D. degree at the University of Manchester with a study of the *Shahnameh*, the famous national epic of Iran. He has published three collections of his own poems, *In the Distance*, *Seeing the World*, and *The Covenant*. With his Iranian wife, Afkham Darbandi, he has translated Farid al-din al-Attar's *Conference of the Birds* from Persian, published by Penguin Classics in 1984. After residing at the Universities of Durham and Newcastle, he emigrated to the United States and is currently teaching Persian language and literature at the Ohio State University in Columbus.

CHARLES DORIA

After studying classics and comparative literature at Harvard University and SUNY, Buffalo, Charles Doria has taught at various institutions, including Rutgers University in New Jersey. An American poet and translator, he has published many scholarly articles on literary topics, particularly the classical period. He has also published three volumes of poetry: *The Game of Europe, Short*, and *Shorter*. Among his translated works are *Origins: Creation Texts from the Mediterranean*; *The Tenth Music: Classical Drama in Translation*; Muhammad al-Mahdi al-Majdhoub's long poem, "Birth," on the birth of the Prophet Muhammad; and eight poems of Salma Khadra Jayyusi, published in *Women Poets of the Fertile Crescent* (1977).

THOMAS G. EZZY

A citizen of both Canada and the United States, Thomas Ezzy was born to a Lebanese-American father and a French-Canadian mother. Having studied French and classics at Holy Cross College in Worcester and English at the University of Toronto, he now lives in Montreal and teaches English language and literature at Dawson College. A poet and writer of fiction, he has published two collections of poetry, *Parings* and *Arctic Char on Grecian Waters*. More recently he has begun research on a social history of the European novel. He has cotranslated a wide variety of selections for PROTA anthologies, including *Modern Arabic Poetry, The Literature of Modern Arabia, Modern Arabic Fiction* (forthcoming), and *Modern Palestinian Literature*.

ANSELM HOLLO

A native of Helsinki, Finland, Anselm Hollo has lived in Sweden, Germany, Austria, England, and, since 1967, in the United States. A poet, translator, editor, journalist, and teacher, he has been the recipient of an NEA Fellowship (1979) and two translation awards from the American-Scandinavian Foundation in New York (1980 and 1988). He is on the faculty of the MFA Poetics and Writing Program at the Naropa Institute in Boulder, Colorado. His most recent collection of poems is *Outlying Districts: New Poems* (1990). Among recent translations is the novel *The Whale in Lake Tanganyika* by the Swedish writer Lennart Hagerfors (1989) and *Franz Werfel: The Story of a Life* by the Austrian biographer Peter Stefan Jungk (1990).

DESMOND O'GRADY

Born in Limerick, Ireland, in 1935, O'Grady studied at Catholic schools in his hometown, then at the Cistercian College in Roscrea. Later he went to Harvard, where he studied for an M.A. degree in Comparative Celtic Studies. He taught at the Berlitz School in Paris for a year in 1955, then went to Rome, where he was senior English master at the Overseas School for several years. In 1975–76 he was poet-in-residence at the American University in Cairo, and in 1978 he became a lecturer in English literature there. These experiences enhanced his cultural relationship with the Arab world and aroused in him a special interest in Arabic literature, particularly the old poetry. He was back at Harvard in the 1980s where he lectured for some time before returning to Ireland. He has many publications, among which are several collections of poetry and some verse translations, which include the famous ode of the pre-Islamic poet, Imru al-Qays. Quite a few of the translated modern poems he published were first done as PROTA translations.

Editors

ROGER ALLEN

Roger Allen is Professor of Arabic at the University of Pennsylvania in Philadelphia. Since obtaining his D.Phil. at Oxford in 1968, he has been active as editor, translator, scholar, and anthologist of Arabic literature, with a specialization on fictional narratives. However, he is interested in all aspects of Arabic literature, and, as a consultant for PROTA, has helped greatly in the task of selection, evaluation, and promotion of the Project's goals. Among his published works are *A Period of Time*, a full-length study and translation of Al-Muwaylihi's *Hadith ᶜIsa ibn Hisham* (2d ed., 1992), *The Arabic Novel: An Historical and Critical Introduction* (2d ed., 1995), and *Modern Arabic Literature* (1987), an anthology of critical writings on over seventy modern Arab litterateurs. He has translated novels and short stories by Najib Mahfuz, Yusuf Idris, Jabra Ibrahim Jabra, ᶜAbd al-Rahman Munif, and many others. He has contributed numerous articles to many books, including two chapters on the novel to *Modern Arabic Literature*, the final volume in the Cambridge History of Arabic Literature series. He resides in Philadelphia with his wife, Mary, and children, Timothy and Marianna.

SALMA KHADRA JAYYUSI

A Palestinian poet, critic, scholar, and anthologist, Salma Khadra Jayyusi graduated in Arabic and English literature from the American University in Beirut and later obtained a Ph.D. degree in Arabic literature from the University of London. She has traveled widely and lived in many places in the Arab world, Europe, and the United States, first as a diplomat's wife, then as Professor of Arabic literature, which she taught at several Arab and American universities. In 1980, realizing how misrepresented and ignored Arabic literature and culture were in the West, she founded PROTA (Project for Translation of Arabic Literature), which she directs. Her poetry and critical writings have appeared in many journals, and her first collection of poetry, *Return from the Dreamy Fountain*, was published in 1960. Her two-volume critical study, *Trends and Movements in Modern Arabic Poetry*, was published in 1977 by E. J. Brill and is due to appear in Arabic in 1995. Under the auspices of PROTA, Jayyusi has edited some thirty volumes thus far, ranging from single-author works to five large anthologies of Modern Arabic literature. Other than the present anthology with Roger Allen, she has edited *Modern Arabic Poetry* (1987), *The Literature of Modern Arabia* (1988), *Anthology of Modern Palestinian Literature* (1992), and *Modern Arabic Fiction* (in press). She has also edited a comprehensive volume of essays, *The Legacy of Muslim Spain*, published by E. J. Brill in 1992, to coincide with the five hundredth anniversary of the end of Muslim rule in Spain. She is currently at work on a new anthology, *End of the Century Arabic Poets,* and has started work on preparing, with a number of specialists, a comprehensive book of essays, *Culture and Literature in North Africa*.

M. M. BADAWI

M. M. Badawi is a Fellow of St. Antony's College, Oxford University, and until his retirement in 1992 was Reader in

Modern Arabic Literature at the university. Born in Alexandria, Egypt, he began his teaching career in English literature at the university of his home city before coming to England. He was a founding editor of the *Journal of Arabic Literature*, the primary specialist journal in the field, published by E. J. Brill since 1970. In addition to his prominent role as an editor and teacher, he has made many important contributions to the library of works on Arabic literature, including *A Critical Introduction to Modern Arabic Poetry* (Cambridge, 1975), *Modern Arabic Drama in Egypt* (Cambridge, 1987), and *Early Arabic Drama* (Cambridge, 1988). A collection of his articles on a variety of topics is gathered together in *Modern Arabic Literature and the West* (London: Ithaca Press, 1985), and most recently he has served as editor of *Modern Arabic Literature* (Cambridge, 1992), the final volume in the Cambridge History of Arabic Literature series.